Encyclopedia of American Business History and Biography

The Automobile Industry, 1920-1980

Edited by

George S. May
Eastern Michigan University

A Bruccoli Clark Layman Book

Facts On File®
New York·Oxford

Encyclopedia of American Business History
and Biography:
The Automobile Industry, 1920-1980
Copyright © 1989 by Bruccoli Clark Layman, Inc., and
Facts on File, Inc.

Library of Congress Cataloging-in-Publication Data

The Automobile industry, 1920-1980 / edited by George S. May.
    p.   cm. — (Encyclopedia of American business history and
biography)
   "A Bruccoli Clark Layman book."
   Bibliography: p.
   Includes index.
   ISBN 0-8160-2083-3 :
   1. Automobile industry and trade—United States—History.
I. May, George S. II. Series.
HD9710.U52A816   1989
338.4′76292′09730904—dc20   89-11671
                                                               CIP

British CIP information available on request

Printed in the United States of America

10 9 8 7 6 5 4 3 2 1

To the memory of John B. Rae

Encyclopedia of American Business History

Railroads in the Age of Regulation, 1900-1980, edited by Keith Bryant (1988)

Railroads in the Nineteenth Century, edited by Robert L. Frey (1988)

Iron and Steel in the Nineteenth Century, edited by Paul F. Paskoff (1989)

The Automobile Industry, 1920-1980, edited by George S. May (1989)

Contents

Foreword

The Encyclopedia of American Business History and Biography chronicles America's material civilization through its business figures and businesses. It is a record of American aspirations—of success and of failure. It is a history of the impact of business on American life. The volumes have been planned to serve a cross section of users: students, teachers, scholars, researchers, and government and corporate officials. Individual volumes or groups of volumes cover a particular industry during a defined period; thus each *EABH&B* volume is freestanding, providing a history expressed through biographies and buttressed by a wide range of supporting entries. In many cases a single volume is sufficient to treat an industry, but certain industries require two or more volumes. When completed, the *EABH&B* will provide the fullest available history of American enterprise.

The editorial direction of *EABH&B* is provided by the general editor and the editorial board. The general editor appoints volume editors whose duties are to prepare, in consultation with the editorial board, the list of entries for each volume, to assign the entries to contributors, to vet the submitted entries, and to work in close cooperation with the Bruccoli Clark Layman editorial staff so as to maintain consistency of treatment. All entries are written by specialists in their fields, not by staff writers. Volume editors are experienced scholars.

The publishers and editors of *EABH&B* are convinced that timing is crucial to notable careers. Therefore, the biographical entries in each volume of the series place businesses and their leaders in the social, political, and economic contexts of their times. Supplementary background rubrics on companies, inventions, legal decisions, marketing innovations, and other topics are integrated with the biographical entries in alphabetical order.

The general editor and the volume editors determine the space to be allotted to biographies as major entries, standard entries, and short entries.

Major entries, reserved for giants of business and industry (e.g., Henry Ford, J. P. Morgan, Andrew Carnegie, James J. Hill), require approximately 10,000 words. Standard biographical entries are in the range of 3,500-5,000 words. Short entries are reserved for lesser figures who require inclusion and for significant figures about whom little information is available. When appropriate, the biographical entries stress their subjects' roles in shaping the national experience, showing how their activities influenced the way Americans lived. Unattractive or damaging aspects of character and conduct are not suppressed. All biographical entries conform to a basic format.

A significant part of each volume is devoted to concise background entries supporting and elucidating the biographies. These nonbiographical entries provide basic information about the industry or field covered in the volume. Histories of companies are necessarily brief and limited to key events. To establish a context for all entries, each volume includes an overview of the industry treated. These historical introductions are normally written by the volume editors.

We have set for ourselves large tasks and important goals. We aspire to provide a body of work that will help reduce the imbalance in the writing of American history, the study of which too often slights business. Our hope is also to stimulate interest in business leaders, enterprises, and industries that have not been given the scholarly attention they deserve. By setting high standards for accuracy, balanced treatment, original research, and clear writing, we have tried to ensure that these works will commend themselves to those who seek a full account of the development of America.

—William H. Becker
General Editor

Acknowledgments

This book was produced by Bruccoli Clark Layman, Inc. James W. Hipp was the in-house editor.

Production coordinator is James W. Hipp. Systems manager is Charles D. Brower. Penny L. Haughton is responsible for layout and graphics. Copyediting supervisor is Joan M. Prince. Typesetting supervisor is Kathleen M. Flanagan. The production staff includes Rowena Betts, Joseph M. Bruccoli, Amanda Caulley, Teresa Chaney, Patricia Coate, Mary S. Dye, Sarah A. Estes, Cynthia Hallman, Kathy S. Merlette, Laura Garren Moore, Sheri Beckett Neal, and Virginia Smith. Jean W. Ross is permissions editor. Susan Todd is the photography editor.

Walter W. Ross and Jennifer Toth did the library research with the assistance of the reference staff at the Thomas Cooper Library of the University of South Carolina: Lisa Antley, Daniel Boice, Faye Chadwell, Cathy Eckman, Gary Geer, Cathie Gottlieb, David L. Haggard, Jens Holley, Jackie Kinder, Marcia Martin, Jean Rhyne, Beverly Steele, Ellen Tillett, Carol Tobin, and Virginia Weathers.

Introduction

Automobiles had progressed greatly as both technology and commercial product in the United States by 1920. The crude, unreliable horseless carriages of the previous century had been replaced by vehicles that were recognizably automobiles, and the industry that produced them had grown from the initial output in 1896 of thirteen Duryea Motor Wagons to a multitude of firms whose car and truck production in 1919 exceeded 1.876 million units. During the same period car ownership figures, which had been optimistically estimated to have numbered 8,000 in 1900, had risen to some 6.7 million, or one car for every sixteen Americans. Clearly a dramatic shift was underway that would alter long-established transportation patterns and habits. But spectacular as the advances had been, they were only the prelude to the developments of the 1920s, which was the decade that witnessed the full-scale emergence of the automobile culture that would dominate the country through the remainder of the century. Sales of passenger cars, buses, and trucks hit a new high of 5,337,087 in 1929, nearly three times the sales recorded ten years earlier. This record was not broken until 1949 as the Great Depression and World War II slowed and then halted production, but by the 1950s the high growth pattern of the earlier years resumed and continued for some two decades during what has come to be regarded as the Golden Age of the American car culture. Although the 1970s and 1980s were troubled times for the industry, as the automobile and its use came under widespread attack, registration figures that totaled more than 175 million motor vehicles by the mid 1980s were an indication that reports of an end to America's love affair with the automobile were somewhat premature.

The 1920s had hardly begun when the country was made aware of the impact the young automobile industry could have on the nation's economy. During World War I automobile output had been cut in half because of the industry's shift to war production and the scarcity of materials available for civilian automobile production. When the war ended in November 1918 the automobile companies prepared for a postwar boom. Already in 1919 the pent-up demand for cars had restored sales to levels reached just prior to the war, and by 1920, as the transition from a wartime to peacetime economy had been fully completed, sales were expected to soar over the 2-million mark, with Ford alone gearing its American and Canadian plants for a 1-million-car year. The trade journal *Automotive Industries* declared that it was impossible to find any companies talking of retrenchment or even stability in reference to their factory capacity. "Alterations and additions that will permit of doubling and trebling the factory output is the rule, and the financial plans of many of the leaders contemplate a combined total that is staggering."

But then the postwar boom collapsed in summer 1920, and the country tumbled into a depression that lasted until 1923. As the economy turned sour the impact on automobile sales was soon evident. Earlier economic slumps, in 1907 and 1910, had provided signs of how sensitive automobile sales were to changing market conditions, but the postwar depression erased any doubts that in bad times an automobile or a truck is a purchase that large numbers of people decide can be postponed. The sudden drop in demand for their vehicles took the companies by surprise, leaving them with huge inventories of unsold cars which they had been counting on to pay for their heavy investments in expansion programs. Not just the motor vehicle manufacturers and their employees were affected by declining sales. Throughout the country, in areas far removed from the centers of car production, those who supplied raw materials and parts for the industry and those who sold the industry's products were likewise hard hit. The economic conditions that had triggered the drop in vehicle sales were thus worsened by the ripple effect this decline had on the health of a widening circle of related business activities.

The postwar depression drove a number of companies out of business, some of them new ventures that had been formed in hopes of cashing in on the expected boom in demand for cars. Other failed companies, such as Saxon Motor Company and Jackson Automobile, had been formed before the war and had a legacy of problems. Their demise was as much due to the increasing difficulties in competing with a handful of strong firms as it was to the depressed market conditions of the early 1920s. But the stronger companies also suffered. Willys-Overland, saddled with heavy debts incurred as a result of John North Willys's ambitious expansion program, managed to survive the depression but never regained the market position which had seen its Overland cars rank second in sales only to Ford's Model T. Two other well-respected names, Maxwell and Chalmers, were saved only after Walter P. Chrysler, brought in by the companies' creditors, put them through bankruptcy. Chrysler shortly dropped the Chalmers name, and although the Maxwell car continued in production Chrysler used it only as a stepping stone to form a new company, bearing his own name, in 1925. When Chrysler three years later acquired the Dodge company, whose founders, the Dodge brothers, had died in 1920, he solidified the Chrysler Corporation's position and his own reputation in history for having put together the last successful entry in the American automotive industry, the third member of what became known as the Big Three.

Chrysler's emergence in the late 1920s was part of the trend toward consolidation that saw the number of companies producing automobiles rapidly shrinking at the very time when, after the country pulled out of the postwar depression, automobile sales were booming. Many famous nameplates with origins in the beginnings of the industry, such Haynes, Apperson, Winton, Locomobile, and Stanley, disappeared from dealers' showrooms. Relatively new companies with names such as Rickenbacker and Wills Sainte Claire, despite their production of excellent cars, went bankrupt by decade's end. By 1929 nearly 75 percent of all car sales were accounted for by three companies: General Motors (GM), Ford, and Chrysler.

The bigger companies prospered while the smaller firms struggled because the former were better equipped to adjust to the changing conditions of the automobile market, and none proved more capable of making that adjustment than GM. The 1910s had been Ford's decade, as the founder and his company perfected the means of mass produc-

ing one, unchanging model and with it had gained control of half of all sales. GM, meanwhile, had offered the public a variety of cars, but it was not until its founder, William C. Durant, was forced out of the company late in 1920 that the firm truly prospered. As a result of Durant's personal financial problems GM was placed under the managerial direction of Alfred P. Sloan, Jr., whose influence on the industry's development equaled, if it did not surpass, that of Ford and Durant. Sloan took the loose conglomeration of manufacturing operations that Durant had put together and devised an orderly method of managing the corporation that would be for many years the model for all large companies. Equally important was Sloan's move to assign each of GM's divisions a distinctive price range in which cars would be sold, from the Chevrolet at the low end to the top-of-the-line Cadillac. At the same time, by keeping the price of the costliest model in each range only a little below that of the lowest-priced model in the next range, Sloan encouraged buyers to trade up and gain the added status that supposedly came with owning a Pontiac, for example, for one who had previously driven a Chevrolet. Such an appeal to people's vanity was also at the heart of Sloan's emphasis on the changing annual model. This marketing strategy, which Sloan did not invent but did institutionalize, emphasized cosmetic changes in the outer appearance of each year's models and encouraged owners to trade their still-serviceable cars for more stylish new ones.

Sloan's strategy stemmed from his realization that the forces that had driven the market from its beginnings were no longer in force. During the industry's early years the manufacturers had been selling a product that people had never owned before. In such a market a manufacturer's main concern was to increase production in order to keep up with the demand. By the 1920s, however, the market for first-time buyers was decreasing as a percentage of total sales. For the growth in sales to continue, manufacturers were faced with the task of convincing owners to replace cars. Sloan's strategy of providing eye-catching new models in an increasingly bewildering variety of styles and prices—what he called a car "for every purse and purpose"—was successful in the buyer's market that developed by the mid 1920s.

In 1927 Henry Ford, who had continued to build the Model T long after it was obsolete, finally realized the new market environment demanded a new approach and a new product. Style and comfort began to be more important to car buyers than the rugged reliability offered by the Model T. At the end of 1927 the Model T was replaced by the Model A, a low-priced car that incorporated the styling changes the public had come to expect of cars in the 1920s. The car's mechanical features measured up to the high standards the public expected of a Ford car, but the Model A, although it temporarily enabled Ford to regain leadership in the low-priced field, did not have the long-lasting impact of the Model T. Instead, the Model A was replaced by the Ford V-8 in 1932, evidence that Ford realized the importance of offering new models to the public. But while Ford, however reluctantly, adopted Sloan's marketing ideas, he rejected suggestions that he implement some of Sloan's managerial reforms. The result was that the Ford Motor Company, under Ford's one-man management direction, dropped to second place in sales behind GM by the mid 1920s and by the end of the decade was facing a serious challenge from newcomer Chrysler for second place in the industry. This downward trend did not reverse until Henry Ford surrendered control of the company in 1945.

Despite the importance of annual model changes and other techniques that GM employed to stimulate sales in the 1920s, nothing did so more than installment buying. The requirement that buyers pay cash for a car had begun to break down prior to the 1920s; John North Willys in 1915 organized the Guaranty Securities Company, which financed purchases of Willys-Overland cars with one-third of the purchase price paid upon delivery and the remaining payments spread over eight months. This idea gained wide acceptance after the war, and by 1922, when a convention of such automobile-financing firms was held, it was estimated that there were as many as 300 such companies "of considerable size." Car payments were now spread over a twelve-month period, and in 1924 even easier terms were offered, permitting down payments of less than the normal one-third and monthly payments extended beyond one year. By 1925 three-fourths of all car purchases were financed on the installment plan, and although the tightening of credit requirements helped to drop the percentage of cars bought on credit to 58 percent in 1927, the figure shortly moved up to the 67-percent range where it would remain. Banks and other financial institutions which had earlier looked upon car loans as too risky were now glad to make money available for such purchases. Some automobile companies followed the example of Willys and created their own financial divisions to provide assistance to their dealers and customers. GM embraced the concept most fully by establishing in 1919 the General Motors Acceptance Corporation (GMAC), which became the giant of the industry. GMAC later accounted for 16 percent to 18 percent of all credit provided for car sales in the United States. Ford resisted this trend for some years but ultimately had to establish a similar credit facility in order to compete with GM.

Although the purchase of consumer products on the installment plan had existed long before there were automobiles, nothing helped to popularize such credit arrangements as did the enormous upsurge in their use to buy cars in the 1920s. The ability to buy cars on installment credit was also instrumental in creating an automobile-centered culture, a change which fundamentally altered American society. The importance of owning a car was demonstrated by the small number of cars purchased on credit that had to be repossessed—only 1 percent to 2 percent in the mid 1920s. "In other words," one banker declared, "the car stays sold, no matter what hardship may attend its keeping. It takes courage of no mean order to confess to the world that you had a motor and have lost it. Therefore the car is the last sacrifice to be offered on the altar of reverses." The installment plan made it possible for many people in the lower-income brackets to own an automobile. For such people who were fortunate to earn $1,000 per year, paying cash for even the cheapest car was impossible, but installment loans made it possible to spread that expense over an extended period. What percentage of the so-called working class took advantage of this opportunity in the 1920s is not entirely clear. By the end of the decade approximately 40 percent of the nation's families did not own a car. Some of these were families that did not feel the need to own one or who, because of some kind of disability, could not use one, but the great majority were people who simply could not afford a car, even under the best of credit terms. On the other hand many who probably should not have bought one still went ahead and did just that, committing one-fourth or more of their monthly income to their car payments. As Robert and Helen Lynd discovered in *Middletown* (1929) their classic sociological study of

Muncie, Indiana, in the mid 1920s there were a surprising number of households in that city that owned a car while still lacking indoor plumbing. But then as one person told another researcher, "You can't ride to town in a bathtub."

It was the increased mobility that the automobile provided to its users, enabling them to go where they wanted when they wanted, that was responsible for the dramatic changes in the way people traveled during the 1920s. The close community ties which had resulted from people having jobs, friendships, shops, and churches all within walking distance of their homes began to give way when cars made it easier to move outside such narrow confines. By 1929 a researcher studying a twenty-block section of Los Angeles discovered that there was "a new definition of a friendly neighborhood. . . . It is one in which the neighbors tend to their own business." One resident said he had "nothing whatsoever to do with [his] neighbors. I don't even know their names or know them to speak to. My best friends live in the city but by no means in this neighborhood. . . . We go auto riding, visiting and uptown to the theaters."

The horse, never widely available to the average city resident, was rapidly disappearing from urban areas by the 1920s. In Chicago, where in 1910 there had been 58,114 horse-drawn vehicles and only 13,725 motor vehicles, only 11,027 horse-drawn vehicles were reported in 1929 in contrast to nearly 500,000 motor vehicles. Already by 1920 the non-farm horse population had dropped to 1.7 million, a decline of almost half from the figure of 1910, and by the late 1930s one estimate placed the number at only 300,000. The horse-drawn carriage was a thing of the past, and although the use of the horse as a dray animal held out longer, with some milk wagons and junk dealers' wagons continuing to be seen into the late years of the century, the rapid development of the motor truck after World War I soon absorbed most of the freight-hauling jobs that had previously been handled by horses.

In rural areas, where the term "horse-and-buggy age" had much greater meaning than in urban districts, the story was somewhat different, with the horse population continuing to rise during the first two decades of the twentieth century and reaching a peak of more than 21 million by 1919. Twenty years later, however, fewer than half that many horses were found in rural areas. Many had been displaced by the rapid adoption of farm trac-

tors, the numbers of which increased from 147,600 in 1919 to 825,900 ten years later. Many more horses disappeared as farmers, once depicted as the staunchest opponents of the automobile, were quick to see in these vehicles the means of breaking out of the limited radius to which they had been restricted by horse-drawn conveyances. By the end of the 1920s the nation's 6 million farms included some 4.5 million passenger cars, a much higher ratio per household than found in the cities. For most farmers the 1920s were not prosperous years, but, as William Allen White declared, the American farmers "refused to become peasants. They will not take their families to town in two-wheeled carts. . . . They demand their picture shows, daily papers, radios and Fords—even at the price of more indebtedness."

Although rural, free mail delivery had been started on an experimental basis in 1896 it was only when the carriers were able to use motor vehicles, not horse-drawn carriages, that daily mail delivery, which had been available in the cities for many years, became available to most of the nation's farm families. In addition, although efforts to upgrade rural schools by combining a number of small one-room districts had begun in the pre-automobile era, the availability of motor buses in the 1920s was primarily responsible for the ability to draw sufficient students from a large enough area to provide the tax base needed to maintain the kind of schools city children had enjoyed since the middle of the nineteenth century. The crossroads country store and country church, like the familiar one-room school, also began to suffer as the farmer made use of his car to take advantage of the broader range of choices and services offered by the larger stores and churches in towns and cities.

At the same time that automobiles brought rural residents closer to the city, they also made the country more accessible to the city dwellers. Already in the latter part of the nineteenth century streetcars and interurbans had enabled housing developments to be opened on the outskirts of many cities. However, the growth of these suburban areas had been limited because their residents were required to live close to the fixed-rail transportation systems they depended on to reach their business and shopping destinations in the central city. In the twentieth century the automobile not only breathed new life into these suburban communities but also created new ones outside cities like Atlanta and

Houston where the lack of interurban service had prevented such settlements from arising. The automobile freed the suburban residents from the restraints imposed by their dependence on public transit lines. Although many continued to use those systems to travel into the downtown districts, parking their car at the suburban station, others drove into the city.

Estimates vary as to how many people were commuting by car in the 1920s, but the numbers were great enough to cause one transit executive in 1926 to declare that the $6 billion that had been invested in these lines could be written off as a loss. Just as steam railroads had destroyed stage coach lines, so too, he said, motor vehicles were wiping out electric railways. By 1927 electric railway mileage was off 10 percent from the peak mileage reached during the boom years of development earlier in the century. Interurban lines, which had flourished particularly in the Midwest and the East, were among the hardest hit and already by the mid 1930s had virtually disappeared in many areas. Similarly, the number of cities depending entirely on streetcars for their public transportation dropped from 369 in 1912 to only 11 by 1940. Motor buses, which transit companies had first looked upon as a competitor, were now adopted because they gave these companies greater flexibility to provide service in a far wider area than had been possible with rail lines.

For years bus riders more than made up for the sharp decline in the number of commuters carried by electric rail cars. But while the majority—sometimes an overwhelming majority—of people entering and leaving the central city district continued to use public transportation, by the 1920s the bulk of the passenger-carrying vehicles in cities were automobiles. The percentage of cars reached 87.2 percent in St. Louis in 1925, for example, when over 70 percent of the passenger traffic was by streetcars and buses. The result of this influx of motor vehicles was an increasingly serious problem of traffic congestion. Already in 1919 visitors to Los Angeles found that cars were "parked everywhere" downtown, "apparently for hours at a time," making it "practically impossible" to travel on cross streets or to find a place to park near their destination. A survey of Atlanta's downtown in 1923 found that of the thirty-five acres of street surface, fourteen were occupied by 2,236 parked vehicles. Attempts to alleviate the problem by providing

more parking, widening main streets, and encouraging people to use public transportation rather than driving their own cars met with little or no success. As a result, by the end of the 1920s the economy of the downtown districts was suffering as businesses began to move to the outskirts of cities where parking was abundant and where these commercial establishments were closer to their employees and customers in the suburbs.

The automobile's impact, however, was not confined to travel associated with the motorist's normal day-to-day activities. It seems doubtful that the demand for automobiles would have come anywhere near the levels that were reached by the 1920s if they had been viewed simply as a means of going to work, shopping, or socializing with acquaintances in the community. It was the expectation that the vehicle would be used for longer trips, whether for pleasure or business, that for most people justified the expense of such a purchase. By the 1920s the railroads, like the streetcars and interurbans, were feeling the effects as those expectations were realized. The growing use of motor trucks began cutting into the railroads' freight revenues, but it was the passenger revenues that were much more severely hit. The emergence of motor bus lines, such as Greyhound, accounted for some of this decline, particularly in short runs between nearby communities, but private automobiles were the major culprit. Traveling salesmen, long among the railroads' most frequent and reliable customers, discovered they could cover their territory more efficiently if they traveled by car and were not restricted by the railroad timetable. As for recreational travel, the same ability to schedule a trip according to one's own preferences, and not those of a carrier, made the automobile attractive. Many trips were taken by car that would not have been taken by train, because the car enabled people to travel in any direction without the advance planning required by rail travel. In addition train travel required payment in advance, while the expense of a car trip was spread out over a series of purchases in relatively small amounts made along the way. And with gasoline companies in the 1920s introducing the credit card, the payment of travel expenses could be postponed until the trip was over. Thus it is not surprising that the number of passengers on American railroads declined steadily after the peak year of 1920, while the number of passenger miles traveled by automobile, which had been only a quarter of rail passenger miles in 1922, was four times greater than rail passenger mileage by 1929.

Such an explosion of highway travel required a complete change in government attitudes towards roads. With the development of railroads in the nineteenth century, roads had come to be regarded only as avenues of local commerce between communities and the nearby farms. The maintenance of roads was delegated to local governments while the state and the federal governments concentrated on assisting the growth of the railroads, which would handle long-distance travel. Bicyclists in the late nineteenth century had been the first to press for roads that were designed for cross-country travel, but it was the motorists and the automobile companies that took up the campaign in the early twentieth century and finally began to see results by the 1920s. Paying for the surfaced, all-weather roads that automobile traffic required was the major obstacle. As long as the traffic on roads had been local, it made sense that the cost of maintaining the dirt roads be borne by the residents, mainly through assessments on property owners. But once those roads became part of a paved system designed to serve through traffic, it was manifestly unfair to continue using local taxes to pay for such improvements. Automobile license fees, which all states were collecting by about 1905, were the first user tax allocated for road work, but they proved totally inadequate. In 1919 Oregon began levying a tax on gasoline, and by the mid 1920s all states had followed suit, with a federal gas tax being added in 1933. The large revenues from the gasoline tax totally replaced other fees as the source of money. These funds helped pay for the networks of primary roads that were developed first by the states and then in the 1920s, as the federal government began investing massive amounts of money into road improvements, became part of a system of numbered U. S. highways spanning the country. A variety of surfacing materials was tried, but concrete was found to be most resilient, and it was in the 1920s that ribbons of such pavement became an increasingly familiar feature of the landscape.

Concrete highways, which were for motor vehicles what steel rails were for railroad trains, were only one of the additions to the landscape that resulted from the growth in automotive travel. The early motorists, as they had toured the country, had turned to camping along the roadside as an alternative to overnight accommodations in hotels which in most cases were not located close to highways and attracted a sometimes rough clientele. By 1915 communities began to open campgrounds for automobile tourists, providing not only a space for them to pitch their tents but also water and sanitary facilities, all at no cost. Because it was hoped the travelers would spend money in town, the campgrounds were usually located near the business areas. In the early 1920s more and more communities began charging fees for campground use in order to discourage transients from staying a long time without contributing to the community's economy. In response motorists in great numbers started to use private campgrounds, better located on the outskirts of town. These also charged fees but provided additional services, including cabins for those who had grown tired of living in a tent. By the end of the 1920s tourist cabins were rapidly replacing camping in popularity with motorists. With the cabins arose a whole range of new commercial establishments that were designed to provide not only lodging but fuel, food, and entertainment for the traveling public. These factors added to the growth of suburban communities already affected by automobile traffic.

The growth of highway construction and residential and commercial development in the suburban areas underscored the importance of the automobile as a dynamic force in the economy. Already in the 1920s the primary automobile industry, its production and sales, was overtaking steel as the most important sector of the economy. At least 10 percent of the annual income of Americans was estimated to be taken up in the purchase of automobiles and trucks and in the purchase of gas, oil, tires, parts, repairs, and other auto-related items and services. The auto industry absorbed 14 percent of the country's iron and steel, 50 percent of its plate glass, 85 percent of its rubber, 63 percent of its upholstery leather, 28 percent of its nickel, 25 percent of its aluminum, 21 percent of its tin, 13 percent of its copper, and 11 percent of its hardwood. Clearly automobile sales were the greatest contributor to the economic boom in the last half of the 1920s. But the reverse side of that picture was the sobering thought that a sharp drop in automobile sales could have disastrous consequences for the economy.

Just how disastrous those consequences could become evident in the final weeks of the decade, following the stock market crash in October 1929.

The automobile industry in 1929 achieved record sales of more than 5 million units, topping the previous record set in 1928 by nearly 1 million cars and trucks. However, fearing that the stock market crash portended a slow-down in the economy, the industry, led by Ford, sought to assure continued good sales by announcing price cuts within days after the bad news from Wall Street. But these moves were no more successful in stemming a sales decline than had been similar tactics attempted at the start of the postwar depression in 1920. Sales in 1930 were off by 2 million units and by 1932 had plummeted to a mere 1,331,860, a drop of 4 million from the 1929 record and the lowest yearly sales since the war year of 1918. Even worse, the wholesale value of the 1932 production was the lowest since 1915. After 1932, sales struggled slowly upward, reaching mid-1920s levels by the mid 1930s, only to slip back sharply again late in the decade, reflecting the break in the nation's recovery that occurred in 1937 and 1938.

The depression wiped out the bulk of the remaining smaller companies, including Pierce-Arrow, Peerless, Jordan, Stutz, Franklin, Marmon, Du Pont, Durant, Duesenberg, Auburn, Cord, Moon, Kissel, Gardner, Graham, Hupmobile, and the two remaining producers of electrics, Rauch & Lang and Detroit Electric. Some of these companies managed to keep going by switching to a different product, as Peerless did when the repeal of Prohibition in 1933 prompted it to begin brewing beer. The Reo company stayed in business by halting production of its automobiles and concentrating solely on trucks. Most of the automobiles that disappeared had been in the high-priced, luxury-car field that had garnered some 10 percent of the passenger-car market in the late 1920s but that was especially hard hit by the collapse of the economy in the 1930s. Aside from the Big Three's most expensive cars and a handful of imports, the only other luxury-car to survive was Packard, whose image was weakened, however, by the company's introduction of a lower-priced "Junior" Packard. The demise of so many luxury car firms also meant that among the hardest hit of the automobile parts suppliers, who, of course, suffered severely with the drop in car production, were the custom body companies who had prospered by supplying special bodies for expensive cars. Nearly all of these firms were gone by the end of the 1930s.

While the number of automobile companies declined dramatically during the depression, the number of automobiles registered in the country fell far less than many had expected. Since an automobile was for most people, unless they owned their own home, their most valuable possession, many had assumed that cars would be sold for desperately needed cash. Instead the depression provided evidence of how important the automobile had become to most Americans. Critical eyebrows were raised when people drove to government offices to receive public assistance funds, but it was for them a matter of pride to retain their car if at all possible.

The Big Three automakers suffered during the depression but, because of the disappearance of so many of the smaller companies, increased their market share to 90 percent, up from the slightly less than 75 percent held at the end of the 1920s. GM, under the astute leadership of Sloan, who moved from president to chairman in 1937 but remained chief executive officer, upped its market share to 40 percent. Although Chrysler himself was no longer in charge day-to-day, the Chrysler Corporation was in capable hands and the company moved into second place in the industry in 1933 and by 1936 had retired the indebtedness incurred when the company was formed in the mid 1920s. Ford suffered the most. The Ford V-8, introduced in 1932, recalled the technological innovations for which Henry Ford had been famous in earlier years, but it was one of the few positive developments for the company. Henry Ford's increasingly unpredictable and outmoded management style contributed to the company's fall to third place in automobile production in 1933, a position in which the firm remained until 1950.

Ford and his fellow industry heads not only dealt with the seriously bad economic conditions but also with the first major attempts to place political restraints upon the freedom they had always enjoyed to run their businesses as they saw fit. The National Recovery Administration (NRA), established shortly after Franklin D. Roosevelt took office as president in March 1933, sought to promote industrial recovery by having members of each industry draw up a code to establish standardized practices among the companies during the depression emergency and cut down on competition that might retard recovery. An automobile code was drawn up, although most of the companies felt that its provisions differed little from what the industry was already doing. Ford refused to allow his company to cooperate with this New Deal measure or to abide by the government-imposed regulations. Not wishing to fight a man who was still the most revered businessman in the country, the Roosevelt administration did nothing to force his compliance. It was secretly relieved in 1935 when the industrial code provisions of the NRA, which did not work anyway, were declared unconstitutional by the Supreme Court.

The Court's decision left standing another provision of the recovery act which guaranteed the rights of workers to be represented in bargaining with their employer by a union of their own choosing. This brought about a fundamental change in the relationships between employees and employers in the automobile industry. Labor unions in the United States, prior to this time, had been mainly confined to skilled workers. But the mass-production orientation of the automobile industry meant that the great bulk of its work force was comprised of unskilled or semiskilled workers, most of whom had had little or no experience with factories or unions and who were content with the good pay they received for a job that required little training. The craft union leadership had little interest in organizing these workers, and the automobile companies were successful in defeating the few attempts that were made to unionize these employees along industrial lines.

The onset of the depression in the 1930s caused many autoworkers to see a union as an agency that could protect them from the cost-cutting actions of the companies and could guarantee them a greater degree of job security. With the more favorable attitude toward union activities that was shown by the Roosevelt administration, labor leaders suddenly began giving more attention to the possibility of organizing workers in mass-production industries. Congress made this organization more possible in 1935 by passing the National Labor Relations Act (NLRA), which reinforced the earlier New Deal guarantees of the rights of labor with provisions that made illegal the heavy-handed means by which the companies had killed earlier organizing efforts. Late in 1936 the fledgling United Automobile Workers (UAW) union, a member of the newly-formed Congress of Industrial Organizations (CIO), launched an illegal sit-down strike at several GM plants in Flint, Michigan. In the weeks that followed, although it did not have the strength

to shut down the entire company, the UAW was able to close enough plants to cause a major decline in GM output. This economic pressure, together with political pressure exerted by President Roosevelt and Michigan governor Frank Murphy, finally led GM to admit defeat on February 11, 1937 and recognize the UAW as the bargaining agent for the company workers who belonged to the union. Most important, GM agreed to stop any further actions to prevent the union from recruiting additional members.

The Flint sit-down strike has been called the most important strike in the history of American labor, for it marked the first victory for the industrial union approach of the CIO and the beginnings of an era in which, in the words of labor historian Sidney Fine, "the decision-making power in large segments of American industry where the voice of labor had been little more than a whisper, if that, would henceforth have to be shared in some measure with the unions in these industries, and the trade-union movement as a whole would enjoy a higher status in American life than it ever had before."

For the automobile industry, the UAW's victory over GM was followed in a few weeks by a similar victory over Chrysler, but while most of the smaller companies also fell in line, victory was not so easily achieved at Ford. Henry Ford relied upon his tough security chief, Harry Bennett, to deal with the union, and on May 26, 1937, Bennett's men brutally beat union organizers who were seeking to hand out literature to workers leaving the Ford Rouge plant. Despite these and other illegal union-busting tactics, and the company being condemned for its actions by congressional committees and the National Labor Relations Board (NLRB), Bennett kept the union out for four years until a walkout of Ford workers in April 1941 finally forced Ford to agree to an NLRB-supervised referendum to determine if employees wanted a union. The result was an overwhelming vote in favor of the UAW, and although Ford, now enfeebled by a stroke he had suffered in 1938, at first threatened to go out of business rather than agree to a union contract, he was persuaded to give the UAW better terms than they had received from any other company. The unionization of the automobile industry was complete, and although prolonged strikes were occasionally needed to reach contract agreements the companies eventually came to see some positive benefits in unionization. The union now had the responsibility of enforcing many difficult contractual obligations on its members, obligations which had previously been the responsibility of the companies' personnel departments.

One reason why the Ford Motor Company may have been willing to accept the union in 1941 was that organized labor was becoming increasingly vocal in criticizing the federal government for awarding military contracts to a non-union company. World War II had been underway in Europe for nearly two years and, although the United States was not yet actively engaged, the buildup of the country's armed forces and the effort to supply arms had led to massive infusions of government funds to industry. From summer 1940 the automobile industry had been a major beneficiary of these war contracts, and with automobile sales by 1941 reaching levels not seen since the record year of 1929, the companies were once again experiencing prosperity.

With the entry of the United States into the war after the December 7, 1941 attack on Pearl Harbor, all civilian automobile production was halted by February 9, 1942. The industry, with its years of experience with the techniques of mass producing materials, was kept fully employed throughout the war by producing trucks, armored cars, other vehicles, and many products used in the war. Some, like the 25,000 tanks produced by Chrysler, bore some resemblance to the industry's peacetime products, but the industry also manufactured 85 percent of the helmets used in the war, 87 percent of the aircraft bombs, 47 percent of the machine guns, and 56 percent of the carbines.

None of the industry's contributions to the war effort attracted as much attention as that related to aircraft production. At one time it had been thought that airplanes would be a logical product for the automotive industry, but with a few exceptions the different nature of airplane manufacturing led to their construction being handled by a separate industry. However, the automobile industry was able to contribute to airplane production by turning out 455,522 aircraft engines, a product somewhat similar to automobile engines. It did build over 22,000 complete airplanes. The more than 8,500 B-24 Liberator bombers produced by Ford between 1942 and 1945 involved one of the most dramatic stories in industrial history. The company was beset by bitter conflicts between rival executive factions that sought to take advantage of the lack of leadership from the aging Henry Ford, who was now unable to function in any consistent executive capacity. In spite of these conflicts the Ford staff somehow exceeded its embattled production chief Charles Sorensen's goal of one bomber an hour.

The end of the war in summer 1945 ushered in a period in which the automobile industry not only had to change over from a wartime to a peacetime economy but had to adjust to market conditions it had not experienced for more than two decades. Because there had been no civilian passenger car production since February 1942 there were few cars on the road less than four years old, and 48 percent were more than seven years old. Car registrations during the war had dropped some 4 million, and many of those that were still registered were but junk. The result of the desperate need for replacements for the nation's automobiles was a seller's market in which almost any car could be easily sold. The smaller companies, which found it easier than the Big Three to shift to peacetime production, enjoyed their best years in a long while, accounting for about 20 percent of new car sales by 1948, twice the market share they had held at the end of the 1930s. Plans were also announced for the formation of several new companies that hoped to take advantage of the extraordinary conditions. But of these only Kaiser-Frazer made any significant impact, and only for a very brief period. By the early 1950s the seller's market had weakened, and the small companies simply could not compete with the Big Three. Efforts to survive by merger only delayed the end for a few years. Studebaker and Packard merged in 1954, but the Packard name disappeared within four years while the last Studebakers produced in the United States came out in 1963. The merger of Nash and Hudson to form American Motors in 1954 lasted longer, but with the purchase of American Motors by Chrysler in 1987 the winnowing process that had reduced the number of domestic automobile companies from many hundreds to three giant firms had been completed.

For the Big Three the postwar years were years of transition. It took them longer to transfer to peacetime production and to replace warmed-over 1942 models which were the best they could offer. By 1949 they had introduced new models, and with their vastly superior production and marketing facilities were on their way to regaining the 90-percent share of the market held before the war. Sales figures during these years repeatedly shattered the records set in the booming 1920s. For GM, Ford, and Chrysler this period also saw the old leadership give way to a new generation. At GM Sloan stepped down in 1945 as chief executive officer, and for more than a decade that position was held by Charles E. Wilson and then Harlow Curtice. These were production men who concentrated on the product rather than on managerial and cost accounting, as Sloan and his financial staff had done. The new emphasis made GM more than ever the trendsetter in terms of styling and mechanical innovation, but the firm's increased market share, up from the 40-percent range in the Sloan years to over 50 percent by the mid 1950s, raised demands by antitrust advocates that the giant firm be broken up. Fears of such a break-up led to a return to power of the financial staff under Frederic Donner in 1958, and actions to curb the power of the production staff and provide protection from anti-trust action.

GM's growth also caused problems for the management at Chrysler and Ford. Until 1950 Chrysler was still being managed by men who had been with the firm since its founding in the 1920s. Under these men the corporation had prospered by offering reliable, well-engineered cars with production costs that were less than those of the competitors. But in the postwar years Chrysler lost the cost advantage as its aging plants could not incorporate the new production techniques introduced by other companies. In addition the flashy styling that characterized the new GM cars and other companies' products caused more and more customers to abandon Chrysler models, which still emphasized the solid but stodgy engineering that K. T. Keller, Walter Chrysler's successor, continued to favor. By the time Keller resigned in the early 1950s the company's sales had dropped it to third place behind GM and Ford. Keller's successors, Lester Colbert in the 1950s and Lynn Townsend in the 1960s and 1970s, tried to regain lost ground through organizational reforms, bizarre styling, and overly-ambitious expansion programs that ultimately saddled Chrysler with a crushing debt. Drastic cutbacks and a government bailout under Lee Iacocca restored Chrysler's financial health in the 1980s by essentially being satisfied with a respectable number three position in the industry.

The Ford Motor Company seemed in even worse shape in 1945 when Henry Ford II took over from his grandfather. But in spite of the mistakes of Henry Ford's last years the public still retained a great deal of respect for the Ford name, which gave Henry Ford II a solid base on which to rebuild the company. In addition the family's control of the company enabled him to remove unproductive management and bring in able outside executives who could modernize the company. Colbert was never able to accomplish the same at Chrysler. The 1949 Ford maintained the high standards set by the Model T, the 1928 Model A, and the Ford V-8, while the Thunderbird in the 1950s and the Mustang in the 1960s strengthened the company by adding touches of glamour and youth appeal rarely found in Ford's past offerings. Mistakes were made, of course, notably the Edsel in the late 1950s. In the 1960s and 1970s Henry Ford II began to show signs of the unpredictable and sometimes irrational managerial style of his grandfather. Nevertheless, when he stepped down in 1979 he bequeathed to his successors a company that would in a remarkably short time become one of the major success stories in the booming American economy of the mid and late 1980s.

For the American consumer the 1950s began a period in which the automobile was once again in abundant supply and, despite the diminished number of automobile companies, in a variety of models never before seen. By the 1960s Chevrolet buyers had a choice of 46 models, 32 engines, 20 transmissions, 21 colors, and some 400 accessories and options. Other GM divisions offered a similar diversity of choices (as did Ford and Chrysler) which virtually guaranteed that no two cars would be exactly alike, leading the corporation's president, John Gordon, to declare that Sloan's goal of "a car for every purse and purpose" had been revised to "a car for every purse, purpose, and person." And indeed the number of people owning cars, either new or used, grew rapidly and spread into socioeconomic classes that had previously been largely excluded from the ranks of automobile owners. The number of households without a car declined from about 40 percent of the total in 1950 to about 15 percent in the 1980s. For the 85 percent that came to have a car, one car was increasingly not enough, with a third or more of these families owning two or more vehicles.

Until the 1950s the reaction to all this growth and to the culture it spawned generally had been favorable. But a more critical tone began to be heard as more and more questions were asked about the contributions of automobiles and the industry that produced them. There is probably truth to the contention of ardent defenders of the automobile that at least some of the criticism was elitist in its origins. It may not have been a coincidence that the noticeable increase in concern over the number of cars on the road accompanied the increase of car ownership by the so-called working classes. They preferred cars to the buses and commuter trains they were forced to use earlier, modes of transportation dubbed the "poor man's automobile."

Similarly it was only after the war, when the application of mass-production techniques to the building industry led to the appearance of huge new suburban developments, that for the first time those in the lower-income brackets had the opportunity to live in areas that previously only the more affluent could afford. Possibly in response, critics began to ridicule what they referred to as "suburbia" and the damaging effects such communities had on the central cities from which they drew their residents. Such developments were directly related to the acquisition of automobiles, which in nearly all cases were essential in traveling to their place of employment. The tract houses of the Levittown suburbs and the commercial developments they attracted did have an adverse effect on the health of most central cities, but they allowed a much larger number of people to live in less crowded circumstances. Also the freedom to move about in their own cars had earlier been largely the privilege of middle- and upper-income families. By the 1950s it was too late to halt the changes in the American way of life that had been brought on by the automobile, which had been accepted with relative equanimity when they first had begun to appear earlier in the century.

Some things could be changed, however. The criticism that the cars of the 1950s had become too big and heavy did lead the automobile companies to introduce in the 1960s slightly smaller cars with more restrained styling. However, the industry's failure to respond in a similar fashion to charges that it did not pay enough attention to safety and environmental concerns finally caused Congress in the 1960s and again in the 1970s to pass laws requiring seat belts and other safety features, as well as devices to reduce engine emissions, be included in all

new cars. The industry lost much public support by continuing to fight the imposition of these measures.

Other changes resulted from external developments, over which neither the industry nor the government had much control. The price of gasoline, which had never been a matter of much concern in the United States, suddenly escalated in the 1970s as oil-producing nations, on which the country had become more dependent, began using their power to control the supply of oil and increase prices. To guard against an oil shortage the federal government in 1975 adopted legislation requiring the automobile companies to double their average fleet fuel efficiency within a decade. The resulting smaller, lighter, aerodynamically-designed cars that appeared in the 1980s presented a dramatic contrast to the big cars that had dominated American automobile production in earlier decades.

The most serious challenge the American automobile industry faced in these later years, however, came from the growth of automobile production in other parts of the world. Most countries had lagged far behind the United States in the widespread adoption of the automobile, but after 1950 western Europe and Japan began to catch up with the United States. This worldwide growth led foreign producers to seek to tap the rich market for cars in the United States. Until this time the American automobile companies had never worried over imports, but in the late 1950s and 1960s the German-built Volkswagen demonstrated the appeal a well-designed and well-marketed import could have. In the late 1960s as the novelty of the Volkswagen Beetle began to wane, the Japanese arrived in the country with Toyotas and Datsuns and soon several other makes whose sales made Japan the leading importer. The price of these small, conventionally designed cars made them attractive to many American buyers. The rise in gas prices that began in the mid 1970s was also a great boon to the sales of the Japanese cars, which were already as stingy in their use of gas in 1975 as the American cars would be required to be ten years later. But perhaps the biggest boost to the continued growth of the volume of Japanese imports was their reputation as extremely well-made, reliable cars at a time in the late 1970s when evidence of the poor quality of American-made cars was widely publicized.

In the 1980s, to blunt criticisms that their exports to the United States were taking jobs away from American autoworkers, the Japanese voluntarily agreed to limit their shipments to the United States to slightly more than 2 million cars a year. At the same time, however, the Japanese companies began establishing branch assembly operations in the United States, which by 1990 could have a combined capacity to produce an additional 2 million vehicles annually. The Japanese will obviously be a major force with which the American automobile industry will have to contend as the centennial of its beginnings approaches in 1996.

Entries in this volume deal with developments in the automobile industry during the period from 1920 to 1980. Because of the desire to avoid as much as possible dividing a topic into two chronological segments to fit the period covered in each of the two automotive volumes, decisions had to be made concerning where to place entries whose subject matter overlapped these periods. With the exception of the entries for GM and Ford, which, because of their size and overall importance, were divided to provide accounts of their developments in the early and later periods, complete company histories appear in the volume covering the period in which the company began production. Thus Chrysler, which had its beginnings in 1925, appears in this volume, while Studebaker, which had its origins in the earlier period, will be found in *The Automobile Industry, 1896-1920*, even though that company continued in operation into the 1960s. Some major background entries,such as those dealing with production and mangagement, have been divided so that each volume contains information on topics pertinent to the period encompassed. In other cases, such as the entry on labor relations, which will be found in this volume and not in that covering the early history of the industry, the entry appears in the volume covering the period in which the most important developments relating to that topic occurred. Since it was decided that biographical entries would not be divided, judgments had to be made as to where to place biographies of individuals whose careers overlapped the two significant periods. Since Henry Ford's major accomplishments occurred before 1920, his biography will be found in *The Automobile Industry, 1896-1920*, even though he was a dominant figure in his company during the first twenty-five years of the period covered in this volume. On the other hand, Charles Kettering's biography appears in this volume be-

cause of the significant contributions he made in the development of research work at GM after 1920, even though Kettering is most famous for introducing the self-starter in the 1912 Cadillac. The cutoff date of 1980 does not exclude the inclusion of material relating to developments after that date when it is needed to provide complete coverage of an individual or topic. However, topics that had their beginnings after 1980 are not included as separate entries. Thus, entries for Honda and other Japanese companies that began assembly operations in the United States after 1980 are not included, although reference is made to these actions in the article on imports.

In an industry as large as the automotive industry, the decision as to who or what should be included has been extremely difficult. An attempt has been made, however, to include individuals and topics that are likely to be of the greatest interest to the largest number of users of these volumes. In this volume, biographies will be found for all who have served as chief executive officers of the three major companies, GM, Ford, and Chrysler, since 1920. All of the presidents of the United Automobile Workers union have also been included. Biographies of some of the leaders of other important companies who were active in the post-1920 era are also included, along with those of individuals who made important contributions to the development of the industry or who achieved special notoriety for their actions. As in the case of the first volume, an attempt has been made to provide coverage of all companies that produced automobiles in any significant quantities and that had their beginnings in the period from 1920 onward. Because of the highly specialized nature of the products of many companies engaged in manufacturing trucks and other commercial vehicles, the coverage of such companies is confined to the producers of the better-known trucks that are most commonly seen on the nation's highways. The enormous number of companies producing parts for motor vehicles precludes any coverage of these companies beyond one that must be, because of space limitations, extremely selective.

—George S. May

Eastern Michigan University

Encyclopedia of American Business History and Biography

The Automobile Industry, 1920-1980

Accessories

by James Wren

Motor Vehicle Manufaturers Association

At the turn of the century the typical horseless carriage consisted of an open carriage to which a -motor, driving chains, and a steering mechanism had been attached. All other equipment either necessary or useful for motoring was not considered to be the business of the seller and only a few of the items were available from the manufacturer at the time of purchase. The majority of accessories were available only from separate automobile-parts companies or from accessory equipment suppliers.

A scant few accessories such as tops, windshields, horns, speedometers, and dry cell batteries were available from the manufacturers but usually only at the time of purchase or when the vehicle was ordered. Access to the manufacturer after the purchase was available only to buyers in large cities where agents were present. The automobile makers were by and large content to concentrate on producing vehicles and letting the supplier and equipment companies provide accessory services.

Within a short time after the horseless carriage was introduced, outlets for extra equipment were established throughout the country. Carriage supply companies, boat equipment companies, hardware stores, and bicycle suppliers were quick to offer equipment and accessories for motor vehicles.

Astute suppliers began to differentiate between classes of accessories by describing them as essential or "necessary" accessories, or "useful accessories." A. L. Dyke, one of the nation's foremost automobile supply houses, defined "necessary" accessories as "those which protect the occupants from accidents or injury" while "useful" accessories were those which "add to the comfort and convenience of the occupants." The necessary accessories required on early motor vehicles were quite numerous. And in addition to the top, windshield, horn, speedometer, and dry cell batteries, accessories such as windshield wipers, bumpers, mirrors, shock absorbers, tire chains, tire-repair kits, chamois for fuel filtering, gasoline gauges, radiator gauges, and tool kits were needed for even minor auto trips. There were also available many antitheft devices.

There were other "useful" accessories which may have been considered necessary by many motorists. Those included storm aprons, caps, goggles, dusters, lap robes, and gauntlet gloves. Many owners also carried a complete array of spare parts and equipment for worry-free driving in remote areas. Often the purchase price of necessary accessories and spare parts was nearly equal to the list price of the car.

As American motor vehicles progressed toward the development of standardized parts and the maturation of the industry lowered prices for basic transportation, the accessory market expanded to include products which offered distinctiveness or provided symbols of status for the vehicle owner. Ford's stark and frugal Model T provides a case in point. While Ford offered few accessories and less variety, numerous companies throughout the country specialized in providing accessories, extra parts, and even special bodies for the car.

The advent of the closed car and the improvement of roads during the early 1920s changed the nature of the accessory market. These changes, along with the appearance of service stations in the countryside, eliminated the need for special driving clothes and the necessity of carrying extensive spare parts. The improved roads made it safer to append more frivolous and less durable accessories solely for the driver's pleasure or comfort.

Also playing a crucial role in the changing market for accessories was the changing market for automobiles. By the 1920s the pool of potential buyers who had never before owned an automobile was shrinking, and more and more automobile manufacturers faced the task of selling replacement vehicles. Alfred P. Sloan, Jr., the president of General Motors, instituted a management and product structure which addressed the problem. One of Sloan's tactics in his "a car for every purse and purpose" strategy was to place more emphasis on style, status, and comfort.

By the onset of the Depression following the 1929 stock-market crash, the basic automobile was fairly well equipped. The automobile had become primarily an enclosed car with roll-down windows, safety windshield, electric horn, shock absorbers, front and rear bumpers, rearview mirror, instrument panel with ammeter, gasoline, oil, and cooling gauges, electric starter, built-in trunk, and an adjustable driver's seat. One major accessory—the radio—introduced in the 1930s has dominated the accessory field since that time. Other luxury or comfort items quickly followed. During the 1930s the manufacturers began publishing accessory catalogs for their product lines. Eventually many of the items became comfort accessories, and the term optional (as opposed to standard) equipment emerged to describe modifications or improvements on existing equipment. Such improvements were the automatic transmission, power-operated convertible tops, power seats, and power windows. Additional power improvements, such as power steering and brakes, debuted in the 1950s.

During World War II and the postwar period of the 1940s and 1950s, a number of fad accessories surfaced. For example colored air deflectors became popular. Called "Breezies" they clipped onto the side vent windows both for decorative and functional purposes. Another fad was tinted sun visors. However, the overwhelmingly popular accessory in the 1940s, which every automobile supply and department store carried, was the automobile seat cover. It was available in a vast array of colors, textures, and materials to add a special decor aura to the interior and to cover the drab mohair upholstery of standard seats. Also during the 1940s, bumper guards, spotlights, steering wheel spinners, and fender curb feelers were popular.

By the 1960s special interior decor, coordinated hues in upholstery, exterior finishes, and performance options were offered by manufacturers; and the outside sale of individual accessory items dwindled. As the early "necessary" accessories became standard equipment on new cars, manufacturers included increasingly more accessories as standard equipment. Accessories began to be standard on luxury cars and would eventually filter down to lower-priced models.

In the 1980s items formerly considered luxury accessories and offered at extra prices have often become standard equipment, included in the purchase price of the automobile. Standard equipment usually now includes accessories such as antennas, automatic transmission, color-coordinated seats, steel-belted tires, body-color bumpers, front and rear bumper guards, computer command controls, window defoggers, front-wheel drive, fuel-injected engine, locking glove compartment, spare tire, standard battery, and other basic items.

After the automobile industry reached maturity in the 1920s, the marketing of automobiles more and more focused on accessories rather than performance. This trend became even more pronounced after World War II and only now seems to be abating.

References:

A. L. Dyke, *Dyke's Automobile & Gas Engine Encyclopedia,* twelfth edition (St. Louis, 1920), pp. 511-515;
Mort Schultz, "Accessories: A Century of Progress," *Popular Mechanics* (December 1985): 46-48, 58.

Archives:

Material concerning accessories is located at the Motor Vehicle Manufacturing Association, Detroit, Michigan.

American Austin Car Company

by George S. May

Eastern Michigan University

The American Austin Car Company was incorporated in Delaware in July 1929. It acquired a factory in Butler, Pennsylvania, and in May 1930 produced the first American Austins, which were modified versions of the English-made Austin Seven. As did companies that had earlier produced such foreign cars as Mercedes and Fiat in the United States, the American Austin Car Company operated under a license granted by the foreign producer.

The American Austin attracted a great deal of publicity because of its size, which was 16 inches narrower and 28 inches shorter than any other American car on the market. The attention was not translated into sales, however, and in 1932, after fewer than 10,000 cars had been produced, the factory ceased operations. A Georgia car dealer, Roy S. Evans, resumed production that same year and continued building cars until 1934 when the parts inventory was exhausted and the company was forced into bankruptcy. Production totaled approximately 19,500 cars and light trucks. Evans secured financial backing and reorganized the company in June 1936 as the American Bantam Car Company. The first American Bantam cars went on display in September 1937. Like the earlier American Austins the Bantam was a small car with an engine that was based on the English Austin. Evans and his designer, Alexis de Sakhnoffsky, incorporated sufficient changes to avoid having to pay royalties to the English company. Unfortunately, the Bantam suffered the same commercial fate as its predecessor and failed to generate much consumer interest. By 1940 sales amounted to only 6,700 units, these attained only by selling at a loss of $50 on each car.

The last Bantams were produced in 1941. In 1940, however, American Bantam won a competition to develop a four-wheel-drive vehicle for military use, based on designs of Arthur W. S. Herrington and Capt. Robert G. Howie of the United States Army. However, American Bantam's limited factory facilities caused nearly all of these vehicles, the famous Jeeps, to be produced during the war by the company's competitors, Ford and Willys-Overland. American Bantam turned instead to the production of two-wheeled trailers and finally became profitable. The company was bought by American Rolling Mills in 1956, ten years after Evans had sold his interests in the company.

To some, the failures of American Austin and American Bantam confirmed the traditional view that Americans would buy only big cars. However, that the first American Austin cost more than the more commodious Ford Model A probably hurt sales during a period when the car's excellent gas mileage performance was rendered unimportant by the cheap and plentiful supply of gasoline. A half century later the little car might have met a much different reception.

References:

Nick Baldwin and others, *The World Guide to Automobile Manufacturers* (New York: Facts on File, 1987);

George Edward Domer, "Good Things Did Come In Small Packages: The History of American Austin and Bantam," *Automobile Quarterly,* 14 (Fourth Quarter 1976): 404-429;

Beverly Rae Kimes and Henry Austin Clark, *Standard Catalog of American Cars, 1805-1942* (Iola, Wis.: Krause, 1986).

American Motors Corporation

by George S. May

Eastern Michigan University

The most important and enduring of the numerous automotive firms bearing the American name, the American Motors Corporation was formed on May 1, 1954, through the merger of the Nash and Hudson automotive companies. The merger was the product of the rapidly changing dynamics of the automobile industry following World War II. The brief seller's market that followed the war ended by the early 1950s, and the smaller independent companies found it increasingly difficult to compete with General Motors, Ford, and Chrysler. George Mason, president of the Nash-Kelvinator company, had foreseen this development at least as early as 1948 when he held discussions with A. E. Barit, president of Hudson, regarding a possible merger. In addition to Hudson, Mason also had his eyes on Packard and, according to some accounts, Studebaker, hoping to merge the four companies and compete with the Big Three by offering cars in all price ranges from the low-priced Studebaker through the Nash and Hudson mid-priced models to the top-of-the-line Packard, while Kelvinator competed in the consumer goods market with GM's Frigidaire division.

Nothing came of the 1948 Mason-Barit merger talks, but by the latter part of 1953 the rapidly deteriorating economic fortunes of Hudson left Barit and his staff little choice but to accept Mason's renewed bid to join forces with the healthier Nash organization. Following an announcement on January 14, 1954, that the directors of the two companies had agreed to a consolidation under the name of the American Motors Corporation (AMC), the stockholders approved the merger. The deal stipulated that three shares of Hudson stock be exchanged for two shares of the new American Motors stock, while each share of Nash-Kelvinator stock was to bring one share of American Motors stock, a further indication of Nash's dominant position in the marriage. The merger officially took ef-

fect on May 1, 1954, with Mason serving as president and chairman of the board of the new corporation while Barit became a director and consultant. Plans to consummate the merger of Studebaker and Packard continued, apparently part of Mason's grand plan to bring about the consolidation of the four auto firms. The merger of Studebaker and Packard was completed in November 1954, but Mason did not live to see it. His death on October 8, 1954, and the disappearance of his strong leadership effectively ended the possibility that the four major independents would merge.

Although it had been announced when American Motors was formed that Nash, Hudson, and Kelvinator would continue to exist and operate as separate divisions with their own dealer networks, economic realities soon modified that plan. The aging Hudson plant in Detroit was closed down in late 1954, and all auto assembly operations were concentrated in the Nash facilities in Kenosha and Milwaukee, Wisconsin, although the AMC offices remained in Detroit. Hudson models that appeared in the 1955 model year were nicknamed "Hash" since they were clearly Nash models with the Hudson name. In addition the survival of a full line of Nash and Hudson models was threatened by Mason's strong commitment to the compact Nash Rambler, introduced in 1950, which George Romney, Mason's successor as head of American Motors, believed in even more strongly. With the new corporation losing money steadily, Romney cut the ties with the past and abandoned the Nash and Hudson names with the 1958 model year. Rather than continue the charade that sought to convince consumers that AMC was offering two distinct lines of cars, all of AMC's models, with one exception, were given the name of the only model which had been doing very well, Rambler. The one exception was a small sports car, the Metropolitan, which was an early example of what would later be called

The 1953 Nash Rambler; the Rambler was the main focus of AMC's efforts to create a market niche for smaller cars

a "captive import" since it had been developed for Nash in the early 1950s by the Austin Motor Company of England and was produced in England for AMC from 1954 through 1961.

The little Metropolitan became a cult favorite of car collectors in later years, but Romney counted on the Ramblers to put AMC into the black. The Rambler Ambassador was a full-size V-8 model, while the 1958 Rambler American was the latest version of the compact model that Romney had been promoting throughout the decade. The combination of Romney's aggressive marketing of the Rambler compact as a sensible alternative to the Big Three's "gas-guzzling dinosaurs" and the desire of many buyers in a time of economic recession to find a less expensive, more fuel-efficient car enabled AMC in 1958, alone among the American auto companies, to register an increase in sales, with production rising to 217,332, nearly double the figure for 1957. With an increase to 401,446 in 1959, AMC became the fourth leading producer, behind Ford, Chevrolet, and Plymouth, and in 1960 as production topped 485,000 cars it supplanted Plymouth as the third largest automaker.

George Romney's gamble on the Rambler name paid off. Nearly all of the company's car sales were accounted for by the Rambler American compact, but its success, which enabled AMC for the first time to show a profit, alerted the Big Three to the increasing interest in smaller cars. All three automakers introduced their own compact models for

the 1960 model year and with the uniqueness of its compact eliminated, AMC's market share faded rapidly in the early 1960s, and the red ink again appeared on its ledgers. George Romney left the company in 1962 for a political career, and his successor, Roy Abernathy, was unable to reverse the downward trend in AMC's fortunes. As the public's interest in compact cars faded, AMC's efforts to compete with the Big Three's "muscle cars" and "pony cars" by introducing the Marlin, the Javelin, and the 2-seater AMX met with only limited success.

At the end of the 1960s, with company sales mired in the 250,000 range, AMC's new chairman, Roy D. Chapin, Jr., son of the principal founder of the Hudson company, sought to return to Romney's concept of offering an alternative to the Big Three. In 1969 AMC offered a new compact, the Hornet, which revived the name of one of the more successful of the last Hudson models. In 1970 AMC was the first American company to introduce what was called the subcompact, a car that was comparable in size with the Volkswagen and Japanese imports. The car, a Hornet with the back end cut off, was labeled the Gremlin. Chapin appeared in television ads touting the new models, a tactic which recalled Romney's vigorous promotion of the Rambler. But the Gremlin was on the market only a short time before the Big Three produced their own subcompacts. AMC lost its chance of receiving the same boost it had enjoyed with its pioneering offer of a compact in the 1950s.

The 1986 Jeep Comanche, an example of the type of vehicle Chrysler was seeking to acquire through its purchase of AMC

Throughout his tenure as chairman from 1967 to 1978, Chapin and the rest of the AMC staff struggled to make the company profitable. The company sold its Kelvinator division in 1968 and two years later acquired the Kaiser Jeep Corporation, a move that was crucial in enabling AMC to survive the difficult years of the 1970s and 1980s. The purchase of Kaiser Jeep not only gave AMC the immensely popular Jeep vehicle but also provided government contracts for the military trucks Kaiser Jeep had been producing. Full-size cars were dropped entirely from the AMC lineup in 1974 as the company renewed its commitment to cars that were not merely copies of bigger companies' offerings. With front-wheel drive and its unusual design, the sub-compact Pacer created some interest in the late 1970s; the Eagle, introduced in 1981, was the first regular American car with the four-wheel drive previously available only in vehicles such as the Jeep.

By 1981, however, hope for AMC's survival rested on the investments the French automaker Renault had been making in the company since 1978, which gave Renault effective control of the firm. In addition to opening AMC dealerships to Renault imports, the investments led to the production of the Alliance and the Encore, Americanized versions of Renault models, at AMC's Kenosha plant beginning in 1982. But the red ink continued to flow, forcing the 1983 sale of the AM General Division, producer of military trucks, for $170 million. Although both the Alliance and the Encore received some critical acclaim from the press, sales of the cars did not live up to expectations, and Renault's hopes of becoming a significant player in the American market were unfulfilled.

In 1987 Chrysler reached an agreement with Renault to acquire American Motors for $600 million. Chrysler's chairman, Lee Iacocca, had for a number of years been looking at mergers or acquisitions as a way of enabling his often troubled organization to survive. American Motors may not have ranked among his top prospects, but the acquisition did give Chrysler the Jeep, by far the most popular vehicle AMC had to offer, as well as a new, state-of-the-art AMC plant in Bramalea, Ontario. There was also some hope for a new prestige model of European design that AMC had been working on and that the new owners introduced late in 1987 under the Eagle division. Although Jeep and Eagle represented a continuation of names long associated with AMC, the American name disappeared, and, despite earlier promises that the Kenosha plant would continue in use, Chrysler announced in 1988 that the aging facility, hopelessly obsolete, would be closed. With its abandonment went the most visible reminder of a company that, under different names, had been in business since the start of the century.

References:

Nick Baldwin and others, *The World Guide to Automobile Manufacturers* (New York: Facts on File, 1987);

"Kenosha Suffers a Blowout in Chrysler 'Race,'" *Chicago Tribune,* January 31, 1988;

Richard M. Langworth, *Hudson: The Postwar Years* (Osceola, Wis.: Motorbooks International, 1977);

Tom Mahoney, *The Story of George Romney: Builder, Statesman, Crusader* (New York: Harper, 1960);

William Serrin, "When You're No. 4, You Sell Harder: The Roy Chapin Chapter of the AMC Story," *Detroit Free Press,* July 12, 1970.

American Trucking Associations

by William R. Childs

Ohio State University

Organized in 1933, the American Trucking Associations (ATA) has been the driving institution of private-public cooperation in the motor truck industry. Its history falls into the twentieth-century pattern of private-public activity that Ellis Hawley has labeled "associationalism." Throughout its history the ATA has focused on three general areas of cooperation: exchange of information to educate truckers, public relations to educate the public, and policy-making activities geared toward shaping regulation of the industry. It has been uncannily successful in controlling disparate interests and guiding them toward effective business and government programs.

Antecedents of the ATA trace back to the 1920s when the trucking business emerged. The structure of trucking was atomistic; numerous kinds of truckers appeared to utilize surplus wartime vehicles. At first truckers competed against one another for freight the railroads did not handle; later truckers competed directly with the railways. Such competition, whether in good times or depressed times, was unstable because numerous entries and exits negatively affected truckers, shippers, and, significantly, manufacturers. In the late 1920s the National Automobile Chamber of Commerce (NACC) attempted to bring stability to trucking by establishing statewide associations designed to curtail the tensions of competition. Such private-sector cooperation, the NACC leaders hoped, would lead to a predictable and steady demand for new trucks, as well as control the used-truck market. They

hoped also to forestall the growing movement on the state and national levels toward government regulation of the new business. The NACC sponsored seminars and published pamphlets designed to educate truckers on sound business practices. By the early 1930s, however, conditions in the industry had not improved, and some leading truckers became convinced that self-education was not enough and that a stronger effort to control trucking was necessary.

In 1933 the intensification of the depression and the New Deal response forced the state trucking associations to nationalize their efforts. Specifically the ATA was organized because some trucking leaders and federal government officials desired one central agency, through which the National Recovery Administration (NRA) would attempt to eliminate, through self-regulating efforts, the chaotic competition of the young trucking industry. The NRA experience did not work out as intended, but the ATA survived the failure. Through the ATA, truckers now had a central institution through which they could learn sound business methods and combine forces to shape federal regulation of their industry.

One personality in particular helped make the ATA a successful private-public institution. In 1933 Ted V. Rodgers emerged from the presidency of the Pennsylvania Motor Truck Association to galvanize the different interests comprising the trucking industry. With little formal education, but with business experience in the coal mines and as a contract trucker for the Great Atlantic & Pacific Tea Company, Rodgers not only led the trucking industry toward stability during the depression, but also helped orchestrate the industry's movement into federal regulation under the Motor Carrier Act of 1935. The ATA's president for its first fifteen years, Rodgers led the cooperative effort with the Interstate Commerce Commission (ICC) to devise a federal regulatory scheme. He continued his leadership role during World War II when the industry worked with the Office of Defense Transportation in the mobilization effort.

The structure of the ATA reflected a mixture of decentralized and centralized administration of associational activities. State associations represented the decentralized branches. Common carriers, private carriers, and contract carriers all had committees within each state organization which focused on the peculiar business problems of their constituents. The state offices furnished educational materials, offered discount services to members (insurance and equipment purchases, for example), and kept members apprised of political developments. State association members, while often at odds on policy issues, nonetheless tended to form a united front against attacks on their industry. This was facilitated by the work of the Washington, D.C., offices which formed the centralizing branch. The Washington staff monitored state activities, funneled information to the state groups, and managed the national lobbying efforts (such as testifying before Congressional committees). Both the state and national offices have invested resources into safety programs, including the sponsoring of "truck roadeos" in which the best and safest drivers competed for

awards. The decentralized-centralized structure has worked rather well, despite occasions when some groups within the ATA were lobbying for policies detrimental to other members.

After the end of World War II the ATA faced problems similar to those encountered in the 1920s and 1930s. Business education and public relations efforts continued. In policy matters the ATA worked to gain antitrust immunity for rate-making bureaus (granted by Congress in the Reed-Bulwinkle Act of 1948); lobbied for the interstate highway system (established in 1956); and unsuccessfully tried to forestall the deregulation movement of the 1970s and 1980s. Deregulation struck at the heart of what the ATA had been doing for nearly fifty years; the delicate balance of organized interests became unbalanced as deregulation aided some members (private and contract carriers, for example) at the expense of others (common carriers). In a sense, then, the ATA in the 1980s faced the same problems that had brought about the organization in the first place. The main difference was that the ATA had firmly established in a half century of activity the notion that private-public cooperation was the most effective method for determining controversies in the political economy.

Reference:
William R. Childs, *Trucking and the Public Interest: The Emergence of Federal Regulation, 1914-1940* (Knoxville: University of Tennessee Press, 1985).

Archives:
Material concerning the ATA is located in Record Group 9, National Recovery Administration, National Archives, Washington, D.C.

Annual Models

by George S. May

Eastern Michigan University

Since the appearance of Alfred P. Sloan, Jr.'s *My Years With General Motors* in 1964 the view that Sloan and General Motors (GM) were largely, if not totally, responsible for introducing the annual model changeover as a marketing strategy has been widely accepted by automotive historians and also by such scholars as Daniel J. Boorstin and David A. Hounshell. In his memoirs Sloan quoted at length from the record of a GM sales committee meeting on July 29, 1925, at which the topic of discussion was "Annual Models Versus Constant Improvement." Richard H. Grant, Chevrolet's sales manager, spoke out in favor of continuing to improve the models but without any thought that such improvements and changes should be geared to providing new models that would be introduced each year at the same time. Sloan admitted that there were "many disadvantages" to the yearly model, but in the mid 1920s, when a nearly saturated market was dictating the necessity of finding new ways of stimulating buyer interest, he declared that he found the idea of new models, introduced regularly each year near the close of the busy spring and summer sales period, to be an attractive method of arousing such interest. As he was GM president his views prevailed.

The impression Sloan gave in 1964 is that GM was pioneering a new idea that then spread through the entire automotive industry and was taken up by many other segments of the American economy. However, although Sloan and GM are entitled to considerable credit—or blame, depending on how one views this marketing approach—for refining the annual model technique, they cannot be credited with having invented a concept that had been well established long before there were any automobiles. Annual trade shows where new products were displayed had been used by numerous industries for many decades to stimulate the public's interest. The carriage industry in the nineteenth century utilized

shows where the companies that participated exhibited their new models, and the bicycle industry followed suit late in the century. At several of the annual bicycle shows in the late 1890s a few horseless carriages began to be shown; separate automobile shows were instituted in New York, Chicago, and other localities in 1900.

Horseless Age in 1904 noted that most manufacturers were waiting until the annual New York automobile show to come out with something new in their cars. The importance to the industry of annual model changes was already evident, with the success of the new cars, the trade journal declared, depending on the ability of the manufacturers to gauge the "fickle public fancy or fashion." By 1909 *Motor* was observing that, although one year's model had differed substantially from that of the following year in the early shows, dramatic changes were no longer the case, and buyers could be assured that the forthcoming 1910 cars would be little different from those of the 1909 model year.

The automobile shows continued to provide the one occasion each year when the new models could be seen and compared under one roof, but manufacturers soon were jumping the gun on the competition and introducing their cars ahead of time. On May 13, 1897, Col. Albert Pope held at a reception in Hartford, Connecticut, what was probably the first press preview of a new car when he unveiled the Pope Manufacturing Company's first models. As time went on, October came to be the traditional beginning of the new model year, but companies were not averse to coming out earlier than that if they felt it was to their advantage. One such introduction was that of Chevrolet's 1988 Corsica and Beretta models, which went on sale to car rental companies in the latter part of 1986 and to the general public early in 1987.

Whatever methods were used to introduce new cars, a trade writer in 1914 declared that the

The 1932 Ford V-8, the car which replaced the Model A and marked Ford's acceptance of the frequent model change

changes from one year to the next were practically nonexistent, but the industry had been so successful in promoting the concept of annual models that it had created "a state of mind toward automobiles that is similar to the state of mind of women toward changes of fashion in dress. 'Last year's car' has come to be as much a phrase of reproach as 'last year's hat.'" The Ford Motor Company was the industry's biggest holdout against the annual model strategy, but most companies were not persuaded by the huge success of the Model T, which remained essentially unchanged year after year after its appearance in fall 1908, that a static model would work for them.

In the industry's early years, when rapid advancements were being made in how the cars functioned and were operated, mechanical improvements were emphasized in distinguishing each new model. The 1912 Cadillac would go down in history as the car that dispensed with the crank by providing the first practical self-starter. Three years later, when the 1915 Cadillac models were introduced, its V-8 engine, the first to appear in an American car produced in any quantity, was another obviously significant feature that distinguished that year's Cadillac from those of previous years. Such mechanical breakthroughs were becoming less fre-

quent by that time, however, and in later years, aside from a few developments such as the perfection of an automatic transmission, whose introduction in the 1940 Oldsmobile became for that car what the self-starter had been for the 1912 Cadillac, the mechanical changes that were incorporated in the annual models were of relatively minor importance and made little impression on the average car buyer.

Already in 1913, when Howard E. Coffin, head of engineering at Hudson, surveyed the industry's new models for the 1914 season, he recognized the limited possibilities that lay in a continued reliance on mechanical changes to convince the public that the new models were better than the old ones. Increased attention, he declared, would have to be given to "annual style changes in body lines." As a result advertisements for the 1916 Hudson stressed not mechanical features but such "innovations" as the Hudson Road Cruiser's sleek "Yacht-like Body," its "Ever-Lustre Finish," and its "Roomier Tonneau." It was such features that GM, under Sloan, a decade later seized upon as readily recognizable means of identifying new models as different from those they replaced. Sloan recognized that the seller's market conditions that had prevailed during the industry's first quarter of a century were coming to an end. No longer could they count on any car they produced being snapped up by people who had never owned a car. Instead they now had to deal with a market in which most of their sales would have to be generated by persuading people to replace their old cars. Through cosmetic changes in the car's outer appearance the difference between the new and the old could be made evident to everyone. It did not matter that under that outer shell the mechanical features remained the same. For twenty-five years the Chevrolet models were powered by the same 6-cylinder engine introduced in the 1929 models, but while the engine, nicknamed the "cast-iron wonder," did not change, the Chevrolet bodies changed drastically during that period, giving the new models the appearance of being more up-to-date. Sloan was quite correct in believing that many people would buy these new models rather than continue to drive their old ones which still were performing quite adequately but which everyone could see were several years old.

GM's effective use of this marketing strategy made it the volume leader in the industry by the latter part of the 1920s. Even Henry Ford had to agree that his Model T looked hopelessly outdated. The vehicle was abandoned in 1927 and was replaced later that year by the Ford Model A, the lines and styling of which were closer to what was expected of cars in the 1920s. The Model A was an outstanding car, but its replacement by the Ford V-8 in 1932 was clear evidence that Ford had been forced to move away from the unchanging Model T marketing approach to that of the rapid change in models that GM and most of the rest of the industry were now following.

The annual model changeover always drew criticism from those who thought it a wasteful practice to encourage people to dispose of cars that were still in fine operating condition. Another criticism of the changeover was that it caused hardship for many automobile workers who were laid off for weeks each year while the factories were geared up to produce the new models. But it was not until the 1950s that the increasingly nonfunctional styling changes to distinguish the new models from those of the previous year brought a strong reaction. The extravagant use of chrome trim was one of the most popular devices, but the tail fins GM introduced in 1948 became the symbol of the era as all three of the big automakers eventually competed to have the tallest of these rear-end protuberances. Subsequent decades saw a return to more restrained styling, especially as regulations that mandated safer, more fuel-efficient vehicles led to an increased emphasis on more functional design. Automakers also worked to cut expenses, causing less emphasis on marked changes in the appearance of each year's new models. Nevertheless, although much of the excitement that had once surrounded the unveiling of the new cars was no longer present by the 1980s, the annual model remained an entrenched part of the industry's routine, and when strikingly new models were introduced, such as Ford's aerodynamically designed Taurus, the technique could still generate an increased volume of sales.

References:

Daniel J. Boorstin, *The Americans: The Democratic Experience* (New York: Random House, 1973);

Joel W. Eastman, *Styling vs. Safety: The American Automobile Industry and the Development of Automotive Safety, 1900-1966* (Lanham, Md.: University Press of America, 1984);

James J. Flink, *The Automobile Age* (Cambridge, Mass.: MIT Press, 1988);

David A. Hounshell, *From the American System to Mass Production, 1800-1932* (Baltimore: Johns Hopkins University Press, 1984);

George S. May, *The Automobile in American Life* (forthcoming, 1990);

Alfred P. Sloan, Jr., *My Years With General Motors* (Garden City, N.Y.: Doubleday, 1964).

Automobile Manufacturers Association

by James Wren

Motor Vehicle Manufacturers Association

The Automobile Manufacturers Association (AMA), the industry trade association, first came into existence in 1900 as the National Association of Automobile Manufacturers (NAAM). The NAAM merged in 1913 with the Association of Licensed Automobile Manufacturers (ALAM), a similar group which had been founded in 1903, to form the National Automobile Chamber of Commerce (NACC). The NACC continued its activities until October 3, 1934, when it became the AMA.

As a trade association the AMA was dedicated to promoting the use of the automobile and also to working for government and market conditions favorable to the development of the industry. It also sought to coordinate the activities of the industry and to act as a clearinghouse for information. The AMA promoted the construction of government-sponsored highways, including the interstate system begun in the 1950s, the standardization of parts, and the establishment of the National Safety Council. The association also conducted public education programs, sponsoring the annual National Automobile Show from 1900 until 1962 except for a hiatus during World War II.

The AMA retained a permanent staff, but its directors and officers were generally chosen from the roster of automobile company presidents and chairmen. Until 1934 the association's offices were located in New York, but upon the formation of the AMA the headquarters moved to Detroit with branch offices being maintained in New York and Washington, D.C. Membership in the association initially consisted of the major automobile manufacturers, excepting Ford and American Bantam, and several smaller firms. Ford, because of Henry Ford's refusal to join, did not join the AMA until 1956. The AMA was financed by dues determined by a percentage of each member's sales.

The association was originally organized into specialized departments under expert managers.

The general manager was responsible to the board of directors and the officers, which included the president, two vice-presidents, a secretary, and a treasurer. In 1967 the duties of the general manager were merged into the office of the president. The New York office was specialized into an Ocean Rate department and the Washington office assigned duties in government relations and international topics.

Although the AMA has coordinated many projects which have benefited the industry, some of its most helpful efforts have come in the areas of automotive and highway safety, standardization, engineering standards, and air pollution. The Automotive Safety Foundation was established in 1937 by the AMA's Traffic Planning & Safety Committee and played a major role in studying the problem of traffic safety. In conjunction with the Society of Automotive Engineers, the AMA helped establish a standard bumper height. The AMA also helped standardize automotive safety equipment through its development of the sealed beam headlamp in 1939; the design was further improved in 1954.

Complementing its activity in the safety area, the AMA continued monetary support for special industry programs. In 1960 the AMA spent $1.706 million to promote traffic and highway safety. In the 1970s the AMA donated $1 million to the Highway Safety Research Program at the University of Michigan. Of course many of the AMA's efforts were undertaken in order to preclude government intervention into what the automobile manufacturers thought of as their legitimate business concerns. But in 1966, with passage of the National Highway Safety Act imminent and motor vehicle safety standards not far behind, the AMA through its engineering committees worked hard to make these standards reasonable to implement.

The AMA continues its efforts to promote the automobile industry and its reasonable regulation under its new name, adopted in 1972, of the Motor Vehicle Manufacturers Association.

Archives:
    Material concerning the AMA and its affiliated organizations is located at the Motor Vehicle Manufacturers Association offices in Detroit, Michigan.

Harry Hoxie Bassett

(September 11, 1875-October 17, 1926)

by Richard P. Scharchburg

GMI Engineering & Management Institute

CAREER: Clerk (1891), assistant treasurer (1891-1893), assistant general manager, Remington Arms Company (1893-1905); assistant superintendent (1905-1906), assistant factory manager (1906-1907), factory manager (1907-1912), general manager, Weston-Mott Company (1912-1916); assistant general manager, Buick division (1916-1919), general manager, Buick division (1919-1920), vice-president and director (1919-1926), president, Buick division, General Motors Corporation (1920-1926).

Harry Hoxie Bassett was the second of three children born to William L. and Mary Babcock Bassett. He was born in Utica, New York, on September 11, 1875, and received his early education at Utica and at Ilion, New York. Just before his graduation in 1891 from high school, Bassett was offered a job as an office boy at the Remington Arms Company. Upon his graduation he was promoted to assistant billing clerk, where he showed an ability to work with figures. He flourished in the position and was soon promoted to be an assistant treasurer.

Bassett continued working at Remington for the next fourteen years, serving from 1893 to 1905 as assistant general manager. At the turn of the century Remington was interested in making parts for the new horseless vehicles that were beginning to be manufactured in increasing numbers. The company had already ventured into the bicycle field and later was to build its own motorcar. At the beginning of the twentieth century industry was undergoing rapid changes in order to accommodate the increasing demand for the motorcar. Bassett was in a good position to take part in such changes at Remington.

Harry Hoxie Bassett (courtesy of Automotive History Collection, Detroit Public Library)

His aptness for figures and his careful study of factory operations and cost analysis soon set Bassett apart from other contract cost estimators. Before long he began to develop cost-cutting methods for the factory and suggestions for process improvements. Another opportunity for Bassett was about to become available.

In 1905 the Weston-Mott Company of Utica, New York, already solidly established in making wire wheels and rims for bicycles, carriages, and other vehicles, was considering building a plant in Flint, Michigan, to better supply automobile axles, wheel rims, and hubs to the new Buick Motor Company, the company's largest wheel and axle customer. Charles Stewart Mott, then general manager and president of Weston-Mott, had been an early and active believer in the future of the motorcar, especially those powered by the internal-combustion engine. Convinced that the motorcar industry would be centered in the Midwest, Mott decided to move his manufacturing operations to Flint, Michigan, at the invitation of William C. Durant, one of Flint's volume producers of carriages who was about to cast his future with Buick. The nascent Buick Motor Car Company had been brought to Flint by James H. Whiting, another carriage maker. The Buick operation was temporarily installed in underutilized buildings owned by the Flint Wagon Works until a building could be constructed.

Knowing that intelligent manpower was needed to staff the new Weston-Mott axle factory in Flint and alerted to the qualities of Bassett through Hubert Dalton, Weston-Mott's superintendent, Mott asked Bassett to join his organization with a prospect of becoming assistant superintendent. Bassett accepted and was placed in charge of the Utica plant. When the Weston-Mott factory was completed in 1906, Bassett was installed at Flint as assistant factory manager; a year later he became factory manager. Weston-Mott's rapid growth caused great difficulty in keeping pace with the orders. A whole new factory manpower development program had to be instituted while the plant operations were still being shifted from Utica.

The new plant in Flint had started operation with a 200-man payroll, but by 1912 this had grown to a 2,300-man list. At the end of the same five-year period Weston-Mott was producing 80,000 axle sets, with its product becoming the standard of the industry. In 1912 Bassett was also promoted to be Weston-Mott's general manager, and under his leadership the latest and best metallurgical practices were habitually tested and used. Case-hardening, machining to ordnance specifications, chrome-nickel steel and related technical items were common practice. Bassett also encouraged new methods and processes, in particular in the building of running gear, so that when he later became assistant general manager of Buick in 1916, this interest and experience naturally was extended to engines and transmissions. In order to keep a step ahead of the competition, Weston-Mott established its own metallurgical analysis laboratory, one of the first in the industry.

When General Motors (GM) was organized in 1908 by William C. Durant, Mott had sold 49 percent of the Weston-Mott stock to GM. Since its formation GM had brought into the new organization the other firms purchasing Weston-Mott axles. When in 1913 Weston-Mott produced almost all of its axles for GM cars, Mott exchanged his remaining Weston-Mott holdings for GM stock. Weston-Mott was merged completely with the Buick organization in 1916, and Mott was elected a director of GM. Mott then offered his considerable abilities for public service, leaving the day-to-day management to Bassett, who became assistant general manager of Buick following the merger.

Bassett stayed with the Buick group and became its general manager on May 1, 1919, following Walter Chrysler's departure from Buick after a disagreement with Durant. In June 1919 Bassett was made a vice-president and a director of GM, in addition to serving as general manager of Buick. In January of the following year he was elected president of the Buick Motor Company. Under Bassett's leadership the emphasis on quality was continued and intensified, the engineering staff being nearly doubled in less than three years. Attention to materials and manufacturing techniques spread to all of the Buick mechanical parts. Buick factory engineering now included the heat treatment of nickel-steel transmission gears, machining of chrome-nickel-steel transmission shafts, and the making of special hard-alloy bronze bearings. Some of these techniques had been developed earlier at Weston-Mott and transferred to Buick by close contact between the engineering staffs of the two companies before consolidation.

The merger of Weston-Mott with Buick brought about a slow, but general, shift of trained personnel, the erection of new processing buildings, development of new departments, and expansion of sales facilities. Bassett's leadership resulted in Buick becoming the leading manufacturer of automobiles in its price range. The year before Bassett joined Buick, production totaled 43,946 cars. In 1917 output totaled more than 100,000 units. By 1926, six years after Bassett became president of Buick, the company was selling more than 200,000 cars a year, an indication of Bassett's executive skill and his ability to lead an organization.

Bassett's training, gained through experience rather than formal education, was well suited for the positions he held during his career. He had an exceptional understanding of men and kept his office open to his employees. He also spent much of his time in the factories, familiarizing himself with his organization and maintaining a personal acquaintance with thousands of the workers. Throughout his working life he was keenly aware of the needs of those who worked in the factories he supervised. For example, he was instrumental in the establishment by GM of the GMI Engineering & Management Institute at Flint. The school resulted from Bassett's interest in the Industrial Mutual Association (IMA), an organization of factory men having a membership of more than 20,000, which maintained comfortable club quarters and furnished mutual benefits to members at cost. The IMA established a trade school as one of its activities, and Bassett studied it carefully. As a result of his observations, Bassett recommended to GM that it take over the college and offer special courses in automotive and mechanical technology and engineering. His recommendations were accepted, and in 1926 ground was broken for what later became the GMI Engineering & Management Institute, an independent, private college granting degrees in mechanical, industrial, and electrical engineering and industrial management.

Besides his connection with the Buick Motor Company and GM, he was a director of the Genesee County Savings Bank and the Workmen's Mutual Bank of Flint. He was also a member of the Flint Country Club, the Detroit Athletic Club, and the Society of Automotive Engineers.

Bassett's talents at management of production were not always confined to Buick. In 1926 he and four other General Motors executives traveled to Germany to make recommendations for a complete reorganization of GM's Opel Division. The group also spent considerable time conferring with executives of General Motors Export Company. They also met in Paris for an automobile exposition in which GM cars were to have a prominent place. On arrival in Paris, Bassett dined with the others in his party, and on the following day he was taken ill and admitted to the American Hospital at Neuilly. Double bronchial pneumonia developed, his condi-

tion steadily worsened, and he died on October 17, 1926.

Not since the death of the Dodge brothers in 1920 had the automobile industry been so stirred by the passing of an individual. Condolences poured in to the Bassett family from Bassett's many friends and associates in the automotive industry. Buick, under Bassett's eleven years of leadership, had become an industry leader. When he became president of Buick in 1920, the Buick plant immediately began an expansion program designed to increase its capacity to 750 cars a day from its limit of 500. Six years later the company was building 1,200 cars daily and was expanding to increase the number to 1,500. This phenomenal expansion was a fitting tribute to Bassett's management ability.

Like many other leaders in the automotive industry, Bassett rose from modest surroundings to become the head of one of the largest automobile manufacturing businesses in the world. Contemporary accounts of his death seldom fail to mention that, in addition to his vast business responsibilities, he was a man who always found time for his friends. He also devoted some of his energies to worthwhile civic projects, efforts which gained him the respect of his fellow townsmen, business associates, and the 23,000 employees who had worked for him.

References:

Terry B. Dunham and Lawrence R. Gustin, *Buick: A Complete History* (Princeton: Princeton Publishing, 1980);

B. C. Forbes and O. D. Foster, *Automotive Giants of America* (New York: B. C. Forbes Publishing, 1926);

C. B. Glasscock, *The Gasoline Age* (Indianapolis: Bobbs-Merrill, 1937);

Arthur Pound, *The Turning Wheel* (Garden City, N.Y.: Doubleday, Doran, 1934);

Bernard A. Weisberger, *The Dream Maker: William C. Durant, Founder of General Motors* (Boston: Little, Brown, 1979).

Archives:

Material concerning Bassett is located in the C. S. Mott Papers and other collections in the GMI Alumni Foundation Collection of Industrial History at the GMI Engineering & Management Institute, Flint, Michigan.

Harry Herbert Bennett

(January 17, 1892-January 4, 1979)

by George S. May

Eastern Michigan University

CAREER: U.S. Navy (1910-1916?); artist (1917), service department and personnel (1918-1945), director, Ford Motor Company (1943-1945).

Harry Herbert Bennett, who probably wielded more power in the Ford Motor Company in the 1930s and the first half of the 1940s than any one person except possibly Henry Ford, was born in Ann Arbor, Michigan, on January 17, 1892. When Bennett first appeared in *Who's Who in America* in the 1940-1941 edition the year of his birth was given as 1893. That year continued to be listed, presumably with Bennett's approval, until the 1946-1947 edition, the last time his biography appeared, when the date was changed to 1892. This discrepancy is typical of many that abound in information about Bennett that help create an aura of mystery and uncertainty about one of the most bizarre figures in American automotive history.

Bennett was the only son of Vern C. and Gene Bangs Bennett. His father was killed in a barroom brawl, an unhappy end that nevertheless fits in rather well with the pride Bennett took in his own reputation as a fighter and tough guy. Bennett's mother remarried a University of Michigan professor and had hopes her son would pursue a career in the arts. As a boy Bennett sang in the choir at Ann Arbor's St. Andrew's Episcopal Church and developed a liking for music which led him in later years to play the saxophone in a band he organized. He is also said to have taken art classes at the Detroit Fine Arts Academy and the Cleveland Art School, and it was as an artist that he was first employed by the Ford company. A more important influence on his career at Ford, however, resulted from his enlistment in the navy when he turned seventeen. While Bennett was in the navy he learned to box. Only 5 feet 6 inches tall, Bennett all his life was very conscious of his small stature. As a boy, he said, he had needed help when he got into scuf-

Harry Herbert Bennett

fles with bigger boys, but the navy taught him how to take care of himself, and he boxed for the fleet as a lightweight, under the name "Sailor Reese."

Bennett's reputation as a fighter had something to do with his employment at Ford, although how and when that took place is one of those cloudy areas that remain to be cleared up. The most familiar story, related in Bennett's ghost-written autobiography, *We Never Called Him Henry,* has Bennett, still in the navy, getting into a street fight in New York while on shore leave. The Hearst newsman, Arthur Brisbane, happened to see the fight, and he rescued Bennett from the police, convincing them that Bennett had only jumped into the fray to help a friend. By chance Brisbane had an appointment to see Henry Ford, and when he brought Bennett along with him Ford was so interested in the story of the battling sailor that he offered Bennett a job as a security man—presumably to begin after he was released from the navy.

Harry Bennett began work at Ford in 1917, not as a guard but as an artist in the photography department. In 1918, however, William S. Knudsen, who was in charge of Ford's war time production of Eagle sub-chaser boats, was looking for someone to check on watchmen whom he suspected of stealing materials. A Ford worker told him, "We have just the man for you—an ex-champion of the U.S. Navy named Harry Bennett." When Bennett was brought to Knudsen's office, Knudsen, who was expecting somebody of impressive size, said with scorn when he saw the small ex-sailor, "I thought you were going to bring me a big prizefighter." A short while later, when Henry Ford came through the Eagle plant with Knudsen, Bennett caught Ford's attention by attacking and knocking down a bigger worker who was accused of having beaten a young boy. Bennett seized other opportunities to impress Ford with deeds of bravado, and he was rewarded by being named head watchman at the vast Rouge complex Ford was building in Dearborn.

Typically Bennett exaggerated the job he had been given, listing his role in the company from 1918 onward as "Director of Personnel." Aside from the fact that job titles were not used in a company whose boss ridiculed the need for organized management, such as General Motors (GM) installed in the 1920s under Alfred P. Sloan, Jr., responsibility for hiring and firing employees, although it ultimately became one of Bennett's duties, was not likely to be given to an inexperienced new employee. Bennett first had to prove himself, and he accomplished that by demonstrating an ability to get things done, no questions asked. Initially, as a number of top executives were leaving or being forced out, Bennett moved ahead by playing up to Charles Sorensen, who he correctly saw had the best chance of winning the struggle to be, next to Ford, the top person in the company. One employee recalled: "If Charlie Sorensen pointed his finger in a direction, Bennett would go into action

without thinking. . . . I remember on one occasion Sorensen sent Bennett after someone he saw standing around apparently idle. He said, 'Go and get rid of that fellow.' Harry came running back boasting, 'I just fired fourteen men going down that aisle.' Very pleased, Sorensen said, 'Good boy, Harry, good boy.' "

By the mid 1920s Bennett was head of what was euphemistically called the Service Department at the Rouge complex. He began hiring men who could be and were used not only for normal watchmen's duties but also to deal with a host of other matters of concern to the company. Clearly, also, Bennett, not satisfied with being Sorensen's man, sought to make Ford aware of how useful he could be to him, and the result was that an increasingly close relationship began to develop between the two men. With the end of Model T production in 1927 and the shift of the main Ford production from Highland Park to the now completed Rouge complex, Ford's regular trips away from Dearborn to Highland Park ended, and Bennett began driving over to Ford's Dearborn home or telephoning him each morning to inquire if Ford needed anything of him. This became an almost daily routine that continued until 1945, as long as Ford retained control of the company.

Like Sorensen, Ford soon learned that he could count on Bennett to do what he was asked to do. "Harry, never try to outguess me," Bennett said the automaker told him shortly after the ex-sailor had been hired. "You mean I should never try to understand you?" Bennett asked Ford, to which Ford replied, "Well, that's close enough." Bennett, however, seems to have tried to interpret what Ford would like to have done, rather than always waiting for a direct order. Thus, one year when they visited the Ford exhibit at the Michigan State Fair and Ford expressed disappointment that it simply displayed Ford products and was not the kind of state-fair exhibit Ford had remembered seeing as a farm boy, Bennett had the cars and machines replaced by livestock, crops in full bloom, and rustic attendants. He drove Ford over to the fair the next day, and when Ford saw the revamped exhibit, he said, "That's nice, Harry."

Bennett's actions were not usually of such an innocuous nature, however. In spring 1927 Bennett and his men, with or without any direct orders, saved Ford from the embarrassment of being put on the witness stand in the libel suit brought by

Aaron Sapiro against Ford for anti-Semitic statements published in Ford's newspaper, the *Dearborn Independent*. A mistrial was called as a result of one juror's remarks that reflected the jury tampering actions initiated by Bennett. Then before a new trial was held, Bennett was part of negotiations that led to the issuance of what some called the "Ford Retractor," in which Ford apologized to Sapiro and to Jews in general for the notoriously anti-Semitic stands his paper had been publishing throughout the 1920s. When Bennett telephoned Ford and tried to read the statement, telling Ford that the wording of the apology was "pretty bad," Ford told him, "I don't care how bad it is, . . . you just settle it up. The worse they make it the better."

It was two events in spring 1932 that solidified the hold Bennett had over Ford. The kidnapping and murder of the Lindbergh baby aroused Ford's fears that his grandchildren might meet the same fate. These were the children of Ford's only child, Edsel, and it would appear that part of the attraction Harry Bennett held for Ford was that he was the kind of man that Ford had always hoped his son would be but which he was not. Ford liked rough, tough-minded men who were unswerving in their loyalty to him. Bennett was just such a man while Edsel, who was about the same age as Bennett, was sensitive and liked to move in high society circles that his father disdained. Though Edsel was often appalled by some of his father's actions, he never stood up to him, even though he was technically president of the company from 1919 to his death in 1943. Now in 1932, therefore, Ford, rather than leaving the care of his grandchildren to their father, placed their security in the hands of Bennett.

Bennett by this time had built up a security force that was composed of a great many thugs, ex-convicts, and other unsavory characters. In his memoirs Bennett sought to shift at least some of the blame for such a hiring policy onto Henry Ford, who he claimed had a "morbid" and even perverted fascination with criminals and crime. This is certainly unfair to Ford, whose interest in criminals seems to have stemmed from his surprisingly enlightened hiring policies that had led him to be far ahead of his competitors. Ford led the industry in hiring large numbers of blacks, in finding a place for disabled workers in the company, and in believing that people who had made a mistake were entitled to have a chance to rehabilitate themselves. It was

Bennett who was fascinated with the criminal element and with the contacts he gained with the underworld, contacts that enabled him in the late 1930s to convince even J. Edgar Hoover and the FBI that he was a valuable source of information for their investigative activities. It was these contacts, both within the Ford Security Department and among organized crime figures in the Detroit area, that undoubtedly made Bennett able to assure the safety of the Ford family, although his methods were often ruthless. William Clay Ford recalled the time his older brother Henry Ford II was threatened by a hoodlum. "Bennett said he'd handle it. Later on, the guy was found floating face down in the river."

Within the Ford company Bennett's security force, said to have been one that a Chinese warlord would have envied, was used to control the workers. Spies and informers singled out those suspected of being labor organizers or of harboring radical political views, suspicions that were likely to lead to their summary dismissal. Other auto companies engaged in similar practices, but none was as widely publicized as those at Ford and no official responsible for such policies was as famous as Harry Bennett.

On March 7, 1932, in the depths of the depression, a Communist-organized "March on Hunger" made its way from Detroit to the Rouge plant. Police and firemen had been unable to disperse the thousands of marchers. Bennett's security men turned the fire hoses on the marchers, but when this had no effect, despite the freezing temperature, Bennett, who was a courageous man, came out to confront the demonstrators. Despite his reputation Bennett's face was not widely known, and one woman shouted, "We want Bennett, and he's in that building." "No," Bennett said, "you're wrong. I'm Bennett." That brought a hail of bricks and pieces of slag, one of which struck Bennett on the side of the head, and as he collapsed, bleeding profusely, he grabbed Joseph York, a Young Communist League organizer with whom he had been talking, and pulled him down. York struggled to his feet, only to be shot and killed, along with three others, as Dearborn police fired into the unarmed demonstrators, wounding twenty others.

Henry Ford was at lunch at the time, and when word of the riot reached him, he rushed over, together with Sorensen and Edsel Ford. But when Ford saw Bennett on the ground, "It was," one onlooker declared, "like it was Edsel lying there. . . .

Bennett, right, with Henry Ford in 1932 (courtesy of Henry Ford Museum and Greenfield Village)

Henry was white as a sheet; there were tears in his eyes." He went with Bennett to the hospital, called him every day to see how he was, and gave him a new Lincoln. After he was released from the hospital Bennett played his injury to the hilt, daubing Mercurochrome on his head bandage for several days in order to keep Ford worked up about the need for still stronger security measures to combat the threat from the Communists and other radicals. Ford photographers are said to have trained their cameras on the mourners who filed behind the coffins of Joseph York and the three other demonstrators who had been killed. Bennett's men then examined the photographs carefully, and any Ford employee who was spotted among the 15,000 marchers was out of a job by the end of March.

With the coming of Franklin Roosevelt's New Deal, a worker's right to belong to a union was soon protected by the federal government, and by early 1937 GM, Chrysler, and other auto companies had given in to demands that they recognize the new United Automobile Workers (UAW). But not Ford. Ignoring Edsel Ford's arguments that a collective bargaining agreement was now inevitable, Henry Ford assigned Bennett the job of dealing with the union. Bennett beefed up his security

forces, and, despite the fact that the intimidating measures he had used to root out union organizers and members were now illegal, he continued these practices. The confrontation culminated in the "Battle of the Overpass" on May 26, 1937, when Walter Reuther and other UAW organizers who were attempting to hand out literature to workers coming out of the Rouge plant were brutally beaten by Bennett's "Service" men. The event, which received national attention through photographs that newsmen escaped with, in spite of the efforts of Bennett's men to destroy all such evidence, further tarnished Ford's already badly damaged image as an enlightened employer. Nonetheless Bennett's methods succeeded in postponing for four years the inevitable recognition of a union. When a strike finally shut down the Rouge plant in April 1941, and Ford agreed to a federally supervised vote of his employees on the question of union recognition, Bennett threw his support behind a new auto union organized by the AFL, believing it would be easier to deal with than the CIO's established UAW. However, the Ford workers overwhelmingly supported the UAW. Bennett then encouraged Ford to refuse to sign a contract with the winning union, creating a threat of renewed violence that was ended when

Mrs. Ford insisted that her husband give in—which he did, agreeing to terms better than the UAW had received from other auto companies.

Although Bennett's labor policies were a dismal failure, his hold over Ford remained unshaken. With the onset of World War II Sorensen, Bennett's principal rival in the company, had to devote all of his attention to the massive task of getting bomber production under way at the huge new Ford Willow Run plant, some twenty miles west of Dearborn. Sorensen's absence left Bennett free to expand his influence into areas previously controlled by Sorensen. By the end of 1943 Sorensen, realizing that his days with the company were numbered, resigned.

Earlier in 1943 the death of Edsel Ford brought Henry Ford back to the position of company president that he had turned over to his son in 1919. This return was only at the insistence of other members of the Ford family that Bennett not get the job. Bennett, however, was appointed to the board of directors. The eighty-year-old Henry Ford's inability to perform fully the requirements of the job provided Bennett with the opportunity to act as de facto chief executive.

Alarm in Washington, D.C., at what was happening at Ford led to Henry Ford II's release from the navy so that he might provide some of the leadership in the company that his grandfather was no longer capable of providing. Ford found upon his return that as long as Henry Ford continued to support Bennett there was little he could do to assume real authority. But Bennett was not content to depend on the aging automaker's backing, which, considering the state of Ford's health, could end suddenly at any time. Shortly after Edsel Ford's death Bennett worked with I. A. Capizzi, his hand-picked choice as the company's chief attorney, to draw up a codicil to Ford's will that placed control of the company for ten years after Ford's death in the hands of a trust, to be dominated by Bennett and board members loyal to him.

When Henry Ford II early in 1944 learned of this codicil, his first inclination was to quit the company in protest, but John Bugas, a former FBI agent who had been brought into the company by Bennett a few months earlier but who had become an ally of the young Ford in seeking to undermine Bennett's authority, persuaded Ford to let him first discuss the matter with Bennett. Bennett was upset when he learned that Henry Ford II knew of the plan to prevent him from taking over the company when his grandfather died, but he told Bugas to come back the next day, "and we'll straighten the whole thing out." The following day Bennett showed Bugas the codicil and then threw it on the floor, burned it, put the ashes in an envelope, and told Bugas: "Take this back to Henry." Apparently, according to Capizzi, the reason for this surprising action was that Bennett realized the codicil probably would not stand up in court. There is some question whether Henry Ford ever signed the document, but even if he had, the fact that over several months he had scribbled Bible verses and other irrelevant material on the paper would have raised serious doubts as to his mental condition when he agreed to the trust.

In April 1944 Henry Ford II was named executive vice-president, putting him technically above Bennett in the company hierarchy, but Bennett still had the advantage of being able to count on the elder Ford to maintain his power. The grandson added a number of executives to those he could count on in an ultimate showdown, but it was his mother and grandmother who finally forced Henry Ford to step aside and let his grandson assume the presidency; Edsel's widow threatened to sell her huge block of Ford stock. Henry Ford capitulated on September 20, 1945, and at the board meeting the next day his letter of resignation was read. As it was being read Bennett got up to leave. He was persuaded to stay and see his control end with the board's vote to accept the resignation and name Henry Ford II the new president.

What happened after the board meeting is not clear. One account has Henry Ford II talking with Bennett in the hall and telling him his services with the company were terminated. Bennett angrily retorted: "You're taking over a billion dollar organization here that you haven't contributed a thing to!" Ford then backed down and said Bennett would be reassigned to other duties. Another version has this exchange taking place in Bennett's office, where Ford later admitted he had gone in some fear for his life since Bennett, who was a marksman, had a gun in his office with which he often liked to amuse himself by firing at various targets. But there is still a third account of how Bennett was let go which has Ford dispatching John Bugas to give Bennett the news. As Bugas entered Bennett's office Bennett shouted at the man he had hired two years earlier, "You son of a bitch!" and he hauled out a

.45 automatic. The ex-G-man, however, had his own gun, and he told Bennett, "Don't make the mistake of pulling the trigger, because I'll kill you. I won't miss. I'll put one right through your heart, Harry." Bennett then adopted a friendlier tone and offered to take Bugas for a ride in the airplane that Charles Lindbergh had taught Bennett to fly earlier in the war. Bugas turned down the invitation and walked out, somewhat concerned, as he later confessed, that Bennett might shoot him in the back.

That evening Henry Ford II went over to his grandfather's house to tell him that Bennett was through. He expected the old man would "blow my head off." Instead Ford, always given to enigmatic statements, said, after a long silence, "Well, now Harry is back where he started from."

In October Bennett resigned as a director of the Ford company. Along with being allowed to resign Bennett was kept on the payroll for a year and a half and was given a pension thereafter. A business partnership he formed with two other men lasted only a few months, and he departed from Michigan, returning only once in 1951 when he was called before a legislative committee investigating criminal activities. Bennett moved to California to his winter home near Palm Springs. The fortress-like home he had built overlooking the Huron River between Ann Arbor and Ypsilanti, with its electrical and mechanical security devices, its gun towers, its armed guards and patrol dogs, its secret doors, hidden rooms, escape tunnels, and separate quarters for Bennett's lions and tigers, was sold. Going with Bennett to California was his second wife, Esther Beatty Bennett, whom he had married in 1937, and their one daughter. (Bennett's first marriage had ended in divorce. He had had three daughters by that marriage.) In 1969 the Bennetts moved from their comfortable California retreat, which had a swimming pool, seven cats, three horses, a picture of Henry Ford, but no phones. The family moved to a ranch-style home in Las Vegas to be nearer the medical care that Mrs. Bennett needed. Bennett busied himself by returning to his old love of painting and by looking after the maintenance of his home and property. By the 1970s arthritis and poor eyesight had slowed him down, and at least one interviewer came away with the impression that the octogenarian's mind was beginning to fail.

Harry Bennett died in a California nursing home on January 4, 1979. It had been more than thirty-three years since his days at Ford had ended,

and the possibility of clarifying some of the details of those days probably died with him. In 1951 his autobiography, *We Never Called Him Henry,* ghost-written by Paul Marcus, appeared in a cheap paperback. "I want to try to set the record straight," Bennett declared, but on a draft copy of the manuscript, which he gave to David C. Smith of Detroit in 1974, Bennett had written: "This Book is so slanted I don't think it should be printed." Several publishers apparently agreed, turning down the manuscript, but, although several passages were deleted as a result of pressure brought by the Ford Motor Company, the book is full of juicy details and anecdotes that have enlivened the unending stream of Henry Ford and Ford family books that have appeared since 1951. Bennett's unhappiness with the book may have resulted from the attempts of Paul Marcus to cast Bennett in too favorable a light. By all accounts Bennett could be a real charmer, and there is some evidence that he was at times more sensitive to the needs and feelings of others than he is usually depicted. But Bennett liked to be known as a hard-boiled person and had told two reporters who had earlier had the idea of writing a flattering biography of him that the person they had described would not be recognized by anyone who knew him. "Why not?" one of the newsmen asked. "Well," Bennett replied, "you don't say I'm a son of a bitch."

Publication:
We Never Called Him Henry, with Paul Marcus (New York: Fawcett, 1951).

References:
George Cantor, "The Ford-Bennett Days: Fear Ruled the Rouge," *Detroit Free Press* (March 19, 1972);

Peter Collier and David Horowitz, *The Fords: An American Epic* (New York: Summit, 1987);

Robert Lacey, *Ford: The Men and the Machine* (Boston: Little, Brown, 1986);

David L. Lewis, "Here, for the First Time Ever, Is Harry Bennett's Mysterious, Legendary Castle: Your Tour Begins Below," *Detroit Free Press* (June 18, 1972);

Lewis, *The Public Image of Henry Ford: An American Folk Hero and His Company* (Detroit: Wayne State University Press, 1976);

"Life with Henry," *Time,* 58 (October 8, 1951): 101-104;

Allan Nevins and Frank E. Hill, *Ford: Decline and Rebirth* (New York: Scribners, 1963);

Nevins and Hill, *Ford: Expansion and Challenge* (New York: Scribners, 1957);

Nevins and Hill, *Ford: The Times, The Man, The Company* (New York: Scribners, 1954).

Archives:

Although Bennett burned his personal business records before leaving the Ford company, much material in the form of business records and oral interviews remains

in the Ford Archives, located in the Henry Ford Museum, Dearborn, Michigan.

Owen Frederick Bieber

(December 28, 1929-)

by Gilbert J. Gall

Pennsylvania State University

CAREER: Wire bender, McInerney Spring & Wire Company (1948-1961); president, United Automobile, Aerospace & Agricultural Implement Workers of America (UAW) Local 687, Grand Rapids, Michigan (1956-1961); international representative (1962-1972), director, UAW Region 1D (1974-1980); vice-president and director, General Motors Department, UAW (1980-1983); president, UAW (1983-).

Owen Frederick Bieber, since 1983 president of the United Automobile Workers (UAW) international union, representing approximately one million autoworkers in collective bargaining, to date has led his union through what many observers see as a transitional era in U.S. automobile labor relations. The first president of the UAW not closely associated with the leadership caucus of former president Walter P. Reuther and the founding era of the union, Bieber assumed the helm of the UAW in the wake of a devastating recession in the automotive industry and disruption of its traditional patterns of collective bargaining. During the first five years of his presidency his priorities stressed the job security needs of UAW members, restoration of traditional economic bargaining strength where possible, unionization of foreign-owned automobile plants in the United States, and promotion of a rationalized national industrial policy.

Bieber was born on December 28, 1929, in North Dorr, Michigan, in the western part of the state. After graduating from Catholic Central High School in 1948, Bieber followed his father into employment at McInerney Spring & Wire Company in Grand Rapids, Michigan, as an automobile seat wire bender. His father, Alfred F. Bieber, was active in the organizing drive that founded UAW Local 687 at McInerney, and his son followed in

Owen Frederick Bieber

his footsteps. Within a year of beginning his job Bieber was elected as a shop steward by his peers—perhaps because his 6-foot-5-inch height gave the impression he could not be easily intimidated. Over the next six years he served in a variety of local union posts: executive board member in 1951, bargaining committee and vice-president in 1955, and finally president of the local in 1956. Between his union activities and his family commitments—he married the former Shirley M. Van Woerkom on November 25, 1950—Bieber found time in short supply.

Even without his imposing stature, Bieber would probably have been noticed by the UAW leadership. Kenneth Robinson, director of UAW Region 1D, in which Local 687 resided, became Bieber's mentor, bringing him along first as a part-time organizer in 1961, a full-time organizer in 1962, an international staff representative and aide in 1964, and finally as assistant director of the region in 1972. When Robinson retired for health reasons in 1974, he designated Bieber as his chosen successor. With the former director's backing and his own reputation as an aggressive grievance handler (his nickname among the rank and file he serviced was "Big Dad") well established, Bieber handily won election as regional director, becoming as well, by virtue of that election, one of the 26 members of the international union's policy-making executive board.

These were formative years, Bieber later acknowledged, years in which his emotional commitment to the union grew. "Something happens to you when you join the UAW," he told the delegates hearing his first address as UAW president. "It's almost as if the union takes a young man or woman by the hand and by the heart, and shows the way to what is right and just and fair and decent." Young people, he noted, "are exposed, first, to the harsh realities of the workplace. . . . Then they are exposed to our union, our movement, and to the understanding that work need not be dehumanizing, unrewarded drudgery . . . that the boss need not reign supreme and unchallenged . . . that a day's labor can be fairly compensated . . . and there can be time away from the job to spend with family and friends." It was a process that many in the hall had gone through, "as the union shaped you and you shaped the union. It is an experience I, too, have gone through." As Bieber's psychological attachment to the UAW grew, so did his involvement in liberal Democratic politics in western Michigan and Grand Rapids' Kent County grow during the 1960s and 1970s. He served as a delegate to the Democratic National Convention in 1968, 1972, and 1976.

During his tenure as director of Region 1D, which covers 62 western Michigan counties, Bieber developed a reputation as a hard-nosed bargainer and a cautious, methodical administrator. Many of the companies with which he dealt in that region were parts suppliers to the automobile industry and subject to strong competitive pressures. Bieber thus cut his mid-level bargaining teeth in an environment quite different from that of the highly oligopolistic major automobile companies—an experience that was later to serve him well when that oligopolistic environment eroded due to increased foreign competition. In 1980 his solid performance led to his election as a UAW vice-president by his coexecutive board members. Bieber and his family, now numbering five children, moved to Detroit and to UAW headquarters at Solidarity House to take up his new responsibilities. UAW President Douglas Fraser quickly put Bieber to the test by appointing him to the directorship of the union's General Motors (GM) Department, the largest and most complex in the organization, at the time servicing some 400,000 members.

Negotiating union contracts in the automotive industry was not an easy task during the early 1980s. The sales figures of the Big Three automobile manufacturers, slipping for years under the increasing penetration of foreign car makers from Japan and Germany, plummeted as the country went into a steep recession. Carmakers' combined losses for 1980 and 1981 were $4 billion and $1.2 billion, respectively. Similarly, automotive employment tumbled: levels of production workers in the industry dropped from over 800,800 in 1978 to 487,700 in 1983. Chrysler, the smallest of the Big Three, nearly went bankrupt in 1979 and would have done so had not the UAW agreed to $243 million in wage concessions.

Thus, in 1982 when Bieber approached his first national contract negotiations at GM, the prospects were not promising. "By the time I got here," he commented to a reporter, "all the good things had passed." In an effort to stanch the hemorrhaging of employment, the UAW agreed to early renegotiation in spring 1982, and Bieber was realistic enough to know that the resulting agreement would contain concessions in wage determination rules and benefits, mainly in exchange for a jointly negotiated profit-sharing plan. The resulting accord also contained some guarantees on income levels for laid-off workers and limited job security experiments. Critics, however, contended that the new GM director was less than impressive in putting the package over to the membership as negotiations were broken off twice due to rank-and-file pressure against concessions. Ultimately, the ratification of the GM contract passed by only 52 percent to 48 percent, though Ford workers easily assented to similar changes.

The unpopularity of the agreement apparently did not extend to Bieber personally. In 1982 he decided to run for UAW president, an office due to open because of the mandatory retirement of the incumbent Fraser in 1983. During the 1982 negotiation rounds the executive board ordered a moratorium on campaigning between the four top contenders: Bieber; Raymond Majerus, the union's secretary-treasurer; Donald Ephlin, the head of the Ford Department; and Steven Yokich, the vice-president in charge of the agricultural implement and skilled trades departments. While Bieber respected the order, Ephlin and Majerus continued to pursue support. When Ephlin saw his candidacy fade, he withdrew, and his backers turned to Bieber, as did those of Yokich when he likewise removed his name from the race. The contest between Bieber and Majerus was hard fought to the very end. In the context of UAW internal politics, they were contending for the endorsement of the executive board, which for years has been tantamount to election at the convention. On the first ballot the candidates tied at thirteen votes each. On the second Bieber pulled ahead thirteen to eleven. On the third round, sensing the inevitable, the executive board unanimously recommended Bieber. In May 1983 25,00 UAW convention delegates cast the official ballots making Bieber the new president of the international union.

In his first remarks as UAW president given to the Dallas convention delegates who had selected him, Bieber charted his vision of the future course of the union. He pointed out the close connection between politics, public policy, and the disadvantageous trade balances that had undermined the domestic automobile market, exhorting his membership to aid in casting out the Reagan administration in the coming 1984 elections. Turning to collective bargaining, he acknowledged that the tough economic bargaining environment had shaken the UAW to its roots, but the new president insisted that the decisions of the last few years were tactical and not philosophical. "We made sacrifices, not because we lacked the guts to take the companies on," he explained, "but because we possessed the wisdom to know we were better off to protect much of what we had and to fight another day from a position of strength." Charging that retreat would not continue in the face of the sharp rebound in recent automaker profits, he said he hoped top automotive executives were listening when he announced that he was "deadly serious when I say it's their turn to do some giving."

Bieber further pledged that the new Japanese-owned automobile assembly plants being built in the United States in the last few years–Honda in Marysville, Ohio, Nissan in Smyrna, Tennessee, and GM-Toyota in Fremont, California–would eventually produce their products with UAW members. Concluding his speech, he informed the conventioneers that he had no doubt that the union "will not just survive, we will prosper because we march as one."

Almost immediately after the end of the convention Bieber received an opportunity to prove that he could persuade automobile company officials that it was their turn "to do some giving." His first challenge was the Chrysler negotiations–the first since the unprecedented concession contract of 1979-1980. Over the course of four years workers had invested over $1 billion in wages and benefits back into the corporation, and pressure was pronounced to achieve an agreement that would again put Chrysler workers in parity with GM and Ford autoworkers. Bieber contended that if the company could grant top executives over $60 million in stock options it could certainly afford to make up the $2.42 average wage difference between companies. Chrysler countered that it was too soon in its program of recovery to bring wages into parity and furthermore that it wanted to get a handle on health care cost containment–possibly through worker contributions or deductibles. Bieber broke off the early negotiation meetings after a month. After the personal intercession of Chrysler Chairman Lee Iacocca the company acceded to parity, disdaining a strike that would interfere with the introduction of its highly touted series of minivans. Concurrently, in fall 1983 Bieber convinced GM to operate its joint, Japanese-managed venture with Toyota–the New United Motor Manufacturing Company (NUMMI)–under an innovative experimental union contract with the UAW. The new UAW president thus quickly achieved impressive results in his first leadership challenges.

The upcoming contract renegotiations with Ford and GM, however, promised to be just as problematical. The automotive industry, capitalizing on the recent tax cuts proposed by the president and passed by Congress, bounced back from the recession with $6.5 billion in profits in 1984. While this may have seemed to portend a return to the previous bargaining patterns of seemingly ever-increasing economic advances for autoworkers, automation and corporate restructuring in the industry presented ever-increasing dangers to job security. Further substantiation of this danger came when a confidential strategic GM memorandum, recommending a paring down of corporate production employment levels by 100,000 through robotics, fell into the hands of union officials and the media. Thus, while it seemed to some in the UAW—particularly rank-and-file leadership activists—that it was time to recoup on unobtained raises, Bieber looked upon the Ford and GM renegotiations as a chance to make meaningful gains in job security for its members.

Concurrent negotiations with both companies began early in mid summer. After a month of discussions Bieber suspended talks and engineered a vote of the executive board giving him the power to choose either one, or both, of the two companies as a potential strike target. Though neither side relished the thought of a walkout, the companies' low inventory levels as they approached their new model year perhaps made them a bit more anxious about the economic impact of a stoppage. After Labor Day the UAW president designated GM as the main target.

Bieber continued to make job security gains the centerpiece of the negotiations in high-level meetings between himself and GM chairman Roger Smith. After contract expiration the UAW adopted the innovative strike tactic of selective stoppages at specially chosen corporation plants: plants where union militancy was greatest and plants that generated the highest GM profits. This strategy kept as many GM-UAW members working as possible, helped vent the frustrations of the rank and file against the corporation where necessary, and eased pressure on the union's strike fund. Late in the month GM and the UAW reached agreement. While there was a wage increase and restoration of some aspects of previous economic benefits, the unique aspect of the accord was the attempt to deal with the issue of job security. GM agreed to establish a "job bank" with $1 billion in funding that would function as a "guaranteed income stream" for any workers displaced by "outsourcing" (either abroad or to nonunion suppliers) or by decisions to automate, to be paid until a replacement position was offered. Ford followed in the fall with a comparable contract, and though the media highly touted the innovative concept, critics did point out that the union obtained no restrictions on where the companies

could produce nor whether the replacement jobs found would be similar in skill and pay. Nevertheless, while the initial ratification voting went against the agreement, when Bieber warned that rejection would mean a renewed strike, the rank and file ratified the pact by a 58 percent margin. Though Bieber did experience relative success in the United States, in Canada his pressure on Canadian UAW Director Robert White to settle within the boundaries of the U.S. pattern of wage restraint—despite strong protest from White's sizable Canadian rank and file—led to a break within the union. In 1985 White disaffiliated from the UAW international union in the wake of an executive board refusal to grant the Canadian wing independent collective bargaining determination.

In 1985 Chrysler negotiations returned with similar pressures to catch up with the advances at the other two automakers. Bieber's objectives stressed the job security advances achieved at Ford and GM and denounced the company's increasing use of "outsourcing" and import sales, while Chrysler Chairman Iacocca argued for cost reductions and combining archaic job classifications for efficiency. Chrysler was very attracted to the flexible and innovative agreement—flexible work assignments, extensive employee involvement in work teams, and lower-than-standard wages—that the UAW negotiated with GM on an experimental basis for the corporation's planned Saturn plant, to be built in Spring Hill, Tennessee, not far from the non-union Nissan plant that had been a UAW organizing objective. Bieber—who had been elected to the Chrysler board of directors to replace the retired Douglas Fraser (a quid pro quo of the concession contract of 1979-1980)—demurred, announcing that the Saturn agreement was an isolated understanding and not a new pattern for the automotive industry. After a week's strike in fall 1985, Bieber emerged with an agreement he termed "parity plus." In addition to wage increases and the institution of profit sharing, the union won similar provisions on wage continuations.

The most recent engagements with Ford and GM have enabled Bieber to expand the "job banks" concept by establishing "fixed employment levels" for skilled and unskilled workers at every company location. If a worker cannot work at his or her normal job when employment levels are below those negotiated, he or she is given a "job bank" assignment at full pay, with seniority rights and full benefits. Automotive industry analysts and press claimed that the new concepts set a pattern which will spread not only throughout the industry but throughout American manufacturing. *Automotive News,* for example, hailed the UAW president's efforts as "an example of negotiations at their best—and leadership at its best." In the 1988 Chrysler pact Bieber for the first time succeeded in linking represented employee compensation to the compensation of management; no bonuses will be paid to corporation executives if Chrysler workers also do not receive bonus payments from their profit-sharing plan in a given year.

All expectations are that Bieber will continue with his "patient, carefully planned and low key" style that seems to be chalking up a fairly admirable record of achievement without engaging in the usual adversarial rhetoric. He has combined tenacious bargaining and a proven willingness to strike with what admirers say are farsighted leadership objectives, both in collective bargaining and in the public-policy arena. Thus, while willing to strike for the needs of his membership, he has tied that militancy to job security in exchange for company-desired agreements on productivity improvements. As a member of the Chrysler board of directors, he voices his concerns that "corporations in our democratic society are chartered to serve the public's interest, not the other way around" and strives to present the union's conception of economic democracy through trade union representation in various forums. Moreover, he never tires of pointing out that creative changes in labor-management relationships can only handle part of the problem. The need for active government involvement in developing industrial policies, in his mind, is critical to the eventual survival of U.S. manufacturing—despite the accusations that national economic planning would be a threat to freedom. "In the UAW," he told the Commonwealth Club of San Francisco, "when we have talked about industrial policy proposals, we have been careful to stress the importance of decen-

tralized planning and democratic guarantees. We've pointed out that planning in the open—with various interests clearly identified—could hardly be less democratic than the economic planning that takes place every day behind the closed doors of corporation board rooms." His tenure promises to be longer, and his potential for a record of accomplishment greater, than that of any UAW president since Walter P. Reuther.

Publications:

"What Better Eligibility for Board Membership?," *Management Review,* 75 (February 1986): 56;
"Updating Labor-Management Relations is Only Part of the Answer," *Journal of State Government,* 60 (January-February 1987): 17-19.

Unpublished Documents:

"Remarks by UAW President Owen Bieber to the UAW Constitutional Convention, May 19, 1983, Dallas, Texas" (UAW, *Proceedings of the Constitutional Convention,* 1983, Archives of Labor History and Urban Affairs, Walter P. Reuther Library, Wayne State University, Detroit, Mich.);
"Economic Democracy and Economic Rights: Free Trade Unions," *Vital Speeches of the Day,* 52 (January 1, 1986): 165-168;
"American Living Standards: Debt and Dependency on Foreign Capital," *Vital Speeches of the Day,* 52 (March 15, 1986): 350-353.

References:

"Bieber, Owen F.," *Current Biography,* 47 (1986): 3-4;
"Interview with Owen Bieber," *Automotive News,* November 16, 1987, pp. E22-E25;
"Owen F. Bieber," in *Biographical Dictionary of American Labor,* edited by Gary M. Fink, second edition (Westport, Conn.: Greenwood Press, 1984);
"Owen F. Bieber," *New York Times,* May 19, 1983, p. 15.

Archives:

Material concerning Bieber is located at the UAW President's Office, Archives of Labor History and Urban Affairs, Walter P. Reuther Library, Wayne State University, Detroit, Michigan. The Bieber files are currently not available, but it is assumed that they will one day be deposited and opened at this official UAW archival repository.

Albert Bradley

(May 29, 1891-September 11, 1983)

by George S. May

Eastern Michigan University

CAREER: Assistant comptroller, assistant treasurer, general assistant treasurer, and vice-president (1919-1942), executive vice-president (1942-1956), chairman (1956-1958), director, General Motors Corporation (1958-1972).

Despite his long years of service in top executive capacities at General Motors (GM), including a two-year term in the 1950s as the chairman, Albert Bradley rarely attracted much attention from the press, leaving researchers with a paucity of information readily available concerning many aspects of his life. His fate illustrates the need that still exists for much more extensive work to be done with the lives of businessmen such as Bradley, whose career did not extend into the production side of the corporation's activities but whose work in finance was vital to the corporation's success.

Bradley was born in Blackburn, England, on May 29, 1891, the son of Walter and Maria Winward Bradley. While Bradley was still a child, the family came to the United States. Details of his early life are lacking, but the fact that he graduated from Dartmouth in 1915 at the age of twenty-four indicates that something out of the ordinary occurred to delay his education. Bradley was a loyal alumnus of the university, serving as a trustee of Dartmouth in the 1950s, and, along with the Alfred P. Sloan Foundation, was a major donor to the establishment of the Albert Bradley Center for Mathematics at the school. He was also a major donor to the Albert Bradley Class of 1915 Fund, which provided scholarships and loans, and in 1969 he funded the creation of the Third Century Professorship to develop new approaches to teaching mathematics.

Bradley was awarded a fellowship in political economy at the University of Michigan, where he obtained his M.A. and Ph.D. in economics in two years. While at Michigan, Bradley became acquainted with William A. Paton, who, during his ca-

Albert Bradley

reer as a professor of economics and accounting at the Ann Arbor school, had a remarkable influence over students who went on to occupy top positions in the automobile industry, including Roger Smith, chairman of GM in the 1980s. After service in the Army Signal Corps and Air Service during World War I, Bradley became perhaps the first of those whom Paton influenced to join GM; Bradley took a position as an assistant to the comptroller in 1919.

Bradley came to GM at a time of great expansion during the second period in which the company was controlled by its founder, William C. Durant. Bradley's background in finance was badly needed. Alfred P. Sloan, Jr., who joined GM only shortly before Bradley and whose educational background was in electrical engineering, declared that Bradley "later was kind enough" to tell him that a system of accounting that Sloan had drawn up "was pretty good for a layman." But because so many of GM's executives had come out of the factory, not college, neither Bradley nor GM for many years would publicize his university background. He only started wearing his Phi Beta Kappa key after William Knudsen, GM's most prominent noncollege executive, left for government war service in 1940. "Until then," Bradley told Peter Drucker, "I'd only get a speech from Knudsen . . . about spoiled rich kids who never did any honest work and who give themselves airs." The financial side of the business was supposed to be under the control of Du Pont officials since that company was the largest stockholder in GM. But John J. Raskob of Du Pont, who served as chairman of GM's finance committee, proved to be even more enthusiastic than Durant in pushing for ambitious expansion programs. When the postwar boom turned into a depression late in summer 1920, the Durant-Raskob expenditures for expansion threatened the corporation's survival. Durant was forced out, and by the end of the year Pierre S. du Pont had taken over temporarily as chief executive officer and had brought in Donaldson Brown from Du Pont to provide more restrained leadership in financial matters, although Raskob continued to serve as chairman of the finance committee.

Bradley became an associate of Brown's, and the two men together became responsible for instituting financial reforms that brought order out of chaos and were a principal basis for the corporation gaining and holding on to the top position in the industry. In personalities the two men were quite dissimilar. Brown, who like Sloan was an electrical engineer by training but who had acquired a formidable grasp of financial matters, was the prototype of the humorless, coldly calculating accountant executive to whom men on the production side would later contemptuously refer as "bean counters." Bradley, on the other hand, was a warm, friendly type, who not only liked to play golf but who was also described as "an enthusiastic bowler," a sport not usually associated with corporate executives. Bradley also had a sense of humor, as he showed in a paper he presented before a professional group on the forecasting program he had set up at GM. In discussing the background needed for such work, he observed, "Apparently no knowledge

of astrology is required or even implied." But in spite of such differences Bradley and Brown, along with Sloan, who succeeded Pierre S. du Pont as head of GM in 1923, shared the view that a strong system of financial controls was needed if they were to avoid the economic problems that had almost destroyed the corporation in 1920.

Essentially Brown concentrated on the development of a plan for controlling the rate of production that would avoid the wild gyrations caused by an attempt to tie that production too closely to the ups and downs of the economy. He came up with a "standard volume" plan that was designed to assure a steady, generous return on investment, regardless of general economic conditions. Bradley meanwhile worked on the more practical problem of developing a forecasting program that would enable Brown's production goals to be achieved. Taking into account the various factors, such as general business conditions, seasonal variations in demand, the growing saturation of the market for cars among first-time buyers, and the activities of GM's competitors, Bradley developed a system of forecasting the coming year's production needs. These were not based on projections of the production divisions, whose leaders always took an overly optimistic view of future sales prospects, but on an increasingly sophisticated analysis of sales reports from all of GM's thousands of dealers. Production schedules based upon those forecasts were then carefully adjusted monthly based upon detailed study of reports of dealers' orders and sales that came in every ten days. Although Bradley's system of forecasting was by no means foolproof, it did enable the corporation to avoid the nearly calamitous consequences that resulted from the failure in summer 1920 to heed the signs of impending economic crisis that should have led to a slowdown in production.

Although Bradley's principal responsibilities would remain in the financial area, where he would ultimately serve as the corporation's chief financial officer, his activities, as Sloan noted, "spread to a large extent over the whole General Motors map." In the late 1920s Bradley was a member of a committee that recommended the purchase of the German automaker Opel. In the post–World War II years he played a key role in supporting the rebuilding of that German subsidiary as well as in the development of a subsidiary in Australia that produced the Holden in 1948. As executive vice-president Brad-

Bradley in 1928 with the General Motors Commission to Adam Opel, A. G., and Opel officials. From left to right: Keith A. Wood, Bradley, Dr. Wilhelm von Opel, John T. Smith, Alfred P. Sloan, Jr., Manfred Wronker-Flatow, Dr. Fritz Opel, F. J. Fisher, and Fritz von Opel.

ley was one of the three officials principally involved in the corporation's war-production activities in World War II.

At the end of the war Sloan, who at the age of seventy had reached the corporation's mandatory retirement age, was ready to step down as chairman and chief executive officer. According to Peter Drucker, Sloan favored the choice of Bradley as his successor. But because it was felt conditions in the immediate postwar period would require the leadership of a production man, the board instead transferred the duties of chief executive officer to the president, Charles E. Wilson. "Maybe not picking Bradley . . . was the right decision," Sloan later told Drucker. "I may have favored him because he did even better the things I did well. Mr. Wilson does different things, and that's what a company needs." Sloan wanted Brown to replace him as chairman, a post that would no longer carry the responsibilities of chief executive, but Wilson and others asked Sloan to stay on. Sloan agreed, the retirement age re-

quirement was waived, and Brown retired. Bradley became the senior financial executive.

During the next ten years the finance staff became increasingly alarmed at the expansion programs carried out under Wilson and his successor, Harlow H. Curtice. Many felt that Curtice went ahead with expensive programs without first asking the advice and gaining the support of the people who would have to arrange the financing of these programs. When Sloan finally stepped down as chairman in 1956, Bradley succeeded him. It was hoped that he could regain some of the influence the New York finance staff had lost to the production staff in Detroit. However, lacking the title of chief executive officer, there was little that Bradley could do. The opportunity the finance staff had been waiting for came in summer 1958 when both Bradley and Curtice announced their retirements. Frederic Donner, one of Paton's students recruited by Bradley in 1926 and Bradley's successor as head of the finance staff, became chairman. Donner succeeded in getting the duties of chief executive officer restored to the chairman's office, where they have remained ever since.

Bradley continued as a director of GM until 1972 and in that capacity served as the chairman of the finance committee until 1969, as well as chairman of the bonus and salary committee until 1968. He died at his Greenwich, Connecticut, home on September 11, 1983, at the age of ninety-two. He was survived by his wife of sixty-three years, Helen Worcester Bradley, by a son and a daughter, and by six grandchildren. A Congregationalist, Bradley had attended the First Church of Round Hill in Greenwich, where memorial services were held on September 15.

Publication:

"Setting Up a Forecasting Program," a paper presented to the American Management Association in 1926 and reprinted in *Managerial Innovation at General Motors*, edited by Alfred D. Chandler (New York: Arno Press, 1979).

References:

Ed Cray, *Chrome Colossus: General Motors and Its Times* (New York: McGraw-Hill, 1980);
Peter Drucker, *Adventures of a Bystander* (New York: Harper & Row, 1979);
Alfred P. Sloan, Jr., *My Years with General Motors* (Garden City, N. Y.: Doubleday, 1964).
"Two to the Top," *Newsweek,* 47 (April 16, 1956): 90.

Brakes

by James Wren

Motor Vehicle Manufacturers Association

The development of braking technology after 1920 was substantial. From the primitive internal and external expanding brakes, which applied mechanical pressure directly on only two wheels and were common in the early decades of the automobile industry, the technology advanced by the 1920s to 4-wheel braking systems. More important than the advance of 4-wheel braking was the appearance of hydraulic braking systems. Developed by Malcolm Loughheed (Lockheed) in 1918, hydraulic brakes quickly became the predominant technology among American automobile manufacturers.

Hydraulic brakes utilized a fluid reservoir in conjunction with a master cylinder or pump which pressurized the fluid through metal tubing to individual cylinders in each wheel. The cylinders forced brake shoes, lined with asbestos or sintered metal, against the interior of the wheel, bringing the car to a stop. The system was based on the theory formulated by Blaise Pascal "that pressure applied to a fluid in an enclosed body is transmitted equally in all directions."

A few developments in the technology took place during the next twenty to thirty years, notably the introduction of mechanisms intended to adjust braking power as the linings wore down. Before 1925, when the Cole Motor Car Company introduced a self-adjusting system, ratchets on the drum enabled the brakes to be adjusted manually. It was not until 1946 that Studebaker introduced the modern self-adjustment system. Another improvement in brakes was the development of power assistance to increase stopping ability. Air brakes, like those used extensively in later years on trucks, were used on a Tincher automobile in 1903. A vacuum system was introduced on the 1928 Pierce-Arrow automobile.

Despite these improvements basic braking technology, as utilized commercially, was stable until the 1970s, when disc, rather than drum, braking systems entered widespread use. But even this was not new technology, having been used as early as 1898 on the Sperry Electric vehicle. Disc brakes were used periodically by other manufacturers during the century.

Throughout the nearly one hundred years of the automobile age, the major problem with brakes was that their sudden application sometimes caused wheel lock, loss of control, and pulling to one side. Most of the developments in braking systems since the 1960s have come in the area of antilock braking systems. Several of the automatic antilock systems were introduced in the 1960s, but these functioned only on rear wheels. In the 1980s more sophisticated, extensive, and effective antilock systems were developed and introduced. Another innovation of the 1980s was the invention of an electrically driven brake booster. These improvements have been coupled to the development of automobile computer technology, which has come to be the driving force behind almost all automobile improvements. Future technologies will undoubtedly depend on, and contain, improvements in computers.

References:
James J. Flink, *The Automobile Age* (Cambridge, Mass.: MIT Press, 1988);

John B. Rae, "The Internal Combustion Engine on Wheels," in *Technology in Western Civilization*, edited by Melvin Kranzberg and Carroll W. Purcell, Jr., volume 2 (London: Oxford University Press, 1967), pp. 127-128;

Andrew White, *Brake Dynamics* (Lee, N.H.: Motor Vehicle Research of New Hampshire, 1963), pp. 41-60.

Archives:
Information on braking technology is located in the technical reference files of the Motor Vehicle Manufacturers Association patent library, Detroit, Michigan.

Ernest R. Breech

(February 24, 1897-July 3, 1978)

by Michael L. Lazare

New Milford, Connecticut

CAREER: Accountant, Fairbanks, Morse & Company (1917); auditor, Adams & Westlake (1920-1922); accountant (1922-1923), controller, Yellow Cab Manufacturing Company (1923-1929); general assistant treasurer, General Motors (1927-1933); president and chairman, North American Aviation (1933-1937); group vice-president (1937-1939), vice-president, General Motors (1939-1942); president, Bendix Aviation (1942-1946); executive vice-president (1946-1955), director (1946-1967), chairman, Ford Motor Company (1955-1960); trustee (1960), chairman, Trans World Airlines (1961-1969).

Ernest Robert Breech was born February 24, 1897, in Lebanon, Missouri, the son of Joseph F. E. and Martha Atchley Breech. His father operated a blacksmith shop specializing in carriages. There Breech worked as a boy, although the study of mechanics was never his first interest. He attended Lebanon High School, where he excelled both in studies and sports. He was a good enough baseball player that the St. Louis Browns of the American League offered him a tryout. Breech, however, turned down the offer because he wanted to study law. Consequently he entered Drury College in Springfield, Missouri. He attained a scholastic average of 93, but insufficient funds forced him to drop out of college

after two years. He moved to Chicago and took a job in 1917 with the accounting department of Fairbanks, Morse & Company, at a salary of $15 a week. He excelled in his job and after three months received a 20-percent raise, to $18 a week.

The job was to have a seminal influence on his career. He told *Life* Magazine in 1955, "I realized that it was here a business stood or fell—on cost controls. That was the nut of any business." His intelligence was quick, and his determination was boundless. While working during the day, he took night courses in accounting at the Walton School of Commerce in Chicago; but he felt he was not moving along quickly enough, so he switched to correspondence courses, which he could finish in half the time it would have taken him in a classroom. In 1921 he took the certified public accounting examination and won a gold medal for receiving the highest grade in Illinois. He was awarded the certification by the University of Illinois at Urbana.

In an interview with *Nation's Business* in October 1966, he was asked what had given him the greatest satisfaction in his business career. His reply was revealing: "If I were to go back to anything, I would have to say that the greatest satisfaction I've had was receiving a letter from the University of Illinois telling me I had passed the C.P.A. examination

Ernest R. Breech

with the highest grade. That was my first success. I think that was probably the happiest day of my life, business-wise. I took the exam against boys who had gone to the universities. I went to night school but then switched over to correspondence course, where I could do a lesson a day instead of a lesson a week. That way, I completed the course in less than half the normal time. Just after the exam I heard some fellows from the larger universities, Illinois, Northwestern, and Chicago, say how they had answered certain questions. It just happened I hadn't answered them that way, and I was worried. So the day I received the letter saying I had passed with the highest grade, I think that was probably, well, the happiest day of my business career. And I have had many a happy day since then."

In 1920 Breech had taken a job as auditor with Adams & Westlake, a Chicago manufacturing firm. As an accountant he specialized in factory cost accounting and wage systems. He often lectured about factory cost accounting at evening classes at the Walton School of Commerce. He became a member of the Illinois Manufacturers Cost Association, a group of young financial executives.

Members took turns addressing the organization about various topics of mutual interest. In 1922 Breech lectured on methods for establishing machine-hour rates. It happened that Irving Babcock, treasurer of the Yellow Cab Manufacturing Company, was in the audience that night. Babcock was so impressed with the young accountant that a few days later he invited him to join Yellow Cab and head the accounting function. Breech declined because he wanted to go into business for himself.

In 1922 he selected a partner, and the two of them opened their own accounting firm. The partner, whose name has not been preserved, specialized in taxation and auditing, while Breech was to concentrate on his specialty, factory cost accounting. However, the partnership dissolved, and Breech told *Nation's Business* magazine, "I soon found out I had made the wrong selection of a partner, and just about that time Babcock called me again. I went to work for Yellow Cab on January 2, 1923, in charge of accounting."

For the next thirty-seven years Breech was involved in the automobile industry. He served as controller of Yellow Cab until 1929. In 1925 the company merged with General Motors Truck & Coach, and Breech handled the financial end of the merger and became controller of the merged company. In 1927 he became a director of the Yellow Truck & Coach Manufacturing Company and was also promoted to assistant treasurer of General Motors, headquartered in New York. General Motors had invested in a new company, Transcontinental & Western Air, Inc. (TWA), and in 1933 General Motors placed Breech on the board of that airline. At that time General Aviation Corporation, a GM subsidiary, was designing a new passenger craft for TWA with Douglas Aircraft Company. The General Aviation design was expensive. Breech said later, "The General Aviation trimotor was designed to be supported by a large aluminum spar–hogged out of a solid bar of aluminum, a very expensive proposition–extending from wingtip to wingtip through the center section." The expense of this design seemed excessive to Breech, and he ordered development of the aircraft stopped even though it was being developed by a member of the GM family. TWA instead chose the Douglas DC-1, whose wings were of cellular, multiweb construction, lighter and therefore more economical than the General Aviation design.

Breech with the Ford management team in 1950. From left to right, Delmar S. Harder, Lewis D. Crusoe, Henry Ford II, Breech, Theodore N. Yntemna, John S. Bugas, and Harold T. Youngren (courtesy of Henry Ford Museum and Greenfield Village)

Always adept at handling details of mergers, Breech in 1933 was given the task of joining General Aviation, North American Aviation, Eastern Air Lines, TWA, and Western Air Express. The surviving corporation was North American Aviation. Breech served as the corporation's president and chairman until 1936. The experience was not successful, however, though certainly through no fault of Breech's. The new company first lost air mail contracts. Then came controversies over "vertical" companies, which owned or controlled both aircraft manufacturers and airline companies, and, one by one, GM sold its airline interests. Breech kept the reins of North American, moved its operations from Baltimore to Los Angeles, and started it on the way to becoming one of the leading aircraft manufacturers of the country. By the outbreak of World War II, North American had 100,000 employees and was a leading manufacturer of war planes.

In 1937 Breech moved back to GM, becoming a group vice-president in charge of the household appliance division and aviation subsidiaries. One of the subsidiaries he became involved with was

Bendix Aviation. As he said later, "[Bendix] needed reorganizing, so I did it." On his forty-fifth birthday, on February 24, 1942, Breech resigned his GM vice-presidency to become president of Bendix, a post he held until June 30, 1946. Again, Breech's genius for success manifested itself. Within a year he had tripled its output; within two years its gross sales had climbed from $40 million to $1 billion. Bendix was selling parts to both GM and Ford.

In the course of his work Breech met Henry Ford II, who was struggling to bring Ford Motor Company into the modern age after having been run as the personal kingdom of its founder, Henry Ford. But changing conditions and the exigencies of readjusting from a wartime economy to meet the growing demands for cars made it too difficult a task for Henry Ford II, who immediately recognized Breech's talents and asked him to help oversee the transition of Ford into a competitive organization. Ford was in deep trouble, and by most estimates had been losing $68 million a year since the end of the war. Henry Ford II had begun to reorganize the company, streamline its affairs, and introduce efficiency into its operations, but the task was too much for a young, relatively inexperienced executive. Ford was impressed by Breech's reputation as a troubleshooter and an executive with a brilliant record of turning companies around. At first Breech turned down Ford's offer. But as he said later, "after going out there on several trips to try to give him advice and help him out, I got more and more involved, until finally I thought, 'I'll hate myself if I don't accept this challenge.'" It was a difficult decision. Bendix was doing well, and Breech was highly respected and at the top of his profession.

Breech discussed the situation with his wife and told her, "Here's a young man only one year older than our oldest son. He needs help; this is a great challenge that if I don't accept I shall always regret." On June 30, 1946, Breech resigned from Bendix, severed all his remaining connections with GM, and joined Ford as executive vice-president and member of the board of directors. He later received a ten-year contract, which would give him the security and latitude to do what needed to be done.

In the 1966 interview with *Nation's Business* Breech commented:

> When we took over [Ford], we found ourselves short on everything but determination. The company faced the postwar markets with run-down plants, obsolete products, almost nonexistent financial control, an inadequate engineering staff and just sufficient cash to meet daily operating requirements. As we looked to the future, we saw we wouldn't be able to last when the competitive market returned unless we made ourselves completely into a strong, modern, going concern. . . . We had to attack every facet of the business. First, we had to get a real engineering department and design what we felt would be really competitive products. We had to establish good financial controls, because Ford Motor had a country store bookkeeping system. We had to consider long-range plans for adequate facilities because our plants were obsolete. We saw only one answer to this, and it was to get profitable again and put our cash flow into new facilities. That took some time.

Breech plunged right into Ford's massive problems. He worked with Henry Ford II to decentralize management, a difficult task given the autocratic rule of the founding Henry Ford. Ford

Breech with his wife, Thelma, in their Detroit home

himself wanted to change the structure of the company. But according to the June 13, 1953, issue of *Business Week,* "The professional managerial 'savvy' required to translate the concept into the elaborate organization" came from Breech. *Business Week* also noted that Breech had a knack for "picking men and for using them most effectively." Breech also aggressively plowed profits back into the company. He embarked on a huge modernizing program, which he called a "betterment program." Under this program Ford embarked on a large-scale building plan: thirteen manufacturing plants around the country, sixteen parts depots, and four engineering buildings. He also remodeled twenty existing facilities. All of this was accomplished with internally generated funds, without the need for long-term and potentially crippling debt. The strategy worked, and Ford moved into an era of postwar innovation and profitability.

Breech was known not only for his financial acumen but for his ability to find, train, and motivate top managers. To *Nation's Business* he explained, "I remarked many times over the years about the need for managers to be leaders, not just bosses—men who can inspire others. I made the remark in my first speech at Ford Motor Co.: 'The role of management always calls for two qualities above everything else: For one, the manager must be realistic; he must be a practical man. But something else is equally important. He must be a man of vision, he must be going someplace, he must have a goal.' "

Breech stressed what would later be known as "participative" management: "The team members must see that they are important cogs in the machine, and I don't mean just the top fellows. They must be made to feel a part of the company, feel a personal interest in it. They must not regard their work as just a job that pays them a wage or salary." Later in his career, when asked if management techniques were interchangeable from one company to another, he replied, "The answer is simple, yes. In manufacturing you must first have a good product. From then on it's good men that count. Machines are nothing without men, competent management men and competent men to run the machines and competent men to design your products and lay out your factories and get good manufacturing processes."

Initially, the relationship between Breech and Henry Ford II was extremely close; the younger man looked to the experienced executive as his mentor who was preparing him for the day when he could truly take over and run the company. As Ford became more confident in his own abilities, he began to assert himself more often, rather than deferring to Breech's judgment. Breech's authority began to be undercut as ambitious executives realized that if a project was rejected by the executive vice-president, they might be able to get it approved by playing up to Ford.

On January 25, 1955, Breech was elected board chairman of Ford, the first person to hold that title. One of his first major accomplishments was the negotiation and signing, on June 6, 1955, of a three-year pact with the United Automobile Workers. Speaking to the Harvard Business School's annual national business conference five days after the contract was signed, Breech said, "It has been Ford policy for years to stabilize production and employment, to minimize layoffs through better planning and to use overtime pay to meet production peaks rather than hire temporary workers." He noted that Ford had been working on a plan of private supplementation of unemployment compensation "that would give substantial added security

to our workers in ways consistent with private enterprise principles. Such a plan should not shackle management's freedom to manage. It should not offer unemployment benefits so great as to remove the incentive to work. The present plan meets every one of those requirements."

Although Henry Ford had created the position of chairman for Breech, perhaps hoping it would strengthen his leadership role, he found it galling after a time to see Breech serve as the spokesman for the company. It was Breech who as chairman addressed the annual stockholders' meeting after the family-owned business went public in 1956, while Ford, who held the seemingly less important post of president, sat there and listened. Increasingly Ford spoke out in committee meetings in opposition to ideas advanced by Breech. As Breech's authority continued to be eroded, it was apparent that his usefulness to the company was ending, but Ford apparently was unwilling to ask him to resign. But at a management conference held at the Greenbrier Hotel, West Virginia, in 1958, Ford told the gathering of Ford executives, "I am the captain of the ship and I intend to remain captain as long as my name is on the bow." Breech was said to have "turned white" at the tone of Ford's remarks. He stayed on for awhile longer, but then early in 1960 he is said to have come to Ford and declared: "Henry, now you've come of age. You want to take over and I want to step aside." Ford replied "Yes, Ernie. I've graduated."

When his retirement officially took effect in July 1960, Breech was said to have reached this decision after "many months of deepest soul searching" which had led him to conclude that he wanted younger men to assume "the heavy demands of day-to-day operational responsibilities both in their best interests and for the long-term good of the company." His legacy was a company that was earning $500 million a year, with $4 billion in new plants and equipment.

For a few months after Breech's departure Ford held the titles of chairman and president before elevating Robert S. McNamara to the president's position late in the year. Then, when McNamara left after only two months to become secretary of defense in the incoming Kennedy administration, Ford, in some panic, approached Breech, implying that he would be welcome to come back to the company. Breech, who was now sixty-three years old and had established himself in an office he had leased in the Ford Parts Distribution Center in Dearborn, told Ford that he was enjoying his retirement. A short time later, however, he took on potentially the most challenging assignment of his career.

TWA was a company with which Breech had been associated early in his GM career and which was in deep trouble. About 78 percent of the voting stock was held by the eccentric Howard Hughes, who had run the airline as his private possession. After quarrels with TWA's creditors and management Hughes had been forced to place his stock in a voting trust, effective December 31, 1960. At that time TWA's creditors, who were desperately looking for able leadership for the airline, selected Breech as one of the three voting trustees.

Under Hughes's leadership TWA had fallen on lean times. Its loss in 1961 amounted to $14.7 million, and the airline was perilously close to bankruptcy. The jet age was well under way, but the airline did not have enough money to buy the airplanes it needed to be competitive. Credit was almost nonexistent. Against these odds, Breech swung into action. He personally called on TWA's major creditors and convinced them that if the airline failed, they would lose their investments, but if they consented to finance Breech's new ventures, the old and new loans would be repaid. He was successful, bankruptcy was averted, and TWA began its recovery. In 1961 Breech was elected TWA's chairman. One of his first acts was to hire Charles C. Tillinghast, Jr., as the airline's president. Breech and Tillinghast began a whirlwind program of advertising and public relations to convince the public, employees, and potential customers that a new TWA was being built. In 1965 TWA generated $50 million in after-tax profits and was first in net profits and second in revenues among American airlines.

The specter of Hughes's management continued to haunt Breech and his executives. There were suits and countersuits as Hughes fought to regain control of what he considered to be his airline. But eventually Hughes severed his ties with TWA, which continued to prosper under Breech and Tillinghast. Breech's reputation as a manager of men continued. One of the young executives at TWA during those years was Floyd B. Hall, who later became president of Eastern Air Lines at a very troubled time in that company's history and was able to return it to profitability, just as his mentor had done at TWA. In 1967, aged seventy,

Breech resigned from Ford's board of directors. In 1969 he became honorary chairman and director emeritus of TWA.

Breech received an award from the Freedom Foundation in 1951 and the annual award of the Brotherhood of Christians and Jews in 1953. In 1955 he was named to an eight-member board to study the peaceful uses of atomic energy. He was a trustee of the John F. Kennedy Center for the Performing Arts in Washington, D.C., and vice-chairman of the executive committee of the Business Advisory Council for the Department of Commerce.

He married Thelma Rowden on November 11, 1917, and they had two sons, Ernest Robert, Jr., and William H. His personality was ebullient at times. The *New York Times* noted that "Breech, for all those brain cells lined up in his head like the buttons on a calculator, knows how to get away from it all and to have fun. He can find time to fish from a rowboat as well as from his cabin cruiser on the Great Lakes. He is something of a raconteur and his associates particularly delight in his use of dialects." Breech told *Nation's Business,* "I know how to have fun. I think too many people take themselves too seriously. They try to be big business executives even when they play. I think that's a mistake. I think you have just got to be yourself and let people judge you on being yourself and have a good time. . . . I don't mind telling good stories at parties and being a ham actor. I have fun doing these things—playing a one-man band, a pogo stick band, or playing at my banjo, which I play terribly, or playing golf."

He suffered a heart attack on June 27, 1978, and died on July 3, 1978, at the William Beaumont Hospital in Royal Oak, Michigan. Henry Ford II, who had continued to have a high regard for Breech, commented at the time of his former associate's death: "He was a business executive of extraordinary talent and energy who made a major contribution to the postwar revitalization of the Ford Motor Company. He was a warm human being with the ability to inspire loyalty and dedication in others."

Breech's record of rescuing ailing companies was extraordinary. His application of sound financial principles and his recognition of the value of sound management worked hand-in-hand to bring him success. In an article in *Look* of April 10, 1951, entitled "America's Secret Weapon," Breech wrote, "Management, first of all, is a matter of spirit—a feeling of resourcefulness and responsibility and enthusiasm for always doing things better. Second, it is people—the millions of Americans who share in the direction of our unsurpassed production machinery. Put them together, and America's secret weapon comes out as the free-wheeling ingenuity and competitive drive of free men, constantly needled by the urge to beat others at the job of providing better things and services and more of them."

References:

Peter Collier and David Horowitz, *The Fords: An American Epic* (New York: Summit Books, 1987);

J. Mel Hickerson, *Ernie Breech* (New York: Meredith Press, 1968);

Robert Lacey, *Ford: The Men and the Machine* (Boston: Little, Brown, 1986).

Donaldson Brown

(February 1, 1885-October 2, 1965)

by George S. May

Eastern Michigan University

CAREER: Worker, electrical department, Baltimore & Ohio Railroad (1903-1904); general manager of Baltimore sales office, Sprague Electric Company (1904-1908); salesman (1908-1912), assistant to general manager (1912-1914), assistant treasurer (1914-1918), treasurer (1918-1921), director, E. I. du Pont de Nemours & Company (1918-1965); vice-president of finance (1921-1937), chairman of finance committee (1929-1946), vice-chairman of board of directors, General Motors Corporation (1937-1946).

Donaldson Brown, who is credited with being the principal architect of the complex system of financial controls that contributed to the rise of General Motors (GM) to dominance in the automotive industry, was born in Baltimore on February 1, 1885. The son of John Wilcox and Ellen Turner Brown, Brown came from one of the old-line Maryland tobacco-growing families. When he later joined the Du Pont Company, his father made him promise that he would not stay with a company run by a family the Browns reportedly regarded as "upstarts." However, Brown not only continued with Du Pont until a few months before his death in 1965, but in 1916 he married Greta du Pont Barksdale, a member of the great Delaware family which is said to have looked upon the Maryland Browns as "poor white trash."

Despite the fact that his fame would rest on his work in the area of finance, Brown received his training in electrical engineering at Virginia Polytech-

Donaldson Brown

nic Institute, from which he graduated in 1902. He did postgraduate work at Cornell University in 1903 and then applied his training in electrical engi-

farm at Port Deposit, Maryland. Early in 1965 his wife died, and in June he retired from the board of the Du Pont Company where he had continued as an active member of the company's finance committee. On October 2, 1965, Brown died. No matter what his family may have thought of the du Ponts in earlier years, Brown had successfully bridged the gap, and at death he was buried in the du Pont cemetery in Wilmington, Delaware.

Publications:

"Pricing Policy in Relation to Financial Control," three articles in *Management and Administration* (1924) reprinted in *Managerial Innovation at General Motors*, edited by Alfred D. Chandler (New York: Arno Press, 1979);

Some Reminiscences of an Industrialist (Port Deposit, Md., 1957);

"Centralized Control With Decentralized Responsibilities," paper presented in 1927, in *Managerial Innovation at General Motors*, edited by Chandler (New York: Arno Press, 1979).

References:

Ed Cray, *Chrome Colossus: General Motors and Its Times* (New York: McGraw-Hill, 1980);

Peter Drucker, *Adventures of a Bystander* (New York: Harper & Row, 1979);

Alfred P. Sloan, Jr., *My Years With General Motors* (Garden City, N.Y.: Doubleday, 1964).

Bumpers

by James Wren

Motor Vehicle Manufacturers Association

Bumper technology and styling changed rapidly after 1920. Instead of the single bar spring steel bumper common during the 1910s, the 1920s brought the adoption of the Biflex bumper, a design which widened the surface over which the car was protected. These multiple bar bumpers were installed on both the front and rear ends of the automobile, a symbol, perhaps, of the increasing traffic on the nation's roads. As manufacturers recognized that the automobile market was changing from one driven by mechanical innovation to one based on aesthetic appeal, bumpers became a styling point as well as a safety mechanism. As a result chrome-plated bumpers were offered on American cars during the 1920s.

In the 1930s and 1940s vertical bumper guards were added to the bumper assembly. By the late 1940s this design was altered to include a horizontal connecting bar between the vertical posts, yielding a configuration known as a Van Auken guard. During the stylistic revolution of the 1950s the front bumper became an integral part of the automobile grille design, and the usually massive unit was heavily plated in chrome.

This emphasis on styling changed in the 1960s. With the passage of the National Traffic and Motor Vehicle Safety Act of 1966, the federal government began the process of mandating safety standards. Standard bumper heights were mandated for 1967 model cars intended for purchase by the government. General production cars were required to meet these same standards for the 1968 model year. By the mid 1970s the standards were tightened to include requirements that the bumper protect automobiles in crashes up to five miles per hour.

With the radical effects on the automobile industry of the 1979 fuel crisis, bumper technology again changed. Struggling to reduce vehicle weight—designers developed new bumper materials. Lighter aluminum polyurethane and Lexan, a polycarbonated plastic, all have been tested as possible bumpers. Lexan, although the most expensive of the three, offers the most flexible use for styling purposes. For this reason high technology plastics hold out the most promise for use in bumpers of the future.

References:

"Bumper History Still in Making," *Automobile Topics* (May 19, 1928): 124-127, 138;

"Crash Program Underway for New Bumpers," *Iron Age* (November 4, 1971): 60-64.

Archives:

Material on bumper technology is available in the technical references file of the Patent Department, Motor Vehicle Manufacturers Association, Detroit, Michigan.

Philip Caldwell

(*January 27, 1920-   *)

by George S. May

Eastern Michigan University

CAREER: Various positions, U.S. Navy (1942-1946); civilian employee (1946-1948), deputy director of procurement policy division, U.S. Naval Department (1948-1953); various positions (1953-1968), vice-president and general manager of truck operations (1968-1970), president and director of Philco-Ford (1970-1971), vice-president, manufacturing group, North American automotive operations (1971-1972), chairman, chief executive officer, Ford of Europe (1972-1973), executive vice-president, international automotive operations (1973-1977), vice-chairman (1977-1979), deputy chief executive officer (1978-1979), president (1979-1980), chief executive officer (1979-1985), chairman, Ford Motor Company (1980-1985); senior managing director, Shearson Lehman Brothers, Inc. (1985-   ).

Philip Caldwell, who in 1979 became the first chief executive of the Ford Motor Company in nearly three-quarters of a century from outside the Ford family, was born in Bourneville, Ohio, on January 27, 1920, the son of Robert Clyde Caldwell, a farmer, and Wilhelmina Hemphill Caldwell. The Caldwell family had lived in Ohio for nearly a century. Some family members had pursued careers in other areas, including one who became a dean at the Massachusetts Institute of Technology and another who went to China as a missionary and became president of the University of Nanking. For those like Caldwell's father, who continued as a farmer in Ohio, the 1920s were disastrous as farmers experienced a preview of the economic hardships that they and the entire country would have to face in the 1930s. For some reason Caldwell never wanted to talk about those boyhood years, as though he were embarrassed by his family's economic problems. He was furious when a *Detroit News* reporter investigated his childhood and wrote

a sympathetic story depicting how the Ford executive had overcome adversity. Ford staffers tried to find out who had leaked this information to the reporter, and when Caldwell met him he told the newsman angrily, "That was going too far. . . . There was no need for that, no need to stir that up again."

Nevertheless, whatever the family circumstances may have been, the Caldwells were scarcely poverty-stricken. Caldwell and his three brothers all went to college, as Caldwells traditionally had done, but Philip, in one of the rare instances in his life in which he deviated from the expected course of action, attended Muskingum College, rather than Wooster, where Caldwells usually enrolled. Caldwell had decided to be a businessman, influenced, he said, by reading the superbly written, detailed profiles of businessmen and companies that appeared in *Fortune* magazine in the 1930s. He majored in economics at Muskingum, where he graduated in 1940. A $300 scholarship helped him to enter the Harvard Business School. His experiences at Harvard were among the first that he later enjoyed recalling. There he met Robert McNamara, like Caldwell a future Ford president, and who, Caldwell declared, "taught me to run a calculator." His professor of industrial management, the legendary Georges Doriot, later recalled that Caldwell had demonstrated as a student an "abnormally analytical" mind. Caldwell, he said, "knows what can be done, and should be done—and he expects it done," qualities that served Caldwell to great advantage in his business career but also drove several colleagues to distraction.

At the beginning of each semester Doriot would ask his class to choose what businessmen they would like to appear as guest speakers. His prestige and the prestige of the school were such that he was always able to get anyone the class wanted,

Philip Caldwell, right, with Henry Ford II, center, and Lee Iacocca as Ford announces Caldwell's promotion to vice-chairman in April 1977 (courtesy of Junebug Clark)

but on December 8, 1941, the guest was not a businessman but a naval recruiter. Caldwell immediately enlisted in the naval reserve, and following the receipt of his M.B.A. in 1942 he was assigned to duty in California. There he worked under a captain whose job it was to prepare preassembled bases to be used in the island-hopping campaign against the Japanese. The job, which eventually took Caldwell to Pearl Harbor, gave him invaluable firsthand experience in the management of operations in a huge organization. After receiving his discharge in 1946 Caldwell stayed on in the navy as a civilian employee. By 1953, when he was given the navy's Meritorious Civilian Service award, he was the top civilian official in charge of procurement.

It was Caldwell's experience in procurement that brought him to Ford in 1953. There his former Harvard instructor, Robert McNamara, was already well up the executive ladder, and James O. Wright, another of the group of ten bright men, including McNamara, who had been hired by Henry Ford II in 1945 to bring some order to the company, was trying to institute logical and efficient procurement procedures. Caldwell declared that the division was indeed a mess, operated by what he termed "glorified shipping clerks." The effective work that he contributed in helping to straighten out this phase of Ford's operations was the first step in giving Caldwell a reputation in the company of one who could handle tough situations.

After a number of different assignments Caldwell began to rise from the pack of junior executives when he was named manager of the truck division in the 1960s. As Caldwell later recalled it, he sat down with two other executives to study what could be done to improve the performance of the division, whose trucks ran well behind Chevrolet's in sales. He had them list twenty-five reasons why people bought a truck and then compile another list of twenty-five points of comparison between Ford and Chevrolet trucks to determine how Ford rated with its competition. The result, Caldwell said, was that the three of them agreed that Ford had a better heater and provided better visibility, but that Chevrolet had the upper hand on the other twenty-three points. From this starting point Caldwell then directed the development of a new truck that five years later replaced Chevrolet as the top seller in the industry. Others, however, told a somewhat different story. The meeting of the three executives, they said, was typical of Caldwell's penchant for detailed analysis of everything, which led him to be called, David Halberstam reports, "the A-J Man because of his insistence upon having options A through J." When it came time to decide on the design of the new truck, weeks went by with no action, until one of Caldwell's superiors went to the shop where plans for the truck were being drafted. There he found Caldwell surrounded by drawings of different trucks pinned to the wall. Sensing that Caldwell was finding it impossible to decide which one to choose, the executive said, "Phil, why don't we just walk over and pick one before we leave the room today?" They did, and the design question was resolved. Regardless of how the matter was handled, the truck was a success, and when Caldwell in 1968 went to Semon Knudsen, the company president, and told him that he had received a job offer from Rockwell, Knudsen quickly got Henry Ford II to name Caldwell to a vice-presidency.

Caldwell's abilities as an administrator were put to their severest test in 1970 when he was asked to leave the now prospering truck division and take over the direction of Ford's Philco subsidiary. Philco had been a money loser since its acquisition in 1961 and was known at Ford as the company's Siberia. "Since the three men who preceded me at Philco never returned, it wasn't exactly an ingratiating assignment," Caldwell later recalled. Believing that it was more important for him to continue to run the truck division, Caldwell scheduled an appointment with Ford. "He was very understanding of my reservations," Caldwell said, "but he told me that Philco was the greatest management challenge the company had to offer." By this time, Ford's view of Philco had reached the point where he told Caldwell: "Either fix it up or get rid of it." Within a year and a half Caldwell had closed or sold several Philco factories, had increased production at overseas plants where costs were much cheaper, and had overseen the improvement of the company products to the point where the subsidiary was making money. The division was sold shortly after Caldwell was appointed to direct Ford's North American automotive manufacturing operations.

The move that probably assured Caldwell's rise to the top, however, came in 1972 when he was named chairman and chief executive officer of Ford of Europe. In 1973 he was placed in charge of all of Ford's operations outside of North America. Ford's overseas branches, particularly those in Europe, had become Henry Ford II's favorites, and aside from the fact that he loved to visit them and revel in the attention he was accorded in those countries, Ford had good reason for liking them: they were money-makers. Despite the adverse economic conditions for the world market following the oil embargo by the Middle Eastern producers in fall 1973, Caldwell pushed through a large-scale expansion of plants and oversaw the introduction of several new models. The most famous of these was the Fiesta, a front-wheel-drive subcompact introduced in 1976 in Europe where it quickly became a big seller. The car was later imported to the United States where it contributed balance to a product lineup heavily weighted with bigger, less efficient models. Although Caldwell, who compared the Fiesta's impact to that of the Model T, publicly refused to allow himself to be referred to as being the father of the Fiesta, some critics within the company contended that he was indeed receiving too much credit for a car that they said he had not supported until the very end. They asserted that production of the car had been made possible by William O. Bourke, who had been named president of Ford of Europe at the same time Caldwell had been named chairman, and who fought Caldwell's delaying tactics.

Bourke, who was five years younger than Caldwell, was another of the rising stars in the Ford organization being tagged by insiders as a future head of the company. A certain coolness developed between Bourke and Caldwell, whom Bourke regarded as little better than the bland, colorless accountant executives whom production men like Bourke liked to call "bean counters." But a more formidable rival to Caldwell was perhaps the best-known "car" man in America, Lee Iacocca. Although he too was younger than Caldwell, Iacocca had been a national figure since the sensational debut of the Ford Mustang in 1964, a car which he was quick to take full credit for having fathered, in sharp contrast with the reluctance Caldwell would later affect with the Fiesta. At the end of 1970 Iacocca had been named president of Ford, and the assumption had been that he was the heir apparent to succeed Henry Ford II as chairman. But on April 14, 1977, Ford announced he was setting up a new three-man Office of the Chief Executive (which newsmen immediately labeled the 1977 Ford Trimotor, after Ford's famous airplane of the 1920s) to run the company. Ford remained as chairman and Iacocca as president, but in between them was the new office of vice-chairman to which Ford appointed Caldwell. Although attempts were made to downplay it, the arrangement clearly meant that Iacocca had been passed over in favor of Caldwell, who would serve as chief executive officer in Ford's absence and who now had the inside track to head the company when Ford, whose health was not good, stepped down as chairman.

There was much speculation as to what had brought about this change in management. It was obvious that Ford had come to dislike Iacocca and that feeling was mutual. Ford, like his grandfather before him, did not like company officials who received more attention from the press and public than he. Iacocca had eagerly sought and received that kind of attention. In turning to Caldwell, it was said, Ford was choosing a person who knew his own place in the system and who would never seek to upstage the chairman. But this was unfair to Caldwell. The fact of the matter was that he had proven himself to be a highly capable administrator, whose successful direction of the truck and Philco operations had been followed by leadership of the Ford overseas activities that had made them the most profitable part of the overall Ford operations. Meanwhile, Ford's North American operations, which were Iacocca's responsibility, had suffered a serious decline in the 1970s, plagued by embarrassing lawsuits over the safety of the Pinto, another car for which Iacocca had been glad to accept credit when it came out in 1970, and increasing suspicions regarding the quality of Ford cars.

The three-tiered executive arrangement was doomed to a short life because of the clash of personalities. "It was a real crack in the face," Iacocca declared later in his memoirs. "Every time there was a dinner, Henry hosted table one, Caldwell hosted table two, and I was showed down to three. It was public humiliation." If there was the expectation that Iacocca would solve the problem by resigning, he did not cooperate by taking such action. Efforts by the board of directors to work out a compromise by which Iacocca would receive more responsibilities and remain with the company were finally ended when Ford told the directors, "No, it's him or me." The next afternoon, July 13, 1978, Iacocca was called into Ford's office and fired. When Iacocca asked what he had done wrong, Ford's classic response was simply, "I just don't like you."

Caldwell replaced Iacocca as president while still holding on to the position of vice-chairman and deputy chief executive officer. Ten months later at the annual Ford stockholders meeting on May 10, 1979, Ford announced that Caldwell would succeed him as chief executive officer on October 1. Ford retained the position of chairman but stepped down in 1980, at which time Caldwell moved into the office, which again included the duties of chief executive officer. Don Petersen succeeded Caldwell as president.

Ford remained on the board of directors until his death in 1987 and continued during that time to be the most powerful person in the organization. But that Caldwell held the title of chief executive officer from October 1979 marked a dramatic break with the company's previous leadership. He was not, as even the *New York Times* mistakenly reported, the first nonfamily member to head the company. It was in 1906, three years after the founding of the company, that the first Henry Ford had gained full control of the company, which had until then been headed by its first president, John S. Gray. But in 1979 that was all ancient history. To some the contrast between the outgoing and the incoming chief executives was the most dramatic story. "Company spokesmen, who have spent much of their time relating the colorful escapades of various members of the Ford family, are hard-pressed to come up with anecdotes about their new chief executive," the *Times* reported. The society pages would not be carrying stories about the Caldwells engaging in the kinds of late-night carousing that were filed by reporters covering the social activities of Henry Ford II. Ford himself had discovered as much early in Caldwell's career at Ford. At a dinner in London, Ford had offered Caldwell some wine. "I don't drink wine, Mr. Ford," he said. "As a matter of fact, my wife and I don't drink beer or any hard liquor. . . . In fact, we don't drink coffee or tea, and we don't smoke." The astonished Ford then asked Caldwell, "Well, then, what the hell do you do?" What Caldwell and his wife, Betsy Chinn Clark, whom he had married in 1945, did do socially was to enjoy their ample wealth (he had received over $1 million in salary and bonuses the previous year) by indulging their liking for eighteenth-century American antiques, which were used to decorate their home in Bloomfield Hills and also his office. They were active in cultural affairs, with Caldwell heading up a successful fund drive for the Detroit Symphony in 1978, and they took pleasure in their three children. As for the company, however, the importance of Caldwell's appointment as chief executive officer was that for the first time Ford was doing what General Motors had been doing for many years, bringing an executive up through the ranks, giving him broad experience in all phases of the business, and then entrusting him with the responsibility to run the company in the last few years before his retirement.

"I'm really sorry about leaving you with all these problems," Ford said to Caldwell as they rode down in the elevator on Caldwell's first day as chief executive; "it's an awful time, and it doesn't seem fair to dump this on someone else." Caldwell, recalling the condition in which the company had been when Ford had taken over in 1945, replied, "Well, you've been through it all yourself." "Yes, I suppose so," Ford said, "but it was different then. Even at its worst, in 1946, we could sell everything we made. But you don't have the market with you anymore. It's changed on us." If history will judge Ford by the success he had in pulling the company through that earlier critical period, history is also likely to credit Caldwell with being principally responsible for overcoming the even greater problems the company faced during the first years that he was in charge. Ford's market share plummeted from 28 percent in 1978 to 15 percent in 1981. Losses totaled over $3 billion during the first three years. Ford's American-made cars accounted for virtually all of that loss, and for a time there were rumors that the company might shut down it's American plants and rely entirely on it's still-profitable foreign operations. But instead Caldwell cut costs ruthlessly by drastically reducing production schedules, shutting down seven plants, and cutting the number of salaried and hourly workers by over 60,000. Fixed costs in 1980-1981 were cut by $2.5 billion while operating costs were reduced by $4.5 billion a year. Meanwhile, although Don Petersen has received most of the credit for directing the development of the new cars that were needed, it was Caldwell who decided that Ford cars should emphasize quality and innovation rather than follow the conservative and uninspiring, and sometimes shoddy, car Ford had produced for many years. "It struck many in the company as supremely ironic that it was he who was responsible for such a sharp break with the past," David Halberstam reports. "As one Ford man said, it was as dramatic a departure as Richard Nixon's decision to visit Communist China. . . ." Others would take on the job of designing such cars, but it was with obvious satisfaction that Caldwell presided early in 1985 at a Hollywood extravaganza to unveil the Ford Taurus and Mercury Sable, the dramatically designed aerodynamic cars that solidified

Ford's recovery. Ford had already begun it's resurgence when total earnings of nearly $5 billion in 1983 and 1984 had wiped out the memories of the losses earlier in the decade.

The Hollywood event marked the end of Caldwell's career as Ford chairman, for Don Petersen succeeded him on February 1, 1985. Robert Lacey felt that the transition marked the final sign that Ford had adopted the GM system. The power had been passed peacefully, without the turmoil and surprise that had so often accompanied such change in Ford's past. But it was not quite that peaceful behind the scenes. Reportedly, Caldwell had wanted to stay on past the age of sixty-five, but Henry Ford, still the major power in the company, had vetoed that idea. Petersen had also not been Caldwell's choice as a successor. The two men had long had difficulty in hiding the animosity between them. In 1984 Petersen had told a friend that he thought he would get the chairmanship. "It just depends on Henry Ford," he said. When queried about Caldwell's role, Petersen replied that "Decisions like this are still made by Henry Ford and I think he feels the company needs to be more product-oriented."

Caldwell, hailed as "Ford's Mr. Turnaround" by *Fortune,* the favorite magazine of his youth, left his position at Ford while still a vigorous man in his mid sixties. He immediately moved into a new career as senior managing director of Shearson Lehman Brothers, Inc. and as chairman of the policy committee of the firm's investment banking group. It is his role, however, in the critical developments at Ford in the 1970s and the first half of the 1980s that is the basis of his business reputation.

References:

James J. Flink, *The Automobile Age* (Cambridge, Mass.: MIT Press, 1988);

"Ford's Mr. Turnaround: 'We have more to do,' " *Fortune,* 111 (March 4, 1985): 83-84;

"Ford's New Trimotor," *Newsweek,* 89 (April 25, 1977): 65;

David Halberstam, *The Reckoning* (New York: Morrow, 1986);

Robert Lacey, *Ford: The Men and the Machine* (Boston: Little, Brown, 1986);

"A Leader Who Isn't a Ford Takes Center Stage," *Fortune,* 100 (October 8, 1979): 15-16;

"Philip Caldwell: New Breed of Ford Leader," *New York Times,* May 11, 1979;

" '77 Ford Trimotor," *Time,* 109 (April 25, 1977): 76-77.

Roy Dikeman Chapin, Jr.

(September 21, 1915-   )

by Robert J. Kothe

Atlanta, Georgia

CAREER: Engineer and salesman (1938-1954), director, Hudson Sales Corporation (1946-1954); director (1954-1987), assistant sales manager, Hudson division (1954-1955), assistant treasurer (1954-1955), vice-president and treasurer (1955-1956), executive vice-president (1956-1967), president, American Motors International Corporation (1961-1965), general manager (1966-1967), chief executive officer (1967-1977), chairman of the board, American Motors Corporation (1967-1978).

Roy Dikeman Chapin, Jr., was born in Detroit on September 21, 1915, to a distinguished automobile family. His father, Roy D. Chapin, was a notable automobile pioneer and one of the founders of the Hudson Motor Car Company. He led Hudson for a number of years and also served in President Herbert Hoover's cabinet as secretary of commerce. Chapin's mother was the former Inez Tideman.

Chapin graduated from Yale with an A.B. degree in 1937. In October of that year he married Ruth May Ruxton, with whom he had four children: Roy D., Christopher King, William Ruxton, and Cecily Penny. After his first wife's death he married Loise Baldwin Wickser in July 1965. They had four children: Alexandra, Robert L., Loise B., and Hope B.

In 1938 Chapin joined Hudson as an engineer, but most of his early career was spent in sales and finance. His experience in production planning and engineering aided him later, however. In 1946 he was named to the Hudson board of directors and remained there until Hudson merged with Nash in 1954 to form American Motors Corporation (AMC). At the time AMC was formed, Hudson held only 1 percent of the American automobile market; Nash, the larger firm, was the stronger partner in the new company, and former Nash employees dominated the merger. Chapin served as treasurer of AMC, and a major part of his job was to secure credit and negotiate terms and loan extensions for the company, which was often in serious financial trouble.

From 1961 to 1965 he was in charge of AMC's international operations as president of American Motors International Corporation, while retaining his title as executive vice-president of AMC. As head of international operations Chapin came in contact with Renault, a major player in AMC's future. At that time Renault, a French automobile manufacturer, assembled AMC cars for overseas markets, where they were sold as luxury vehicles.

AMC did reasonably well in the late 1950s and early 1960s. Under George Romney's leadership it concentrated on compact cars, an area of the market where the major American automobile manufacturers were not especially active. Romney left the company in 1962 to pursue a political career, and Roy Abernathy, Romney's successor, was not able to maintain the firm's market share. Sales dropped to about 1 percent of the market in the mid 1960s.

Robert B. Evans, an heir to a family fortune and a businessman who had made a career out of buying and turning around faltering companies, purchased about 200,000 shares of AMC stock in late 1965. At that point he became its largest individual stockholder. Even so, his total ownership was still only 2 percent of the outstanding shares, and he did not have a controlling interest. Still, Evans moved rapidly to extend his influence on AMC. In March 1966 he was named to the company board and by fall had been named chairman of the board. Evans, who was unhappy with Abernathy's performance, looked to Chapin, a longtime friend, as a possible replacement. Through Evans's influence Chapin was named general manager in 1966 and took over as chairman of the AMC board and chief executive officer in January 1967.

Over the next few years AMC, despite severe financial difficulties, brought out a number of remarkable cars that employed novel engineering and design. The Hornet, Gremlin, and Pacer were attempts to create, and serve, niches in the automobile market not filled by the rest of the industry. The Pacer, for example, employed a radical, sometimes labeled perverse, design to create a wide, relatively roomy small car.

AMC, despite an often-strained relationship with the United Automobile Workers (UAW) during Chapin's leadership, was able to negotiate favorable contracts with the union which helped the firm survive. In addition, Chapin forced AMC to diversify. Perhaps his greatest contribution to the company was the purchase of Jeep from Kaiser in 1970. Buoyed by a rising interest in off-road vehicles, although the majority of Jeeps spent very little time off the road, Jeep was a consistent money-maker for the firm. When the federal government moved to break GM's virtual monopoly on urban buses, AMC moved strongly into that market. The company also acquired several plastics manufacturers and a garden tractor manufacturer. Despite these forays into other fields, the corporation still depended on passenger cars still for about half of its revenues.

But the firm lacked the resources to compete in the rapidly changing market of the 1970s and sought a merger with a healthier partner. Renault, heavily subsidized by the French government and eager to enter fully into the American market, was a logical choice. In 1977 Renault merged with AMC, and Chapin began the process of turning over control. Chapin retired as chief executive officer in September 1977 and was replaced by Gerald Meyers. He remained as chairman of the board until he announced his retirement from the day-to-day operation of AMC in September 1978. He remained on the board and served AMC as a consultant as well. Chapin continues to serve on a number of corporate boards in retirement, including Gould, American Natural Resources, Michigan Consolidated Gas, and Whirlpool.

Renault was not successful and by 1985 was looking for a way out of its investment with AMC. Chrysler was interested in the company, and Chapin was brought out of semiretirement to be part of the team negotiating with Chrysler. The deal was finalized in early 1987, and Chapin retired from the board in September.

Chapin is truly part of the automobile aristocracy. He attended Yale, lives in Grosse Pointe Farms outside Detroit, and maintains a summer home on Martha's Vineyard. He enjoys hunting and fishing on his California ranch. He also has a strong sense of social responsibility, serving on the board of Detroit Renaissance, the organization set up in the wake of the 1967 Detroit riots with the hope of rebuilding the city.

He spent his entire career with Hudson or the corporation that succeeded it, and for most of that time the companies were struggling for survival. As chairman he was faced with the difficult, perhaps impossible, task of trying to keep the last of the independents alive. Chapin displayed remarkable skill in managing the company and more importantly in negotiating with banks, unions, and merger partners.

Archives:

A large collection of Roy D. Chapin, Jr.'s papers covering his years with Hudson and AMC are at the University of Michigan.

Checker Motors Corporation

by George S. May

Eastern Michigan University

After the demise of Studebaker in the first half of the 1960s, American Motors Corporation (AMC) was commonly referred to as the sole surviving American automobile producer, aside from the Big Three. There were, of course, specialty companies that produced handfuls of replicas of famous models of the past or custom-made vehicles. These were rightfully classified as outside the mainstream of the industry. But in addition to AMC there actually was one other long-established motor vehicle manufacturer, Checker Motors, that was producing tiny numbers of passenger cars during these years and continued to do so until 1982.

The Checker name originated with a Chicago taxicab company of that name that in 1920 began buying taxicab versions of a car built in Joliet, Illinois, by the Commonwealth Motor Company. Commonwealth, established in 1917, was the successor to several other companies dating back to the DeSchaum Automobile Company of Buffalo, founded in 1908. The Checker cab bodies were furnished by the Markin Auto Body Corporation of Joliet, and in 1921 the head of that company, Morris Markin, took over the Commonwealth company. The following year he discontinued passenger-car production and changed the company's name to the Checker Cab Manufacturing Company. In 1923 Markin moved the company to Kalamazoo, Michigan, taking over factories previously used by the Handley-Knight and Dort automobile companies.

Kalamazoo previously had been the site of a number of automobile companies, but Checker was the only one to last for any length of time. With production of 1,000 taxicabs a year by 1925, Checker claimed to be the country's "largest exclusive cab makers," distinguishing itself from other manufacturers, such as John D. Hertz, who manufactured both passenger cars and cabs. Like Hertz, whose taxicabs were used by his Yellow Cab companies, Checker cabs were used by local cab companies

CHECKER CAB MANUFACTURING CORPORATION
Kalamazoo, Michigan

(Prices upon application)

CHECKER TAXICAB—K

COLOR........	Optional	LUBRICATION ..	Forced feed and splash
SEATING	Six	CRANKSHAFT..	Four bearing
WHEELBASE...	127 inches	RADIATOR	Cellular
WHEELS......	Steel disc	COOLING......	Water pump
TIRES........	7.00—18 (32 x 7.00) inches	IGNITION......	Storage battery
		STARTER......	Two unit
BRAKES.......	Foot, hydraulic, expanding on four wheels. Hand, contracting on transmission	FUEL FEED..	Vacuum
		CLUTCH	Multiple disc
		SPEEDS.......	Three forward, one reverse
ENGINE.......	Six cylinder, vertical, cast in block, 3⅜ x 4½ inches; head removable; valves in side; horsepower 27.3, N.A.C.C. rating	DRIVE........	Spiral bevel
		REAR SPRINGS.	Semi-elliptic
		REAR AXLE...	Three-quarter floating
		STEERING.....	Cam and lever

STANDARD EQUIPMENT—Instrument panel with speedometer, ammeter, tank gasoline gauge, air cleaner, oil filter, gasoline strainer, electric horn, automatic windshield cleaner, spare wheel, shock absorbers, stop light, spot light, front and rear bumpers, cowl ventilator, cowl lamps, depressible headlight beams, heater, ventilating windshield, dome light, door tell-tale light, fender mirror, tools and ash tray.

The 1929 Model K

using that name. Checker cabs were also used by a subsidiary of the company, the Parmelee Transportation Company, which by the 1930s was said to be the country's largest operator of cabs.

In 1933 the Checker company became part of Erret L. Cord's far-flung network of businesses when it was announced he had acquired a majority stock interest in the company. Markin remained as president of Checker. In August 1937 the Securities and Exchange Commission, after a year-long investi-

A Checker cab in service in New York City in the 1970s (courtesy of Museum of Modern Art, New York, Helaine R. Messer)

gation, charged Cord and Markin with having manipulated the stock of Checker, Parmelee, and Chicago Yellow Cab, which Checker also controlled, for their personal financial benefit. Both men denied the charges but agreed to abide by a court order enjoining them from engaging in any further trading activities in violation of the securities laws. The same day the order was issued Cord disposed of all of his varied interests. Markin retained his position with Checker, and that company was the only one of Cord's former automobile holdings to survive the collapse of his business empire.

During World War II and for some years afterward Checker benefited from war contracts to produce 4-wheel-drive vehicles and army trailers. After the war it also produced buses and from 1958 to 1974 produced a twelve-passenger stretched version of its taxicab, the Aerobus, which was widely used to carry air travelers to and from airports.

Although some Checker taxicabs reportedly were available as "pleasure cars" as early as 1948, it was not until 1959, a year after the name of the company had been changed to Checker Motors, that passenger cars, known as Marathons, officially were sold. The cars were based on the company's Model A8 taxi, introduced in 1956. The 4-door sedans used the 6-cylinder Continental engine that Checker had purchased for its cabs for many years, but from 1964 the company shifted to 6-cylinder

and 8-cylinder engines which were purchased from Chevrolet (a few Chrysler V-8 engines were used in 1963-1964). Production of the passenger car never numbered more than a few thousand per year, as Checker's total production of cars and cabs in the 1960s at its peak did not exceed the 8,000-unit range. Marathon sales seem to have been confined to several large cities, such as New York, and to a few people who enjoyed owning and driving a car that, because of its origins as a taxicab, emphasized interior roominess and durability. Although Ghia, the Italian design firm, did develop a prototype in 1970 of a new, more up-to-date model, the company chose to stay with the existing model, essentially unchanged since 1956.

By the early 1980s production of the cabs and cars was down to about 3,000, and the company was losing money. Sales were affected in part by the fact that there was a good deal of truth in the company's claim back in 1925 that "no Checker Cab has ever worn out." In contrast to other American cars, the replacement market was not an active one for Checker. In addition, economic conditions growing out of the much higher cost of gasoline created a demand for more fuel-efficient cars than were the 4,000-pound Checkers. With the taxicab business, the staple of the company over the years, being lost as cab companies preferred to buy less roomy but more efficient standard Detroit cars, David Markin, who had succeeded to the presidency after his father's death in 1971, announced in July 1982 that Checker was ending vehicle production after some sixty years.

References:
Nick Baldwin and others, *The World Guide to Automobile Manufacturers* (New York: Facts on File, 1987);

"The Checker Cab: Checking Out," *Newsweek*, 99 (April 19, 1982): 73;

"Death of a Supercab," *Time*, 119 (April 19, 1982): 66;

John A. Gunnell, ed., *Standard Catalog of American Cars, 1946-1975* (Iola, Wis.: Krause Publications, 1979);

Larry B. Massie and Peter J. Schmitt, *Kalamazoo: The Place Behind the Products* (New York: Windsor Publications, 1981).

Walter Percy Chrysler

(April 2, 1875-August 18, 1940)

by Richard P. Scharchburg

GMI Engineering & Management Institute

CAREER: Locomotive mechanic (1892-1912); works manager (1912-1916), president and general manager, Buick Motor Company (1916-1920); executive vice-president, General Motors Company (1919-1920); executive vice-president, Willys-Overland (1920-1921); president, Maxwell-Chalmers Motor Car Company (1920-1925); president (1925-1935), chairman of the board of directors, Chrysler Corporation (1925-1940).

Walter Percy Chrysler was a locomotive mechanic turned automobile manufacturer who founded the Chrysler Corporation with the money and experience gained as general manager of Buick Motor Division and executive vice-president of General Motors (GM). His life began in a Kansas railroad town, and through hard work he achieved the American dream, becoming one of the creative geniuses of American industry.

In the mid nineteenth century, western Kansas enjoyed the fruits of being linked with the rest of the country by means of the Union Pacific (UP) Railroad. Henry Chrysler, an engineer on the UP, settled with his wife Anna in the village of Wamego, Kansas.

On April 2, 1875, the Chryslers' second child was born and was named Walter Percy. During Chrysler's early years the family remained in Wamego, but they later moved to Ellis, Kansas, which, because it was headquarters for the UP repair shops, held far greater opportunities for education and employment for the Chrysler children. In the atmosphere of this booming railroad town, Chrysler was raised like most boys of that time,

Walter Percy Chrysler (courtesy of Motor Vehicle Manufacturers Association of the U.S., Inc.)

and his school days were filled with the rough-and-tumble adventures associated with growing up in small-town Kansas.

At home he performed the usual chores of a young boy growing up in a nineteenth-century small town—chopping wood, milking the family cow, and then peddling the surplus product door-to-door. He also worked in a grocery store after school and on Saturdays, earning $10 a month. Later he sold flowered calling cards and silverware to the ladies of Ellis; he was seldom idle. As he grew older his interests turned more and more to machines, and Chrysler spent most of his spare time in the UP repair shops watching locomotives being repaired. He asked countless questions of the mechanics which showed a keen, observant, and thoughtful aptitude for mechanics. He tried his hand at small jobs coaxed from any genial mechanic who would give him a chance and also learned to make his own tools, keep them in repair, and to use them carefully and expertly. Chrysler accomplished all of this before graduating from high school and while working his many jobs and chores.

Chrysler progressed at the usual rate through high school where he did well in mathematics, especially algebra. His mother, worried his attention to railroad mechanics would be at the expense of schoolwork, was no doubt overjoyed when he finally completed his studies and received his diploma from Ellis High School.

Since Chrysler's older brother Ed had gone to work in the railroad shops, Walter's father thought one mechanic in the family was enough. He wanted his son to continue his education at Quincy College, but Walter refused to go. His father was resolute, declaring that "You can't learn machinery, and that's all I've got to say. You cannot get to be an apprentice until I say the word, and I won't recommend you." But Chrysler, as stubborn as his father, went to the railroad shops and succeeded in being hired as a sweeper at 10¢ an hour. Not only did he have to sweep the greasy floors but he was also required to assist in cleaning the flues of the boilers in the steam locomotives. He later recalled that "I carried miles of boiler pipe, and swept the floor and did all the other kinds of work that fell to the lot of a janitor."

More important than the dirty job, hard work, and low pay was the opportunity to observe the machinists at work and to explore the mysteries of the giant locomotives. After six months he approached the master mechanic about becoming an apprentice machinist. The master mechanic expressed his approval and was successful in gaining Chrysler's father's consent in 1892 for Chrysler to begin his four-year apprenticeship. All apprentices

were required to pass an entrance examination, which he did with ease, attributing success to his background in algebra—the one subject in which he excelled during his high school education.

Chrysler was not content to do only the jobs assigned him but was eager to build things—an eagerness which animated him throughout his life. When only eighteen he revealed his energy and ambition by constructing a miniature steam locomotive, complete in every detail, including air brakes, and capable of developing speed. The 42-inch-long locomotive finished, he next built a track 220 yards long and gave demonstrations which attracted adults as well as all the local children.

In 1895, after completing his apprenticeship, Chrysler became a journeyman machinist. Again opposing his parents' wishes, he left home and took jobs anywhere he saw an opportunity to learn. He moved from job to job for several years until he was promoted from machinist to foreman at the Denver & Rio Grande Western Railroad in Salt Lake City. During this time he completed a correspondence course in electrical engineering from the International Correspondence School.

In 1901 Chrysler returned to Ellis and married Della Forker. The marriage was not viewed favorably by the townspeople. Writing in 1924 about Chrysler, the *Kansas City Star* quoted one resident who remembered saying at the time of their marriage, "It is too bad for Della, isn't it? Why couldn't Walter have gone into a bank or been a doctor instead of deciding to spend his life fiddling around engines?" By 1924 the Ellis resident's derisive comments had already been proved mistaken many times over.

In 1903 Chrysler began again to travel extensively looking for work; only now he traveled with wife and child. He took jobs as general foreman and finally as master mechanic on the Chicago & Great Western Railroad, where he steadily advanced to be superintendent of motive power. He distinguished himself by being the youngest man, only thirty-three, ever to hold the superintendent's position, which oversaw nearly 10,000 machinists.

While employed by the Chicago & Great Western Railroad, Chrysler would often travel to Chicago. On one of these excursions in 1908, the year Henry Ford introduced the Model T and William C. Durant incorporated GM, Chrysler visited an auto show and began to cultivate his interest in automobiles. Although his first interest in automobiles, as it had been in railroads, was mechanical, Chrysler understood that automotive travel was different:

> As I visualized its [the automobile's] future, it far outran railway development, which in a sense had reached its zenith, because the automobile provided flexible, economical, individual transportation which could be utilized for either business or pleasure. It knew no limits except a right-of-way, it was bounded by no greater restrictions than individual effort and will. To me it was the transportation of the future and as such I wanted to be a part of it. That was where I saw the opportunity.

At the 1908 Chicago Auto Show Chrysler became intrigued by the beauty and mechanical sturdiness of one of the cars, a Locomobile Phaeton. Painted white with red upholstery and a khaki top, it was one of the earliest models to feature four doors. He could not drive an automobile, he could not afford the $5,000 cash asked for the car, nor was he interested in it primarily as a mode of transportation. He wanted it so that he might take it apart and study it as a fascinating new piece of machinery. The pistons in this new machine—driven not by steam but by expanding hot air instantly heated by ignited gasoline vapor—gave every man his own locomotive, one that would not be tied to rails. The possibilities for the future were unlimited.

Chrysler's total savings in the bank were only $700, and he had a wife and two children to support. Yet he could not suppress his curiosity, and he was able to convince a banker friend to loan the $4,300 he needed to buy the car. When the banker described Chrysler's willingness to wipe out his savings and incur the huge debt as "madness," Chrysler retorted, "Just ask yourself what this country will be like when every individual has his private car and is able to travel anywhere."

The Locomobile came by rail to Oelwein, Iowa, where the Chryslers were living. He hired a team of horses to haul the car from the freight depot to the barn behind their home. During the next several months, Chrysler spent every spare hour taking the Locomobile apart and putting it together again until he knew its inner workings. Only then did he allow Mrs. Chrysler to coax him into taking her and the children for their first ride. That journey nearly ended in disaster several times, because Chrysler had been too busy studying the engine to teach himself to drive. His first try at driving ended up in a neighbor's garden; the second try was more

successful but still a harrowing experience for him and his family. After a 4-mile ride at 20 miles an hour they all arrived safely back at the barn.

In 1910 Chrysler moved to Pittsburgh to join the American Locomotive Company. By 1912 he was earning $12,000 annually, double his starting salary. Chrysler's outstanding work caught the eye of James J. Storrow, a director of American Locomotive, who was also chairman of the finance committee of the financially troubled GM. In 1912 Storrow asked Chrysler to go to Flint, Michigan, to meet Charles W. Nash, president of the Buick Motor Company. Impressed by Chrysler's record, personality, and his progressive ideas of production, Nash promptly offered him the post of works manager at Buick. Nash warned him, however, that "We can't pay you more than $6,000 a year"— exactly half his pay at the locomotive manufacturing company. "I'll accept," answered Chrysler to an astonished Nash. This was the opportunity to break into the automotive industry for which Chrysler had been quietly, but impatiently, waiting.

After taking the position at Buick, Chrysler quickly used his experience to improve production efficiency. On an introductory tour of the Buick plant Chrysler made mental notes of time—and material-wasting practices then common at the Buick plant. One of Chrysler's first steps at Buick was to institute a program whereby the cost of a new car model could be precisely estimated in advance instead of being set after the fact. In order to accomplish this, the cost of drilling every hole, making every casting, machining all parts, and fabricating car bodies had to be known. This method was new to the automotive industry but had been used for years in locomotive production and proved to be a move toward more efficient organization.

Chrysler was familiar with metalworking, but the workmen in the Buick plant were from the carriage trade of woodworkers, in which procedures were slow and inefficient. By the old carriage-building methods each automobile frame took four days to produce. Each frame was diligently sanded, painted several times, and dried for twelve hours between coats. By Chrysler's reasoning this was a waste of time and material since no one saw this fine finish after the car was completed. As a first step, production time was reduced to two days by eliminating several coats of paint and reducing drying time by increasing the temperature in the drying rooms.

The Chrysler Six, the company's first production model, was introduced in early 1924 (courtesy of the Chrysler Corporation)

The Buick plant was in a building with many posts placed throughout which supported the roof. These were a hindrance to the workmen and reduced the amount of space available to move the automobiles during assembly. To solve this problem Chrysler braced the roof with stronger trusses and had the posts removed. Until Chrysler's arrival at Buick each car was almost completely assembled in one spot in the factory. The various crews of workmen carried the parts to each car, assembled that part, and then moved on to another area. To save time and movement Chrysler installed a track made of two-by-fours throughout the plant. After the wheels and springs were attached to the frame, the assembly was pushed along this track to the workmen, who fastened their part and passed the car onto another station. This version of mass production saved Buick large amounts of money and further enhanced Chrysler's reputation.

With Chrysler's developments and improvements installed, the production at the Buick plant was increased to 550 cars a day. The innovation of painting parts before they were assembled was also started at this time, a procedure which enabled Buick to stockpile parts and reduce bottlenecks in the assembly line. A new method of applying the paint was also developed. Based on the principle of the atomizer, using air pressure to spray the paint, this method of applying the finish to automobile bodies was eventually used throughout the industry.

In 1915 Chrysler was still being paid the same salary as in 1912. Because he had saved Buick millions of dollars, effected many economies, and increased production, Chrysler walked into Nash's office, rested his knuckles on Nash's table, and demanded, "Charley, I want $25,000 a year, or I'm going to leave." (Chrysler later laughingly remarked that Nash probably had the change from the first nickel he had ever earned.) Shocked by Chrysler's demand, Nash told him that he would have to look into the matter. In a few days Nash told him that the raise had been approved. "Well, thank you; and by the way: Next year I want $50,000," was Chrysler's reply.

However, in 1916 there was a shift in control of GM from the banker group, headed by James J. Storrow and Charles W. Nash, to the company's founder, William C. Durant. As a result Chrysler was offered the presidency of Buick at an annual salary of $500,000. Chrysler did not immediately accept the position, as Storrow and Nash had invited him to join them in a venture which involved taking over the Packard Motor Car Company in Detroit. Their plan failed to mature, and Chrysler was glad he still retained Durant's generous offer to remain at Buick. Chrysler had been cautioned by Nash about Durant's habit of interfering in matters that were someone else's responsibility, so when he did accept, Chrysler demanded absolute management control of Buick. Durant, at the time, agreed to his terms.

While Chrysler was president of Buick and, later, executive vice-president of GM, the corporation purchased many thousands of car bodies from Fisher Body Corporation. As GM absorbed a larger and larger proportion of Fisher's output, Chrysler suggested that GM acquire as large a financial interest as possible in Fisher Body. Chrysler's associates recognized the wisdom of the move, but the Fisher brothers, when first approached, were cool to the idea. After three months of negotiations GM acquired 60 percent of Fisher Body stock, which gave GM control over one of their most important components and assured as many bodies as their car production demanded.

When Chrysler arrived at Buick he scrapped the leisurely carriage-making methods that slowed production, redesigned the plant's floor space, installed one of the first moving production lines, and increased the factory's output from 45 to 550 cars a day. By the time he left in 1920, he had overseen the construction operation of a vast new plant, seen that Buick cars had attained a reputation for sound design and manufacture, and increased Buick's net income in 1919 to $48 million, over 50 percent of GM total for that year. While at Buick, Chrysler accumulated some $1.14 million in GM stock. In 1919 he was promoted to executive vice-president of GM in charge of automotive operations, retaining also his Buick position for the nearly 2 years he remained at GM before leaving.

While at Buick, Chrysler had frequently endured Durant's interference in operations despite Durant's agreement to respect Chrysler's autonomy. In 1920 Chrysler's frustration reached a boiling point when Durant sold a Buick sales branch in Detroit to a friend and had hired away a superintendent from a Buick drop-forge plant without so much as consulting Chrysler. On both occasions Chrysler had stormed to Durant's office in Detroit, was forced to wait while Durant answered telephone calls, and eventually had bluntly told his boss to stop meddling. A third breach of his management understanding with Durant was too much for Chrysler. While attending a luncheon at the Flint Chamber of Commerce, the president of Buick was astounded that a new $6-million plant for supplying frames to Buick would be built in Flint. The toastmaster, Durant's old partner Dallas Dort, called on Chrysler, who was engaged in tough bargaining for frames from a supplier in Milwaukee at very favorable prices, to comment. Furious at the latest interference from Durant, Chrysler told the startled Flint audience that "not so long as I stay here will General Motors have a frame plant in Flint." He stormed out of the meeting, leaving a stunned and silent audience.

The following day, at a board meeting, Chrysler confronted his boss with angry questions and on March 20, 1920, resigned. Alfred P. Sloan, Jr., who occupied an office next door to Durant, later recalled, "I remember the day. He (Chrysler) banged the door on the way out, and out of that bang came eventually the Chrysler Corporation." In spite of their business disagreements, Chrysler and Durant remained close friends until Chrysler's death in 1940.

In 1919 national motor vehicle output had swelled to 1,651,625 passenger cars and 224,731 trucks and buses. A millionaire at forty-five, Chrysler discovered that he could not break the habits of a lifetime. He continued to get up at 6 A.M., and his Flint home was usually filled with friends and business acquaintances who talked of nothing but mechanical inventions and automobiles. Della Chrysler rebelled at the constant stream of males coming and going at all hours with their greasy shoes and smelly cigars, dropping ashes everywhere they went in the house. She soon announced to Walter that she wished he would go back to work. Already chafing under the inactive life, he did not have to wait long for an opportunity to do just that.

Chrysler's old mentor at American Locomotive, James J. Storrow, along with other individuals, called on Chrysler to help rescue the financially ailing Willys-Overland Company. Chrysler agreed to take on the challenge for an annual salary of $750,000, plus perquisites which boosted his total yearly compensation to $1 million.

John North Willys had successfully built the company from the tottering Overland firm making only 465 cars in Indianapolis in 1908 to a production of 141,000 cars in 1916. He made the mistake, however, of abandoning full-time management of Willys to engage in war work and moved his offices to New York. Disastrous strikes in the Ohio plants, plus bloated inventories and excess material orders, had almost ruined the company, which was $46 million in debt by the time Chrysler joined the company in 1920.

Chrysler eagerly attacked Willys-Overland's problems, which represented precisely the sort of challenge he liked. By his skill in organizing and in setting up thrifty and efficient operations, Chrysler succeeded quickly in reducing the company's indebtedness to $18 million. What the company needed, however, was an entirely new car with more market appeal, and Chrysler wanted to begin the process of developing such a product. But Willys, who still retained the presidency, believed that the company's problems could be solved better by refining the old model rather than by designing and engineering a completely new car. Chrysler was determined to develop a new car, and became aware that his objective would not be realized within the Willys firm.

While he was still engaged with the problems with Willys, Chrysler was persuaded to take on yet another faltering enterprise, the Maxwell Motor Car Company and its subsidiary the Chalmers Motor Car Company, which were $26 million in debt. In addition to trying to save Willys-Overland and Maxwell-Chalmers, Chrysler was also laying the foundations for his future by developing a close engineering relationship with the Zeder-Skelton-Breer engineering group, which was eventually to form the basis of Chrysler Corporation's engineering leadership.

Maxwell was a highly respected name in the automotive world; Jonathan Dixon Maxwell, one of the pioneers of the automobile industry, had collaborated with Elwood Haynes in building the first Haynes car in 1893. He later moved on to Olds Motor Works, then left in 1902 to start the Northern Automobile Company in Detroit. In 1903 the Maxwell-Briscoe Motor Company was founded in partnership with Benjamin Briscoe. Managing to survive the collapse of United States Motors, of which it had been a part, Maxwell was taken over and ably managed by Walter E. Flanders, and by 1915 the company ranked sixth in output among all automobile manufacturers in the United States. That same year Flanders engineered a leasing agreement with the Chalmers Motor Car Company, chiefly to obtain access to the Chalmers manufacturing facilities on Oakland Avenue in Highland Park. In 1916 Chalmers introduced the Model 6-30, which provided the company with its best production year ever. However, only minor mechanical improvements were made in the Maxwell during the next three years, and the departure of Walter Flanders in 1918, along with an outdated product, sealed the company's fate. World War I and the boom that followed it, together with what appeared to be an impending shortage of materials, had tempted the company's leadership to overextend. Also, with the public eagerly buying any car that the maker could deliver, more than one manufacturer had neglected to improve his product to keep pace with the times.

Suffering on both of these counts, and also possessing inept leadership, Maxwell became embroiled in a complicated controversy with Chalmers. As such, conditions at Maxwell-Chalmers were far from ideal when Chrysler joined the company.

But Chrysler did not agree to join Maxwell-Chalmers without stipulations. He demanded that the company be reorganized, with himself as president in complete control, and that $15 million in new working capital be provided by the same men to whom the company already owed $26 million. No better proof exists of the banker's confidence in Chrysler's ability than that the financiers agreed to the terms. Following Chrysler's plan, a reorganization committee purchased the assets of the old company at auction and organized the new Maxwell Motor Car Corporation early in 1921. Fundamentally the major problem at Maxwell was the same as at Willys: the car of the moment had some major flaws that had completely destroyed public confidence in the product.

The idea for an all-new, 6-cylinder car had never been far from Chrysler's thoughts since meeting three brilliant young automotive engineers named Zeder, Skelton, and Breer in 1920. Fred Zeder, a graduate of the University of Michigan, Owen Skelton, from Ohio State, and Carl Breer, from Stanford University, formed a near-perfect engineering team. Chrysler knew that these three men were crucial to his revitalization plans.

Zeder, Skelton, and Breer (ZSB), with an organization of approximately fifteen engineers, left Detroit on July 14, 1920, to join the Willys Corporation at its new plant located in Elizabeth, New Jersey. Chrysler did not employ the ZSB group only to design a "hurried replacement car" for the Willys product line, but rather to form an engineering department to prepare a newly designed "Light Six" for production and marketing by Willys. Presumably little engineering would be required for the new Willys Six since it was to be the same car as was then being built in Toledo at Willys-Overland except for the addition of two more cylinders and a longer wheelbase. Both cars had semi-elliptic springs placed in a "v" formation extending ahead of the front axle and to the rear of the rear axle. This type of wishbone suspension delivered a very fine ride due to the flexible chassis. However, because of very low gas mileage and high breakage rates in chassis, frames, and bodies, the car was unpopular, and sales fell sharply.

Not until the ZSB organization had examined the design and tested the experimental cars was there any understanding of the flimsiness of the car. Their adverse report was given to Chrysler in spring 1921 by A. B. (Tobe) Couture, who tested most of the experimental cars and was stationed at Elizabeth prior to the arrival of the ZSB group. A meeting with the bankers in control of Willys was called, and since the nature of Couture's report was so adverse, Chrysler declared before these bankers that the car would not be built.

Quickly following the rejection of the first "Light Six," there was a revival of a so-called "hurried replacement car" to try to ease the tension and embarrassment of the whole situation. The fine, large new factory, paid for out of the millions which John North Willys had obtained from top Boston and New York bankers, was a considerable embarrassment lying idle and unused except for research. In August 1920 a business downturn led to huge layoffs at Willys-Overland in Toledo, and Chrysler's goal was to ease pressure on Willys-Overland through canceling current commitments for parts and materials which were no longer needed.

Along with the engineering and production problems at Willys, Chrysler also faced declining sales at Maxwell-Chalmers. Nationally, sales of cars dropped precipitously during the postwar slump of 1920-1921, and even the popular Ford Model T dropped from a production of 990,658 to 479,077 cars in one year, despite a price reduction of $125 per car. Maxwell had 26,000 unsold, and apparently unsellable, cars scattered throughout the country. The cars were falling apart, and most Maxwell dealers were in dire financial straits. The cars were plagued by a mechanical defect which caused the rear axles to buckle at the first sign of stress. Chrysler first analyzed the mechanical weakness and installed the necessary braces to carry the cars over the bumpy roads. At the same time the cars were being strengthened, Chrysler mounted an advertising campaign to bolster Maxwell sales by trumpeting "The Good Maxwell" across the nation.

The 26,000 "braced-up" Maxwells were then marked down to bargain prices at which they were sold with a profit of only $5 each. More and better-engineered Maxwells were soon introduced, and by 1922 Maxwell sales increased to 48,850, and the company earned a net profit of $2 million. But Chalmers, which had been made a subsidiary of

Maxwell in the reorganization, lost $1 million, and the company was liquidated in 1923 in order to concentrate assets to Maxwell. Large payments were made on Maxwell's indebtedness after the 1921 downturn ended, and in four years under Chrysler's management Maxwell paid off a large portion of its debts and generated some $5 million in cash.

In the meantime the ZSB was still busy trying to develop a 6-cylinder car for Willys. When testing resumed on the modified car, the results revealed that the suspension was riddled with problems. The car's springs would break unless stiffened, and when that was accomplished the supporting frame ends would also break. If they stiffened both to the point of desired endurance, the ride resembled that of a lumber wagon. In still further tests they found the entire frame and suspension distinctly inferior, and if they remedied one fault several appeared to take its place. As the engineers tested the engine they discovered problems with the cooling system. Additional mechanical defects were also discovered in the intake manifold and the crankshaft.

The results of the ZSB tests did not reveal a car able to attain even minimal standards in daily use. It was a discouraging situation since patterns, dies, tools, and fixtures were all set, waiting a go-ahead for production. The choices offered to Chrysler were two: make as many improvements as possible in the present design; or begin all over again to design an entirely new automobile, incorporating the specifications that Chrysler desired and with which the new engineering team felt comfortable. In summer 1921 he gave the go-ahead to do both.

This decision added yet another potential problem. The ZSB team believed that conducting the new design work in the same plant as the modifications would cause morale problems among the workers. As a result the new design group was moved to an off-site location in Summit, New Jersey, about twelve miles from the Elizabeth plant. It was there on the upper floors of the Beechwood Hotel that the entirely new automobile gradually took shape. Owen Skelton took up residence in the hotel to be near the project and recalled that his bedroom "became a drafting room where the first design of the original Chrysler Six engine took form." This "two-pronged" effort produced two distinctly different cars: one which was immediately intended for production as a Willys Six, and another which was to become the Chrysler Six.

The first Plymouth, introduced in 1928, confirmed Chrysler's position as one of the industry giants (courtesy of the Chrysler Corporation)

The new car design utilized an "L" head engine with a 7-bearing crankshaft, 6 cylinders in line, an updraft carburetor at the center of the manifold with hotspot intake providing uniform distribution of vaporized gasoline, a Hotchkiss rear axle, and semi-elliptic front and rear springs. By late summer 1921 the car was being tested by drivers who turned in about 800 miles per day over the course laid out on roads extending from the New Jersey coast into Pennsylvania and finally through New Jersey's Orange mountains. This prototype was tested for 30,000 miles, after which it was torn down and found to be in perfect condition.

During the first six months of 1921, while the ZSB developmental work continued, negotiations continued among Chrysler, the bankers, and John Willys over production of the newly designed car. A few days before July 4, 1921, Chrysler called Zeder, Skelton, and Breer to his office and said, "Boys, it is all set; I am taking my family for a boat trip over the 4th, and when I return we will be building the car at Elizabeth." But Chrysler did not expect Willys to bring out the "Chrysler" car because, at his direction, the Maxwell Corporation had made an offer to Willys for the purchase of the Elizabeth property (including the "Chrysler" car). After the holiday nothing happened. The only word passed was that someone was blocking the sale, perhaps suspicious of Chrysler. For the next several months Chrysler seemed to lose interest or perhaps

was preoccupied with the affairs of Maxwell in Detroit. Strangely, John Willys was never seen again around the Elizabeth plant, seemingly tired of the whole deal. Suddenly, and to Chrysler's surprise, Willys announced on November 30, 1921, that the Willys Corporation would be taken over by receivers and the assets liquidated at public auction. Chrysler's connection with Willys ended with the November 30 announcement.

At this time the Zeder-Skelton-Breer Engineering Company was incorporated and continued to operate as engineering consultants using space and facilities rented at the Elizabeth plant for $100 per month. The ZSB company took on outside jobs to pay the way for their rather large engineering organization. At no time, however, did they stop work on the "Chrysler Six."

During the early months of 1922 Chrysler was neither seen nor heard around the Elizabeth plant. One evening Zeder and Skelton invited Chrysler to have dinner at the Robert Treat Hotel in Newark; he accepted but appeared restless and after a pleasant visit seemed anxious to return to New York. It was only after much persuasion by Zeder that Chrysler consented to drive to Elizabeth. They showed Chrysler the latest developments of the "Chrysler Six," and, showing his old determination and excitement, he did not return to New York until long after midnight. But Chrysler had not been as idle as his silence may have suggested. Chrysler was still pursuing a plan for the future of the "ZSB Chrysler" which involved the Maxwell Corporation's purchase at the upcoming public auction of the Elizabeth plant, along with the rights to manufacture the experimental car then nearly ready for production.

But Durant appeared again to frustrate Chrysler's plan. As expected, the court-appointed receivers decided to sell not only the plant but also the rights to manufacture the car developed for Willys. A minimum bid of $2 million was expected. Chrysler had been planning quietly to make a serious offer to purchase the plant and plans for Maxwell. He was not prepared, however, for the spirited bidding undertaken on the behalf of Durant. When the final gavel sounded, Chrysler had been outbid by Durant, who paid $5.525 million for the package. The Durant Corporation set up manufacturing in the Elizabeth plant for the Star car and eventually brought out the ZSB- designed car—with a slightly enlarged engine—as the Flint.

Again disappointed and thwarted, Chrysler set to work with an engine that Zeder and company had been designing in secret at the Summit, New Jersey, site. Forced to vacate the Elizabeth plant laboratory in 1922 following the sale to Durant, Zeder moved his engineering group into a loft on the fourth floor of a building at 26 Mechanic Street in Newark. Here Chrysler and the engineers consolidated their gains and went to work at once on a third new car. Chrysler was excited again about the prospects and visited the shop often, contributed many ideas, and worked with ZSB in planning every detail of how the newest Chrysler would be built.

On November 11, 1922, Chrysler approved the specifications for the Chrysler Six and contracted with ZSB Engineering to set up production facilities. He said, "Now we are going to build the car; it is your job to get it ready for production; I don't know where it will be built, but I know of some factories we can have." Late in 1922 Durant Motors was tooling up to manufacture the Flint, but the experimental models were not performing up to Durant's expectations. Durant asked Tobe Couture of ZSB to refine the experimental cars; as a result ZSB was given the job of redesigning and developing the engine for the Flint, an assignment which also gave ZSB access to the dynamometer laboratory at the Elizabeth plant and a splendid oppor-

tunity to develop and test the new Chrysler engine on their own time.

In April 1923 Chrysler was invited to come to the Elizabeth laboratory to see a version of the new engine on dynamometer test. As it had been months since Chrysler had visited the Elizabeth plant, Skelton arranged to have the electric sign, which Willys had installed and the Durant Corporation had never removed, illuminated to spell CHRYSLER. Chrysler was delighted with the nostalgic tribute but was even more impressed with the smoothness and performance of the new engine, immediately giving orders to proceed with the final design of the car. He made one stipulation: five experimental cars would have to be running by September 1, 1923. As a result the design, procurement of all material, and building of five experimental cars had to be accomplished in about four months.

On June 6, 1923, ZSB arrived in Detroit and took space on the second floor of one of the Chalmers plants on Jefferson Avenue. From then on progress was made, and the first experimental cars were built by the September deadline. The cars were first built with only 2-wheel brakes, but after testing Chrysler made the decision to incorporate hydraulic 4-wheel brakes, the first in the automotive industry among mass-produced cars.

The new car stirred so much interest in the industry that the Studebaker Corporation made a determined effort to buy a controlling interest in Maxwell. This effort progressed so far that some of the Studebaker principals came to Detroit and were given a demonstration of the machine by Couture. Chrysler was in a predicament because Maxwell stock had risen from around 10 to 18 and selling represented a good deal for the stockholders. However, Chrysler wanted the car bearing his name and imposed terms that the Studebaker interests did not choose to meet. Chrysler was determined not to lose again his car to another automobile company.

Just before Thanksgiving Day, 1923, Zeder, Skelton, and Couture drove the first Chrysler Six Phaeton equipped with 4-wheel brakes east to Washington, D.C., then to Newark, and on to Chrysler's home at Great Neck on Long Island. It was a banner day for everyone who had been working since 1920 to develop the car that would bear Chrysler's name. On December 26, 1923, the Chrysler Motor Corporation of Michigan was chartered to produce the car, which would be marketed through the Maxwell organization.

Cars were coming off the production line by December 20, and before Christmas the Chrysler Six line of cars was shown to leading bankers, material and parts suppliers, automobile dealers, and other selected individuals at the Jefferson Avenue plant, and reports indicate that the car was enthusiastically acclaimed. But there were still problems; most of the money advanced to Maxwell in 1920 had been spent increasing production and correcting the mechanical and engineering defects in cars. The new Chrysler Corporation of Michigan needed capital before full-scale production could begin.

Chrysler planned to show the first Chrysler Sixes at the January 1924 New York automobile show. According to tradition, Chrysler's decision was made at the last minute, and the automobile show, according to its rules, would not allow the Chrysler automobiles to be shown since the cars had no production record for the previous year. Not to be deterred from his objective, Chrysler supposedly requested his sales manager, Joseph Fields, to engage the entire lobby of the Commodore Hotel and have a private showing there. Evidence reported in the March 1983 issue of *Wheels* indicates that the traditional account of the introduction of the 1924 Chrysler car may contain several inaccuracies. Because of overcrowded conditions at the armory in the Bronx, where the main automobile show was being held, several other car and automobile accessory manufacturers also took advantage of the spacious main floor of the Commodore for their displays. The January 12, 1924, *Automobile Topics* reported that "... the Commodore Hotel, headquarters for many automobile and accessory manufacturers ... was the scene of several private and 'overflow' exhibits. Automotive exhibits included the Stutz, Rollin, Chrysler, and Federal Truck...." The *Wheels* article quotes the *New York Times* for January 6, 1924: "The most important new car [Chrysler] of the year is on exhibition at the Commodore Hotel and in space 35 [actually 34] at the Automobile Show." On December 27, 1923, *Automotive Industries* announced that six body styles of Chrysler Sixes were being produced at the Chalmers plant in Detroit; therefore the roadster model, which Chrysler and others said was the only car available for display during the show, was probably only one of several Chrysler cars actually brought to New York. Additionally, the official catalogue for the 1924 New York Auto Show lists Chrysler cars in area 34 along with Chalmers cars. Chrysler may well have perpetrated a public relations hoax in the automobile industry with his dramatic story of the debut of the Chrysler Six. Nonetheless, 1924 Chrysler cars were featured as medium-priced with a high power, high speed, high compression engine, 4-wheel hydraulic brakes, air filter, and air cleaner—more standard features than many higher-priced cars. The Chrysler roadster could be purchased for $1,525, and other body styles were comparably priced from $1,325 for the Phaeton to $1,895 for the Imperial Sedan.

Though the announcement and showing of the Chrysler Six at the 1924 automobile show drew huge crowds and was widely acclaimed in the trade publications, Chrysler was really seeking approval from the bankers. The bankers were suitably impressed with the car and the public's reaction to it, the last helping to solidify their noncommittal attitude toward the new Chrysler Six. Especially impressed was Edward Tinker of Chase Securities Corporation, with whom Chrysler began preliminary negotiations on a $5-million loan while at the show. At one point Chrysler and Tinker haggled in the backseat of one of the display cars, surrounded by a crowd of curious faces. Acceptable terms were reached, and, after working all night, the contracts were signed at 6:00 A.M. the next day. In Chrysler's own words, "A very little while later the contract was executed and what was already, in my heart, the Chrysler Corporation, but still called Maxwell, was out of the woods. We had our money, we had our car, and we had a live organization." Seventeen months later the old Maxwell organization was liquidated, and the modern Chrysler Corporation came into being on June 6, 1925.

With financing assured, Chrysler rushed to place his car into production. The production schedule reached 100 units a day within three months of the construction of the first car. By the beginning of June, production was running at 150 cars a day, and in September the Chrysler outsold the Maxwell line. Within twelve months of its appearance, 32,000 Chrysler Sixes had been sold, a record for the first year's production of a new car. By fall 1925 nearly 3,800 dealers were selling Chrysler cars. By 1926 the new corporation had risen from twenty-seventh to fifth place in the industry. Four new models were introduced that year, and by

1927 the firm was fourth in the industry in new car sales with registrations of 192,000 vehicles.

The year 1928 was the most momentous in the early history of the Chrysler Corporation. In the space of twelve months the corporation successfully launched two completely new lines of cars: Plymouth and DeSoto. This alone would have taxed the energies of an ordinary manufacturer in the depression era, but Chrysler dared do something even more difficult: it bought out and absorbed a rival company several times its size.

The company was Dodge Brothers, one of the largest and most respected companies in the auto industry. Founded in 1914 by John and Horace Dodge, who started in the automobile business by manufacturing motors and transmissions for Ford, Dodge was the third largest automaker and possessed a strong product and a loyal dealer group. The Dodge plant in Hamtramck, Michigan, was one of the largest and most completely integrated automobile factories in the world, covering 58 acres and employing approximately 20,000 workers. Acquisition of its facilities was Chrysler Corporation's main goal in the purchase.

Chrysler moved with care and deliberation, and negotiations with Dodge, begun in spring 1928, were not concluded until July 30. Chrysler knew that the merger would succeed far better if it had the goodwill and support of a majority of the Dodge shareholders, and one of the points that he insisted upon throughout the bargaining was that the terms must be acceptable to the holders of 90 percent of every class of Dodge stock. The final terms provided that Chrysler Corporation would pay for the Dodge properties with 1,253,557 shares of Chrysler common stock, then at about $80 per share on the market, and also would assume Dodge notes amounting to $59 million. On the day of closing the agreement that put the transfer into effect, a number of Chrysler executives under the leadership of K. T. Keller moved into the Dodge offices at Hamtramck. Throughout the factory signs appeared, reading: "Chrysler Corporation, Dodge Division." The next morning the plant opened under Chrysler management. Chrysler later maintained that "Buying Dodge was one of the soundest acts of my life." In acquiring the Dodge properties Chrysler accomplished three things: the increase of its physical size by at least a factor of five; the movement into third place among the world's automobile manufacturers; and the laying of groundwork for still further

growth. Despite the Great Depression beginning in 1929, the corporation managed to pay off the last of the Dodge bonds in 1935, five years ahead of schedule. Throughout the depression Chrysler Corporation never failed to pay dividends to its shareholders.

Even before the purchase of Dodge, however, Chrysler planned another car that would be within reach of more people. As early as 1926 Chrysler engineers had been laboring over the blueprints and specifications for the newest car to be added to the Chrysler product line. The name of it was to be Plymouth, symbolizing the endurance and strength, the rugged honesty, enterprise, and determination of the Pilgrims. First showings of the Plymouth took place in early July 1928, with Amelia Earhart taking center stage to introduce the Plymouth to the American car-buying public. In Chicago thirty thousand people jammed the Chicago Coliseum to catch a glimpse of the latest Chrysler product. Its delivered price of $670 and $725 (depending on body style) made it appealing to the mass market. By mid July a flood of orders had disrupted factory production schedules, and it became apparent that more factory space was necessary. Chrysler at once began to plan and build a new plant. Although construction began in the dead of winter, four crews working around the clock completed the job in three months. By March 1929 the new plant was ready, and the Plymouth manufacturing and assembly lines moved in.

The DeSoto Six, another new car introduced in 1928, was the corporation's answer to filling the gap between large cars and the popular 4-cylinder models. For the first time in the moderate-price class, DeSoto included as standard equipment such features as improved insulation, a rigid frame with four cross-members, and transmission gears of chrome alloy steel. Introduced shortly after the Dodge purchase in July 1928, the new DeSoto sold 80,000 units in its first year and, as a result of demand resembling that for the Plymouth, increased production facilities were urgently sought. In fall 1936 the DeSoto Division, which had first operated in the Dodge plant in Hamtramck and later in the Chrysler Jefferson Avenue plant, settled in quarters of its own on the west side of Detroit. The new plant was tooled for making 500 cars per day, and nearby the company built the industry's most modern stamping plant for sheet metal parts. This state-of-the-art manufacturing complex became one of the showplaces for automobile production and one of Detroit's major tourist attractions.

In 1929 Chrysler Corporation was one of the Big Three automobile companies, and in spite of the depression which hit hard at the pocketbooks of Americans, the company never reduced research or investments earmarked for development of better-engineered cars. Nor did it cancel investments in new model development. The depression took its toll within American and world business, but Chrysler Corporation strengthened its place in the industry and gained a reputation for being vigorous, tough, and competitive. In 1933 it was the only automotive firm to surpass its sales record of the 1929 boom year. By 1933, due in large part to Chrysler's aggressive management, the Chrysler Corporation had moved into second place in the industry ahead of Ford. Throughout the depression years Chrysler continued the momentum of the corporation's growth and managed to repay the $50 million borrowed in 1925 and most of the Dodge indebtedness as well. Engineering and research, headed by Zeder, continued to be the foundation upon which Chrysler continued to build the future of the corporation.

In 1934 Chrysler caught the industry and the public by surprise with the introduction of the Chrysler and DeSoto Airflow cars. The Airflows embodied a new concept of weight distribution that reduced vibration frequencies to a range comfortable to passengers. Engineers moved the engine forward over the front axle and increased the weight of the front springs, softening their action to reduce vertical shock from rough spots and eliminate pitching. With the engine forward it was possible to shift the entire car body ahead and place the rear seat in front of the rear axle, thus producing a smoother, more comfortable ride. The car's riding qualities were further enhanced by using smaller wheels and larger tires—the forerunner of today's low-pressure radial tires. The Airflows also featured, for the first time, unit body construction which provided greater strength, rigidity, and safety for the passengers.

In 1934 Chrysler added more to riding comfort when Plymouth, Dodge, and the Chrysler Six were introduced with individual front-wheel suspensions, permitting the front wheels to rise or fall independently. The airstream models introduced in 1935 by Chrysler and DeSoto had all-steel bodies—an advancement pioneered by Dodge.

Sometime in 1929 Chrysler had decided to bring his son, Walter, Jr., into the business. Walter, Jr., grew up in New York and wanted to live there. Because he was eager to work but had little interest in automobile manufacturing, his father decided to construct the Chrysler Building and turn it over to him to manage. On a visit to Paris, Chrysler had been impressed with the Eiffel Tower—the world's highest structure at the time. So when instructing architects for the Chrysler Building he simply said, "Make this building higher than the Eiffel Tower." Chrysler immersed himself in the building project with the same thoroughness that he did everything in which he was interested. He made changes in the building's design and in the colors of the tile for the lobby; he gave advice on how to plumb the elevator shafts to eliminate noise and permit speeds of 1000 feet per minute; he spent hours down on his hands and knees on the floor of his office with the blueprints and the other drawings by the architects; he made the final choice for marble in the corridors and the veneers that were used in the elevators; and he was involved in nearly all the major decisions relating to the design, construction, and interior decorating of the 77-story building that bore his name. Then he promptly turned over the management and operation of the building to Chrysler, Jr., saying, "You better learn something about the building. It's yours; not mine." Chrysler, Jr., learned about his building by working in the basement scrubbing floors, then cleaning offices, and literally moving from the ground up to the executive offices.

Following completion of the Chrysler Building, Chrysler began to delegate more and more of the responsibility for daily operations of the corporation to his team of executives. He began to spend more time with his wife and family and commenced work on his autobiography, *Life of an American Workman*. After more than ten years of guiding the corporation with the combined talents of an organizer, merchandiser, financier, manufacturing expert, and pacesetter, Chrysler resigned the presidency of the firm on July 22, 1935. He retained the post of chairman of the board until his death. On May 26, 1938, without any warning, Chrysler suffered a severe stroke from which he never fully recovered. This necessitated his divesting himself of all affairs of Chrysler Corporation, and on August 18, 1940, he quietly died at his home on Long Island of a cerebral hemorrhage.

The firm, which was Chrysler's dream, continued to grow on the foundation built by his genius because, as he put it: "Any great industrial corporation lives and grows only through the devoted services of many who pool their intelligence and energy for a common effort." Chrysler's efforts, at least, were generously rewarded. When he turned the presidency over to K. T. Keller in 1935, he owned $9 million of stock in the $169-million corporation. He maintained an office in New York on the fifty-sixth floor of the impressively designed Chrysler Building and commuted from his Long Island estate on his yachts *Zowie* and *Frolic III.*

Most of the credit for the Chrysler Corporation's foundation and early growth was due to Chrysler himself, but he never claimed to have done it all. His experience at GM had convinced him of the importance of choosing good subordinates. But the Chrysler Corporation was not decentralized like GM under Alfred P. Sloan, Jr.; neither was it the one-man operation that Ford had become. All major product and marketing decisions were made at the corporate headquarters, but in other areas like engineering and production the people in charge of these functions were in complete control and accountable to him personally rather than through an extensive staff system as in the case of GM. The Chrysler style involved the hiring of the best talent available for building the Chrysler team and then giving people the opportunity and room to succeed. The three men who had helped to develop the Chrysler car were very much a part of the organization, Zeder as vice-president in charge of engineering, Breer and Skelton as directors. So was treasurer B. E. Hutchinson, the financial genius who had done the figuring in Detroit while Chrysler was dickering with bankers in New York. And when the Dodge purchase was consummated, the management of what became the Dodge Division of the corporation was put in the capable hands of Kaufman T. (K. T.) Keller, who later became Walter Chrysler's successor as president. Chrysler took calculated risks, but he was also an organization man who left the corporation he created ably managed by some of the most capable and effective automobile executives in Detroit.

Publication:

Life of an American Workman (New York: Dodd, Mead, 1937).

References:

B. C. Forbes and O. D. Foster, *Automotive Giants of America* (New York: B. C. Forbes Publishing, 1926);

C. B. Glasscock, *The Gasoline Age* (Indianapolis: Bobbs-Merrill, 1937);

Richard M. Langworth and Jan P. Norbye, *The Complete History of Chrysler Corporation, 1924-1985* (New York: Beekman House, 1985);

Theodore F. MacManus and Norman Beasley, *Men, Money and Motors* (New York: Harper & Brothers, 1929);

Michael Moritz and Barrett Seaman, *Going for Broke: The Chrysler Story* (Garden City, N.Y.: Doubleday, 1981);

Arthur Pound and Samuel T. Moore, eds., *They Told Barron* (New York: Harper & Brothers, 1930);

John B. Rae, *American Automobile Manufacturers* (Philadelphia & New York: Chilton, 1959).

Archives:

Unfortunately no Chrysler papers or other primary source materials are known to exist. The Chrysler Corporation's historical collection in Detroit does contain some manuscript material, most notably three typescripts by Owen Skelton, A. B. (Tobe) Couture, and Carl Breer, all of whom are prominent in the history of the Chrysler Corporation.

Chrysler Corporation

by George S. May

Eastern Michigan University

Walter P. Chrysler is rightly hailed as one of the automobile industry's most important leaders because of his establishment in 1925 of the last American automobile company that survived over a long period and which is still in business today. But it is not fair to contrast the success of the Chrysler Corporation with the failure of such contemporary creations of the 1920s as Durant Motors or Wills-Ste. Claire or the later Kaiser-Frazer company. The founders of these companies started from scratch, whereas Chrysler had the advantage of being able to use an existing automobile company upon which to build the Chrysler Corporation. The later growth of Chrysler was also aided by the acquisition of other established automotive firms.

The Chrysler Corporation had its origins in 1921 in the financial troubles of the Maxwell and Chalmers companies, troubles which led the companies' creditors to hire Chrysler to salvage the firms. Chrysler negotiated a restructuring of the companies' debts, orchestrated friendly bankruptcy proceedings, and emerged in 1922 as head of a reorganized Maxwell company. Chrysler continued to produce the Maxwell car, although the Chalmers, which had been absorbed into the new company, was dropped after 1923. The future of the company, Chrysler believed, lay with a new car that was being developed with his support by the engineering team of Fred M. Zeder, Owen Skelton, and Carl Breer. When the prototype of the car, bearing Chrysler's name, was exhibited early in 1924, the attention it received enabled Chrysler to obtain the necessary financing to produce it. Sales quickly outstripped those of the Maxwell, and in 1925 the Maxwell company was reorganized as the Chrysler Corporation, with the Maxwell car shortly being dropped in favor of the four Chrysler models that had been developed.

The Chrysler's high-compression engine, 4-wheel hydraulic brakes, and other innovations established the company's reputation for engineering excellence, and by 1927 sales of 192,000 cars placed the new company fifth in the industry. However, to challenge the two biggest producers, General Motors (GM) and Ford, Chrysler realized he needed a greater diversity of products. The opportunity he had been seeking came in 1928 when he was able to acquire the Dodge Brothers company. Besides acquiring the Dodge car, which, like Chrysler, had a reputation for being well-built, Chrysler also acquired one of the industry's top dealer organizations and the additional manufacturing facilities he needed. Two new cars, the medium-priced DeSoto and the low-priced Plymouth, were quickly added, and by 1929 the Chrysler Corporation, with sales of 450,543 cars, was ranked third in the industry. It has remained among the top three American automakers ever since.

Building upon the solid reputation its early cars had won for the company and the range of choices it offered the buyer, the Chrysler Corporation weathered the storm of the depression, pushing ahead of Ford for the first time in 1933 and maintaining that position nearly every year thereafter until the 1950s. In 1935 Walter Chrysler officially transferred management of the company to his long-time associate, K. T. Keller. By this time the company, only ten years old, was free of debt and seemingly well-positioned to continue to grow and even challenge GM for the leadership in the industry.

Chrysler never quite realized the potential that its early record appeared to indicate. The reasons for this failure began to become evident after World War II, during which the production facilities were used to turn out an impressive volume of guns, airplane engines, tanks (which Chrysler continued to produce until it sold the division in 1982), and other war materials. In the immediate postwar years, however, Chrysler failed to make the adjustments needed to compete with Ford and GM. With

Walter P. Chrysler with the first Chrysler car in late 1923 (courtesy of Archives of Chrysler Corporation)

the death of Henry Ford, whose increasing inability to provide effective leadership had been much of the cause of his company falling behind Chrysler in the 1930s, the Ford Motor Company was rejuvenated under Henry Ford II, who in 1945 and 1946 brought in outsiders trained to provide the kind of managerial and financial direction that GM had for twenty years used to attain its position. By the end of the 1940s, with its new organizational plan in place and its first new postwar models in production, Ford began to improve its relative position in the industry. Meanwhile GM, under its new chief executive officer, Charles E. Wilson, expanded production facilities to meet the demand for the striking new models which would maintain or increase the corporation's hold on nearly half of the automobile market.

It was the unfavorable comparisons that were being drawn by 1950 between Chrysler's cars and those of its competitors that first indicated that the company was in trouble. While other companies followed GM's lead and introduced lower, longer, sleeker models, Chrysler continued to market tall, boxy cars that looked increasingly outdated. In an era when hats were beginning to be worn less frequently, Keller stubbornly insisted that his company continue to produce cars designed for people who

did not want to have to take off their hats when they got into their automobiles. Chrysler cars continued to have a solid reputation for their engineering and construction, and this reputation was reinforced in the early 1950s when the introduction of a new high-performance V-8 "Firepower" engine gave Chrysler the lead in the horsepower race. But styling had always taken second place to engineering in the Chrysler organization and the postwar models, when contrasted with GM's flashy models, were referred to as "schoolteachers' cars."

At first the problem did not seem serious. A three-month strike in 1950 was a convenient explanation for why Chrysler that year, for the first time since 1936, had fallen behind Ford in vehicle output. The company bounced back in 1951 to regain the number two spot, but then in 1952 it slipped back to third, where it has remained ever since. Ford widened its lead in 1953 and 1954, by which time that company was even setting its sights on the number one position. Lester Lum "Tex" Colbert, who had succeeded K. T. Keller as president in 1950 when Keller, in order to devote his time to directing the United States's guided missile program, had moved into the chairman's job, realized something drastic had to be done to reawaken the public's interest in Chrysler's cars. Virgil Exner, an

Advertisement for the 1925 Chrysler Six, the basis of Chrysler's early success

experienced stylist who had worked on GM and Studebaker cars, had been hired in 1949, but his ability was stifled by the entrenched control the engineers had always exercised over all aspects of the car's design. Colbert, with Keller's somewhat reluctant support, placed the weight of his authority behind Exner. As a result, the corporation's cars, which had been the industry's most conservatively styled, became among the most exotic cars of the late 1950s. The new designs helped sales rebound for several years, but Colbert, who poured hundreds of millions of dollars into Exner's new models, slashed the normal time needed to move a car from the developmental to the production level. The result was that quality control suffered and so did sales, as customers discovered that Chrysler's thirty-year reputation for building finely crafted cars was no longer as well-deserved as in the past. By the end of the 1950s Chrysler's market share, which stood at 23.1 percent in 1951, had fallen to 11 percent.

The old-fashioned design of Chrysler cars in 1950 was only the most visible evidence of the real problem at Chrysler. That problem rested with Chrysler's management and what it perceived as the company's future in the automobile industry. At the start of the decade the top management consisted largely of aging executives who went back to the very beginnings of the company. K. T. Keller; Fred M. Zeder, the vice-chairman; Owen Skelton, the engineering director; B. E. Hutchinson, the man in charge of finances; and others in the upper executive ranks had performed brilliantly in the company's early years but were nearing retirement. The company they left was no longer on its way up but had dropped to third place in the industry. They had failed to maintain the momentum that had propelled Chrysler in the 1920s and 1930s. The most important question that the new generation of leaders faced was over the basic direction of the company: should they try to reverse the downward trend and once again aim for the top, or should they decide that the company did not have

*The 1934 Chrysler Airflow, one of the company's great failures and an influence on the design
of the Volkswagen Beetle*

the resources necessary to challenge GM and Ford.

For many years the competency of the new leaders to make those judgments was widely questioned. Colbert, who replaced Keller at the top of the organization in the 1950s, had been with Chrysler since 1933 and had wide experience at many levels of the company's organization before becoming president in 1950. But he always labored under the handicap of being known as the first head of Chrysler who was not a "car" man like Chrysler and Keller. Instead, before joining Chrysler, he had been a cotton buyer and a lawyer. He tried to rebuild Chrysler not only by changing the image of the company's cars but by launching an ambitious expansion program, building new factories and purchasing the Briggs Body Company. Accomplishing this, however, required Colbert to seek outside financial help, and the result was that Chrysler began to be burdened by a debt load that would eventually threaten the company's ability to survive. Colbert's efforts to replace the centralized system of management of the Chrysler-Keller era with one modeled after GM's, which allowed division heads great freedom to operate within certain broad guidelines established by central committees, were opposed by the old guard, who did not want to relinquish any of their power. Colbert was not strong enough to override this opposition, and as a result, in the late 1950s he again returned to a centralized management.

Internal dissension and Chrysler's eroding economic position forced Colbert out in 1961. His replacement, Lynn Townsend, was a man with a much more dominating personality, but his qualifications to head the company were also called into question. The fact that he had only been with the company for four years was a sign of another Chrysler weakness—its failure to engage in an aggressive program to recruit talented young individuals who could fill junior executive positions and ultimately occupy the top positions. Thus, like Exner, who had been hired from outside the company, Townsend, an executive with the Detroit accounting firm that audited Chrysler's books, was hired by Colbert in 1957 to fill the job of comptroller shortly after Hutchinson retired. Townsend immediately brought in financial experts from Ford to install some of the financial controls that had been one of the important reforms Ford had installed ten years before.

Because of his accounting background, Townsend was somewhat unfairly ridiculed by his critics as a "bean counter," who was even less in the Chrysler-Keller mold than Colbert and was interested only in the bottom line. It was true that Townsend's approach to the financial problems the company faced was to institute a severe cost-cutting program, but he also deserves credit for efforts to restore the public's confidence in the quality of Chrysler workmanship. In the mid 1960s Chrysler offered a warranty far beyond anything the competition had to offer. He also turned away from the extreme styles that had come to characterize Chrysler cars under Virgil Exner. Once again, however, the changes were not affected by a stylist promoted from within the organization but by Elwood Engel, brought in from Ford. Similarly, Virgil Boyd of

Lee Iacocca driving the first Chrysler K-car off the assembly line on August 8, 1980 (courtesy of Chrysler Corporation)

American Motors and Stewart Venn of Ford were hired to breathe new life into Chrysler's sales organization and dealer network.

Townsend's view was that Chrysler should not be satisfied to be third but should instead continue to strive to be better. To do that he constantly emulated Ford and GM. A credit subsidiary was set up to provide financial help to dealers, just like those GM and Ford had been providing for years. An overseas presence, such as the other two companies had maintained for decades but which Chrysler had lacked, was established by acquiring control of several foreign automobile companies. Non-automotive activities in such areas as the space program, chemicals, marine engines, and air-conditioning were aggressively pushed, along with a huge program to build new plants and expand existing facilities.

By the mid 1960s Chrysler, which had been competing with only about 60 percent of the models produced by GM and Ford when Townsend took over, had increased the number of its models

until it was competing in more than about 90 percent of the product line. Chrysler's market share rose to 16 percent, twice the low point to which it had fallen in the early 1960s, earnings were higher, and Wall Street, hailing Townsend as the man who had turned Chrysler around, made the company's stock one of the hottest issues in the bull market of the 1960s. But the good times were short-lived. Townsend's expansion programs had been made possible only by a huge increase in Chrysler's debt level. When sales of the 1969 models dropped precipitously and dropped further at the onset of a recession in 1970, Chrysler was in deep financial trouble. Townsend was forced to institute another cost-cutting program in order to carry off a restructuring of the company's debts. Improved economic conditions in the country gave the company a respite in 1972 and 1973. But then the Arab oil embargo in 1973-1974 was followed by a much deeper recession that affected the sales of all automobiles but was felt especially at Chrysler, where the earlier cost-cutting measures had not permitted it to develop the small, fuel efficient cars that were now in great demand.

With huge inventories of Chrysler's big models piling up, Townsend again resorted to belt-tightening measures in the winter of 1974-1975. But losses continued, and he came under heavy attack at the annual stockholders' meeting in spring 1975. He survived the attack but announced in July that he was taking early retirement. Succeeding him was John Riccardo, another accountant whom Townsend had brought into the organization in 1959, and whom he had been grooming as his successor. After being hired in 1959, Riccardo moved rapidly from one job to another until he was named president in 1970; he took over Townsend's position as chairman in fall 1975.

Within a few months improved economic conditions again changed Chrysler's losses to profits as car sales picked up sharply. But Riccardo recognized that Chrysler's financial condition was precarious, and he moved to cut back on some of Townsend's ambitious programs. The foreign subsidiaries that Townsend had acquired had proved more of a liability than an asset, and by 1978 Riccardo had sold off virtually all of the overseas holdings as well as the air-conditioning unit and some other domestic non-automotive ventures. Meanwhile, reacting to the demand for fuel efficient cars, Chrysler introduced late in 1977 the Dodge Omni and Plymouth Horizon, the first small, American-made front-wheel drive cars to compete directly with the imports, especially those from Japan, that had been taking an increasingly large share of the market. These Chrysler models, plus the somewhat larger front-wheel drive K-cars that were in the developmental stage and would go into production in 1980, provided the company with the cars it needed to survive in the changing market conditions of the 1980s.

Riccardo was confident that Chrysler's fortunes would improve when the K-cars arrived. Unfortunately the Omni and Horizon were not enough to counter the unfavorable reactions to the other 1978 models, and losses again returned. Appeals for financial assistance were received coolly by bankers who had too often in the past been told Chrysler's rosy prospects lay just a short distance down the road. When Moody's and Standard & Poor's downgraded Chrysler's credit rating in spring 1978, hopes of additional help from private sources faded. Riccardo's efforts to enlist help from the fed-

eral government also met with little favorable response.

In summer 1978, therefore, Riccardo did what had become a natural reaction at Chrysler to a difficult problem: he brought in an outsider. In this case the outsider was probably the best-known automotive executive in the country, Lee Iacocca. In July 1978 irreconcilable differences between Iacocca and Henry Ford II led to Ford firing the man who had served as president of the Ford Motor Company since 1970. Within days Riccardo was in contact with Iacocca, and by November he was installed as Chrysler's new president. Riccardo recognized that the company's efforts to stave off bankruptcy needed to be revitalized by bringing in a fresh face, not identified with the failures of the past thirty years. Riccardo planned to stay on through 1979 before relinquishing the chairman's job to Iacocca, but warnings by Washington officials that there was little hope of securing federal help until Iacocca was in complete charge caused Riccardo to step aside late in summer 1979.

In Iacocca, Chrysler once again was led by a "car" man. Iacocca claimed to have known little about the inner workings of Chrysler before taking his new job, but he soon decided that the company's main problem was that it had been too long run by men who did not really like cars. He quickly fired nearly all the top Chrysler executive force and brought in a small army of former colleagues at Ford to install the orderly, systematic administrative setup to which he had been accustomed at Ford. He had been astonished to discover that such a system, which Ford had utilized for thirty years and GM for over a half century, did not exist at Chrysler. Chrysler, he said, was being "run like a small grocery store."

But although the new organizational chart at Chrysler now resembled that which was in place at the other two companies, Walter Chrysler would still have felt comfortable because the real power at Chrysler still rested in the hands of one man. Iacocca *was* the Chrysler Corporation, and, because of his reputation and his irresistible charisma, he was able to accomplish that which Riccardo had been unable to do. By the end of 1979 he had secured the adoption of an enormously complicated bailout plan, backed by $1.5 billion in federal loan guarantees, to save Chrysler from bankruptcy. There is little doubt that this plan could not have been pulled off without Iacocca, and it was unquestionably his leadership that maintained the morale of the company as it struggled through years of billion-dollar losses amid a severe national recession.

For a time Iacocca thought Chrysler's salvation lay with a merger with another company. He first approached Volkswagen, but the German company, which itself had struggled in the 1970s, was not interested. Iacocca then pursued the idea of a merger with Ford, with Chrysler and Dodge cars surviving as divisions of the bigger company. Although the idea appealed to some financiers, it was quickly vetoed by Ford. Eventually, as the economy improved and the K-cars contributed the booming sales that Riccardo had forecast, Chrysler began to prosper by 1983. It showed a profit once again and paid off its government loans seven years ahead of schedule.

Iacocca was acclaimed as a miracle worker. In 1987 Chrysler bought control of American Motors from Renault. The acquisition added a promising new European-designed car, the Eagle, to the Chrysler lineup, which had consisted only of Plymouth, Dodge, and Chrysler since DeSoto had been scrapped in 1959. Chrysler also acquired the enormously popular Jeep. On balance the merger seemed to fit in with Iacocca's realistic approach, which was to make Chrysler as competitive as possible while at the same time recognizing that there was little possibility that Chrysler could unseat either Ford or GM in the ranking of the three remaining American automobile firms.

The big question regarding Chrysler at the end of the 1980s was the company's plans following Iacocca's retirement. The uncertainty was over whether the organization he had established was strong enough to make the adjustments required when he was no longer serving as Chrysler's chairman. Similar questions have hounded the company throughout its existence.

References:

Lee Iacocca with William Novak, *Iacocca: An Autobiography* (New York: Bantam Books, 1984);

Steve Jefferys, *Management & Managed: Fifty Years of Crisis at Chrysler* (New York: Cambridge University Press, 1986);

Richard M. Langworth and Jan P. Norbye, *The Complete History of Chrysler Corporation 1924-1985* (New York: Beekman House, 1985);

Michael Moritz and Barrett Seaman, *Going for Broke: The Chrysler Story* (Garden City, N.Y.: Doubleday, 1981);

Robert B. Reich and John D. Donohue, *New Deals: The Chrysler Revival and the American System* (New York: Times Books, 1985).

Lester Lum Colbert

(June 13, 1905-   )

by George S. May

Eastern Michigan University

CAREER: Cotton buyer (1921-1929); attorney, Larkin, Rathbone & Perry, New York City, (1929-1933); resident attorney (1933-1942), member of operations committee (1933-1961), vice-president, Dodge (1935-1945), operating manager (1942), general manager, Dodge Chicago plant (1943-1946); president, Dodge (1946-1951), vice-president (1949-1950), director (1949-1961), president (1950-1961), chairman, Chrysler Corporation (1960-1961); chairman, Chrysler Corporation of Canada (1961-1965).

Lester Lum "Tex" Colbert, who in 1950 became Chrysler's third president, was born on June 13, 1905, in the small town of Oakwood, Texas. He was the third child and only son of Lum Herbert Colbert, a cotton farmer, and Sallie Driver Colbert, who was a schoolteacher prior to her marriage. Colbert, even as a youth, was a hard worker, taking a part-time job for a local druggist while he was still in grade school. When he was thirteen his father brought him into the cotton business, and by the time he was sixteen Colbert was working as a cotton buyer. He earned enough to pay his way through the University of Texas, graduating after three years with a degree in business administration in 1925.

With a $5,000 nest egg resulting from his continued success as a cotton buyer, Colbert entered Harvard law school, his mother and one sister having persuaded him that training in the law was a necessity. Cotton trading continued to be his main interest, as was indicated when he dropped out of law school for a time in 1926 to cash in on booming cotton prices. His legal studies seem to have been designed primarily to give him some pointers regarding the law that he could use in the cotton market, rather than to prepare him for a career as an attorney. In 1929, however, when he completed his work at Harvard, Colbert found the prospects for profits in cotton trading were less promising, and he accepted a job as a law clerk with the Wall Street law firm of Larkin, Rathbone & Perry.

The job as a clerk proved to be Colbert's stepping stone to a career in the auto industry. The partner who hired Colbert, Nicholas Kelley, was a legal adviser to Chrysler, as well as a director and vice-president of the corporation. Colbert's resulting contacts with Walter Chrysler led to the young attorney being assigned the task of helping Chrysler's son-in-law organize Tish Inc., producers of paper handkerchiefs. Impressed by Colbert's work, Chrysler in 1933 persuaded him to become the Dodge division's resident attorney.

Moving from New York to Detroit, Colbert was taken under the wing of K. T. Keller, Chrysler's production chief who would succeed Chrysler as president in 1935 when Chrysler became chairman of the board. Although Colbert carried out various assignments in keeping with his position as resident attorney, including assisting Nicholas Kelley, who was brought in to handle Chrysler's negotiations with the new United Auto Workers in 1937, Keller had other plans for him. Colbert's critics, when he took over direction of Chrysler in the 1950s, ridiculed him as a lawyer whose management of a tissue company made him ill-suited to run an automobile company. But Colbert, under Keller's direction, had nearly two decades of wide-ranging experience in all aspects of Chrysler's management. Shortly after he arrived in Detroit in 1933 Colbert was placed on the operations committee, and he attended the weekly luncheon meetings that dealt with production matters. For two years, more or less at Keller's insistence, Colbert took night classes in drafting and mechanics, and the experience led Colbert to decide "that this was much more to the cut of my jib than practicing law."

Lester Lum Colbert (courtesy of Junebug Clark)

When Keller assumed the Chrysler presidency in 1935, Colbert was made vice-president of the Dodge division, as well as of a host of the corporation's other wide-ranging list of subsidiaries, including the Plymouth and De Soto divisions. However, it was with Dodge that Colbert demonstrated that Keller had been justified in his assessment of the Texan's managerial potential. In 1942 Colbert was named operating manager of the huge new government-financed plant that was being built in Chicago, where Dodge would produce engines for the B-29 bombers. When spring mud caused a slowdown in construction, Colbert, drawing on his Texas background, procured twenty-five horses from a local riding academy to enable the supervisors to better oversee the work. He became the plant's general manager in 1943 and directed the successful wartime production of 18,413 engines, keeping ahead of schedule in spite of constant and innumerable design changes, and cutting the cost of the engines from an initial $26,000 to only $12,000 per unit.

After the war Colbert was promoted to president of Dodge operations, and under his direction Dodge's car and truck output was increased from the prewar daily figure of 1,700 to 2,800 units. In addition Colbert visited most of the 4,000 Dodge dealers to spur them on, although in the immediate postwar years, when the nation was clambering for new cars, high-pressure salesmanship was scarcely needed to sell cars.

In 1948 Henry Ford II, who was in the midst of his efforts to rebuild and revitalize the Ford company, offered Colbert a position, which Colbert turned down, no doubt aware that he was in line to succeed Keller as head of Chrysler. In 1949 he was named to the board of directors and was made vice-president of the corporation. On November 3, 1950, after Keller accepted an appointment to lead the United States guided missile development program, Colbert replaced Keller as president, with Keller assuming the position of chairman, which had been left vacant since Walter Chrysler's death in 1940.

The corporation that Colbert took over late in 1950 appeared to the casual observer to be in fine condition. During the first nine months of the year it had earned profits of over $105 million, or $12.09 a share. With the outbreak of the Korean War the previous summer, hundreds of millions of dollars in contracts for various war materials had been received. A bitter three-month strike earlier in 1950 had caused Chrysler's output of cars and trucks to drop behind Ford's into third place in the industry for the first time since 1936. But Chrysler's nine-month total of 1,385,000 cars and trucks was more than any previous full year's production, and by the start of 1951 the corporation's weekly output had once again moved ahead of Ford. Barring an escalation of the Korean conflict into another world war, which would lead to an end of civilian car production, the combination of war contracts and a continuing strong demand for civilian vehicles seemed to leave Colbert with few worries.

The new Chrysler president claimed that he never lost any sleep over his work in any event. "Business doesn't worry me," he said. "It's a downright pleasure!" At the end of the workday Colbert rarely took any work to his comfortable home in Bloomfield Hills, the favored location for the newer generation of Detroit auto executives. Instead, he was said to spend many evenings going over his three children's homework and relaxing with his wife, Daisy Gorman Colbert, whom he had known since childhood and had married in 1928. He did little reading, but every night before going to bed he took a long walk, a practice he had acquired from Keller. "Somehow," he said, "when I'm walking, my mind clears. A lot of problems I've had during the day seem to fall into place."

Whether he worried about them or not, Colbert was well aware that Chrysler faced some serious problems. At age forty-five he still had twenty years ahead of him in which to deal with those problems before he would reach what was becoming the mandatory retirement age in the industry. Colbert had an excellent grasp of what needed to be done to strengthen the company, and he had the opportunity to exert as positive an effect on the corporation's future as either of his two predecessors. Unfortunately, few of his programs were successful, and in 1961 he was forced out as chairman of a company torn by internal strife and its share of the automobile market drastically reduced, leaving it third

in sales behind the other two prospering Big Three automakers.

Certainly one of the foremost problems Colbert faced at the end of 1950 was the need to overhaul Chrysler's management. Within two years the bulk of the corporation's top executives would be retiring, including vice-chairman Fred M. Zeder and engineering director Owen R. Skelton, who, along with the already retired Carl Breer, had formed the legendary engineering team that had designed the original Chrysler car introduced in 1924 and all of the company's cars since that time. They and the rest of the retiring executives went back to the earliest days of the company under Walter Chrysler. Colbert decided that the massive number of retirements provided a good opportunity to revamp the entire management system. McKinsey & Company, a management consulting firm, developed a massive report that recommended Chrysler adopt a system much like that under which General Motors (GM) had been operating for thirty years. Walter Chrysler and Keller had learned, from their experience as staff members at GM, of the importance of offering the customer a choice of cars and thus by the end of the 1920s had created a company whose Plymouth, Dodge, DeSoto, Chrysler, and Imperial lines were designed to compete with GM's Chevrolet, Pontiac, Oldsmobile, Buick, and Cadillac. However, while GM under Alfred Sloan allowed the managers of its divisions great freedom to operate, within certain guidelines set by the corporation's central committees, Chrysler and Keller maintained tight controls over all aspects of the company's operations in a manner not unlike the authoritarian, one-man domination of Henry Ford over his company.

Colbert followed the consultants' recommendations and launched an ambitious program to decentralize operations and to appoint vice-presidents who had real authority to run their own divisions. But he ran into stiff opposition from the old guard, especially in the Central Engineering Department, which resisted his efforts to convert the department into a policy-making body that would advise the engineering staffs in the divisions rather than controlling all engineering activities, as it had under Chrysler and Keller. Colbert finally backed down in 1956 and returned to the centralized approach of the past, leaving division managers by 1958 with decision-making power only over cost control and purchasing.

Meanwhile, Colbert was engaged in a massive expansion program designed to better position Chrysler to maintain its strong position in the industry. New assembly plants, transmission factories, a stamping plant, increased glassmaking facilities, and a new proving ground were opened, and when Walter O. Briggs died in 1952 and inheritance taxes prevented his heirs from continuing his business, Colbert was able to buy the Briggs Body Company for $35 million, acquiring twelve body plants in Michigan, Ohio, and Indiana and adding 30,000 employees to the company's rolls. Chrysler for years had been Briggs's major customer, but now it became Briggs's sole customer, in the same manner that GM had acquired the full resources of the Fisher Body operations when it had taken over full control of that firm in the mid 1920s. To accomplish this expansion, however, Colbert was forced to turn to the Prudential Insurance Company in 1954 for a 100-year, $250-million loan agreement, an early sign of Chrysler's need for financial help, which would ultimately saddle it with a near fatal debt.

Colbert also sought to implement the recommendation of McKinsey & Company that Chrysler become an international company. Unlike GM and Ford, which had for decades had strong overseas manufacturing divisions and subsidiaries that contributed significantly to those companies' earnings, Chrysler, aside from its plants in neighboring Canada, had done virtually nothing to develop operations outside of the United States. Now, however, Colbert sought to rectify that by seeking to acquire Rolls-Royce, but his bid was quickly rejected by that company. Colbert also approached Heinz Nordhoff, head of Volkswagen, who in the immediate postwar years had viewed acquisition by an American company as the most practical way in which the war-devastated German firm could survive. But by the 1950s Volkswagen, under Nordhoff's brilliant direction, was succeeding on its own, and Colbert again came up empty in his bid for a well-known foreign company. Unfortunately, Colbert then decided to pursue several smaller, more marginal firms, the first example being the 1958 acquisition of a 25-percent interest in Simca, a barely profitable French carmaker. Acquisitions such as Simca, along with other purchases, continued in the 1960s and left Chrysler with several foreign carmakers, which proved to be far greater liabilities than they were assets for the parent corporation.

The most visible problem Colbert faced in 1950 was the Chrysler products themselves. Had the demand for Chrysler's cars continued upward in the 1950s, Colbert would have been forgiven his failures in other areas. But such was not the way the market reacted—and again it was not because Colbert was unaware of what needed to be done.

The basic difficulty Colbert faced was demonstrated early in 1951 when he hosted a party at Chrysler's headquarters to introduce the new models. The extroverted Colbert mingled with the 450 reporters, "with rarely a slip on a first name," and when it was time to eat "he held a chrome tray overhead like a gong, whacked it with a spoon, and led the parade of guests to the dining room." And what were the features that made the new cars newsworthy? They included a number of engineering innovations, the most important of which was a new V-8 "Firepower" engine—what would soon be known as the Chrysler "hemi" (for its hemispherical combustion chamber), a high-performance engine that put Chrysler out in front in the horsepower race that GM had touched off with its 1949 Cadillac and Oldsmobile. The new Chrysler models were in keeping with the company's longtime reputation for turning out well-built, superbly engineered cars, but by the 1950s exterior styling changes, not less visible technical improvements, were what was attracting the attention of more and more buyers. In contrast to the new GM and Ford cars, Chrysler's styling was dull. Since 1934, when they had been burned by the customers' rejection of the aerodynamically styled Chrysler and DeSoto Airflow models, Chrysler's designers had maintained a conservative approach. While others in the postwar era were designing longer, lower, sporty models, Chrysler continued to turn out high, boxy cars that conformed to Keller's belief that there were still millions of people who wanted to get into and sit down in a car without having to take off their hats. Although conceding the excellence of their engineering, car enthusiasts ridiculed Chrysler's functionally designed models as "schoolteachers' cars."

Colbert realized that to stay competitive Chrysler was going to have to adopt a more modern approach to styling. But that approach was hampered by the fact that Keller was still chairman. However, as Chrysler's market share declined to third place in sales in 1952 and fell more precipitously in 1953 and 1954, even Keller saw the need for change. After examining the latest sales figures, he declared:

"I have seen the error of my ways. Christ, we can't afford another mistake."

The man to whom Colbert and Keller turned for help was Virgil Exner, a highly talented stylist who had been given most of the credit for the radically new look of the 1947 Studebaker. Keller had hired Exner in 1949, and although it is not entirely clear how Exner's ideas meshed with Keller's traditional views as to how a car should be styled, Exner was exactly the person Colbert needed to make the changes the new president saw were required. In the early 1950s Exner designed several show cars that made the rounds of Chrysler dealers and held the promise of more exciting production models in the future. But his influence on the look of the Chrysler consumer products of those years was minimal because much of the work on them had been started before he arrived and because he was resented by some of the older engineering and design staff members who regarded him as an outsider. But beginning with the 1955 model year, Exner's influence was evident in the look of the cars that abandoned the dowdy look of the models of previous years in favor of the fashionably longer, lower, sleeker look. The new styling was labeled "The Forward Look," as an effort was made to depict Chrysler as no longer behind the times but instead as moving out ahead of its competitors.

The new models were also said to have "The Hundred Million Dollar Look," to indicate the money Chrysler was pouring into the new styling effort. Colbert enthusiastically backed Exner, and when Keller, who still had grave reservations about the new styling trends, retired as chairman in 1956, leaving Colbert in undisputed control of the company, Colbert poured hundreds of millions of dollars into new model development. As Exner, who once had been one of the more restrained of the new generation of stylists, felt some pressure to keep up with the competition in the use of ornamentation, Chrysler's styling, which had been the industry's most conservative, became perhaps the most bizarre of the last half of the 1950s. For a time it paid off, as Chrysler sales soared, only to slip badly again in 1958 and 1959, when the corporation's market share, which had stood at 23.1 percent in 1951, slipped to 11 percent. The decline was in part due to the recession of 1957-1958, which affected industry sales in general, but sales were also hurt by the fact that Colbert had cut down drastically on the time allotted for pre-

production, quality control, and engineering. The quality and performance of the cars suffered badly.

With the improved economic conditions of 1960, Chrysler rebounded to achieve a 14 percent market share, only to fall back again with its 1961 models to an 11 percent share. Stockholders' discontent led to a rapid series of executive changes. Already, in April 1960, Colbert had elevated a close associate of many years, William C. Newberg, to the presidency, with Colbert becoming chairman, a post that had been left vacant after Keller had retired four years earlier. But Newberg was quickly forced out when it was revealed he had financial interests in several companies that sold parts to Chrysler. Colbert again assumed the presidency, while continuing to serve as chairman, but even his fortunes were declining. Newberg blamed Colbert for his dismissal and became his bitter enemy. The two men even engaged in a fistfight in the locker room of a Detroit-area country club. At the annual stockholders' meeting at Chrysler's Highland Park headquarters in mid April 1961 a stockholder read a letter from Newberg in which he declared that Chrysler would never be strong again as long as it remained "under the czarist rule of Mr. Colbert." The only management policy Colbert had, Newberg wrote, was to institute "frequent and unpredictable change that throws off balance not Chrysler's competitors, but Chrysler itself." When Colbert expressed his regret that Newberg did not have the courage to appear at the stockholders' meeting in person, a stockholder declared that Colbert's selection of Newberg as his successor "doesn't reflect very well on your judgment, sir." Colbert's excuse that Newberg had failed to apprise him of his outside interests was met with a chorus of boos. A former executive cried, "Who are you trying to fool, Mr. Colbert? You've got your head in the sand and your flanks exposed to attack. You do all your planning with one hand on the panic button and the other in the till."

Colbert controlled enough proxies to survive the tempestuous meeting, but rumors that the directors had asked him to step aside were soon confirmed when he retired as president and chairman on July 27, 1961. In order to enable him to qualify for his executive pension Colbert was transferred to the chairmanship of Chrysler of Canada, a position he held until his final retirement from Chrysler in 1965. Colbert's wife died in 1970. He remarried in 1972, and although maintaining an office in the Detroit suburb of Birmingham he eventually made his home in Naples, Florida. Aside from his continuing involvement with his alma mater, the University of Texas, as a director of its development board, Colbert's active career both in the automotive industry and outside of it—as a director of New York's Hanover Bank, chairman of Detroit's United Fund, member of the National Industrial Conference Board, and one of the overseers of Harvard's law school—ended in 1961. His career as head of Chrysler had been a turbulent one, and his critics were undoubtedly correct in faulting his judgment. But in light of Chrysler's subsequent history Colbert probably deserves to be viewed in a more favorable light. His administration may have ended in failure, but that should not deny him credit for having seen that drastic measures were necessary if the corporation was to survive. The much-touted comeback engineered by his successor, Lynn Townsend, also turned sour after a time, leading to Townsend's early departure as head of the corporation in 1975. It was three years later that the drastic surgery Colbert had sought to carry out began to be performed with some success under the leadership of another dynamic executive, Lee Iacocca.

References:

Richard M. Langworth, *Chrysler and Imperial: The Postwar Years* (Minneapolis: Motorbooks International, 1976);

Michael Moritz and Barrett Seaman, *Going for Broke: The Chrysler Story* (Garden City, N.Y.: Doubleday, 1981);

Robert B. Reich and John D. Donahue, *New Deals: The Chrysler Revival and the American System* (New York: Times Books, 1985);

Robert Sobel, *Car Wars: The Untold Story of the Great Automakers and the Giant Battle for Global Supremacy* (New York: Dutton, 1984);

Time, 57 (January 29, 1951): 89-96.

Edward Nicholas Cole

(September 17, 1909-May 2, 1977)

by Robert J. Kothe

Atlanta, Georgia

CAREER: Laboratory assistant, technician, design engineer, Cadillac division (1933-1943), chief design engineer, Cadillac division (1943-1944), assistant chief engineer, Cadillac division (1944-1946), chief engineer, Cadillac division (1946-1951), works manager, Cadillac division (1951-1952), chief engineer, Chevrolet division (1952-1956), general manager, Chevrolet division (1956-1961), vice-president, Car and Truck division (1961-1965), executive vice-president, Operations Staff (1965-1967), president and chief operating officer, General Motors (1967-1974); chairman, Husky International (1974-1977); chairman and chief executive officer, Checker (1977).

Edward Cole's four-decade career with General Motors (GM) was extraordinary. When he joined GM in 1933 the Model T was still the automobile most familiar to many Americans, and the industry still had a dozen or more important independent producers. Serious foreign competition was limited to a few specialized niches in the market. Pollution from exhaust fumes was thought to be a nuisance at worst. When he retired from GM in 1974 the industry was radically different, and Cole had played a major role in reshaping it.

Cole's career and personality were complex. Although he was generally considered to be an outstanding engineer, Cole was involved with some of GM's most unsuccessful cars and engineering projects. He was an able corporate politician, but the chairman of the board position eluded him. He decried government interference in industry but hoped to enlist government aid in the airfreight project he was involved in late in his life.

Edward Nicholas Cole was born in Berlin, Michigan, on September 17, 1909. During the patriotic frenzy of World War I, which saw sauerkraut renamed Liberty Cabbage, the town's name was changed from Berlin to Marne, although the race car track is still known as the Berlin Raceway. Cole was the oldest son of Franklin Benjamin Cole, a dairy farmer, rural mail carrier, and contractor, and Lucy Catherine Blasen Cole. Cole had a brother, Earl F., and a sister, Audrey.

Cole's project, the 1960 Chevrolet Corvair, which was the primary focus of Ralph Nader's book Unsafe at Any Speed *(1965) (courtesy of General Motors Corporation)*

Cole seems to have had a typical small-town upbringing, attending local public schools, playing football and baseball in high school, and being named valedictorian of his tiny graduating class. Cole milked his father's twenty cows every morning before going to school. During the summer he demonstrated and sold Ford tractors. Cole owned a 1917 Saxon motorcar that he "souped up" and a series of used Model T's. He did not buy a GM product until he started working at the company.

After high school graduation Cole enrolled at nearby Grand Rapids Junior College, taking pre-law classes. The largest city in western Michigan, Grand Rapids was best known for its furniture factories, but it was also an important supply center for the automobile industry. Cole found temporary employment with several different automobile body makers located in the city.

In 1927 Cole abandoned the law as a possible career and instead enrolled in the General Motors Institute (GMI) in Flint, Michigan. Study at GMI was cooperative, with academic terms alternating with work at a sponsoring GM division. Cadillac, headquartered in Detroit, was Cole's sponsor, and in April 1933, shortly before he was to graduate from GMI, he was offered a job in Cadillac's Detroit engineering laboratory. He accepted the job and never took his degree. That same year Cole married Esther Engman, with whom he had two children, David Edward and Martha Ellen.

Cole was assigned to the engineering department at Cadillac. Over the course of a few years he

advanced from laboratory assistant to technician to design engineer, working primarily in engine noise reduction and cooling. He also had a minor role in the development of the automatic transmission at Cadillac. Cole recalled that while working in the engineering laboratory he incorrectly attached some piping to an engine and transmission on a test stand. The unit leaked, spraying the observers with oil. Cole was soon transferred to another project.

During World War II he was first assigned to the development of a new engine for the M-5 Light Tank, 12,500 of which were produced by Cadillac. In 1943 Cole was named Cadillac's chief design engineer for army light tanks and combat vehicles.

In 1944 he returned to automobile design and production as assistant chief engineer for Cadillac. Two years later he was promoted to chief Cadillac engineer. Cole's most important assignment in this period was the development of a new Cadillac V-8 engine for the 1949 models. The short-stroke engine was a striking success and served as a model for a generation of GM engines. During this period Cadillac experimented briefly with a design for a rear-engine car. While Cadillac abandoned the project, it did give Cole some experience with what was, for an American car, a radical design.

With the approach of the Korean War, Cole returned to the design and production of armored vehicles, being assigned to the Cleveland Tank Facility. For some time Cole had been working, in addition to his regular duties, on a new design for a light tank engine. His design served as the basis for an air-cooled, horizontally opposed engine that would become the standard engine for the T-41 tank.

Cole returned to Cadillac in 1951 for a brief stint as works manager. In May 1952 Cole was named chief engineer for the troubled Chevrolet Division. Ford automobiles were threatening Chevrolet's market share, and Chevrolet's division manager, Thomas Keating, was determined to take decisive action to recoup the division's market position. Cole and his design team were given two years to develop a new V-8 engine for Chevrolet. The resulting 265-cubic-inch engine was 35 pounds lighter than Chevrolet's classic "stovebolt six" and capable of producing more than 180 horsepower. It was extremely successful and remained the basic design of small V-8 GM engines for many years.

In July 1956 Cole was appointed general manager of Chevrolet. Shortly after his appointment Cole ordered the development of one of the most significant cars in American automotive history. The Corvair, designed to be GM's import fighter, would reflect many of Cole's ideas.

It was, without question, the most innovative American car intended for mass production in years. The Corvette sports car, also introduced while Cole was at Chevrolet, was, with the exception of its plastic body, much more conventional in design and was not really intended for a mass market. The Corvair, however, was intended to retake the small-car market from the foreign, mostly European, producers that were gaining a foothold in the United States. The Corvair's list of engineering features was dazzling, and many of the features showed Cole's influence. For one, the Corvair was the first American-built, modern rear-engine car, a layout that offered an exceptional amount of interior space and a nearly flat floor. It was also the first GM vehicle equipped with 4-wheel independent suspension. Its horizontally opposed 6-cylinder 140-cubic-inch, air-cooled aluminum engine was a radical design, although it certainly reflected some of Cole's earlier work with tank engines. The engine produced a reasonable amount of power and fair gas mileage. In later models the engine proved to be very responsive to fine tuning, and some remarkably fast Corvairs were produced. The cars enjoyed some success in racing, especially in road rallies and hill climbs.

The Corvair was introduced in September 1959 as a 1960 model, and first-year sales were a brisk 229,985 units. But early in the development of the car, handling problems had cropped up. An early prototype rolled over with Frank Winchell, a Chevy engineer, at the wheel. Ford later reported similar problems with two early models they acquired for testing. Cole, who had been heavily involved in the design of the car, felt the swing axle was safe as designed. There was disagreement within the staff, and a solution to the problem, entailing some changes to the suspension, was rejected for cost reasons. After Cole left Chevrolet a stabilizing bar was added to the rear suspension, and in 1965 a redesigned rear suspension was introduced.

Cole left Chevrolet in late 1961 to become group executive vice-president in charge of the Car and Truck division. He could look back at a successful tour at Chevrolet. In an industry where a percentage point of market share means millions of dollars the division's market share had rebounded from 23 percent to 26 percent. To many, Cole seemed to be a prime contender for the president's office at GM.

But in 1964 Cole was divorced from his first wife. Shortly after, in December, he married Dollie Ann McVey. There was a good deal of speculation that, in the conservative environment of the Detroit automotive establishment, he had lost any chance of reaching the top at the corporation. He eventually had three children as a result of this second marriage: Anne Murray, Robert Michael Joseph, and Edward N.

His personal life and its problems seem not to have mattered in July 1965 when Cole was named to succeed Louis C. Goad as head of the operating staff and to occupy one of six executive vice-presidential slots. This promotion put him in direct line for the presidency of the corporation.

Five months later Ralph Nader's book, *Unsafe at Any Speed,* was published. In the book Nader assailed the American automobile industry and attacked the Corvair in particular for GM's indifference to safety and health. He called the Corvair "one of the nastiest-handling cars ever built" and accused the company of ignoring the car's alleged safety problems in the interest of greater profits.

GM had, in fact, started receiving complaints about the Corvair's handling almost from its introduction. The most serious charges were that the car was unpredictable and would suddenly flip over at moderate speeds under certain fairly common conditions. Ultimately more than 500 lawsuits were filed against the company claiming injury or death as a result of the design of the car. The company never lost any of these cases in court although a number of them were settled out of court, in some cases for substantial amounts.

Perhaps as damaging to the company's reputation were Nader's claims that GM had tried to buy him off and, failing in that, had hired private detectives to investigate him in an effort to discredit his views. Nader did prove that he had been followed and won a large settlement from GM. While Cole was not part of the detective scheme, Nader claimed that Cole had suggested that Nader be offered a position at GM as a means of buying his silence.

The publicity of the lawsuits and Nader's book cut deeply into Corvair sales. Despite improvements in the rear suspension and the introduction of some sporty models, sales continued to fall. Sales in 1965 were 209,000 units, but in 1966 only 86,000 units were produced. By 1968 only 12,887 Corvairs were sold.

Was the Corvair unsafe? The answer is perhaps less important than the change in the public's perception of the industry, caused, in part, by Nader's book and charges. Distrust of the leaders of the automobile industry led to tighter government control and greater involvement in the industry by the federal government. Cole also presided over the recall of more than 6 million GM cars for the repair of faulty motor mounts in 1971. Much as in the Corvair case, the company initially denied that there was any problem with the mounts. When the mounts failed, the resulting movement of the engine often locked the accelerator partly open. Cole made the comment, which was widely reported, that anyone who could not handle a car at 25 miles an hour should not be driving.

On October 30, 1967, Cole succeeded James M. Roche, who moved up to chairman of the board, as president and chief operating officer of GM. He was chosen for the position from among many able executives, including Semon Knudsen, who, shortly after being passed over, left the company to become Ford president.

In his new post Cole faced major political, technical, and economic challenges. One of Cole's prime objectives was to implement a renewed policy of centralization and standardization among the GM divisions. The divisions enjoyed relative autonomy in the operations, design, and purchasing areas, and the central staff was determined to increase efficiency by reducing the inevitable duplication of efforts that this caused. To achieve this, Cole and his staff dismantled a number of private kingdoms that had grown up in the divisions.

Another critical task was the development of a new small car. In keeping with the renewed interest in centralization and standardization at the company, the new project was to be a corporate car—not a Chevrolet or a Buick but a GM small car. Cole had begun work on the project when he was head of the operating staff, and he continued in charge of the project as company president. Cole was the chief engineer for the project, and Bill Mitchell was the chief stylist.

The project car was named XP887 and clearly reflected Cole's engineering interests. The car utilized radical new engine design made from an aluminum alloy, specially developed by Reynolds, with a 17 percent silicone content that would have all of the advantages of that material, primarily light weight and faster production, but would solve the durability problems common to engines made from aluminum. The intended price for the car was $1,800, about the price for a Volkswagen Beetle at that time, and its projected weight was about 2,000 pounds.

A new factory, using the latest production technology, was added to an existing facility in Lordstown, Ohio. Quality control was intended to be the best of any American car. There was a computerized system to spot and report defects early in the assembly process and a large number of Unimate welding machines to ensure, it was thought, high-quality welding. But the pace planned for the line was rapid, 100 units an hour. Most U.S. assembly lines ran at little more than half that speed, and the speed of the Lordstown line eventually caused serious labor problems.

The car was introduced on September 10, 1970, as the 1971 Chevrolet Vega. The same year the United Automobile Workers (UAW) struck GM in a bitter sixty-seven-day confrontation that cut into the first-year production of Vegas. Vega sales that year were 245,000, about 70,000 fewer units than Ford sold of its rival Pinto, a vehicle with a much more conventional design.

Lordstown was struck again in 1971, this time in a local disagreement over work standards, after production, originally a Chevrolet division responsibility, had been turned over to the General Motors Assembly Division (GMAD). The dispute between labor, claiming unreasonable work loads, and the company, claiming poorly motivated workers, came to symbolize the chronic labor problems of the 1970s. It was called the Lordstown Syndrome. In a typical story from the management side, a foreman asked an assembly-line worker why he worked only four days a week, invariably taking off a Friday or Monday. The worker replied, "Because I can't make it on three." The UAW, on the other hand, claimed the line traveled so fast that the workers could not keep up and were forced to skip some cars, with the obvious negative effect on quality.

The Vega was a trouble-prone car, with its aluminum engine causing the most serious problems. If the vehicles were not meticulously maintained, they would overheat, and the aluminum block would warp and cause a rapid loss of oil. Without oil the engine self-destructed. Later models were equipped with a cast-iron engine that was much more durable.

Cole was a hands-on engineer, always involved in the details of design and product. Even as the president of GM he was well known for his tendency to be directly involved with products and testing. One of the team members on the Vega project said that GM did not have a president, just a chief engineer. As a result the Vega was, to a large extent, his car, and his influence and political ability ensured that it would be built much as he wanted.

As the chief operating officer of GM, Cole was a product innovator. Perhaps his greatest contribution to automotive technology was his leading role in the development of the catalytic converter as the major component in automobile exhaust pollution control. As pollution laws became stricter, the various methods used to clean up auto exhaust were having serious negative effects on automobile performance. Fuel economy was suffering, as was speed and power. Cole asked GM's AC Sparkplug division to develop a catalytic system that would serve as the primary means of emission control for GM cars and light trucks. In the converter a metal interacts with the exhaust to change the fumes to less undesirable chemicals. Introduced in 1975, just after Cole retired, the converter has allowed automobile performance to improve greatly while controlling exhaust pollution. Cole was also a vocal supporter of improved safety devices for cars, including air bags for passenger safety.

Cole was a progressive engineer interested in the application of new technology and was once described as a "kick the hell out of the status quo" engineer. He championed research into the rotary engine, often called somewhat inaccurately the Wankel engine after the holder of some basic patents. The rotary engine, with few parts and a compact configuration, seemed ideal for use in compact cars. GM spent $170 million developing the engine before it determined that problems with pollution, fuel economy, and durability were too difficult to overcome.

In 1974 Cole was sixty-five and ready to retire from GM. He had been passed over for the chief executive officer's position and chairman of the board. He also was unhappy with the constant conflict between the engineering and the financial sides of the business, as well as increasing government interference in the industry. In an interview near the end of his career Cole was asked about the free enterprise system. He replied, "there's a hell of a lot of enterprise, but little of it is free."

Once he was free of the responsibility of speaking for the corporation, Cole also relished the opportunity to reply directly to one of his chief critics, Ralph Nader. A debate, of sorts, was arranged for the October 29, 1974, Phil Donahue television show. The debate was recorded in Detroit's Art Institute and was a rare case of an individual, who had been part of the highest level of decision making at GM, speaking without corporate restraints to the industry's harshest critic. The results were predictable, however. Nader called some of the cars that Cole was involved with "Stylistic Pornography" and restated his charges about the Corvair. Cole called the Corvair "the best handling car GM ever built." They discussed the cost-effectiveness of bumper standards, and Nader raised the possibility of asbestos hazards from automobiles. Nader thought automobile profits were too high, and Cole said they were too low.

When he retired from GM in 1974 Cole was still an active and vigorous man. He became interested in developing an elaborate airfreight system and purchased an interest in and became chairman of a Michigan-based company called Husky International. The key to his new system was to be a huge new freight aircraft, twice the size of a Boeing 747, with a payload of 400,000 pounds. The plane did not exist, but he hoped to enlist the aid of the government in its design and creation.

In 1977, in partnership with Victor Potamkin, an enormously successful automobile dealer, Cole purchased a large interest in Checker, the Kalamazoo-based manufacturer of taxicabs. The Checker was designed specifically for use as an urban taxi and had a number of features well-adapted for that use, such as a small turning radius and easy repairs of body damage, but by the early 1970s the design was dated and it had been replaced, to a large extent, by production cars. Cole and Potamkin planned to design and produce a radically new cab based on the Volkswagen Rabbit, utilizing extensive modifications to the body to increase passenger space and luggage room. They intended to offer the vehicle with a small diesel engine of either Perkins or Mitsubishi origin. But whatever plans had been made for Checker were cut short when Cole was killed at the controls of his own plane, a British-built twin-engine Badger, in a crash just outside of Kalamazoo on May 2, 1977.

In many ways Cole had been the prototypical auto executive. He had the rural working-class background common among automobile executives, lived in the proper suburb of Bloomfield Hills, Michigan, and loved working with cars. His son said that whenever he drove home a test vehicle, often the product of a rival company, they could count on him spending hours in the garage examining and often partly disassembling the car before he would come into the house.

While there were failures under his leadership, overall the corporation had weathered a difficult period in fairly good shape. Oil prices and the cost of driving shot up, causing rapid changes in the industry. Urban unrest and demands for equal employment opportunities for minorities had changed the environment of the factory forever. Perhaps Cole's greatest fault may have been a fascination with and a lack of sufficient caution in accepting new and novel technology. But in an era in which GM, and the industry in general, was increasingly becoming dominated by accountants, Cole, the product-oriented car man, was a refreshing throwback to an earlier age when the men who built the cars had been in control.

Convertibles

by James Wren

Motor Vehicle Manufacturers Association

When automobiles were first developed, and continuing into the twentieth century, few models had tops of any kind. But as production and sales increased and automobile travel became less a novelty, folding carriage tops were added to shield the passengers from sun, wind, and rain. When curtains were added to the carriage tops, the style, known as the touring car, dominated body design.

In 1904 the E. R. Thomas Company offered a model which featured a removable hardtop and called it a convertible, the first known use of the term in reference to an automobile. With the introduction in the 1920s of the closed car equipped with roll-down windows, the touring car faded from popularity. The convertible became the prime alternative to the closed sedan and coupe, recalling the openness and freedom of the touring car and also adding stylishness. Some measure of convenience was added to convertibles in 1938 when Plymouth introduced a power-operated top.

The popularity of the convertible and its attendant style had great effect on the design of other automobiles. After World War II, and especially during the early 1950s, automobile manufacturers introduced the hardtop, a body design offering the lines and styling of a convertible with the convenience and comfort of a closed car. The improved technology of accessories, particularly the air conditioner, and the changing role of the automobile in society, from recreational and luxury item to a necessity, hastened the decline of the convertible. Its higher price and the inherent inconvenience of having to raise the top in inclement weather were further factors in the style's diminishing popularity.

The decline of the convertible continued through the 1960s and accelerated during the gasoline crises of the early and mid 1970s. Production of the style by the major American manufacturers ended in 1977 with the Cadillac Fleetwood Eldorado. But with the return of lower energy prices and economic prosperity in the early 1980s, the convertible made a comeback as a production vehicle. Chrysler, partly as a publicity measure to highlight its new models and its return to profitability, introduced a convertible Le Baron in 1982. Thus the convertible has proved to be one of the automobile industry's most resilient designs.

Erret Lobban Cord

(July 20, 1894-January 2, 1974)   by George S. May

Eastern Michigan University

CAREER: Various West Coast automotive business activities (c. 1912-1920); sales, Moon Motor Car Company (1920-1924); general manager (1924-1926), president (1926-1933), chairman, Auburn Automobile Company (1933-1937); president (1929-1933), chairman, Cord Corporation (1933-1937); chairman, Aviation Corporation (1933-1937); various business and political activities (1937-1974).

Erret Lobban Cord, whose name is attached to one of the most famous cars ever built but whose astonishing business activities in the 1920s and 1930s carried him far beyond the confines of the automobile industry, was born in Warrensburg, Missouri, on July 20, 1894. His parents, Charles W. and Ida Lobban Cord, moved to Los Angeles where Cord graduated from high school. He immediately was involved in a variety of automotive activities—operating one or more garages in Los Angeles, making racing cars out of junked Fords and driving them on dirt tracks on the West Coast, running truck lines through Death Valley, and selling new and used cars.

It was his ability as a car salesman that ignited his career. He went to Chicago in the early 1920s and became a salesman for Moon cars. "I saved about $100,000," he recalled some years later. "Then I started looking around. I wanted to do something with that $100,000." What he found was the Auburn Automobile Company of Auburn, Indiana, an old company that was deeply in debt, had an output in 1923 of only 175 cars, and did not appear to have long to live. Cord persuaded Ralph Bard, head of a Chicago group that had acquired control of the company, to allow him to become general manager, with no pay, on the condition that if he succeeded in turning things around he would be given the chance to acquire a controlling interest in the company. Cord quickly launched a sales blitz that cleared the inventory of unsold Auburns,

rushed out new models, and enabled the company to show a profit once again. By 1926 Cord was the president and in control of Auburn. "They all thought Auburn was a little bum," he said, "but we established dividends in 1927 at $4 [a share] and 8 percent in stock."

It was the Auburn stock that may well have been of more interest to Cord than the cars. He had brought with him to Auburn as his right-hand man Lucius B. "Lew" Manning, a Chicago broker. Auburn stock began to be traded on the Chicago Stock Exchange in 1925 and was soon one of the hot stocks of the day, moving to the New York Stock Exchange and generating profits that had as much to do with Cord's rapid expansion of his business activities as did the profits from sales of his cars. Much like William C. Durant, who had been hired to save the floundering Buick operation and then, when he had made a success of that business, had not been content with it alone but had instead moved on to acquire control of a host of other companies, Cord was not satisfied simply to manage Auburn, whose sales rose to more than 22,000 units by 1929. In 1926 he acquired the Duesenberg Company in order to add a top-of-the-line luxury car to his Auburn models, which sold for surprisingly low prices considering the classic lines of such cars as the boat-tailed Auburn Speedster, introduced in 1928. Cord assured his company of an adequate supply of engines by buying Lycoming Motors. He also acquired the bodies he needed by gaining control of the Limousine Body Company of Kalamazoo, and also added two engineering plants in Connersville, Indiana.

In 1929 Cord formed the Cord Corporation to serve as a holding company for his various interests. By that time he had branched out into the aviation field, purchasing the Stinson Aircraft Corporation, producers of commercial planes. Lycoming was soon producing engines for airplanes as well as

The 1935 Auburn 851 Speedster

automobiles. The onset of the depression did not stop Cord, who had wisely avoided the kind of stock-market speculation that led to the downfall of other promoters, including Durant. Instead he increased his holdings in the aviation area, maneuvering to gain control of Aviation Corporation late in 1932 after a fierce fight with the Lehman-Harriman interests. Lew Manning was installed as the president of the corporation, which operated airlines. In August 1933 Cord acquired the New York Shipbuilding Corporation, builders of ocean liners as well as naval vessels. This was followed shortly afterward by the announcement that Cord had gained control of the Checker Cab Manufacturing Corporation, which, through a subsidiary called the Parmelee Transportation Company, ran the country's biggest taxicab operation.

Meanwhile, all was not going well for the automotive elements in Cord's far-flung business empire. In 1929 appeared the first car carrying Cord's name, a pioneering American front-wheel-drive model priced at $3,000 to go along with Cord's Duesenberg Model J, which was modestly touted as "The World's Finest Car" when it was introduced a few months earlier at a price of nearly $20,000 in some custom coach versions. The Cord L-29 proved to be a disappointment and was discontinued by 1932 after sales of only 4,400. By that time the depression was having its effects on car sales throughout the industry. The Duesenberg was never intended to be a high-volume car, but even wealthy buyers who might not have blanched at its price tag in the 1920s now had to think twice about buying one of the Model J's or the even more expensive su-

percharged Duesenberg SJ models, introduced, incredibly, in the very depths of the Depression in 1932. Auburn sales had fallen off to 14,000 in 1930 and had then rebounded to twice that figure in 1931 when Cord abandoned its range of models and introduced just one medium-sized 8-cylinder car. The addition of a 12-cylinder model proved to be a mistake, and by 1933 sales had dropped off to a mere 6,000.

Elsewhere Cord had other troubles. The government was investigating airmail contracts granted to Cord's Aviation Corporation, and there were attacks by people such as New York Mayor Fiorello LaGuardia, a one-time pilot, on the wages Cord, who sought to undercut fares charged by other airlines, paid to his pilots. Other allegations led to a congressional probe into some of Cord's shipbuilding activities. Then suddenly, in May 1934, Cord took his family and moved to Europe, turning over the direction of his business interests to Lew Manning. He was reported to have left because of kidnapping threats against his two young daughters, but there was at least the suspicion that he also may have been trying to escape from the investigations, one of which reputedly included the Internal Revenue Bureau.

After two years in England Cord and his family returned to the United States in summer 1936, a little over half a year after Gordon Buehrig's "coffin-nose" Cord, the second car to carry the businessman's name, made its sensational debut at the New York Automobile Show in November 1935. (Originally, the car was to have been a Duesenberg model, with August Duesenberg reportedly having

The 1937 Cord 812 (courtesy of Peter Roberts Collection)

worked on the mechanical features. Cord, who presumably must have been sent photographs or artists' sketches of the car, is said to have liked it so much that he gave orders that it be named after him.) But the new Cord was no more successful in the marketplace than the earlier Cord L-29, and its disappearance from the showrooms by the latter part of 1937 coincided with the end of the business empire Cord had built up over the preceding decade. Cord's downfall came with an investigation by the Securities and Exchange Commission (SEC) into his stock dealings. After a year-long probe the SEC in August 1937 charged Cord with having manipulated the stock of the Auburn company in 1935 and 1936, and Cord and Morris Markin, president of the Checker Cab Manufacturing Company, with having manipulated the stock of the Checker Cab, Parmelee Transportation, and the New York and Chicago Yellow Cab companies. The amount of stock in all of these companies was small, and thus it was possible to influence the price of the stock through their purchases. In one case Cord and Markin bought 70,000 shares of Checker Cab at $7 a share. Their action created an artificial sense of great activity in the stock which drove the price up and enabled them shortly to sell 6,000 shares at an average price of $59 a share.

On August 7, 1937, Judge Charles E. Woodward of the United States District Court in Chi-

cago, acting upon the SEC complaint, enjoined Cord and Markin from "further violation" of the Securities Exchange Act of 1934. Both men denied the charges but consented to the injunction, they said, in order to avoid prolonged and costly action in the courts. Markin retained his presidency of the Checker Cab company, but that same day Cord sold his entire interest in the Cord Corporation for over $2.6 million to a syndicate composed of the New York investment house of Emanuel & Company, the investment banking firm of Schroder, Rockefeller & Company, and some individuals that included Cord's old associate, Lew Manning. The Cord Corporation holding company was dissolved. The aviation components were reassembled under the umbrella of the Aviation Corporation, but Cord's automobile companies were placed in receivership in 1938 and auctioned off.

Cord, who was still only forty-three years old, moved back west, settling in Nevada in 1939. There he built sizable holdings in real estate, and in the 1950s, becoming a power in the local Democratic party, he was elected to the state senate. He died of a heart attack in Reno on January 2, 1974. He was survived by his second wife, Virginia Kirk Tharpe, whom he had married in 1931. They had two daughters. Cord's first wife, Helen Marie Frische, whom he had married in 1914, had died, leaving him one son.

A slight, bespectacled man who scarcely looked the part of the hard-driving promoter, Cord once declared that a challenge, once conquered, was "no longer fun. You want to tackle something else. All you can do by staying where you are is make more money, and that isn't fun." He might have been wiser to have remained with the automotive businesses he started in the mid 1920s. Regardless of the outcome of his subsequent business ventures, Cord left a legacy of classic car styling and design in the Auburns, Cords, and Duesenbergs produced during his regime that probably cannot be matched by anyone else in American automotive history.

References:

"Cord: Ex-Auto Racer Gives Up A Ship-Auto-Airplane Empire," *Newsweek*, 10 (August 14, 1937): 32;

"Cord Corp. May Change Name," *Business Week* (August 14, 1937): 21, 24;

"Cord out of Cord," *Time*, 30 (August 16, 1937): 51;

John T. Flynn, "Other People's Money," *New Republic*, 92 (August 25, 1937): 75-76;

Karl Ludvigsen and David Burgess Wise, eds., *The Complete Encyclopedia of the American Automobile* (Secaucus, N.J.: Chartwell Books, 1979), pp. 9-15, 53-55, 65-70.

Powel Crosley, Jr.

(September 18, 1886-March 28, 1961)

by George S. May

Eastern Michigan University

CAREER: Salesman, Kleybolte Bond Company (1907-1908); various positions (1908-1916); organizer, American Automobile Accessories Company (1916); organizer and president, Crosley Corporation (1921-1945); president, Cincinnati Baseball Club Company (1934-1961); organizer and president, Crosley Motors, Inc. (1945-1952).

Although the career of Powel Crosley, Jr., had so many twists and turns that he once described himself as having fifty jobs in fifty years, and although his major successes in business were in radio and home appliances, his first love was always automobiles. The son of Powel and Charlotte Utz Crosley, he was a lifelong resident of Cincinnati, Ohio, where he was born on September 18, 1886. He graduated from Cincinnati's College Hill Public School in 1901 and the Ohio Military Institute in 1905. Although he studied first engineering and then law at the University of Cincinnati, he did not go on to complete the work for a degree. Instead he pursued his growing passion for cars.

His father, a lawyer who would have preferred his son to engage in a more proper career than cars, which he regarded as a passing fad, had sought to discourage the boy's interest by betting him he could not build a car that would run between two well-known locations in Cincinnati. Crosley won the bet, however, by building a vehicle that covered the distance at 5 miles an hour. After becoming better versed in the mechanics of automobiles, Crosley in 1907 borrowed $10,000 and formed a company to produce the Marathon Six, a 6-cylinder car that he planned to sell for $1,700. Like nearly all such ventures of that period, Crosley's company probably would not have lasted long in any event, but the Panic of 1907, which made it too difficult to obtain additional investment capital, quickly put him out of business.

Over the next nine years Crosley went from one job to another, never earning more than $20 a week, he claimed, until he was over thirty years of age. He went to Indianapolis in 1908 where he worked for a time for Carl Fisher, then as assistant sales manager at the Parry Automobile Company and advertising manager for the National Motor Vehicle Company. From Indianapolis he went on to Muncie in 1910 and then back to Cincinnati, where he was a salesman for several advertising companies. Between 1912 and 1914 he made three more unsuccessful efforts to enter the business of manufacturing automobiles, before returning to a job selling advertising.

Powel Crosley, Jr., and the 1939 Crosley

In 1916 Crosley was selling novelties. Determined never again to work for someone else, he jumped at the chance to join one of his clients in organizing the American Automobile Accessory Company, a mail order business. Combining his salesmanship and mechanical abilities, Crosley within a couple of years had built up a million-dollar business by marketing, among other things, gadgets of his own making, and had bought out his partner.

Crosley credited the interest of his nine-year-old son, Powel Crosley III, in obtaining a radio set with moving him into the field of communications at the start of the 1920s. He organized the Crosley Corporation in 1921, and, using his own ability to assimilate some of the technical aspects of the new communications medium and the talents of two engineering students he hired from the University of Cincinnati, the company had become by 1922 the world's largest manufacturer of radios. That summer he also launched radio station WLW, which was for many years one of the most powerful stations in the country. In the 1930s he expanded his manufacturing activities into refrigerators and other

appliances, and in 1939 he introduced a little 2-cylinder, 1,150-pound automobile.

Development of the car was halted by World War II, but in June 1945 Crosley sold all of his business interests, except the Cincinnati Reds baseball team, which he had acquired in 1934, and his automobile division, for $19 million to Aviation Corporation, which had once been owned by Erret L. Cord of earlier automotive fame. Crosley in 1945 organized Crosley Motors, Inc., and announced plans to produce a "really salable bantam car." The following year the first postwar Crosley car came off the assembly line at the company's plant in Marion, Indiana. After nearly forty years Crosley was achieving his ambition of manufacturing an automobile, and, as *Life* observed, when Crosley eased his 6-foot 3-inch, 205-pound body "through the 45-inch door of a Crosley fresh off the assembly line and uncoils under the steering wheel, he comes into new focus, a man at peace with his convictions and pleased with his handiwork."

Although Crosley's final attempt to produce cars was longer lasting than his earlier short-lived ventures, its ultimate fate was the same. Although

The 1946 Crosley

the tiny car, which weighed 100 pounds less than the prewar version and was over a foot shorter than a Volkswagon Beetle, was obviously bucking the trend toward ever bigger cars that dominated American automobile production in these years, Crosley was convinced that there would be enough customers to enable him to succeed if he reduced the price of the car to $500. But he could never approach that figure. He never came closer to his initial production goal—150,000 cars a year—than the 28,000 figure reached in 1948. He added a sports car and tiny station wagons and trucks in 1947 and sold his cars through department stores and service stations. "Why buy a battleship to cross a river?" he argued, but with price tags that never sank below $800, few people were buying when the same money could buy a much bigger car. By 1949 Crosley Motors was losing $1 million per year. "I tried to save it," Crosley said in 1952. "In the last few years I lent the company about $3 million of my family's money." By 1952 production had declined to less than 150 cars a month when a shortage of materials caused operations to be shut down. Shortly afterward, in July, Crosley traded his majority stock interest in the company for stock in Gen-

eral Tire & Rubber Company. That company was interested only in obtaining the company's factory, making it clear that it had no intention of continuing with the failing automobile effort.

"The load became too much for us to carry," Crosley declared. He now devoted his time to his beloved Cincinnati Reds, his farms in Indiana and Georgia, and his private life, which was almost as complicated as his business life. He was married four times. His first wife died in 1939 after they had been married for twenty-nine years. His second marriage ended in divorce in 1944 after only one year. He married again in 1952, only a few months after the sale of his automobile interests, and this third wife died three years later. In 1956 he married for the fourth time, this one ending in divorce in 1960. The following year, Crosley died. His business career had been crowned by many successes, and his Reds had one World Championship to their credit while he owned the team, but in the one area which he had always favored above all others he had been ahead of the times. Had he lived at a later period when the public's tastes in cars and the price of gasoline had both changed considerably, an

American-made automobile that got 50 miles to the gallon would have created a sensation.

References:

"Crosley to General Tire," *Newsweek*, 40 (July 28, 1952): 45-46;

"Latest Purchase: Crosley," *Business Week* (July 26, 1952): 30-31;

"Love's Labor Lost," *Time*, 60 (July 28, 1952): 70;

Gerald Piel, "Powel Crosley, Jr.," *Life*, 22 (February 17, 1947): 47-54.

Cummins Engine Company

by George S. May

Eastern Michigan University

The largest American manufacturer of diesel engines, the Cummins Engine Company of Columbus, Indiana, was organized in 1919 by Clessie L. Cummins and William G. Irwin. Cummins, a mechanical genius who earlier had organized the Cummins Machine Works after having been employed by two automobile companies in Indianapolis, had built a diesel engine that Sears, Roebuck indicated it was interested in selling. Cummins obtained the capital he needed to put the engine into production from Irwin, the leading banker and industrialist in Columbus and for whom Cummins had once worked as a chauffeur.

At the time of the company's founding diesels were used primarily as industrial and marine engines. Cummins was convinced, however, that the engines could be used to power trucks, an idea that others had rejected because of the weight of existing diesels. Throughout the 1920s Cummins worked on the development of an adaptation of the heavy marine diesels to truck and automotive use. In 1930 he drove a Packard, powered by a 4-cylinder diesel that he had installed, from Indianapolis to New York. Over the distance of 792 miles the car averaged a little over 31 miles an hour and, with diesel fuel costing less than a nickel a gallon, made the trip at a cost of $1.38. The following year a truck powered by a Cummins diesel was driven from New York to Los Angeles. Through these and other demonstrations Cummins succeeded in attracting not only attention but buyers for his engines, and the company, which had showed no profits during its first seventeen years, acquired a near monopoly on the production of high-speed, lightweight diesel engines which revol-

utionized the trucking industry by the latter part of the 1930s.

Successful use of Cummins diesels during World War II touched off a rapid growth in the postwar years. With the expansion of intercity truck freight service, Cummins provided the heavy-duty diesels required to haul the twin trailers that became common. Although truck manufacturers such as General Motors (GM) and Mack built their own engines, Cummins competed successfully with them. The head of International Harvester's truck division declared: "Whenever you thought of diesel power, you thought instinctively of Cummins." In a business that was risky, with half of the newly developed diesels proving to be commercial failures, Cummins, the pioneer, maintained its leadership because of the reputation it had achieved for the quality of its engines. In 1952 the Cummins Diesel Special had the fastest speed at the Indianapolis 500, demonstrating that diesels could compete with lightweight gasoline engines. The stunt, which further solidified Cummins's hold on the heavyweight truck market, was promoted by J. Irwin Miller, the grandnephew of William Irwin, who died in 1943. Miller took over the direction of the company as Cummins, who had been president until 1948 and had then become chairman of the board, stepped aside in 1950 to become honorary chairman. In 1954 Miller established the Cummins Engine Foundation, which was responsible for much of the support for the extraordinary outburst of new buildings of modern design in Columbus, and made the city a mecca for people wishing to see the work of such noted architects as Eero Saarinen, I. M. Pei, Harry Weese, and John Carl Warneke. Beginning in 1962 Cummins do-

The Cummins Diesel Special, designed for the 1952 Indianapolis 500

nated 5 percent of its pretax profits to the foundation and to other charitable and worthy causes.

Cummins's profits suffered at times, as other companies competed more effectively and as Cummins for some years was slow to respond to changing market conditions. There was a growing need for very high-horsepower diesels as the legal requirements on the permissible weights and sizes of trucks were raised; there was also need for lower-horsepower engines in lighter trucks employed in heavy stop-and-go city traffic. But Cummins survived these problems. In the 1950s and 1960s it established numerous overseas plants and also made some attempts to diversify into other products. But the manufacturing of diesel engines and their components and replacement parts remained by far the principal activity of the company, whose operating revenues increased from $10.305 billion in 1976 to $23.037 billion in 1986. Although sales of diesels for industrial purposes were a substantial element in these revenues, engines for the heavy-duty, on-highway truck market accounted for the largest number produced. In 1986 every major American truck manufacturer offered Cummins engines either as standard or optional equipment, with seven of these companies producing over 90 percent of the heavy-duty trucks sold in the country that year.

References:

Thomas O'Hanlon, "The Cough in Cummins Engine," *Fortune,* 78 (August 1968): 109-111, 136, 140;
James A. Wren and Genevieve J. Wren, *Motor Trucks of America* (Ann Arbor: University of Michigan Press, 1979).

Harlow Herbert Curtice

(August 15, 1893-November 3, 1962)

by Richard P. Scharchburg

GMI Engineering & Management Institute

CAREER: Clerk, Horner Woolen Mills (1912-1914); bookkeeper, Standard Rule Company (1914); bookkeeper (1914-1915), comptroller (1915-1917), assistant general manager (1918-?), vice-president (?-1929), president, AC division (1929-1933), president, Buick division (1933-1948), director (1940-1962), executive vice-president (1948-1953), president, General Motors Corporation (1953-1958).

Harlow Herbert Curtice was elected president of General Motors (GM) Corporation in 1953, succeeding Charles E. Wilson, who had resigned to become secretary of defense under President Dwight D. Eisenhower. In addition to his duties as GM president Curtice also served as chairman of the corporation's powerful and influential operations policy and administration committees as well as a member of the finance committee. He was the first president under whom GM generated corporate earnings of more than $1 billion. Curtice was also the last GM president to hold simultaneously the office of chief executive officer, that office being shifted to the chairman of the board following Curtice's retirement in 1958.

Curtice was born on August 15, 1893, in the village of Petrieville, Michigan. He was educated in Eaton Rapids public schools and received his high-school diploma in 1912. During his adolescence Curtice spent his summer vacations attending to shipments of fruit bought by his father, a commission merchant, from local growers. He also took care of his father's bookkeeping. Curtice's first job outside of the family business was as a shipping clerk at the Horner Woolen Mills in Eaton Rapids in 1912. The mill was small and opportunities were limited, so Curtice decided to further his education by attending a two-year business course at Ferris Institute in Big Rapids, Michigan. His first job following college was in 1914 at the Standard Rule Company in

Harlow Herbert Curtice

Flint, Michigan. The job was short-lived, because Standard Rule was sold to the Lufkin Rule Company a few months later and operations moved from Flint. Curtice then took a bookkeeping job with the Champion Ignition Company, which in 1917 became the AC division of GM. When the comptroller left in 1915, Curtice took his place.

At age twenty-four Curtice was drafted into the army and sent to France to fight in World War I. In the service he supplied equipment for horse-drawn units of artillery. Following his discharge he returned to AC, where he earned rapid promotions to assistant general manager, vice-president, and then, in 1929, at thirty-five years of age, to president.

During his rise at AC, Curtice managed to meet and marry Dorothy Briggs of Sherman, Texas. The couple was married on May 5, 1927; their European honeymoon was interrupted by Curtice's desire to be on hand for Charles Lindbergh's arrival in Paris after his transatlantic flight. He was anxious to witness this historic event because Lindbergh's plane, the Spirit of St. Louis, was equipped with AC spark plugs. Despite this intrusion of work on their honeymoon, the Curtices were happily married.

Curtice did outstanding work and began to build the reputation that carried him to the highest position in the GM hierarchy. His first major success was in expanding the scope of AC's business. Curtice accomplished this by enlarging the AC product line to include oil pumps, oil and gasoline filters, speedometers, air cleaners, tachometers, ammeters, water temperature gauges, instrument board panels, electric gasoline gauges, radio spark plugs, vacuum pumps for operating windshield wipers, and fuel pumps.

Curtice was also successful in persuading automobile companies other than GM to use AC products. He was known to have been especially pleased that he was able to convince Ford to buy from AC, something that Albert Champion, the original company's founder, had tried to accomplish for years. So successful were his diversification plans that during the worst of the Great Depression AC was able to increase its employment even while the majority of Flint's businesses floundered. Curtice took pride in this accomplishment.

In 1933 Curtice received a request from John Lee Pratt, then vice-president in charge of accessories at GM, to see him in Detroit at Curtice's convenience. He was not met by Pratt but by William S. Knudsen, executive vice-president of GM. Knudsen told Curtice of the impending breakup of GM's troubled Buick-Oldsmobile-Pontiac (B-O-P) sales and manufacturing organization and of Curtice's potential role in the regrouping of GM. The B-O-P arrangement had been formulated in April 1932 to save money during the Depression. Originally B-O-P served only as a sales organization, but later, after a partial merger of production management under William Knudsen, it became a largely independent operation.

B-O-P management functioned as follows: Irving J. Reuter, Oldsmobile manager, came to Flint as president and general manager of Buick and Oldsmobile. Other executives joined Buick, Oldsmobile, and Pontiac as numerous executives were retired. Apart from this personnel turnover virtually the only significant development under B-O-P was the increase in the number of interchangeable parts, especially between Buick and Oldsmobile cars and between Chevrolet and Pontiac. These changes reduced the cost of tooling, and, with the accompanying decrease in the executive staffs, the experiment was initially cost-effective.

Toward the end of B-O-P, which lasted only eighteen months, tool and die makers in nearly all automobile plants, as well as in other shops, organized the Mechanics Educational Society of America (MESA) and engaged in widespread strikes, including one at Buick in October 1933. This corresponded with a general organizational drive by the American Federation of Labor (AFL) in the Flint plants. The AFL did not, however, support the MESA strike, and production continued, although the output of 1934 models was delayed. The B-O-P assembly was never popular with the majority of people in any of the automobile plants, particularly not at Buick, the employees of which were fiercely loyal to independent Buick management and production. Some critics even charged that Buick had had to "carry the whole load" for the B-O-P organization. On the other hand, the other operations accused Buick of getting the "lion's share of consolidated manufacturing operations." A well-intended plan to solve the corporation's sales slump and improve the profit margin, the B-O-P arrangement was doomed by the internal bickering and rivalry. When the news of the impending B-O-P shake-up leaked, the reorganization plan was accelerated. On October 21, 1933, B-O-P was dissolved and the individual divisions were placed under separate management. Curtice became president of Buick on October 23, 1933.

In 1933 Buick division production had dropped to 46,924 cars—the lowest output in nearly twenty years and less than one-sixth of the company's 1927 peak of 250,116. The Depression, then near its worst, combined with cars which had failed to remain competitive, caused Buick to tumble from its accustomed position of industry leadership. The gloomy atmosphere failed to dim Curtice's enthusiasm when he took on the challenge at Buick.

Although he had been trained in the field of accounting and finance, Curtice possessed a custom-

Curtice, left, with Alfred P. Sloan, Jr., center, and Charles E. Wilson in 1956 (courtesy of General Motors Institute Alumni Foundation Collection of Industrial History)

er's eye for styling, a fair amount of engineering sense, production experience, and a flair for salesmanship. With a self-imposed "higher speed and lower price" objective came a new, quickly tooled line—the 1934 Series 40. Built on a 117-inch wheelbase and boasting a 233-cubic-inch straight 8-cylinder engine which developed 93 horsepower, the new cars sold in the $855 to $925 price range. Higher-priced Buick models included the Series 50 and Series 90 in the $1,110 to $2,170 price range. The company's sales volume doubled in 1934, and the resurgence of the division appeared to be on the way. Production that year rose to 78,757 from the previous year's all-time low.

But one good year did not satisfy the new president. He still worked twelve and often fourteen hours daily and expected the same from key assistants. The following year he named W. F. Hufstader to be general sales manager, one of the wisest personnel decisions made during the early months of his presidency. Hufstader was an experienced salesman who began his automotive career with Pierce-Arrow in New Jersey. In 1920, following service in World War I, he moved to Flint and took a job as publicity director for the chamber of

commerce. In 1922 he joined the sales force of the Dort Motor Car Company and for the next eleven years drifted through a succession of sales jobs with such automobile companies as Mason Truck, Graham Brothers, Dodge, Buick, and B-O-P. Terry B. Dunham and Lawrence R. Gustin's *The Buick: A Complete History* calls Hufstader "a great 'dealer's man'—he understood their problems, he talked their language, he was a terrific salesman himself."

Together Curtice and Hufstader developed a unique plan to distribute Buick cars directly from the Flint factory without going through dealers. It quickly became popular, and many Buick customers came to Flint to see Buicks manufactured and then drove away with their new purchases. Some loyal Buick customers were known to plan family vacations around their car purchase. Next Curtice coordinated the manufacturing, engineering, and sales staffs with one objective: to restore Buick to its former prominence.

In line with Buick's reputation for reliability, dependability, and sound engineering, the company needed a car priced more in reach of the general public. Curtice decided that a lower priced, high performance, smaller automobile was needed to improve

Buick's sales and profit position. Facing stiff opposition from the GM finance committee, whose approval was required to authorize product development and production, Curtice found an ally in Charles Stewart Mott. Good fortune found Mott chairing the finance committee the day the decision was to be made regarding Curtice's new ideas for Buick. Alfred P. Sloan, Jr., was the leading critic of Curtice's plan, but Mott came to the defense of the Buick manager:

> If Mr. Curtice is to be criticized, and I think he should be criticized, the criticism is that this car should have been put into production a year or two ago and, if it is not put into production now, the Buick business will diminish, and its production and reputation will be passed by other automobile builders.

As proof of Curtice's perception of the market and of Mott's confidence in him, Buick production climbed to 179,533 units in 1937, boosting Buick's percentage of the industry's volume to 4.9 percent. The record shows that in the final analysis, during Curtice's presidency, Buick averaged more than 8 percent of industry sales and production volume for the four years preceding America's entry into World War II. Curtice brought power and speed (and, not incidentally, profits) back to Buick.

The year 1936 also saw the introduction of the Buick Special, a model that gave exceptional performance for its price of $865. Production of Specials that year reached 78,757 units. Next Curtice issued GM's chief stylist, Harley Jefferson Earl, a simple challenge: "Design a Buick that you would like to own." The result was the Roadmaster, which was added to the other names in the Buick line of cars: Special, Super, Century, and Limited. The final lineup of 1936 models boosted production to the 168,596 mark, and at the end of the year a GM central office executive gave Curtice the words he had been waiting to hear: "I'm glad to say that Buick is off relief."

In September 1936, amidst rumors of a record year for Buick production, Curtice released the past year's figures to the public. The figures were based on a statistical survey of the company's employment and wage rolls covering the twelve months ending July 31, which coincided with the beginning and end of the production of the 1936 models. The survey revealed that during the year local Flint payrolls had mounted to just over $24 million, an increase of more than $9 million and 50.5 percent

over the previous year. Average employment over the same period was 13,561 men, as opposed to 9,329 during the previous year.

On September 20, 1936, Curtice announced that production was under way "in volume on the 1937 line" and that improvements and expansion plans for Buick plants in Flint would amount to $30 million. He estimated an increase in production of 30 percent for 1937, citing 30,000 advance orders from Buick dealers for 1937 models as justification for increasing production. By October 24 Buick reported orders at 40,000 units, over 10,000 above the amount received by the same time during the previous year. Three shifts at the Buick plant produced 19,525 cars in October 1936, the largest output for a single month during that year—and still there were 30,000 outstanding and unfilled orders on hand at the factory and an additional 20,000 on file in zone points. It would appear Buick was headed for another record year. A November 15, 1936, article in the *Detroit News* quoted Curtice as saying "Nothing can stop business in 1937." But Curtice's remarkable powers of prognostication failed to take into account grievances festering among many GM employees at Fisher Body in Flint and elsewhere.

On December 30, 1936, the newly organized members of the United Automobile Workers (UAW) began the sit-down strike at the Fisher Body plants in Flint which would eventually shut down Buick final assembly operations. This resulted in the immediate layoff of 5,000 Buick workers and, by January 20, 1937, the entire Buick plant being closed due to shortages of parts from other GM facilities effected by other strikes. As a result of the shutdown, another 10,000 workers were idled, jeopardizing Curtice's hopes for record 1937 production.

On February 11, 1937, the Flint strike ended with the workers gaining recognition of the UAW from GM's reluctant management. Buick employees were quickly called back to work on all three shifts, and final assembly resumed on February 17. Production soon reached unparalleled levels, and although deliveries to dealers rapidly climbed, Curtice announced that the company would enter March with the largest number of unfilled orders in its history, with an estimated 60,000 orders on hand and at dealer distribution points. In spite of the interruption in production caused by shortages of bodies and parts during the strike, model-year production reached 220,346, which exceeded 1936 by 51,750 units. It seemed that Curtice's drive for success could surmount most obstacles.

The next revolutionary move by Curtice came in 1938 when Buick introduced cars with four-wheeled coil-spring suspension, an optional semi-automatic transmission, more power, and new styling that expressed his preference for a long, high hood line. Running boards, already fading in 1939, were scarcer still on the torpedo-style 1940 models, which concealed the running boards under the doors. In those years, Buick also introduced its distinctive hood design, opening from either side by means of an outside latch which, like the running boards, was incorporated into the styling.

In 1941, at Curtice's direction, Buick introduced still more power under the hood with a 165-horsepower engine in the Century and Roadmaster models. Both were clocked at better than 101 miles per hour at the GM Proving Grounds. The 1942 Buicks looked as swift as they were. For that war-shortened model year, Curtice also modernized the styling. Buick was the first American automobile producer to extend the front fender line all the way back to the rear fender. The idea was so radical that Fisher Body refused to put the fender on the doors. Undaunted, Curtice had the piece bolted onto the doors at the Buick plant. This striking Buick look, with its wide, low grille, was resumed after the war, carried through 1948, and greatly influenced many postwar car designs. Buick's rush to the top of the automotive market reached its apex in 1941, when a record total of 377,428 cars were produced.

By late 1940, with the threat of war increasing, Curtice offered Buick's manufacturing facilities to William S. Knudsen, the coordinator of the United States defense preparedness program for President Franklin D. Roosevelt. Knudsen accepted Curtice's offer and handed Buick a challenging assignment. The country needed Pratt & Whitney aircraft engines—thousands of them for the giant 4-motored Liberator bombers which, with the Flying Fortresses, were the nation's top long-range bombers. Automobile production methods were adapted to the engine program to give the army the 1,000-a-month volume it desired. In March 1941 ground was broken for Buick's new engine plant at Melrose Park, Illinois, and six months later the huge building was virtually completed. The first engine was completed and accepted by the government in January 1941, several months ahead of

schedule. During the war the plant continued ahead of schedule and made 74,797 engines, enough for 18,699 Liberator bombers.

Buick halted automobile output on February 2, 1942, and turned its total production capacity to badly needed war material, the manufacture of which Curtice personally oversaw. More than thirty other war assignments were eventually assigned to Curtice and Buick. Buick plants were converted for truck, tank destroyer, and engine production.

One important achievement under Curtice's leadership was the development and production of the M-18 "Hellcat" tank destroyer. Buick's tank program began in early 1942 with efforts to develop the T-70 tank destroyer, but the army kept altering specifications. As a result, a heavier vehicle was needed, as well as a large power plant, a different design, and operational changes. The final army-approved plans specified a 16-ton vehicle capable of a speed of 60 miles per hour and equipped with a 76mm cannon and machine guns. Later the designation of the T-70 tank destroyer was changed to M-18, but it was commonly known by its nickname, Hellcat. Powerful and mobile, the Hellcat was among the first Allied weapons to prove a worthy match for heavy German tanks. Later, on January 26, 1949, Curtice received from President Harry S Truman the Medal of Merit for his "outstanding and meritorious conduct" in aiding wartime production.

Long before V-J Day, Curtice began the planning process of converting Buick back to peacetime production. A study commissioned in 1944 projected an annual production level of 500,000 Buicks after the war and also proposed that $48.3 million in conversion and expansion of production facilities would be required. For Buick, the decade following the war was among the most innovative of any in its history. The torque-converter transmission, hardtop styling, and tinted glass were all pioneered by Buick. Although smooth—there were no gears to shift—dynaflow transmission was sluggish at first. Buick engineers improved it with pitch-switching stator blades and later with additional gear ratios. Today most automatic transmissions follow the design lead set by Buick. Some have called the decade following World War II the "Second Golden Age" of the automobile industry. It was the era of "more car per car," as makers introduced a long list of options—power steering, power brakes,

Curtice, center, with his wife and Charles F. Kettering

automatic transmissions, and air conditioning. These innovations were introduced on Buicks.

During Curtice's fifteen years as president of Buick, production reached 2.25 million automobiles. He had also been responsible for extending the Buick into the higher-priced class where the division took about 40 percent of the market. In 1948 Curtice was named executive vice-president of GM in charge of general staff activities, which included styling, engineering, manufacturing, research personnel, employee relations, public relations, and business research. He was, in addition, given many committee assignments.

On December 1, 1952, Curtice became acting president of GM during C. E. Wilson's confirmation hearings for the post of secretary of defense. After Wilson was confirmed, Curtice was named president on February 2, 1953, by the GM board of directors. Questioned at the time, he modestly attributed his success to "hard work." Judging from the record, that was no exaggeration. Mott, at a dinner given in Curtice's honor, stated, " . . . every business has to have a head, to sort the wheat from the chaff, to hold up a standard to work to, and to make decisions of prime importance. You [Curtice] are head of Buick and you have done all three

things, and we are here to tell you of our appreciation and friendship."

Curtice's elevation to the presidency of GM marked the beginning of a new era in the company's corporate management philosophy. Until then GM presidents had been individuals with experience chiefly in manufacturing, engineering, or production—men skilled in the mechanics of automobiles. Curtice was GM's first professional manager, and he made a decided impact on the postwar business and industrial world.

As GM president, Curtice managed the world's largest manufacturing corporation. He had a boundlessly optimistic confidence in GM and its products, as well as in himself and his ideas. He instituted an almost immediate shift in corporate strategy. Wilson had kept a wary eye on GM's market share, preferring to maintain it near 45 percent and thus avoid attention from the government's antitrust division. It soon became obvious that Curtice intended to make and sell cars without regard to market percentage. Curtice, as a salesman, was determined to sell as many automobiles as the public could be enticed to purchase, the government of the United States notwithstanding. He made no public effort to contain his optimism about the world in general, the U. S. economy in particular, and GM specifically. "At General Motors," he proclaimed, "we don't have any bad years. We have better years, then good years, then better years." The sales and profit records he consistently established were proof that his proclamations were not entirely idle boasts or marketing hype.

In 1955 GM had, under Curtice's leadership, the best year of any corporation, foreign or domestic, in history. Sales totaled over $12.4 billion, and net income exceeded $1.1 billion, up over 54 percent from 1954. *Time* magazine honored Curtice by naming him its "Man of the Year" for 1955, because "in a job that required it, he has assumed the responsibility of leadership for American business." On February 12, 1955, Michigan State College (now University) awarded Curtice an honorary doctor of law degree, and the University of Michigan awarded him an honorary doctor of engineering degree four months later. Both citations refer to his leadership and service to American industry. It seems he had arrived at the high point of his career.

The main reason for GM's tremendous performance in 1955, of course, was due in large part to the general prosperity—there is no doubt that what had been good for the country had also been good for GM. The pace of business and the surge in personal income and spending generated the biggest of all automobile markets—an 8-million-automobile year. But GM had to do more than simply ride the boom to make its gains; it had to meet history's fiercest competitive drive among the automotive industry's Big Three. Ford, with 30.9 percent of the 1954 market against GM's 50.7 percent, was bent on narrowing the gap in 1955. Chrysler, down to 12.9 percent, completely redesigned its line in an attempted comeback.

To keep competition—and production—rolling within GM, Curtice operated on the theory that "standing still in the auto business was the surest way of rolling backward." Two years before, while others worried about recession, Curtice confidently announced that GM was going ahead with a two-year, $1-billion expansion program. Because of this investment, Curtice was given credit for restoring business confidence throughout the country.

Presiding over GM's expansion program, Curtice became the nation's best-known business prophet, chiefly because he was more optimistic about the economy than almost anyone else. His annual predictions, combined with the extent of GM's

own unprecedented spending, stimulated confidence throughout the economy in general. Curtice's predictions, in fact, were probably intended as much for inspiration as for augury.

Whether he was the herald or the prophet of the business boom—or both—he was usually right. But in addition to his pronouncements he also listened to others and remembered what he heard; but when he finally was ready to make a decision, he usually made it quickly and had few second thoughts—with the possible exception of how he would convince others it was right. In GM's management system Curtice was no dictator; most major decisions had to be approved by GM's board of directors and its three top policy committees, those for finance, operations, and administration. As Curtice once put it: "I have to sell my ideas to them." Most of the time his persuasive sales technique won approval, and he was seldom forced to back down, which earned him considerable leeway to take major steps based entirely on his own judgment. For example, during the course of a 1954 European trip, Curtice liked the overseas automobile market prospects so well that he arbitrarily hiked the GM appropriation for European expansion by $50 million. The expanded program was approved without question (although Albert Bradley, chairman of the finance committee, reportedly cabled Curtice in mock despair: "Come home before we run out of money").

In the job as president and chief executive officer, which paid nearly $700,000 in salary and bonuses, Curtice set the pace for his subordinates. He was particularly intolerant of complacency, which he firmly believed might become an "occupational disease" in a company as large and successful as GM. He constantly drove his executives to greater achievement, cautioning them against being satisfied with the status quo. For instance, when Buick executives seemed a little self-satisfied in 1955 at having won 10 percent of the automotive market for the first time, Curtice reminded them that they were still losing some nine out of every ten automobile deals.

The nature of Curtice's job demanded just such executive leadership; managing GM in the 1950s was a task so large and multifaceted that it had no real parallel. Curtice's working day began at 8:00 AM, and would often last until 6:00 or 8:00 PM. While president, he usually spent only weekends with his family. On Mondays he commuted to Detroit either by car or by one of the eighteen GM planes at his disposal. He spent most nights in the executive suite just down the hall from his fourteenth-floor Detroit office, and when he returned home on weekends he usually had a briefcase stuffed with reports which he had not read during regular office hours.

For extended periods of each year, Curtice was often on the road, appearing at the Motorama in various cities, touring GM's European plants, or attending monthly board meetings in New York. Even at home in Flint he kept busy, often visiting the Buick plant on Saturday mornings. This pattern was established early in his career.

It was also under his presidency that GM approved the development of its technical center in Warren, Michigan. "It is our hope and expectation," he said at the dedication on May 16, 1956, "that this great technical center will enable GM not only to carry on its tradition of the inquiring mind but even to speed the processes whereby many more new developments may be brought into being for the good of all."

Curtice recognized the importance of a strong dealer organization and led in the establishment of a series of GM Training Centers across the country. These facilities covered subjects ranging from dealer management operations to new mechanical techniques for repairing and servicing cars. Thousands of people from GM dealership service departments took advantage of the factory-authorized training opportunities.

As Curtice moved up the corporate ladder of success, the characteristics that became the hallmark of his presidency were his ability to sense customer tastes and to predict a product's appeal. His widely recognized talent as a salesman guided his years as president and launched a sustained marketing blitz that lasted long after his retirement in 1958. Ed Cray, in his history of GM, writes: "Of all the corporation's presidents—Durant, du Pont, Sloan, Knudsen, and Wilson before him—Curtice was to be the most influential in shaping Automobile America and the least recognized for that influence."

By the end of Curtice's tenure as president of GM, Chevrolet had been securely installed as the number-one manufacturer of cars and trucks and had captured 26 percent of the market, which helped to elevate the corporation's market share to 52 percent. This tempted government antitrust ac-

tion against GM. Unlike Wilson, no self-imposed restraints limited Curtice's ambition to drive GM to dominate each field it entered. In a perpetual balancing act between increasing sales and the antitrust threat, he plunged ahead to the sixty-fifth year of his life and mandatory retirement from GM. As the final act of his career, in 1958, he approved the decision to go ahead with a compact car project—the ill-fated Chevrolet Corvair recommended by Edward Cole, general manager of Chevrolet division.

Since he had moved to Flint in 1914 to take his first job with GM at Champion Ignition Company, Curtice had called this city home. He and his wife Dorothy and daughters Catherine Dale, Dorothy Anne, and Mary Leila lived in a modest but comfortable house in the city's southwest section. Curtice readily lamented that, like most top executives, he had less time than he would have liked for family life or relaxation. He had felt it necessary to give up golf, but did take an occasional hunting trip and usually a three-week vacation each year on Cape Cod with his family. When he could he always tried to join the Saturday afternoon poker game at the Flint City Club.

His interest in civic, business, and social activities in Flint was keen throughout his life. He was chairman of the board of the Genesee County Savings Bank, trustee of the Clara Elizabeth Maternal Health Fund, a president of the Flint Community Association, a member of the Flint Chamber of Commerce, the Flint City Club, and the Flint Golf Club.

Curtice was an avid sports enthusiast and became interested in a young Detroit fighter, Joe Louis. As Buick's president he directed the advertising department to sponsor the then unknown fighter's radio bouts. After dinner at home, when television became available, he and his wife often watched the fights. He was also a football fan, particularly of the University of Michigan. While attending a Michigan game in 1937, he later recalled, "We'd just be comfortably seated, when someone would come along with a pail asking for donations to send the band to the next game." When he rose to an executive position at the corporate level, he saw to it that GM sponsored at least one annual trip for the Michigan band. He justified the expenditure by saying, "I think it builds good will all around."

Curtice is also justly credited with providing momentum and leadership for Flint's College and Cultural Development (CCD) in its early period.

The development now includes the Sloan Museum, the Sarvis Food Center, the Whiting Auditorium, the Bower Theater, the Longway Planetarium, the Flint Institute of Art, the Flint Public Library, the Flint Institute of Music, the Charles Stewart Mott Community College, and, until its recent move to a new campus, a branch of the University of Michigan. He never admitted the part he played, but his announcement on November 23, 1954, that GM was giving $3 million to the CCD gave the campaign for funds an auspicious beginning. Curtice and his wife Dorothy also contributed $25,000 each in personal sponsorships.

Curtice retired on August 31, 1958, but remained an active member of the board of directors until his death. He died unexpectedly on November 3, 1962, of an apparent heart attack at his Flint home. His sudden death was a shock to the world of commerce, which had long looked on him as an articulate and effective spokesman for business. Even in retirement he had been called to Washington many times to testify before congressional committees. Congressional leaders regarded him with a respect accorded few businessmen who appeared before them—he always cooperated, supplied requested information, and answered questions directly.

In the final analysis Curtice's whole career might be summed up as a continuing demonstration of how to stump the experts, at least those "experts" who specialize in explaining why things will not work or cannot be done. Yet he had no magic formula for success. "Do it the hard way!" he once told graduates of Olivet College in Olivet, Michigan. "Think ahead of your job. Then nothing in the world can keep the job ahead from reaching out for you. . . . Be bold, knowing that finally no one can cheat you but yourself." There was nothing complicated or even new about that philosophy, but it worked magnificently for Curtice.

References:

Ed Cray, *Chrome Colossus: General Motors and Its Times* (New York: McGraw-Hill, 1980);

Terry B. Dunham and Lawrence R. Gustin, *The Buick: A Complete History* (Wyomissing, Pa.: Automotive Quarterly, 1980);

Robert Sheehan, "How Harlow Curtice Earns His $750,000," *Fortune* (November 1947): 93;

Alfred P. Sloan, Jr., *My Years With General Motors* (Garden City, N.Y.: Doubleday, 1964);

Clarence H. Young and William A. Quinn, *Foundation for Living: the Story of Charles Stewart Mott and Flint* (New York: McGraw-Hill, 1963).

Archives:

Scrapbooks, GM news releases, and news clippings relating to Curtice are located in the files of the GMI Alumni Foundation Collection of Industrial History at GMI Engineering & Management Institute, Flint, Michigan.

Daimler-Benz AG

by George S. May

Eastern Michigan University

Formed in 1926 through the merger of the two German companies whose founders, Gottlieb Daimler and Carl Benz, had built the world's first workable internal-combustion gasoline automobiles in 1885 and 1886, Daimler-Benz has been best known in the United States for its automobiles. However, the company has been for many years the world leader in production of heavy-duty trucks, which also carry the famous Mercedes-Benz name.

In June 1980 Daimler-Benz began assembling trucks at a plant in Hampton, Virginia, using knocked-down parts which it manufactured in Brazil. The resulting Mercedes-Benz trucks added to the approximately 4,000 imported trucks which Daimler-Benz was already selling in the country. These, however, were lightweight models, and, in order to gain a foothold in the more lucrative market for the larger trucks with a gross weight of at least 33,000 pounds, Daimler-Benz in March 1981 reached agreement with Consolidated Freightways to buy its Freightliner subsidiary for nearly $20 million. Differing European and American standards governing the production and regulation of heavy-duty trucks made it impossible for Daimler-Benz to export those it built for the European market to the United States. Although it agreed to pay Consolidated considerably more than the book value of its subsidiary and to share some of Freightliner's profits for six years, Daimler-Benz's acquisition of Freightliner, which had an excellent reputation as a producer of top-of-the-line trucks, was still a less costly means of entering the market than it would have been to start from scratch.

The acquisition aroused speculation that the Germans might also seek to acquire White Motor, which had filed for bankruptcy in September 1980.

Daimler-Benz in 1977 had acquired a subsidiary of White's, Euclid, manufacturers of heavy-duty, off-highway hauling equipment, and there had been some discussion of acquiring the remainder of White's truck operations. Together with Freightliner this would have given Daimler-Benz a 16-percent share of the American market. Instead, Sweden's Volvo acquired White in September 1981.

Daimler-Benz sold off Euclid in 1983; nevertheless, by 1985 its presence in the American market had been greatly improved. Freightliner, which retained its separate identity, increased its output to over 16,000 units, double what it had been earlier in the decade. Meanwhile, over 5,000 Mercedes-Benz trucks were assembled that year at the Hampton, Virginia, plant, a figure that nearly equaled the total number of trucks the company had exported to the entire world thirty years before. These trucks were sold through Mercedes-Benz truck dealers and also through Freightliner's network of dealers, another reason why Daimler-Benz had been interested in acquiring the American company.

References:

Nick Baldwin, *Trucks of the Sixties and Seventies* (London: Frederick Warne, 1980);

Andrew C. Brown, "Hard Times for Truck Makers," *Fortune*, 104 (September 7, 1981): 80-89;

"Daimler-Benz Ups Its U.S. Truck Power," *Business Week* (March 23, 1981): 40-41;

Nick Georgano, *World Truck Handbook*, new edition (London: Jane's Publishing, 1986);

Beverly Rae Kimes, *The Star and the Laurel: The Centennial History of Daimler, Mercedes and Benz, 1886-1986* (Montvale, N.J.: Mercedes-Benz of North America, 1986).

John Zachary DeLorean

(January 6, 1925-)

by Kevin M. Dwyer

George Washington University

CAREER: Automotive engineer, Packard Motor Company (1952-1956); director, Pontiac Advanced Engineering Department (1956-1961), chief engineer (1961-1965), general manager, Pontiac (1965-1969); general manager, Chevrolet (1969-1972); group executive for North American car and truck operations, General Motors (1972-1973); president, National Alliance of Businessmen (1973-1974); owner, DeLorean Motor Corporation (1974-1983).

John Zachary DeLorean was among the most innovative engineering and administrative minds of his era and perhaps in automotive history. A "car man's car man" in the parlance of Detroit, he worked for three American automotive corporations and founded another company overseas. But DeLorean made his mark upon the automotive establishment at the General Motors (GM) Corporation. DeLorean, who was dynamic and effective, but unconventional, was followed by controversy as he rose through the ranks of the world's largest industrial corporation. Ultimately, philosophical and behavioral differences led to DeLorean's fall at GM and his subsequent demise as an engineering and administrative force within the industry.

DeLorean was born on January 6, 1925, to immigrant parents on Detroit's lower east side. His father, Zachary, came to America as a teen from Alsace-Lorraine. His migration continued in the United States, and he held a variety of jobs throughout the Midwest, finally settling down as a millwright at a Ford foundry in Detroit. A gifted but little-educated craftsman unable to advance above line work at Ford, Zachary DeLorean took to drink to allay his frustrations. His problem drinking eventually split the DeLorean household. DeLorean's mother, Kathryn Pribak, had relatives in Los Angeles, and she and her four sons shuttled between California and Detroit during several unsuccessful

John Zachary DeLorean

attempts at marital reconciliation. Born in Austria-Hungary, but arriving in the United States young enough to benefit from public education, Kathryn DeLorean lived to see many of her son's successes but not his eventual downfall.

Family instability and a resulting transient existence disrupted DeLorean's middle schooling, but after resettlement in Detroit he was admitted to Cass Technical High School on academic probation and began to show promise. From there DeLorean won a music scholarship to Detroit's Lawrence Institute of Technology, but the army draft interrupted his studies for two years active service stateside as World War II wound down. Upon his discharge DeLorean took a job as a Detroit Public Lighting Commission draftsman and also as a seasonal employee at a Chrysler assembly plant. He learned to function on four and five hours of sleep while moonlighting as a dance band director, earning enough to complete his studies at Lawrence Institute with a B.S. in mechanical engineering in 1948. DeLorean developed his talent for marketing through cursory experience in sales, first as a life insurance salesman and later as a sales representative for a Detroit automotive parts supplier. He quickly tired of selling but benefited from the self-confidence he acquired from the experience. He returned to engineering after his admission to the Chrysler Institute, where in 1952 he took his M.A. in industrial engineering. At the age of twenty-seven he began his executive apprenticeship at the Packard Motor Company.

A smaller, less bureaucratized automobile manufacturer, the Packard Motor Company provided DeLorean multi-departmental exposure to automobile manufacturing operations. At Packard he was able to guide projects to completion, and his talent became quickly apparent. With cars he found, in his words, "the central focus of my life since its start," and his knack for the business resulted in his rapid ascent at Packard. By 1956 he was restless at Packard and ready to move on. New Pontiac general manager Semon E. Knudsen was at the same time scouting young talent to shore up his slipping GM division. In fall 1956 he lured DeLorean over to head Pontiac's fledgling advanced engineering department.

Son of the legendary GM president William S. Knudsen, S. E. Knudsen made a marked professional impression on DeLorean. They were philosophically similar in their approaches to the business (both emphasized the primacy of the product) and adept at troubleshooting existent product and systems flaws and also at anticipating future trends, notably the rise of the potentially profitable but as yet unexploited youth market. The Knudsen team planned to restore the sagging morale and the profitability of what had become "an old lady division" by designing, building, and, as they saw it, inevitably selling better cars. Featuring Elliott M. "Pete" Estes as chief engineer and DeLorean as his first lieutenant, Knudsen's team functioned extraordinarily well. Fusing solid business sense with creativity, product and marketing innovations made Pontiac the industry's hottest division. After bottoming out in 1958 as sixth of seven nameplates in sales with a 4.9 percent market share, by 1961 Pontiac had pulled to third, behind Ford and Chevrolet, with a 6.4 percent share.

DeLorean played a significant role in the turnaround and was one of its principal benefactors.

Often the sponsor and frequently the originator of many product innovations, DeLorean's stint at Pontiac was his most productive as an engineer. The patenting of the overhead cam engine is his most lasting achievement. Stylistically, the DeLorean-inspired "Wide Track Look" made Pontiacs unique. The cars were streamlined and set on a wider wheel base that gave a distinctively sleek, low-riding look to the Bonneville and the Catalina. Bulky chrome was removed in favor of the cleaner lines that replaced the old Indian head logo as the Pontiac trademark. Their popularity with amateur and professional racing enthusiasts aided the division in its image reconstruction, for which DeLorean deserved and was quick to accept much of the credit.

In the early 1960s Pontiac sought to expand its product lines. Although cheap gasoline maintained and reinforced the American desire for bigger cars, and bigger cars typically meant bigger industry profits, Pontiac ventured into the compact market which conventional wisdom had written off as unprofitable. The Pontiac Tempest, featuring DeLorean's patented Tempest power train, generated excitement and received industry-wide praise in fall 1960, taking the 1961 *Motor Trend* car of the year award. The Pontiac success was the talk of the industry. GM management was, however, decidedly less enthusiastic, as the majority of buyers won over to the Pontiac division came at the expense of Chevrolet, the corporation's largest division, which accounted for between one-third and one-half of GM's annual car sales.

Management rewarded the success in the traditional way, and the members of the Pontiac team all moved when Knudsen was promoted to head Chevrolet. DeLorean became Pontiac's chief engineer under general manager Pete Estes, and the success continued with DeLorean setting the styling trends for the rest of the domestic industry. Attuned, as Knudsen had been, to the youth market, DeLorean continued designing cars that tapped into it successfully. In the process he drew increasing attention and recognition as the industry's leading design man. In 1965, for the third time in six years, *Motor Trend* car of the year award went to Pontiac for overall "styling and engineering leadership," with specific appreciation of the Tempest compact, the luxury/sport Gran Prix, the full-size Catalina, and the luxury Bonneville, as well as the hallmark DeLorean, the GTO, America's first "muscle" car. Continued success brought continued advancement;

in 1965 Estes was given the dubious promotion to head Chevrolet, and top management, somewhat befuddled, turned over the Pontiac reins to the forty-year-old DeLorean.

Pontiac continued to thrive under DeLorean's stewardship. Sales continued to climb, increasing a healthy 27 percent between 1964 and 1968 from 688,000 units to 877,000 units. The Gran Prix and Firebird accounted for half of the gain. The Gran Prix, a DeLorean design, went virtually unsupported by top management, but after selling 40,000 units after its introduction late in 1962, management took notice and endorsed the project. The combination of Knudsen's anticipation of the youth market and DeLorean's success at catering to it had perfectly positioned Pontiac to ride the cultural and demographic youth wave. But personnel aside, the Pontiac recovery was made possible by the division's size. It could respond quickly to executive initiative. Whether the same would hold true at Chevrolet was something top management wanted to find out, and in 1969, it appointed the firebrand DeLorean the general manager of the increasingly unmanageable Chevrolet colossus.

On his first day at his new post, February 15, 1969, DeLorean found the GM flagship division in serious, worsening trouble. Return on investment at Chevrolet sank to 10.3 percent for model year 1969, down from well over 50 percent in 1964. Between 1962 and 1968 its market share dropped from 31.6 percent to 24.2 percent, which, at roughly $100 million per percentage point, cut deeply into the corporation's profit margin. Chevrolet had been beaten consistently to the punch by its perennial challenger, Ford, most noticably at the small end of the market. Ford had the momentum. The introduction in 1960 of the Ford Falcon and then of the Mustang in 1964 revealed new markets to which Chevrolet was slow to respond. Chevrolet's answer to the Mustang, the Camaro, took four years to develop. Product quality also lagged, and by 1968 Chevrolet resale value had fallen from $250 over Ford's to parity. In sales, Ford narrowed the gap with Chevrolet from 600,000 units in 1962 to within 200,000 units by 1968. Estes, whom corporate management had promoted out of the general manager's slot to make room for DeLorean, compared the division to "a big monster," and he complained to his one-time first officer and now successor that "you can twist its tail and nothing happens on the other end for

months and months. It is so gigantic that there isn't any way really to run it. You just sort of try to keep track of it."

DeLorean's various on-site inspections confirmed Estes's frustrated summation. Ironically, DeLorean the nonconformist saw that the main order of business at Chevrolet was to impose structure. The division was financially and structurally expansive and undisciplined; organizational chaos proceeded with growth, but since profits had until recently been sound, management failed to react. Departments routinely outspent their growing annual budgets, a fifteen-year habit at Chevrolet engineering. Capital investment for research and development and for plant expansion and retooling, allocated to respond rather than to direct, was haphazard. To compound matters, in responding to what it perceived to be popular demand, GM management had imposed a product system which increased product lines and model options. From 1963 to 1967 the variety of Chevrolet car lines increased from 29 to 50, its truck lines from 124 to 292. To meet the tastes of the individual consumer, components other than standard issue could be bought, as an option, from the dashboard to the suspension system. Although this raised corporate profits, it also tied production schedules in knots. As DeLorean put it: "We could build one million Chevrolets and not have two alike." The add-on technique was also applied to the management systems. Divisional and corporate management retained the basic form employed by Alfred P. Sloan, Jr., with various departments and subdepartments expanded or created proportionate to the growth of GM sales. While GM offered the customer more lines and more options, the corporation remained dependent upon a management structure designed to produce one line of cars.

The 1970 model year loomed badly for Chevrolet, an outlook which worried management because of its ramifications for corporate finances. GM president James Roche charged DeLorean to accomplish at Chevrolet what he had helped to do at Pontiac, and, because all past attempts to abate the Chevy slide had failed, he gave DeLorean uncommon operational autonomy. For management there was little risk in hiring DeLorean to run Chevrolet. His success would be to the corporation's benefit; his failure would result in his own demise. As general manager, he would be accountable for the red ink that some rival executives thought inevitable.

A stockpile of DeLoreans in 1982, as the company neared its demise

DeLorean began his tenure with a break from traditional practice, crisscrossing the country to meet with dealers, parts suppliers, plant managers, and line workers. His travels encouraged unfriendly colleagues in top management to criticize him for spending too much time away from the office. Within the division, his new initiatives did little for his popularity among departmental staff and supervisors accustomed to the present chaotic and inefficient, but familiar, operations. Much as he had done for the design lines of a Pontiac, DeLorean attempted to streamline operations at Chevrolet. He updated strategies for marketing and design and decentralized authority to "drive decision making down to the lowest level possible." He succeeded in cutting 10 percent of the division management, reducing layers of management from five to three. To increase the division's dealer responsiveness, DeLorean drastically cut model lines and custom features options and centralized the order procedure by making the division the order point.

As Chevrolet's "forward response" to customers and dealers improved, so did its sales. Although sales in 1969 were depressed industry-wide, Chev-

rolet accounted for half of GM's sales. The long-awaited introduction of the compact Chevy Vega in 1970, a car imposed by corporate management rather than developed from within the division and thus accompanied by a substantial advertising budget, contributed to the recovery. A United Automobile Workers (UAW) strike in 1971 was costly, but the company was on the rebound. By 1972 manufacturing operations had been made more efficient, and in some quarters budget allocations were not fully spent. Combined sales of cars and trucks hit a record 3 million for the 1972 model year, a pace which continued throughout 1973. Restoring Chevrolet to its comfortable position, however, removed DeLorean's reason for being there, and corporate adversaries were quick to exploit that fact.

Never the loyal foot soldier, DeLorean's resistance to falling in with the corporate ranks garnered resentment and suspicion. In the homogenous GM corporate culture, his individualism raised accusations of disloyalty, and the flamboyant image he cultivated seemed to substantiate the charges. He had long since rejected the standard executive blue or grey suit in favor of fashionably colored Italian clothes. He wore his hair to his collar with sideburns. Roger M. Kyes, DeLorean's boss during his divisional general managerships and also his chief corporate nemesis, remonstrated him constantly for his outward nonconformity and urged him to "get on the team." Shortly after DeLorean's assignment to Chevrolet Kyes told him: "You weren't my choice for general manager. I am stuck with you, But you are goddamn well going to do this thing my way or you're going to be gone." The GM rule of management conduct dictated a low profile; attention was to be focused on the corporation, not on executive personality, and here, DeLorean's personal life compounded the problem. Married and divorced twice, his engagement and eventual marriage to model Cristina Ferrare defied the expected anonymity and increased his public exposure.

Although DeLorean had been considered as a possible successor to Edward N. Cole as GM president, the autonomy he had been given to revitalize Chevrolet was gradually withdrawn as the division recovered. Once the division returned to strength, top management refused to approve DeLorean's product and systems innovations. Frustrated, he began privately complaining about corporate interference and micromanagement. As a result he was promoted in spring 1972 to group executive for North American car and truck operations. The move, in effect, put him under top management's nose on the fourteenth floor of the GM building. After his compact "K-project" and a $1 billion cost-cutting program were rejected by his superiors, DeLorean's outward rebelliousness became more pronounced. He wore his hair longer and sported blue jeans and open collars under blazers. Clearly a substantial rift between the executive and the corporation had developed, and both began to realize that they might be better off without each other.

Within top management, the anti-DeLorean faction plotted his demise. Portions of a very critical speech he gave at an in-house conference were leaked to a Detroit paper. His relations with the corporation continued to decline thereafter, and in April 1973 he agreed to resign from GM. Thus ended DeLorean's unprecedented seventeen-year rise within GM from division engineer to high-level executive. He received generous severance pay and a Cadillac dealership in Florida. He soon made his complaints with GM public, telling *Fortune* magazine in September 1973 that GM had "no forward response" to popular demand, that management was

"tending a machine . . . just watching instead of running it." In 1975 Playboy Press published DeLorean's saga, written by Patrick J. Wright, entitled *On a Clear Day You Can See General Motors*, which was exceptionally critical of his former employer.

In 1973 and 1974 DeLorean served as president of the National Alliance of Businessmen. A nonpaying position, it instead provided a vehicle for DeLorean's criticisms of inefficient big business and kept him in the public eye. After finishing his term, he founded a private engineering and research consulting firm, the DeLorean Corporation, amassed large real estate holdings in New York and California, and became a part owner of baseball's New York Yankees and football's San Diego Chargers. The consulting firm kept DeLorean in touch with the automobile industry and provided a base for his return to the production end. In the late 1970s he began soliciting investment capital for an independent venture, a production sports model that would compete with those of the Big Three.

The DeLorean Motor Corporation was slow in producing anything, although it received considerable financial backing. Great Britain invested $90 million to have the factory built in Northern Ireland, but cost overruns and other problems delayed the production of the cars. When the first vehicle rolled off the production lines late in 1981, there were problems with quality. In addition the cars were extravagantly priced, in part to pay for extravagant executive spending. Although the luxury/performance market was profitable, the company neither produced nor sold the cars in sufficient quantity to make money.

In an effort to raise funds to save his failing company DeLorean allegedly became involved in a new venture: narcotics trafficking. An FBI sting operation in 1982 snared DeLorean in a $60 million drug deal, and he was arrested. His legal troubles ended in 1985 when the charges were dropped because of entrapment, and his third wife, Cristina, divorced him quickly and quietly thereafter. Presently DeLorean is maintaining a low profile, which he was unable to do at GM, and pursuing real estate interests, primarily in California.

References:

Ivan Fallon and James Srodes, *Dream Maker: The Rise and Fall of John Z. DeLorean* (London: Hamish Hamilton, 1983);

David Halberstam, *The Reckoning* (New York: William Morrow, 1986);

Hillel Levin, *Grand Delusions: The Cosmic Career of*

John DeLorean (New York: Viking, 1983); J. Patrick Wright, *On a Clear Day You Can See General Motors* (Grosse Point, Mich.: Wright Enterprises, 1979).

Frederic Garrett Donner

(October 4, 1902-February 28, 1987)

by George S. May

Eastern Michigan University

CAREER: Accountant, Reckitt, Benington & LeClear (1923-1926); member, financial staff (1926-1934), assistant treasurer (1934-1937), general assistant treasurer (1937-1941), vice-president (1941-1956), director (1942-1974), executive vice-president (1956-1958), chairman, financial policy committee (1956-1967), chairman of the board and chief executive officer, General Motors Corporation (1958-1967); chairman of the board, Alfred P. Sloan Foundation (1968-1975); director, Communications Satellite Corporation (1975-1987).

Few officials in the history of General Motors (GM) served so long and with such importance in shaping the corporation's policies while remaining as little known to the public as Frederic Garrett Donner, a GM board member for thirty-two years and chief executive officer during the company's critical period from 1958 to 1967. But this obscurity suited Donner, who, being a financial man, did not crave the publicity accorded the engineering men associated with the automobile industry.

Donner was born on October 4, 1902, in Three Oaks, Michigan, the only child of Frank N. and Cornelia Zimmerman Donner. Three Oaks was a town of 1,500 people in southwestern Michigan. Its chief claim to fame was that in return for having the highest per-capita subscription of any community in the country to a national Spanish-American War monument, it had been awarded a cannon captured by Admiral George Dewey. The town's principal employer was the Warren Featherbone Company, where Donner's father was an accountant.

Even as a boy Donner was developing some of the traits that would characterize the business ex-

Frederic Garrett Donner

ecutive of later years. A boyhood friend recalled that Donner adhered to a regular routine, each day allotting specific times for study, work, and play, with regular attendance at the Congregational Church's Sunday School. Despite the time set aside for play, athletic pursuits do not seem to have been of much more interest to the young Donner than they were to the adult businessman. Reading remained his favorite form of recreation throughout his life, with history being his special favorite because it helped him, as he said, "to learn how mistakes have been made in the past. And success."

Donner graduated in 1919 from the local public high school. The school's destruction in a fire earlier that year at a reported loss of only $20,000 is another indication of the small size of Donner's hometown. He entered the University of Michigan, where his parents took care of all of his expenses. "A boy can't become an honor student unless you pay his way," his mother declared. The son justified their confidence by graduating with honors in 1923 with a degree in economics. Donner impressed one professor, William A. Paton, a legendary conservative economist at the Ann Arbor school, with his "great skill in writing and an excellent vocabulary," which Paton saw as proof that the young man "could think clearly." Thus, several years after Donner had graduated, when Paton was asked to single out "a bright young accountant with an analytical frame of mind" for a job with GM, he recommended Donner, who was working in Chicago at the accounting firm of Reckitt, Benington & LeClear. When Donner learned that the job with GM involved "dealing with projections and forecasting rather than what had happened in the past," he quit his Chicago job and in March 1926 began his forty-one years of active employment with GM as a member of its financial staff in New York City.

Donner joined GM near the beginning of the period when Alfred P. Sloan, Jr., was reshaping the corporation into the organization that would dominate the American, and indeed the world, automobile industry until late in the twentieth century. When Sloan took over direction of GM after the departure of the company's founder, William C. Durant, at the end of 1920, a major objective of the managerial reforms he began to institute was to develop tighter centralized controls over the operations of the corporation's far-flung divisions. Although Sloan sought to continue to allow division managers considerable freedom to run their plants as they saw fit, events at the onset of the postwar depression that began in 1920 had demonstrated the dangers of allowing the divisions too much latitude. Several of the divisions had proceeded with full-scale production of cars when economic conditions dictated cutbacks. Seeing the need to look to the future to project market demands in the rapidly chang-

ing, highly competitive market of the 1920s, Sloan soon ceased to rely on the division heads, who always tended to be too optimistic in their forecasts. Instead he brought in Donaldson Brown, who, although trained as an engineer, had become treasurer at Du Pont because of his success in analyzing and assessing that corporation's finances.

Brown has been described by Ed Cray as one of "the first of a new generation of financial specialists, men who cared little about machines and manufacture and even less about such intangibles as excitement or the romance of industry. . . . They cared not whether the companies for which they worked produced steel thimbles or steel tanks; the principle of sound investment was the same—if it could but be discovered." Because Du Pont had become by far the largest holder of GM stock and had a direct interest in seeing the automaker's fortunes improve, Sloan was able to hire Brown as vice-president in charge of finances. Brown proceeded to work on plans that were designed to assure GM of profitability in good times as well as in bad. Meantime, Albert Bradley, whom Brown had hired as GM's first statistician, worked on forecasting future demand in order to establish production schedules. It was Bradley, who had a doctorate in economics from the University of Michigan and had joined GM as the assistant to the controller in 1919, who had asked William Paton for a recommendation of a bright young economist and who had hired Paton's choice, Frederic Donner. It was Donner's job for several years to work on the monthly forecasts and also the annual pricing studies. At a time when Henry Ford, disdaining the need for such financial controls and analysis, continued to run his company without scientific management techniques, Donner was part of a new analytical approach to management that helped GM by the end of the 1920s supplant Ford as the number one automaker.

In the late 1920s and early 1930s Donner also researched corporation benefit plans, which brought him to the attention of Edward R. Stettinius, Jr., vice-president in charge of personnel. Later in the decade the scope of Donner's activities within the corporation again expanded as he became involved in studies of dealer relation policies. He directed the preparation of much of the material on this controversial subject that was presented to the Senate Temporary National Economic Committee in 1939. These studies resulted in improved relationships with the dealers by establishing procedures for hearing dealer complaints and for reviewing contract cancellations. Ford and Chrysler took similar actions, but only after the subject of the relations of dealers with the big auto companies had come under investigation by Congress and by the Federal Trade Commission.

By the mid 1930s Donner was making his mark as one whose future in the corporation was bright, although one of his supervisors from these early years said that Donner annoyed some of his fellow workers because "he expected everyone to be as smart as he was." He was rewarded with a series of promotions that were unusual for someone his age. On January 1, 1934, he was named assistant treasurer of GM and was promoted to general assistant treasurer in 1937. On July 1, 1941, he became vice-president in charge of the financial staff, and on January 5, 1942, at age thirty-nine, he was elected to the board of directors, merely a confirmation of his position as one of the corporation's top executives.

Donner's most notable achievement during World War II was to set up bank credit arrangements under the "V-loan" procedure, a program to finance the expansion of GM's war production. Under Donner's plan, a revolving line of credit of $1 billion was made available to GM through some 400 participating banks, reportedly the largest such credit arrangement ever extended to one company. As a result GM's working capital expanded from a prewar figure of just over $434 million to about $950 million by mid 1945.

In 1946 Sloan, after a quarter of a century as the de facto chief executive officer, stepped down. Now seventy years old, Sloan remained as chairman of the board, but the responsibilities of chief executive officer were transferred to the office of the president. That office had been held since 1941 by Charles E. Wilson, and Wilson's new responsibilities shifted the center of power from the financial staff in New York, where Sloan had been based, to the production-oriented staff in Detroit, where Wilson was headquartered. Wilson believed that in the postwar period the main emphasis would need to be on expanding plant facilities and boosting factory productivity, and it was in these areas that Wilson and Harlow H. Curtice, who succeeded him as president in 1953, had the most experience. While Wilson and Curtice led the drive to increase GM's production, Donner had the major responsibility for raising the capital needed to carry out these pro-

grams. To accomplish this, Donner oversaw the offering of 1 million shares of preferred stock in 1946, a 2 for 1 common-stock split in 1950, a public offering of $300 million of debentures in 1953, and the raising of $350 million in 1955 through the sale of additional shares of common stock, the last effort said to have been the largest industrial financing ever undertaken.

The corporation's financial staff, never very happy about the increased power of the production group, became increasingly upset during Curtice's presidency at his tendency to commit millions of dollars to new projects without first consulting those in charge of overseeing the corporation's finances. Curtice's style harked back to the impulsive, one-man managerial approach of Durant. Sloan's carefully crafted committee system and the controls it was intended to exert over corporate policy and decisions were not popular with Curtice, who said, "The best committee is the committee of one."

In April 1956 Sloan retired as chairman, and he was succeeded by Albert Bradley. Donner moved up to fill the position of chairman of the financial policy committee, formerly held by Bradley, and was also elected executive vice-president. Bradley was unable to restore greater balance in the dealings between the financial staff and Curtice and the production staff. But the chance for the financial group to regain some of its lost power came in summer 1958, when both Bradley and Curtice announced their retirements. On August 23, 1958, Donner was elected to succeed Bradley as chairman, as well as Curtice as chief executive officer. John F. Gordon was elected to succeed Curtice as president, a move that was seen by insiders as evidence that Donner and the financial staff were determined to maintain the upper hand over the operations staff by promoting a man who, although he had been general manager of Cadillac, had not been considered a leading candidate for the presidency and who would therefore be grateful to Donner for making him the surprise choice for the job.

As Donner assumed his new duties he received for the first time widespread attention in publications other than the automotive trade journals. Donner and his wife, the former Eileen Isaacson, a schoolteacher from Grand Rapids, Michigan, whom he had married in 1929, lived in an apartment on New York's Fifth Avenue in the winter and in a twenty-two room house on Long Island in the summer. He belonged to the University Club in New York, the Recess and Detroit clubs in Detroit, and two Long Island country clubs. Rather typically, however, none of these personal details appeared in Donner's brief biography in *Who's Who in America,* which omitted even a mention of his birth date, birthplace, or the names of his parents. Instead, all that was included were the bare facts concerning his university education and the business offices he had held. A coworker declared: "What he really thinks about all the time, day and night, is this corporation."

In contrast with the flamboyant, outgoing Curtice, Donner was perceived as a reserved, coldly calculating accountant who viewed nearly everything in strictly financial terms. "How much are we paying that man?" was likely to be the first thing he asked after meeting a young GM executive for the first time. In an interview with a *Time* magazine reporter shortly after taking over as chairman, Donner sought to project a somewhat different image. The photograph of a smiling Donner that appeared with the article was in itself markedly different from the dour face that usually accompanied stories about him. "I am not taciturn; I am not shy," Donner told the reporter. "I am not afraid of people, and I don't even own a slide rule. People build up an image of a financial man that has no relation to reality. It will take a little time to get across the true picture." Obviously sensitive to the criticism that his experience was limited to GM's financial staff and that he was the first head of the corporation since the 1920s without hands-on experience in running a factory, Donner declared that "most people have a false idea of what the financial end is. At GM it can mean personnel, engineering, research, sales, even styling–and for me, it now means all of them."

Although he would never be mistaken for the backslapping, gregarious Curtice, Donner quickly took charge of affairs and demonstrated that he was "far more than a mere book balancer." He proved to be a forceful individual with definite ideas concerning all aspects of the business, an individual whose dominance over the corporation would equal, if not exceed, that of Curtice or any of his other predecessors. In the new regime Donner served as chairman of the finance committee and continued to devote much of his time to that side of the business. Gordon headed the executive committee that dealt with production, matters

in which Donner generally deferred to the judgment of Gordon and later to that of James M. Roche, who succeeded Gordon as president in 1965. However, on those occasions when Donner differed with the president, there was never any doubt that the chairman was the final authority on what was to be done. According to John DeLorean, who served as chief engineer and then head of Pontiac during Donner's term as chairman, Donner was an authoritarian. "He would rarely tolerate views opposed to his." Donner's response to any attempt to bring up a subject that had been dealt with earlier would be a blunt "We already decided that!" Even if new information were available that might warrant a second look at the matter, Donner's comment ended further discussion. Others depicted Donner in a more favorable light, as one who respected the committee system established earlier by Sloan. "He's not arbitrary," a member of the finance committee declared, "but he is positive and strong. He can be reversed, but you have to have damn good reason for reversing him." A member of the board of directors said that Donner "always does his homework and so do we. He won't tolerate anybody who doesn't."

When Donner took over as chairman in summer 1958, the country was in the midst of a severe recession that had contributed to a drop in car sales from a record of about 9 million units sold in 1955 to a low of just over 5 million in 1958. Donner angrily rejected the charge that the auto industry had helped bring on the recession by being too generous in offering credit to customers in the mid 1950s. He blamed the recession on an overheated economy that had been the result of "business excitement," although he admitted that auto dealers, enthusiastic about the new cars that appeared in the mid 1950s, the newest and freshest-looking models seen in years, "may have overtraded." Within the corporation, however, Donner and his associates blamed Curtice for the economic problems that confronted the company. At the retirement party for Donner in October 1967 Gordon attacked the condition of GM under Curtice. DeLorean characterized the outburst as an unprecedented attack by one corporate executive on a previous executive before an audience of corporate managers. "When Fred and I took over this corporation in 1958, it was in trouble," Gordon said, as nearly as DeLorean could recall his remarks. "Executive morale was low. People were horribly depressed. We were coming apart inside. It was like that because Harlow Curtice let it get that way. He almost wrecked this company." Gordon declared that he and Donner, who, DeLorean said, also attacked Curtice after Gordon had concluded, had sized up the problems "and by busting our rears with hard work . . . were able to turn this company around."

Although the tone of Gordon's and Donner's remarks represented an unwarranted attack on the reputation of a man many in their audience still revered as a strong leader who had been vitally interested in the company's products, Curtice was not blameless in GM's problems. He continued producing the big, high-powered, heavily chromed and finned models that had been so popular earlier in the decade and instead of heeding signs that consumer preferences were shifting. The new 1959 models that were introduced a few weeks after Donner took office were a legacy of the Curtice regime, and they represented a continuation of the big car emphasis. However, in Curtice's defense the planning of the 1960 models that appeared in fall 1959, and which marked the beginning of a turn to somewhat smaller, more tastefully styled cars, had begun under Curtice. And Donner, on the other hand, gave little indication that he opposed the kind of models for which GM had been famous when he took office in 1958. Instead he declared that reports claiming the public was now more interested in low-cost transportation than in fancy cars "were just rationalizations for not buying a car. Lots of this sort of attitude would change overnight if economic conditions change."

The fact that sales of the small imported cars, especially the Volkswagen Beetle, and of American Motors' compact Rambler rose during a period in which other car sales slumped was a phenomenon that Donner admitted he found rather puzzling. "I don't know for sure what it means," he told a reporter in September 1958, "but I can tell you this— before we move at GM, we will be sure." In the meantime, he said, they were in no hurry to introduce a small car. However, Donner knew full well that GM had committed itself months earlier to the rear-drive Chevrolet Corvair that would be one of the 1960 models introduced in fall 1959. Donner's failure to acknowledge that a small car was in the offing resulted in part from a seemingly unrelated concern—the threat of antitrust action against the auto giant that was, along with the problems of the

economic recession, one of the issues Donner had to deal with as he took charge.

The Supreme Court had ruled in 1957 that Du Pont must divest itself of its 25 percent holding in GM because of the monopolistic implications of a situation in which a company that sold GM most of the paints and fabrics used in its vehicles had the largest single block of voting stock in that corporation. This action also renewed interest in the proposal that GM itself should be broken up to create greater competition in the auto market. Already in 1955 Sloan had been called before a Senate committee and had defended GM from the charge that its sheer size gave it an unfair competitive advantage, and early in 1958 Donner had been a witness before a committee chaired by Senator Estes Kefauver that looked at GM's ability to determine the price range at which all cars would have to be sold. Donner, who annoyed even some of the Republican senators by what they regarded as his cold, even disdainful treatment of the committee, accompanied Curtice to the hearing, and Donner and his financial staff blamed Curtice for having stimulated much of the support that had developed for breaking up GM. Where Sloan and Wilson are said to have sought to hold down GM's market share to around 45 percent, Curtice had pushed sales and by 1955 had grabbed 50 percent of the market. Curtice's term as chief executive officer, from 1953 to 1958, coincided with a period in which several of the remaining small auto companies ceased to exist as separate entities, leaving only American Motors, a merger of Hudson and Nash, and Studebaker-Packard as competitors to the Big Three in auto production. That American Motors by 1958 was producing only the small Rambler and that Studebaker-Packard was about to introduce its own compact car in fall 1958 had caused even Curtice to hesitate to give the go-ahead signal for the Corvair because of fears that its appearance would lead to charges that GM was seeking to kill off the last of the independents.

No matter how he may have felt about Curtice's aggressive marketing tactics, Donner gave no indication when he took over the corporation that the company would cut back in the face of the antitrust storm. Did the corporation "feel a responsibility not to compete so hard as to drive marginal producers out of business?" he was asked. "And when did you stop beating your wife?" Donner shot back. "If you are thinking of Studebaker-

Packard, we didn't drive them to their present condition. They drove themselves there. Did you ever stop to wonder what they did with the profits of the lush war years, if they reinvested them in the business?" Asked about the suggestion that GM should voluntarily limit itself to a share of the market that was less than 50 percent, he replied that "Nothing sets me off so much as the suggestions that we ought to tell our people that there are limits on the effort they should make," Donner replied. "Nothing could pull a corporation down faster. I have never seen us with a percentage of the industry that we could not be proud of." Another executive was quoted at the same time as saying, "We've never turned away any business yet, and I can't see where we ever will."

Donner could take justifiable pride in much of what was accomplished during his nine years as chairman. Aided by the return of better economic conditions, GM regained the momentum that it had lost during the recession of 1957-1958. Chevrolet, whose position as the top selling car in the country had been seriously threatened by Ford in the late 1950s, regained its healthy lead during the early 1960s. The other divisions also did well, especially Pontiac, which replaced Plymouth as the third best-selling car during much of the 1960s. Interest in small cars faded, allowing GM to concentrate on the bigger, more profitable models. With the declining interest in small cars, American Motors, which had briefly enjoyed unheard-of sales for its compact Rambler, once again was struggling to survive, while Studebaker-Packard finally folded, ending car production in the United States in 1963 and at its Canadian plant in 1965. GM's market share, meanwhile, topped the 50-percent figure reached under Curtice, while sales and profits by 1965 reached record levels. Although there was still talk of breaking up GM, as import sales grew rapidly in the late 1960s, those who were concerned about the impact of those sales argued that GM's size made it a more effective competitor than the smaller companies that would result from the company's breakup.

Donner's most dramatic administrative reform was a clever move to make it more difficult to press antitrust actions against GM. In 1965 he created the General Motors Assembly Division, consolidating most of the car assembly operations under one management. It would no longer be so easy to talk about setting up a car division such as Chevrolet as a separate company if Chevrolet no longer managed the plants in which its cars were assembled. But the reform was also related to two of Donner's other major concerns. In theory, at least, the new assembly division was more efficient and cost-effective than similar assembly activities under five different car divisions. This conformed to Donner's goal of increasing profits by cutting costs. In addition the move was intended to reduce the power of the automobile divisions and to strengthen the hand of the financial staff. Although stories in the press depicted Donner as a staunch defender of the "System" established by Sloan forty years before, Donner's actions in reality served to upset the delicate balance Sloan had sought to maintain between centralized controls and guidelines and decentralized authority granted to division managers to run their operations. The production men fought Donner's changes, but well before the end of his term it was clear that he had won.

Yet Donner could not have been very pleased with other developments during his tenure. Despite record sales, the auto industry in general and GM in particular had come under increasingly heavy attack for its failure to pay enough attention to the harmful effects automobiles had on the environment and to the ways in which automobiles could be made safer. It was in connection with the latter issue that in 1965 Donner and the newly installed GM president, James Roche, were called to testify before a Senate subcommittee, headed by Sen. Abraham Ribicoff, which was looking into the need for the involvement of the federal government in the safety question. The two executives appeared before the committee on July 20, 1965, and it is Donner's performance at the hearing that will likely be the one feature of his long career for which he will be best remembered. Neither he nor Roche seem to have regarded Ribicoff, a freshman senator, as a very serious threat. Nevertheless, in an attempt to defuse any negative comments regarding GM's record on safety, the corporation a week before the hearings announced a $1 million grant to MIT to study the relationships between highways, automobiles, and car drivers as contributing factors to automotive safety. It also announced it was making certain safety features—ones that Ford had been offering for nine years—standard equipment in all GM cars.

Donner opened with a prepared statement in which he presented the standard industry argument that the question of safety was constantly being studied, and new features that contributed to greater safety were constantly being tested. Before they were installed in cars, however, the public had to accept them. The items could be offered as options, but until a substantial number of customers chose those optional features, Donner was opposed to making them standard equipment. The Ribicoff committee hearing came at a time when considerable support had arisen for government regulations mandating the inclusion of certain safety features in all cars. Donner made it clear that he did not approve of such tampering with the operations of the competitive marketplace.

When the time came for committee members to ask questions, Ribicoff inquired if the GM executives were familiar with a study made by the Cornell Aeronautical Laboratory in 1963 that showed that in accidents the doors on GM cars were torn off at a far higher rate than the doors on Ford or Chrysler cars. Surprisingly, neither Donner nor Roche nor the company's vice-president for engineering were familiar with the report, even though the vice-president acknowledged that it was well known in the company that Cornell made these kinds of studies. Sen. Robert Kennedy commented that he found it rather shocking that Cornell made the information from these studies available to the corporation, but "not one" of these top executives "knows anything about it. It does seem to me that that is not giving it the highest priority, or the kind of priorities that it deserves."

Kennedy then went on to try to determine how much money GM spent on safety research each year. Donner did not know, and Roche finally guessed that the figure was about $1.25 million. Kennedy then wanted to know how much profit GM had made the past year. Donner objected that this was unrelated to the subject of safety, which was the ostensible subject of the hearing. Kennedy nevertheless insisted that he wanted to know what profit had been earned. "I will have to ask one of my associates," Donner replied. Published stories about Donner had always pointed out his passion for having exact figures, on all aspects of the corporation's business, ready to bring up in meetings at all times. It was part of what DeLorean called "Donner's style of management by intimidation" to ask an executive a production figure for the last month, for example, and, when the executive cited an approximate figure, to rattle off the exact number. "Look how I know this goddamn business, people!" was the point DeLorean thought Donner was

trying to make. "Look what a mind I have!" But now the chairman, perhaps flustered by a grilling for which he was unprepared, could not recall how much profit GM had made in 1964, even though he carried around with him a two-inch thick packet of note cards filled with data.

James Roche, a kindly man who is said to have been one of the few GM executives who had developed a warm friendship with Donner, stepped in to declare that the corporation had made $1.7 billion. "You made $1.7 billion last year?" Kennedy asked. "That is correct," Donner replied. "And you spent $1 million" on safety research, Kennedy asked. "If you gave just 1 percent of your profits, that is $17 million." Kennedy continued to press for more precise figures on how much had been spent each year on research into safety features and testing new pieces of safety-related equipment. But none of the three GM executives was able to provide the information. The *Wall Street Journal* called their performance "dismal," and quoted one senator as saying "I really wouldn't have believed they could be so bad."

The lack of interest Donner and his colleagues had shown in the importance of the safety issue, when combined with an equally dismal performance by the Chrysler executives when they appeared before the committee (only Ford made a favorable impression), probably tipped the scales in favor of a law requiring the companies to include seat belts and other safety features in all their cars. But all doubts that such action would be taken were removed in late 1965, when Ralph Nader's *Unsafe at Any Speed* appeared, charging that the companies knowingly built cars that contained features potentially hazardous to the safety of the car's occupants. Although Nader attacked the design of many cars, he zeroed in on the Chevrolet Corvair. A few weeks later an incredible story broke in the nation's newspapers regarding the clumsy efforts GM had made to uncover information that would discredit Nader, who, it was feared, might be called as an expert witness in some of the numerous damage suits filed against the corporation for deaths and injuries suffered in Corvair accidents. Fortunately for Donner, he was in New Zealand and Australia at the time, and thus it was left for Roche to appear once again before Senator Ribicoff's committee, for whom Nader had acted as an adviser. In front of the television cameras, Roche was made to apologize for the manner in which GM's hired investigators had infringed upon Nader's privacy rights. The investigation had been launched by the corporation's chief counsel, without the knowledge, apparently, of either Roche or Donner, but it left a stain on the auto giant's reputation that would take a long time to erase.

Donner retired as chairman and as an active employee in October 1967. Despite the efforts that had been made when he took the office nine years before to project a warmer, more open image, Donner had remained aloof, rarely granting interviews. But he did tell one reporter as his term was coming to an end, "I am not ashamed of General Motors." The corporation was his life, and although he was retired, he remained on the board of directors until 1974, and his presence was very evident. Roche succeeded him as chairman. When Roche was ready to retire in 1971, Donner made sure that the mantle was passed to Richard Gerstenberg, a longtime colleague of Donner's on the finance staff, while Thomas A. Murphy, another accountant, was moved up to be next in line when Gerstenberg reached the mandatory retirement age in 1974. The moves assured the continued dominance of the corporation by the financial staff through the rest of the decade.

Besides his continued involvement in GM affairs, Donner also served from 1968 to 1975 as the chairman of the board of the foundation established by Sloan. He also was appointed by President Lyndon Johnson to be one of the three directors of the Communications Satellite Corporation. His wife died in 1983, and his son, too, had died before Donner's death at his home in Greenwich, Connecticut, on February 28, 1987. Private funeral services for the onetime member of the Three Oaks Congregational Church Sunday School were held on March 2 at St. Stephen's Episcopal Church in Port Washington, New York.

GM's current chairman, Roger Smith, declared that Donner's contributions to the company "are beyond measure. The corporation flourished under his chairmanship, establishing new records in dollar sales, earnings, dividend payments, and worldwide sales. His primary concern was that GM build for the future." There was no mention of the problems and the strains that Donner had had to deal with, but he himself once declared: "We're always under strain. This business wouldn't be any fun if it wasn't for strain. It would be like selling soap or matches."

References:

Alfred D. Chandler, Jr., *Giant Enterprise: Ford, General Motors, and the Automobile Industry* (New York: Harcourt, Brace & World, 1964);

Ed Cray, *Chrome Colossus: General Motors and Its Times* (New York: McGraw-Hill, 1980);

Time, 72 (September 8, 1958): 84-85;

Time, 72 (September 22, 1958): 79;

Time, 79 (May 18, 1962): 85-90;

J. Patrick Wright, *On a Clear Day You Can See General Motors* (Grosse Point, Mich.: Wright Enterprises, 1979).

Duesenberg Incorporated

by Northcoate Hamilton

Columbia, South Carolina

Duesenberg Incorporated was the most famous of the companies bearing the Duesenberg name. Formed in 1926 as a wholly owned subsidiary of Erret Loban Cord's Auburn Automobile Company, the firm concentrated on building and selling the luxury automobiles which made the Duesenberg name synonymous with elegance and performance. Yet Duesenberg Incorporated was merely the culmination of a lifetime of research, production, and failure by the Duesenberg brothers, Frederick and August.

The Duesenbergs were born in Lippe, Germany, and in 1885, after their father's death, they traveled to the United States with their mother and their five brothers and sisters. In 1897 Frederick Duesenberg started a bicycle business, from which he, like so many automobile pioneers, would later enter the automobile industry. While Frederick was becoming famous as a world-class bicycle racer, he also became intrigued with the motorcycle. In 1899 he built a highly efficient gasoline engine for the motorcycle, a design which directly began his career as an engine designer.

In 1902 Frederick sold his bicycle business and took a job with the Rambler Motor Car Company in Kenosha, Wisconsin. There Frederick came in direct contact with automobile technology and began his research into constructing engines for use in race cars. In 1905 he, with August, designed such an engine, the Mason, and founded the Mason Motor Car Company to produce it. In 1906 the company and the engine were sold to the Mason-Maytag Motor Company, for which Frederick and August both worked until 1913. The brothers designed for Mason the famous "walking beam" overhead-valve engine which was used in the company's racing cars.

In 1913 the Duesenbergs opened their own business in St. Paul, Minnesota, building engines for race cars, boats, and racing hydroplanes. Many

The Duesenberg engine, one of the most renowned in the automotive industry

of their boat engine designs were produced by the Loew-Victor Manufacturing Company of Chicago, an association which led to the formation of the first Duesenberg Motors Corporation. J. R. Harbeck, managing director of Loew-Victor, invested the money for the firm, which was organized in 1916. A factory was built for the company in Elizabeth, New Jersey, and first production began six months after the United States entered World War I. The business of the factory was to manufacture airplane engines for use in the war, but only 60 of the 2,000 contracted for had been completed when the war ended. The remaining contract canceled, the Duesenbergs left the company in 1919 to begin development of a straight 8-cylinder engine for use in luxury automobiles.

Frederick Duesenberg at the wheel of the SJ in 1932

In March 1920 the Duesenberg Automobile and Motors Company was established and a new factory built in Indianapolis. There the brothers produced the Duesenberg Model A, the first car utilizing both a straight 8-cylinder engine and hydraulic front-wheel brakes. The first Model A's did not reach dealers until December 1921, and deliveries totaled about 150 cars in 1922. Prices for the Model A ranged to about $6,500.

The company failed in 1924, and a new firm, the Duesenberg Motor Company, was formed in 1925. Production of the aging Model A design continued, but only about 200 cars were produced in 1925 and 1926. As did many firms in the mid 1920s, Duesenberg Motor Company found itself without the capital to develop the new models it needed to compete in the rapidly changing automobile market. That capital was made available by Cord, who was the owner of Auburn Automobile Company. In 1926 Cord purchased the Duesenberg firm for $1 million, forming Duesenberg Incorporated and giving the Duesenbergs free rein to develop new models. The Model J, the new design, was announced in 1928 and claimed a horsepower rating of 265. Even at the lower horsepower levels

it probably attained, the Model J was the most powerful car in the world. It was the Model J which fashioned the Duesenberg's public reputation, and prices ranged from $8,500 for a chassis to over $25,000 for a custom-body model.

Cord planned to build the Model J in batches of 500, but the first batch was never completed. Only 480 of the Model J's were built, and it took ten years to sell even these. Of course, the Great Depression dampened sales greatly, and most deliveries of the car took place before 1932, when the Depression reached its low point. The company, beginning in 1932, offered a new model, the SJ, which was a supercharged version of the Model J. Only 36 of these were ever built, and Frederick Duesenberg's death in 1932 ended the firm's history of innovation. Cord's entire empire collapsed in 1937, and the nearly idle Duesenberg plant was sold to the Marmon-Herrington Truck Company.

Despite the failure of the Duesenberg firm, the cars it produced were highly realized, marking the high point of American luxury car production. The standards of the Duesenberg automobile were so high that when attempts were made to revive the name and the car in the 1960s and 1970s, the

Duesenbergs carried price tags from $20,000 to $100,000. Regardless, the Duesenberg remains for many the quintessential automobile.

References:

Nick Baldwin and others, *The World Guide to Automobile Manufacturers* (New York: Facts on File, 1987);

Griffith Borgeson, *Erret Loban Cord, His Empire, His Motor Cars: Auburn-Cord-Duesenberg* (Wyomissing, Pa.: Automobile Quarterly, 1983);

Beverly Rae Kimes and Henry Austin Clark, *Standard Catalog of American Cars, 1805-1942* (Iola, Wis.: Krause, 1986);

Louis William Steinwedel and J. Herbert Newport, *The Duesenberg* (New York: Norton, 1982).

Pierre Samuel du Pont

(January 15, 1870-April 5, 1954)

by George S. May

Eastern Michigan University

CAREER: Various positions (1890-1899), financial director (1902-1909), acting president (1909-1915), president, E. I. du Pont de Nemours (1915-1919); director (1915-1944), chairman (1915-1929), president, General Motors Corporation (1920-1923).

Pierre Samuel du Pont is the only example in American automotive history of a major figure from a different industry taking over the leadership of an existing major automobile company and having an important influence on its development. From Albert Pope, the bicycle manufacturer in the 1890s, to Henry Kaiser, shipbuilder, in the 1940s, businessmen with nonautomotive backgrounds had become important figures in the automobile industry by organizing new companies. Du Pont's involvement resulted from investments he and his company made in General Motors (GM), investments that ultimately led him to assume executive responsibility in order to protect that investment.

Du Pont was born near Wilmington, Delaware, on January 15, 1870, the second of eleven children born to Lammot and Mary Belin du Pont. Du Pont's father, second in control of the Du Pont powder-making company, was killed in 1884, and at age fourteen Pierre du Pont became the head of his family. After graduating from the Massachusetts Institute of Technology in 1890, he returned to work in the family business. Dissatisfaction with the unwillingness of the elder members of the extensive du Pont clan to agree to changes he suggested in the company's management led him to leave in 1899 to pursue other business interests. He re-

Pierre Samuel du Pont

turned in 1902 and, together with his cousins, T. Coleman du Pont and Alfred I. du Pont, bought the family firm for $12 million. Under their direction the E. I. du Pont de Nemours Powder Company by 1904 controlled 70 percent of American explosives facilities. While Coleman du Pont was the president and Alfred du Pont was in charge of operations, Pierre du Pont handled the financial end of the business and helped devise an efficient method of administering the firm. As the two cousins began turning their attention to other interests, du Pont in 1909 became the acting president and then officially the president from 1915 to his retirement in 1919. He guided the company during a period of enormous expansion during World War I and gained control of the company through the purchase of the holdings of Coleman du Pont. Alfred du Pont challenged this action in court, and, although Pierre du Pont won the case, the feud continued to split the family for many years.

Meanwhile, in 1914, at the urging of his close business associate, John J. Raskob, du Pont had purchased 2,000 shares of GM stock. Raskob, who bought 500 shares, argued that it was important for du Pont to diversify his holdings and that GM stock represented an excellent buy. Its low selling price of $70 a share was a reflection, he said, of the fact the company had never paid a dividend and was not a true indication of the company's earnings record, which Raskob predicted would lead to the stock doubling in value within a year. In fact, the stock's price rose to $350 by September 1915 and to $558 by December.

Most of this increase was the result of a bitter fight for control of the company into which Pierre du Pont found himself being drawn. GM's founder, William C. Durant, had been forced to relinquish control of the company in 1910 in return for obtaining the necessary financial help from an Eastern banking syndicate to save GM from collapse. The term of the loan was for five years, with the bankers holding control of the company during that period through a voting trust. The bankers, headed by James J. Storrow, assumed they controlled enough stock to remain in power after the loan had been paid off in fall 1915. However, Durant sought to regain the company by buying up trust certificates, and, as the date of the termination of the voting trust approached, it appeared he might be successful in his objective. At least that was the information conveyed to du Pont by the New York banker, Lewis G. Kaufman, a Durant ally who also handled the Du Pont company's New York banking transactions. Kaufman persuaded du Pont to attend the GM board meeting on September 16, when the voting trust would be ended and, he said, Durant would resume control of the company.

At the September meeting du Pont discovered to his surprise that he had been misled. Durant did not have a majority of the stock, and the meeting dragged on for hour after hour with neither the Durant forces nor the rival bankers' group able to agree upon a slate of directors to be submitted to the stockholders at the annual meeting in November. A compromise was finally reached, although there are differing accounts as to who initiated it. Of the fifteen directors to be nominated, the two factions had already agreed on twelve nominees, with six being put up by the Durant faction and six by the bankers. Although Pierre du Pont was one of the six nominated by the Durant group, his standing in the business world apparently led the bankers to accept the agreement, which broke the deadlock by having du Pont name the remaining three directors, who would represent a supposedly neutral point of view. He chose Raskob, who was with him at the meeting, another business associate, J. Amory Haskell, and du Pont's cousin, Lammot Belin. The slate was approved at the November meeting, and du Pont was chosen as the chairman of the board, while Charles W. Nash, who had become president during the period of the voting trust, remained in that office.

Fall 1915 was a period of stability for the Du Pont Company, and the calm provided du Pont, who told Haskell that he did not intend to be "a 'dummy' director," with the opportunity to develop an active interest in GM. Any thought that he might act as a peacemaker to draw together the two rival factions in the company was soon dispelled, however, when Durant aggressively pursued ingenious new initiatives that left no doubt by spring 1916 that he had acquired the majority stock interest that he had been seeking. The bankers were out and so was Charles Nash, whose earlier close ties with Durant in the Durant-Dort Carriage Company might have caused Durant to keep him on as president had Nash not allowed his name to be used in the bankers' attempt to block Durant's takeover. As a result Nash was forced to resign and was succeeded as president by Durant on June 1, 1916. At Durant's request du Pont continued as chairman.

Once he was back in control of GM Durant launched ambitious new expansion programs, and in 1917 he was able to persuade the du Pont Company to invest $25 million of its war profits in GM stock. Raskob strongly supported Durant's bid for

Du Pont in 1915, near the time of his first purchase of General Motors stock (courtesy of Hagley Museum and Library)

these funds, telling his fellow Du Pont executives that, among other advantages, the dominant stock holding they would gain in GM "will undoubtedly secure for us the entire Fabrikoid, Pyralin, paint and varnish business of [the GM divisions], which is a substantial factor," words that would come back to haunt Du Pont years later when they were used to support the government's charge that the company's acquisition of stock in GM represented a violation of the antitrust laws. However, more important in securing the company's approval of the investment was the fact that Pierre du Pont strongly approved it. With additional investments made in 1918 the Du Pont Company by the end of that year owned 26.4 percent of GM stock.

The dominant stake that Du Pont held in GM forced Durant to pay more attention to the company and its interests. In effect, while operations, which were handled by the Executive Committee, remained under Durant's control, the financial matters of the business were handled by the Finance Committee, which was chaired by John Raskob and composed entirely of people from Du Pont, except for Durant. However, Raskob failed to exercise the necessary restraining influence over Durant's expan-

sion plans and the kinds of expenditures needed to carry them out. In fact Raskob sometimes pushed for new programs that went beyond those Durant proposed. The commitment of huge amounts of money to finance these expansion programs, when combined with Durant's inability or unwillingness to recognize that the business had grown far too big for one man's control, spelled deep trouble for the company when the postwar boom turned into a postwar depression in fall 1920.

Pierre du Pont, meanwhile, had stepped down as president of the Du Pont Company in 1919, and, although he continued as chairman of GM, he had begun to turn to other personal interests, assuming that his and the Du Pont Company's interests in the auto company were well protected. The onset of the depression in 1920 and its severe impact on car sales by itself would have forced du Pont eventually to take a more active role in the affairs of the company. Any uncertainty as to the scope of that involvement was removed in November 1920, when du Pont learned that, in addition to GM's serious financial difficulties, Durant was on the brink of bankruptcy. On November 26, 1920, du Pont related the events of the preceding two weeks and his discovery of the full extent of Durant's problems in a letter to his brother, Irénée du Pont, who had succeeded him as president of the Du Pont Company. The fact that Irénée du Pont had been present at several meetings with Durant during the period covered in the letter and that du Pont addressed his brother as "Dear Sir" is an indication that the purpose of the lengthy letter was to officially record the du Pont version of events, which did not always jibe with Durant's. There is no disputing, however, that Durant for months had been engaged in a large-scale move to buy GM stock, in a one-man effort, he claimed, to halt the downward slide in that stock's price. These purchases had been made largely by borrowing from various brokers and banks. In November some of these loans began to be called in, and it was then that Durant met with du Pont and Raskob on November 11 and for the first time indicated that "he was worried about his personal accounts." When he was pressed about the seriousness of his problems, he was evasive, but as du Pont delved more deeply into the matter he was shocked to discover that it would take at least $20 million to cover Durant's indebtedness if and when sense could be made of his totally disorganized accounts. The prospect of the GM president declaring personal bankruptcy and the effect such a declaration would have on the financial world's view of GM's soundness led to a series of complicated negotiations whereby the Morgan banking interests and the du Pont interests provided the money needed to rescue Durant. Durant's stock in GM was the collateral for the loan. In addition Durant was forced to resign his position as president on November 30, 1920. Durant severed his ties with the company he had created twelve years earlier.

With the additional stock it had acquired as a result of the Durant affair, the Du Pont Company now controlled about 36 percent of GM common stock. As there was an overriding need to restore public confidence in the company after the blows it had suffered from the disastrous drop in its sales and the resignation of Durant, Pierre du Pont acceded to appeals that he succeed Durant as president. He continued to serve as chairman, but in that period the job of chairman was much less important than it would be in later years. The president in effect served as the chief executive officer, although that was a term not yet in use, and du Pont's associates argued that, despite the fact that he did not have any extensive background in the automobile business, only he had the requisite stature in the business world that could offset the damaging effects of the news of Durant's departure.

"I was very loath to accept the position [of president]," du Pont later declared. "I had recently retired from business, but I said that I would do whatever they thought best, and I was put in as president with the distinct understanding that I was only to stay there until a better posted man could be found to take the job." He served as president until May 10, 1923, when he resigned, and the board, at his suggestion, chose Alfred P. Sloan, Jr., as his successor. Sloan joined the GM sphere of influence in 1916 when the Hyatt Roller Bearing Company he headed had become part of a merger that Durant arranged of auto parts manufacturers. The merged firm was officially acquired by GM in 1918. The relationship between Sloan and du Pont which, because of the personalities of the men was always rather formal, became closer in the period after the war as they became aware of their shared ideas as to strategies needed to correct the problems that led to the company's near collapse in late 1920. When du Pont became president, one of his first actions at the end of December 1920 was to appoint Sloan,

Du Pont with John Jacob Raskob in 1950 (courtesy of Hagley Museum and Library)

who had been serving as vice-president of the parts and accessories division, as well as a director of the company and a member of the Executive Committee, to a new four-man Executive Committee including himself, Raskob, and J. Amory Haskell. The new committee was intended to implement the reforms necessary to build a company that would be capable of competing effectively as the market for cars rebounded from the postwar slump.

Du Pont's role in effecting the changes that turned Durant's sprawling, disorganized empire in a few years into the giant of the industry was, as his biographers put it, "to act as a catalytic agent." He naturally drew upon his experience at Du Pont, bringing in a host of upper- and middle-level executives from that company, who, like him, knew little about automobiles but who knew a great deal about what it takes to run a modern large manufacturing operation. Perhaps the most important of these executives was Donaldson Brown, whom du Pont made vice-president of finance at the start of 1921. During the next several years it was Brown who installed the tight system of financial controls that he had developed at Du Pont, the lack of which at GM had been one of the company's major problems. The other major defect in the GM organization had been the absence of an effective method of managing the diverse operations. Because du Pont had presided over the development of such an effective system of management at the Du Pont Company, many have assumed that the system adopted at GM in the 1920s, which bears some resemblance to the Du Pont managerial structure, was, like Donaldson Brown's financial controls, a result of the Du Pont influence. But the organizational plan that began to be implemented when du Pont became president was one that Sloan had drafted a year earlier and which Durant had failed to put into effect. Sloan in later years was naturally rather sensitive about the charges that his plan was little more than a copy of the du Pont plan. The evidence indicates that, despite some similarities, the two plans were developed independently from one another and that Sloan is entitled to much of the credit for creating the model for large corporate management in the twentieth century. In any event Sloan was the most important of the GM executives that du Pont inherited. The effectiveness with which du Pont combined the transplants from the Du Pont Company, the figures from the banking world, and the holdovers into a strong, dynamic management was his principal legacy to GM.

After he stepped down in 1923 from the job of president, which he had always looked upon as temporary, du Pont continued as chairman of the board until he resigned that post in 1929. He remained a member of the board until 1944. His brother, Lammot du Pont, who had been a director since 1918, succeeded him as chairman, but with the du Ponts now confident in Sloan's ability to run the company and to maintain its number one position in the industry, his function was simply to monitor and protect the Du Pont financial stake. In 1937 Sloan took over as chairman, and the position was given the status of chief executive officer.

After the 1920s du Pont was able to pursue the other interests he had put on hold when he stepped into the breach at GM. He achieved his long-time ambition of developing the magnificent gar-

dens at his Longwood estate. He also conducted a vigorous campaign to improve the quality of public education in Delaware. His public service to his home state also included a term as State School Tax Commissioner in the mid 1920s and as State Tax Commissioner in 1937 and again from 1944 to 1949. He died of an aneurysm on April 5, 1954. His wife, who was also his first cousin, Alice Belin du Pont, survived him. They were married in 1915 and had no children.

Shortly before his death, du Pont testified in the antitrust proceedings the government had brought to force the Du Pont Company to divest itself of its massive GM stock holdings. The case was still undecided at the time of du Pont's death, but within a few years the divestiture was ordered, and, as du Pont's biographers observe, "General Motors [had] become similar to most large American corporations where the managers do not own and the owners do not manage." Du Pont's tenure as head of GM provides some good reason for believing that the change that had occurred was not necessarily for the better.

References:

Alfred D. Chandler, Jr., and Stephen Salsbury, *Pierre S. du Pont and the Making of the Modern Corporation* (New York: Harper & Row, 1971);

Ed Cray, *Chrome Colossus: General Motors and Its Times* (New York: McGraw-Hill, 1980);

Arthur J. Kuhn, *GM Passes Ford, 1918-1938: Designing the General Motors Performance Control System* (University Park: Pennsylvania State University Press, 1986);

Alfred P. Sloan, Jr., *My Years With General Motors* (Garden City, N.Y.: Doubleday, 1964);

Study of the Anti-Trust Laws, United States Senate, Committee on the Judiciary (Washington, D.C.: GPO, 1954).

Archives:

A huge collection of du Pont papers are housed in the Hagley Museum and Library, Wilmington, Delaware. They provide information about du Pont and his business and family relationships. John J. Raskob's papers are also in this collection.

Du Pont Motors

by George S. May

Eastern Michigan University

The appearance on the market in 1919-1920 of a Du Pont automobile attracted special attention because of the well-publicized connection between Pierre S. du Pont and the Du Pont munitions and chemical manufacturing company with General Motors (GM). E. Paul du Pont, the founder of Du Pont Motors, Incorporated, of Wilmington, Delaware, was a member of the prolific Delaware du Pont clan. He was also the cousin of Pierre du Pont, then chairman of GM and soon to become its president. But both du Ponts made it clear that the two automobile concerns were entirely separate. Paul du Pont, in fact, had been among those in the family who had sided with Alfred I. du Pont in his unsuccessful court fight to overthrow the control of the Du Pont company that Pierre du Pont had gained through stock purchases, a fight that had left long-standing divisions within the family.

Paul du Pont had established the Delaware Marine Motors Company which built engines for the navy during World War I. After the war he turned his attention to automobiles and had the good sense to hire executives with considerable experience in the automobile industry. The car they designed was aimed at the high-priced, prestige end of the market, a fact that was emphasized when the first Du Pont model was introduced late in 1919 at the annual custom-car Salon Show in New York's Commodore Hotel rather than at the New York Automobile Show. The engines were produced in du Pont's former marine engine plant in Wilmington, bodies were built in Springfield, Massachusetts, and the assembling of the car took place in Moore, Pennsylvania.

Although the various Du Pont models were attractive cars, Paul du Pont soon discovered, as did many others, that it was becoming increasingly difficult to break into the automobile industry by the 1920s, particularly in the luxury class where there was already an abundance of well-established firms in business. By the mid 1920s production, which had always been limited, was down to about one car a month. The plant in Moore was abandoned and assembly operations were moved to Wilmington. In 1927 Paul du Pont wrote to his cousin, Alfred du Pont, seeking investment in the company, but Alfred replied that although he liked the Du Pont car, he could see little future for such small companies in an industry which would more and more be controlled by big firms such as GM and Ford.

Despite being turned down by his cousin, Paul du Pont was able to find the resources to bring out the best known of all the Du Pont cars in the late 1920s—expensive models offering a wide choice of body styles from the leading coach-building companies. Operations in 1930 were moved to Springfield, Massachusetts, to the factory of the Indian Motorcycle Company, which du Pont had purchased. But the depression ended any further hopes of keeping the business going. The last models were built in January 1932. All told, in a little over twelve years Du Pont Motors built 547 cars. Paul du Pont continued the Indian Motorcycle Company until he retired in 1945.

References:

Nick Baldwin and others, *The World Guide to Automobile Manufacturers* (New York: Facts on File, 1987);

Marquis James, *Alfred I. DuPont: The Family Rebel* (Indianapolis: Bobbs-Merrill, 1941);

Beverly Rae Kimes and Henry Austin Clark, *Standard Catalog of American Cars, 1805-1942* (Iola, Wis.: Krause, 1985).

Durant Motors

by George S. May

Eastern Michigan University

Within six weeks after he was forced out of General Motors (GM), William C. Durant was back in the automobile business with Durant Motors, Inc., chartered on January 12, 1921, in the state of New York. Investors, recalling the spectacular success Durant had earlier enjoyed in promoting Buick, GM, and Chevrolet, quickly scrambled to buy shares in Durant's latest venture. Within a year Durant Motors was reported to have over 146,000 stockholders, more than any other American company except American Telephone & Telegraph. Some of Durant's former colleagues at GM, in fact, were fearful that his real intent was to use the stock of his new company as a means of regaining control of GM, as he had done in 1915-1916 using Chevrolet. However, although Durant did toy with the idea of launching a full-scale drive to persuade GM stockholders to exchange their shares for shares of Durant Motors, which for a time was selling for a higher price, the prospects for success in such a deal seemed so unpromising that he turned his attention to building up the new company.

In the early years of Durant Motors it appeared that Durant had created a new automobile empire that would be capable of competing with the giants in the industry. Plants were acquired in Long Island City, New York; Elizabeth, New Jersey; Muncie, Indiana; Flint and Lansing, Michigan; and Oakland, California; and new ones were built in Flint and near Toronto. The medium-priced Durant was the company's first car on the market, with 55,000 of them sold in 1922. The low-priced Star was introduced that year to compete with the Ford Model T, and 130,000 were sold in 1923. Plans for the Princeton, which would compete with luxury cars like Packard, were announced, and, although that car never got into production, Durant's acquisition in 1922 of Locomobile gave him one of the most famous names among high-priced cars. The company's purchase in 1922 of Flint's Mason

William C. Durant, founder of General Motors and Durant Motors

Motor Truck Company gave Durant an entry into the commercial vehicle field.

But by the middle of the 1920s, when automobile sales in the country were booming, Durant Motors was in trouble. The new plant he had built in Flint was much too large for what was needed to produce the Flint, another of the company's new cars that was supposed to compete with Buick. In desperate need of cash, Durant in 1926 sold the plant, at barely 25 percent of what it had cost to build, to GM. The Long Island factory was sold to Ford in 1927, but these and other moves were not enough to halt the decline of Durant Motors well before the depression of the 1930s. The depression finished off the pitiful remnants of the company, with

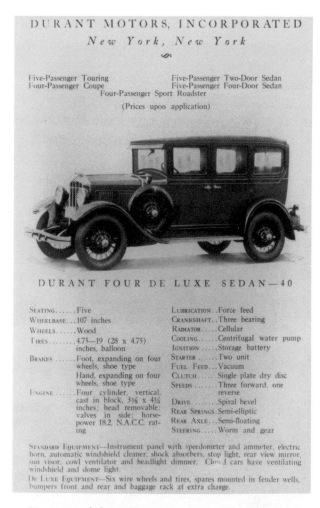

Features of the 1929 Durant Four De Luxe Sedan-40

the last cars being produced in January 1932, and the company liquidated in 1933. All told, Durant Motors total sales may have amounted to 1.5 million cars.

A number of elements contributed to the collapse of the company. Durant admitted that his plans were too ambitious and had been implemented too quickly. His earlier work with Buick and Chevrolet had demonstrated that he was at his best when he could concentrate on a single car but that he got into trouble when he tried to keep track of several different operations. Locomobile, the only established car company he was able to acquire, was past its prime and was a liability from the outset. Introducing new cars that could compete effectively with established lines was difficult, as Durant found out with the Star, which, despite good initial sales, was hopelessly outclassed in a battle with the Model T. But most important is the fact that Durant, after the first two or three years, did not devote the kind of attention to the company that he had to his earlier automobile companies. In Durant's days at GM men like Walter Chrysler and Alfred P. Sloan, Jr., who were frequently frustrated by Durant's constant interference and unwillingness to let them run their divisions, would have been delighted at the lack of control Durant exercised, but there were no Chryslers or Sloans in the Durant Motors organization. Thus, when Durant spent more and more time pursuing his passion for the stock market, there was no one with his experience and entrepreneurial skills to provide the direction needed if the company had any chance of surviving.

References:

Nick Baldwin and others, *The World Guide to Automobile Manufacturers* (New York: Facts on File, 1987);

Lawrence H. Gustin, *Billy Durant: Creator of General Motors* (Grand Rapids, Mich.: Eerdmans, 1973);

Beverly Rae Kimes and Henry Austin Clark, *Standard Catalog of American Cars, 1805-1942* (Iona, Wis.: Krause, 1985);

Bernard A. Weisberger, *The Dream Maker: William C. Durant, Founder of General Motors* (Boston: Little, Brown, 1979).

Harley Jefferson Earl

(November 22, 1893-April 10, 1969)

by George S. May

Eastern Michigan University

CAREER: Designer, Earl Automobile Works (1918-1919); general manager, Don Lee Coach & Body Corporation (1919-1926); consultant (1926-1927), director of styling (1927-1940), vice-president of styling, General Motors (1940-1959); president (1945-1958), chairman, Harley Earl Associates (1958-1969).

Harley Jefferson Earl, the most famous American automotive designer, or stylist as those in Earl's profession came to be called, was born on November 22, 1893, in Hollywood, California. He was the son of Jacob W. and Abbie Taft Earl, who had moved from Michigan to Hollywood in 1889 and established a carriage works. The Earl Carriage Works was a success, but by 1908 Jacob Earl, like many carriage makers, recognized future trends and reorganized the business as the Earl Automobile Works. The new business at first made accessories for cars but turned to custom body work in 1911, a decision, as it turned out, that would determine Harley Earl's business future.

Little information exists in print on Harley Earl's boyhood years. His family was well-to-do, which enabled Earl to attend Stanford University. An illness that grew out of an injury suffered in a track-and-field competition led to his withdrawal from school, and he never returned. He instead became increasingly involved in the family business and by 1918 had taken over its management from his father. The skills Earl had developed as a designer were now applied to designing the entire car, not simply the body. The Earl Automobile Works had already cashed in on Hollywood's changing economy by building vehicles to be used as props in motion pictures. Earl also built custom cars for movie stars, including Fatty Arbuckle, for whom Earl designed what was for its day a "streamlined" car costing the comic actor $28,000, and Tom Mix, whose customized automobile came equipped with

a leather saddle that Earl mounted on the roof for the cowboy actor.

Another of Earl's clients was Don Lee, who was later known for the regional radio network bearing his name but who was at this time the West Coast Cadillac distributor for whom the Earl Automobile Works did custom work. In 1918 Lee acquired the Earl business, and in 1919 he hired Earl to be the general manager of the new Don Lee Coach & Body Corporation. By 1920 Earl's work was attracting more and more attention, with one national observer of custom cars citing the Don Lee company as one of two Pacific Coast custom operations that had been going about their business at "their own gait ... without reference to customary motor car modes, and the results have been interesting, to say the least." Inevitably Earl's customized Cadillacs also came to the attention of General Motors officials. One report has Alfred P. Sloan, Jr., GM president, and the Fisher brothers, who built bodies for GM cars, noticing Earl's work when it was displayed at New York's Commodore Hotel Salon Show, where the world's leading custom car designers each year exhibited their creations. Sloan, however, credited a visit to the Don Lee shop by Lawrence P. Fisher, who had been hired by Sloan in 1924 to manage the Cadillac division, as the contact which established Earl as the man who could provide GM cars with the visual appeal that Fisher and Sloan had come to believe was essential to boost sales. Fisher, who was familiar with the methods employed by automobile body designers, was surprised to find that Earl, unlike other designers, did not confine himself to the body but instead dealt with the entire car, "shaping the body, hood, fenders, headlights, and running boards ... into a good-looking whole." It is probable that others who were involved in creating custom cars had also been designing parts of the entire car that were usually the responsibility of the chassis engineers. Simi-

Harley Jefferson Earl with three of his experimental gas-turbine vehicles at the Arizona Desert Proving Ground in August 1958

larly, Earl's use of clay models, rather than the traditional wood and metal models, in the development of his design ideas, which also struck Fisher as a new approach, was being used by the New York custom body design firm of Le Baron, Inc., and possibly by others. But the assumption that Earl was the first to use this technique is another example of the extent to which his long tenure as the world's biggest automaker's chief stylist has caused the work of others to be overlooked. But there is no denying that Earl was a highly talented artist who so impressed Fisher that he was persuaded to come to Detroit early in 1926 to work for Cadillac on a new car.

That car was to be part of Sloan's plan to offer a car "for every purse and purpose." There was a gaping hole between the price of the average Buick and that of the Cadillac, and thus Sloan proposed a car that would be priced about halfway between GM's two most expensive cars. It would be produced by Cadillac and for economical reasons would use the Cadillac chassis, but, so as not to detract from the status of the Cadillac, it would have its own name, La Salle. It was Earl's job to establish the identity of the car as a truly new breed, not

simply a warmed-over Cadillac, by providing the La Salle with a distinctive look.

Earl responded to this assignment with what is probably his finest piece, a car that was introduced in March 1927 and is one of the jewels of the period from the late 1920s through the 1930s, which is regarded as the golden age of American automotive design. Earl's La Salle had graceful, rounded contours that gave it the look of the custom cars that Earl had been designing for individual customers but which had not been seen in production cars which retained the square, boxy look that was a carryover from the earlier horseless carriage design. Earl also sought to give the La Salle the longer, lower look that would be the most constant element running throughout his career as an automotive designer. "Why?" he asked rhetorically in an article in 1954. "Because my sense of proportion tells me that oblongs are more attractive than squares, just as a ranch house is more attractive than a square, three-story, flat-roofed house or a greyhound is more graceful than an English bulldog." By later standards the 1927 La Salle still looks "top-heavy and stiff-shouldered," as Earl

The 1927 La Salle, Earl's first design for GM and his most famous (courtesy of Harrah's Automobile Collection, Reno, Nevada)

would subsequently admit, but it marked the beginning of a trend that reduced the height of a typical GM car from 75 inches in 1926 to 51 inches by 1963. In addition to this actual reduction, Earl created an illusion of change when he added a decorative strip along the La Salle's beltline "to eat up the overpowering vertical expanse of that tall car."

Lawrence Fisher, delighted with Earl's La Salle design, asked Earl for suggestions to improve the 1927 Cadillac. It was too late to make any significant change in the car, which was about to go into production. Earl suggested different paints could make a difference. "Put a lot of color and some wire wheels on them and doll them up." Thus again an illusion of a different model was created as Cadillac, which had never offered more than three choices of colors in a model, announced that the 1927 Cadillac would provide the buyer with a choice of five hundred color and upholstery options. The development earlier in the decade of Duco lacquers by GM and DuPont researchers had made it economically feasible to offer cars in a far greater range of colors than the black which had been the only choice Ford offered for a good many years in its Model T's. In rather typical fashion Earl became closely identified with this change because he made such bold use of the opportunity the new paints provided.

Sloan was so impressed with Earl's work for Cadillac that he persuaded him to become the director of a new department that would oversee the styl-

ing of all of the corporation's products and was called the Art and Colour Section. Several automotive companies for some years had employed their own body designers, rather than leaving such matters to the body companies they dealt with, but none had been on the scale of GM's new section. Although both Chrysler and Ford soon followed GM's example and created their own styling sections, these remained small for many years compared with the Art and Colour Section, which grew rapidly from its original staff of fifty workers at the start of 1928 and was reorganized a decade later and renamed the Styling Section. Most important, no other automobile company during these years had a chief stylist who was as visible and dominant as Earl, whose importance to the corporation was indicated when he was named a vice-president on September 3, 1940, "the first stylist to be given such a position, and indeed," Alfred Sloan believed, "the first designer in any major industry to become a vice president."

The preeminent status that Earl achieved among automotive stylists—and among industrial designers in general—was partly attributable to his physical appearance, which was, like his cars, dramatic. At 6 feet 4 inches, unusually tall for men in the first half of the twentieth century, Earl towered over his staff and associates, and he took full advantage of his physical bulk by giving meticulous attention to his appearance. He seemed always to be suntanned, and he spent half an hour in the morning shaving and an equally long time deciding which of his many suits to wear, each one designed to enhance his overpowering personality. His office closet included a duplicate wardrobe so that he could stay unwrinkled throughout the day, and, according to one associate, his handmade English shoes "looked as if they had trees inside them even when he was wearing them."

This was all part of a careful plan to cultivate a certain image and reflected the showmanship Earl had learned in his days in Hollywood, as did the suspenseful means he used when unveiling his latest designs for the approval of the General Motors executives or the public. For years, however, the quarters in which Earl's staff was housed were less than ideal, and when Sloan in the 1940s began to press for the construction of a new facility to house all of the corporation's research activities, including the Styling Section, it was Earl who argued in favor of a center that would be architecturally and aesthetically distinctive in opposition to the more mundane, less expensive approach favored by some of the other executives. Sloan was convinced, and he directed Earl to find the architect for the job. It was Earl who brought about the selection of Eliel and Eero Saarinen, whose breathtaking General Motors Technical Center in Warren, Michigan, completed in 1956 at a cost of $125 million, is one of the landmarks of twentieth-century architecture. The structure's styling auditorium, which utilized a dome sheathed in aluminum, provided a fitting setting for Earl in his last years at the head of the corporation's styling work.

Although Earl was in total control of his section, operating in an autocratic, intimidating fashion, rejecting or accepting staff suggestions in a deceptively quiet voice, he ran into considerable opposition in his early years from the car divisions and Fisher Body. These other groups resented the fact that he was taking control over matters of design from their engineers. Recognizing that it would take some time for Earl and his staff to win acceptance, Sloan let it be known that the transplanted Californian had his full support. Nevertheless personality clashes developed, even with the Fisher brothers, despite the fact that it was Lawrence Fisher who had first brought Earl to Detroit. Earl blamed the engineers at Fisher Body for butchering the design of the 1929 Buick when they put it into production, creating a slight bulge beneath the car's beltline that led to it being ridiculed as the "preg-

nant Buick." According to Earl's longtime associate and successor as GM's chief stylist, William L. Mitchell, Earl referred to the Fisher brothers, who were small in stature, as the "Seven Dwarfs." They dressed conservatively and wore homburgs–"what a contrast," Mitchell said, "to this 6' 4" man, who had a bronze complexion. He'd wear bronze suits, suede shoes–flamboyant was the word, and *outspoken* . . . he'd cuss those Fisher brothers out. . . . He didn't have any respect, because he was hired by Sloan." Nevertheless, in spite of Sloan's support, Earl often faced opposition from the engineers and production men who objected to some of the designs because of production difficulties or high costs. This was especially true with design changes for the high-volume Chevrolet where an "arty bumper" that Earl proposed was rejected in the late 1930s because it cost 3¢ more to produce than an ordinary bumper. Mitchell declared that Earl's main reason for introducing prototypes, known as "dream cars," was not simply to prepare the public for possible design changes in the future but to "wake up the manufacturers and corporate managers to what could be done without meetings and committees, which ultimately boiled a good design down into mediocracy."

Because of these negative internal forces, and because of the adverse reaction to the 1929 Buick, the first complete car that Earl's new section had designed, Earl followed a relatively conservative design approach in the 1930s. Only the 1938 Cadillac Sixty Special is usually included, along with the earlier 1927 La Salle, on any list of the great production cars of this classic era. Instead the period was dominated by the work of other stylists, such as Amos E. Northup's 1931 Reo Royale, 1932 Graham Blue Streak, and 1938 Graham Spirit of Motion; Chrysler's engineer-designed 1934 Chrysler and DeSoto Airflow models; the 1936 Lincoln Zephyr, designed by John Tjaarda and Eugene T. "Bob" Gregorie, with much input from Edsel Ford; the 1939 Continental, designed by Bob Gregorie; and Gordon M. Buehrig's Cord, which dispensed with running boards two years before Earl's similarly designed 1938 Cadillac. But by the time Earl died in 1969 the *New York Times* had forgotten this and in its obituary declared that in the 1930s Earl had "rubbed his thumb across a sketch of a proposed new model, and erased the exterior running board from the American scene."

Earl's first "dream car" for GM, introduced in 1938

If the prewar years had been ones in which other stylists were in the forefront of innovation, the postwar years unquestionably belonged to Earl. The late 1940s and the 1950s were years in which, apart from a few exceptions such as the 1956 Continental Mark II of Gordon Buehrig and John Reinhart, designers moved away from classical lines to more bizarre styles. Designs became so extreme that Stephen Bayley calls this era the "Golden Age of Gorp." Leading the way was Earl. He continued his practice of making the cars longer, wider, and lower until by 1959 the Series 75 Cadillac measured over 20 feet from bumper to bumper. With the 1954 Chevrolet Nomad station wagon Earl realized that he had lowered it to the point that he could see clear across the roof, which was thus "now visible as a part of the car's conformation. . . . we had to give this unbroken roof expanse a decorative treatment. We grooved it." Although he said he was not particularly fond of chrome trim, dealer surveys revealed that the public liked chrome, and so by the late 1950s, Mitchell declared, "We were putting on chrome with a trowel."

But the styling touches for which Earl is most famous, and which now came to symbolize the cars of the 1950s, resulted from his fascination with others' designs. His 1927 La Salle was inspired by his viewing of the great Hispano-Suiza at a Paris automobile show, and his cars of the late 1940s were inspired by his sight of the Lockheed P-38 fighter at Selfridge Field near Detroit in the early years of World War II. The P-38 influence began to be seen in the "Futuramic" 1948 Oldsmobile with airplane motifs that included simulated air scoops under the headlamps that were modeled after the fighter plane's engine nacelles. But it was one of the 1948 Cadillac models in which Earl introduced the first tail fins, inspired by the P-38's twin tails. Customers at first seemed not to like them, and GM president Charles Wilson ordered Earl to redesign the car's rear end. But Wilson's opinion changed when "Cadillac owners realized," Earl declared, that the fins "gave them an extra receipt for their money in the form of a visible prestige marking for an expensive car." As the idea caught on, the tail fins became bigger. They soon began appearing on other GM cars besides the Cadillac, and by the mid 1950s the competition began coming out with their own tail-finned cars. Chrysler, under its stylist Virgil Exner, made a valiant effort to win the race to have the biggest and tallest tail fins, but none could surpass the awesome rear end of the 1959 Cadillac Eldorado, a feature that has made that car one of the most sought after by car collectors in recent years.

After thirty-two years as the head of GM styling Earl retired on December 1, 1959. In 1945 the corporation had allowed him to establish his own design firm, Harley Earl Associates, on condition that the firm should not be involved in the design of any product that competed with GM. Now after 1959 Earl could devote his full time to this business, again with the condition that Harley Earl Associates or Earl himself was not to engage in any work for other automobile companies. A newspaper headline in 1964 that announced "Earl Joins Ford" thus sent momentary shock waves through General Motors until a reading of the story revealed that Earl's firm was merging with W. B. Ford Design Associates. However, although Walter B. Ford II, founder of that design firm and chairman of the new firm of Ford & Earl Associates, was not one of the automobile Fords, he had married the sister of Henry Ford II, Josephine Ford, and his firm did do some work for the Ford Motor Company. Earl is said to have had only a "minimal association" with the firm of Ford & Earl, but Earl's son James, who had worked with his father in Harley Earl Associates, served as president of the firm.

Although Earl had enjoyed some success in designing airplane interiors, the products he dealt with in his nonautomotive design career, such as carpet sweepers and biscuits, must have seemed little more than things to do to fill his time after his retirement from the job that clearly had been his first love. After what amounted to a second retirement following the merger of the design firms in 1964, Earl spent most of his time at his residence in Palm Beach, Florida, and it was there in March 1969 that he suffered a stroke that resulted in his death on April 10. He was survived by his wife of fifty-two years, Sue Carpenter Earl, and two sons, James Milton Earl and J. Courtney Earl, the last a Pontiac car dealer in Delray Beach, Florida.

In the ten years since he had left GM there had been a strong reaction away from the overblown creations that had been Earl's last contributions to automotive design. A variety of factors brought a return to more restrained and functional styling, but for many the period that ended with Earl's retirement marked the end of the last great era of automotive design. For these people, as Stephen Bayley says in the one full-scale attempt to assess Earl's work, "Harley Earl *was* the American car." Earl, Bayley declares, had worked in a time when ownership of a new car was the epitome of the American dream. His "contribution was an optimistic one: he subscribed to the pleasure principle. Now that we know there is nothing in the world as boring as a flush door, it is easier even than it was in the fifties to be moved by that faith in the magic of machines which allowed Harley Earl to say, 'You can design a car so that every time you get in it, it's a relief–you have a little vacation for a while.' "

References:

Stephen Bayley, *Harley Earl and the Dream Machine* (New York: Knopf, 1983);

Gordon M. Buehrig and William S. Jackson, *Rolling Sculpture: A Designer and His Work* (Newfoundland, N.J.: Haessner Publishing, 1975);

Ed Cray, *Chrome Colossus: General Motors and Its Times* (New York: McGraw-Hill, 1980);

F. Graham Dickens, Telephone interview with George May, November 17, 1988;

George S. May, *The Automobile in American Life* (forthcoming, 1990);

May, "Ford & Earl Associates, Inc.," in his *Michigan: An Illustrated History of the Great Lakes State* (Northridge, Cal.: Windsor Publications, Inc., 1987), p. 222.

Engines

by James Wren

Motor Vehicle Manufacturers Association

Sometime during the fourteenth century a linstock was placed at a touchhole and the first cannon was fired. More significantly, the first internal-combustion engine was born. That momentous explosion in a cylinder created power which propelled the cannonball. Despite the destructive nature of that work, the concept of the internal-combustion engine changed the course of the world. Nearly five centuries later an offspring of that cannon, the gasoline-powered internal-combustion engine, was adapted to carriages and wagons and a revolution in personal transportation began.

In the mid 1800s work on the internal-combustion gas engine began in earnest, William Barnett of England conceiving the 2-cycle engine in 1838. In the Barnett engine the gas, which was compressed outside the piston, displaced the exhaust gases as they entered the cylinder at the end of the stroke and were compressed in the cylinder of the motor before ignition occurred. By that method an impulse was produced at each forward stroke. In 1854 the Italians Barsanti and Mattencci invented the free-piston atmospheric engine. Other variations appeared, but none were commercially acceptable.

Finally in 1860 Etienne Lenoir, a Belgian mechanic working in France, patented the first commercially acceptable gas engine, acceptable because it was noiseless, dustless, started and stopped easily, and used a coil for ignition purposes. The Lenoir engine was installed successfully in a boat and in a motor carriage. Within two years another major breakthrough was achieved by the French when Alphonse Beau de Rochas drafted plans for a 4-cycle engine for perfectly utilizing the force of the expansion of gas in an engine. However, a 4-cycle free-piston engine was introduced some years later by Otto and Langen of Germany and was so commercially successful that the cycle became known as the Otto cycle. The patented Otto Silent Gas Engine of 1876 dominated the engine field until 1890 when the patent expired. The Otto engine included flame ignition, a governor, and a clutch gear.

A notable American engine development of 1872 was the Brayton engine with a precombustion chamber which could use liquid or gaseous fuel. The Brayton ready engine and George Brayton's subsequent oil engine were America's first commercially successful gas engines. However, the Brayton would not prove to be commercially adaptable to an automobile.

By the late 1890s, when horseless carriages first appeared in America, the 2- and 4-cycle engines were well-recognized power sources. Cooling was attained by air or water, lubrication was applied by sight feed, and the fuel feed system used gravity with either wick or spray type carburetor. Hot tube and spark ignition were used, and the trembler spark and jump spark systems were both prevalent.

Concurrently with the development of the internal-combustion engine, the search for a suitable fuel resulted in many experiments with fuels such as kerosene, naptha, stove gas, alcohol, acetylene, oil, illuminating gas, carbonic gas, and of course gasoline. Electric and steam power sources also had their supporters. The public in general was more familiar with steam power; they were enamored by the silence and cleanliness of electricity, and they were dubious about the noisy, malodorous, and erratic gasoline engine.

However, when huge oil deposits were found in Texas and the inexpensive Curved Dash Olds runabout appeared in 1901, the gas buggy was quickly thrust into the forefront of the American transportation revolution. Because of the poor road system in America, the small runabout automobile became the typical American automobile in the late 1890s and early 1900s. Although the 1- or 2-cylinder gas engines were adequate enough to propel small horseless carriages, generally they were slow, inefficient, and extremely heavy. Peak engine speeds were less than 1000 rpm, and huge cast-iron pistons in large cylinders provided average horsepowers from 1 to 10. The engines were placed upright or horizontally under the car either amidships or in the rear. Drive to the rear wheels was by means of a chain. There were several manufacturers such as Autocar who used shaft drive to the rear wheels, and that drive system eventually dominated as the engine was moved to the front and under a hood.

As the runabout style gave way to the larger touring car the gas engine also grew in size. Multiple cylinders began replacing the single cylinders, and by 1905 4-cylinder engines with horsepowers ranging up to 20 and 30 were becoming common. The 4-cylinder engine was livelier, faster, and more powerful. By 1910 over 80 percent of the models offered 4-cylinder engines. The cylinders were usually cast individually or in pairs and bolted to the crankcase. Generally, cylinder heads were cast integrally with the cylinders rather than using detachable cylinder heads, which were precluded because of the lack of a suitable gasket material. When copper-asbestos gaskets eventually became available, many manufacturers adopted the detachable cylinder head.

The poppet valve was in general use, and a common arrangement was the T-head where intake and exhaust valves were located on opposite sides of the cylinder block with separate camshafts and manifolds. The T-head arrangement, however, suffered from predetonation. The more popular L-head valve arrangement was also used as early as 1910 and arranged the intake and exhaust valves on the same side. Although some manufacturers opted for the overhead valve arrangement at an early date, cooling was very difficult.

By the mid 1910s multiple cylinders continued to increase primarily because of their smoother operation and diminished noise and vibration. The 6-cylinder engine had overshadowed the 4 by 1914, and even larger models were soon introduced.

Cadillac in 1915 pioneered the use of the V-8 engine in a widely produced car. Earlier the Sturtevant car had used a horizontal 8-cylinder engine in 1905 but the model was short-lived. In 1916 Packard unveiled its famous Twin Six 12-cylinder engine with aluminum alloy pistons. Other manufacturers such as National, Pathfinder, and Enger also introduced 12-cylinder engines. Hudson contributed a milestone engine improvement in

1916 by adding counterweights to the crankshaft for improved engine balance.

Despite wide use and improvements the twelve-cylinder movement was short-lived as World War I altered priorities in the automobile industry, and many automotive companies were involved in the development and production of Liberty aircraft engines.

By the 1920s 6-cylinder engines were used in most models but a move toward straight 8-cylinder engines was noted in the more expensive models. Complementing the introduction of the new straight 8 model was the increased use of rubber engine mounts, aluminum pistons, engine balancers, and hydraulic valve lifters. Compression ratios were also increased, and some manufacturers added weight to the crankshaft and shortened the piston stroke. The effect of the numerous engine improvements resulted in faster, more powerful engines with horsepower ratings slowly climbing.

By the late 1920s and early 1930s an era of large, custom car building renewed interest in larger multicylinder engines as new V-8, V-12, and V-16 engines developed. With the demise of the Model T in 1927 the 4-cylinder engine all but disappeared, especially in widely produced cars. Ford introduced a V-8 engine in 1932. Further development in engine mounting was notable with Chrysler's rubber engine mounts, which dramatically reduced vibration and movement of the engine. Higher cylinder temperatures resulted from increased compression ratios and spurred design changes to improve cooling and durability. The water jacket area was increased and extended to reduce piston temperatures, and valve seat inserts were also introduced. Engine development was more or less stabilized by the late 1930s, and when World War II began, automobile industry engine development was also directed toward large tank and aviation engines.

Based on technology and designs developed during the war, emphasis on the development of a lightweight, more durable short stroke engine was stressed. In 1948 the high-compression, short-stroke overhead-valve V-8 engine was introduced by Oldsmobile and later by Cadillac. By the mid 1950s a horsepower race was beginning and automobile manufacturers' products grew larger with more powerful, high-horsepower engines, intended for travel over new super highways at 80 mph cruising speeds. Engines with larger bore and stroke and compression ratios of 7.25 and 7.5, with ratings of 135 hp at 3600 rpm and 160 hp at 3800 rpm respectively, were common. Well into the 1960s horsepower numbers in the 300 and 400 range were commonplace.

Several manufacturers offered V-8 engines with side valves in the early 1950s, but when Ford opted for the overhead valve in the mid 1950s, the vast majority of engines used overhead V-8 designs. In the late 1950s the use of aluminum in engines increased as the power-to-weight ratio came under close scrutiny. Both American Motors (AMC) and General Motors (GM) introduced aluminum engines, but quality problems and performance were disappointing.

The Ford lightweight cast-iron engine of the 1960s was a notable development in engine manufac-

turing. By the late 1970s concern over fuel shortages and fuel economy increased interest in small V-8 and V-6 engines. The 4-cylinder engine was revived in the early 1980s as fuel economy became a national concern, turbocharging becoming a method to provide for more response and power in the small engine. The V-6 turbocharged engine also gained in popularity, and as computer controls improved ignition, combustion, and fuel economy the larger engines once again found favor with the public. Since the late 1890s hundreds of engine concepts have been introduced. Rotary, radial, pancake, compound, sleeve valve, rotary valve, piston valve, gas turbine, free piston, wobble-plate, and rotating cylinder type engines are but a few of the numerous but futile attempts to unseat the reciprocating engine in its straight- or V-cylinder configuration.

Environmental Protection Agency

by Kevin M. Dwyer

George Washington University

Among the many calls for government action having root in the 1960s, the demand for a cleaner environment brought forth considerable effort in the form of federal regulation. The perceived need for industrial responses to rising public environmental concerns culminated in establishment of the Environmental Protection Agency (EPA) by Congress in 1971. Charged with the supervision, preservation, and, when necessary, the restoration of a clean environment, the EPA is the largest independent regulatory agency of the federal government.

The EPA consolidated under its jurisdiction an array of federal environmental protection programs from various government agencies. From the Department of Health, Education and Welfare it assumed clean air and solid waste disposal programs, as well as clean water programs from the Department of the Interior. The power to monitor pesticide research, regulate usage, and set various federal standards, which had been functions of the Department

of Agriculture and the Food and Drug Administration, now also fell to the EPA, as did the monitoring of radiation levels, formerly the task of the Atomic Energy Commission. Under the direction of William Ruckelshaus, its first chief administrator, the EPA initiated programs to reduce pollution on a variety of fronts.

EPA's earliest programs, concerning air pollution, directly affected the automotive industry. Automobile manufacturers complained, with some justification, that their industry had been unfairly targeted. But since motor vehicle exhausts accounted for more than 40 percent of all pollution emissions and constituted the single greatest source of air pollution, the propriety of targeting them was never seriously challenged. As the U.S. Air Pollution Control Office projected that motor vehicle emissions in 1970 would result in the dispersion of 57.42 million metric tons of carbon monoxide, 14.94 million tons of hydrocarbons, 7.29 million tons of nitric oxides, and 1.08 million tons of particle pollutants into the air, not much popular sympathy for manufacturers' protests was forthcoming.

The EPA, though by far the largest and best coordinated, was not the first governmental attempt to limit automobile emissions through regulation. After studies by California Technological Institute chemist Arie Jan Haagen Smit established the connection between automobile emissions and Los Angeles's infamous "smog" problem in the 1940s, environmentalists successfully lobbied the California state legislature to adopt pollution controls in 1959. Following nearly a decade of failed overtures to automobile makers, the California emissions control standards, which took effect in 1963, mandated more efficient combustion to maximize fuel consumption, thus reducing waste in the form of exhaust. With national ecological consciousness on the rise following the release of Rachel Carson's *Silent Spring* (1962), Washington, D.C., became the focal point of national environmental initiatives. In 1965, using the California law as a model, Congress passed the Vehicle Air Pollution and Control Act, which set emissions control standards to take effect on October 1, 1968, for the 1969 model year.

Politicians kept ecology on the political agenda as support and public awareness of environmental issues grew. Senator Edmund Muskie of Maine in 1970 challenged the automotive industry specifically to "force technology" to respond to the demands of the voter / consumer for cleaner air and to reduce emissions by 90 percent. Muskie's challenge resulted in the passage of the Clean Air Act of 1970. President Richard Nixon, while privately suspicious of environmentalists and generally ambivalent to their concerns, nevertheless made good political capital of environmental issues. In his 1970 State of the Union address Nixon labeled automobiles the "worst polluters of our air" and endorsed a proposed federal agency to protect and preserve the environment.

But following its establishment, the EPA met with staunch resistance from many industries and localities. With opposition to its standards coming from management and worker alike and from cities and towns economically dependent upon smokestack and heavy manufacturing industries, implementation of EPA standards was often delayed. Since the EPA was given no means to enforce its dictates, they were often ignored, a fact evidenced by the compliance of only 29 states with the EPA's 1979 air pollution reduction targets for 1983.

For the automotive industry, however, compliance with EPA standards resulted from a source unrelated to government regulation: the marketplace. As cheap oil and gasoline became a thing of the past with the 1973 energy crisis, fuel economy became a higher consideration for car buyers. In this area American manufacturers lagged considerably behind their foreign competition. New techniques, often borrowed from Europe and Japan, which resulted in better fuel mileage and cleaner carburation were installed in American makes by the mid 1970s. These included retarded spark-advance, redesigned combustion chambers, heated air intake systems, as well as more sophisticated devices like fuel injection, catalytic converters, and reduced engine sizes and modifications for unleaded fuel consumption. Yet the global marketplace forced the industry's response in this area because the EPA lacked the power to enforce standards. However, the EPA's regulatory power over the automobile industry was later increased with the passage of the 1975 Energy Policy and Conservation Act. A response to oil shortages, the act charged the EPA with testing and rating the gasoline mileage of all cars sold in the United States. The EPA also sets annual emissions testing standards for state vehicle inspections.

While the imposition of EPA standards and the phasing out of leaded gasoline have successfully reduced automobile emissions, the dangers of air pollution remain constant. The global problem of acid rain, which will threaten the oxygen-producing tropical rain forests of South Asia and South America in the 1990s, is caused by industrial emissions, of which automobile exhaust produces 84 million tons of a total of 140 million tons annually.

EPA-mandated modifications raised the prices of motor vehicles but did not retard sales, as the industry feared and predicted. The cost of the industry's response to the ecological demands of the voter was one which the market seemed willing enough to bear and consumers willing to pay. Registrations of automobiles in America remained a constant third of the world's total from 1970 to 1981, although American production ratios declined against the world totals from 29 percent in 1971 to 23 percent in 1983.

Both popular and governmental concern over the environment receded in the early 1980s. Despite "superfund" programs for cleaning up hazardous waste dumping sites, EPA funding has often been substantially cut. Its performance has thus far been commendable in a variety of areas: many lakes and rivers formerly stagnant are being rejuvenated and support plant and wildlife once more; various harmful pesticides have been banned despite strong opposition from agribusiness; and reductions of carbon monoxide, sulfur dioxide, and particle air pollution

by 20 percent, 30 percent, and 12 percent, respectively, indicate progress.

Reference:

George Moss, *America in the Twentieth Century* (Englewood Cliffs, N.J.: Prentice-Hall, 1989).

Albert Russel Erskine

(January 24, 1871-June 30, 1933)

by Alan R. Raucher

Wayne State University

CAREER: General auditor and department manager, American Cotton Company (1898-1904); treasurer, Yale & Towne Manufacturing Company (1904-1910); vice-president for advertising and sales, Underwood Typewriter Company (1910-1911); treasurer (1911-1915), president, Studebaker Corporation (1915-1933).

Though without training in engineering or much experience in the automotive industry, Albert Russel Erskine rose quickly and for nearly two decades dominated the Studebaker Corporation as its president. At the peak of the automaker's success in 1923, he led Studebaker to rank third in assets behind Ford and General Motors (GM). But in the nadir of the Great Depression ten years later Studebaker collapsed into receivership, at least partly the result of his mismanagement.

The son of William Michael and Ursula Dudley Erskine, Albert Erskine was born on January 24, 1871, in Huntsville, Alabama, and attended public and private schools there. After gaining experience as a bookkeeper, from 1898 to 1904 he worked in St. Louis and then New York as an auditor and department manager for the American Cotton Company, which supervised 300 cotton gins across the South. At the age of thirty-two he married Anne Lyell Garland of Huntington, West Virginia. They named their only child Albert Russel Erskine, Jr.

The year after his marriage Erskine moved into precision manufacturing. From 1904 to 1910 he served as the treasurer of the Yale & Towne Manu-

Albert Russel Erskine

facturing Company, a pioneer in scientific management, and became a certified public accountant. In

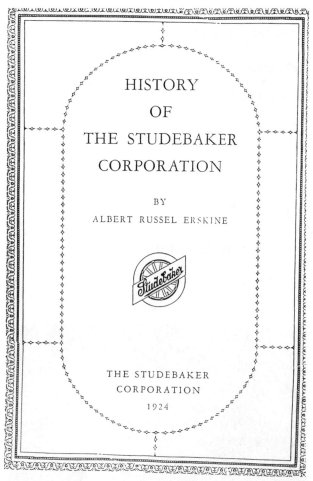

Title page to Erskine's history of Studebaker

1910 he moved to the Underwood Typewriter Company as its vice-president in charge of advertising and sales. The following year he became the treasurer of the Studebaker Corporation, newly organized by Frederick S. Fish, a son-in-law of the family that had manufactured wagons and carriages in South Bend, Indiana, since 1852. In 1915 Erskine became its president, replacing Fish, who became chairman.

During the early years of his tenure as president of Studebaker, stockholders regarded Erskine as a miracle worker, and the directors granted him wide latitude in policy-making. With that freedom he pursued a strategy of expansion while aiming to make Studebaker one of the industry's progressive leaders. His installment credit plan introduced in 1916 enabled Studebaker, with medium-priced cars, to compete with manufacturers selling cheaper models. During World War I he pursued military contracts, even with low profit margins, to increase new plant capacity. Under his leadership Studebaker enjoyed high levels of sales and profits during

the slump of 1920-1921, when even GM lost money.

In South Bend, Erskine stood at the top of the corporate hierarchy. From profit sharing and investment in Studebaker stock and local real estate, he built a personal fortune estimated at $12 million to $15 million. His palatial estate, Twyckenham Manor, rivaled the residences of Detroit's automotive tycoons. From South Bend's only truly grand office he shaped the economic destinies of about 15,000 families in the St. Joseph valley. Nominally a Presbyterian but without strong religious sentiment, he supported the local Catholic university, Notre Dame, as well as local philanthropies.

Genial, kindly, highly emotional, Erskine brimmed with self-confidence. Perhaps reflecting his small-town origins he followed a paternalistic business style, especially toward labor relations. Yet his motto, "We eat obstacles for breakfast," expressed the outlook of a bold risk taker. Like too many business leaders of that era, however, he allowed optimism to become reckless gambling.

During the 1920s, while the automotive business changed rapidly, Erskine pursued a broadly conceived plan to make Studebaker one of the industry's giants. In an effort to expand quickly in the early 1920s he tried to buy the Maxwell Motor Company but lost out to Walter P. Chrysler, who then built his own successful company. Although a domineering personality Erskine realized that he needed a strong team of executives. Therefore, in the mid 1920s he staked the corporation's future with two newly appointed vice-presidents, Los Angeles car dealer Paul G. Hoffman and production specialist Harold S. Vance.

With Hoffman and Vance in support, Erskine continued his policy of expansion. In 1926, while Vance supervised the consolidation and modernization of facilities at South Bend, the company launched a new model inspired by the small, fuel-efficient cars Erskine had seen in Europe. Advertised as "The Little Aristocrat of Motordom," the new Erskine failed to attract the market its creator envisioned. Two years later Erskine tried a different tactic by buying the Pierce-Arrow, one of the grand automobiles of that era. The car gave him the prestige he craved but also lost money for Studebaker.

When Studebaker suffered declines in car sales, the combination of Erskine's temperament and his command of the policy-making apparatus proved disastrous. Unrestrained by a compliant board of directors, during the prosperous 1920s Erskine had squandered Studebaker's capital with overly generous dividends that boosted the price of its stock in which he speculated. With his boom mentality he had rejected pessimistic economic forecasts as destroyers of public confidence and as excuses for business retrenchment. Thus when sales slumped in 1929 and 1930, he was slow to cut Studebaker's managerial costs, including his own salary and profit sharing. Worse, he continued to dissipate capital reserves with foolishly high dividends.

During the early 1930s the financial situations of Erskine and of Studebaker followed the downward course of the national economy. Erskine responded in the political arena by lashing out against excessive government spending that he claimed prolonged the depression. He responded in the corporate arena by negotiating a merger with the White Motor Company, a truck manufacturer based in Cleveland. Intended to bring Studebaker badly needed capital, the merger was opposed by a minority of White stockholders, who obtained a court order blocking the move. Short of cash to meet immediate obligations and unable to find banks willing to lend more, Studebaker was placed into receivership in March 1933 by U.S. District Court Judge Thomas W. Slick.

Humiliated by his removal from Studebaker's presidency Erskine felt that he had betrayed a trust. Moreover he had squandered in speculation his own personal fortune based on Studebaker stock and South Bend real estate and still owed $700,000 in federal taxes. A few days after telling his protégé Paul G. Hoffman that he intended to commit suicide so that his family could collect his insurance, he ended his own life at age sixty-two with a bullet through the heart. Hoffman made the public announcement. His widow and his son survived him.

Publication:

Albert Russel Erskine, *History of the Studebaker Corporation* (South Bend, Ind.: Studebaker Corporation, 1924).

References:

Stephen Longstreet, *A Century on Wheels* (New York: Holt, 1952);

Alan R. Raucher, *Paul G. Hoffman, Architect of Foreign Aid* (Lexington: University Press of Kentucky, 1986);

Kathleen Smallzried and Dorothy Roberts, *More Than You Promise* (New York, 1942).

Archives:

Material concerning Erskine is located in the Studebaker Papers at Discovery Hall Museum, South Bend, Indiana.

Edsel Bryant Ford

(November 6, 1893-May 26, 1943)

by George S. May

Eastern Michigan University

CAREER: Secretary (1915-1919), director (1915-1943), treasurer (1919-1943), president, Ford Motor Company (1919-1943).

Edsel Bryant Ford, who from 1919 until his death in 1943 had the title of president of the Ford Motor Company but rarely possessed the power associated with his position, was born in Detroit on November 6, 1893, the only child of the great industrialist Henry Ford and his wife Clara Bryant Ford. When Edsel Ford was born his father was an employee of Detroit's Edison Illuminating Company, but in less than three years the elder Ford had begun his career in the automotive industry. That career was the central element in the life of the Ford family and was ultimately the source of tragedy and heartbreak in the relationship between father and son. After Edsel Ford's death his name was remembered mainly for a car that was launched with great fanfare but totally rejected by consumers.

Except for his dark complexion, which he inherited from his mother's side of the family, Edsel Ford bore a striking resemblance to his father, with the same slight build and cleanly sculptured, handsome features. As a child he and his father were very close, Henry Ford doting on his son and spending spare moments playing with him. On the rare occasions the two were apart, they exchanged loving letters expressing their deep affection for one another. It was the automobile, however, that held them together when the son became an adult and the warm father-son relationship began to cool.

Edsel Ford grew up with the automobile, although claims that he was taken on outings in Henry Ford's first car within weeks after his birth had to be abandoned when the Ford Motor Company, and even Henry Ford, eventually had to admit that Ford's first car had been built and driven in 1896, not 1893 as they had initially maintained. But at least by his tenth birthday, Edsel

Edsel Bryant Ford, left, with his son, Henry Ford II, in 1934 (courtesy of Ford Motor Company)

Ford was driving a car, and before long he was tinkering with car mechanisms in a workshop his father built for him.

When it was time for Edsel Ford to enter school, he was enrolled in the Detroit public schools. Once he had completed the elementary grades, however, the family's newfound prosperity, resulting from the success of the Ford Motor Company, founded in 1903, was reflected in his transfer to the private Detroit University School. His excellent academic record at the college preparatory school and the family's financial status qualified him for any of the elite eastern universities to which most of his classmates were headed. But while college may have been the son's expected destination it was not in Henry Ford's plans.

Henry Ford, whose formal education had been confined to a one-room country school, was convinced his son would learn all he needed by working for the Ford company. This was perhaps the first major instance in which Ford interposed his authority to prevent his son from doing what he wanted to do. However, Edsel probably did not object too strenuously in this case. There had never been any question that his future lay with the company. For years he had hurried to the Ford factory after school and during vacations and had delighted his father by showing an intense interest in its affairs. Thus, when he graduated from the Detroit University School in 1912, he may have welcomed the opportunity to fulfill his destiny by going to work full-time for Ford rather than waiting until graduating from college four years later.

Edsel soon demonstrated real administrative ability and a wide-ranging understanding of all aspects of the business which, when combined with a pleasant and even-tempered personality, won him a high degree of respect and affection from the company's employees. But although Edsel was capable, his father accounted for his rapid rise to the top. "Identified with father in mfr. of automobiles from the beginning of active career" was the way he put it in his modest, thirteen-line biography in *Who's Who in America,* and it was his inability or unwillingness to break away and establish his own identity that doomed him to remain in his father's shadow.

In 1915, following the resignation of James Couzens, Edsel Ford, not yet twenty-two years old, was promoted to company secretary, as well as being named to the board of directors. Couzens, a powerful personality who had never hesitated to stand up to Henry Ford, something his successor proved incapable of doing, had quit because of his objections to Ford's antiwar pronouncements following the outbreak of war in Europe in 1914. Although Ford subsequently modified his views and accepted contracts for war materials, his efforts to prevent Edsel from serving in the armed forces provoked widespread public criticism. After the United States entered the war in 1917, Edsel was quoted as saying that he was "perfectly willing to be drafted with the rest of the young men of this community," but his father intervened and insisted that he ask for a draft exemption. Dutifully the son did as he was directed, and after considerable difficulty the request was granted. The exemption was given

in part on the grounds that Edsel's work was essential to the war effort and in part because he was now married and, with the birth of Henry Ford II in September 1917, qualified for deferment because of his dependents. Although a few applauded him for honestly avoiding military service rather than buying a commission and getting a safe assignment far from the battle front, Edsel, by bowing to his father's wishes, lived with the knowledge for the rest of his life that many thought of him as a draft dodger.

At the end of December 1918, Henry Ford suddenly resigned as president of the Ford Motor Company, and his son was elected to succeed him. The surprising action stemmed from Ford's annoyance at the opposition he received from the minority stockholders, especially the Dodge brothers, who had brought suit to force him to pay higher dividends. Early in 1919 Ford announced that he planned to form a company that would produce a new car that would be better and cheaper than the Model T. It is doubtful he intended to do this, but the stockholders, aware of Ford's unpredictability, could not be sure. The prospect of an improved Ford car that would send the value of their stock in the old Ford company tumbling led them to accept offers that agents, secretly working for the Fords, made to buy their shares. Edsel acted as the frontman in his father's little charade, and by July 1919 the purchase of all the minority stockholding interests had been completed; the Ford Motor Company was totally owned by the Ford family. The financial well-being of Edsel and his family was assured by the fact that he was now the owner of the 41 percent of the company stock that had been previously in non-Ford hands. But his father remained the majority stockholder.

Once the minority stockholders were gone, nothing more was heard of Henry Ford's plan to introduce a new car. At the same time he made no move to resume the company presidency. Instead, he expressed his confidence in the ability of his son to carry on. The elder Ford remained on the board of directors and was, of course, ready to provide advice, but Edsel was now in charge, and Henry Ford declared that he looked forward to having more time to pursue some of his other interests. Of course no knowledgeable observers believed Ford, and when the company faced a financial crisis during the postwar depression in summer 1920, it was Ford, not his son, who received the plaudits of Wall

Henry and Edsel Ford in front of a Model A Fordor (courtesy of Henry Ford Museum and Greenfield Village)

Street for the draconian measures that were taken to pull the company through.

Henry Ford's control of his company, in fact, had never been stronger. The earlier departures of Couzens and the Dodge brothers were followed immediately after the war by the departures, forced or otherwise, of such top executives as C. Harold Wills, John Lee, Frank Klingensmith, and William Knudsen, leaving a staff that was dominated by Ford loyalists such as Charles Sorensen and Harry Bennett. Edsel, who came to favor policies that often differed from those of his father, found himself without the support he needed to try to convince his father of the advantages of his ideas. For a time in the 1920s he sought to build up a power base with the help of his brother-in-law, Ernest Kanzler, an aggressive, energetic attorney whom Ford had hired to manage the Ford tractor operations. Kanzler's success led him to the Highland Park automobile operations and in 1923 to a vice-presidency and a director's seat in the company. However, by that time Ford was increasingly annoyed with Kanzler, who he thought was seeking to drive a wedge between him and his son by encourag-

ing Edsel in his differing ideas. Kanzler agreed with Edsel that changes were needed in management policies, but this proposal smacked of the orderly managerial style that General Motors (GM) had adopted and that Ford despised. But the final straw came early in 1926 when Kanzler sent Henry Ford a detailed memo setting forth the reasons it was time to discontinue the Model T in favor of a new model more in tune with the times, a change for which Edsel had been arguing without success for some time.

Later that year Edsel returned from a European trip to find that his brother-in-law was no longer with the company. Whether Kanzler had resigned or been fired is not clear, but what is clear is that Edsel did nothing to express to his father his opposition to the move. This reticence was typical of the way in which he dealt with his father. On one occasion in the early 1920s, Edsel had been persuaded that the sales and accounting staffs needed more space, and he had authorized work to begin on a new office building. Ford had been away at the time, and when he returned and saw the construction work he asked his son for an explanation.

Henry and Edsel Ford at a factory building site (courtesy of Ford Motor Company)

When Henry Ford asked, "Space for who?" the son made the mistake of singling out the accountants, whom his father had never liked. When the accountants arrived at work the next day, they found their existing offices on the fourth floor of the administration building had been emptied and their jobs abolished. "Edsel," Ford told his son later that day, "if you really need more room you'll find plenty of it on the fourth floor." On another occasion Ford disagreed with his son's decision to build coke ovens at the Rouge plant but acquiesced. Days after they were completed Ford had them torn down. As he told one person, he thought Edsel was "too soft," and these actions were apparently his way of trying to toughen him up. But if that was the intent, he did not achieve his goal. In the case of the fired accountants Edsel managed to find other places for them in the organization, but he did not stand up to his father for overruling his decision in that case or in numerous others. Instead he continued to express his loyal support of his father's business ideas. "I do not merely accept his beliefs," he said in a ghost-written article in 1929, "I feel as strongly about them as he does."

The one area in which Edsel was allowed a relatively free hand was in the styling of some of the cars. Although he was thoroughly familiar with the car's mechanical features, his interest in the car's appearance was an outgrowth of the very considerable artistic talent he had shown since he was a child. As long as the Model T remained in production he had little success in persuading his father to agree to changes that would update the styling of that plain old workhorse, but one reason why Ford agreed to buy the failing Lincoln Motor Company in 1922 was undoubtedly to give his son something on which to lavish his design ideas. Under Edsel's direction the Lincoln was soon transformed into one of the leading luxury cars in an era in which American-made luxury cars abounded. Although GM receives most of the credit for placing a new emphasis on car styling by establishing a separate department in 1927, headed by the flamboyant Harley Earl, to deal with the look of their cars, Edsel deserves to be recognized as a pioneer in this field. Not only did he build up a styling staff, small by GM standards, composed of some very talented people, but he took a personal, hands-on interest in the work to an extent that was not true of any other top American automobile executive of that, or perhaps any other, day.

When Ford finally realized the need to replace the Model T, it was Edsel who saw to it that the Model A, introduced at the end of 1927, had an elegant look that attracted buyers who previously would have rejected a car with such a low price tag. This was followed by the Lincoln Zephyr, introduced late in 1935 and regarded by many as the first successful streamlined car, and in 1939 by the Continental, Frank Lloyd Wright's choice as the most beautiful car of all time. Although the well-known stylists John Tjaarda and Eugene T. "Bob" Gregorie supervised the development of the Lincoln Zephyr and Gregorie that of the Continental, Edsel was in every sense their collaborator, keeping a close watch on both projects, approving each step in the design process, and never hesitating to introduce his own ideas into the creation of two of the most famous products of that golden age of American car design.

Edsel's artistic interests also led him to support the painter Charles Sheeler in a critically acclaimed series of studies of the Ford Rouge plant and in 1932-1933 to finance Diego Rivera's Detroit

Diego Rivera's 1932 portrait, Edsel B. Ford *(courtesy of the Detroit Institute of Arts, bequest of Eleanor Clay Ford)*

Institute of Arts murals that were likewise centered on the Ford Rouge operations but from a far different perspective than Sheeler's. When Rivera's colorful murals were unveiled, many in Detroit were shocked by the Marxist overtones of the work, but Edsel, showing a stubborn resolve that he unfortunately never showed in his dealings with his father, gave his full support to the Mexican artist and refused to allow any tampering with what has come to be regarded as one of the masterpieces of twentieth-century art.

Edsel's involvement with the Rivera mural grew out of the work of Dr. William J. Valentiner, director of the Detroit Institute of Arts, who had worked during the 1920s to cultivate the automaker's interest in great art. Valentiner convinced Edsel to become one of the museum's principal benefactors and also to acquire a great private art collection. These acquisitions represent still another difference between Edsel and his father, standing as they do in sharp contrast with Ford's homespun collecting activities that led to the opening in 1929 of the Henry Ford Museum and Greenfield Village. That Henry Ford located that center of Americana

in Dearborn near his Fair Lane estate and the heart of the Ford Motor Company operations was still another example of the difference between the father, who had remained loyal to his hometown, and the son, who chose to live elsewhere after his marriage to Eleanor Clay in 1916.

The family of Eleanor Clay, who was the niece of the late J. L. Hudson, Detroit department store magnate, represented somewhat older money than the Ford's, and she introduced her husband to Detroit society. Henry and Clara Ford at first seemed to like their daughter-in-law, but they were unhappy with the young couple's decision to live in Detroit's fashionable Indian Village section rather than on the property adjacent to the Fair Lane estate where the parents had always hoped their son would build his home. The rift widened in the late 1920s when Edsel moved his family to the even more elite Detroit suburb of Grosse Pointe Shores, where they took up residence in a new home that was far more elaborate than Fair Lane. Edsel's lakefront property had once been owned by his father, who at one time had thought of moving to that

The 1958 Edsel, a memorial to Edsel Ford and the most famous failure in automotive history

wealthy suburb. He had abandoned the idea probably because he felt, quite correctly, that he and his wife would not fit in with the neighborhood. The fact that Edsel, under his wife's tutelage, came to enjoy the company of Detroit's social aristocracy from which Henry Ford remained aloof caused relationships between the two families to become increasingly cool.

The tensions of the depression years caused Henry Ford to turn to Harry Bennett as a confidante. Fearing that his grandchildren might be kidnapped, Henry Ford turned to Bennett to provide the protection they needed, even though Edsel was perfectly capable of handling such matters. In the more liberal political climate fostered by the economic hardships of the 1930s, Ford, rather than heeding the advice of his more moderate son, relied on the strong-arm tactics of Bennett to beat back the attempts to unionize Ford workers. These violent and image-costly tactics succeeded in holding off only until 1941 what Edsel had argued in 1937 was the inevitable recognition that the company would be forced to grant to a union.

By the end of the 1930s Edsel's health was suffering as a result of the increasingly strained relationship with his father. As the country moved toward full involvement in World War II, Edsel was seen as

the stabilizing force in the company. The conflict between Bennett and Sorensen over present power and future position in the company added to the already chaotic situation at Ford, chaos fomented by Ford's senility and weakened health. Some long-time employees remained at Ford only because it appeared that Ford would soon retire or die and that Edsel would take over. "You always figured there was one person who was a perfect gentleman," a Ford engineer who had worked on the Model A's engine said of Edsel, "and that some day he was going to run the place, and that it would be a fine place to work when he was running it. You stuck around because of him." But the father would outlive the son. When Edsel underwent surgery in January 1942 for the stomach ulcer condition he had developed in the late 1930s, the doctors discovered rapidly spreading cancer. Apparently, because they felt that the situation was hopeless, they did not tell him the true nature of his illness. Late that year he was readmitted to the hospital for undulant fever, which had resulted from drinking unpasteurized milk from the Ford farms. Although this widely publicized cause of Edsel's final illness did certainly drain him of the energy he so much needed as he tried to carry on his exhausting wartime duties with the company, it was undoubtedly the cancer that finally compelled him to remain bedridden in his Grosse Pointe mansion in spring 1943 and that was the major cause of his death on May 26, 1943.

Ford, who had refused to take seriously his son's illness, declared that Edsel had brought it all on himself by adopting the high style of his society friends. Nevertheless, the loss of his only son was a blow from which he never recovered. According to Bennett, Ford "couldn't keep away from the subject." At one point, Ford apparently reacting to charges by Edsel's widow that he was responsible for his son's death because of his treatment of him, asked Bennett, "Harry, do you honestly think I was ever cruel to Edsel?" When he was not satisfied with Bennett's response he demanded "an honest answer." "Well, cruel, no; but unfair, yes," Bennett, replied. "If that had been me, I'd have got mad." At that Ford declared, "That's what I wanted him to do. Get mad."

After Edsel's death his widow used the one weapon that would persuade Ford to alter his methods: the 41 percent of Ford stock that her husband had controlled since 1919. Knowing that her father-in-law never again wanted outsiders to have any voice in the management of the company through their ownership of stock, Eleanor Clay Ford apparently blocked Ford's desire to pass the presidency on to Harry Bennett by threatening to sell her family's stock holdings. As a result the eighty-year-old Ford resumed the presidency that he had surrendered to his son twenty-four years before. Since he was clearly not up to the demands of the job, Eleanor Ford's brother-in-law, Ernest Kanzler, used his contacts in Washington to secure Henry Ford II's release from his duties as an officer in the navy so that he could take up a position as vice-president and heir apparent to the Ford Motor Company during these critical war years. Two years later when Henry Ford had still not acted to step down so that his grandson might take over, Eleanor Ford again succeeded in pressuring him by declaring that if he did not she would put her block of stock on the market.

Edsel Ford had four children. At a time when the belief that daughters in families of such wealth and standing as the Fords should not work was still quite strong, there was never any thought that Josephine Clay Ford would have any position in the family business. Such was not the case with her three brothers who, it had always been assumed, would become Ford executives. Benson Ford worked for the company before Pearl Harbor and after the war served in a number of capacities with little distinction. His younger brother, William Clay Ford, played a more important role in the company. Inheriting his father's artistic talent, he succeeded in reviving the Continental in the mid 1950s. To a very considerable degree, however, his ambitions and those of his brother Benson were frustrated by the fact that the oldest son, Henry Ford II, made it clear that there was room for only one Ford at the top. But if there was more than a little touch of the grandfather in Henry Ford II, there was also much of the father in a son who within a few years after taking over in 1945 had fulfilled Edsel's dream of seeing the family business reshaped into a modern, fully competitive organization.

References:

Peter Collier and David Horowitz, *The Fords: An American Epic* (New York: Summit Books, 1987);

Robert Lacey, *Ford: The Men and the Machine* (Boston: Little, Brown, 1986);

David L. Lewis, *The Public Image of Henry Ford* (Detroit: Wayne State University Press, 1976);

Allan Nevins and Frank Ernest Hill, *Ford: Decline and Rebirth, 1933-1962* (New York: Scribners, 1963);

Nevins and Hill, *Ford: Expansion and Challenge, 1915-1933* (New York: Scribners, 1957);

Nevins and Hill, *Ford: The Times, The Man, The Company* (New York: Scribners, 1954).

Archives:

Edsel Ford's personal papers were originally part of the Ford Archives set up at the time Allan Nevins was commissioned to write his three-volume work on the Fords and the Ford company. In 1964, when control of these archives was about to be transferred to the Edison Institute, the overall corporate name for the various activities comprised by the Henry Ford Museum and Greenfield Village, some of Edsel Ford's papers were removed and apparently destroyed on orders from Henry Ford II, who also later had the medical records of his father and other Ford family members housed at the Henry Ford Hospital destroyed. However, although the latter action will probably leave some questions regarding the state of Edsel Ford's health in his last years never to be satisfactorily answered, there remains a vast amount of material in the Ford Archives upon which a future biographer of Edsel Ford should be able to reconstruct a reasonably complete account of this complex man's life.

Henry Ford II

(September 4, 1917-September 29, 1987)   by John B. Rae

Harvey Mudd College

CAREER: Director, Ford Motor Company (1938-1987); ensign, United States Naval Reserve (1941-1943); vice-president (1943-1944), executive vice-president (1944-1945), president (1945-1960), chairman of the board and chief executive officer (1960-1979), chairman, Ford Motor Company (1979-1980).

Henry Ford II, automobile executive, was born on September 4, 1917, in Detroit, Michigan, and died in Detroit on September 29, 1987. He was the oldest of the four children of Edsel and Eleanor Clay Ford, the others being two sons, Benson and William Clay, and a daughter, Josephine Clay. As the eldest of Henry Ford's grandsons and Edsel's sons, Henry II was marked from birth as the prospective future head of the Ford Motor Company, but as he grew up he became aware that this position was clouded by conflict between his grandfather and his father. The young man resented what he saw as his grandfather's mistreatment of his father and clearly intended that in his own business career he would follow his father's ideas rather than his grandfather's; yet he was always conscious of being Henry Ford II, with a name to live up to.

His parents saw to it that he had the kind of education Edsel had been denied. He attended the Detroit University School, then Hotchkiss, an exclusive private school in Connecticut, and went from there to Yale University. Henry II's educational record was undistinguished. He remained at Yale for four years from 1936-1940 but left without a degree, largely because his senior thesis proved to be the work of a professional thesis agency. He allegedly left the receipt from the agency in the document when he submitted it, but he himself insisted that he was not that foolish. During the summers he worked in the Ford Motor Company, as did his brothers when they became old enough, and when

he became twenty-one in 1938 he was elected to the company's board of directors.

During his last year at Yale, Ford married Anne McDonnell, daughter of a wealthy Wall Street broker. They had three children, Charlotte, Anne, and Edsel Ford II. After he left Yale, Ford went to work full time at the Ford Motor Company, along with his brother Benson, who had done poorly at Princeton. They were moved about various departments in order to familiarize them with the operation of the company, an experience that was soon to prove important for both Ford and the company. It gave Ford a fuller understanding of the disarray into which the Ford Motor Company had fallen. Its founder was approaching senility, suffering from strokes, and completely under the influence of the infamous Harry Bennett. The company's organization was chaotic, and it had fallen behind Chrysler as well as General Motors (GM) in total sales. Labor relations were extremely bad. A year later, in 1941, there was a prolonged strike, ending with the company accepting the United Automobile Workers as the bargaining agent for its employees, even though Henry Ford was so far removed from reality that he insisted that all Ford workers were "loyal" and had no desire to have a union. There was a bitter struggle for power between Bennett and Charles E. Sorensen, the manager of production, with Sorensen more or less the ally of Edsel Ford, although he was certainly not in sympathy with Edsel's desire for a more humanitarian style of management.

His experience at this time intensified Ford's dislike of his grandfather. He could see firsthand how his father, Edsel, although nominally the president of the Ford Motor Company, was denied any effective authority and was treated with contempt by his father and with open antagonism by Bennett. The elder Ford even objected to having his grandsons in the River Rouge plant, but no action was taken. It did not matter, because immediately after

Henry Ford II, center, with Lee Iacocca, left, and Philip Caldwell as Ford explains the new executive struc-
ture on April 14, 1977 (courtesy of Ford Motor Company)

the attack on Pearl Harbor both Henry II and Benson volunteered for service. Henry became an ensign in the United States Naval Reserve and was stationed at the Great Lakes Naval Station. Benson entered the army with some difficulty because of poor eyesight but eventually rose to the rank of captain. This was unquestionably what both Henry II and his brother wanted to do, but they were also influenced by the criticism that had been directed at Edsel during World War I, when he had been deferred from the draft on the ground that he was needed at the Ford Motor Company, which seemed a lame excuse in view of the complete domination of the company by his father. However, Henry II's naval career was short-lived. On May 26, 1943, his father, Edsel, died at the age of forty-nine, from what historian Allan Nevins has described colorfully as "stomach cancer, undulant fever, and a broken heart." The cancer originated in stomach ulcers, products of the endless frustration with which Edsel had been forced to live. The fever came from raw milk produced at the family farm in Dearborn; Henry Ford, suspicious of the process,

would have nothing to do with pasteurization.

Edsel Ford's death left the company leaderless. Henry Ford resumed the presidency, but he was eighty years old and in failing health. In view of the company's vital role in the war effort, its management could not be left in this situation. It was, therefore, decided that Henry Ford II should be released from the Navy and brought back to assist with, or perhaps take over, the management of the Ford Motor Company. The alternative was for the government to take charge.

Henry Ford II was not to attain his position without a struggle; indeed, when he first returned to the Ford Motor Company his position was quite uncertain. His grandfather, far gone in dotage, was still determined to run the company himself and resented his grandson's presence. Bennett, given his influence over the old man, saw himself as the successor to the presidency after Henry Ford died. When Bennett saw that this ambition was meeting resistance, he convinced Henry Ford to add a codicil to his will establishing a board of trustees, with Bennett as secretary, to manage the company for ten years after the elder Ford's death. Bennett later dramatically burned this document, saying that the codicil was invalid anyway because the old man had scrawled biblical and other texts all over it. Undue influence would probably have been easy to establish also, and there is some doubt that Ford ever signed the document.

Bennett regarded Henry II as an inexperienced youth who was incapable of managing the Ford Motor Company and who might well be brought under his thumb as his grandfather had been. This was a serious miscalculation, because Ford was not disposed to subordinate himself to anyone. He knew a great deal about the operation of the company and was taking steps to remedy some of its problems by associating with executives like Mead Bricker, an honest production man, and John Bugas, a former FBI man who had investigated the handling of some Ford war contracts and then had gone into the Ford Service Department. Bugas was placed in charge of labor relations. Nevertheless Ford's position was unsatisfactory as long as he lacked complete authority in the company. He became vice-president in 1943 and in 1944 became executive vice-president. The promotions clarified his status and gave him definite powers, but the contest between him and Bennett continued. One of the major victims was Charles E. Sorensen, whom Bennett contrived to make the scapegoat for the early failure of the giant Willow Run aircraft plant to live up to its highly advertised expectations. For a time the plant was referred to as "Will-it Run?" Sorensen was forced out after a record forty years at Ford.

Since Ford was a major producer of war materials, there was concern in Washington. Government officials realized that the elder Ford was no longer capable of managing his company, and they distrusted Bennett, with ample cause. There was even talk of taking the company over for the duration of the war. Internally, it was difficult to make plans for the return of peace. It was obvious that something would have to be done, and the obvious something was to replace Henry Ford I with Henry Ford II as president of the Ford Motor Company.

At this stage Harry Bennett made the biggest blunder of his career: he ignored the women of the Ford family. Clara Bryant Ford, Henry I's wife, had long resented Bennett's influence over her husband and was not going to let him cheat her grandson out of his inheritance. Eleanor Clay Ford, Edsel

Ford's wife, hated Bennett, holding him responsible for her husband's premature death, and threatened to sell the stock that Edsel had bequeathed if Edsel's son did not receive his due. Since this came to over 40 percent of the voting stock in the Ford Motor Company, the threat was a powerful weapon, powerful enough so that Henry I finally gave way to his wife's importunities and reluctantly agreed to resign the presidency of the company. Henry II agreed to accept it on condition that he would have a free hand to make changes, and on September 21, 1945, the board of directors, with a very angry Bennett present, elected Henry Ford II president of the Ford Motor Company. Bennett left the company shortly afterward.

Ford had assumed a challenging responsibility. The Ford Motor Company was losing $10 million a month, its accounting system was archaic, and cost and inventory controls were nonexistent. Labor relations were at best an armed truce. It would take time and effort to dissipate the Bennett legacy of fear and distrust. These problems and others had to be dealt with while the company was making its transition from concentration on military production to the situation posed by the postwar world. Provisions had to be made for reconversion to peacetime production, for deciding on what the Ford postwar models ought to be, and for dealing with the labor unrest that loomed as soon as the war was over.

The new head of the Ford Motor Company was fully aware of his company's problems and had formulated ideas for solving them. He was also well aware that he was still inexperienced and needed help, and he had a definite concept of the kind of help he wanted. Part of the help he received, however, came quite unexpectedly, in the form of a group of ten Air Force officers who had agreed to try to work together after the war. They had performed brilliantly in the Air Force's Office of Statistical Control, which was responsible for making sure that the proper quantities and types of materials were delivered to the right places at the right times, and they believed that the same techniques would be valuable in postwar business. Their leader was Charles B. (Tex) Thornton; the others were George Moore, William R. Andreson, Charles E. Bosworth, J. E. Lundy, Robert S. McNamara, Arjay Miller, Ben D. Mills, Francis C. Reith, and James O. Wright. Their ages ranged from twenty-six to thirty-four. After some uncertainty they of-

Ford with Ernest Breech (courtesy of Henry Ford Museum and Greenfield Village)

fered their services to the Ford Motor Company in November 1945 and were accepted. They were promptly dubbed the "Whiz Kids"; they did not remain long as a consolidated group, but they would give the Ford Motor Company an effective system of financial controls, and two of them would rise to its presidency. The decision to hire them was made by Henry Ford II.

However, Ford had still wider ideas. He admired the organization that Alfred P. Sloan, Jr., had given to GM, and he wanted his company organized in the same way. To achieve that, he realized that he needed executives with GM experience. On the recommendation of his father's long-time friend, Ernest Kanzler, Ford approached Ernest R. Breech, who had been a vice-president of General Motors and was then president of the Bendix Aviation Corporation, which was partially owned by GM. After considerable negotiation Breech decided to accept the challenge at Ford and became executive vice-president of the Ford Motor Company on July 1, 1946. He had hoped to become president of GM, and his disappointment when Charles E. Wil-

son was chosen instead played a strong role in his decision to move to Ford.

Breech recruited other GM executives, notably Lewis D. Crusoe, trained as a finance man but also interested in production, and Delmar S. Harder, who was to be in charge of manufacturing and who is credited with coining the term "automation." In 1949 Crusoe became head of the newly organized Ford Division, which had complete responsibility for the manufacture and sale of Ford-division cars and was the keystone of the company's reorganization plan.

While these administrative changes were taking place, and to a large extent because of them, the Ford Motor Company made progress. The company was soon beginning to show profits, and these increased steadily. The labor unrest of the immediate postwar years was resolved peacefully, with the new era at Ford displayed in an address by the company's president to the Society of Automotive Engineers in January 1946. In it Ford endorsed collective bargaining and called for industrial statesmanship on both sides of the bargaining table. The speech was well received; it certainly symbolized a major change at Ford. Subsequently the Ford Motor Company pioneered agreements establishing a minimum retirement income for employees with thirty years service (1949) and supplementary unemployment benefits when workers were laid off (1955).

The company's international operations were also reorganized. A European tour in 1948 convinced Ford that the effects of World War II required termination of the arrangement where Ford of Britain supervised all the company's European activities. British Ford was left undisturbed, but the other European properties were brought under the control of a new International Division, with its head office in Dearborn.

When the Ford Motor Company celebrated its fiftieth anniversary in 1953, it was a well organized, efficiently operating, highly profitable concern. Its head was a respected businessman, admired for what he had achieved in the company. He was also active in community affairs and in 1953 was appointed by President Eisenhower as an alternate delegate to the United Nations, an assignment that he performed conscientiously.

In 1955 the Ford Motor Company went public, probably the greatest single accomplishment of Henry Ford II's stewardship. The issue of public ownership arose because of the Ford Foundation, which due to the company's escalating profits had grown to become easily the biggest and wealthiest of the private philanthropic foundations. Yet the foundation had a major weakness; it had no real control over its finances. Its assets consisted almost entirely of close to 90 percent of the common stock of the Ford Motor Company, very valuable stock as things stood but all of it class A, or non-voting, stock. The trustees of the foundation considered it undesirable to have their assets concentrated in a single security. In theory the Ford family could have voted to plow all profits back into the company and cut off the foundation's income. That was highly unlikely; Ford was chairman of the foundation's board and deeply interested in its work, and he endorsed the idea of going public.

The resulting negotiations were necessarily complex. There was a very large amount of money involved if this much Ford stock was to be put on the market. The family, Ford included, wanted to retain control of the company, but the public could not very well be asked to buy stock that gave them no voting rights whatever. In the end a reclassifica- tion of stock was worked out in which the family's 12.1 percent of stock retained 40 percent of the voting power. Ford shares went on the market in January 1956 and were instantly oversubscribed.

There were difficulties in the company also. There was friction between the production-oriented executives that Breech brought in and the Whiz Kids, referred to contemptuously by the production people as "bean counters" with no interest in or knowledge of the actual making of cars. These lines later became blurred; Crusoe and Reith joined forces in the Ford Division, while Breech and McNamara became allies. Thornton became disgruntled with his prospects early and left Ford to move to California and found Litton Industries. There is some indication that Ford possessed his grandfather's penchant for setting his subordinates at odds, or enjoying seeing them at odds. It was not pronounced as yet, but the Henry Ford I streak in his character would later appear in more emphatic form.

One of the first problems that Ford had to attend to after becoming head of the company was an unsatisfactory arrangement with Harry Ferguson, a brilliant and cantankerous Ulsterman whose goal was to mechanize small farms. This mechanization was to be achieved by designing a small tractor with a linkage that would allow several instruments to be attached interchangeably. Ferguson initially believed that the Fordson tractor would serve his purpose, but this prospect vanished when the manufacture of Fordsons was discontinued. However, Ferguson's efforts brought him into contact with Henry Ford I, and in 1939 they arrived at a highly publicized, unwritten "handshake" agreement whereby the Ford Motor Company would build tractors of Ferguson's design which would be marketed under the Ferguson name through a company called Harry Ferguson, Inc.

This operation proved to be a money-loser for the Ford Motor Company, and Henry Ford II and Breech decided to terminate it and have the company make and market its own tractors. They tried first to revise the agreement with Ferguson but did so without success. The situation was especially awkward because no written agreement existed and only Harry Ferguson could now claim to know what the details of his actual settlement with the senior Ford had been. Whatever the agreement may have been, Ford and Breech cancelled it in 1948; in the meantime a Ford subsidiary called Dearborn Motors was created to market the new Ford tractors.

Ford with Harry Bennett (courtesy of Henry Ford Museum and Greenfield Village)

Dearborn Motors served another purpose. Since Ford Motor Company stock was not yet publicly traded, it had not been possible to offer Breech and others the stock options that are customary for top management in American business. Dearborn Motors partially filled this gap.

Ferguson responded to the cancellation of his agreement by suing the Ford Motor Company for $250 million, charging that Ford had violated antitrust laws by conspiring to put him out of business and that the new Ford tractors infringed on his patents. Ford met Ferguson several times without effect in an effort to avoid expensive and time-consuming litigation. In April 1952 the case was settled by a consent decree that gave Ferguson $9.25 million for patent infringement but rejected the antitrust charge. Ferguson then moved into the Canadian agricultural implement firm of Massey-Harris and converted it into Massey-Ferguson. When the Ford Motor Company put its stock on the market in 1955 the need for Dearborn Motors disappeared, and it was dissolved. Subsequently, Ford withdrew from tractor manufacture for the second time.

Then there was the Edsel, probably the most highly publicized failure in the history of the American automobile, and perhaps also the most misunderstood failure. The decision to build the car was quite reasonable under the circumstances that existed in the mid 1950s. The Ford division enjoyed outstanding success with the Thunderbird of 1954, which outsold its GM counterpart, the Corvette. Optimism about the company's prospects ran so high that signs in Ford plants reading "Beat Chevrolet" were changed to "Beat G.M." It seemed desirable and feasible to expand the Ford offerings beyond the existing Ford, Mercury, Lincoln, and Continental lines, and market research in 1954 indicated that there was a place for a new car in the range between the Lincoln and the Mercury, competing with GM's Oldsmobile and Buick lines. Studies were also made of a stripped-down, low-priced car, but this offered poor prospects. The industry and the American public were in the era of the big car, with high horsepower, exaggerated tail fins, elaborate use of chrome, and many accessories.

The name for the new car was selected after an elaborate search, including suggestions from the

American poet Marianne Moore, produced nothing acceptable. There was some hesitation in the Ford family about using the name "Edsel," but Ford finally agreed to it as a well-deserved tribute to his father, and the project was launched with much enthusiasm and vigorous advertising. What went wrong could hardly have been foreseen. In the three years between the Edsel's preliminary design and final production, the American economy went from a peak in 1955 to recession in 1957. Car sales fell sharply from their 1955 level. Consequently, when the Edsel was introduced, there was little demand for high-priced cars. The car itself suffered from awkward styling and in a short time its production was stopped, at a cost to the Ford Motor Company of some $250 million. Ford's part in all this was indirect; he had approved the plans of Crusoe and Reith. The company could stand the loss, and did, but it was a bitter disappointment to Ford that the car dedicated to his beloved father's memory should become a symbol for a fiasco.

These difficulties had little effect on the growth of the Ford Motor Company. As the 1950s came to an end, it was a solidly established, profitable organization, a far cry from what it had been when Henry Ford II became its president. He had changed also. From the young man who knew that he had to have help to rebuild his company he had become an executive with confidence in his ability to manage the organization he had created. He was also very conscious of being Henry Ford II and wanted it clearly recognized that the Ford Motor Company was under Ford control. As did his grandfather, he objected to having any Ford executive appear to be a rival, and the first obvious target for this feeling was Ernest Breech.

Breech had been made chairman of the board in 1956, a promotion which appeared to have been a well-deserved reward. However, it created some question as to who was the actual head of the company, and Ford found it irksome that Breech as board chairman was likely to be called on to be spokesman for the company. There was no dramatic conflict between the two, just a gradual deterioration of relations until early 1960, when Breech resigned, telling Ford that he realized he was no longer needed. Ford then took the position of chairman of the board and chief executive officer. There would be no further question about who was head of the Ford Motor Company.

The departure of Breech signaled a significant change in the management of the Ford Motor Company. When Ford took over from his grandfather and undertook the rehabilitation of the company, his model was the Sloan organization at General Motors, and it remained so. There was no change in the formal structure at Ford after Breech left. The vital difference, of which Ford may have been unaware, was that Sloan had predicated his system on the belief that GM was too big to be run by any one man, and so he provided the executive and finance committees to direct the top executives on basic policy. There was nothing comparable at Ford. From 1960 on, it was established that ultimate authority in the Ford Motor Company was held by one man–Henry Ford II.

When he became board chairman, he appointed Robert S. McNamara as president. It looked like an ideal combination. McNamara was probably the ablest of the Whiz Kids, and certainly the most impersonal, an Admirable Crichton type of man who lived entirely in a world of figures and who could be depended on not to upstage the head of the company. As it happened, the combination was never really tested. McNamara had been in office only a few weeks when he left for Washington to become secretary of defense under John F. Kennedy and, later, Lyndon Johnson.

McNamara's departure left a void in the company that Ford had trouble filling. The next president was a one-time Ford ally against Bennett, John Dykstra, but Dykstra retired in 1963. His place was taken by Arjay Miller, the only other Whiz Kid to rise that far in the Ford organization, but Miller did not satisfy Ford either and was dismissed in 1968. Part of the difficulty could have been due to pressures in Ford's private life. He had become involved with a jet-setting Italian, Cristina Vettore Austin, whose first husband had been a British naval officer, and in 1965 he divorced Anne McDonnell and married Cristina. Both were excommunicated; Ford had become Catholic when he married Anne.

None of this appreciably affected the work of the Ford Motor Company. The entire American automobile industry was facing new challenges as the 1960s began. One was an increasing intervention of governmental authority in areas such as highway safety and atmospheric pollution, interventions that affected the design of motor vehicles. Henry Ford was basically sympathetic; in 1956 Ford had put out a car that emphasized safety features, only to

Ford meeting with workers at the company's Rouge plant in 1945 (courtesy of Ford Motor Company)

find that the buying public at that time was not interested. However, because of this demonstrated commitment to safety, Ford was asked to be the industry's spokesman before the committee of the United States Senate that was investigating these matters, and John Bugas was appointed special representative in Washington for this purpose.

Bugas convened a committee representing the automobile companies, which came up with a recommendation to the effect that since the industry was now aware that some action must be taken, no legislation was necessary. Ford disagreed with this response, but he did not want to repudiate Bugas publicly. His own more sensible belief was that if safety and antipollution equipment were going to be required, it should be done by legislative action, which would make it mandatory for all motor vehicle manufacturers and would therefore remove the subject from the area of competition. This, of course, was what happened with the passage of the National Traffic and Motor Vehicle Safety Act in 1966 and the Vehicle Air Pollution and Control Act in 1965.

The second challenge was the rise of the small car, particularly foreign imports, which had become a noticeable part of the American automotive scene by the end of the 1950s. This was to prove a long-term problem, for which there was no remedy in legislation, and the American automobile industry's response was not one of the brighter episodes in its history. It was not that the potentiality of the compact was ignored. At the end of World War II both Ford and General Motors made studies of the prospects of a small car and both concluded, quite accurately at the time, that the savings in cost would be negligible and that the American public preferred larger cars. Several other experiments were made at the time, but none succeeded until the American Motors Rambler in the mid 1950s, by which time the German Volkswagen was becoming a force in the United States market.

There was no particular Ford Motor Company tradition in the small-car field. Ford was quite willing to accept imports, within limits. His own company had been pushing the sale of its small British car in the early 1950s, less because it expected a large market than because Ford wanted to do what he could to alleviate Britain's severe shortage of dollar exchanges. As were the other leaders of the American automobile industry, Ford was firmly opposed to any move toward protectionism that could only lead to mutually costly trade wars, and, also like the other leaders, he shared the complacent attitude that if the imports did become a market threat, defined in those days as a 5-percent share, then the big American companies would build their own compacts and "drive the imports into the sea."

The 5 percent mark was reached and passed before the end of the decade, and the Big Three took action. GM introduced a compact, the Corvair, in 1959, but it was called unsafe. Ford's entry of the same year, the Falcon, had a good reception and sold well, as did the somewhat larger Fairlane which appeared in 1961. Ford also tried to market its small German-built Taunus, but this car did not appeal to American buyers. The influx of imports declined for a couple of years and then climbed; the problem simply refused to go away. Ford himself was not especially interested in compact cars. He is reported to have remarked that "mini cars mean mini profits," an accurate reflection of the attitude of all the American automobile manufacturers toward compact cars. If he did say it, it was a reversal of the decision that had made his grandfather great: to accept a low-unit profit per car and instead seek high-volume production and sales.

At this stage of his career Ford was displaying the complex characteristics that would mark him for the rest of his life. He remained dedicated to the management of the Ford Motor Company, always with the provision that he must be recognized as top man. He was also acutely conscious of being head of the Ford family. In his personal life he gave extravagant parties and drank heavily and publicly. He and his second wife spent much time in Europe, where as head of the Ford Motor Company he was lavishly feted. In his social life he displayed a streak of coarseness, which may have been a factor in the friendly relations he developed with President Lyndon Johnson, who had the same quality.

Yet his social consciousness survived. When a major race riot convulsed Detroit in 1967, Ford threw the resources of his company into programs for increasing minority employment and worked with Detroit officials to seek out and try to remedy the causes of the unrest. If the immediate results were limited, that was because the problem was overwhelming.

Through it all he retained his grip on the affairs of the Ford Motor Company. In the first half of the 1960s he approved the repurchase of the publicly owned shares of Ford's profitable European enterprise and the acquisition of the Philco Corporation, which put Ford into the radio and electronics business. The new Philco Division absorbed the Ford Aeroneutronics Division, which had been created in 1956 in an effort to enter missile and space activities. Ford did not stay long in the field of radio and electrical equipment, but the operation eventually became Ford Aerospace and Communications, located in Southern California.

Ford continued to admire the GM management structure, and after Miller's departure he again went to GM for assistance. This came in the person of Semon E. "Bunkie" Knudsen, the son of William S. Knudsen. He became president of the Ford Motor Company in 1968, to the accompaniment of much publicity about how his father, William S. Knudsen, had been one of the great builders of the Ford Motor Company in its early days and had then gone to GM and made Chevrolet into Ford's successful competitor. Now his son was taking the Knudsen name back to Ford. S. E. Knudsen had been conspicuously successful as head of GM's Pontiac and Chevrolet divisions and had become available to Ford because he was disappointed at being passed over for the presidency of GM.

He lasted just a year and one-half at Ford. His appointment antagonized Lee Iacocca, the head of the Ford Division, who was already aiming at the presidency himself, and he undoubtedly worked to undermine Knudsen. The main trouble, however, was that Ford resented the publicity given to Knudsen, and there was a gulf that neither of them understood between the GM and the Ford philosophies of management. At GM presidents and board chairmen came and went; there was no ruling dynasty, whereas Ford never forgot that the Ford Motor Company was his by inheritance, and he would accept no rival to his authority. At GM the division heads were given a good deal of leeway, and Knudsen was adhering to this pattern when he authorized actions in Ford's absence that ordinarily would have required approval by the company's chief executive officer. Ford made it clear that, whatever the practice may have been at GM, this was not the way to do things at Ford.

Fifteen months of improvisation followed and then Ford appointed Iacocca president, where he remained for an astonishing seven years. Iacocca firmly believed himself to be the man best qualified to be the CEO of the Ford Motor Company, and he had a flair for self-advertisement. He despised Ford as a drunkard who was incompetent to manage the company. Ford disliked Iacocca, but for the time being Iacocca's unquestioned ability was needed.

The decade of the 1970s was a difficult one for the American automobile industry. The influx of small import cars continued to grow, with the Japanese now in the lead and steadily increasing their share of the American market. When the Arab oil embargo was imposed in 1973-1974, sales of the large American cars declined sharply. Even when the embargo was terminated, an increase in the price of gasoline imposed by OPEC (Organization of Petroleum Exporting Countries) put a premium on cars with low fuel consumption. The industry also had further restrictions imposed by the Energy Policy and Conservation Act of 1975, which required all new automobiles to attain a maximum fuel consumption of 27.5 miles per gallon by 1985. Three Ford models—Pinto, Maverick, and Mustang—that Iacocca had sponsored, helped the company to face the crisis, although the Pinto later involved Ford in massive damage suits because it was alleged to have a tendency to burst into flames if hit from behind. The litigation proved expensive; still worse was the allegation that Ford officials had known the Pinto was unsafe but had declined to add to the cost of the car by making the necessary changes. The company was better served by its International division, which was Ford's special pride. Through these critical years the International division accounted for over 40 percent of the Ford Motor Company's total earnings.

The worldwide presence of the Ford Motor Company was most impressive. British Ford, which was not included in the International division, was the second largest maker of motor vehicles in the United Kingdom. Under the International division's supervision were Ford installations in Argentina, Australia, Belgium, Brazil (including Willys-Overland of Brazil, bought by Ford in 1967), Denmark, Finland, Mexico, Singapore, South Africa, Spain, Sweden, and Venezuela. In the 1970s Ford added connections with the booming Japanese automobile industry through a partnership with Nissan and Toyo Kogyo to form the Japanese Automatic Transmission Company, which used Ford patents, and the acquisition of a 25-percent stock interest in Toyo Kogyo, maker of the Mazda. This last move was done by merging Ford of Japan with Toyo Kogyo. The Japanese company then built the Ford Courier pickup truck and also made components such as transaxles for Ford cars.

But there were distractions that took Ford's attention away from business affairs. One, much to his credit, was his deep involvement with the Detroit Renaissance Center. Another, less happy, was the impending breakup of his second marriage. A third concern was his deteriorating health. In 1976 an angina attack put him in the Henry Ford Hospital for six weeks, and his doctors warned him that it was time for him to slow down.

The angina attack was important for the Ford Motor Company because Ford realized that if he were to die suddenly, Iacocca, whom he had come to dislike, would be left in full charge. Consequently he created a triumvirate consisting of himself, Iacocca, responsible for North American operations, and Philip Caldwell, head of the International Division, with the proviso that when Ford himself was away Caldwell would be in charge. When this arrangement produced friction, as it was bound to do and probably was intended to, Ford fired Iacocca in 1978. Iacocca then went to Chrysler and became famous for rescuing the company from impending bankruptcy with the aid of government guaranteed loans of $1.5 billion.

The question bound to be asked is why the other members of the Ford family, in particular Ford's brothers, were not called in to assist him in the management of the family firm. The answer is that they were eclipsed by Henry's powerful personality. Benson, the nearest to him in age, never achieved anything. He did poorly in school and never held anything more than nominal positions at Ford. He became an alcoholic and died in 1978. William Clay Ford, eight years younger than Henry, also suffered from alcoholism but recovered, worked in various managerial positions, and eventually became vice-chairman. Like Benson he was always overshadowed by his older brother, but he found an outlet for himself in becoming owner of the Detroit Lions football team. By the time Henry was ready to step down William was too old to be considered for the top position and was not especially interested in it anyway. Their sister Josephine

Henry Ford II, standing, with his brothers Benson, left, and William Clay (courtesy of Ford Motor Company)

married an architect named Ford, no relation whatsoever, and lived her own life.

In addition to his commitments to his company and his family, Ford held a strong sense of responsibility to his community. Edsel Ford had believed that a man of wealth had an obligation to contribute to the betterment of his community, views very much in accordance with Andrew Carnegie's *The Gospel of Wealth*. Ford shared his father's attitude. For a time Ford flirted with politics but showed no real disposition to run for public office. Nonetheless, he remained open to the possibility of an appointive position.

His service at the United Nations during the Eisenhower administration has been alluded to. He was also chairman of the board of trustees of the Ford Foundation, giving up the position in 1956 but remaining a trustee. He took this action because he felt that he could not do justice both to the responsibility of being president of the Ford Motor Company and board chairman of the Ford Foundation.

He was nominally a Republican and gave a formal endorsement to Richard Nixon in 1960. However, he soon became friendly with President Kennedy and still more so with President Johnson.

If Ford hoped for some major appointment from this association, he was disappointed. He would have liked to be ambassador to Great Britain, but his heavy drinking and his occasional publicized crudeness at social functions ruled out any such prospect, even with Johnson. The best Johnson could do was appoint Ford president of an organization called the National Alliance of Businessmen, whose function was to formulate programs for cooperation between business and government to deal with the problem of the hard-core unemployed. It was probably also intended to drum up business support for Johnson's faltering administration. Ford resigned this position when Johnson's term expired. President Nixon then made him chairman of the National Center for Voluntary Action, which had a similar purpose. Neither appointment was more than a formality or made any great demands on Ford's time and energy.

In any event the natural theater for Ford community activities was Detroit, where the family had grown up and the company had been founded. One of the earliest of these community efforts has attracted little attention outside the historical profession, but it is one for which historians owe a deep debt to Henry Ford II. This was a decision, early in the 1950s, to have the history of the Ford family and the Ford Motor Company written under the direction of a historian of recognized stature. The man selected, Prof. Allan Nevins of Columbia University, met that standard completely. The arrangement for the history provided that the Ford Motor Company make a grant to Columbia University to complete the work. Professor Nevins and his staff were employed and paid by Columbia and did most of their work there. The outcome was a monumental three-volume work carrying the Ford story from its beginning to 1962. (A fourth volume is in preparation, carrying the story into the 1980s.) The history was based on exhaustive research on the American automobile industry, on Ford company and family records, and on hundreds of taped interviews. It is the only genuinely scholarly history ever supported by an American automobile company, and it makes the Ford Motor Company one of the very few business concerns with the wisdom to present the story of business to the public factually and accurately.

While this project was in progress Henry Ford I's mansion in Dearborn, Fairlane, was sold to the Ford Motor Company and was used for a time to house the Ford Archives. Fairlane had no sentimental attachment for Henry Ford II; he reportedly said that he would not mind if the place was torn down. However, it was to serve a more useful purpose. In 1956 the property was given to the University of Michigan for use as a Dearborn campus. The archives were moved to the Henry Ford Museum, still the only archives of an extant American automobile company to be open to qualified scholars.

These were preliminaries, evidence that Henry Ford II had interests beyond the making of cars and money. What really aroused his social conscience was the plight of Detroit as dramatically demonstrated in the destructive riots of 1967. Detroit's problem was no different and probably no worse than that of other cities with decaying centers, but the rioting stimulated an irresistible demand for action and for cooperation between business and government to find solutions for the city's problems.

The Ford Motor Company responded, as has been mentioned, by taking steps to try to increase minority representation in its work force. Ford himself went further. However, his first major move was made in all-white Dearborn rather than in Detroit, and it had the earmarks of real estate development rather than community rehabilitation. This was a large shopping center, begun in 1971 and named Fairlane because it was sited on a piece of the Ford family land that had been used to grow soybeans. The Fairlane Mall attracted some of Detroit's most important stores, including J. L. Hudson and Lord & Taylor, and Hyatt built a multistory Regency Hotel on the property. Fairlane, covering 277 acres, was by far the largest of Detroit's suburban shopping complexes. It was built by a branch of the Ford Motor Company, the Ford Motor Land Development Corporation, and proved to be highly profitable.

The Fairlane shopping center was of considerable benefit to Detroit suburbanites, but it did nothing for the inner city, and that was not enough for Henry Ford. From his very real concern came the concept of the Detroit Renaissance Center, and it was largely through his exertions that the idea was carried to completion. This was a project for completely rebuilding thirty-one acres of run-down waterfront property, adjacent to the tunnel under the Detroit River to Canada. To finance the project Ford assembled a consortium of fifty-one Detroit or Detroit-oriented business firms and exerted all his power and influence, as well as the personal charm

that he possessed and could display when he chose, to get contributions. He was perfectly willing to put pressure on firms that did business with the Ford Motor Company. One steel company executive is alleged to have observed that the appropriate logo for the Renaissance Center would be a twisted arm.

It was completed in 1977 at a cost of $477 million, of which $86.6 million came from the Ford Motor Company, this during the period when Ford, like other American automobile manufacturers, was struggling with the aftereffects of the Arab oil embargo and facing both reduced earnings and a falling market for large, high-powered cars.

The Renaissance Center was the largest single construction project in the history of Detroit. Its core is a tall, twin-towered office structure that dominates the Detroit skyline, along with a large hotel and supplementary stores and other business enterprises. The Center was not a financial success. Nevertheless it helped revitalize downtown Detroit by attracting visitors (an average of 275,000 annually in the Center's Westin Hotel) and still more by stimulating other construction projects that have given the downtown area more of an entertainment and residential character. It has enabled Detroit to attract conventions and other meetings on a scale that previously was impossible.

While the Renaissance Center was being constructed, Ford fell into disagreement with the Ford Foundation. The problem initiated with his brother Benson, who was responsible for supervising the affairs of the Henry Ford Hospital, their grandfather's one important philanthropy. The hospital suffered from the decay that was blighting Detroit's center city; by the 1970s it was short of money and its facilities were deteriorating. Benson Ford was not the man to deal with this problem. He suffered from heart trouble and alcoholism, and his wife was dying of cancer. Cristina Ford became aware of the hospital's situation and suggested appealing to the Ford Foundation. When Benson told her that he had done so and had been turned down, she enlisted her husband's assistance.

The president of the Ford Foundation at the time was McGeorge Bundy, one of the liberal intellectuals who had gathered about John F. Kennedy and who had been unable to stay with Lyndon Johnson. He joined the Ford Foundation in 1966, using the organization for purposes outside those of the family. When Ford appealed for help for the hospital, Bundy continued to resist. Bundy eventually relented and approved a grant of $100 million for the Henry Ford Hospital. In his somewhat abrasive manner, Bundy added the message that this was a terminal grant: the Ford Foundation would give no more money to the Ford family for the Henry Ford Hospital.

At the end of 1977 Henry Ford resigned as a trustee of the Ford Foundation. The hospital incident may have been the catalyst for this decision, but it is evident that he had been disturbed for some time by Bundy's policies. In his letter of resignation he noted that the foundation's resources were a product of American business and suggested that the system that had made the foundation possible was probably worth preserving.

The middle 1970s were a watershed period in Henry Ford II's life. Early in 1975 he was stopped for a traffic violation in Goleta, California, and arrested on a charge of drunken driving. In the car with him was a woman named Kathleen DuRoss, a widow from Detroit whom he had met some time before. The incident had two important features. It was of course front-page news, but Ford refused all comment with one of his favorite dicta: "Never complain, never explain." More important, it revealed that his marriage with Cristina was disintegrating. A year later it was announced that they were separating, and after prolonged negotiations they were divorced in 1980. The cost of the settlement was estimated at between $5 million and $10 million. Shortly after the divorce Henry married Mrs. DuRoss, who survived him.

Early in 1976 Ford was hospitalized for six weeks with heart trouble. Later in the year his mother died. They were deeply attached to each other, and she had been a steadying influence on him, so that he felt her loss keenly. The consequence of these events resulted in his decision in the following year to share power in the Ford Motor Company with Philip Caldwell and Lee Iacocca.

It was still more a device for easing himself out in a series of planned steps. In 1979 he resigned as chief executive officer of the Ford Motor Company, turning that post over to Caldwell. A year later he stepped down as chairman of the board, again with Caldwell as his replacement. Donald Petersen became president of the company, which meant that for the first time in its history the Ford Motor Company had no member of the Ford family in either of its top executive positions. Ford re-

mained on the board of directors and continued to exert great influence. In 1982, at age sixty-five, Ford officially retired from the company. Although he was now an outside director, the bylaws were amended to allow him to chair the powerful finance committee.

The transition was undoubtedly painful for him. He was very conscious of being the custodian of the Ford family heritage, and he could not have been pleased about being unable to turn the responsibility over to another Ford. His brother, William Clay Ford, was vice-chairman of the board, but was not considered CEO material. Ford's son, Edsel Ford II, was doing quite well in the company and was an obvious future choice to become its head, although Henry had made the point on an earlier occasion that there were no crown princes in the Ford organization. Ironically Edsel was regarded as too young and inexperienced to take over from his father, but in 1980 he was thirty-one, older than his father had been when he became president of the Ford Motor Company in 1945. But Ford needed high-quality management as the 1980s began. As were the other American motor vehicle manufacturers, the company was faced with a declining market for the vehicles it was making and with an enormous need for capital investment in new production techniques. The Ford Motor Company lost $1.5 billion in 1980 and was undertaking to spend twice that much for the development of the Ford Taurus, steps approved by Ford as chairman of the finance committee of the board of directors. In spite of the horrendous financial burden it had taken on, the Ford Motor Company of 1980 was definitely in better shape than it had been in 1945. Nevertheless, Edsel Ford II was not chosen as his father's replacement.

Henry Ford II contracted pneumonia in summer 1987 and died on September 29, 1987, in the Henry Ford Hospital, at the age of seventy. Although he has a secure place in the history of American business, he could not compete with his grandfather as a pioneer in introducing the automobile and making historic changes in the techniques of production. His own achievement was of a different order. From his childhood it had been taken for granted, and he had taken it for granted, that he would eventually become head of the Ford Motor Company. But no one could have anticipated, least of all Henry II himself, that he would find himself in that position at the age of twenty-eight, with a slender background of training and experience, facing difficulties that could well have appeared insurmountable. The company was rapidly sliding toward bankruptcy, it had fallen to third place among American automobile manufacturers, its management was disorganized and torn by bitter internal dissensions, and its labor relations were atrocious. The measure of Henry II's stature as a businessman is that he took charge of the Ford Motor Company and transformed this situation, then continued building it so effectively that at the time of his death Ford was the most profitable of the American motor vehicle manufacturers.

It is possible to offer the argument that Henry Ford II was actually just a figurehead, nominally in charge because of his birth, and that the real credit for the revival and growth of the Ford Motor Company should go to able lieutenants like Ernest Breech, John Bugas, Robert McNamara, Lee Iacocca, and others. Iacocca has in fact made this argument, but it is a specious one. Harry Truman would have known better. The crucial individual in any organization is the one at whose desk the buck stops, and in the Ford Motor Company from 1945 to 1980 that was unmistakably Henry Ford II. He appointed these lieutenants, and he discharged them. When they succeeded, their achievements were generally recognized, sometimes to the exclusion of the head of the company; yet if they had failed, Ford would have been held responsible for bad judgment. He should at least be given credit for picking the right people.

References:

Peter Collier and David Horowitz, *The Fords: An American Epic* (New York: Summit Books, 1987);

David Halberstam, *The Reckoning* (New York: Morrow, 1986);

Booton Herndon, *Ford: An Unconventional Biography of the Men and their Times* (New York: Weybright & Talley, 1969);

Lee Iacocca, *Iacocca: An Autobiography* (New York: Bantam Books, 1984);

Robert Lacey, *Ford: The Men and the Machine* (Boston: Little, Brown, 1986);

Allan Nevins and Frank E. Hill, *Ford: Decline and Rebirth, 1933-1962* (New York: Scribner s, 1963);

John B. Rae, *The American Automobile Industry* (Boston: Twayne, 1984);

Lawrence J. White, *The Automobile Industry Since 1945* (Cambridge, Mass.: Harvard University Press, 1971).

Archives:

The Ford Archives are located at the Henry Ford Museum in Dearborn, Michigan. They have materials relating mainly to the period of Henry Ford II's youth and early years as a Ford executive. The bulk of the records dealing with his years as head of the company are in the Ford Motor Company Industrial Archives, Redford, Michigan, and can be used only with permission from the company.

Ford Motor Company

by George S. May

Eastern Michigan University

In 1920, seventeen years after it had been founded, the Ford Motor Company was by far the world's largest automobile manufacturer, and its Model T, the only model the company had offered since shortly after the car was introduced in 1908, accounted for about half of all new car sales in the United States. Like all automakers, Ford's sales dropped sharply with the onset of a postwar depression late in summer 1920, but they soon rebounded. By 1922 and 1923 sales in the annual range of 2 million gave Ford close to 60 percent of the domestic market. With a new Model T selling for under $300, the sturdy 4-cylinder car continued to be the favorite of first-time car buyers, providing a solid basis for the company's claim that this was "The Car that put America on Wheels."

With Henry Ford's buyout of the company's minority stockholders in 1919 Ford was completely owned and controlled by the family whose name it bore. The extent to which the family has continued to control the company, long after the individuals who founded other companies and their families ceased to exercise any control in those businesses, has been one of the features that has set it apart from its competition. Edsel B. Ford became president early in 1919 and continued to hold that office until his death in 1943, but despite the title there was never any question that his father was the one who ran the company. Already hailed as the father of mass production, Henry Ford earned new respect from a surprising quarter, Wall Street, for the way in which he overcame serious financial problems at the start of the 1920s. Ford had borrowed heavily in 1919, and, with the decline in car sales late in 1920, the danger arose that the company would not be able to repay the debt on time. Ford slashed prices by about 20 percent, ripped out 60 percent of the telephones, and cut the ranks of the office staff by 50 percent and the number of foremen by 75 percent. Still short of money, he used up his entire stock of parts in winter 1920-1921 to produce tens of thousands of Model Ts and ship them to the dealers. The cars had not been ordered by the dealers, who had trouble selling those they already had in stock, but faced with the prospect of either paying for the new cars or losing their dealership, nearly all dealers borrowed the money from local banks and took delivery. The resulting flow of money provided Ford with more than enough funds to pay off his loans. Dealers were understandably upset, but a Dow Jones release praised Ford for having "displayed a degree of financial astuteness totally unexpected." Before the decade was over, however, assessments of Ford's leadership were being revised as his company slipped from its number one position and was in danger of falling to the third spot in industry production figures.

Although a number of reasons help explain this decline, they all relate to Henry Ford's leadership. In the process of securing complete control, Ford had forced out or fired such capable executives as James Couzens, William Knudsen, C. Harold Wills, Norval Hawkins, and Frank Klingensmith, who, together with such stockholders as the Dodge brothers, had helped to counter Ford's often impetuous and irrational style of management. With their departure few remained who dared to oppose Ford's wishes. Edsel Ford recognized that the company had grown much too big to be run by one man, but his father rejected any suggestion that they should adopt the managerial and organizational reforms that were being implemented at General Motors (GM) to replace the one-man management approach of the departed William C. Durant. Edsel Ford could not or would not stand up to his father, revealing a weakness that ironically drew Ford closer to Charles Sorensen and Harry Bennett, executives who had the strengths that Ford recognized his son did not possess but

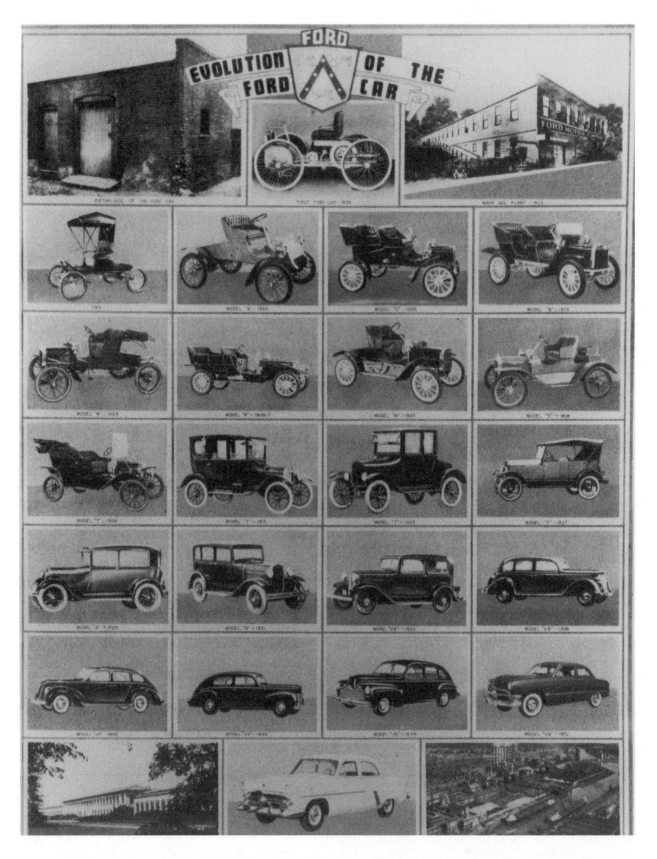

Ford cars from 1896 to 1952 (courtesy of the Henry Ford Museum, The Edison Institute)

who he knew could be counted on to do whatever he asked them to do.

Thus Ford, refusing to recognize that market conditions were changing, remained confident that the Model T would continue to be the basis for the company's growth. Meanwhile, GM concentrated on developing a variety of models with features and comforts that customers were seeking. This strategy was implemented as first-time buyers, who had dominated the market, were being replaced by those who were looking for a replacement car and basing their decision on criteria such as styling and comfort. GM earnings surpassed Ford's in 1925, and by 1927 Chevrolet's sales, under the direction of Ford alumnus William Knudsen, were challenging the Model T's dominance of the market for the lowest-priced cars. Ford finally realized a change had to be made. He halted Model T production and virtually shut down the company for six months while he and his staff developed a replacement for the obsolete model.

The car they came up with at the end of 1927, the 4-cylinder Model A, had the look and the feel that the public expected in a car by that time, and it enabled Ford to regain its leadership among the big-volume, low-priced cars—but only temporarily. Chevrolet quickly brought out a 6-cylinder model and regained the lead. Henry Ford was slowly recognizing that he could no longer rely on one, basically unchanging model year after year. The Model A gave way in 1932 to the Ford V-8, but without a variety of models in other price ranges to go with this basic model, Ford in 1933 fell to third place behind the newcomer Chrysler, which had followed GM's lead by offering cars from the low end to the high end of the price ranges. Ford did indeed have the Lincoln, which it had acquired in 1922, but although that car, under Edsel Ford's direction, became an elegant luxury car, its sales were no threat to those of GM's top-of-the-line Cadillac. The medium-priced Mercury, introduced in 1938, was further indication of Ford's reluctant acceptance of the GM marketing strategy. Mercury sales were respectable, but they again were not a serious challenge to the well-established medium-priced models produced by GM and Chrysler.

The depression of the 1930s, which greatly affected Ford sales, as it did those of all automakers, brought demands for some restraints on the companies' freedom to operate as only they saw fit. More

than any other industry leader, Henry Ford was adamant in his refusal to accept these changes. He refused to have anything to do with the code drawn up under the National Industrial Recovery Act of 1933, which sought to bring about recovery by mandating that the companies agree to certain standard operating procedures. The same act and the later Wagner Act of 1935 protected the rights of workers to join and be represented by a union. After a bitter strike GM, in February 1937, agreed to recognize the new United Automobile Workers (UAW) union. The other companies, except Ford, soon followed suit. Henry Ford's decision to turn over labor relations to Bennett kept the union out for four years, but the brutal methods Bennett employed destroyed the image Ford had earlier enjoyed of pursuing an often surprisingly enlightened labor policy. Finally, after a strike in spring 1941, Ford workers, in a government-supervised vote, overwhelmingly chose to be represented by the UAW. Henry Ford at first refused to agree to a contract with the union, saying he would rather go out of business. But then, at his family's urging, he consented to a contract that gave the UAW better terms than it had received from other automobile companies.

Such inconsistent behavior had always been a Ford trait, but such behavior became more common after Ford suffered a mild stroke in 1938. The stroke, when combined with Ford's advancing age—he was eighty years old in 1943—made it more and more difficult for him to exercise real direction over the company's activities. Edsel Ford's death in 1943, which led Ford to resume the presidency of the company, only served to intensify the battle within the company's executive ranks to take advantage of Ford's incapacity and gain control over operations. The chief protagonists were Bennett and Sorensen, and by 1944 Sorensen, who had served Ford faithfully for forty years, realized that he had lost the war and resigned. Yet, in spite of the turmoil in the executive offices, the company was still able to produce a vast array of war material during World War II, including more than 8,500 Liberator B-24 bombers produced at a huge new plant at Willow Run, near Ypsilanti, Michigan.

It was the fear on the part of government officials that the company's leadership problems after Edsel Ford's death might hamper its ability to fulfill its war contracts that led to Henry Ford II, the founder's grandson, being released from the navy in 1943 so that he could assume an executive role with the

The 1929 Model A Roadster

company. From 1943 to 1945 a struggle ensued as Bennett sought to use the influence he had gained over Henry Ford to ensure his continued control of the company. In 1945, however, pressure exerted on Ford by his wife and his son's widow finally persuaded him to step down as president and permit his grandson to take over.

Henry Ford II ran the Ford Motor Company for the next thirty-four years, and even after his retirement he remained a dominating influence over company policy until his death in 1987. The company he took over was in terrible shape after years of mismanagement. Although its records were in such disarray that it was impossible to compute exact figures, Ford was estimated to be losing money at the rate of $11 million a month. Some analysts doubted the company could survive the dislocation resulting from the adjustment back to peacetime production that followed the end of the war in summer 1945. These fears were probably exaggerated. With the return of a seller's market in the immediate postwar years, Ford could sell as many cars as it could produce. But over the long haul drastic reforms needed to be made. For twenty years the company had been riding on the reputation it

had gained from Henry Ford's early accomplishments. Now the grandson placed his own mark on the company by instituting the managerial reforms that were needed for Ford to be able to compete when normal market conditions returned.

After firing Bennett and much of the leftover executive staff from his grandfather's days, Henry Ford II brought in outsiders to revamp the company's antiquated management system. Late in 1945 he hired ten air force officers who had worked together in the service and were trained in financial and statistical analysis techniques. Dubbed the "Whiz Kids," they were told to study methods of modernizing the company's operations. More important, however, was Ford's success in persuading Ernest R. Breech, a top executive with GM, to become the executive vice-president and, with the aid of many GM staffers whom Breech brought with him, to install the kind of administrative plan that had accounted for GM's rise to the top of the industry in the 1920s. When the 1949 model Fords appeared, the first new postwar car developed by the new staff, the success of the design signaled the success of Henry Ford II's efforts to rejuvenate the com-

Ford's River Rouge Plant in Dearborn, Michigan (courtesy of Henry Ford Museum and Greenfield Village)

pany. Fears of its imminent collapse could now be put to rest.

By 1952 Ford had moved ahead of Chrysler into second place, a position it has maintained ever since. For a time in the 1950s some of the Ford executives had visions of pushing the clock back thirty years and unseating GM from the number one spot. The cars of the Ford Division gave Chevrolet a strong run in the competition to be the top-selling car on the market. And, following Chevrolet's lead, the division no longer relied on only one model. Ford cars now came in a variety of models, some of which were not necessarily cheap. Ford again followed Chevrolet's lead in 1954 by introducing a sports car, the Thunderbird. Although the Thunderbird did not long continue as a sports car, its evolution into what was called a "personal car" provided Ford with a car priced at a much higher level than buyers had been accustomed to seeing attached to a Ford. In the mid 1950s the company also revived the Continental, a famous car which had been developed under Edsel Ford's direction in the late 1930s. Lincoln and Continental provided Ford with an impressive presence in the luxury car field, although their sales were but a pale shadow

of Cadillac's booming sales during this period. In the area between the most expensive and the least expensive models, however, Ford was still weak, and in the mid 1950s a new entry was prepared to fill the gap between the Mercury and the Lincoln and the Continental. The resulting car, the Edsel, proved to be the most celebrated failure in the history of the American automotive industry, and it was abandoned by the company within two years after its 1958 debut. The failure strengthened the hand of those company officials who had felt it was a mistake to try to go head-to-head with GM, and under their direction the company in subsequent years would concentrate its efforts on maintaining and upgrading its existing lines rather than attempting to match GM model for model.

The failure of the Edsel was a special disappointment to Henry Ford II because it had been intended to keep alive the memory of his father, but in other ways the son's administration reflected the influence of his father's thinking. Edsel Ford had opposed the hard-line approach to dealings with labor that had been carried out by Bennett, with Henry Ford's backing, and in the postwar years under Henry Ford II the company's relationships with the

UAW were greatly improved as management showed a willingness to engage in mutually beneficial negotiations with the union. The younger Ford also showed a much greater sensitivity in dealing with some of the problems the industry faced than his grandfather had shown in the 1930s. In 1956, when concern for automotive safety was becoming increasingly widespread, the new Ford models included seat belts and many other features designed to provide greater safety to the occupants of the cars, long before such features appeared in the cars of the competition. Robert McNamara, head of the Ford Division, was responsible for pushing these features, not Henry Ford II, who, when he looked at the comparative sales of Ford and Chevrolet, is reported to have remarked that "Ford is selling safety and Chevrolet is selling cars." Nevertheless, when he appeared before a Senate committee in 1965 concerning a move to establish a federal agency to require companies to include certain safety features in all their cars, Ford and his company, alone among the Big Three, made a favorable impression by not indicating an adamant opposition to such requirements.

But while Henry Ford II clearly showed that he was Edsel Ford's son, he also gave more and more evidence that he was Henry Ford's grandson. The GM system of management had been installed under his direction, and in 1955 the total control the Ford family had over the company had been ended when the public was able to buy voting shares in the business. However, the Fords retained 40 percent of the voting stock, enough to give it effective control of the company. As the eldest of Edsel Ford's children, Henry Ford II began to assert the power that he felt he deserved because of that position and his name. Unease and conflict began to return to the company's executive ranks as the grandson, like the grandfather before him, made it clear that he did not like to be overshadowed by officers who received more publicity than the head of the company. By the 1970s the company was suffering. It failed to respond quickly enough to the new inter-

est in smaller cars that was emerging, in part, at least, because Henry Ford II did not like small cars. The quality of Ford products was badly damaged by several government-ordered recalls and lawsuits. Finally there was the clash between Lee Iacocca, Ford president, and Henry Ford II, the company chairman, which led to Iacocca's firing in 1978, in spite of the efforts of some outside directors to try to work out a compromise that could have retained Iacocca's services for the company.

However, unlike his grandfather, Henry Ford II recognized when it was time to step aside. In 1979 he turned the duties of chief executive officer over to Philip Caldwell, who became the first non-Ford to head the company since 1906. Ford stepped down as chairman in 1980, with Caldwell taking over this position and Don Petersen assuming Caldwell's former position as president, although Caldwell remained as chief executive officer in his new position. Henry Ford II remained a director, and it is doubtful if any company policy to which he had strong objections could have been adopted. But the success of Caldwell and Petersen in the 1980s in restoring confidence in the quality of Ford products, and in bringing it through the difficult economic conditions of the early 1980s to record profits that in 1986 surpassed those of GM for the first time since 1924, marked the triumph of the professional managerial approach at Ford. Fords continue to be involved in the company that carries their family name, but it is unlikely that any of them will exercise the kind of personal, one-man domination that Henry Ford and his grandson had over the company.

References:
James J. Flink, *The Automobile Age* (Cambridge, Mass.: MIT Press, 1988);

Robert Lacey, *Ford: The Men and the Machine* (Boston: Little, Brown, 1986);

Allan Nevins and Frank Ernest Hill, *Ford: Decline and Rebirth, 1933-1962* (New York: Scribners, 1963);

Nevins and Hill, *Ford: Expansion and Challenge, 1915-1933* (New York: Scribners, 1957).

Douglas Andrew Fraser

(December 18, 1916-   )

by Gilbert J. Gall

Pennsylvania State University

CAREER: Metal finisher, Chrysler Corporation (1935-1947); president, United Auto, Aerospace, and Agricultural Implement Workers (UAW), Local 227 (1943-1947), international representative, UAW (1947-1951), administrative assistant to the president, International Union, UAW (1951-1959), codirector, Region 1A, UAW (1959-1962), member-at-large, executive board and director, Chrysler Department, UAW (1962-1970), vice-president, UAW (1970-1977), president, UAW (1977-1983); university professor of labor studies, Wayne State University (1983-   ).

Douglas Andrew Fraser, president of the United Automobile Workers (UAW) international union from 1977 through 1983, led his union through one of the most difficult periods in its history. Assuming the presidency upon the retirement of Leonard Woodcock, Fraser took control of one of the most powerful industrial unions in America (1.4 million members in 1977) at a period in which the automobile industry was setting records in terms of units produced. In short order, however, a sharp increase in competition from foreign automakers (assisted by an energy shortage), advanced automation of car production, and the most serious recession to hit the U.S. economy in years threw the industry and the union in turmoil, disrupting traditional collective bargaining patterns. Fraser was thus forced to lead the UAW through an initial period of retrenchment and then through the beginning stages of what some observers have termed a transitional era in the industry's labor relations. The UAW president's willingness to accept change has been epitomized by his comprehension of the competitive business problems of the automotive industry and his unprecedented election to the Chrysler board of directors in the early 1980s.

Fraser, a man with a relaxed and often earthy style, was born in Glasgow, Scotland, on December 18, 1916, the son of a skilled trade unionist who was an active member of the Scottish Socialist Party. He moved to the United States with his family in 1922 and settled in Detroit, Michigan. Tagging along to labor meetings with his activist father made an impression on the young Fraser, as did the economic deprivation of the Great Depression and his father's unemployment during those years. Leaving Chadsey High School in Detroit in his senior year (he never graduated), Fraser's union sentiments and willingness to act on them were clear at the start. When asked years later what it was like working in a nonunion situation, Fraser pinpointed the emotional attraction of unionism. "The best way to describe it, to use an old-fashioned word," he said, was "that there was no *dignity*. You couldn't question any decisions and you couldn't dissent." In acting on his commitment he found himself fired from his first two jobs for union activity. In December 1936, in the midst of the sit-down strike wave that established the UAW in the industry, he took a job as a metal finisher in the Dodge Main plant (of Chrysler Corporation) because of its training program. Not long afterward he moved on to the company's DeSoto plant.

It was at DeSoto where Fraser began his career as a union official. He joined Local 227 of the UAW and advanced through the ranks as a steward, chief steward, recording secretary, and finally local union president in 1943. Thus, it was only with a bit of puffery that one of his early election flyers touted him as the best presidential candidate for his local because he "eats . . . breathes and *lives* unionism." As he said years later, "We were young and aggressive, and we got by and we learned. We were a little wild, but I think you had to be in those days." After serving in the army from 1945 to 1946, he returned to his union activities in the midst of a bitter political struggle for the presidency of the international union.

Douglas Andrew Fraser, second from right, facing camera, with the UAW lobbying team (courtesy George Tames, New York Times Pictures)

In 1946 Walter P. Reuther challenged incumbent president R. J. Thomas, who came up through a Chrysler local, for the UAW's highest office. The Addes-Thomas faction (so termed because its real leader was secretary-treasurer George Addes) combined nonaligned militant trade unionists with the union's Communist and far-left wings. The socialist-leaning Reutherites were considered to be ardent anti-Communists, and the competition foreshadowed the cold war battles against Communists in the Congress of Industrial Organizations (CIO), generally culminating in the expulsion of party-dominated industrial unions by CIO president Philip Murray in 1948. During the struggle in the UAW, Fraser sided with the Addes-Thomas caucus and somehow escaped the political repercussions after Reuther's victory in 1946 and his consolidation of power upon reelection in 1947. Fraser was appointed an international representative and subsequently participated in Reuther's eventual displacement of Communist influence in the union. Of that period he recalled the difficulty of the internal bat-

tles. The "Communists were well trained; they were good speakers; they had a sense of how to organize. . . . We were no match for them when we were kids," he judged, "but I think we got a little better than they did because we weren't hampered by their rigidity of thought."

Fraser's assignment as an international representative involved servicing Chrysler locals. In 1950 his performance as a negotiator during a 104-day strike against Chrysler attracted Reuther's attention to Fraser's skills and talents. Always on the lookout for leaders of promise, Reuther asked Fraser to become his administrative assistant—which he did—in 1951. From that position he participated intimately in the innovative and landmark bargaining victories won from all three automobile companies by Reuther and the UAW during the 1950s. "I stayed with Walter for eight years," said Fraser, of that time, "and I really loved working for him. You could get things done." Moreover, his mentor had a significant impact on his thinking. Fraser concluded that when he "went to work for Walter" he was "pretty doctrinaire" about union-company relationships. It was the UAW president, he believes, who "taught me flexibility." His job as Reuther's assistant, however, limited the scope of his contributions. He aspired to have more of an impact on union policy, and, when an opportunity presented itself in 1959, he won an election for a regional codirector's post in Region 1A. In 1962 he successfully ran for an executive board position as member-at-large.

It was following this election, during the 1960s, that his bargaining skills came to the forefront as he served as the chief Chrysler negotiator and liaison with the union's sometimes restive skilled trades workers. In 1964 he negotiated the pathbreaking concept of early retirement for workers with sufficient years of service to the company. In 1966 he became involved in a dispute between black assembly-line workers and skilled trades members of the union due to his promotion of increased minority recruitment programs, a longtime interest. The essence of the skilled trades workers' complaints was the narrowing of the gaps between skilled and unskilled. Fraser mediated the disagreements and succeeded in assisting the skilled trades workers in obtaining a constitutional amendment giving them the power to veto proposed contracts. The next year, in 1967, he was responsible for the first Chrysler U.S.-Canadian wage parity agreement. In these engagements with the corporation, as in internal union politics, Fraser managed to emerge with the respect of the opposition. According to a *New York Times* labor reporter, he was "an exceedingly tough-minded unionist, like most men who rise through the ferocious fighting that can characterize union politics." He "confronted his union rivals with intense vigor, in both private and public." The same would have to be said for his relations with automobile executives, where the force of his personality worked in his favor. "His word is enough for us," a Chrysler vice-president of industrial relations once said of him. "He gets into plant problems like no other union leader I know."

Shortly after Fraser had been elected as one of the six UAW vice-presidents in April 1970, Reuther was killed in an airplane crash in northern Michigan. Afterward, Fraser campaigned for the presidency but withdrew his name in favor of General Motors (GM) department head Leonard Woodcock, also a vice-president, when a poll of the executive board favored Woodcock by 13 to 12. Immediately,

in a spirit of unity, he nominated Woodcock to serve the last two years in Reuther's term. Although disappointed, he had more than enough challenges to occupy his time. In addition to heading the Chrysler department, he now directed the skilled trades and office, technical, and professional organizing departments. An ardent liberal Democrat, he also considered a race for the U.S. Senate but decided against it because his record as a strong supporter of civil rights and his pro-school-busing stand—especially unpopular in Michigan at the time—would probably have led to his defeat.

In the 1970s union leadership began to face quite different challenges from those encountered during the founding decades. The job of ensuring a decent standard of living and due process had largely been accomplished. Established union leaders now represented a young, better-educated, and restless automobile production work force often militant enough to engage in wildcat strikes. In bargaining Fraser used these developments as arguing points in his advocacy of improving the deadly tedious job structures prevalent in the auto industry. He pressed Chrysler executives to "humanize" jobs, insisting that not only would it be good for the workers but that it would decrease rampant absenteeism and turnover as well and lead to better productivity. In the 1973 bargaining round—during which he and Woodcock established the historic "30 - and - Out" early retirement pattern and substantial improvements in health and safety conditions after a nine-day strike—his arguments seemed to be borne out as Chrysler workers engaged in a series of wildcat strikes in protest of working conditions. Although Fraser agreed with the wildcatters about the conditions, he repudiated their unauthorized tactics.

Soon, however, that militancy dissipated as the industry's job security became even more tenuous. In the 1976 negotiations, his last as vice-president, Fraser received a preview of the bargaining conditions he would have to deal with as president of the international union. The oil-related recession of the mid 1970s had resulted in substantial layoffs. Fraser focused on shortening working time through increased time off and restrictions on compulsory overtime in hopes of stimulating callbacks. He also succeeded in enriching the Supplemental Unemployment Fund for those who were not to be quickly brought back.

Fraser's support of UAW president Woodcock placed him in a good position to succeed to the union's presidency when the latter retired in 1977. At the 1977 Los Angeles convention Woodcock returned the favor to Fraser when he nominated him as the executive board's candidate for president. With little difficulty Fraser won election as the sixth president of the UAW.

In his acceptance address, the new union president only spoke sketchily about collective bargaining initiatives and instead discussed in general terms the difficulties of representing workers in an industry facing sweeping change. "My generation of leadership is in the habit of telling younger people how difficult it used to be in the '30s and '40s—and it was difficult physically," he told the delegates at the beginning of his remarks. "But society today is much more complicated. Your job in the local union and ours in the International Union is much more complex than it ever was before," he pointed out. And one "of the reasons is that things change more frequently now, and when they change they change more profoundly." How the union would deal with those changes—in bargaining with automotive companies, in dealing with government regulation of the industry, in politics—was still open in terms of specifics. But he was sure the UAW would be able to meet the challenge, even though many of its founding generation would soon pass from the scene. Discounting the arguments that the next generation of union leadership was not as idealistic as his because it had not experienced the sacrifices involved in establishing the union, he told the assembly that he did not believe it. Commitment "and dedication is an intellectual process," he argued, not an experiential one, "and I believe that the future leaders of our union will be as talented, as dedicated, as committed, and as idealistic as we are." In closing he exhorted his fellow unionists to maintain the union's historic commitment to social justice beyond the immediate work force it represented—with the unrepresented North Carolina worker struggling to live on $100 a week, with the black teenager in Cleveland who cannot find a job, with the elderly who can barely feed themselves on Social Security, and with the assembly worker "in the Ford plant in Spain who is still oppressed" and who does not enjoy the benefits of the American Ford workers. "That, after all," he insisted, "is what the UAW has been doing for the last 40 years. So let me say this finally, that on this very important moment in my life I offer you my commitment and all of my energy, and whatever talent that I possess,

and I dedicate it to this great institution called the UAW."

By now, at age sixty-one and possessed of a shock of white hair, Fraser's accessible manner and approachability marked him as a union president comfortable and at home in the company of rank-and-file workers. Moreover, his honesty enabled him to critically analyze his union and the automobile companies, as well as the labor movement and business generally. In his inaugural address he signaled that he realized that sweeping change was upon American business, and consequently the labor movement, and that he believed that one of the challenges of labor leaders would be to adjust creatively to those changes in a way that was consistent with union principles.

Realizing that challenge, however, was only the first step, and the next six years tested Fraser's leadership skills to their utmost. The next major bargaining rounds were scheduled for 1979, so the first two years of his presidency were limited to his efforts to reaffiliate the UAW with the American Federation of Labor (AFL)-CIO. The UAW had left the AFL-CIO, the umbrella organization advancing political action for most American international unions, in 1968. Reuther had disaffiliated his union from the federation, charging that the AFL-CIO's executive council under President George Meany's leadership lacked social vision and a desire to organize the unorganized. Fraser began negotiations on reaffiliation soon after he assumed office, desiring to add lobbying strength for labor in Washington. The new UAW president's proposals were structured around a proposed reaffiliation at the national level, with an option being left open for UAW state organizations to join their AFL-CIO counterparts if they desired. In addition Fraser wanted to ensure that the UAW would maintain an independent political voice through its Community Action Program (CAP). Ultimately the discussions succeeded, and the UAW rejoined the AFL-CIO under the presidency of Meany's successor, Lane Kirkland, in 1981.

More difficult, though, was the deteriorating situation in the automotive industry, which by the arrival of the 1979 negotiations had begun to fall apart. Bargaining at Ford and GM, both of which faced declining sales, proceeded somewhat predictably: the union won some gains in indexing pension benefits for current and future retirees, in improving the cost-of-living formula, and in reducing work time. It was at Chrysler, however, where Fraser confronted his first major challenge as UAW president, as it became apparent that the third-largest automobile manufacturer was on the verge of bankruptcy.

The combined shock of the oil embargo and increased foreign market penetration by most automobile imports sent car sales into a tailspin. In 1978 the automotive industry produced 9.3 million domestic vehicles. By 1982 sales had declined to 5.7 million units. Hundreds of thousands of autoworkers were placed on indefinite layoff as the troubles in the automotive industry became exacerbated by the sharpest recession to hit the American economy in decades.

Chrysler executives, strapped for cash and facing $1.1 billion in losses, turned to the U.S. government for the $1.5 billion in loan guarantees to enable the corporation to avoid bankruptcy. The UAW under Fraser threw its considerable clout behind the initiative, and in 1980 Congress, with the support of the Carter administration, passed the Chrysler loan guarantee bill. One of the conditions for that law, however, was a provision that UAW-represented Chrysler workers give up hundreds of millions of dollars in already-negotiated wages and benefits. Having convinced himself that Chrysler was indeed on the precipice, Fraser led in the renegotiation of concessions both then and again in 1981, when the union gave up another $622 million. In exchange workers received stock options that would accumulate to 16 percent in a few short years. Even more significantly, as a quid pro quo for union assistance, Fraser was named as a member of the Chrysler board of directors in 1980. While company management insisted that Fraser's seat was *not* an official UAW seat, in his proxy statement to shareholders Fraser insisted he was accepting the position as a representative of the Chrysler workers.

That Fraser was able to do so in a union long known for militant, adversarial rhetoric, and in a way in which he won the respect of other Chrysler board members, says much about his leadership abilities. This experience, starting with Chrysler in 1980 and continuing into the 1982 bargaining with Ford and GM, convinced him that international competitive pressures were forcing vast changes to which he and his union must respond. "One of the difficulties with institutions generally–government, educational institutions, management–is a seeming inability to change," he later said in an interview. "There's no flexibility, only rigidity. And that was

true of the labor movement also." In his view, flexibility would have to mean an expansion of the areas in which American manufacturers and the UAW could fruitfully cooperate to advance productivity by advancing workplace democracy. And realistically, he later acknowledged that "I suppose it came about not intellectually, but probably out of necessity because of the adversity we faced, and we reached the conclusion that if we're going to be competitive, we're going to have to cooperate in many areas."

The Chrysler experience, though, was only the first step. In the 1982 negotiations Fraser encountered concession demands from both Ford and GM. With the economy in the depths of recession, mass layoffs in the automotive industry in all three automakers, and the specter of plant closings and more outsourcing of production looming in the background, the UAW president made the best of a bad situation by negotiating concessionary agreements in the face of significant internal union opposition, particularly at GM. The UAW president used the unwanted opportunity to make advances in what he considered important areas. In bargaining these agreements the UAW stressed a variety of job security and retaining arrangements and expansion of employee involvement decision making on the shop floor, in addition to negotiating profit-sharing plans. On the political front, under his direction the UAW advanced the concept of trade content legislation, common in many other countries, to halt the advance of foreign-manufactured automobiles and automotive parts. Though it did not pass Congress (succeeding only in the House), the pressure the campaign produced forced even the conservative, free-trade oriented Reagan administration to negotiate voluntary automobile-import quotas with the Japanese government. In addition the UAW became a strong contributor to policy debates on the desirability of a national industrial policy for the United States.

Even though the 1982 contracts generated a good deal of intraunion turbulence, Fraser remained convinced that the course he steered the union toward was the correct one. "We're now involved in international competition; we're never going back to the old ways," he contended. The challenge for his union in the future, he thought, was to continue to find ways through bargaining in which it could continue to "democratize" labor relations. Unions "can no longer be content merely to react and protest company decisions after they have made the decisions, after they are irreversible, and you can't do anything about them," he told a UAW gathering. "The principle involved here is that workers must have a greater voice in their own future and their own destiny," and that meant involvement from top to bottom.

Of course, not unexpectedly, his codirectors on the Chrysler board did not always see the issue in just that way. Although his demeanor in corporate board meetings won him respect among the other members, he did not miss any opportunity to be the voice of Chrysler workers in top-level management decision making. "A lot of times business uses labor as a crutch ... to hide their [*sic*] own failings," he told an interviewer. "A lot of the competitive difficulties are because of poor management. I'm not saying they're all to blame, and I'm not saying that labor unions are faultless," he said. "All I'm saying is that everyone's contributed to the problem."

As a board member he could point this out, participate in strategic corporate planning, and have needed access to financial information. Moreover, he strove to inform the company's directors of the human impact of their decisions to close plants and lay off workers, so effectively that one board member said that "you could feel the shock go through the board room" when he did so. "I've talked to a lot of board members since then," the UAW president later recounted, "and they said they had just never thought of it. I thought to myself, 'That tells the whole story.'" While conceding that his role on the board was a form of "tokenism" and that the impact of his arguments was circumscribed, he insisted that there was value in having union representation at the highest echelons of the enterprise. "The role the labor union now plays [without such representation] is just inadequate to present and protect the workers' interests and jobs."

In 1983 Fraser retired from union leadership. In his last speech to the UAW convention electing his successor, Owen Bieber, he ruminated over the events of the past six years as well as the challenges ahead. At the close he told of how proud he had been to be a member of the UAW, a union that had never forgotten that it was its "brother's keeper" even as it expanded its "capacity and courage to change with the times." And in a personal note, he said, "when I pass the torch of the presidency ...

as I said in the testimonial dinners that we've had, this union owes me nothing, and I owe it everything. This union has been my school and my college and my education. This union has opened the door to worlds that I never dreamed of... It wasn't me who went through the door, it was you ... because you let me be a leader of this great institution. You have enabled me to lead a rich and rewarding life, and you've enabled me to experience that greatest of all feelings—of helping those that [*sic*] can't help themselves and giving me the power to right some wrongs."

Fraser, upon leaving the UAW, took up an active career as a university professor of labor studies at Wayne State University, where his second wife, Winifred Fraser, is an associate dean. Assuming the presidency of the UAW at the height of an automobile-industry boomlet, he led the union through some of its most challenging moments since its founding in the 1930s. Although critics charged that he was overly friendly and understanding to automobile corporations and business concerns, there can be no doubt that he responded in an innovative way to the adversity besetting the industry, using the granting of concessions as a lever to foster a somewhat different climate in labor relations. Judging that in a global economy automobile labor relations could not much afford the luxury of being reflexively adversarial, he focused on achieving job security gains even as he pursued his objective of broadening workplace democracy in U.S. automobile factories, on both the shop floor and in corporate boardrooms, a course that his successor has likewise continued.

Publication:

"My Years on the Chrysler Board," *Across the Board*, 23 (June 1986): 33.

Unpublished Documents:

"Keynote Speech, UAW President Douglas A. Fraser, Los Angeles, California, 18 May 1977," UAW, *Proceedings of the Constitutional Convention*, 1977 (Archives of Labor History and Urban Affairs, Walter P. Reuther Library, Wayne State University, Detroit, Mich.);

"Report of the President, Douglas A. Fraser," UAW, *Proceedings of the Constitutional Convention*, 1983 (Archives of Labor History and Urban Affairs, Walter P. Reuther Library, Wayne State University, Detroit, Mich.).

References:

"Douglas A. Fraser," *Biographical Dictionary of American Labor,* edited by Gary M. Fink, second edition (Westport, Conn.: Greenwood Press, 1984);

Kirkland Ropp, "Douglas Fraser: a Unique Perspective," *Personnel Administrator,* 32 (September 1987): 82;

William Serrin, "Working for the Union: An Interview with Douglas A. Fraser," *American Heritage,* 36 (February-March 1985): 56.

Archives:

Material on Fraser is located in the records at the UAW President's Office: Douglas A. Fraser Files, Archives of

Joseph Washington Frazer

(March 4, 1892-August 8, 1971)

by Mark S. Foster

University of Colorado at Denver

CAREER: Dealer, Packard Motor Company (1916-1919); assistant treasurer, General Motors Acceptance Corporation (1919-1923); vice-president and general sales manager, Pierce-Arrow Finance Corporation (1923-1924); assistant to the vice-president, Maxwell-Chalmers Motor Company (1924-1927); general sales manager, vice-president, Chrysler Corporation (1927-1939); president, Willys-Overland, Inc. (1939-1944); chairman of the board, Graham-Paige Motors Corporation (1944-1945); president (1945-1949), board of directors, Kaiser-Frazer Corporation (1945-1953); chairman of the board, Sterling Engine Company (1951-1954).

Despite an upper-middle-class background and education at elite Hotchkiss and Yale, Joseph W. Frazer entered the automobile business at the bottom, as a mechanic's helper, and near its infancy in 1912. He learned many important phases of the business at an early age: design, production, accounting, finance, and sales. During the 1920s and 1930s he offered many innovations in installment financing and sales, first with General Motors Acceptance Corporation (GMAC) and later in association with several companies headed by Walter P. Chrysler. Frazer was closely involved with development of several important segments of Chrysler Motors, including the Plymouth and DeSoto divisions. In 1939 he was elected president of Willys-Overland, which during World War II concentrated on producing jeeps for the military. Between 1939 and 1944 corporate sales increased from $7 million to $170 million. In August 1945 he and Henry J. Kaiser organized Kaiser-Frazer Corporation with Frazer as president and Kaiser chairman of the board. Between 1946 and suspension of conventional motor

Joseph Washington Frazer

vehicle output in 1955, Kaiser-Frazer produced almost 750,000 cars. In 1947 and 1948 the organization briefly became the fourth largest car manufacturer in the United States. Although Frazer maintained his position as a member of the board until 1953, Frazer and Kaiser disagreed over corporate policy in 1949, and his active participation in the automobile industry ended at mid century.

Frazer, a direct descendant of Martha Washington, was born in Nashville, Tennessee, on March 4, 1892. His father, James S. Frazer, was an attorney for the Louisville & Nashville Railroad. Unfortunately the elder Frazer died when Joseph was just six weeks old; yet he left his family in comfortable financial circumstances. Frazer was sent to the Hotchkiss School in Connecticut, then to the Sheffield Scientific School at Yale. A husky six footer, he played football in college. Growing restless with book learning and academic theory, the twenty-year-old left Yale for Detroit in 1912.

Frazer obtained a job at Packard Motor Company's plant as a mechanic's helper at 16¢ per hour. Even working six twelve-hour days, he may have needed some help from home. Frazer never forgot the exhaustion he felt late on his shifts: "they didn't get much out of me those last two hours of the day." In later years, when he employed thousands of men, his vivid recollections of factory life induced him to take a liberal view toward workers. Meanwhile he longed for relief from manual labor, and his polished social skills and family connections landed him a job as a salesman for Packard in New York City. He enjoyed sales and soon earned an income permitting him to marry college sweetheart Lucile Frost of Chicago in 1914. The couple returned to Nashville, where Frazer became a partner in his brother's automobile agency. But in 1916 he was ready once again to strike out on his own, this time with his own Packard dealership in Cleveland.

The World War I years were tumultuous in the automobile business, with many plants converting to war production. At the end of the war Frazer returned to Detroit; in 1919 his more specialized training commenced. He joined the export division of General Motors Corporation (GM), and later that year became assistant treasurer of GMAC, which was initiating installment buying for consumers. In the early 1920s Frazer served as liaison officer between GMAC and the Chevrolet division. One biographer notes that "[he was] an energetic and successful salesman . . . from the first, a pioneer in the evolution of automobile sales paper and one of the leading architects of the general financial structure of the industry."

Frazer's talents in automobile financing quickly attracted recognition within the automobile industry and in national banking circles. In 1923 New York banking interests asked GM to "loan" Frazer to Pierce-Arrow's Buffalo, New York, office.

There he organized that company's finance operations, and he was promoted to vice-president and general sales manager. In 1924 he joined Walter P. Chrysler at Maxwell-Chalmers Motor Company. Although they remained associates for fifteen years, Frazer ruefully recalled their initial endeavor, selling "about as poor a vehicle as was ever sold as an automobile." Before they sold 1924 models, Frazer hoped to unload unwanted 1923 cars. Years later Frazer challenged an interviewer: "Did you ever try to sell anybody a 1923 Maxwell?"

Chrysler thought highly of his thirty-five-year-old sales associate. In 1927 Frazer joined Chrysler Corporation as general sales manager and rose through the ranks quickly. Frazer enjoyed job security during the depression but hardly thought of it in those terms. He had the almost impossible job of trying to sell cars in a rapidly shrinking market. Despite hard times, he proved his mettle and became vice-president of sales at Chrysler. A means of stimulating automobile sales previously demonstrated by Alfred P. Sloan, Jr., at GM was offering a wide range of models and prices. Frazer helped implement a similar strategy at Chrysler, overseeing the Plymouth and DeSoto divisions. Plymouth, a low-priced entry, helped keep Chrysler afloat during the depression. In 1930 it accounted for 28 percent of corporate sales; three years later Plymouths were 72 percent of unit sales.

In 1939 the forty-seven-year-old Frazer was in his prime, a seasoned industry veteran, steeled by his experience helping a major producer survive hard times. He might have rested on his laurels, but he accepted when Willys-Overland offered him a position as president. The Toledo-based company had little capital, large debts, thousands of unsold 1938 models, and uninspired offerings for the new year. In less than a year Frazer turned the company around; late in 1939 it recorded its first quarterly profit in two years. By the end of 1939 monthly production reached 4,000 units; better yet, in the first four months of 1940 sales exceeded the 1939 total by 150 percent. Willys-Overland sold economy, claiming that it produced "the lowest-priced standard size car in the world."

World War II brought entirely new challenges, but they marked Frazer's happiest and most productive years. Like other car manufacturers, Willys-Overland converted to military production. In 1939 the firm had sales of just over $7 million; five years later business reached $170 million. Although the company did not invent the general purpose vehicle known as the "jeep," Frazer's publicity agents effectively connected it to Willys-Overland, and it accounted for most of the company's wartime contracts. Frazer also served the Office of Production Management (OPM) and later the War Production Board (WPB) as one of a select group of eleven automobile industry advisers. The military asked Frazer to help the Warren (Ohio) City Tank & Boiler Company, which was having trouble meeting its contracts. He took over both management and ownership of the concern in January 1944. In less than a year output quadrupled; having done the job at Warren, Frazer joined Graham-Paige Motors Corporation.

Frazer hoped to use Graham-Paige to fulfill larger ambitions. Like other experienced automobile executives who had labored many years for others, Frazer dreamed of producing cars bearing his name. To have a legitimate chance of success, Frazer had to raise money from bankers and find plants capable of producing tens of thousands of units each month. It was an enormous gamble.

Despite his solid credentials, Frazer received little encouragement from eastern bankers, so he headed west. In California he conferred with Amadeo P. Giannini, founder of Bank of America. Giannini had little interest in underwriting a Detroit-based company, preferring to encourage western industrial development. He advised Frazer to look up shipbuilder Henry J. Kaiser, who had a large, aggressive organization, access to private capital, and experience in dealing with government officials. Kaiser also had big ideas about entering the automobile industry. Frazer was wary about following Giannini's lead; he and Kaiser had exchanged public barbs in 1942 after the latter urged automobile manufacturers to start planning for peacetime production. Frazer had labeled Kaiser's suggestions "half-baked" and "stupid." But in the summer of 1945 each realized he needed the other to have a realistic chance of challenging the Big Three. On August 9, 1945, the Kaiser-Frazer company was incorporated in Nevada.

For several reasons there was a narrow window of opportunity for those desiring to enter the automobile industry after World War II. The Big Three, with most of its machinery and plants tied up in wartime production, required several months to reconvert to automobiles. During the war the government had built many plants which would be available for lease or sale at bargain rates. Labor leaders in Detroit were eager to encourage competitors for the Big Three; although their motives were readily transparent, they were in a position to assist new producers. Perhaps most important, the industry had not experienced "normal" markets since 1929. Wartime prosperity filled the pockets of prospective buyers with war bonds and overtime pay which they were anxious to spend on consumer goods. In a word, it was a sellers' market; car buyers would buy anything on wheels, and producers knew it.

The partners had to devise corporate strategy quickly. During the war Kaiser had dreamed of mass-producing a small, "poor man's" car in the $400 price range. But Frazer had designs for conventional, medium-priced cars, and time was of the essence. Frazer's strategy prevailed, primarily because they could get conventional cars on the market far more quickly. The partners moved with impressive speed. By late 1945 they had leased the gigantic Willow Run plant thirty miles outside of Detroit and had successfully marketed the first of three stock issues which eventually brought in $53 million in capital. The first issue was sold at $10 a share; by the time the first issues sold out, the price per share hit $24, which was destined to be its all-time peak.

Many industry insiders scoffed at Kaiser-Frazer. Frazer was a member of the club, but critics viewed Kaiser as an upstart entrepreneur, who succeeded as a businessman only with the help of millions of dollars in government contracts and loans. When the partners leased Willow Run, Detroit veterans snickered that they should name their models "Willit Run?" But in 1945 and 1946 all signs appeared positive. Newsmen had nicknamed Kaiser the "Miracle Man" for his production feats during World War II; certainly his name was magic in 1945. Frazer was a solid, experienced automobile man who knew how to assemble a dealer organization. They expected to lose money in 1946, the first year of actual production. Kaiser-Frazer produced only 11,754 cars and lost $19 million.

The next two years marked the heyday of Kaiser-Frazer. On September 25, 1947, the partners celebrated their 100,000th car; by then, Willow Run was churning out more than 15,000 automobiles per month. In 1947 Kaiser-Frazer produced 144,507 cars and earned $19 million. Although profits dropped to $10 million in 1948, output jumped to 181,316 vehicles. Kaiser-Frazer moved past every other independent producer and briefly assumed fourth place in the automobile sweepstakes. During 1947 and early 1948 their units sold well, and the partners appeared on the verge of seriously challenging the Big Three.

Unfortunately, their dreams collapsed all too soon. In retrospect it is clear that their star was falling by mid 1948. Production was at an all-time peak, but inventories were beginning to pile up. By then the Big Three were gaining enormous momentum. Customers clearly favored Chevrolets, Pontiacs, Fords, and Chryslers. Kaiser-Frazer dealers had to offer far more generous trade-in allowances in order to compete at all. Corporate results were catastrophic in 1949. Output dropped more than two-thirds from its 1948 peak, dealers had difficulty unloading a mere 58,281 cars, and the company lost over $30 million. Despite heroic attempts after 1949 Kaiser-Frazer was doomed. Corporate leaders introduced an early "compact," the "Henry J," but it was ahead of its time and failed to capture the public's fancy. By 1955, when Kaiser-Frazer suspended production of conventional automobiles and sold most of its machinery, the company had lost a total of $123 million.

By then Frazer's participation in corporate affairs had long since tapered off. Kaiser and his men had taken over the company, and Frazer, seeing the handwriting on the wall long before his less experienced partner, permitted himself to be eased out. In retrospect Frazer might have gotten the better of it. Reasons for the company's failure certainly transcended differences between the two men. Kaiser later admitted that corporate strategists had raised far too little capital when public confidence was high; the company simply did not have the funds required to compete with the Big Three in research, design, and development of new models. Frazer shared the blame for starting with insufficient capital. But Kaiser made the mistake of pushing for all-out production in 1948 despite declining sales. Kaiser and his men presided over the decline of the company. Edgar F. Kaiser, Henry's older son, took over as president in 1949; Frazer remained a director until 1953 at a handsome salary of $75,000, but after 1950 his participation in corporate affairs was largely symbolic.

Frazer was unfortunate in that he was remembered more for his one great failure than for his many successes. The breakup of the partnership was an unhappy occasion; although the two remained on civil terms, the same could not be said for the dozens of high-level executives loyal to one or the other. Frazer, a physically vigorous man, was only fifty-seven when he stepped down as president of Kaiser-Frazer; he was not ready to retire. He served as chairman of the board for Sterling Engine Company from 1951 to 1954 and also held management positions in the Standard Uranium Company and the Frazer-Walker Aircraft Corporation.

Yet from the mid 1950s on Frazer basically relaxed and enjoyed life. He and Lucile had one daughter, Aerielle. The former football player remained husky all his life, and he enjoyed outdoor activities. He played golf but admitted that he never broke one hundred. His main outdoor avocation was farming, which he enjoyed on a genteel level. He "ranched" in Arizona and owned an Ohio farm where he raised walking horses. Frazer was Republican in politics and Episcopalian in religion. The former Yale man enjoyed an aristocratic life-style, holding memberships in numerous social clubs in Detroit, New York, and Newport, Rhode Island. He and Lucile owned a villa in Newport, where they spent most of their time in later years, enjoying the company of the rich and famous. Frazer died of cancer in Newport on August 8, 1971, at age seventy-nine.

References:

"Adventures of Henry and Joe in Autoland," *Fortune*, 33 (March 1946): 98-99, 101-103;

Mark S. Foster, "Challenger from the West: Henry J. Kaiser and the Detroit Auto Industry," *Michigan History*, 70 (January/February 1986): 30-39;

"Kaiser-Frazer Cashes In," *Fortune*, 36 (December 1947): 94-96;

"Kaiser-Frazer: The Roughest Thing We Ever Tackled," *Fortune*, 44 (July 1951): 74-77, 154-162;

Richard M. Langworth, *Kaiser-Frazer: The Last Onslaught on Detroit* (Princeton, N.J.: Princeton Publishing, 1975).

Archives:

The Henry J. Kaiser papers are located at Bancroft Library, Berkeley, California.

Freightliner Corporation

by George S. May

Eastern Michigan University

Freightliner Corporation was established by Leland James as a subsidiary of Consolidated Freightways of Salt Lake City, the trucking company that James had founded in 1929. Freightliner evolved from the interest James had in acquiring a light-weight truck that could still haul the largest load legally permitted. Not satisfied with what was available, he decided to build his own. Using lightweight aluminum construction, the prototype of the truck was developed in 1940. After the war construction of the cab-over-engine model began at a plant in Portland, Oregon. By 1948 some of the vehicles were being sold to other truckers who had become interested in the new trucks that Consolidated had on the road. Consolidated Freightways in 1951 entered into an agreement with White Motor to sell the trucks through White dealers under the White-Freightliner name. White also assumed the responsibility of providing after-sales service to the purchasers of the trucks. The agreement ended in 1977 when Freightliner set up its own network of dealers. Through an arrangement with Volvo, these dealers also offered light-and medium-weight models manufactured by that Swedish company. In 1981 the link between Volvo and Freightliner was cut, and the company was sold by Consolidated Freightways to Daimler-Benz for a reported figure of about $225 million. The purchase gave Daimler-Benz, the world's largest manufacturer of heavy-duty trucks, greater access to the American market, both through the sale of Freightliner trucks, which retained their separate identity, and through the use of Freightliner dealers as outlets for imported Mercedes-Benz trucks.

Since their first appearance in the 1940s, Freightliner trucks have undergone relatively few changes. Conventional models were added in 1973 to a product line that had been until then exclusively of the forward-control, cab-over design. Some 80 percent of the parts were interchangeable between these two types. With weights that differed by only 100 to 200 pounds, both retained the advantage of being able to carry a greater payload than any other trucks in their class—those with gross weights of 33,000 pounds or more. Freightliner trucks were favorites with owner-operators, who constituted the bulk of the company's customers, because although they were expensive, their large payloads meant more dollars per trip while the luxurious interiors provided comforts that lessened the hardships of the long hauls.

Sales, which had slumped badly at the end of the 1970s, rebounded in the 1980s, with over 16,000 units produced in 1985, an eight-fold increase over production figures of the early 1960s. In addition to its main Portland plant, Freightliner also had factories in Chino, California; Indianapolis, Indiana; Mt. Holly, North Carolina; and Vancouver, Canada. A factory in Hampton, Virginia, where Mercedes-Benz trucks were assembled, had also been made part of the Freightliner organization when it became a Daimler-Benz subsidiary.

References:

Nick Baldwin, *Trucks of the Sixties and Seventies* (London: Frederick Warne, 1980);

"Daimler-Benz Ups Its U.S. Truck Power," *Business Week* (March 23, 1981): 40-41;

Nick Georgano, *World Truck Handbook*, new edition (London: Jane's Publishing, 1986);

James Wren and Genevieve Wren, *Motor Trucks of America* (Ann Arbor: University of Michigan Press, 1979).

General Motors Corporation

by Northcoate Hamilton

Columbia, South Carolina

The founding of the General Motors (GM) Company on September 16, 1908, began the formal process of building the largest automobile manufacturer in the world. Within two months GM had acquired the assets of the Buick Motor Car Company and the Olds Motor Vehicle Company, setting in motion the consolidation among automobile manufacturers that has been the dominant characteristic of the industry. But of course GM did not spring fully grown as the corporate giant of the present day. Rather, the venture was an exceedingly risky investment in a risky industry. Of the nearly 1,000 companies which entered the business prior to 1927, fewer than 200 were viable long enough actually to produce a commercially suitable vehicle. That GM was able to survive, and even to prosper, is monument to the intelligence and determination of the several individuals who guided its founding, development, and maturation.

The man behind GM was William Crapo Durant, an automaker and entrepreneur with a flair for risky, visionary projects. By the end of 1909 Durant had gathered under the GM umbrella twenty-two independent businesses, including Buick, Olds, Cadillac, Oakland, Ewing, Marquette, Welch, Scripps-Booth, Sheridan, Cartercar, Elmore, Ranier, Rapid, and Reliance. The rapid, almost impulsive, acquisition of smaller car companies was the most significant characteristic of Durant and the early GM. As many of the firms were weak and financially shaky, GM suffered from the resulting strain on finances.

Durant lost control of GM twice, the first time in 1910 as a result of the company's wretched financial condition. A banker's trust took over management of the firm, and Durant left to found Chevrolet. In 1916 Durant returned to GM, with his Chevrolet company acquiring the larger company. In 1918 GM in turn acquired Chevrolet and, with Durant again in control, began another spate

William C. Durant, founder of General Motors

of acquisitions. Included in these purchases were Samson, a tractor manufacturer; Northway Motors; Champion Ignition; Guardian Frigerator, which later become Frigidaire; Hyatt Bearings; and Dayton Engineering Laboratories. Although most of these companies brought great benefits to GM, especially Champion, Hyatt, which brought Alfred P. Sloan, Jr., and Dayton, which brought Charles F. Kettering, the added financial burden portended disaster when the economy slumped in 1920.

One of Durant's great problems was his mania for autocratic control. During the early years of GM, this management style had been beneficial, giving Durant the power to make needed decisions. But it also gave Durant the opportunity to make serious mistakes. In addition the growing size of the company made it increasingly difficult to coordinate the various divisions or even to gather information. Although assets had increased from $135 million in 1918 to over $575 million in 1920, the underlying weakness of the company was revealed in the 1920 depression by GM's plummeting sales.

Durant's dealings in the stock market caused complementary problems. As the market faltered, Durant invested more and more cash in order to support and stabilize GM stock. When the bankers learned that GM was in serious trouble and that Durant was also near bankruptcy, the company's founder was persuaded to leave GM. His exit was made much easier to take by the banker's agreement to provide $30 million to Durant in order to pay his debts.

In Durant's place, Pierre S. du Pont took over GM. This new beginning in 1920 marks the true emergence of the modern GM. With du Pont in charge, and Du Pont interests gaining a large percentage of ownership in the company, GM received over $100 million in needed funds from the House of Morgan. In addition the company also instituted a much needed reorganization plan. Formulated by Sloan, and similar to an earlier structure introduced at Du Pont, the system of decentralization and financial control created at GM in the early 1920s was the most influential management innovation of the century. Sloan envisioned a corporation in which each division was relatively autonomous but also had specific market targets. Chevrolet, for example, was targeted for the low end of the market while Cadillac, with a reputation for quality dating back to 1904, was marketed for the luxury car segment. The rest of the GM divisions, Oakland, Oldsmobile, and Buick, and later Pontiac and La Salle, filled market holes in between.

This plan not only aimed at maximum market coverage and penetration but also corresponded to Sloan's accurate divination of changing market conditions. By the 1920s the American automobile market was beginning to change from one dominated by first-time buyers. Sloan correctly reasoned that for the industry, and particularly GM, to continue to prosper, ways had to be found to stimulate the replacement market. Sloan's organizational plan was one method, in that it instituted a clear class structure to GM's automobile lines. This class structure was upwardly mobile, meaning that a buyer could theoretically purchase additional stature by moving from a Chevrolet to a Pontiac and from that line to a more expensive car.

Sloan also institutionalized the annual model change, through which an older car could be identified as such and would, Sloan thought, therefore be an incentive to buy a new model. But Sloan knew that "planned obsolescence" could not rest on mechanical innovation. In 1927 GM created its Art and Colour Section, led by the famed stylist Harley Earl, which helped to create the aesthetic, rather than mechanical, emphasis of the annual model change. Sloan's changes contributed to GM's emergence as the industry leader. In 1926 GM sold over 1.25 million vehicles. In 1927 Chevrolet alone outsold Ford, the number two manufacturer.

GM took the lead not only in styling and sales but also in research and financing. Kettering oversaw the GM Research Corporation and led the search for innovations such as the self-starter, antiknock gasoline, the octane rating, and others. Another product innovation, Duco lacquer paint, was introduced by Du Pont but directly benefited GM by aiding Earl's styling efforts. In 1919 GM created the GM Acceptance Corporation (GMAC), which extended credit to dealers and customers. GMAC provided installment credit, which allowed buyers to pay for cars on time, ranging from twelve to twenty-four months. All of these factors contributed to the glut of automobile sales in the 1920s and the increasingly unsustainable level of those sales as the decade neared its end.

Increasing competition, expanded production capacity, bloated credit, narrowing profit margins, and a saturated market all spelled trouble for the automobile industry. The depression, which began in earnest in 1933, proved the final catalyst for the consolidation of the industry into an oligopoly. Production of automobiles in 1932 declined 75 percent from 1929 levels. This market tightening came on the heels of a decade which had already reduced the number of automobile-producing firms from 108 in 1923 to 44 in 1927. GM, however, emerged from the depression unscathed. It did not emerge unchanged.

The depression, and the rise of Franklin Roosevelt and the New Deal, placed a new emphasis on labor relations in the automobile industry. The National Labor Relations Act (NLRA) was passed in

The GM headquarters in Detroit (courtesy of the library of the Campbell-Ewald Company)

1935 after the Supreme Court ruled the National Industrial Recovery Act (NIRA) unconstitutional. The NLRA, known as the Wagner Act, gave workers the right to unionize and prohibited "unfair labor practices" by management. Autoworkers, who had long been unsuccessful in organizing the industry and who were emboldened by the NLRA, began a long effort to unionize the work force of the industry leader, GM. In December 1936 the United Automobile Workers (UAW) closed down GM's Fisher Body plant in Flint, Michigan, by using the illegal but effective tactic of a sit-down strike. When the Michigan governor, Frank Murphy, refused to intervene in favor of the company's legal rights, GM surrendered to the union on February 11, 1937. After GM capitulated, Chrysler soon followed. Ford held out until 1941.

Shortly after the Flint sit-down strike, on May 3, 1937, Sloan moved from the presidency of GM to the position of chief executive officer. As long as Sloan occupied the position of ultimate power at GM, which he did until 1956, the delicate balance between the engineering and financial sections of the

company was more or less maintained. Harlow H. Curtice, a former bookkeeper and GM president from 1953 to 1958, made decisions heavily weighted in favor of the financial side of the business, but he made these decisions largely outside of the decision-making structure so painstakingly built by Sloan. When Sloan retired and was replaced by Albert Bradley, an accountant, the GM hierarchy was dominated by men centered in the financial division.

During the decades following World War II, demand for cars was so strong that mechanical innovation played very little part in the industry. As a result the "bean counters," as the financial men were derisively known, were very successful in generating high profits by merely increasing production. Research, quality, and technology all were deemed less important than the bottom line. Had the world remained the same, this approach might have reaped nothing but benefits. But the world changed. In the 1960s inflation and higher labor costs drove the price of cars higher, and some lower-cost imports, notably the Volkswagen Beetle, began

Alfred P. Sloan, Jr., in suit, shaking hands, and William S. Knudsen, with hat in hand, greeting workers at a GM plant in southern California

to make large inroads in the American market. GM and the other American manufacturers, except American Motors, did not aggressively fight the foreign manufacturers. Once again the world situation changed in a way that worked most negatively on GM's strategies.

The Arab oil embargo of 1973-1974 and the price shock of 1979 fundamentally altered the automobile market. Smaller cars, which GM and other manufacturers had rejected as being unpopular with the big-car-fixated public, became best-sellers because of their lower price and high mileage ratings. This change in the domestic market also corresponded with the rapid industrialization of much of the rest of the world. The effect on American manufacturers, including GM, is gleaned from the fact that American manufacturers took 76.2 percent of the world market in 1950 while only occupying 19.3 percent in 1982.

During the 1960s and 1970s GM and the other domestic manufacturers gained a reputation for corporate irresponsibility and mechanical shoddiness. Ralph Nader's exposé of the Chevrolet

Corvair in his book *Unsafe at Any Speed* (1965), and the admission by GM that Nader had been harassed by private detectives hired by the corporation, helped increase this perception. Frederic G. Donner, GM's chief executive officer, and James Roche, the corporation's president, were called to testify in 1965 before a U.S. Senate committee chaired by Abraham Ribicoff. During the hearing GM was chastised for spending so little of its research and development money on automobile safety. The somewhat overripe political environment of the 1960s led the government to impose strict and wide-ranging regulations on safety equipment, regulations which added to the burdens of the manufacturers.

GM's problems in the late 1960s and early 1970s were perhaps best exemplified by the development and introduction of the Chevrolet Vega, GM's long-delayed and -awaited small car. The product of GM president Edward Cole's vision and millions of research funds, the Vega was introduced in 1970 to lukewarm sales, questions about its quality, and labor unrest. The Lordstown, Ohio, factory where the Vega was produced and new labor techniques were used became a hotbed of worker dissatisfaction. Strikes in both 1970 and 1971 helped dampen sales of the car, and the quality problems doomed the car to be much less successful than GM had hoped.

The 1979 oil price shock exacerbated the problems faced by the American automobile industry. In addition to almost bankrupting Chrysler and raising grave doubts about Ford's future, the economic dislocation of the price rise, quickly followed by the 1982 recession, shook GM to its foundations. Far from controlling 50 percent of the domestic market as it had in the 1950s, GM was faced with accepting a 35-percent share of the market as its upper limit. And entering the late 1980s GM had yet to formulate an entire line of cars seriously competitive with the Japanese, the Europeans, and even with the rebounding Ford and Chrysler. In fact, in 1986, 1987, and 1988, Ford earned more profits than GM, a spectacular feat considering Ford's smaller size. But Roger Smith, GM's chief executive officer since 1981, scheduled to serve until 1989, began the process of finding cars which would return GM to its accustomed place of industry leadership. In 1985 GM announced the formation of the Saturn Corporation, a wholly owned subsidiary slated to produce a high-technology small car. The cornerstone of the Saturn, which is planned to be built in Spring Hill, Tennessee, is a groundbreaking agreement with the UAW. Productivity is to be increased and labor costs slated to be more predictable. Unfortunately, as the 1980s end, rumors abound that the Saturn will never be built. Regardless, GM recorded record profits in 1988, but its problems could not seriously be considered as being ended.

References:

Ed Cray, *The Chrome Colossus: General Motors* (New York: McGraw-Hill, 1980);

Ralph C. Epstein, *The Automobile Industry: Its Economic and Commercial Development* (Chicago: A. W. Shaw, 1928);

Federal Trade Commission, *Report on the Motor Vehicle Industry* (Washington, D.C.: GPO, 1939);

James J. Flink, *The Automobile Age* (Cambridge, Mass.: MIT Press, 1988);

Lawrence R. Gustin, *Billy Durant: Creator of General Motors* (Grand Rapids, Mich.: William B. Eerdmans, 1973);

Arthur Pound, *The Turning Wheel* (New York: Doubleday, 1934);

Richard P. Scharchburg, *W. C. Durant: The Boss* (Flint, Mich.: GMI, 1973);

Lawrence H. Seltzer, *A Financial History of the American Automobile* (Boston: Houghton Mifflin, 1928);

Bernard A. Weisberger, *The Dream Maker: William C. Durant, Founder of General Motors* (Boston: Little, Brown, 1979);

Lawrence J. White, *The Automobile Industry Since 1945* (Cambridge, Mass.: Harvard University Press, 1971).

Archives:

Material on GM and GM employees is located in the GMI Alumni Foundation Collection at GMI Engineering & Management Institute, Flint, Michigan.

Richard Charles Gerstenberg

(November 24, 1909-)

by George S. May

Eastern Michigan University

CAREER: Timekeeper, Frigidaire division (1932-1934), accountant, Fisher Body division (1934-1949), assistant comptroller (1949-1955), treasurer (1956-1960), vice-president in charge of finance staff (1960-1967), executive vice-president, finance (1967-1970), vice-chairman (1970-1971), chairman (1972-1974), director, General Motors Corporation (1967-1980).

Richard Charles Gerstenberg, whose tenure as chief executive officer of General Motors (GM) was one of the shortest but also one of the most critical periods in the company's history, was born on November 24, 1909, the son of Richard Paul and Mary Julia Booth Gerstenberg. He was born in Little Falls, New York, which, by coincidence, was also the birthplace of John Riccardo, who became Chrysler's chairman the year after Gerstenberg retired at GM. However, Gerstenberg grew up in the neighboring town of Mohawk, where his father was an inspector at the Remington Typewriter Company.

After graduating from high school Gerstenberg was accepted at Notre Dame, but he chose instead to enroll at the University of Michigan. The Ann Arbor university was the alma mater of Albert Bradley and Frederic Donner, the top men on GM's finance staff under whom Gerstenberg would eventually serve. While at Michigan, Gerstenberg helped to support himself by taking various jobs, and he graduated with a degree in business in 1931. With the country sliding deeper into the Depression Gerstenberg began his job search.

When Gerstenberg had left for college, his father had said to him, "I wish there was some way you could get a good education so you could get a good job with a big company and take things easy." Jobs of any kind were rare in summer 1931, however. Gerstenberg returned to Mohawk but found that there was nothing there for him in that

Richard Charles Gerstenberg

town of only 2,900 people. He then traveled to Detroit to be near his girlfriend and future wife, Evelyn Hitchingham, and also an older friend from Mohawk, H. Whitney Clapsaddle, who was an accountant in the comptroller's office at GM. When a neighbor of the Hitchinghams was injured in his job at a foundry, Gerstenberg replaced him, shoveling sand until the man was able to return to work. Gerstenberg then did some research for a University of Michigan professor while paying frequent visits to Clapsaddle's office in hopes of finding employment. Finally on April 1, 1932, on one of these visits, Wallace Kileen hired him.

Gerstenberg recited these details during the recession of the mid 1970s as an example of how persistence could pay off, even in bad times. He had received some help from his hometown, where an official at the Remington company had written a letter of recommendation to Kileen, declaring that "Young Dick is one of the ablest boys that Mohawk ever turned out, and he will be an asset to your company." (Showing the letter to a reporter in 1974, Gerstenberg said he "always kind of hoped that I would turn out and live up to his expectations.") The job was that of a timekeeper with the Frigidaire division of GM in Dayton, Ohio, at a salary of $125 a month, good wages in the Depression, although after a few weeks he was put on hourly wages, reducing his salary. Back in Mohawk, Gerstenberg said, his hiring "was a big event . . . one of their guys got a job with General Motors." But no one could have realized that the timekeeper's job was the first step that would lead Gerstenberg to the top position available in the biggest manufacturing company in the world.

In 1968, about four years before he became GM's chairman, Gerstenberg appeared before a Senate subcommittee headed by Sen. Abraham A. Ribicoff. Two other present or future GM chairmen, Frederic Donner and James Roche, had appeared before Ribicoff earlier. As had been the case when they had appeared, automotive safety was the subject on which Gerstenberg was asked to testify, in this case the prices charged for motor-vehicle safety equipment. In response to one question of a complicated technical nature Gerstenberg replied, "You are talking to old Gerstenberg the bookkeeper, Mr. Chairman. I am not an engineer." From then on any discussion of the GM executive in the press was likely to include a reference to "old Gerstenberg the bookkeeper." The self-description, although it may have been made in a jesting way, actually summed up rather accurately Gerstenberg's unspectacular career in the financial side of the business.

After two and a half years at Frigidaire, Gerstenberg was transferred to an accounting job at the Fisher Body division in Detroit, a move that provided the opportunity to marry Hitchingham in December 1934, with whom he had two children, a son and a daughter. It was not until World War II that Gerstenberg began to attract the attention of the top-level corporation executives, attention he gained when he helped to win approval from the Office of Price Administration for company price increases. "I spent months in Washington working on

the detailed end of the assignment," he recalled. "I really got a short course in the cost and pricing problems of General Motors in those days." After the war a report that he prepared attracted the attention of Frederic Donner and led to his appointment in 1949 as assistant comptroller. Seven years later he was named treasurer, and in 1960, with Donner now chairman and chief executive officer, Gerstenberg was promoted to vice-president in charge of the finance staff, a post that Donner had held in the 1940s. Gerstenberg's elevation in 1967, at age fifty-eight, to executive vice-president of finance was another sign that he was Donner's choice to succeed James Roche as chairman when Roche reached the mandatory retirement age of sixty-five in 1971.

As Roche's retirement drew nearer much speculation as to his successor centered on Edward Cole, who had taken over as president in 1967 when Roche moved from that job into the chairman's office. Cole was a production man, well known as an engineer who was responsible for such successes as the 8-cylinder Chevrolets of the mid 1950s as well as the innovative but ill-fated Corvair of the 1960s. Some thought Cole had two strikes against him for a personal life that had twice strayed from the norm expected of top GM executives: first, when he divorced his wife, and second, when he married an outspoken woman who did not fit the stereotyped image of the traditional GM executive's wife. But it is doubtful that Cole was ever seriously in the running for the chairman's job. Donner, who, although retired as an executive, was still the most powerful figure on the board of directors, was determined to see that the position of chief executive officer remained in the hands of men whose background was in the financial, not the production, side of the business. In 1970 Gerstenberg was moved into the newly created job of vice-chairman of the board and chairman of the finance committee, making him clearly the heir apparent to the chairman's job. He was elected to the chairman's post in December 1971, taking over on January 1, 1972. Cole continued as president, but a coolness in their relationship became quite noticeable. This strain resulted no doubt from both the competition for the top post and the differences growing out of their respective backgrounds in the company.

Gerstenberg was already sixty-two when he took over as chairman (his ninety-one-year-old father lived to see his son get the good job that he had hoped for). In less than three years he stepped down, scarcely enough time, one would think, for him to carry through any initiatives that would have any great impact. However, his choice as chairman had widespread support in the industry. "All of our profit margins have been eroding," another Big Three executive declared, "and we respect Dick Gerstenberg as a broad-gauge guy who will do the industry some good." Gerstenberg, in fact, had already accomplished a great deal for the industry before becoming chairman by serving on President Richard Nixon's Commission on International Trade and Investment Policy. Gerstenberg was credited with being the principal architect of the commission's recommendation which became the basis for Nixon's "New Economic Policy" in the last half of 1971. First by placing a 10-percent surcharge on all imports and then by devaluing the dollar, this policy suddenly made the price of American cars far more competitive with the imports, fueling a strong resurgence in American car sales in fall 1971 that pushed domestic automobile production over 9 million in 1972 for the first time in history and brought record or near-record profits to the automakers.

But although Nixon's actions had pushed the price of foreign cars up by as much as 40 percent, sales of imports kept pace with domestic car sales. One of the major problems Gerstenberg faced as chairman was the Chevrolet Vega—the highly touted small car that was supposed to have enabled GM to compete with the Volkswagen and the Japanese cars. Not only was the Vega not doing the job, but it was becoming a growing source of embarrassment to the company. In dealing with this and other problems, *Forbes* in June 1973 declared that Gerstenberg "was a refreshing contrast" to the corporation's leaders of the past who "rarely conceded that anything could go wrong in [that] best of all possible businesses." Gerstenberg readily admitted that GM "faced huge problems" and that the company did not possess all the answers. But he was not ready to concede that the firm's critics were right. When asked about the record number of recalls of GM cars, the Vega being the most notorious example, and how these reflected on the quality of workmanship and materials, Gerstenberg's response was to say: "I think it's a sign of stiffer standards. We've also got a much more complex product today than we ever had." As for the stories of labor unrest at the Lordstown, Ohio, plant where Vegas

were produced, he declared that "the newspapers and others wrote about it way out of proportion to its importance." The basis for the labor difficulties at Lordstown, he asserted, grew out of the fact that they had consolidated two existing plants, and there were always problems resulting from the reassignments and manpower reductions caused by such a consolidation.

On labor issues as a whole he was encouraged that the rates of absenteeism and labor turnover in GM plants had declined for the first time in ten years. He admitted that the changing work attitudes of the young people made it necessary to be sure "that supervisors in our plants are properly equipped to handle all these people in today's atmosphere." GM was doing that "in the vast majority of our plants today. . . . The vast majority of our people are damned good people. They want to do a good job." As for relationships with the United Automobile Workers (UAW), Gerstenberg declared that the union had to find better ways of resolving differences than through strikes and that he had been encouraged to see Leonard Woodcock, the UAW president, express the same sentiment. About the idea of submitting differences to compulsory arbitration, as the steel industry and the steel workers' union had agreed to do, Gerstenberg was doubtful. "I would hope we could find another way of doing it," Gerstenberg replied. "We kind of like to settle those things ourselves."

In summer 1973 GM and the automobile industry in general were still riding the crest of record sales and profits. The price of gasoline was rising, but Gerstenberg did not foresee an energy crisis. There was an energy problem, to be sure, but the head of the company best known for its big cars did not see gas prices forcing them to stop producing the large cars which consumed large amounts of fuel. "A lot of people are going to insist on having them. They're going to be willing to pay for the extra fuel to use them."

All that changed a few months later with the Arab oil embargo that quickly doubled gas prices. By 1974 GM was saddled with a huge inventory of large cars that suddenly nobody wanted and few of the small, fuel-efficient cars that were in great demand. Although Thomas A. Murphy and Elliott "Pete" Estes, who in late 1974 succeeded Gerstenberg and Cole as chairman and president respectively, have usually been credited with instituting GM's decision to "downsize" its entire line of cars, Gerstenberg is more entitled to the credit. Brock Yates quotes an unnamed GM executive who was present at Executive Committee meetings where the subject came up as saying that the idea first came from an outsider on the board of directors who traveled frequently in Europe and was always "harping on the fact that the automobiles in virtually every country in the world were smaller and more efficient than ours." Nobody paid the man any attention until Gerstenberg became interested, and it was the board chairman who then "pushed the whole idea. Ed Cole and most of the Executive Committee fought like hell. They wanted to increase fuel mileage simply by using lightweight materials and keeping the traditional, big sized cars. Believe me, there was plenty of desk pounding and cursing before Gerstenberg got his way." Already before the oil embargo Gerstenberg pointed out that a shift to smaller cars had been underway for some years, and they had to plan for an acceleration of this change as fuel prices went up. As for the effect of a shift away from the big cars, which were more profitable to make and sell, Gerstenberg, keeping a bookkeeper's eye on the bottom line, declared that "we ought to be smart enough to find a way" of building smaller cars "and not further encroach on our profit margin." By the time he retired in 1974 he was predicting that within four or five years small cars would account for considerably more than half of all sales.

At the end of November 1974, in his last week as chairman, Gerstenberg was, as always, upbeat. "I feel good about the future," he told a *New York Times* reporter, and to emphasize his optimism he pounded his fist on his desk. True, the industry was in the midst of one of its worst slumps since the depression, but, he said, "We'll come back. We always have and we always will." As he prepared to clean out his desk, he disagreed with other retiring automotive executives, notably his colleague Cole, who had said that they no longer found the industry to be as challenging or as interesting as it had been when they started out. The suggestion was that if they had known what lay ahead for them they would have gone into another line of work. Gerstenberg disagreed forcefully. "Hell, no," he said. "If I had to do it all over again I don't know of anything I would have done different from what I did. No, this has been an exciting thing." Gerstenberg refused to criticize the industry or GM. Loyalty to GM is a fact of life to Gerstenberg as is his unstinting support for the automobile business that "has been so good to me."

References:

Ed Cray, *Chrome Colossus: General Motors and Its Times* (New York: McGraw-Hill, 1980);

Forbes, 111 (June 15, 1973): 53-56;

Fortune, 89 (March 1974): 21;

Emma Rothschild, *Paradise Lost: The Decline of the Auto-Industrial Age* (New York: Random House, 1973);

Time, 98 (December 20, 1971): 69-70;

Brock Yates, *The Decline and Fall of the American Automobile Industry* (New York: Empire Books, 1983).

Graham-Paige Motors Corporation

by George S. May

Eastern Michigan University

Graham-Paige, organized in 1927, was, along with the later Kaiser-Frazer Corporation, the only new automobile company formed after Chrysler's appearance in 1925 to have any success in producing automobiles. Also like Kaiser-Frazer, Graham-Paige's success was not long lasting. (American Motors, formed in 1954, was not in the same sense a new company but was simply a merger of two existing companies which continued to produce already established lines of cars.)

Joseph B., Robert C., and Ray A. Graham, natives of Washington, Indiana, where they had been born in 1882, 1885, and 1887 respectively, were already successful businessmen with an impressive record in the automotive industry when they bought the Paige-Detroit Motor Car Company for $4 million on June 10, 1927. Their earlier Graham Brothers truck manufacturing company had been one of the most important in that field, but in 1925 and 1926, after several years in which their trucks were handled exclusively by Dodge dealers, Dodge exercised options it had obtained to purchase complete control of the brothers' truck business. The three brothers formed the Graham Brothers Corporation as a holding company for their older business interests but then reentered the automotive industry with their purchase of Paige-Detroit. That company, formed in 1909, once had a reputation as a producer of fine cars, but the firm had fallen on hard times by 1927. The new owners continued to produce cars under the Paige name through the remainder of 1927, and revived the name briefly in 1931 for commercial vehicles, but like Walter Chrysler, who abandoned the use of the Maxwell name shortly after using that company as the base on which he created his Chrysler Corporation, the Grahams wished to see their name appear on the cars their company would produce. They formed the Graham-Paige Motors Corporation, with Joseph serving as president, Robert as vice-president,

An advertisement for Graham-Paige's 1929 automobiles

and Ray as secretary-treasurer, while their father, Ziba, was a director. The Paige name was never dropped from the name of the company, but beginning in 1931 the cars bore the Graham name alone. The public found it hard to adjust to the change and continued to refer to the cars as Graham-Paiges.

The Graham brothers started well with their new automotive venture, producing 73,195 of their first Graham-Paige automobiles, which came in 4-, 6-, and 8-cylinder versions, in 1928, which was a record for a newly introduced automobile. Production in 1929 reached more than 77,000 cars, exceeding the first year's total, but the profits that had been shown on the books the previous year had been replaced by losses. These were the result of various poorly located, money-losing dealerships that were owned by the company, but before this problem could be corrected, the onset of the depression at the end of 1929 created financial problems from which Graham-Paige, like so many other smaller automakers, was never able to recover. Production fell off to only 33,560 cars in 1930, falling further by 1932 to less than 13,000. As economic conditions began to improve, Graham-Paige production and sales figures picked up slightly in mid decade only to fall off again, until less than 9,000 cars were produced in all of 1938, 1939, and 1940. Production ceased entirely in September 1940.

The Grahams put up a valiant fight. Although their initial cars were of a rather undistinguished design, the Grahams recognized, as did many other automakers, that style was becoming the most important factor in determining people's choice of an automobile. In 1928 Ray Graham commissioned the industrial designer Norman Bel Geddes to design a series of new cars, each progressively more radical in appearance, which they could introduce over a five-year period. Bel Geddes, who had designed settings for the brothers' annual company banquets, came up with a remarkable set of plans that were among the first to introduce aerodynamic elements to car styling. However, the onset of the Depression forced Graham-Paige to drop its plans to proceed with these cars, and its efforts to sell the plans to other companies were unsuccessful. These efforts to sell failed either because the companies could not afford to put these cars into production or because they may have shared the views of some Graham-Paige officials that the designs were too futuristic for the tastes of that day.

Graham-Paige did, however, bring out in 1932 a car that would be not only its best known offering but also one of the most famous cars of the entire period. This was the Graham Blue Streak, designed by Amos Northup, the stylist for the Murray Body Corporation, with some details added by the equally well-known designer Raymond Dietrich. Like the earlier proposed designs of Bel Geddes, Northup's design reflected the rising interest in streamlining features, but its most influential element was Northup's treatment of the automobile's

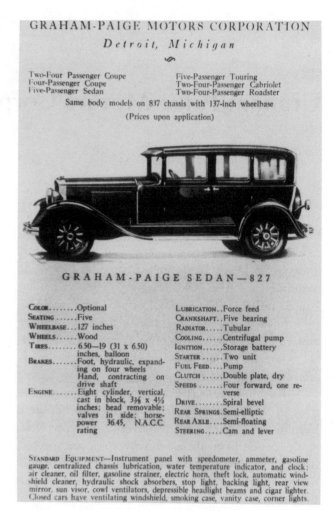

GRAHAM-PAIGE MOTORS CORPORATION
Detroit, Michigan

Two-Four Passenger Coupe	Five-Passenger Touring
Four-Passenger Coupe	Two-Four-Passenger Cabriolet
Five-Passenger Sedan	Two-Four-Passenger Roadster

Same body models on 837 chassis with 137-inch wheelbase

(Prices upon application)

GRAHAM-PAIGE SEDAN—827

COLOR	Optional	LUBRICATION	Force feed
SEATING	Five	CRANKSHAFT	Five bearing
WHEELBASE	127 inches	RADIATOR	Tubular
WHEELS	Wood	COOLING	Centrifugal pump
TIRES	6.50—19 (31 x 6.50) inches, balloon	IGNITION	Storage battery
BRAKES	Foot, hydraulic, expanding on four wheels Hand, contracting on drive shaft	STARTER	Two unit
		FUEL FEED	Pump
		CLUTCH	Double plate, dry
ENGINE	Eight cylinder, vertical, cast in block, 3⅜ x 4½ inches; head removable; valves in side; horsepower 36.45, N.A.C.C. rating	SPEEDS	Four forward, one reverse
		DRIVE	Spiral bevel
		REAR SPRINGS	Semi-elliptic
		REAR AXLE	Semi-floating
		STEERING	Cam and lever

STANDARD EQUIPMENT—Instrument panel with speedometer, ammeter, gasoline gauge, centralized chassis lubrication, water temperature indicator, and clock; air cleaner, oil filter, gasoline strainer, electric horn, theft lock, automatic windshield cleaner, hydraulic shock absorbers, stop light, backing light, rear view mirror, sun visor, cowl ventilators, depressible headlight beams and cigar lighter. Closed cars have ventilating windshield, smoking case, vanity case, corner lights.

Features of the 1929 Sedan-827

outer parts as one cohesive shell, including the addition of valances or skirting to the fenders which was the most copied part of his design. Later, in 1938, another of Northup's designs for the Graham "Spirit of Motion" model added to the company's deserved reputation as a styling innovator, although the unusual appearance of the front end of this car led to the somewhat unflattering nickname "sharknose." The name may have owed its origins to Gordon Buehrig's 1936 "coffin-nose" Cord, the dies for which were acquired by another Detroit firm, Hupp, and, with some changes, were used for the Hupp Skylark. Hupp was now in such bad shape that it hired Graham-Paige to produce the Skylark and also permitted Graham-Paige to use its own adaptation of the Cord dies for a car which it called the Graham Hollywood.

But styling alone was not enough to sell cars in the 1930s. Depressed by the drop in his company's fortunes, Ray Graham committed suicide in 1932. The two surviving brothers struggled through the rest of the decade with various efforts to find ways of keeping the company going. Robert Graham retired at the end of the decade, and in January 1942 Joe Graham retired as president. By that time the company's management had begun reorganizing its operations for the war contracts that carried it through to 1944. At that time the veteran automobile official Joseph W. Frazer became head of Graham-Paige after buying a huge block of stock from Joe Graham. Frazer made the company part of his plans to introduce a new car in the postwar period, plans that were shortly merged with those of Henry J. Kaiser. Briefly in 1946 Graham-Paige resumed production of cars, before the company's stockholders early in 1947 voted to turn over the company's automotive assets to the Kaiser-Frazer Corporation. In 1950 the word "motors" was dropped from the company's name as it became a closed-investment corporation, with headquarters moved from Detroit to New York. Graham-Paige in 1962 became the Madison Square Garden Corporation, so named for the investment firm's best-known acquisition. It in turn subsequently became a subsidiary of Gulf & Western. As such the one-time automaker again found itself having some link with automotive activities since Gulf & Western owned several automotive parts manufacturers.

References:

Nick Baldwin and others, *The World Guide to Automobile Manufacturers* (New York: Facts on File, 1987);

Jeffrey I. Godshall, "The Graham Brothers and Their Car," *Automobile Quarterly*, 13 (First Quarter 1975): 80-103;

Beverly Rae Kimes and Henry Austin Clark, *Standard Catalog of American Cars, 1805-1942* (Iola, Wis.: Krause, 1985);

George S. May, *The Automobile in American Life* (forthcoming, 1990).

Gray Motor Corporation

by George S. May

Eastern Michigan University

The Gray Motor Corporation of Detroit had two links with the Ford Motor Company, with whose Model T the company's Gray automobile was intended to compete. The company's and the car's name was derived from John S. Gray, the Detroit banker who was, until his death in 1906, the first president of Ford and who had provided financial backing to O. J. Mulford to form the Gray Motor Company to manufacture boat engines. The motor company later became a part of Benjamin Briscoe's United States Motor combine.

When United States Motor collapsed in 1912 Mulford regained control of the motor company, which made engines for cars and trucks during the next several years. After the war Frank F. Beall and William H. Blackburn, formerly with Packard and Cadillac respectively, joined the firm, which was reorganized in spring 1920 as the Gray Motor Corporation. The company planned to manufacture a medium-priced 4-cylinder car, but when Frank L. Klingensmith became the president in 1921 he introduced plans to produce a small, low-priced car designed to compete with Ford, where Klingensmith had served as treasurer until he was forced out after World War I by Henry Ford.

The first Grays appeared at the end of 1921. In fall 1922 one of the cars set a new transcontinental record when it averaged 33.8 miles per gallon on a trip from San Francisco to New York, enabling the company to advertise that its "Aristocrat of Small Cars" provided "World Record Economy." However, projected annual sales of 250,000 were never remotely approached, with less than 10 percent of that number being sold by early 1924. Klingensmith resigned in January 1925. Both the size of the cars and their price were increased somewhat for the 1925 and 1926 model years, and a truck was added to the company's product line. These changes had no positive effect. In summer 1926 the company's factory and equipment were auctioned off as Gray became another of the casualties illustrating the disadvantages any newcomer faced in the 1920s in trying to compete with the larger, established automobile companies.

References:
Nick Baldwin and others, *The World Guide to Automobile Manufacturers* (New York: Facts on File, 1987);

Beverly Rae Kimes and Henry Austin Clark, *Standard Catalog of American Cars, 1805-1942* (Iola, Wis.: Krause, 1985).

H. C. S. Motor Car Company

by George S. May

Eastern Michigan University

In the fall 1919, three years after he sold his stock in the Stutz Motor Car Company, Harry C. Stutz, together with his former partner at Stutz, Henry G. Campbell, formed a new car company located, like Stutz, in Indianapolis. Following the example of Ransom E. Olds, who formed the REO company after leaving the Olds Motor Works, the new company was identified by Stutz's initials so as to avoid confusion with his earlier company. However, it was easy to see a family resemblance between the sporty and expensive H. C. S. models that began appearing by summer 1920 and the famous Stutz models with which they were competing. Advertising references to the H. C. S. as "The Car Born with a Reputation" were obviously attempts to capitalize on the renown Harry Stutz had gained from his association with his first car. The victory of a car labeled the H. C. S. Special at the Indianapolis 500 in 1923 was an even more obvious attempt to duplicate the success that had come to Stutz with the victory of his entry at the 1911 Indianapolis 500. However, although initial sales were good, buyers shortly seemed to prefer the original Stutz and not the initialed version. In October 1924 Stutz formed the H. C. S. Cab Manufacturing Company, and, although some H. C. S. passenger cars were produced as late as 1925, taxis were now the main product. The new venture was not a success, however, and it was placed in receivership in 1927, three years before Harry Stutz died.

References:
Nick Baldwin and others, *The World Guide to Automobile Manufacturers* (New York: Facts on File, 1987);
Beverly Rae Kimes and Henry Austin Clark, *Standard Catalog of American Cars, 1805-1942* (Iola, Wis.: Krause, 1985).

Julius Peter Heil

(July 24, 1876-November 30, 1949)

by Genevieve Wren

Creative Automotive Research

CAREER: Drill press operator and welder, Milwaukee Harvester Company (1890-?); welder, Falk Corporation (?-1901); owner, Heil Rail Joint Welding Company (1901-1906); president (1906-1946), chairman, Heil Company (1946-1949); governor, Wisconsin (1939-1943).

Julius Peter Heil played a major role in developing truck technology during the first half of the twentieth century. Born in Dusemond-on-the-Mosel, Germany, on July 24, 1876, Heil immigrated to the United States with his family in 1881. The Heils initially settled in New Berlin, Wisconsin, but soon moved to Prospect Hill, Wisconsin, where Heil received a grade-school education.

Heil's parents died when he was fourteen, and he took a job as a drill press operator with the Milwaukee Harvester Company. He later worked as a welder with the Falk Corporation, a Milwaukee-based company with extensive business dealings in South America. Heil traveled widely in South America, welding steel track for municipal railway systems, and in the process becoming an expert welder.

After his return to the United States in 1900, Heil founded his own company, the Heil Rail Joint Welding Company, in 1901. In addition to welding steel track, the company began to develop riveted steel tanks for transporting kerosene and other petroleum products by wagon. Slowly this aspect of the business began to take on more importance.

In 1906 Heil reorganized the company, increasing its capital and changing its name to the Heil Company. He served as the new firm's president until 1946, when he became its chairman of the board. The business expanded rapidly, especially after the 1907 development of a petroleum-carrying tank trailer with a capacity of 200 gallons.

As a result of the new business, the firm's manufacturing capacity was strained, and in 1908 a new 18-acre plant was constructed on a site in Milwaukee. The same year the Heil Company began producing structural steel for building construction. In 1910 Heil began research to develop welding techniques which would allow the firm to build tanks on a much larger scale. These innovations led to the construction of a frameless, trailered petroleum tank with a 5,600-gallon capacity. The tank was notable for its smooth exterior skin, made possible by Heil's technique for interior welding. He also developed specialized truck bodies, including dumps and hoists, and also machines for airplane loading, garbage collection, and coal transportation.

Some of Heil's other developments included electrically welded compartment tanks; hydraulic hoists; tin-lined steel milk tanks; hydraulic, stainless-steel milk-truck tanks; dehydrating machines; road scrapers; and bulldozers. In 1930 Heil utilized aluminum in building a tank trailer, realizing a small increase in payload capacity while reducing weight by more than 50 percent. During the 1920s and 1930s, Heil expanded production by buying two new plants, one in Hillside, New York, and a second plant in Milwaukee. By 1949 the company employed more than 3,000 workers and was known as one of the world's great truck manufacturers.

But Heil's interests were not limited to manufacturing. In 1938 he was elected as a Republican to be the governor of Wisconsin and was reelected in 1940. His administration oversaw the enactment of the Wisconsin Employment Peace Act, reorganized the welfare and tax agencies, modernized the state's accounting system, and aggressively promoted sales of dairy products.

Heil died on November 30, 1949, leaving his wife, Elizabeth Conrad, whom he had married on June 4, 1900, and their son, Joseph, who continued in the family business.

John Daniel Hertz

(April 10, 1879-October 8, 1961)

by George S. May

Eastern Michigan University

CAREER: Reporter, *Chicago Record* (c.1895); partner, Walden W. Shaw Livery Company (1908); founder, Yellow Cab Manufacturing Company (1915); founder, Chicago Motor Coach Company (1922); founder, People's Motorbus Company (1923); founder, Hertz Drive-Ur-Self Corporation (1924); founder, Omnibus Corporation of America (1924); founder, Yellow Coach Manufacturing Corporation (1924); chairman, Yellow Truck & Coach Manufacturing Company (1925-1929); partner, Lehman Brothers (1934-1961).

John Daniel Hertz, whose multifarious business activities defy orderly classification, was one of the more innovative figures in American business history, although he is best remembered for his work in the automotive field. He was born on April 10, 1879, in Ruttka, a village then part of the Austro-Hungarian empire and now part of Czechoslovakia. He was the son of Jacob and Katie Schlesinger Hertz; the family moved to Chicago in 1884. Hertz attended public school in Chicago, but at eleven he ran away from home and for a time supported himself by working as a newsboy. He was found by his father, but he remained home only for a short time and ceased attending school after the fifth grade.

Precise and accurate information about his rise in business is hard to obtain. He drove a livery wagon for a time. He was also interested in athletics and after a brief career as a boxer took on the management of two professional fighters. At the same time his interest in sports led to a position as sports reporter for the *Chicago Record* beginning around 1895. Because he had no experience and knew little or nothing about writing he was paid by the word, but he turned in so many stories that he received more pay than the staff reporters.

Sometime around 1900 Hertz turned to selling cars, and although in the first year he earned only half of what his income had been as a sports re-

porter, his commissions rose spectacularly when he began promising customers that he would come to their help anytime, day or night, and would aid them in repairing their cars. In 1905 Hertz joined the Walden W. Shaw Livery Company of Chicago, which subsequently began to sell automobiles. Hertz in 1908 purchased a one-third share in the business and began to shift the emphasis from the sale of new cars to that of a "chauffered livery," or taxicab, operation. At first Hertz used trade-ins for his cabs, but in 1910 he bought nine new Thomas Flyers and painted them a bright yellow, thereby launching the Yellow Cab business. He chose the color because he had read an article that indicated such a color would most readily attract the attention of potential cab patrons.

Hertz studied taxicab services in Europe, and he decided to concentrate on providing basic service, without luxuries, at a low price. When standard cab rates were $5.00 an hour, he charged $2.50, and his mileage rate was 30¢ for the first mile, as opposed to the normal 70¢. Hertz's Yellow Cabs were soon operating in hundreds of other cities in addition to Chicago, and Hertz, only in his thirties, was said to be a millionaire.

In 1915 Hertz established the Yellow Cab (or Taxicab, a term that was used interchangeably in references to the company) Manufacturing Company of Chicago. It apparently served as the headquarters for the cab business but, as the name suggests, also reflected Hertz's move to manufacture his own taxicabs, rather than using the products of the automobile manufacturers. But the Yellow Cabs that began to be produced in 1915, and would be produced by the thousands in the years that followed, were built by the Walden W. Shaw company. After World War I the Shaw company decided to produce passenger cars as well as taxis, but the model it turned out in 1920, first called the Shaw and then the Colonial, did poorly. Hertz gained complete control of the Shaw company in 1921, and he made some changes in the car, renamed it the Ambassador, and tried to promote its sales by advertising that the car was associated with Hertz's well-known and reliable cab operations.

The Ambassador, initially a big, 6-cylinder car, continued to be sold until 1926 when it was renamed the Hertz, by which it was known until its production ceased late in 1927. Beginning in 1924, however, Hertz was using these cars mainly for one of his latest ventures, the Hertz Drive-Ur-Self Corporation, which he had organized that year. What he intended was "a system designed after the old livery stable plan ... where a man might go hire a 'rig' for a day's pleasure or business travelling." Before long there were Hertz rent-a-car offices in eight hundred cities, each office originally being locally owned and operated under a license from Hertz. Hertz decided by 1927 that it was not economically feasible to manufacture his own cars for these rental offices, and thus, beginning in 1928, he used cars purchased from automobile manufacturers.

Hertz's decision in this case was also undoubtedly influenced by the fact that Hertz Drive-Ur-Self had become a part of a company organized in 1925 in which General Motors (GM) held the majority stock interest. The Yellow Truck & Coach Manufacturing Company was the outcome of still another of Hertz's automobile interests, this one being the building and operating of motor buses. In 1922 he had organized the Chicago Motor Coach Company and in quick succession he had also acquired control of both the People's Motorbus Company of St. Louis and the Fifth Avenue Coach Company of New York. He merged these bus companies into the Omnibus Corporation of America in 1924. He was not content, however, to rely on outside suppliers for his buses and so in 1924 he formed the Yellow Coach Manufacturing Corporation in Chicago, staffed by officials from the Fifth Avenue Coach Company, which had been making its own buses for nearly a decade.

When Yellow Coach Manufacturing received contracts later in 1924 from outside bus firms, as well as those that Hertz controlled, this attracted the attention of GM, whose president, Alfred P. Sloan, Jr., is said to have told his directors of a new bus he had just seen and had asked "why the hell G.M. wasn't making busses." Discussions with Hertz took place, out of which emerged in 1925 Yellow Truck & Coach, which included Hertz's Yellow Cab Manufacturing Company, Yellow Coach Manufacturing Company, and the Hertz Drive-Ur-Self Corporation, but not the Yellow Cab operations themselves. GM contributed its GMC truck division, valued at $11 million, plus $5 million in cash. It received in return 57 percent of the voting shares in the company. The company's operations were soon centered in Pontiac, Michigan, close to various GM divisions that supplied the company with many of its parts. Despite its majority control, however, GM wisely left the management of the company in the hands of the experienced bus manufacturers whom Hertz had brought into the Yellow Coach company.

Hertz served as chairman of the Yellow Truck & Coach Manufacturing Company, but he stepped down in 1929 to pursue other interests. He continued to head the Omnibus Corporation of America, which in the mid 1930s operated 1,600 buses in New York and Chicago. He remained involved in the cab business, developing a new Black & White cab system with service in New York, Philadelphia, Buffalo, Cleveland, and other cities. His wide experience in transportation matters led to his serving as an advisor on such matters to the War Department in World War II, as he had in World War I. In 1934 he became a partner in the New York investment banking company of Lehman Brothers. *Fortune* magazine in 1936 said that Hertz had once been notorious for his fierce temper. At times he became so angry that he would pound his glass-top desk until the glass was completely shattered. "Today Mr. Hertz is a banker. His temper is only a scorching memory."

In 1953 GM, which had by that time absorbed the Yellow Truck & Coach Company, sold the Hertz Drive-Ur-Self business to a group representing Hertz's Omnibus Corporation of America. Hertz was the largest car rental business in the country, and with the rapid expansion of air travel its continued growth was assured. GM disposed of the business in part because its control of what was in effect a captive market for GM cars would provide additional evidence for those who were already arguing that the corporation's dominance in the automotive field violated United States antitrust laws. The Omnibus Corporation disposed of its buses and was reorganized in 1954 around the car rental business; it was renamed the Hertz Corporation.

After 1954 Hertz held no office in the company that now bore his name.

Hertz died in Los Angeles on October 8, 1961. He was survived by a son and two daughters and by his wife of fifty-eight years, Frances Kesner Hertz. Mrs. Hertz had become well-known in her own right as a result of another of her husband's innumerable interests, horse racing. Serving as a jockey's valet at a track in Indiana had been one of the jobs Hertz had taken as a youth. This had developed into a life-long interest in horse breeding and horse racing. When he became wealthy from his business activities he established an 1,800-acre estate northwest of Chicago where he built one of the country's largest thoroughbred horse breeding operations. He raced his horses in his wife's name, and the colors were, predictably, yellow silks, with a black circle on the sleeves, and a yellow cap. At a race at Saratoga in 1927 he saw one horse try to bite another as they approached the finish. "The one who tried to bite interested me," Hertz said, "because he was the fighter." He bought the two-year-old, named Reigh Count, and the horse won the Kentucky Derby the following year. Fifteen years later, Reigh Count's son, Count Fleet, racing under the Hertz colors, won racing's Triple Crown. Eight years later, Count Fleet's son, Count Turf, brought the Hertzes their third Kentucky Derby triumph. Thus it was that *Sports Illustrated* noted the death of Hertz as "Racing's Loss." He was, the magazine declared, "a man capable of running a highly successful car rental business and a highly successful Thoroughbred racing stable without letting the commercialism of the first corrupt the sportsmanship of the second."

References:

Ed Cray, *Chrome Colossus: General Motors and Its Times* (New York: McGraw-Hill, 1980);

Beverly Rae Kimes and Henry Austin Clark, *Standard Catalog of American Cars, 1805-1942* (Iola, Wis.: Krause, 1985);

"Racing's Loss," *Sports Illustrated*, 15 (October 23, 1961): 12-13;

"Yellow Truck & Coach," *Fortune*, 14 (July 1936): 61-67, 106-115.

Paul Gray Hoffman

(April 26, 1891-October 8, 1974)

by Alan R. Raucher

Wayne State University

CAREER: Car salesman, Studebaker Corporation (1910-1917); first lieutenant, U.S. Army (1917-1919); owner and operator, Paul G. Hoffman Company (1919-1925); vice-president in charge of sales (1925-1933), receiver (1933-1935), president, Studebaker Corporation (1935-1948); administrator, Economic Cooperation Administration (1948-1950); president, Ford Foundation (1950-1953); chairman, Studebaker Corporation (1953-1954); chairman, Studebaker-Packard Corporation (1954-1956); director, United Nations Development Program (1959-1971).

Paul Gray Hoffman, car dealer and Studebaker executive, was born on April 26, 1891, in Chicago and spent his childhood in the comfortable suburb of Western Springs. His father, George Hoffman, was a successful inventor, corporate executive, and entrepreneur. His mother, Eleanor Lott Hoffman, provided Paul, her favorite among three children, with affection and encouragement. From his family he acquired the modern pragmatic outlook of business management and the self-assurance to make the most of it.

Hoffman began his business career in 1909 after one year at the University of Chicago, where he was more interested in fraternity life than in his classes. With the experience acquired by driving and repairing his father's car, at age eighteen he found a job as a porter with a car dealership in Chicago. He worked briefly in the service department and then found the road to success by selling cars. Friendly, unpretentious, and persuasive, within two years he was earning $300 to $400 a month selling cars for a local Studebaker dealership.

When his father moved to southern California in 1911 Hoffman also relocated there, joining the sales staff of a Studebaker dealership in Los Angeles. In his new locale, where the population swelled

Paul Gray Hoffman

with transplanted midwesterners, he enjoyed phenomenal success as a salesman. He became the Studebaker sales manager for Los Angeles and Orange counties in 1915 and for the entire southern California district two years later. During that time he met Dorothy Brown, another transplanted midwesterner who had New England roots and was, like his mother, a Christian Scientist. They married after she graduated from Wellesley College in 1915. The marriage of forty-six years produced four children—they adopted two others and also provided for one ward—and only ended when she died in 1961.

Although married and a father when the United States entered World War I, Hoffman enlisted in the army. Without leaving the country he rose from private to first lieutenant. After eighteen months in the service he returned to civilian life determined to launch his own business. He spurned Studebaker's offer to make him manager of its New York distributorship and a member of the board at a salary of $50,000. Instead, he persuaded Albert Russel Erskine, Studebaker's flamboyant and power-

ful president, to sell him the southern California distributorship for $60,000.

He took a calculated risk and acquired his own business with capital borrowed from relatives and friends. Conditions worked in his favor. The rapidly growing but diffuse population in the Los Angeles area created a large market for cars. His arrangement with Studebaker practically guaranteed profits by giving his firm a 3 percent commission from the sale of every Studebaker in southern California. More important, he knew how to take advantage of the opportunities.

At his car dealership he applied systematic modern business methods. He trained his sales and service personnel. After studying market conditions, he employed Harley J. Earl, the future chief designer for General Motors, to customize factory models to suit local tastes. Keen to use the best and latest advertising methods, he invested $35,000 in 1921 to help launch KNX radio. For several years the station, which CBS bought in 1936 for $1 million, broadcast from Hoffman's showroom on Hollywood Boulevard.

By the age of thirty-four Hoffman had built up his dealership, Studebaker's second largest, to assets of $1.5 million. Its high profits made him a millionaire with a personal portfolio of diversified investments. Wealthy and locally powerful friends thrust other money-making opportunities before him. A sense of civic duty as well as self-interest led him to involvement with public affairs. He became involved in local Republican politics and also led the campaign to solve traffic congestion problems in Los Angeles by expert planning of street and highway construction.

In 1925, just when he was emerging to local prominence, Hoffman left behind his comfortable and successful life in southern California. Studebaker's president, Albert Erskine, appealed to his sense of obligation and love of a challenge and persuaded him to become vice-president in charge of sales and a member of the board. Turning over operation of his dealership to a trusted associate, Hoffman moved his large family to South Bend, Indiana, the site of Studebaker's headquarters and its manufacturing facilities. Erskine soon made it clear that he regarded Hoffman, who assumed a wide range of responsibilities, and another new vice-president, Harold S. Vance, as Studebaker's future leaders.

Besides overseeing Studebaker's sales efforts, Hoffman sought to create a favorable and distinctive corporate image. With the slogan of the "Friendly Factory," he contrasted its good record of labor relations with the brutal pace on the production lines of its competitors. According to his publicity, Studebaker proved itself a progressive and socially responsible corporation by sponsoring academic efforts to upgrade traffic safety. Those sorts of activities gave Hoffman much greater public visibility than Studebaker's size and his own rank should have warranted.

Hoffman's successes while he was vice-president could not, however, overcome the painful reality about Studebaker. The depression of the 1930s, which had a devastating impact on car sales throughout the entire industry, revealed fatal flaws in Erskine's policies. By pursuing expansion while paying excessively high stock dividends, he had dissipated Studebaker's capital reserve until it lacked the cash to continue operations and to meet immediate obligations. In March 1933 creditors sought protection in U.S. District Court. Judge Thomas W. Slick removed Erskine from the management and placed Studebaker in receivership, with Hoffman, Vance, and Ashton G. Bean, the president of White Motors, to serve as receivers.

For two years Hoffman and Vance operated Studebaker under the receivership while trying to reorganize the corporation. Clearly dominant among the receivers, Hoffman concentrated on boosting car sales and reassuring dealers. Accompanied by Vance, he frequently traveled to New York to persuade investment bankers and other underwriters to refinance the corporation. After Judge Slick finally approved a reorganization plan in January 1935, it was Hoffman as president of the new Studebaker who signed an advertisement that boldly announced its return to full-scale competition.

His tenure as Studebaker's president from 1935 until April 1948 marked the high point of Hoffman's automotive career. He and Harold Vance, who served as chairman, formed a leadership team that lifted Studebaker from bankruptcy to profitability. Quite different in temperaments and life-styles, they possessed talents that complemented each other in ways that benefited Studebaker. Extroverted, persuasive, and highly skilled at interpersonal relations, Hoffman gave Studebaker the kind of positive public exposure it needed to

win over investors, car dealers, employees, and customers.

Hoffman and Vance operated Studebaker with the firm conviction that it could compete successfully within the automotive industry dominated by General Motors, Ford, and Chrysler. In articles and signed advertisements, in speeches and testimony before Congressional committees Hoffman argued that the small progressive automaker could overcome the advantages large competitors enjoyed from economies of scale. By giving better attention to personal relations the "Friendly Factory" could stimulate innovation, good workmanship, and superior service for customers. Through efficiency and attention to rapid changes in the market it could find profitable niches not filled by large automakers encumbered by slow-moving and impersonal bureaucracies.

To apply that niche strategy Hoffman first hired a market research firm and learned that Studebaker could compete in the low price mass market with a lightweight, fuel-efficient car as long as it was not undersized. While Studebaker engineers worked on developing such a car, Hoffman hired, on a fee basis, the industrial designer Raymond Loewy. The car that emerged, the 1939 Champion, featured a conservative but modern appearance and better equipment than competitors in that price field. It quickly won praise from automotive experts and, more important, sold well. Until it ceased car production early in 1942, Studebaker enjoyed an increase in sales that outstripped the gains made throughout the industry. Studebaker's leaders earned both profits and favorable publicity.

The managerial strategy pursued by Hoffman and Vance required a cooperative relationship with Studebaker's workers. Unlike other leaders in the industry during the 1930s, they did not resist unionization. In February 1934 they met directly with leaders of a newly formed local union and granted virtual recognition. Their labor relations policies reflected not only Studebaker's economic vulnerability but also their belief that workers had legitimate grievances and interests that unions could represent without hurting the corporation.

Using the slogan of the "Friendly Factory," Hoffman emerged as a strong advocate of the human relations approach to labor management. He argued that such policies motivated all employees to give their best creative efforts and to cooperate in the teamwork needed for high quality work performance. According to Hoffman, known to many employees by his first name, Studebaker produced better cars than its competitors because it treated employees better.

In addition to the recognition he received for the way he led Studebaker, Hoffman also built a reputation as the automotive industry's "apostle of safety." During the 1920s he had shown unusual sensitivity to the threat to car sales posed by public concern over traffic problems and accidents. While a vice-president of the Automobile Manufacturers Association, he persuaded other industry leaders in 1936 to finance a campaign for traffic safety. The following year they agreed to create the Automobile Safety Foundation (ASF) with Hoffman its first president. Clearly created to head off criticism that could hurt car sales, the ASF focused on promoting highway construction and driver education as the best ways to reduce traffic accidents. By heading the ASF Hoffman again identified both himself and Studebaker with progressive business practices.

The start of World War II forced Hoffman and Vance to face new challenges. When United States entry into the war ended civilian car production, the Studebaker team went personally to Washington to obtain military contracts. Then, while Studebaker profited handsomely and expanded production capacity during the war, they boldly planned for a rapid reconversion to peacetime operations. Correctly predicting a postwar consumer boom, they wanted to reenter the market quickly with a distinctive, modern model that could capture the fancy of car buyers and make them loyal to the Studebaker brand name.

Under their leadership Studebaker launched into an eager market the postwar era's first entirely new model, the 1947 Champion. Its engineers created a fuel-efficient car that offered motorists improved safety and handling. Raymond Loewy provided distinctive styling that emphasized efficient functionalism and driver visibility. With that car Hoffman and Vance led Studebaker to new sales records and record profits, enabling them to pay stockholders extra dividends. Their confidence in Studebaker's future seemed well justified when Hoffman's involvement in public affairs led him to leave the corporation in April 1948.

Involvement in public affairs was, of course, nothing new for Hoffman. From personal convictions and from a desire to establish Studebaker's public image as a progressive corporation, he had spent much time away from South Bend working for a variety of causes. During World War II he had helped to establish the Committee for Economic Development (CED). While serving as its first chairman, he acquired a strong interest in foreign relations, becoming convinced that peace and prosperity would depend upon the expansion of international trade. By 1946 he had also come to believe that the Soviet Union represented the major threat to that goal.

It was no surprise, therefore, when President Truman nominated Hoffman to administer the new Marshall Plan. Truman needed a Republican businessman in order to win Congressional backing. Hoffman, who had often testified before Congressional committees, fit the position perfectly. A lifelong Republican identified in the press as a progressive business leader, he fully supported the Truman Administration's foreign policy while the cold war emerged. His appointment won quick Congressional approval.

For five years, between 1948 and 1953, Hoffman worked outside the automotive industry. The first two and a half years he spent successfully administering the Marshall Plan. The rest of that time he spent as the first president of the enormously wealthy Ford Foundation, until a clash with Henry Ford II forced a discreetly camouflaged firing. The public announcement claimed that Hoffman resigned in order to return to Studebaker as chairman. At the time he hoped that the position would not absorb much of his time so that he could continue his activities on behalf of civil liberties within the United States and peace abroad.

Welcomed back in 1953 by Vance, Hoffman quickly discovered that Studebaker faced a combination of problems that together threatened its survival. First of all, with cheap gasoline and new affluence, most car buyers preferred large and powerful cars that offered comfort and the appearance of high status. Vance had failed to react rapidly enough to that trend. Hoffman, too, continued to believe during the 1950s that Americans still needed smaller, less powerful, and safer cars. But with Studebaker sales and dealer morale sagging, he knew that the company had to change its strategy. Toward that end, he hired outside market research experts and persuaded Vance and other top officials to accompany him to meetings with dealers across the country to learn their views.

Hoffman discovered that Studebaker was also suffering from very serious internal deficiencies.

Under Vance it had failed to keep pace with technological change in automotive production. Furthermore, Vance had bought labor peace at a high price: union contracts provided overly generous wages, and management failed to enforce work rules. As a result of that laxity, Studebaker paid high labor costs but received low productivity; its car prices were too high and its quality control too low. During the mid 1940s, while he was still president, Hoffman had warned union officials that high labor costs endangered Studebaker's future and thus workers' jobs. Having returned as chairman, he responded to the situation by hiring outside experts on manpower management and by meeting with union officials and production supervisors.

Even while he tried to correct the problems Studebaker faced on the production side and on the marketing side, he realized that it was simply too small to operate successfully within the new automotive industry. Always a firm believer in the benefits of competitive capitalism, he discovered that the end of the sellers' market created the kind of intense price competition which small automakers could not survive. Nash-Kelvinator under George Romney also recognized that situation and responded by taking over Hudson Motors to form American Motors. Hoffman, who had opposed merger as late as 1949, concluded that Studebaker, too, needed to join with another automaker. Over the objections of Studebaker president Harold Vance, he started negotiations with the Packard Motor Company.

Packard, a small automaker based in Detroit, attracted Hoffman for several reasons. For one thing it sold a well-respected car in the profitable high price range where Studebaker lacked cars. Unlike Studebaker, it had invested in modern production technology. And also unlike Studebaker, it was run by a young and aggressive president. Hoffman believed that Packard president James Nance could make a success of a merger.

Actually arranging the merger proved to be an arduous task for Hoffman. During a 150-day period he maintained an exhausting pace negotiating with Packard and with Studebaker's unionized employees. For a time Studebaker workers blocked the merger by rejecting a new and less generous union contract. Nevertheless, when the new Studebaker-Packard Corporation finally emerged in October 1954 as the automotive industry's fourth largest

firm, Hoffman felt confident about the future. He was mistaken.

Studebaker-Packard disappointed all parties concerned. James Nance, its president, blamed Hoffman and Vance for Studebaker's economic plight. He reversed their policies regarding car design and labor relations and otherwise ignored them, except to obtain military contracts from their political connections with President Eisenhower. Vance, chairman of the executive committee, severed his ties with Studebaker-Packard in 1955.

Hoffman, though without executive authority, remained as chairman for two years. While Nance's new policies failed to reverse declining sales and labor problems, the corporation teetered on the brink of collapse. Then in 1956 Curtiss-Wright bought out Studebaker-Packard, and Hoffman finally ended his long connection with the automotive industry. Soon afterward Lathrop Hoffman, the only Hoffman son to follow his father in the business, closed the Studebaker dealership that once bore the name Paul G. Hoffman.

Sixty-five years old and independently wealthy, Hoffman was yet unwilling to retire. For a while he busied himself with the management of the Hoffman Specialty Manufacturing Corporation, which his father had started in 1913. Mostly he concentrated on international affairs. During the exciting 1956 session of the United Nations (UN) General Assembly he served on the United States delegation under ambassador Henry Cabot Lodge. Then in December 1958 UN secretary-general Dag Hammarskjöld appointed him to head a new agency created to assist the economic development of poor countries.

In 1959 Hoffman moved into a New York apartment and started a highly successful career as an international bureaucrat. His wife Dorothy, who stayed behind at their home in Palm Springs, California, died in 1961. The following year Hoffman, who had stopped attending the Episcopal church during the 1920s, married an old friend and business associate, Anna Rosenberg, in the Unitarian church. With her support he continued at the UN until retiring in 1971 at the age of eighty. After a series of strokes and heart attacks he died in New York in 1974, leaving an estate of about $4 million. The year before, President Nixon had awarded the Medal of Freedom to Hoffman, a businessman with a strong sense of social responsibility and a commitment to world peace.

References:

Crane Haussamen, *The Story of Paul G. Hoffman* (Santa Barbara, Cal.: Center for the Study of Democratic Institutions, 1966 ;

"Paul G. Hoffman," in *Biographical Dictionary of American Business History*, edited by John Ingham (Westport, Conn.: Greenwood, 1983);

Alan Raucher, *Paul G. Hoffman: Architect of Foreign Aid* (Lexington: University Press of Kentucky, 1985);

R. Raucher, "Paul G. Hoffman, Studebaker, and the Car Culture," *Indiana Magazine of History*, 79 (September 1983): 209-230.

Archives:

Hoffman's papers are located in the Harry S. Truman Library in Independence, Missouri. The Studebaker papers are located in the Discovery Hall Museum in South Bend, Indiana. Additional Hoffman material is found in the Oral History Office of Columbia University.

Lido Anthony Iacocca

(October 15, 1924-   )

by James J. Flink

University of California, Irvine

CAREER: Management trainee (1946-1947), truck salesman, Chester, Pa. (1947-1949), zone sales manager, Wilkes-Barre, Pa. (1949-1953), assistant sales manager, Philadelphia district (1953-1956), district sales manager, Washington, D.C. (1956), national truck marketing manager, Ford Division (1956-1957), national car marketing manager, Ford Division (1957-1960), head of car and truck sales, Ford Division (1960), vice-president and general manager, Ford Division (1960-1970), president and chief operating officer, Ford Motor Company (1970-1978); president, chief operating officer, and director (1978-1979), chairman of the board and chief executive officer, Chrysler Corporation (1979-present).

The public recognition and approbation accorded Lee Iacocca is unparalleled in contemporary business history. No executive in the automobile industry has been as widely acclaimed or personally identified with corporate achievements since Henry Ford; William C. Durant, the creator of General Motors (GM); and Walter Chrysler, the founder of the firm Iacocca would head a half century later. In contrast, Iacocca's own choice as the most significant automotive entrepreneur of all time, Alfred P. Sloan, Jr., shunned public attention and eschewed personal credit for the phenomenal business success of GM under his leadership.

Lido Anthony Iacocca was born on October 15, 1924, in Allentown, Pennsylvania. He was the second child and only son of Nicola and Antoinette Iacocca, immigrants from San Marco, Italy, a small

Lido Anthony Iacocca (courtesy of Junebug Clark)

town twenty-five miles northeast of Naples. Nicola immigrated to the United States in 1902 at the age of twelve. He quit a job in a coal mine in Garrett, Pennsylvania, after only one day, "the only day in his life that he ever worked for anybody else." He soon moved to Allentown and became an apprentice shoemaker. In 1921 on a trip back to San Marcos to bring his widowed mother to America, he married Antoinette, the seventeen-year-old daughter of a shoemaker. Nicola quickly became a successful small entrepreneur in Allentown. By the time Lee was born, Nicola had opened a hot dog restaurant. Next he began to operate a fleet of thirty rental cars under a national franchise, opened several movie theaters, and speculated in real estate. However, hard times came to the Iacoccas with the Great Depression: the family went from moderate wealth to near poverty and almost lost its house. Antoinette helped out in the restaurant and took a job sewing shirts in a silk mill so that the Iacoccas could survive.

"The Depression turned me into a materialist," Lee Iacocca writes. "I was after the bucks." His goal upon graduation from college in 1945 was "to make ten thousand a year by the time I'm twenty-five and then . . . to be a millionaire." He reports putting most of his money even today into very conservative investments and that "no matter how I'm doing financially, the Depression has never disappeared from my consciousness. To this day, I hate waste."

Iacocca's 1984 autobiography reveals much about the man. He is admittedly ambitious and aggressive. He is outspoken in his disdain for inherited social position and wealth—especially inherited business leadership, as exemplified by Henry Ford II. He extols the ideal of the self-made man and his own exemplification of that ideal. He is intensely proud of his family background—the accomplishments and values of his immigrant parents, his Italian-American ethnicity, and his Catholic upbringing. He is extremely conscious of class and ethnicity; and he is understandably sensitive to discrimination and slights. Iacocca's self-portrait, above all, unwittingly reveals the egotism at the core of his personality. Maynard M. Gordon observes, for example, that the autobiography displays "an overriding ego bordering on self-righteousness."

"My parents always made my sister, Delma, and me feel important and special," Iacocca reveals. "Nothing was too much work or too much trouble." He felt very close to his father. "I loved pleasing him," he recalls, "and he was always terrifically proud of my accomplishments." Nicola left deep impressions on Lee, who credits his father with being responsible for his instinct for marketing

and for forcing him to perform up to his potential in everything he did.

Iacocca contracted rheumatic fever in 1939 at age fifteen. Although he did not suffer any permanent heart damage, he had to give up sports. While bedridden for six months, he turned to books. Being a good student was always important to him, and he was active in the high school drama club and the debating society. His medical history resulted in a 4-F draft deferment status in World War II. Gordon believes that this gave Lee "an unconscious 'chip' to shoulder later on when he tangled at Ford with the crew of Air Force 'Whiz Kid' officers recruited by Henry Ford II." Iacocca himself relates that his medical deferment "seemed like a disgrace, and I began to think of myself as a second-class citizen. . . . I buried my head in my books."

He graduated twelfth in a high school class of more than nine hundred. He had straight A's in math and had won the prize for being the best student in Latin three years running. He recalls that he was well prepared for college with "a solid background in the fundamentals: reading, writing, and public speaking. With good teachers and the ability to concentrate, you can go pretty far with these skills."

After being turned down for a scholarship to study engineering at Purdue, Iacocca entered Lehigh University at Bethlehem, Pennsylvania. He was motivated to excel by pressure from his father, "typical among immigrant families, where any kid who was fortunate enough to attend college was expected to compensate for his parents' lack of education." Nicola had been disappointed that his son had not graduated first in his high school class and assumed he was "playing around" when he failed to make the dean's list during his first semester at Lehigh. Nonetheless Iacocca developed strict priorities and exemplary study habits. He switched his major from mechanical to industrial engineering, and his grades began to improve. He finished his senior year with straight A's and graduated with a 3.53 average. By his senior year he had switched from engineering and science to business courses, in which he did much better. He also took four years of psychology courses, which he says "were probably the most valuable courses of my college career." He attributes to them his ability "to figure people out pretty quickly. . . . That is an important skill to have, because the most important thing a manager can do is to hire the right new people."

Iacocca wanted to work for Ford even before he graduated from Lehigh, and during the spring of his senior year a Ford recruiter visited the campus. Ford at that time annually selected one student from each of fifty targeted universities to enter its management trainee program. Iacocca was selected from Lehigh. Before entering the program, however, he was awarded a fellowship to do graduate work in mechanical engineering at Princeton. He accepted the fellowship after receiving assurances from the Ford recruiter that a space would be held open for him in the management program the following year.

He found Princeton "a delightful place" with a laid-back pace. He took his electives in political science and in the developing field of plastics. His thesis project was to design and build a hydraulic thermometer. Anxious to begin his career at Ford, he completed his thesis project in two semesters rather than the usual three. But he received his M.A. degree from Princeton in spring 1946 only to find that "nobody at Ford had ever heard of me" and to learn that the training program already had its fifty recruits for the year. He explained his predicament on the phone to the head of the training program, who recognized the unfairness of the situation and accepted him as recruit number fifty-one, provided he could get to Dearborn immediately. The next day Nicola drove Iacocca to Philadelphia, where he boarded the train for Detroit.

In 1946 Henry Ford II was just beginning a revitalization of the Ford Motor Company that is historically even more significant than the lauded turnaround of Chrysler by Iacocca in the early 1980s. Henry Ford II was discharged from the navy, ultimately to take over as president from his senile grandfather on September 21, 1945, a few weeks after the Japanese surrender. The untimely death of Edsel Ford from cancer in 1943 had removed the only check within the firm on the first Henry Ford's mental incompetence. Edsel had been bullied to the end by his father, who held up Harry Bennett, a former boxer with underworld connections and head of the Ford security, as a model worthy of emulation. Bennett's power within the firm had grown as the old man's mental capacities had eroded. Under Bennett's Ford security, fear and demoralization had become a way of life at Ford. The elder Ford had developed the hallucination that World War II was a conspiracy between President Franklin D. Roosevelt, GM, and the du Ponts to

Iacocca in 1956, the year he was promoted to Ford headquarters (courtesy of National Automotive History Collection, Detroit Public Library)

gain control of his company. The combined threats of Edsel's widow, Eleanor Clay Ford, and her mother-in-law, Clara Bryant Ford, to sell their shares of Ford stock to the public finally persuaded the old man to step down in favor of his grandson.

Henry Ford II began his revitalization of the company by firing Bennett. Although Bennett carried a gun and was reputed to be dangerous, Ford confronted him personally. He explained to John Bugas, a former FBI agent who offered to handle Bennett, "If I don't do it, people will always know that at a critical moment when it was my responsibility, I let someone do my dirty work for me." This is strikingly incongruent with the portrayal of Ford in Iacocca's autobiography as someone who characteristically had others do his "dirty work."

Ford hired as a group ten former officers headed by Charles B. "Tex" Thornton from the Air Force Office of Statistical Control. They represented the brightest Officer Candidate School graduates selected to complete a special statistics course at the Harvard Business School and soon became known as the Whiz Kids. Six ultimately became vice-presidents, and Robert S. McNamara and Arjay Miller rose to the Ford presidency. Another, J.

Edward Lundy, as head of Ford finance, came to be probably the most powerful individual in the Ford Motor Company next to Henry Ford II himself.

To be on the safe side and in order not to rely totally on the Whiz Kid group, Ford in 1946 brought in a complete management team from GM, headed by Ernest R. Breech, the president of Bendix Aviation and former general assistant treasurer at GM. As Ford president and chief operating officer, Breech instituted the committee system and financial controls innovated under Sloan at GM that the first Henry Ford had eschewed.

The 100-horsepower 1949 Ford Model B-A, the first fully redesigned postwar Ford car, introduced the "marshmallow" ride with its "Hydra-Coil" front suspension and set a styling trend still in evidence with its "envelope body" that eliminated conventional fenders and running boards. Ford sales doubled from 549,000 in 1948 to 1.2 million in 1950 with the introduction of the Model B-A. Its market success enabled Ford to recapture second place in the industry from a faltering Chrysler Corporation.

Although the Ford Motor Company was regenerated by the Model B-A and "Sloanist" financial controls, the ideal of GM-style depersonalized management by committee foundered on the reality that Ford remained a family-controlled firm. As Iacocca points out forcefully in his autobiography, all decisions were subject to veto by Ford family spokesmen who were on the board of directors—Henry Ford II and his brother, William Clay Ford.

The Ford Foundation was conceived in 1936 as a legal device to maintain family control of the Ford Motor Company, while avoiding Roosevelt's so-called soak-the-rich taxes. The foundation received a 95 percent equity in nonvoting common stock, while a 5 percent equity of all voting common stock was retained by the Ford family. Had this not been done, the heirs of Henry Ford would have paid federal inheritance taxes estimated at $321 million and would have lost control of the company in selling the stock necessary to raise the money. By the end of 1955 the foundation had disposed of some $875 million of the Ford fortune and announced plans to diversify its investments by selling off nearly 7 million shares of its Ford stock, which had to be reclassified as voting shares to be listed on the New York stock exchange. Short of funds to maintain its life-style, the Ford family also

wished to go public. The result was that 60 percent of the Ford voting common stock ended up in the hands of the public or of key Ford executives. That still left two-fifths in the hands of the Ford family, more than enough to exercise effective control of the firm. Ironically, after being fired as Ford president by Henry Ford II, Iacocca, who was by then the president of Chrysler, was the largest individual holder of Ford stock outside the Ford family.

Iacocca's rise to the Ford presidency was unorthodox. Not only did he lack background in finance at a time when Ford was emulating GM in coming to be increasingly dominated by "bean counters," but he even failed to complete his training as a student engineer at Ford. Halfway through the eighteen-month program he decided that engineering no longer interested him. He was "eager to be where the real action was—marketing or sales." He quit and landed a low-level job in truck fleet sales in the Ford district sales office in Chester, Pennsylvania. His rise to the Ford presidency from this inauspicious beginning is incredible.

In Chester, Iacocca came under the influence of two salesmen—Murray Kester, the zone sales manager for Wilkes-Barre, Pennsylvania, and Charles R. Beacham, the Ford regional sales manager for the entire East Coast. Kester was "a great storyteller" who got his material from his brother-in-law, Henny Youngman. Iacocca describes Kester as "a real pro at training and motivating salesmen," and from him he learned "a great deal about the retail car business." Kester taught Lee how to ask the right questions of a buyer in order to make a sale and the importance of closing the deal before the customer walked out the door.

Like Iacocca, Beacham had been trained as an engineer before he switched to sales. Indeed, Beacham hired Iacocca because he considered his engineering background to be an asset in selling heavy trucks to knowledgeable buyers. Iacocca credits Beacham with "more impact on my life than any other person than my father. . . . He was the closest thing I've ever had to a mentor."

The genial Georgian was "a street fighter and a strategist, always thinking ahead about what he could do next." He emphasized "street smarts, the things you just *know*, the basic lessons that can't really be taught." For example, Beacham advised Iacocca before his first sales trip to the South both to slow down his speech and to "tell them you have a funny first name—Iacocca—and that your fam-

The first production Mustang, introduced at the New York World's Fair in April 1964 (courtesy of National Automotive History Collection, Detroit Public Library)

ily name is Lee." The strategy worked, and Iacocca was accepted. Beacham refused to accept excuses for failure. He sometimes began sales meetings by listing all the recent excuses why cars were not selling, "so nobody would be tempted to use any of them." He reinforced Iacocca's materialistic bent. "Make money," Beacham advised him. "Screw everything else. This is a profit-making system, boy. The rest is frills."

Beacham recognized early that Iacocca was a born salesman, and cars were added to his line. Iacocca personally disposed of one Pennsylvania dealer's entire used-car inventory in three weeks by contacting the owners of the oldest cars in the vicinity on the assumption that they would be at the point of trading in on newer models. Such stellar performance earned him a promotion to zone sales manager for Wilkes-Barre in 1949, then to assistant sales manager for the Philadelphia district in 1953. He emulated Beacham's demand for strict loyalty and no-nonsense, no-excuses treatment of the sales staff under him. Staffers were ordered to provide weekly lists of dealers with weak sales to be called upon, and Iacocca personally reviewed the results on sales the following week.

New-car sales slackened as the post-World

War II seller's market turned into a buyer's market after the Korean War. Additionally, Ford sales were suffering in the mid 1950s from a safety campaign that failed to appeal to style-conscious consumers. To counter these conditions Iacocca conceived a sales campaign for the Philadelphia district summarized by the slogan "56 for 56." A 1956 Ford could be purchased under Iacocca's plan for 20 percent down and three years of easy $56 monthly payments. The campaign "took off like a rocket." Within three months the Philadelphia district moved from last to first place in Ford sales. Robert McNamara, then vice-president and general manager of the Ford Division, was so impressed with the success of "56 for 56" in Philadelphia that he adopted the plan and the slogan as part of Ford's national marketing strategy. McNamara later estimated that "56 for 56" was responsible for selling 75,000 additional cars. This brought "Beacham's boy" the recognition at Ford World Headquarters that would launch his rapid rise to succeed McNamara as head of the Ford Division.

Iacocca had been promoted to manager of the Washington, D.C., Ford sales district and after a long courtship was scheduled to wed Mary

McCleary, the receptionist at the Ford regional office in Chester, on September 29, 1956. After several months of searching, the couple had finally located a suitable house in Maryland and spent the considerable sum of $2,000 in having it recarpeted. A week before the wedding Charlie Beacham, who had been promoted to head of car and truck sales for the entire Ford Division, called him to announce: "You're getting moved. . . . I'm sorry, but if you want to get paid, your paycheck will be in Dearborn." McNamara tried to soften the jolt. He explained to Iacocca that the company would buy the house from him and "take care of the rugs in your bonus."

Iacocca was brought to Dearborn as national truck marketing manager under Beacham. Within a year Beacham switched his responsibility to national car marketing manager. In March 1960 Iacocca took over both jobs. Then on November 10, 1960, at age thirty-six, he was promoted to vice-president and general manager of the Ford Division, as McNamara moved up to the Ford presidency for a short stint before becoming secretary of defense in the Kennedy administration in January 1961.

"My years as general manager of the Ford Division were the happiest period of my life," Iacocca recalled. "In those days, I couldn't wait to get to work in the morning. At night I didn't want to leave. We were continually playing with new ideas and trying out new models on the test track." The Mustang was by far the most significant of these ideas and was the crowning achievement of Iacocca's career at Ford. "Because the Mustang did so well, making so much profit on so little investment, the question of whose car it actually was, who deserved the credit for it, would be debated in the auto industry for years to come," writes David Halberstam. "Outside the industry, Iacocca, who controlled the publicity for the car, was always considered the father of the Mustang. . . . Within Ford, however, Don Frey, the product manager, was seen as the brains behind it. It was Frey who had the specific idea for the car itself, an inexpensive sports model for the young, and did much of the original design. Iacocca took Frey's idea, made it acceptable to the reluctant finance people, and finally brought around the rest of the company, including the dubious Henry Ford II."

Yet it can be argued that Iacocca's contribution was even more important to the Mustang's suc-

cess than Frey's original idea. Bob Hefty, the Ford public relations executive in charge of the Mustang campaign, later observed, "no top executive in any business organization in history had given as much of his personal time and as much time from other pressing work to the introduction of a new product" as Iacocca did to the Mustang. Gary L. Witzenburg concludes in his comprehensive history of the Mustang that Iacocca considered the car "his personal product and guided its development every inch of the way."

Upon becoming general manager of the Ford Division, Iacocca set up a committee to explore the idea of producing a small car for the youth market. Frey was a key member. Others were Hal Sperlich, Frey's special projects assistant; Bob Eggert and Frank Zimmerman from marketing; public relations manager Walt Murphy; advertising manager John Bowers; Jacques Passino, special projects racing manager; and Sid Olson, from the J. Walter Thompson advertising agency, which handled the Ford account. The committee called itself the Fairlane Committee because it met after business hours at Dearborn's Fairlane Inn rather than on company time at Ford World Headquarters. Iacocca explains that the committee met evenings at the motel because "a lot of people back at the office were just waiting for us to fall on our faces." He was looked upon as "a young Turk . . . who hadn't yet proved himself," and his associates, although talented, "weren't always the most popular people in the company."

The committee met for fourteen weeks. The primary idea it came up with was, in Iacocca's words, "to take a car called the Falcon and make something of it, and that became the Mustang." A special marketing study had indicated that there was strong demand for a small, inexpensive, sporty car from young people and that half of the cars to be sold during the 1960s would be bought by customers between eighteen and thirty-four years of age. These findings made the question not whether the car envisioned should be built but how quickly and at what cost this could be done. In contrast with the all-purpose family car that thus far had been the automobile industry's mainstay, this first "pony car," Iacocca explained at the time, was "the first of the [Ford] long-term plans to put something together for the kids."

The age gap between buyers of Ford and GM cars was widening as younger buyers switched to

Iacocca with his most famous Ford cars, the Mustang, rear, and the Mustang II

Chevrolet and Pontiac models featuring performance. This was in large part the result of Chevrolet and Pontiac "back door" violations of a 1957 Automobile Manufacturers Association (AMA) pact that banned factory participation in speed contests and advertising based on horsepower claims. The 1961 stock car season was dominated by Pontiac with an unprecedented thirty-one wins, versus eleven for runner-up Chevrolet and only seven for Ford.

Keenly aware of the advertising value of racing, Iacocca's motto became "race on Sunday, sell on Monday." He explained at the time that "after Ford wins a race, Ford sales go up. The customer who has seen the race doesn't necessarily buy a high-performance package. What counts is that he buys a Ford." Development of the pony car thus meant the full-scale return of Ford to racing. In June 1962, a few months prior to formal corporate approval of the Mustang project, Henry Ford II, then president of the AMA, renounced the association's 1957 ban on racing. The Mustang was intended to exemplify a new Ford product policy called "total performance."

The way was cleared for the implementation of total performance with the departure of McNamara for Washington in January 1961. Unquestionably, the Mustang never would have been built had McNamara remained Ford's president. The only feature of the car of which he would have approved was that it was small. He was an opponent of high performance and racing, and his product policy emphasized safety and no-frills basic transportation.

The 1960 Falcon was McNamara's outstanding success. It was the most conventional and cheapest of the first generation of American compact cars introduced in 1959 to stave off increasing penetration of the American market by low-priced imports, particularly the Volkswagen (VW) Beetle. The 85-horsepower, stylistically bland Falcon gave good fuel economy, was relatively trouble free, and was so inexpensive to repair that insurance companies offered discounts to Falcon owners. Yet unlike the cramped imports, the Falcon could accommodate six passengers, which made it a family car. McNamara sold a record 417,000 units during the Falcon's first year. As Iacocca says, "This achievement was unprecedented in automotive history and more than enough to earn McNamara the presidency of Ford."

Despite this phenomenal market success and the fact that the Falcon outsold the far more radically designed Chevrolet Corvair by a wide margin, the Fairlane Committee was far more impressed with the sporty Corvair Monza coupe. The Corvair, which had not yet been singled out by Ralph Nader as being unsafe, featured unitized construction, 4-wheel independent suspension, and a novel rear-mounted, flat-6-cylinder, air-cooled, 80- or 95-horsepower aluminum engine. The engine was especially an attraction to many Volkswagen owners wishing to trade. But it was also the car's Achilles' heel. The unconventional rear mounting and air cooling severely limited the size engine that the Corvair could accommodate, so the car could not meet the expectations of performance-conscious consumers. Despite this handicap, the sporty-looking Monza had sold fairly well to young buyers, indicating an unexploited niche in the market for a similarly sporty but more powerful small car.

Before this niche could be filled, it was necessary to kill off McNamara's pet project—a small, fuel-efficient, front-wheel-drive car called the Cardinal that he "conceived to be the American response to the Volkswagen." The Cardinal was scheduled to be introduced in fall 1962, and $35 million had already been spent on its development when Iacocca took over as general manager of the Ford Division. Iacocca flew to Germany to check on the progress being made on the Cardinal but was underwhelmed. He thought that it was "too small and had no trunk," that its great fuel economy "wasn't yet a selling point for the American consumer," and that "the styling was lousy." The Cardinal might be "a fine car for the European market. . . . But in the United States there was no way it could have sold the three hundred thousand units we were counting on." Iacocca canceled the Cardinal for the American market over the objections of Arjay Miller, then Ford controller, and John Bugas, then head of Ford international operations. "The Cardinal is a loser," he told Henry Ford II. "To bring out another lemon so soon after the [1958-1959] Edsel would bring this company to its knees. We simply can't afford a new model that won't appeal to younger buyers."

The Cardinal nevertheless was brought out in Germany as the Taunus and became the first car to cut significantly into the VW sales in its home market. The Cardinal's front-wheel drive was later adopted for use in small, fuel-efficient cars by Volkswagen and several other European producers. As even Iacocca admits, "A decade later, after the OPEC crisis, the Cardinal would have been a world beater." Whether McNamara was "ahead of his time," as Iacocca contends, or whether the Cardinal would have duplicated the success of the Falcon and perhaps even the Mustang in the American market must remain a matter of conjecture. It is clear, however, that the canceling of the Cardinal project put Ford behind in meeting the technological and marketing challenges that resulted from the 1973 and 1979 oil shocks. The great market success of the Mustang in the late 1960s therefore must be balanced against this longer-range loss.

Free from the Cardinal commitment and free to develop his own small sporty car, Iacocca first considered bringing back the 1955 Thunderbird two-seat roadster, with extra space to accommodate four passengers. The original T-Bird had been designed as "a personal sportster" but lacked the performance capabilities of a true sports car. Although it had sold a total of only 53,000 units over three years, the T-Bird still had outsold the Chevrolet Corvette, a true sports car vastly superior in performance and handling. The Thunderbird had grown in all relevant dimensions to become by 1958 a conventional four-passenger car. The Budd Manufacturing Company still retained the original T-Bird dies and was willing to return them, but it was decided that it would be poor company policy to bring back a discontinued model.

An attempt simply to dress up the Falcon also failed. It was not a sporty car to begin with and could not be made into one with a minor facelifting. After eighteen clay models of proposed designs for the new car had been rejected, Ford styling chief Gene Bordinat held an unprecedented open design contest among his three top studios. The contest was won by a design for a car called the Cougar submitted by Dave Ash, who is generally given credit for the design that became the production Mustang.

The production Mustang combined a long hood with a short rear deck, which gave the car an illusion of power and speed. Engine options ranged from the standard 101-horsepower, 170-cubic-inch 6-cylinder to an optional 271-horsepower 289-cubic-inch V-8 that had to be ordered with a 4-speed transmission. The base price of the car was only $2,368, but buyers ordered it with an average of $1,000 worth of options. This proved Iacocca's cynical contention that "people want economy so badly they don't care how much they pay for it."

The major problem in getting corporate approval for developing the Mustang was that at the time it generally cost $300 million to $400 million to bring out an entirely new car. A retooling cost of $250 million already had been approved for the 1965 Ford models, and the initial sales projection for the Mustang promised that only 86,000 units could be sold. "The answer lay in using components already in the system," Iacocca explained. "The engines, transmissions, and axles for the Falcon already existed, so if we could adapt them, we wouldn't have to start from scratch. We could piggyback the new car onto the Falcon and save a fortune. In the end, we would be able to develop the new car for a mere $75 million." Thus the Mustang was essentially McNamara's Falcon with, in Iacocca's words, "a whole new skin and greenhouse." In the opinion of Ford product planner Don Place, this was "like putting falsies on Grandma." Because the Mustang was essentially a Falcon under the hood, it took only one day short of eighteen months from official approval of the project, rather than the usual three years, for the first Mustang to roll off the assembly line on March 9, 1964.

Leon Mandel calls the Mustang "the most sensational introduction of modern times." The Mustang made its debut on April 16, 1964. Over that week and the following weekend many full-page ads appeared in newspapers and magazines. The Mustang and Iacocca made the covers of both *Time* and *Newsweek*. Feature stories on the car and the man behind it appeared in every automotive publication and in *Business Week, Esquire, Life, Look, Playboy, Popular Mechanics, Popular Science, Sports Illustrated,* and *U.S. News and World Report.* "Virtually every publication of significance had carried the Mustang message to hundreds of millions of people, both through paid advertisements and news stories," Gary Witzenburg writes. "No new car in history had ever received the publicity and attention that the media lavished on Ford's sporty small car, and much of the credit for this incredible PR job went to Lee Iacocca himself."

The Mustang sold 418,812 units during its first year to beat the Falcon's previous all-time industry record. Over its first two years of production

Iacocca, left, with Henry Ford II in May 1975 (courtesy of Junebug Clark)

the Mustang generated $1.1 billion in profits for Ford, leading to promotions for everyone connected with the project. Awards for the Mustang's styling included the prestigious Industrial Designer's Institute Award and the Tiffany Gold Medal Award "for excellence in American design." Consequently, Iacocca, in Mandel's words, became "a legend at barely past forty."

The legend, however, was largely of Iacocca's own making. And it was built on record sales of a car that really offered nothing new technologically and that in fact fell short of the performance and handling capabilities that its styling promised. Semon E. Knudsen probably best characterized Iacocca's enormous success. "Lee is a fantastic huckster," said Knudsen. "The only difference between Lee and the old medicine salesman is that the medicine man ran around in a horse and wagon, while Lee runs around in a private jet and a limousine. But Lee is still selling snake oil over the television."

The Mustang had made Iacocca the odds-on favorite to become the next president of the Ford Motor Company. Then fate intervened. On January 31, 1968, Knudsen resigned as an executive vice-president for overseas and Canadian and nonautomotive and defense operations at GM. The automotive world was stunned when on February 5, after secret negotiations with Henry Ford II, Knudsen became Ford president, and Arjay Miller, who had held the job for five years, was summarily kicked upstairs to a newly created vice-chairmanship. Ford explained to Iacocca that "the addition of a high level GM man to our team at Ford would make a big difference." He assured Iacocca, "You're still my boy. But you're young. There are things you have to learn."

Knudsen was twelve years older than Iacocca and far more experienced. He was the son of William S. Knudsen, undoubtedly the top production engineer in automotive history. The elder Knudsen had set up the Ford branch assembly plants beginning in 1912 and had left Ford to join Chevrolet in 1922. It was under his leadership that Chevrolet outsold Ford after 1927.

Knudsen received an engineering degree from MIT in 1936, then gained practical knowledge of production on the floors of several Detroit machine shops before joining GM in 1939. At GM he worked at a wide variety of manufacturing posts, including assembly-line labor, before rising to general manager of the Detroit Diesel Engine Division in 1955. A year later he became general manager of the Pontiac Division and was elected a vice-president of GM. In 1961 he was named general manager of Chevrolet, and in 1965 he was named group vice-president for overseas and Canadian operations and was elected to the GM board of directors.

Knudsen had been passed over for the GM presidency in November 1967 in favor of Edward N. Cole, the father of the Corvair. Knudsen claims that he resigned a few months later not because of "sour grapes" but because he had become disaffected by the increasing centralization and lack of product development at GM. Henry Ford II could not have hoped to hire an automotive executive with a more rounded background or a more impressive record of accomplishments. But Knudsen's tenure as Ford president lasted only eighteen months, and he was fired by Henry Ford II on September 12, 1969. Knudsen was given no reason for the firing other than the vague statement, "Things just didn't work out." Iacocca recalls "great rejoicing and much drinking of champagne."

Whatever reasons there may have been for the firing, Knudsen's job had been made impossible by Iacocca's daily undercutting of his position. Maynard M. Gordon observes that "Iacocca has never denied that he and his loyal teammates in Ford's upper echelons kept Knudsen from functioning as effectively as he might have liked." Designer Lawrence K. Shinoda, who followed Knudsen from GM to Ford, believes that Knudsen "did not bring enough troops" from GM and "failed to use the big hammer" to put Iacocca in his place.

A particular sore point with Iacocca remains what he alleges Knudsen did to the Mustang. Racing enthusiast Knudsen, according to Witzenburg, wanted to outdo GM in performance cars by making the Mustang, "*the* killer street car for mid-year review." Witzenburg alleges that Knudsen wanted "a street Mustang that would be the closest thing possible within the confines of mass production and limited cost to the Trans-Am racing cars . . . and he wanted it fast." Shinoda points out that very little attention had been given to the Mustang's handling, which needed improvement, and that its engine, designed with only peak horsepower in mind, needed a flatter torque curve. A Mach I sports package, with standard 351-cubic-inch and optional 400-cubic-inch engines, was featured in the redesigned car. As compared with Iacocca's original car, the 1971 Mustang was 8 inches longer, 6 inches wider, 600 pounds heavier, and cost $1,000 more. Sales had declined from 550,000 in 1966 to only 150,000 in 1970. "Within a few years of its introduction," Iacocca lamented, "the Mustang was no longer a sleek horse. It was more like a fat pig."

It is inconceivable that Knudsen could have radically changed the Mustang during his brief time as Ford president over the opposition of Ford Division general manager Iacocca. Knudsen's Mustang was in fact a variation of a concept car designed by Don De La Rossa, an Iacocca loyalist. David Halberstam offers an explanation. "Iacocca was pushing bigger and flashier cars," Halberstam reports. "The Mustang, once slim and sporty and relatively simple, had grown bigger and heavier, until its earlier enthusiasts could no longer recognize it. . . . (In his book Iacocca blamed Knudsen for doing that, but the memory of almost everyone else who worked there [at Ford] in those years is different. It was Lee who kept adding weight to the Mustang.) Iacocca, like Henry Ford II, adopted the formula of GM, which kept producing bigger and more expensive cars for its customers as they presumably became richer and more important. . . . The larger

Iacocca's official photograph as the new Ford president in 1970 (courtesy of National Automotive History Collection, Detroit Public Library)

[unit] profit was in the bigger cars."

Henry Ford II did not immediately elevate Iacocca to the Ford presidency to replace Knudsen. Instead he set up a three-man office of the president composed of Iacocca as head of Ford North American operations, Robert Stevenson as head of Ford International, and Robert Hampson as head of Ford's nonautomotive operations. The troika lasted fifteen months before Henry Ford II decided to give the job to Iacocca alone on December 10, 1970.

When Iacocca took over, Ford profits were only 3.5 percent of sales versus returns of 5 percent or more in the early 1960s. Iacocca was determined to improve the profit margin by reducing operating expenses. One of his first moves was to institute a program to cut operating expenses by $200 million within three years. At the same volume of sales this would translate into a gain of almost 40 percent in profits. By 1974 more sophisticated computer programming and improved scheduling, for example, reduced the time required for the annual changeover of the Ford factories to produce the new models from two weeks to a single weekend, when the assembly lines were idle anyway. Shipping costs were reduced a miniscule .5 percent by trimming a fender design 2 inches and packing the freight cars more

tightly. Another program called "Shuck the Losers" sold off some twenty operations that either lost money or made only minimal profits. Searching out ways to increase profits by cutting expenses was a new area for Iacocca, whose experience up to then had been only in sales and marketing. He relates that his success in saving money finally earned him "the respect of the one group that had always been suspicious of me–the bean counters."

Iacocca was a hard-nosed, authoritarian manager who insisted on strict accountability and accepted no excuses for failure. He installed throughout Ford a top-to-bottom system of quarterly review of staffers by their superiors. "Lee got his reputation for total awareness of every staffer's performance on the job through his own black book on the executives reporting directly to him," Gordon observes. "They in turn were to keep tabs on their own underlings. . . . This technique, constantly grading and reviewing, was linked to a requirement for setting and meeting quarterly goals." His own insistence on the periodic review of the goals and employee performance dated from his years as assistant sales manager of the Philadelphia district. It nevertheless took him several years as president to institutionalize his system fully at Ford. By the mid 1970s, however, "every first-of-the-quarter week came to be known as 'crunch time' around Ford because Iacocca was not an easy boss to con. . . . If the executive on the firing line blamed someone else, Iacocca asked why the problem hadn't been communicated. If the executive admitted guilt, Lee raised hell and asked the errant Fordnik to reassess his goals for the next quarter."

Unfortunately for Iacocca, his own performance and goals were increasingly criticized by chairman of the board Henry Ford II. Relations between the two men became strained and turned ugly. To Ford, Iacocca became "that goddam wop." To Iacocca, Ford became "that dumb spoiled bastard." The distance between them was insurmountable. One of Ford's public relations men later explained that "Mr. Ford always regarded Mr. Iacocca as a rather vulgar Italian." Halberstam believes that "the only thing they had in common was appreciation of Iacocca's ability to make profits at the Ford Motor Company. Iacocca had his soaring ambition, he wanted to have it all; but Henry Ford saw him as merely a hired hand, a skilled and highly paid hired hand, to be sure, but nothing more. . . . The social transgressions might have been forgivable had

Iacocca been less ambitious. . . . But Henry Ford had come to think that Iacocca . . . wanted not just to run the company but to make it his."

Iacocca believes in retrospect that he "should have thought a little more about the company's history. . . . All I had to do was review history and my autobiography was staring me in the face." People close to Ford did not stay long in his favor. He had divorced two wives, Anne and Cristina; and he had become "infamous for dropping his number two men under unpleasant circumstances." Breech was fired a year before his planned retirement because he was no longer needed. Knudsen, Miller, and Bugas had been arbitrarily dismissed. Bugas was concerned when Iacocca got too close to Ford. "He falls in and out of love with both men and women," Bugas explained. "Usually it lasts a few years. Never more than six. For a time they can do no wrong. And then comes the time when they can do no right."

Ford's side of the story remains to be made public. Gordon reports that Ford revealed to his biographer, David L. Lewis, that "ample reasons existed for lowering the boom on Iacocca, whom he had hoped would take the hints and resign." Henry Ford II died on September 29, 1987, and his biography is not to be published until five years after his death. Until then we have only Iacocca's version of what transpired.

For his part Iacocca alleges that "in 1975, Henry Ford started his month-by-month campaign to destroy me." The Ford Motor Company had lost $12 million during the fourth quarter of 1974, its first losing quarter since 1946. First quarter 1975 losses would come to $11 million more. On February 3, 1975, Iacocca returned from a trip to the Middle East, as a member of a *Time* delegation of business leaders, to be informed that Ford had cut $2 billion from future product programs, including small cars and front-wheel-drive technology. Iacocca contends that this put the company four or five years behind in bringing out the Tempo/Topaz. A few weeks later Iacocca was forced to fire Paul Lorenz, an executive vice-president, for paying a $1 million "commission" to an Indonesian general in return for a contract to build fifteen ground satellite stations. Iacocca alleges that Henry Ford II approved the payoff and that there was a cover-up within the company "at least as impressive as anything that went on during Watergate."

In August Ford began an investigation into the travel and expense accounts of top Ford executives that Iacocca contends was inspired by Watergate and ended up costing the company close to $2 million. The "audit" started with an interrogation of Wendell Coleman, head of the San Diego branch sales office, who was in charge of the expense accounts for the February 10, 1976, dealers' meeting in Las Vegas. It ultimately consisted of some fifty-five interviews with Ford executives, outside suppliers, and advertising agencies.

The investigation came to focus on Bill Fugazy, operator of a New York travel and limousine service, who ran the Ford dealer incentive program. Halberstam describes Fugazy as "in effect Iacocca's man in New York. . . . The friendship was close. When Iacocca checked into New York, he checked in with Bill Fugazy." Serious complaints had been lodged against Fugazy directly with Henry Ford II by other travel agencies, whom Fugazy constantly underbid on Ford contracts at the last minute, and by the Ford finance people, who found Fugazy's accounts especially difficult to understand. Fugazy was a friend of Roy Cohn and had perjured himself on Cohn's behalf in the trial of "a major Las Vegas gambler." And Fugazy was talking "in terms less than admiring" about Kathy DuRoss, the future Mrs. Ford, whom Henry was then dating. Even Iacocca's friends were "uneasy about the Fugazy liaison. . . . Fugazy always seemed to know so much about the company, too much." Iacocca refused to be counseled. "Early on," Halberstam writes, "Ford had tried to warn Iacocca off the Fugazy friendship, but Iacocca had been curiously adamant. . . . When it became clear that this was not some small problem with Henry but a genuine sticking point, some of Iacocca's friends, men who took his side almost everytime, urged him to listen to his superior and to put some distance between himself and Fugazy. But that made him more intractable than ever." Iacocca fails to acknowledge these concerns in his autobiography. Rather, he alleges that Ford simply had developed the "ridiculous" notion that Fugazy was "mixed up with the Mafia." Iacocca's perception was accurate, however, that the real subject of Henry's probe was not Fugazy but himself.

Iacocca and his people reportedly were absolved, and Henry Ford II is said to have had more indiscretions in his expense account than they in theirs. Ford was not satisfied with the results, however, and he ordered Iacocca to sever all company connections with Fugazy. Halberstam concludes that the audit was "a terrifying experience for those caught up in it" and gave notice that Iacocca's "power was about to be curtailed." For no apparent reason, Ford ordered Leo Arthur Klemenson, president of Kenyon & Eckhart, the Lincoln-Mercury ad agency, to fire Bill Winn, one of Iacocca's closest friends. Then Ford forced Iacocca, under the threat of losing his own job, to fire without cause Hal Sperlich, one of Iacocca's loyal cadre. Sperlich had gained a reputation as one of the top product planners in the industry, and he had played critical roles in the development of the Mustang and the Fiesta, which made Ford millions. But his commitment to small, front-wheel-drive cars made him persona non grata to Henry Ford. After being fired in November 1976, Sperlich became vice-president for product planning at Chrysler in March 1977. Iacocca interpreted the firings as personal assaults on himself.

Iacocca explains that he did not resign because he had spent his "whole adult life at Ford" and could not imagine working anywhere else. More to the point, Iacocca "liked having the president's perks" and had become "seduced by the good life." At an annual salary of $360,000 plus bonuses, he was making $970,000—more than even the chairman of number one General Motors. "I wanted that $1 million so much," Lee recalls, "that I wouldn't face reality."

Early in 1977 Henry Ford brought in the management consultant firm of McKinsey & Company to reorganize his top administration. After several months of study an "office of the chief executive" was created that interposed Philip Caldwell between Ford and Iacocca, as vice-chairman and chief executive officer in the absence of the chairman. Caldwell was a corporate conservative who had worked his way up within the firm to vice-president and chairman of Ford of Europe. The most notable accomplishment in his rise had been turning money-losing Philco into a profitable operation that could be sold. He was, in Halberstam's words, "a good manager for a troubled company," and the Ford Motor Company "was in trouble again. Its costs were out of line, its products lacked quality, and they had lost their appeal."

Iacocca could not cope with the situation, and his ego began to cause even greater problems. Hosting table three rather than table two at company din-

ners was to him "public humiliation, like the guy in the stockade at the center of town." According to Iacocca, "The entire management shift was no more than an ornate and expensive way to defuse my power in a socially acceptable way. . . . It was ridiculous that Caldwell, who used to work for me, was suddenly above me for no apparent reason except malice." Having to report to Caldwell was humiliating enough. Then on June 9, 1978, Bill Ford became an additional member of the office of the chief executive, making Iacocca "fourth in the pecking order." Iacocca relates, "I put out the word that I wasn't going to take it." This was a foolish and hollow threat, for the fact was that the Fords controlled the company.

On June 12 Henry Ford informed the nine outside directors that he was about to fire Iacocca, but they balked at losing an executive who had been so valuable. A peace was arranged during which Iacocca met with several board members to try to iron out the problems. Ford remained adamant, however, and announced his intention to fire Iacocca again, at a dinner meeting with the outside board members on July 12. "It's him or me," he told recalcitrant board members before storming out of the room. "You have twenty minutes to make up your minds." That same night Keith Crane, publisher of *Automotive News*, the industry trade weekly, phoned Iacocca to break the news. The next day he was informed by Henry Ford II at a forty-five-minute meeting that he was no longer needed. Bill Ford, the company's largest individual stockholder, also was present. The word "fire" was never used. Characteristically, Henry gave no real reason for wanting Iacocca out. "It's personal," he said. "Sometimes you just don't like somebody."

An agreement was reached that Iacocca would resign effective the earliest date that he could without forfeiting any benefits—October 15, 1978, his fifty-fourth birthday. Over the last five years, from 1972 to 1977, he had made $4.2 million in salary and bonuses at Ford. The severance agreement provided for $400,000 in cash, plus $22,500 a month for a year, plus retirement benefits of $178,000 a year until age 65, and $175,000 a year after that. "I got about 75 percent of what I was entitled to," Iacocca says.

Iacocca clearly believed that the Ford Motor Company would come upon hard times with his departure. He relates, for example, that he told off Henry Ford II in a parting shot: "Your timing

Iacocca, right, with Michigan senator Donald Riegle, left, and Michigan representative, and later governor, James Blanchard (courtesy of Chrysler Corporation)

stinks. We've just made a billion eight for the second year in a row. . . . But mark my words, Henry. You may never see a billion eight again. And do you know why? Because you don't know how . . . we made it in the first place!"

Iacocca's prediction proved to be wrong. Caldwell succeeded Henry Ford II as chief executive officer on October 1, 1979, and as U.S. chairman on March 13, 1980. Over an eighteen-month period in 1980-1981 Caldwell trimmed Ford's fixed costs by $2.5 billion. The front-wheel-drive Escort/Lynx, introduced in 1980, quickly rose to the top of the sales charts to become the best-selling car in the world. Donald E. Petersen, the Ford president under Caldwell, supervised the introduction of six new models in twenty months at a development cost of $10 billion. The models broke sharply with conventional design concepts and made Ford the styling pacesetter in the automobile industry. *Motor Trend* named as its "car of the year" the Ford Taurus sedan for 1986 and the Ford turbocharged Thunderbird for 1987. Petersen also put a new emphasis on manufacturing quality at Ford, and *Consumer Re-*

ports has rated Ford cars as the most improved. Petersen became Ford chairman and chief executive officer in 1985 upon Caldwell's retirement. In 1986 Ford surpassed GM in profits for the first time in sixty-two years and repeated the performance in 1987. The Ford Motor Company obviously has done extremely well without Iacocca. One can only speculate whether it might have done as well or even better with him.

"The best ballplayer in the business is now a free agent," said an *Automotive News* editorial on Iacocca's firing. Job offers poured in from companies in a variety of businesses, including International Paper, Lockheed, and Radio Shack. Renault wanted to hire him as a worldwide consultant, and New York University wanted him to become dean of its business school.

During summer 1978 Iacocca conceived the idea of putting together a worldwide consortium of automobile companies, called Global Motors, to challenge GM. Although different partners would work, the logical choices for inclusion in the combination seemed to be Volkswagen, Mitsubishi, and

Chrysler. Chrysler was chosen because he thought that it could provide "a solid engineering base." He asked Salomon Brothers, a New York investment banking firm, to research what the contemplated merger might involve. They reported that American antitrust laws were a major obstacle. "In the process," Iacocca relates, "I learned a great deal about several car companies, including Chrysler. To be more precise, I learned a great deal about their balance sheets. But as I would soon find out, there's a hell of a difference between what a company looks like on paper and how it actually operates."

Coming to Chrysler was first suggested to Iacocca at a lunch in New York City given by board members Richardson Dillworth and Louis Warren, and was then discussed in general terms with Dillworth and Chrysler chairman John J. Riccardo at a secret meeting at the Hotel Ponchartrain in downtown Detroit. Riccardo and Chrysler president Eugene Cafiero had been openly feuding while the corporation bled to death. A bleak picture of Chrysler's situation was painted by Riccardo at two subsequent meetings at the suburban Northfield Hilton. But the picture was not nearly bleak enough to convey the reality, for even top management lacked information on what was going on in the corporation. Iacocca thought that Chrysler "could be turned around in a year.... When I signed on for my new job," he relates, "I couldn't imagine that anything in the automobile business could be *that* bad. I was wrong."

The agreement was that Iacocca would come in as president and chief operating officer to replace Cafiero but that on January 1, 1980, he would take over from Riccardo as chairman and chief executive officer. As it turned out, Riccardo was forced to retire even earlier because of illness, so Iacocca moved up to the Chrysler chairmanship on September 20, 1979. His initial salary was $360,000, the same as at Ford, which necessitated a $20,000 raise for Riccardo to keep even. Additionally, Iacocca received options to buy 400,000 shares of Chrysler stock and $1.5 million in installments to replace the deferred compensation and severance pay from Ford that he forfeited by joining Chrysler. Iacocca retained his Ford pension and $3 million in Ford stock.

On November 2, 1978, the day that Iacocca became Chrysler president, the corporation posted a third-quarter loss of almost $160 million, the largest quarterly deficit in its history. Headlines in the *Detroit Free Press* proclaimed: CHRYSLER LOSSES ARE WORST EVER, and LEE IACOCCA JOINS CHRYSLER. He was given a huge vote of confidence when Chrysler stock closed up three-eighths for the day.

After the death of Walter P. Chrysler in 1940 leadership in the firm that bore his name had passed to K.T. Keller, an engineer, then in 1956 to Lester Lum Colbert, a lawyer. In the 1960s and 1970s the corporation was headed by the accountants Lynn Townsend and Riccardo. Chrysler's deserved prewar reputation for technological innovation and engineering excellence was preserved into the postwar period. The corporation led American industry, for example, in the introduction of disc brakes (1949), the hemispheric combustion chamber (1951), power steering (1951), hydraulic shock absorbers (1952), improved torsion bar suspension (1957), and the alternator (1960). The 1956 Chrysler "Torqueflite" automatic transmission was arguably the finest ever built. Chrysler also led the industry in 1962 in offering extended warranties. Paradoxically, however, Chrysler products gained a reputation for poor quality. A Chrysler production executive recalls that in the 1960s and 1970s the corporation was "building and shipping junk."

Chrysler made a belated, ill-fated attempt to emulate Ford and GM by becoming a multinational enterprise. An ambitious overseas expansion program was mounted with the purchase of a controlling interest in Simca in 1958. By 1973 Chrysler owned 100 percent of Simca, Barrieros in Spain, and Rootes Motors, producer of the Hillman and Humber, in the United Kingdom. Subsidiaries were established in Australia and Japan. Assembly facilities were acquired in Argentina, Colombia, and Venezuela.

Simca and Rootes were both in financial trouble and in poor competitive positions, which explained their low acquisition prices. Chrysler made the classic blunder of adding their weaknesses to its own. Chrysler-U.K. was losing so much money by 1975 that the parent company, in deep financial trouble itself, threatened to begin liquidation, an option that was staved off only when the British government agreed to a bailout.

Despite this bailout, and the claim of Chrysler-U.K. in 1976 that its financial position was viable, Chrysler-U.S. announced the sale of its European subsidiaries to Peugeot-Citroen (PSA) as part of a general retrenchment program in August 1978,

Iacocca and the first Chrysler K-car (courtesy of John Collier, Detroit Free Press)

shortly before Iacocca came aboard. The Latin American facilities were sold the following year, the subsidiaries in Australia and Japan in 1980 for 15 percent of Mitsubishi stock. Since then Chrysler has had operations only in North America, whereas Ford and GM have operations on all continents.

In contrast with family-controlled Ford, no one held more than a 1 percent equity in Chrysler. Yet Chrysler alone among Detroit's Big Three failed to institutionalize Sloanism. GM management practices, as noted, began to be implemented at Ford in 1946 and had been popularized in Sloan's 1964 autobiography. Nevertheless, in 1978 Chrysler still had not emulated GM by instituting even a rudimentary committee structure, clear lines of authority, or a system of financial controls. Iacocca was horrified to learn that Townsend and Riccardo "hadn't brought in any serious financial analysts" and that "nobody in the whole place seemed to fully understand what was going on when it came to financial planning and projecting." No one was responsible for cost control. Overproduction for dumping to dealers at regular sales was a company policy. Manufacturing was not geared to marketing. Design was not

geared to manufacturing. A self-perpetuating managerial bureaucracy had left Chrysler with highly paid, unnecessary executives. Thirty-five vice-presidents ran their operations as personal fiefdoms. Iacocca was dumbfounded that "after thirty years of postwar, scientific management . . . in 1978 a huge company could still be run like a small grocery store."

He saw that the management problem was compounded because "for years, Chrysler had been run by men who really didn't like the car business. . . . Engineering, which had always been Chrysler's ace in the hole, became a low priority under Lynn Townsend. When profits started to fall, it was engineering and product development that paid the price." As a consequence, by 1978 the Chrysler Corporation was in debt to 400 banks and on the verge of bankruptcy. Iacocca berated his friend Hal Sperlich and asked, "Why didn't you tell me it was this bad?"

It became clear to Iacocca by summer 1979 that "only drastic measures could save the Chrysler Corporation. . . . We no longer had the means to save ourselves from drowning." Merger talks with

Toni Schmueker, the head of Volkswagen, had broken down after VW studied the Chrysler balance sheet. A proposal from John Z. DeLorean to merge his faltering DeLorean Motors with Chrysler was rejected for the reason that it would merely put two losers together, as was a research and development tax shelter proposed by DeLorean on the ground that it spelled trouble with the IRS. Chrysler's losses were mounting as the economy in general and the automobile industry in particular felt the impact of the oil shock following the 1979 Iranian Revolution.

Filing for bankruptcy under chapter 11 of the federal bankruptcy law was unthinkable. Consumers would cancel orders out of fears about warranty coverage, availability of parts and service, and resale value. This would create a domino effect. The banks would refuse to finance dealer purchases from the factory. Suppliers would demand payment in advance. It was estimated that about half of the Chrysler dealers and many of the thousands of Chrysler's small suppliers would be forced into bankruptcy themselves. "What would the largest bankruptcy in American history have done to the nation?" Iacocca asks. "A study by Data Resources estimated that the demise of Chrysler would ultimately cost the taxpayers $16 billion in unemployment, welfare, and other expenses."

Ideological free-enterpriser Iacocca relates that "the last thing I wanted to do was turn to the government. But once I made the decision, I went at it with all flags flying." He rationalized going to the government for aid on the basis that "government helped us get into this mess, so government should be willing to help us get out."

Chrysler had been hit particularly hard by the imposition of federal standards on automotive safety (1966), emissions (1965 and 1970), and fuel economy (1975) because it had to spread the development costs to meet them over far fewer units than GM or Ford. The antiquated American antitrust laws prohibited the Big Three from pooling their resources to meet the standards, whereas Japanese companies could work cooperatively. Iacocca estimated in 1984, for example, that $19 billion in research and development costs on automotive safety alone since 1966 had been spread by GM over 5 million units, Ford 2.5 million units, and Chrysler only 1 million units a year and that even greater economies of scale had accrued to GM and Ford in the manufacturing of the mandated equipment. Chrys-

ler also had argued unsuccessfully for meeting the emissions standards through fast burn/lean burn technology. Meeting the standards for mandatory adoption of the catalytic converter further weakened Chrysler's competitive position, because as the least vertically integrated of the Big Three, it had to purchase its catalytic converters while GM sold them at a profit. As a result, equipping a conventionally powered car with the total emissions system required by 1977 cost $200 a unit at GM versus more than $400 at Chrysler. Iacocca noted "the sheer volume of staff time and paperwork necessary to report on our EPA regulatory confirmation. In 1978 alone [Chrysler] had to file 228,000 pages to the EPA!" Despite the poor management of Chrysler, in Iacocca's opinion, "what ultimately brought the company to its knees was the relentless lash of more and more governmental regulation."

Riccardo first lobbied for a freeze on government regulations and for a refundable $1.5 billion tax credit to reimburse Chrysler the money it had spent on meeting safety and emissions standards. Several state governments had given other automobile manufacturers special tax breaks, and the federal government had set a precedent in 1967 by giving a $22 million special tax credit to American Motors. Nevertheless, Riccardo's arguments fell on deaf ears.

The idea of asking for a loan guarantee was suggested first by G. William Miller, who resigned as chairman of the Federal Reserve Board on August 6, 1979, to join Jimmy Carter's cabinet as secretary of the treasury. In his first official act Miller announced that he thought government help for Chrysler was in the public interest and that, while he rejected giving the firm a special tax credit, the administration would consider a loan guarantee. Upon investigation, Iacocca learned that loan guarantees were "as American as apple pie. Among those who had received them were electric companies, farmers, railroads, chemical companies, shipbuilders, small businessmen of every description, college students, and airlines." Conspicuous examples during the 1970s were the federally guaranteed loans extended to Lockheed Aircraft, New York City, the Washington, D.C., Metro, and five steel companies. Still, the idea of a loan guarantee for Chrysler, the country's tenth-largest industrial corporation, proved to be controversial. It came under particularly heavy criticism from such probusiness sources as the Business Roundtable, the National Association of Manufacturers, the *Wall Street Journal,* and conservative Republican politicians. But the bill was endorsed by the Carter administration and steered through Congress by Speaker of the House Tip O'Neill. The Italian caucus and the black caucus were major supporters. A national advertising campaign turned the tide of public opinion in Chrysler's favor. And particularly effective lobbying campaigns were carried on by Douglas Fraser, president of the United Auto Workers (UAW), and by the Chrysler and Dodge dealer organizations.

Just before Christmas the Loan Guarantee Act was passed 271 to 136 by the House and 53 to 44 by the Senate. The act permitted Chrysler to survive at about half of its former size. It created a Loan Guarantee Board authorized to issue up to $1.5 billion in loan guarantees over the next two years, to be repaid by 1990. These loan guarantees were fully secured by Chrysler's assets, which were conservatively estimated by the government at $2.5 billion in liquidation value, so no public funds were ever at risk. Other stipulations were that current lenders to Chrysler were required to extend $400 million in new credit and $100 million in credit on existing loans; foreign lenders were required to extend an additional $150 million in credit; suppliers had to provide $180 million, $100 million of which had to be in stock purchases; state and local governments with Chrysler plants had to provide $250 million; Chrysler had to raise $300 million through the sale of assets and issue $50 million of new stock; concessions of $462.2 million were required from UAW employees, and pay cuts or freezes of $125 million from nonunion employees. Iacocca tried to set an example of "equality of sacrifice" by reducing his own salary to $1. Prior to receiving the first $550 million in guaranteed loans in June 1980, Chrysler issued to the Loan Guarantee Board warrants entitling the bearer to purchase 14.4 million shares of Chrysler stock, then priced at $5, for $13 a share. Obtaining the consent and cooperation of all parties to meet the stringent conditions set by the government undoubtedly was the toughest selling job and most spectacular success of Iacocca's career.

Loans guaranteed by the federal government totaling $1.2 billion were fully repaid in 1983, seven years ahead of schedule. With Chrysler stock at $30, the Reagan administration put up the warrants at auction to the highest bidder. Chrysler bought them back and retired them at a cost of $311 million. Over the three-year period of the loan guarantees Chrysler also paid $404 million in interest, $33 million in administrative fees to the government, and $67 million to the lawyers and investment bankers.

Losses of over $1.7 billion in 1980 and $475.6 million in 1981 were transformed into profits of $170.1 million in 1982, $700.9 million in 1983, and a record $2.38 billion in 1984. Chrysler's debt/equity ratio in 1984 was 19.7 percent, down from 69.8 percent in 1982 and the lowest ratio in seventeen years. Chrysler's share of the North American market reached 11.6 percent in 1984. The corporation's relationships with lending institutions and its labor force were becoming normalized for the first time in years.

Iacocca's greatest business triumph was dulled by his deepest personal loss. Only two months before announcement of the loan guarantee payback, Mary McCleary Iacocca died, on May 15, 1983, of complications arising from diabetes. She had suffered heart attacks in 1978 and 1980 and a stroke in spring 1982. "On each of these occasions when her health failed her," Iacocca remembers, "it was following a period of great stress at Ford or Chrysler." She was "a tower of strength," who had sustained Lee through the Ford firing and the dark days of the loan guarantee battle. "The Lord makes everything turn out for the best," she had counseled him. "Maybe being fired from Ford is the best thing that ever happened to you."

In 1986 Iacocca received total compensation from Chrysler of $20,542,491. This included his base salary of $727,972, a $975,000 cash bonus, and $35,000 from the company contribution to his employee savings plan. The lion's share, however, came in the form of stock and stock options. Iacocca had exercised his options to buy Chrysler stock now worth $9,558,912. And under the terms of his 1983 contract, he had been promised as an outright gift, if he was still chairman on November 2, 1986, 337,000 additional shares, which had doubled in value to $9,280,607. Iacocca's 1986 total compensation at Chrysler compared with $4.336 million total compensation for Ford chairman Donald E. Petersen and $3.825 million total compensation for GM chairman Roger Smith. Iacocca had become the highest-paid executive in the history of the automobile industry and the fourth-highest-paid business executive of all time, after Federal Express chairman Frederick W. Smith, Toys R Us chairman

Charles P. Lazarus in 1982, and Mesa Petroleum chairman T. Boone Pickins in 1984. This was Iacocca's reward for the Chrysler turnaround.

The recovery had resulted in a far leaner and tougher corporation. In addition to selling off its operations abroad to raise operating revenues, Chrysler sold Chrysler Defense, Inc., the nation's only maker of military tanks, to General Dynamics for $348 million. Twenty plants were closed, and the remaining plant facilities were modernized. White-collar personnel was trimmed from 40,000 in 1978 to 21,000 in 1983, while salaries were reduced up to 10 percent. Concessions by the UAW averaged $10,000 a worker during the first nineteen months of the loan guarantee as labor productivity was raised 50 percent. Chrysler's fixed costs were cut in constant dollars from $4.7 billion in 1979 to $3.54 billion in 1983, and the firm's break-even point was reduced from 2.4 million to 1.1 million units. In an unprecedented move, to ensure the cooperation of the workers, Douglas Fraser, the president of the UAW, was made a member of the Chrysler board of directors.

Sales increased with introduction of the fuel-efficient, front-wheel-drive K series and the popular Caravan, Voyager, and Dodge Mini Ram minivans. *Motor Trend* named the Aries and the Reliant as its cars of the year for 1981. Chrysler also made news by bringing back the convertible on a K-car frame. The model sold well despite the fact that the open-car design had become outmoded with car stereos and air conditioning. Between 1979 and 1983 Chrysler claimed a 36 percent improvement in the quality of its cars, based on a decline in consumer complaints and warranty repairs. It also claimed the lowest number of recalls of any automobile manufacturer.

The revitalized Chrysler Corporation, only eight years after almost going bankrupt itself, announced on March 9, 1987, that it had signed a tentative agreement with Renault to buy the French government-owned company's 46.1 percent controlling interest in American Motors, to exchange cash and Chrysler stock for the remainder of AMC's outstanding shares, and to assume $767 million in AMC debt. The acquisition increased Chrysler's plant capacity and dealer outlets and added the 4-wheel-drive Jeep to Chrysler's line.

Chrysler's recovery was accomplished mainly by former Ford executives brought in by Iacocca. Very few of the people in top Chrysler management

had been able to adjust to Iacocca's methods. Over a three-year period he fired thirty-three of the thirty-five vice-presidents. One of the two who remained was Sperlich, who rose to the Chrysler presidency under Iacocca. Sperlich deserves credit in particular for bringing the concept of the minivan to Chrysler from Ford, where it had originated in the late 1960s as an idea of designer Don De La Rossa and been championed in particular by Sperlich and design chief Gene Bordinat. Henry Ford II had shied away from making a commitment to the so-called Mini/Max at the time because it required a totally new design with front-wheel-drive and transaxle, hence was very costly to develop. Subsequently, however, Sperlich was able to develop the vehicle at very low cost at Chrysler by using the K-car platform, in the same manner that the Mustang had been developed from the Falcon. The replacement of separately developed lines of cars at Chrysler with the piggybacking of different design on a common platform was indeed the major way that the corporation gained great economies of scale under Sperlich and Iacocca. Ironically, Cafiero had lost his job to Iacocca for proposing the identical strategy.

William Ford had made the mistake of giving Iacocca permission to take with him his confidential black books, in which the careers of some three hundred Ford executives had been closely monitored. He used the books to raid Ford of executive talent. One of the most highly rated finance people was Gerald Greenwald, at forty-five the head of Ford of Venezuela. Iacocca induced him to join Chrysler as controller. Greenwald in turn recruited from Ford finance Robert S. "Steve" Miller, who played an "absolutely critical" role in placing the federally guaranteed loans with several hundred banks. Greenwald went on to become Chrysler vice-chairman.

Of major importance in the comeback was the "professor-emeritus troika" of retired Ford executives brought in by Iacocca. They were, in Gordon's words, "the toughest cookies to toil for Ford or anyone else around Detroit." Gar Laux had headed Ford sales and marketing before he retired in 1968 at age fifty-one to open a Cadillac agency in partnership with golfer Arnold Palmer in Charlotte, North Carolina. Hans Matthias had been in charge of manufacturing at Ford before retiring in 1972 to form his own manufacturing consulting firm in Detroit. Paul Bergmoser had been in charge of Ford purchasing before early retirement to Palm Springs in 1967 at age sixty. The three assumed comparable functions at Chrysler. Laux revitalized the demoralized dealer and sales organizations. Bergmoser systematized purchasing, smoothed out relations with suppliers, and was Chrysler's president for a short time. Matthias was responsible for updating the production process and improving quality. His other important contribution was pinpointing for advancement to key management positions two capable Chrysler executives whose careers had been dead-ended—George F. Butts, who became vice-president in charge of manufacturing quality, and Stephen Sharf, who became executive vice-president. Glenn E. White, vice-president for personnel and organization, was the only other old-guard Chrysler executive to remain part of Iacocca's new top management team.

Another member of the Ford team that Iacocca took with him to Chrysler was Kenyon & Eckhardt, the New York advertising agency that had been associated with Ford since 1945. Kenyon & Eckhardt had originated the "Sign of the Cat" ads that gave Mercury top consumer recognition among all makes of car and were responsible for the "Ford Has a Better Idea" slogan. On March 1, 1979, Chrysler announced that Kenyon & Eckhardt had been given a five-year contract to take over all of Chrysler's corporate advertising at a guaranteed annual billing of $120 million, a reduction from the $150 million that Chrysler had been paying to Young & Rubicam and Baton, Barton, Durstine & Osborne. This was the largest single account change in advertising history. Iacocca thought that Kenyon & Eckhardt were the best in the business, and he announced that he felt as though he had "just bought the New York Yankees." Agency people were placed on the Chrysler product planning and marketing committees, and Kenyon & Eckhardt, in Iacocca's words, "became an integral part of Chrysler, the closest thing to a house agency we could have. In effect, they became our marketing and communications arm."

The corporation's problems were constantly in the news during the congressional hearings on the loan guarantee, and Iacocca became a nationally known figure. Kenyon & Eckhardt convinced him that it was essential for him personally to tell the Chrysler side of the story. "We have to tell the public that we're a new company, different from the old Chrysler bunch," Iacocca was told by De-

troit agency head John Morrissey. "The best way to get that message across is to feature the new boss." Iacocca was at first reluctant, because he was "convinced that any corporate chairman who appears in his company's ads has got to be on an ego trip." He also was concerned that "appearing in television commercials would be seen by the public as a final act of desperation that would cause the entire enterprise to backfire." But in retrospect, "It's clear that my appearing in the television ads was an essential part of Chrysler's recovery." The ads identified Chrysler personally with its chairman in the public mind and made Iacocca a minor television celebrity. In the most famous of the commercials, he pointed his finger at the viewer and challenged, "If you can find a better car—buy it."

For a self-described materialist, who from the beginning of his career was only "after the bucks," Iacocca has amassed an amazing record of honors and has been involved in civic and charitable activities. He has received honorary doctorate degrees from Lehigh University, the University of Michigan, the Massachusetts Institute of Technology, Duke University, Muhlenberg College, Alma College, the Lawrence Institute of Technology, Babson Institute, La Salle University, Hillsdale College, and George Washington University. He is an honorary trustee of Lehigh University and the chairman of its Asa Packer Society. He is an honorary chairman of the Catholic University of America's Centennial Campaign, chairman of the Committee for Corporate Support of the Joselin Diabetes Foundation, cochairman of the governor of Michigan's Commission on Jobs and Economic Development, and was chairman of the Statue of Liberty—Ellis Island Foundation. He is a member of the Conference Board, the Detroit Press Club Foundation, New Detroit, Inc., the Detroit Symphony Board of Directors, the Executive Board of the Art Center College of Design, the Founders Society of the Detroit Institute of Arts, the Economic Club of Detroit, the National Academy of Engineering, and the Society of Automotive Engineers. The millions of dollars in royalties from his best-selling autobiography have been donated to charitable causes.

Still, what Iacocca's reputation will be from a historical perspective remains uncertain. "We have a tendency in this country to idolize success, often without looking too hard at how it was achieved," John F. Lawrence warns. "The problem with this in business is that it often distorts our judgment about how durable the accomplishments will turn out to be." Lawrence believes that "Iacocca has a real shot at business immortality if he produces a company that is as viable eight years from now as it is today. The job ahead, however, will involve tougher decisions on products and marketing strategies than those he has had to make to date. It is going to take a lot more than acquiring another company; it is going to take a lot of risk-taking without taxpayer support." Observers further wonder what would happen to Chrysler in the event of Iacocca's departure after nearly a decade of his authoritarian management style and the narrow identification of the corporation with his person.

Iacocca's energies clearly are being dissipated away from Chrysler by his considerable involvement in charitable and civic activities and his remarriage in 1985, which ended in divorce late in 1987. He is reported to be increasingly involved in Florida real estate investments with his friend Donald Trump, a New York developer. In 1985 his Italian estate began exporting a red table wine from Tuscany to the United States, appropriately labeled Villa Nicola for his immigrant father. Although he has consistently denied his interest in running, rumors have made him a potential candidate for the Democratic party's nomination for president of the United States.

Publications:

Iacocca: An Autobiography, with William Novak (New York: Bantam Books, 1984);

Talking Straight, with N. R. Kleinfeld (New York: Bantam Books, 1988).

References:

James J. Flink, *The Automobile Age* (Cambridge, Mass.: MIT Press, 1988);

Henry Ford, in collaboration with Samuel Crowther, *My Life and Work* (Garden City, N.Y.: Doubleday, Page, 1922);

Maynard M. Gordon, *The Iacocca Management Technique* (New York: Dodd, Mead, 1985);

David Halberstam, *The Reckoning* (New York: Morrow, 1986);

Semon E. Knudsen, taped interview with James J. Flink, June 9, 1987;

John F. Lawrence, "Iacocca Still Must Pass the Test of Time," *Los Angeles Times,* May 31, 1987;

Leon Mandel, *American Cars* (New York: Stewart, Tabori & Chang, 1982);

Lawrence K. Shinoda, taped interviews with David R. Crippen, October 29, 1985, March 12, 1986, and June 10, 1986. Edsel B. Ford Design Center, Henry Ford Museum and Greenfield Village;

Gary L. Witzenburg, *Mustang: The Complete History of America's Pioneer Ponycar* (Princeton, N.J.: Princeton Publishing, 1979).

Imports

by George S. May

Eastern Michigan University

Although a handful of European-made Benz automobiles that were imported in the first half of the 1890s were the first production cars to be sold in the United States, the domestic automobile industry, launched later in the decade, quickly gained firm control of the market. Tariffs levied on imported cars, which during the 1910s reached 45 percent, were by the 1920s quite low compared with rates charged in many other countries. For a half century foreign cars, with the exception of very limited numbers of such luxury makes as the Rolls-Royce, were an insignificant element in American automobile sales. In 1936, for example, only 1,007 new and used automobiles were imported while 341,326 American-made motor vehicles were exported. Exports rose to 475,914 in 1937, more than a third as many vehicles produced by all of the world's automobile manufacturers outside of the United States and Canada.

Following World War II the rate import sales suddenly began to accelerate. In Europe, the only major center of auto production outside of North America, and where motor cars had always been regarded as the province of the rich, a new emphasis emerged on the mass production of small, inexpensive cars. Until the European economy and standard of living rebounded from the devastating effects of the war, the reviving European automobile industry looked to exports as a major source of sales. As it happened the extreme shortage of new cars available to meet the voracious market that existed in the United States after the war persuaded Americans to look at the low-priced European cars, which in the prewar years had been dismissed as too small and low-powered to fill the needs of American motorists.

By 1949 import sales exceeded 12,000 units in the United States, a tiny figure in a year in which total car sales topped 5 million but nevertheless a marked increase over prewar sales. Modest increases characterized import sales until 1955 when they began to rise at unprecedented rates. By 1959, with more than 600,000 units sold, imports accounted for slightly more than 10 percent of all cars sold that year. Luxury models and sports cars were no longer the import leaders they had once been. Instead, the increasing interest of Americans in the lower-priced imports caused concern among the domestic producers, who saw these foreign cars for the first time competing strongly in that segment of the market where the American companies had always enjoyed dominance.

Although several French and Italian companies, such as Renault and Fiat, were exporting their small cars to the United States by the late 1940s, the British, who were at the time the second largest manufacturers of cars in the world, seemed to have the best chance of gaining a strong foothold in the American market. The high regard with which Americans viewed the Rolls-Royce, Jaguar, and MG caused them to expect the same high quality in such British economy cars as the Hillman Minx, Morris Minor, and Austin A-40. But the initial enthusiasm with which these imports were received in the early 1950s soon cooled when these cars proved subject to breakdowns and could not generate the speed to which Americans were accustomed. Repair costs and the delay in getting parts, which often had to be shipped from Great Britain, more than offset the advantages of the excellent gas mileage of cars that cost nearly as much new as a full-size Chevrolet or Ford.

The decline in British import sales after 1953 was offset by the rising popularity of the German-made Volkswagen (VW), which became the first import to make a sizable dent in the market for low-priced cars. Although it was of prewar origins the Volkswagen did not appear in the United States until 1949, when the first efforts were made by the reconstructed German manufacturer to tap the

The MG-TD, one of the series of MG vehicles which popularized sportscar imports

American market. Initial reactions to what was dubbed "Hitler's car" were negative, but gradually a realization emerged that in spite of its odd appearance, its small size, and its noisy air-cooled rear engine, the Volkswagen was a well-built car which, unlike other small European cars, performed very well when driven as Americans liked to drive their cars. An American Volkswagen organization was set up in 1954 and 1955 to import the car in much greater numbers and sell them through a network of dealers carefully trained to meet Volkswagen's exacting service standards. This dealer and service training overcame one of the major problems earlier imports had faced in winning customers. Before Volkswagen, foreign models were sold by domestic car dealers as a mere sideline, and service was inconsistent and unreliable.

Sales of the Volkswagen, which had totaled only about 1,000 by 1953, came close to 30,000 in 1955 and increased steadily each year thereafter, hitting 120,000 in 1959. Demand for the car was so great that some customers, rather than waiting many months for delivery, turned to some of the other European imports, enabling these models to greatly increase their share of the market. As a result Volkswagen's share, which for a time had accounted for about half of all import sales, sank to only 20 percent by 1959. But the true measure of the consumer's respect for the Volkswagen was evident in 1960 when sales of Renaults, British Fords, Fiats, Simcas, and other small European cars declined sharply in the face of the appearance of the first compact models from the American Big Three automakers. That same year Volkswagen sales in-

creased by nearly 40,000 units. Through the next several years Volkswagen continued to run counter to the overall trend in terms of small-car sales. By 1965 its sales of 383,000 constituted two-thirds of all import car sales for that year. But then in the late 1960s Volkswagen sales leveled off, and in 1971 they began a decline that led to the German company in 1975 losing the position it had held for two decades as the leading importer to the United States.

The Big Three had always tended to discount the importance of Volkswagen sales by citing evidence that it was something of a counterculture car because it was so totally unlike the standard American car. These people were not likely customers for the American cars, and so the domestic automakers dismissed them as out of the mainstream and took comfort in the fact that in the mid 1960s, for every American who bought a Beetle, twenty-four others bought an American compact, intermediate, or full-size car. But the Japanese noticed the same thing, and it was in the late 1960s that increasing numbers of their cars began to appear in the United States. Like the Volkswagen the Japanese cars were smaller than American cars of the day, but unlike the German car they had the look and the feel that made them comfortable to those accustomed to driving Fords or Chevys or Plymouths.

Although the Japanese automobile industry originated early in the twentieth century, its growth before the war had been very limited and had been confined largely to commercial vehicles. By 1967 the Japanese had used this experience to become the world's largest producers of trucks. But aided

The 1967 Volkswagen Beetle; the Volkswagen's low price and stable design made it a fixture in the American market for more than thirty years

by government policies that virtually prevented the importation of foreign cars, the Japanese companies began to build more passenger cars, which, because of the high cost of gasoline in Japan, were small, fuel-efficient vehicles. As the Japanese economy boomed and credit restrictions which had discouraged installment sales were eased, domestic sales of these cars provided the greatest stimulus to the growth of the Japanese automobile industry, which by the early 1970s had supplanted Germany's as the world's second largest.

Foreign markets, which became increasingly important as the domestic market in Japan began to become saturated, were not neglected in the earlier years despite the problems the Japanese automakers had in meeting the surging demand for cars among their own people. In 1957 and 1958, when their combined annual production was less than 40,000 cars, Japan's leading companies, Toyota and Nissan, shipped their cars to the United States. These Toyotas and Datsuns, as Nissan's vehicles were called until the 1980s, proved unsuited to the American market. Their styling seemed old-fashioned by American standards, and their engines, designed for the narrow roads of Japan

which restricted speed, gave out after only a few miles of being driven at expressway speeds in California, where the cars first were imported. But while the cars were a failure, the rugged little Datsun pickup trucks were successful. By the end of the 1960s Japanese trucks, led by Datsun, nearly monopolized the import-truck market, which had previously been dominated by the Volkswagen Combi pickup.

The success of the Datsun pickup prepared the American public to accept the redesigned Japanese cars that began to appear in the mid 1960s. Leading the way was the Toyota Corona, which looked like a traditional, although downsized, American car, with surprising interior roominess and an engine that *Consumer Reports* described as combining "first-rate performance with fuel economy which was better than the VW's." By 1970, when Toyotas and Datsuns were joined by Mazdas, Subarus, and Hondas, the Japanese accounted for a quarter of import sales, up from a mere 3 percent in 1965.

Import sales, which, aside from those of the Volkswagen, had slumped in the early 1960s, were on the upswing in the late 1960s and in 1970 exceeded 1.23 million, or 15.3 percent of all sales in the United States. The alarmed domestic producers rushed out new models, called subcompacts, which were comparable in size to the imports. But in the early 1970s, unlike the early 1960s when the American compacts had stemmed the flow of small cars into the country, the new subcompacts did not result in decline in the sales of the imports. The imports instead kept pace with the overall growth in the auto market, maintaining the same 15-percent share of sales. Sales of the Volkswagen dropped off as Americans grew tired of its unchanging look after twenty years, but Japanese cars took up the slack, pushing Japan ahead of Germany by 1972 as the leading exporter of cars to the United States.

The sharp rise in oil prices that resulted from the actions of the oil-exporting nations beginning in 1973, and the depressing effect this had on the nation's economy, proved to be a bonanza for foreign carmakers who had experience in producing small, fuel-efficient, and relatively inexpensive cars. The American Big Three, on the other hand, with the bulk of their production still geared to big cars, now hard to sell, could not meet the demand for the cheaper compact and subcompact models. By 1975 imports accounted for over 18 percent of car sales in the U.S. The Japanese, garnering over half these sales, were the biggest beneficiaries. Improved economic conditions later in the decade led to better sales for the American full-sized and medium-sized models, but the biggest gainers continued to be the subcompacts. The American manufacturers continued to be slow in stepping up their development and production of smaller cars, leaving the way open for further gains by the Japanese. The imports also benefited from their better gas mileage figures, while the contrast between the quality of workmanship and materials found in the imports and the American makes was dramatized by the numerous recalls and lawsuits to which the domestic models and their manufacturers were subjected. Fears of a new world oil shortage that surged in 1979 again sent the demand for the larger American cars plummeting. During the next three years the domestic industry suffered its worst decline since the 1930s while Japan, with the cars the times demanded, in 1980 moved ahead of the United States in world automobile production and increased its sales in the United States to nearly 2 million cars, more than twice their sales in 1975 and about 80 percent of all import sales that year.

The return of better times by 1983 helped the Big Three to regain much lost ground, but imports were by now a fact of life in the domestic market. By the mid 1980s the Yugo from Yugoslavia and the Hyundai from South Korea were new entries in the small-car field, undercutting the Japanese imports, which still, however, dominated the field. At the other end of the spectrum prosperous times greatly aided the sales of such European luxury and prestige makes as France's Peugeot, Italy's Alfa Romero, Sweden's Volvo and Saab, Germany's Audi, Porsche, and BMW as well as the well-established Mercedes-Benz, Rolls-Royce, and Jaguar. By 1986 imports commanded nearly 25 percent of the market and reached the $3 billion mark in sales.

In the 1980s, however, a growing number of cars of foreign origin were not imported but were being manufactured in the United States. Earlier in the century very limited numbers of such cars had been produced domestically but usually by American companies licensed to manufacture them by the foreign producer. But in 1978 Volkswagen, seeking to rebound from the economic problems it had weathered earlier in the decade, began assembling its small Volkswagen Rabbit models at a plant in New Stanton, Pennsylvania, while at the same time Renault acquired a controlling stock interest in American Motors. Renault used this acquisition not only to open AMC showrooms to imported Renaults but in 1982 to begin to produce these French cars at AMC's Kenosha, Wisconsin, plant.

Despite promising beginnings neither of these attempts to establish subsidiary operations in the United States enjoyed continuing success, and in 1987 both Volkswagen and Renault abandoned them. The Japanese, however, had followed the European companies' lead and with far greater success. Honda, which had begun building motorcycles at a plant in Marysville, Ohio, in the late 1970s, began producing its Accord models, one of the most popular of the imports, at that assembly plant in 1982. Other Japanese companies were not far behind, and by the end of the 1980s nine assembly plants had been built in the United States and Canada. By 1990 these plants were to have an estimated annual capacity of more than 2 million vehicles. With the bulk of the jobs going to American workers, and at least some of the parts produced by American suppliers, the plants helped to offset the criticisms that the Japanese imports were depriving American autoworkers of jobs. However, the impact of these Japanese subsidiaries was to make them a major factor in the North American auto industry, much as Ford and General Motors branches and subsidiaries had been in Europe and elsewhere in the world since the early years of the century. The days when American companies completely controlled the American automobile market were clearly at an end.

References:

Alan Altshuler and others, *The Future of the Automobile: The Report of MIT's International Automobile Program* (Cambridge, Mass.: MIT Press, 1984);

James J. Flink, *The Automobile Age* (Cambridge, Mass.: MIT Press, 1988);

David Halberstam, *The Reckoning* (New York: Morrow, 1986);

James M. Laux and others, *The Automobile Revolution: The Impact of an Industry* (Chapel Hill: University of North Carolina Press, 1982);

George S. May, *The Automobile in American Life* (forthcoming, 1990);

MVMA Motor Vehicle Facts and Figures '87 (Detroit: Motor Vehicle Manufacturers Association, 1987);

John B. Rae, *Nissan/Datsun: A History of Nissan Motor Corporation in the U.S.A. 1960-1980* (New York: McGraw-Hill, 1982).

Jeep

by Robert J. Kothe

Atlanta, Georgia

The Jeep name belongs to the Chrysler Corporation as a result of its 1987 purchase of American Motors Corporation (AMC). AMC had acquired the company in 1970 from the Kaiser company, which had acquired it in 1953 when it took over Willys-Overland. Currently the name can only be used correctly to describe vehicles produced by Chrysler or its predecessors. It is often incorrectly used to refer to any relatively compact 4-wheel drive vehicle.

The Jeep had its origins in the early days of World War II. The need for a relatively small vehicle with off-the-road ability was clear to the army, and it requested designs from a number of companies. The winning basic design was submitted by the American Bantam Car Company, a small firm located in Butler, Pennsylvania, and the producer of a compact passenger car.

The development of the design was awarded to Willys-Overland, a much larger company. Bantam was ultimately awarded a small contract for the production of the vehicle and turned out around three thousand during the war. The Jeep, as designed by Willys-Overland, incorporated the basic running gear from the Willys commercial vehicle. While Willys was the major producer, Ford—which had submitted its own unsuccessful design for a small, all-purpose vehicle—also built a vehicle virtually identical to the Willys Jeep.

The World War II Jeep had an 80-inch wheelbase, was 132 1/4 inches long, and 62 inches wide. It weighed 2,315 pounds, was rated for an 800-pound, "quarter ton" payload, and designed to pull a 1,000-pound trailer. The engine was a 4-cylinder, L-head design with 134.2 cubic inches of displacement.

The exact origin of the name Jeep is not known. Perhaps the most logical explanation is that it was derived as an abbreviation of part of the official army designation, "general purpose vehicle" or GP. Another theory is that the name came from a cartoon character in "Popeye" that was capable of extraordinary feats.

During World War II the Jeep legend was born. Like the cartoon character the Jeep was thought to be capable of unbelievable feats. It could pull through deep mud, snow, sand, and loose coral, carry three times its rated payload, and pull many times its stated trailer capacity. Jeeps were used as tractors to pull everything from field pieces to B-17 aircraft, were fitted with machine guns and used as scout cars, and the hoods were used as temporary altars for religious services in the field. Fitted with a special body, Jeeps were a rough-riding but virtually unstoppable ambulance.

By the end of the war 660,000 Jeeps had been produced. Many were abandoned on the battlefield or sold to the local population. In the Philippines

The 1944 World War II Jeep

they spawned both an industry—the production of spare parts to keep them going—and a form of folk art in the vibrantly decorated bodies that were often installed on Jeep frames.

In the United States surplus Jeeps were converted by the thousands to snowplows and utility vehicles. Since they could be acquired by colleges, local governments, local schools, and civil defense agencies at essentially no cost, they were a common sight on college campuses and in government fleets for many years. The United States Department of Agriculture (USDA) investigated their usefulness on farms and reported that the Jeep was suitable for light plowing. They tested a Jeep pulling a 16-inch plow cutting a 7-inch furrow in a cotton field. The USDA reported it took 1.72 hours to finish an acre, and the vehicle produced a drawbar pull of 862 pounds.

In its July 1946 issue *Consumer Reports* wrote that the Jeep "appealed to the suppressed desires of every road-bound motorist or anyone with a streak of mountain goat in him." The rest of their review was less complimentary. They found the vehicle difficult to get in and out of, as well as other negatives.

The Jeep was emulated by a number of other manufacturers, most notably the English Rover Company which produced the Land Rover. Later the Japanese produced similar vehicles. Willys-Overland

started producing a civilian version, the C (civilian) J (Jeep), after the war as well as continuing to make vehicles for the military. In 1953 Kaiser Motors Corporation acquired Willys-Overland and continued Jeep production at the old Willys Toledo plant. In 1970 Kaiser sold its Jeep operations to AMC.

A new model military Jeep, the MC-M38, was introduced for the Korean conflict. It was equipped with a 24-volt electrical system. It was soon replaced by the MD-38A1. The civilian models underwent gradual changes, such as the L-head engine being replaced by an F-head, and the brakes being improved. In 1964 a Buick V-6 was offered as an optional power plant. The early Jeeps were geared for power rather than speed and, in addition, were equipped with small engines. Jeeps were hard pressed to keep up with highway traffic, so the increased power was necessary on modern roads. After 1971 the wheelbase was lengthened to accommodate the larger engines that AMC wanted to install.

The name Jeep was also applied to a variety of vehicles in addition to the original vehicle. A larger station wagon, the Wagoneer, which would develop into an often luxuriously equipped model in later years, was introduced in 1962 as was a pickup, the Gladiator. Two larger trucks, the FC 150 and the FC 170, were produced between 1957 and 1964. These models were cab-over-engine designs. The inexpensive Jeepster, also called the Commando and the Jeepster Commando, was introduced in 1966. The name has also been applied to fleet vehicles used by the Postal Service, although these were being phased out in the late 1980s.

The smaller Jeep models—the CJ and military models—with substantial ground clearance are well suited for their off-the-road role, but their high center of gravity adversely affects highway handling and makes them more prone to roll over than normal passenger cars under most circumstances. Periodically during the 1970s and 1980s the company was the target of lawsuits and articles in the media concerning the alleged dangerous nature of the vehicles. Recent military models did not meet safety standards for highway use and were routinely destroyed rather than being sold as surplus vehicles.

The military continued to use evolutionary models of the Jeeps well into the 1980s. They are now being replaced with the Hummer, a much more sophisticated, and expensive, off-the-road vehicle. Current civilian models, while they have greatly changed mechanically, retain much of the original appearance of the first Jeep.

The 1970s and 1980s were difficult years for AMC. Its partnership with the French automaker Renault provided capital and some new models, but the company rarely made a profit. The Jeep division, however, was profitable during most of this period, despite increasing Japanese competition in the 4-wheel-drive markets.

The Jeep name and its dealer network were two of the major assets that Chrysler acquired in its 1987 merger with AMC, giving Chrysler a large part of the domestic 4-wheel-drive market as well as access to foreign markets.

Henry John Kaiser

(May 9, 1882-August 24, 1967)

by Mark S. Foster

University of Colorado at Denver

CAREER: Founder of many companies which later became publicly held corporations, Kaiser was president or chairman of the board of the following: Kaiser Paving (1914-1956); Six Companies, Inc. (1931-1945); Kaiser Steel (1942-1956); Kaiser-Frazer Corp. (1945-1955); Kaiser Aluminum & Chemicals (1946-1956); Permanente Cement (1939-1956); Kaiser Industries (1956-1967); and many other companies.

Between 1914, when he founded his first small company, and his death in 1967, Henry John Kaiser became one of the most prominent entrepreneurs in the United States. He was never an inventor like Thomas Edison; nor was he an innovator on the order of Andrew Carnegie or Alfred P. Sloan, Jr. Unlike John Rockefeller and Henry Ford he never dominated a single industry. But his versatility and the breadth of his achievements exceeded those of but a handful of rivals. As a farsighted advocate of industrial growth, Kaiser was a key figure in the economic maturation of the American West. He built hundreds of miles of roads, and he and his partners also constructed some of the largest federal dams in the region. During World War II Kaiser's West Coast shipyards employed more than 200,000 workers and produced one-third of the nation's cargo ships. During the war he also built the region's first large steel mill, and he greatly expanded that facility in the postwar period. Although he continued to promote regional development, Kaiser's influence spread much farther. His aluminum operations challenged Alcoa's empire. The Kaiser Health Plan became the largest Health Maintenance Organization (HMO) in the nation. Kaiser was involved in home construction, cement and building materials, tourism and resort development, nuclear power, radio, television, and many other enterprises. Although he succeeded in almost everything he attempted, Kaiser's ten years in the automobile industry comprised his single great business failure.

Kaiser was born in Sprout Brook, a small village in upstate New York, on May 9, 1882. His parents, Frank and Mary, were emmigrants from Steinheim, Germany. Their economic status was very modest. Frank Kaiser was a cobbler and earned a precarious living selling handmade shoes when ready-made shoes were taking over the market. Henry, the youngest of four children, had three sisters; he was by most accounts a happy, well-adjusted child. Kaiser's formal schooling ended at thirteen, when he gained full-time employment at the J. B. Wells dry goods store in Utica. For three years he clerked and sold dry goods. In the meantime he became fascinated with cameras and provided photographic services on a part-time basis.

At seventeen Kaiser left J. B. Wells for full-time work in photography. With Eastman-Kodak pioneering advances in photographic equipment in nearby Rochester, the late 1890s were exciting years for a young man to enter the business. Kaiser believed photography would be his life's work, and he spent a year as an assistant in a photography store in Utica, followed by a year as a traveling salesman of photographic supplies throughout New York State. In 1901 he learned of an opportunity to become a partner in a photography store and studio in Lake Placid, New York. It was a modest operation and the owner, nearing retirement, sold out within a year, giving Kaiser his first business. But Lake Placid was then a small town, promotion of tourism was quite primitive, and there was little business during long, cold winters. Kaiser decided to follow the tourists to Florida; between 1903 and 1905 he opened a string of photography shops scattered along the east coast of Florida.

Courtship and betrothal changed the direction of Kaiser's life in 1906. Bess Fosburgh, a young woman of good breeding and prosperous background, entered his life. Kaiser proposed marriage but her eminently proper father, a Virginia lumber magnate, considered photography an inconsequential enterprise. Edgar Fosburgh set rigid conditions before the marriage took place, including the requirement that Kaiser had to enter a "real" business. For reasons still unclear Kaiser traveled to the Pacific Northwest and established himself in Spokane, Washington, where he took a clerical job with McGowan Brothers, a wholesale hardware company. Kaiser quickly moved up the ladder and in a few months had a lucrative sales position. He promptly saved a down payment, borrowed enough

Henry John Kaiser (courtesy of Motor Vehicle Manufacturers Association of the United States, Inc.)

to buy a small house, and returned east to marry, which he did on April 8, 1907.

Kaiser made many hardware sales to building contractors and soon became interested in that business. In 1910 he left McGowan Brothers to work for Hawkeye Sand & Gravel, a local materials supplier. After learning a good deal about building aggregates, he joined J. F. Hill Company, a road-building and general construction company. For two years Kaiser learned the construction business, while supervising grading and surfacing of streets and highways throughout the region. He did well financially, earning about $8,000 in 1913, his last year with Hill. Top level management entrusted Kaiser with large jobs, including contracts belonging to its subsidiary, Canadian Mineral Rubber Company.

But in 1913 managerial infighting at J. F. Hill brought on a swift decline in corporate fortunes. Assigned to roadbuilding jobs in and around Vancouver, British Columbia, Kaiser was abruptly fired for refusing to take sides. Although his paychecks were cut off, Kaiser won many admirers in southern Canada by finishing the jobs he had been assigned. Kaiser was primed to strike out on his own; the thirty-two-year old formed Kaiser Paving under Canadian law in 1914.

Kaiser quickly gained a reputation for fast, high-quality work in street paving and road-building. The World War I period provided excellent opportunities for aggressive roadbuilders. With rapid public acceptance of mass-produced automobiles in the United States governments quickly increased budgets for improved streets and highways. Kaiser benefited directly, as he expanded his operations into the entire West Coast region. Many of his early jobs were small, and he sometimes lost money; but as his reputation grew, he won larger contracts. In 1921 he moved his modest business headquarters to Oakland, California, where they remained.

During the 1920s most of Kaiser's work was in roadbuilding, but he also built earthen dams and set up sand and gravel operations to provide materials for his jobs. Kaiser also began building a vital network of capable, loyal managers and professional associates. His skill at interpersonal relations earned him the respect of more experienced construction men, who in turn helped advance Kaiser's career. In 1927 Warren Brothers Company of Massachusetts, a nationally renowned firm with which Kaiser had worked closely on previous western contracts, offered him a $19 million subcontract to build a two-hundred-mile section of a trans-Cuba highway. The task was formidable, as Kaiser's section traversed many miles of swampland. Equally challenging was getting along with laborers holding a very different work ethic and with government officials who were genuinely puzzled by Kaiser's refusal to pay bribes.

As Kaiser's work in Cuba wound down, the United States plunged into the depression. In addition to the highway job in Cuba, Kaiser and his men performed other tasks: levee repair work along the Mississippi River, laying hundreds of miles of petroleum pipeline in the Southwest, and numerous other small contracts. But in the early 1930s Kaiser, like other contractors, was worried about his future. In hard times construction work was a tempting target for budget cutters in the public sector. Fortunately the federal government was beginning a major program of huge public works. One of these projects, the Hoover Dam, was opened for bidding in 1930. The contract was so large and the job so complex that no single contractor risked bidding it alone. Kaiser joined a consortium of contractors named Six Companies; his partners included the most high-powered contractors in the West: Mac-

Donald & Kahn, Utah Construction, Morrison-Knudsen, and others. On March 4, 1931, bids were opened in Denver, and Six Companies won the job with a bid of $48.9 million.

The Hoover Dam job changed Kaiser's career in very unexpected ways. The partners divided responsibilities, and Kaiser's main task was serving as liaison between the contractors and bureaucrats in the Department of the Interior and in Congress. Kaiser's job was vital; he had to keep money flowing into corporate coffers. But it was basically public relations, and he had little to do with actual construction of the dam. Between 1931 and completion of the Hoover Dam superstructure in 1935, Kaiser spent many months in Washington. He learned how the federal government worked, and he became expert at maneuvering himself and his partners into position to receive government contracts and loans. Kaiser used this knowledge to great advantage throughout his career. In the late 1930s Six Companies was twice reorganized under different combinations of partners and successfully bid major portions of both the Bonneville and Grand Coulee dams on the Columbia River. These and other giant tasks kept Kaiser and his men busy into World War II.

But Kaiser was not too busy to seek other work. Ironically, failure to win the bid in 1939 to build Shasta Dam in northern California launched the fifty-seven-year-old into yet another career as a major producer of construction materials. For years Kaiser had been plagued by high prices charged by a West Coast cement combine. When he lost the Shasta Dam job he determined to win the contract to supply cement for the dam. Kaiser underbid the West Coast combine by more than 20 percent. Federal officials were reluctant to award Kaiser the bid because he did not have a cement plant, but they eventually yielded. Within months Kaiser and his men built a huge plant south of San Francisco in Santa Clara County. In the early 1940s Kaiser became a major force in this industry; his Permanente Cement operation supplied much of the cement for military installations in the Pacific during World War II.

The war years marked Kaiser's emergence as a public figure, even a national hero. With the outbreak of war in Europe, Kaiser sensed much earlier than most American businessmen the near inevitability of this nation's eventual involvement in the conflict. Most industrialists, their confidence pro-

The 1951 Henry J, right, and its companion car, the 1953 Allstate, which was marketed and sold by Sears (courtesy of Baron Wolman and Lucinda Lewis © 1982)

foundly shaken by the depression, were extremely wary of expanding production capacity at their own expense. Adopting very conservative positions, analysts in several heavy industries insisted that they could meet any increases in demand with existing plant capacity. Kaiser believed otherwise. Between 1939 and 1941 he testified forcefully that government policymakers should insist upon immediate plant expansion in magnesium, steel, aluminum, and other producer goods. If existing manufacturers failed to accept the challenge, Kaiser offered to help fill critical voids.

Kaiser's concern about industrial production was in part an outgrowth of his heavy involvement in the shipbuilding industry after 1939. During the late 1930s he and his construction partners had built millions of dollars worth of harbor improvements on the West Coast. These projects introduced him to prominent shipbuilders. Kaiser eventually joined with John A. McCone and Stephen D. Bechtel to win a contract to build thirty cargo ships for the British late in 1940. By late spring 1941 Kaiser and his engineers had erected a huge shipyard in Richmond, California. After Kaiser and his partners met the British order well ahead of schedule, the United States Maritime Commission awarded them a steady stream of contracts, mainly for cargo ships. By 1944 the huge shipyard operation at Richmond employed nearly 100,000 men and women,

and Kaiser's team developed similar operations in the Portland/Vancouver region on the Columbia River. During World War II the "Kaiser" yards on the West Coast yielded 1,490 vessels, including fifty small aircraft carriers and nearly one-third of the cargo ships produced in the United States. Kaiser's remarkable shipbuilding feats won him profound admiration from journalists, who dubbed Kaiser the nation's "Miracle Man" and America's "Number 1 Industrial Hero." President Roosevelt was so impressed with Kaiser that he seriously considered asking him to be his running mate in 1944.

Many rival entrepreneurs seethed at what they perceived as hypocritical publicity-seeking on Kaiser's part. When steel shortages became a major bottleneck in meeting cargo ship contracts, Kaiser urged federal officials to grant him permits to build his own steel plant on the West Coast. Eastern steel men were incensed when Kaiser publicly lectured them about their alleged dereliction of duty. In their eyes this upstart entrepreneur had become a public hero only because of huge government contracts; he had never competed in "real" private enterprise. Kaiser threatened their turf, and they vigorously opposed his repeated efforts to win government approval for his own plant. Throughout 1940 and 1941 Kaiser's "war" with Big Steel increased in intensity. Eastern steel men successfully blocked Kaiser's initiative, and his frustration grew.

Pearl Harbor changed the situation overnight. Within weeks Kaiser had his authorization, and he also secured tens of millions of dollars in government loans from the Reconstruction Finance Corporation (RFC) to build a large steel plant in Fontana, fifty miles east of Los Angeles. Setting aside their differences during the national emergency, Big Steel provided technical assistance to Kaiser to set up the Fontana plant. Kaiser and his men needed only nine months to build a steel plant and begin producing ingots.

Unfortunately short-term cooperation by Big Steel did not mark emergence of a permanent truce between Kaiser and many conservative businessmen. In mid July 1942 Kaiser used a ship-launching in Portland to suggest building a fleet of 5,000 huge cargo planes, which could fly men and materiel over Axis submarines then wreaking havoc on Allied shipping. If the aircraft industry could not do the job, Kaiser offered his services. The national press picked up Kaiser's proposal and played it to the hilt; due in part to media pressure, ten days later Kaiser presented his ideas to President Roosevelt. In fact the aircraft industry was performing miracles of its own in meeting military needs. Although existing aircraft manufacturers and their military contacts managed to sidetrack this initiative, Kaiser's critics saw the episode as shameless publicity-seeking. Just four weeks before the Fontana plant produced its first steel Kaiser presented an address before the National Association of Manufacturers (NAM) that further irritated many businessmen. On December 4, 1942, when most entrepreneurs were still gearing up for wartime production, Kaiser urged his listeners to start preparing for the eventual return of peace. Specifically Kaiser urged automobile manufacturers to announce their 1945 models very soon. Kaiser was already doing everything for the war effort that he was permitted to do; he had energy left over, and in his view, planning for the future was simple common sense. To rivals it was another example of unconscionable grandstanding. Joseph W. Frazer, president of Willys-Overland, labeled Kaiser's suggestions "half-baked" and "stupid."

It is ironic that Frazer lambasted Kaiser's NAM speech; less than three years later they were partners in the automobile business. The war years marked Kaiser's emergence as a visionary; anticipating a postwar economic boom of unparalleled magnitude, he dreamed of filling an impressive variety of consumer needs. One of his chief goals was to mass-produce "poor man's" cars bearing his own name. In 1945 Frazer was a seasoned automobile executive with more than thirty years of experience, and he possessed similar dreams. Each man had something the other needed. Kaiser had the "muscle" of a large, aggressive organization, with access to private capital and expertise in dealing with government agencies; Frazer had experience and a good reputation in the industry. Kaiser's foremost banking associate, Amadeo P. Giannini, founder of the Bank of America, arranged a meeting between the former adversaries in July 1945.

Two weeks later they announced incorporation of Kaiser-Frazer in Nevada. For years the automobile industry had been dominated by the Big Three: Ford, General Motors (GM), and Chrysler. Between the 1890s and the stock market crash of 1929 Detroit had been a burial ground for more than 100 would-be automobile companies. Most failed or were soon absorbed by larger companies. Mounting a challenge to the major producers would be a formidable undertaking. But the partners sensed a window of opportunity for new competition in 1945. The Big Three had converted their huge plants to wartime production, and it would be many months before they could begin turning out automobiles in large numbers. Union leaders in Detroit were interested in promoting competition in the industry, and they indicated willingness to cooperate with newcomers. Most important, the industry had not experienced "normal" conditions since the onset of the depression. World War II rationing, plus boom times in the defense industry, had created millions of potential customers who had accumulated thousands of dollars in savings. They would buy anything on wheels, and the producers knew it. Kaiser and Frazer sensed that if they could get new cars onto the market quickly, they might successfully challenge the Big Three's domination.

Kaiser and Frazer made a fatal mistake at the outset; they underestimated public enthusiasm for the venture and failed to exploit fully the opportunity to raise enough capital to compete effectively over the long haul. Three separate stock issues sold out quickly and brought in $53 million. The initial offering, at $10 per share, was oversubscribed by a multiple of six, and the price per share rose to $24 before the company yielded its first car. Kaiser later acknowledged that they should have raised three or four times the amount they did.

At the time, however, the error was not apparent. In late 1945 and early 1946 most signs were favorable. The partners moved with impressive speed to find a plant. They leased the enormous Willow Run plant west of Detroit from the federal government on extremely favorable terms: $500,000 for the first year, $850,000 the next, and $1.25 million for the last three years of a five-year lease. Next they lined up dozens of pieces of expensive, hard-to-obtain production machinery. But many other challenges had to be met. Supplies of axles, engines, and dozens of specialized auto and body parts had to be found. Reliable sources of sheet metal and other basic materials were required. A reliable management team had to be set up. Thousands of skilled and semiskilled workers had to be recruited and union contracts signed. Doubters in Detroit bet on whether or not Kaiser-Frazer would even survive until production began. When the first units dribbled out of the cavernous plant, wags urged the partners to name them "Willit Run?" But fair-minded observers were generally impressed with the partners' early moves.

Kaiser and Frazer had to agree on a production strategy quickly in summer 1945. Kaiser dreamed of a vehicle in the $400 price range, but he had little more than a vision and a few plaster models. Frazer, with his experience and more fully developed plans, urged production of conventional, full-sized models. Realizing that Frazer's strategy promised significant numbers of cars more quickly, Kaiser accepted his partner's plan. Estimating a break-even point of 75,000 units, the partners were not surprised when Kaiser-Frazer lost $19 million in 1946 on output of 11,754 cars. Kaiser and Frazer expected better times in the near future, but stockholders were not so sanguine. Even before Willow Run turned out its first units in August 1946, the stock price dropped to $15.

The next two years marked the heyday of Kaiser-Frazer. Although investor confidence wavered and the stock dipped to $7 in summer 1947, the partners had every reason to feel optimistic. In September they celebrated production of their 100,000th automobile, and Willow Run was turning out over 15,000 units each month. Better yet the cars sold well. In 1947 Kaiser-Frazer produced 144,507 units and earned $19 million. The next year production increased to 181,316 cars, and Kaiser-Frazer enjoyed the prestige of being the largest independent producer in the country. Profits

dipped to $10 million in 1948; company officials voiced optimism, but insiders were nervous about the trend.

In the long run the doubters were correct. Between 1949 and suspension of conventional vehicle production in the United States in 1955, the company experienced a seemingly unending series of reversals. By fall 1948 Kaiser-Frazer had trouble selling cars. The Big Three were catching up with demand, and consumers clearly preferred their models. Kaiser-Frazer dealers had to offer increasingly generous trade-in allowances to compete at all. Even so, longer and longer lines of unsold cars stacked up on lots near Willow Run. Even more worrisome, the Big Three firms were spending tens of millions on research and design of new models, which augured even stiffer future competition. Kaiser-Frazer and other independents did not have the resources to match those efforts.

By 1949 Kaiser-Frazer's suddenly precarious position in the industry was painfully evident. Although production dropped by more than two-thirds to 59,281 cars, dealers could not sell even that modest number. A cursory glance at the models suggested why: having made few improvements Kaiser-Frazer was trying to sell the same basic models that buyers had snapped up two years earlier. By late 1949 the glut of unsold units in company lots reached crisis proportions. Investor confidence sagged further, as the stock dropped to $3.50 per share. In 1949 the company lost $30 million.

The partners managed to gloss over basic philosophical differences when times were good, but hard times exacerbated their fundamental conflict. Many of their joint decisions represented uneasy compromises rather than genuine harmony. Both men hired teams of managers personally loyal to them. Inherent disunity in upper management inhibited Kaiser-Frazer's ability to respond effectively to crises. Top management was so dispirited in 1949 that it considered folding operations. In retrospect that might have been a wise decision. Frazer resigned the presidency and was replaced by Kaiser's older son, Edgar. Although Frazer remained a director most of his loyalists were soon eased out by Kaiser's men. Despite brave and in many ways resourceful efforts to reverse corporate fortunes, Edgar Kaiser and his men presided over the rapid decline of the company. Henry Kaiser retained a very active role in large corporate decisions. In 1950 the company introduced an inexpensive compact, the

"Henry J," but it did not catch on. The timing was wrong; in the 1950s consumers wanted size and luxury.

Ironically Kaiser-Frazer declined just when it began to produce excellent cars. The Kaiser Dragon was a lovely sedan, and the Kaiser-Darrin sportscar was a gem. But production numbers spiraled steadily downward. Tax credits and military contracts to build C-119 cargo planes during the Korean War prevented even larger losses in the early 1950s, but the downward trend was clear. In 1953 the company sold the Willow Run plant to GM, merged with profitable Willys-Overland and consolidated operations in Toledo, Ohio. The new combine specialized in Jeeps and four-wheel drive vehicles and suspended production of conventional cars in 1955. Henry Kaiser pulled a coup in selling much of the Toledo machinery to Argentine dictator Juan Peron in 1954 and setting up automobile plants in Argentina and Brazil that turned out 500,000 cars over the next decade. In such politically unstable countries Kaiser and his managers wisely insisted that majority ownership be held by local investors. However, by the mid 1950s Kaiser-Frazer had lost a staggering $123 million in domestic operations.

A further irony was that Kaiser-Frazer's collapse occurred when most of Kaiser's other enterprises were achieving record-level expansion and profits. Kaiser Steel never challenged Big Steel in national markets but became an important supplier in rapidly expanding western markets. Kaiser Aluminum, an outgrowth of Kaiser's magnesium production contracts during World War II, became a force in national markets. Due in part to the Justice Department's desire to encourage competitors against Alcoa, Kaiser Aluminum gained more than 25 percent of the domestic market by the early 1960s and challenged Reynolds Metals for the number two position in this highly profitable field.

The collapse of Kaiser-Frazer and the parallel emergence of several publicly held corporations in the Kaiser empire induced the founder to create a large holding company in 1956. Kaiser Industries consolidated most of his operations under one roof and facilitated access to private financial markets when corporate leaders needed more resources for expansion. By paying in full a $91 million balance on the RFC loan on the Fontana Steel plant in 1950, Kaiser gained grudging respect from all but his most hostile critics. Owners of Kaiser-Frazer stock did not lose everything; they were allowed to exchange their holdings on a four-for-one basis for Kaiser Industries shares.

The 1950s marked other important changes in Kaiser's business and personal life. Bess Kaiser, his wife of forty-four years, died in 1951 after a lengthy illness. Kaiser wasted little time in remarrying, creating a minor scandal in the process. Just three weeks after Bess's death the sixty-nine-year-old married her thirty-four-year-old nurse, Alyce Chester. In 1954 Kaiser semiretired to Hawaii, where he launched yet another "career" by promoting tourism, constructing a large resort hotel on Waikiki Beach, building a cement plant and a planned city, Hawaii Kai, located ten miles east of Honolulu. He also entered radio and television and sponsored the highly successful series, "Maverick." The Hawaii years also provided him more time to promote the Kaiser Health plan and hospital program. Founded originally as a prepaid health plan for Six Companies employees at Grand Coulee Dam by Dr. Sidney R. Garfield in 1938, the program mushroomed during World War II, when "Kaiser" doctors treated tens of thousands of shipyard workers on the West Coast. Despite furious opposition from American Medical Association opponents, who labeled the Kaiser Plan "socialized medicine," Kaiser and the doctors opened the plan to the public after the war. By the time Kaiser died in 1967 the health plan was the largest HMO in the nation, with 1.5 million members.

In 1962 Kaiser enjoyed his eightieth birthday party at the impressive new high-rise corporate headquarters building in Oakland. Kaiser had always abused his body. At a shade under six feet, he occasionally ballooned up close to 300 pounds and was usually about 100 pounds overweight. Despite his obesity he enjoyed good health and spirits up to his last months. Shortly after his eighty-fifth birthday his health finally failed, and he died at his home in Hawaii on August 24, 1967. Kaiser died when American business appeared to command the free world. He never anticipated the late-twentieth-century decline; indeed, Kaiser engineers had helped countries in the Pacific Basin, including Japan, rebuild and modernize their industrial bases. As one of America's late-nineteenth- and early-twentieth-century self-made men, Kaiser maintained unbounded faith in the nation's economic future. In certain respects, his death symbolized the end of a simpler, more optimistic era.

References:

"Adventures of Henry and Joe in Autoland," *Fortune*, 33 (March 1946): 98-99, 101-103;

Mark S. Foster, "Challenger From the West: Henry J. Kaiser and the Detroit Auto Industry," *Michigan History*, 70 (January/February 1986): 30-39;

"Kaiser-Frazer Cashes In," *Fortune*, 36 (December 1947): 94-96;

"Kaiser-Frazer: The Roughest Thing We Ever Tackled," *Fortune*, 44 (July 1951): 74-77, 154-162;

Richard M. Langworth, *Kaiser-Frazer: The Last Onslaught on Detroit* (Princeton, N.J.: Princeton Publishing, 1975).

Archives:

The Henry J. Kaiser papers are located in the Bancroft Library, Berkeley, California.

Kaiser-Frazer Corporation

by Mark S. Foster

University of Colorado at Denver

Kaiser-Frazer Corporation was in the domestic automobile business for ten years, from 1945 to 1955. During that span the company produced just under 750,000 vehicles. Despite this modest long-term achievement, for a brief period in 1947 and 1948 the company not only earned profits in an extremely competitive enterprise but exceeded all other independent manufacturers in production and sales. Undercapitalized and overextended, Kaiser-Frazer was in an extremely vulnerable position when the Big Three caught up with consumer demand. After 1948 the company's decline was dramatic and swift.

As partners, Henry J. Kaiser and Joseph W. Frazer were an odd couple. Raised in very modest circumstances, Kaiser in many respects embodied the Horatio Alger stereotype. By 1945 he had amassed a personal fortune in general construction, shipbuilding, cement, steel, and other basic building materials. His shipbuilding feats during World War II had made him a media star; admiring newsmen labeled him the nation's "Miracle Man." But many rival businessmen disliked him, charging that he succeeded only with the help of millions of dollars worth of government contracts and loans. By contrast, Frazer was a direct descendant of Martha Washington and was raised in comfortable surroundings. Although educated at private schools, Hotchkiss and Yale, Frazer dropped out of college in 1912 to take a manual labor job at Packard Motors. Frazer quickly rose to important managerial positions and by the mid 1940s was a solid, respected automobile executive who had spent his entire ca-

reer in that industry. Ironically Frazer's first contact with Kaiser was a direct confrontation. In a national address in 1942 Kaiser urged automobile producers to begin planning for postwar production; Frazer replied for the automobile industry, labeling Kaiser's suggestions "half-baked" and "stupid."

Kaiser and Frazer had little in common beyond the fact that each dreamed of mass-producing cars bearing his own name. In 1945 that shared vision brought them together. Frazer had experience and many contacts in the automobile industry. Kaiser had the muscle of a large, aggressive organization with access to private capital and expertise in dealing with government officials. In July 1945 the two men met in San Francisco. Two weeks later Kaiser-Frazer Corporation was incorporated in Nevada.

Few neutral observers gave the new combine much of a chance for success. Detroit was a graveyard for automotive entrepreneurs. Between the 1890s and the late 1920s over 100 automobile companies had been organized. Most either failed outright or were absorbed by larger, more successful companies. But in 1945 there appeared to be a window of opportunity for new producers. The Big Three had dedicated their plants to wartime production and required many months for reconversion to car manufacturing. Union leaders in Detroit were eager to encourage new competitors; they promised cooperation with newcomers like Kaiser and Frazer. Most important, the industry had not experienced normal markets since 1929. The Great Depression brought a decade of hard times; during

The 1947-1948 Kaiser four-door sedan

World War II there were no cars available. By 1945 prospective buyers often had thousands of dollars in savings and war bonds and drove twenty-year-old cars. They would buy anything on wheels, and car manufacturers knew it.

Had Kaiser and Frazer not been inveterate optimists, they might never have started work; but they moved with impressive speed. Between August 1945 and production of their first vehicles a year later, they overcame dozens of formidable challenges. The partners needed capital, and they successfully floated the first of three stock issues which, combined, brought in $53 million. They also arranged exceedingly generous five-year lease terms from the Reconstruction Finance Corporation on the cavernous Willow Run plant, located thirty miles from Detroit. They paid only $500,000 the first year, $850,000 the second, and $1.25 million for each of the last three years. They could not hope to develop a fully integrated company like Ford. Before production commenced, dozens of expensive, sophisticated, and hard-to-obtain production machines had to be located and installed. Reliable sources for raw materials and specialized automobile parts had to be found. They had to recruit thousands of skilled

and semiskilled workers and negotiate union contracts. A hundred problems lay concealed in the jungle of Detroit, ready to ambush the partners if they slipped.

Investors were impressed by their initial moves; by the time the first issues sold out, corporate stock jumped from an offering price of $10 to $24 per share. The cars produced came in two basic models, named after the partners. Industry veterans ridiculed their efforts when the first Kaisers and Frazers dribbled out of the huge facility in fall 1946. Critics claimed that they should call their models "Willit Run?" In fact they had astounded many doubters by producing any cars at all. The partners anticipated losing money their first year, and this expectation was fulfilled; in 1946 Kaiser-Frazer produced only 11,754 cars and lost $19 million.

Stockholders, expecting instant miracles, were disappointed at the short-term results. By the time Kaiser-Frazer yielded its first units in August 1946, the price of the company's stock had dropped to $15. Just over a year later, however, it was the partners' turn to crow. In September 1947 the company celebrated production of its 100,000th car, and Willow Run was yielding over 15,000 vehicles per

A promotional stunt for the 1951 Kaiser-Frazer line, staged at The Willow Run Factory (courtesy of Motor Vehicle Manufacturers Association)

month. Kaiser-Frazer stock had dipped as low as $7 per share in summer 1947; in October, with profitable year-end results on the horizon, it rebounded to $17. In 1947 the firm produced 144,507 cars and generated a profit of $19 million. The next year marked further increases in production; output jumped to 181,316 cars. Profits slipped to $10 million in 1948. Company officials voiced optimism, but insiders worried about the trend.

Unfortunately, 1947 and 1948 were Kaiser-Frazer's only profitable years. Between 1949 and suspension of conventional vehicle production in the United States, the firm suffered a seemingly unending series of reversals. Warning signs were apparent during fall 1948. Although the Willow Run plant was turning out record numbers of cars each month, Kaisers and Frazers were stacking up on dealers' lots and in Detroit. Even more worrisome, the Big Three were meeting backlogged demand for their preferred models and were spending tens of millions of dollars in research and design of even more

appealing future models. Kaiser-Frazer, along with other independents, could not invest similar sums needed to compete. Company dealers had to offer increasingly generous trade-in allowances in order to sell hard-to-move models.

By 1949 Kaiser-Frazer's declining position in the industry was painfully evident. Production dropped by more than two-thirds to 59,281 cars. Dealers struggled to sell even that modest number. A cursory glance at the models suggests why; Kaiser-Frazer had made few improvements and was trying to market the same basic models that customers snapped up two years earlier. By late 1949 the glut of unsold Kaisers and Frazers reached crisis proportions; the annual report exceeded analysts' worst fears as the company lost $30 million.

Investor confidence was sagging; in September 1949 the stock dipped to $3.50 per share. Relations between the two partners thrived at a superficial level when times were good, but hard times brought a crisis in corporate leadership. The issues

The 1953 Henry J

dividing them were complex. Essentially each man believed he was more fit to run the business. Also, both men had brought in teams of managers personally loyal to them. Certainly disunity at upper managerial levels inhibited Kaiser-Frazer's prospects for responding forcefully to threats to its survival. Top management was so dispirited in 1949 that it seriously considered folding operations.

In retrospect that might have been a wise decision. Frazer resigned from the presidency, and Kaiser's older son, Edgar, succeeded him. Although Frazer retained a seat as a director, most of his loyalists were eased out of their posts by Kaiser men. Despite brave, and in many ways resourceful, efforts to reverse corporate fortunes after 1950, Edgar Kaiser presided over the rapid decline of the company. The firm introduced a very early inexpensive compact, the "Henry-J," in 1950, but it was not well received. Their timing was a decade early; in the 1950s consumers wanted size and luxury.

Unfortunately, Kaiser-Frazer entered its final decline just when it began producing excellent vehicles. The Kaiser Dragon was an exceptional sedan and the Kaiser-Darrin sports car was a gem. But production numbers steadily declined. Tax credits and military contracts to build C-119 cargo planes during the Korean War prevented losses from increasing every year between 1950 and 1955, but the trend was clear. In 1953 Kaiser-Frazer sold the Willow Run plant to General Motors, merged with profitable Willys-Overland Motors, and consolidated operations in Toledo, Ohio. Although the new firm concentrated on jeeps and specialized in 4-wheel-drive vehicles, production of conventional automobiles ended in 1955. By then, corporate losses had mounted to a staggering $123 million.

Technically that was the end of Kaiser-Frazer Corporation. The failure of the automobile enterprise was one of several factors which induced Henry Kaiser and his advisors to organize Kaiser Industries, a holding company for his other huge operations in steel, cement, aluminum, construction, engineering, and other fields. Kaiser-Frazer shareholders were allowed to exchange their holdings for Kaiser Industries on a four-for-one basis. Kaiser managed to salvage something from his automobile operation by selling much of the machinery at the Toledo plant to Argentine dictator Juan Perón, and Kaiser's men helped set up large automobile plants in both Argentina and Brazil. By the time of Kaiser's death in 1967, the South American plants had turned out more than 500,000 vehicles. In later years Kaiser Industries publicists put the best face on Kaiser's automobile endeavor, claiming that corporate leadership in compacts, foreign investments, and design somehow transcended the many millions of dollars lost. In his candid moments Kaiser blamed himself for not raising three or four times more start-up capital than he did; with $150 or $200 million he and Frazer might have had enough capital to compete with the Big Three in research, design, and production over a long-term period. Most observers were more blunt, however, calling the automobile venture Kaiser's single great failure.

References:
"Adventures of Henry and Joe in Autoland," *Fortune*, 33 (March 1946): 98-103;

Mark S. Foster, "Challenger From the West: Henry J. Kaiser and the Detroit Auto Industry," *Michigan History*, 70 (January/February 1986): 30-39;

"Kaiser-Frazer: The Roughest Thing We Ever Tackled," *Fortune*, 44 (July 1951): 74-77, 154-162;

Richard M. Langworth, *Kaiser-Frazer: The Last Onslaught on Detroit* (Princeton, N.J.: Princeton Publishing, 1975);

Lawrence J. White, *The American Automobile Industry Since 1945* (Cambridge, Mass.: Harvard University Press, 1971).

Kaufman Thuma Keller

(November 27, 1885-January 26, 1966)

by Richard P. Scharchburg

GMI Engineering & Management Institute

CAREER: Machinist, Westinghouse Machine Company (1906-1910); chief inspector, Detroit Metals Products Company (1910); general foreman, Metzger Motor Car Company (1910); laborer, Hudson Motor Car Company (1911); chief inspector, Maxwell Motor Car Company (1911); troubleshooter, Cadillac, Buick, Oldsmobile, and Oakland Motor Car Companies (1911); general superintendent, Northway Motor Company (1912-1916); general superintendent, Cole Motor Company (1916-1917); general master mechanic, Buick Motor Company (1917-1920); engineering staff (1920-1921), vice-president of Chevrolet Motor Company (1921-1924), general manager of Canadian Operations, General Motors Corporation (1924-1926); vice-president in charge of manufacturing (1926-1928), general manager, Dodge Division (1928-1929), president, Dodge Division (1929-1935), president (1935-1950), chairman of the board, Chrysler Corporation (1950-1956).

Hired away from General Motors (GM) by Walter Chrysler in 1926, Kaufman Thuma "K. T." Keller was solidly schooled in the automotive industry from the earliest days of his working career and justly earned a reputation for extraordinary skill in the supervision of the technical aspects of automobile manufacture. Acquainted with Chrysler while they both worked at Buick, Keller started his career at the Chrysler Corporation as vice-president of manufacturing. In the course of his thirty years at Chrysler he was a major force in building the company into one of the Big Three automobile manufacturers. His special pride was the excellence of Chrysler's engineering department, which for years

Kaufman Thuma Keller (courtesy Detroit Free Press)

was preeminent in the industry. Keller became president of the company in 1935 and served as president and chief executive officer from 1940 to 1950; his greatest exploit was his conversion of the company to war production and its rapid postwar reconversion. In addition to his role at Chrysler he headed the Pentagon's guided-missile program from

1950 to 1953, and by insisting on the production of actual operating missiles rather than theoretical models, he brought operational missiles into production sooner than expected. He retired from Chrysler in 1956 to enjoy his interests in his family, golf, art, photography, fishing, and travel. He died in London, England, on January 26, 1966, while on a study tour with a group of governors and trustees of the Detroit Institute of Art. He was eighty years old. He was buried at Woodlawn Cemetery in Detroit.

Kaufman Thuma Keller was born on November 27, 1885, on the family farm near Mount Joy, Pennsylvania, the son of Zachariah and Carrie Thuma Keller. Later in life he shortened his name to "K. T." Like many small-town boys, he had chores around the farm as part of his daily routine and as a youth attended school in the nearby village of Mount Joy. A physical sturdiness manifested itself early in life and served him well in the demands that he placed on himself throughout his career. That his physical size did not deter his mental development is best reflected by the fact that he graduated at the top of his high-school class at the age of sixteen.

During his high-school years, when not needed around the house, Keller worked in several small factories, where he received his first experience in dealing with mechanical objects. Full of restless energy, he also raised pigeons, and through their sale and his other jobs he managed to save enough to enable him to attend a business school in Lancaster, Pennsylvania, in 1901. There he took courses in commercial law, shorthand, typing, and bookkeeping.

In 1904, at age eighteen, Keller traveled to England as a secretary for a Baptist minister and lecturer on religion. The three years he spent traveling no doubt added to his education, but Keller decided that the only way for him to increase his future prospects was to return home. He found a job—at $75 a month—in the office of the factory manager of the Westinghouse Machine Company in East Pittsburgh, Pennsylvania. Remaining in the office position for about a year, he decided that he preferred to work with mechanical objects. He entered an apprentice machinist program with Westinghouse at only 20¢ an hour, a considerable cut in wages from his previous salary. This was only the first of several decisions that Keller made to reduce

his salary in order to follow his desire to gain knowledge and experience.

Keller was a hard worker, and with his natural thirst for knowledge he impressed his supervisors at Westinghouse. While still an apprentice he was made assistant general foreman of the department which was then making automobile engines for the Chalmers Motor Company of Detroit. His pay was raised to 22¢ an hour until his two-year apprenticeship was over, when it rose to 75¢ an hour in recognition of his skill as a machinist and his ability to direct the efforts of other workers. More important to Keller's career than the pay raise was his initial contact with the automobile industry.

Detroit was rapidly becoming the head of the developing automotive industry, and by 1910, the year Keller finished his apprenticeship, he no doubt saw possibilities in the nascent industry. He moved to Detroit and quickly found a job as chief inspector of the Detroit Metals Products Company, a maker of axles and one of a host of new ventures organized by skilled mechanics to serve the needs of automobile manufacturers. As a machinist he was paid $125 a month, and a few months later he moved to the Metzger Motor Car Company as general foreman of their machine shop at a considerable raise in pay. Barney Everett, one of the owners, once stated that Keller was the best man he ever hired. But his rapid rise affected his attitude and, in his own words, he became "position-minded" rather than "job-minded." When the quality of his work began to diminish Keller was promptly fired.

It took some time for the lesson to sink in. But as he walked the streets of Detroit from one employment office to another, unable to get a job, he began to worry less about a position and more about work. His savings ran low, and at the end of ten weeks he still was unemployed. Of necessity he became a regular patron of pawnshops, and one morning after subsisting on a single meal for several days, he pawned the only possession with which he could part, an extra hat; it brought him 35¢. Ever-present hunger took over his reason, and he spent the entire 35¢ on a single meal which left him absolutely penniless, possessing only the clothes on his back. His fortunes had reached rock bottom.

The next day, with his stomach empty and everything pawnable gone, he again set out looking for work. Applying at the Hudson Motor Car Company, he was told that there was a job available, but that it paid only 40¢ an hour—as a common laborer. Keller jumped at the chance to work even though the job involved heavy repairs and chassis testing.

Keeping watch for a better opportunity, Keller learned that the Maxwell Motor Car Company was looking for a chief inspector at its Tarrytown, New York, plant. He was hired at a salary of $50 a week. With a borrowed $50 for expenses he traveled to Tarrytown. On the way he stopped at Pittsburgh to visit Adelaide Taylor, whom he had dated when he worked at Westinghouse. Three months later he returned to Pittsburgh and they were married. The couple returned to Tarrytown, and Keller settled into his job as chief inspector at Maxwell Motors.

Keller's luck improved as his attitude changed. Henry L. Barton, whom he had known since his apprenticeship days at Westinghouse, had become associated with GM. Barton sent word that if Keller were interested there might be a job for him at GM. Although Barton offered him $50 a month less in salary than he was receiving from Maxwell, Keller welcomed the chance to return to Detroit. He was well aware that the future of automobile manufacturing was there.

By 1912 GM was already becoming a giant in the auto world. William C. Durant had been forced out of the firm in 1910, and Charles Nash was serving as president of GM. Walter Chrysler was president and general manager of Buick, GM's most profitable division. Once again the opportunities for Keller to gain additional experience were more valuable to him than the loss of salary. His duties were to circulate among the company's various machine shops, especially Cadillac, Buick, Oldsmobile, and Oakland, in an effort to install production methods appropriate to each of their operations. Many divisions at first resented his presence, but as soon as the results of his suggestions began to show up in increased efficiency and production, his advice was frequently sought. In 1912 he was appointed general superintendent of Northway Motors, a GM subsidiary.

In 1917 Keller came into contact with Chrysler, a contact which was the most important event in Keller's automotive career. Chrysler, while at Buick, had become acquainted with Keller's work and invited him to become Buick's general master mechanic. Although little information is available

about Keller's activities while at Buick, it is known that he was responsible for start-up of Buick's Liberty Engine production in World War I. As the division prospered so did the fortunes of Chrysler and Keller. Chrysler left Buick in early 1920, eventually to form his own automobile company; in the same year Keller was transferred to the GM central office as a member of the engineering staff. In 1921 he was promoted to vice-president in charge of manufacturing at Chevrolet. Three years later he was sent to Canada to be general manager of GM's Canadian operations.

Meanwhile Chrysler himself had been busy in the automobile industry. Working briefly with the declining fortunes of Willys and Maxwell-Chalmers, he founded his own automobile company in 1925. As production and sales skyrocketed Chrysler began to build a management team talented enough for the Chrysler Corporation that he had planned. In early 1926 Keller received a wire from Chrysler to meet him in Chicago. Keller was offered a job with the infant company and after only a few questions decided to cast his future with Chrysler. There was really little risk involved in Keller's move because the statistics of Chrysler's growth were nothing short of phenomenal. By the fall of the first year of production Chrysler had signed nearly 3,800 dealers. Within twelve months of their appearance, 32,000 Chrysler Sixes had been sold. When Keller first joined Chrysler his title was vice-president in charge of manufacturing. Actually his title did not accurately describe his job, which was more production-oriented than administrative. But with a management philosophy and mechanical knowledge gained from experience, Keller eagerly worked at any and all tasks assigned to him by Chrysler. During Keller's first year with Chrysler four new models were introduced: a 4-cylinder Series 50; a 6-cylinder Series 60; the Series 70, which was a new version of the Chrysler Six; and a big, new Chrysler Imperial, Series 80 (the numbers represented the top speed of each model). By 1927 the firm was fourth in the industry in new car sales with registrations of 192,000 units. Keller was still learning his job but was placed under extreme pressure when in 1928 Chrysler pulled off one of the largest deals in automotive history.

John and Horace Dodge, natives of Niles, Michigan, were trained as machinists by their father and came to Detroit around the turn of the twentieth century. There they opened a machine shop, where in 1901 they made their entrance into the automobile industry by agreeing to produce transmissions for Oldsmobile. In 1903 they began to supply engines and parts for Ford. In 1914 the Dodge brothers began manufacturing their own car, and by the mid 1920s the company was in third place in the automobile industry with a strong product and a loyal dealer group. The "Dependable Dodge" was respected nationally, and the Dodge main plant in Hamtramck was one of the largest and most completely integrated automobile factories in the world, covering 58 acres and employing approximately 20,000 workers.

Following the deaths of both of the Dodge brothers in 1920, the company, valued at $52 million, was left to their widows. In 1925 the Dodge widows decided to sell the company to the powerful financial firm of Dillon, Read & Company for a reported $152 million. But the Wall Street management faltered in not continuing the Dodge tradition. They were primarily interested in quick profits, and the company and its product languished as it maneuvered products and prices in an attempt to maximize profits with little concern for matters relating to the company's future. Sales fell steadily, and by spring 1928 Clarence Dillon was eager to rid himself of the unprofitable investment. Chrysler, on the other hand, was eager to develop or acquire a car to compete with Ford and Chevrolet. With Dodge available, acquiring the company seemed the wisest and speediest course of action. Dodge had the product, the plant, and most importantly the dealer organization that would insure instant success and thus rapid realization of Chrysler's objective. He carefully began to effect a friendly takeover of the Dodge interests. The final terms provided that the Chrysler Corporation would pay for Dodge with 1,253,557 shares of Chrysler common stock, then worth about $80 per share on the market, and also assume Dodge debt amounting to $59 million.

On the afternoon of the day the papers that put the transfer into effect were signed, a number of Chrysler executives under the leadership of Keller moved into the Dodge offices in Hamtramck. Throughout the factory, signs appeared reading "Chrysler Corporation, Dodge Division." The next morning the plant opened under Chrysler management. There were, of course, many problems to be solved with the integration of Dodge, but Keller and his highly motivated management team, consist-

ing of B. E. Hutchinson and Joe Fields and a hand-picked staff of trusted associates, completed the task in record time. In three months Keller and his team had so increased efficiency that less than 70 percent of the floor space was required for Dodge operations.

Although Keller was now devoting most of his time and energy to Dodge, he was still responsible for production of all Chrysler cars and two new products, the Plymouth and the DeSoto Six. He was given the presidency of Dodge in 1929. Keller's management style was simple: "Once having picked a man to head a factory, you must accord him adequate authority and responsibility. You must not dictate to him that he must do this, that and the next thing in such-and-such a way. Give him elbow room. But keep closely in touch with him and his activities."

In the same year that Keller assumed the presidency of Dodge, Chrysler Corporation arrived as one of the Big Three automobile companies. The corporation's cars of that year pioneered the down-draft carburetor and rust-proofed fenders and other sheet-metal parts. Despite the depression Chrysler in the 1930s never reduced research or investments needed for better-engineered cars. Nor did it cancel investments in new models. The 1933 Plymouth was introduced late in 1932 as a six-cylinder model with "Floating Power" motor mounts, a safety steel body, free wheeling, hydraulic brakes, a double-drop rigid X-member frame, and a low center of gravity. New Plymouth car sales outstripped its manufacture, and before the year's end output rose from 1,000 to 1,200 cars a day. Even though the depression took its toll on American and world business, Chrysler prospered by maintaining a reputation for engineering and research, the foundation upon which the company had been built.

After more than ten years of guiding the corporation with a management team whose philosophy meshed perfectly with his, Chrysler resigned the presidency of the firm on July 22, 1935, but retained his position as chairman of the board. As expected, Keller was selected to be president. Over the years Keller had shown Chrysler more than production genius and executive ability. He was a compulsive worker, as proven during hectic days in 1928 when Chrysler had added Plymouth to the line and had directed the campaign to establish the Plymouth as a formidable competitor to Ford and Chevrolet. Competent, profane, full of studious curiosity, Keller

Keller, standing, third from right, with Walter Chrysler, in car, Fred M. Zeder, second from right, and B. J. Hutchinson (courtesy of Chrysler Corporation)

had simultaneously handled the complex problems of the Dodge plant—sales, labor, the thousands of trivial matters that pour over the desk of a big corporation executive—in stride. In Chrysler's mind there was no doubt that Keller had the mental and physical force to steer the company, which in 1934 had sales of over $516 million and had employed 59,000 workers. Keller had also shown other qualities that were expected of executives: the stamina to hold up under hard work; and the singleness of purpose that eventually made the plant the focus of their lives. *Fortune* magazine commented that Keller's rise to the presidency was the outcome of "a situation that has long obtained. In Keller the corporation has another Chrysler whose likeness to his prototype is both obvious and reassuring." Five years later *Fortune* reported, "Chrysler Corp. has made, since its formation in 1925, over $350 million. Of this about $200 million has been made in the past five years—in other words since K. T. Keller became president." Keller quipped in 1940 to the press that his recipe for success was: "Put out a good product; if it's lousy, you better quit."

He certainly never quit.

During the early years of his presidency Keller steered Chrysler through some rough business conditions, including massive sit-down strikes which resulted in the recognition of the United Automobile Workers (UAW) as bargaining agent for workers in the auto industry. Notwithstanding, Chrysler's sales hit their prewar top in 1937: almost $770 million. During the first six months of 1939, after a miserable depression year in 1938, Chrysler's sales jumped to $342,788,293, up a phenomenal 82 percent from the same period a year earlier. Profits generally set records after he assumed the presidency, and production of cars and trucks exceeded 1 million units annually. The record is clear; under Keller's stewardship the Chrysler Corporation emerged from the depression strong, even though in some years production was only at 40 percent of capacity. By the end of 1936 Keller had retired the Dodge bonded indebtedness.

By 1940 approximately one out of every four passenger cars sold in the United States was a Chrysler and the company had advanced ahead of Ford from third to second position among American auto-makers. In August 1940, the month of Chrysler's death, the board of directors abolished the office of chairman and designated Keller as president and chief executive officer. But from this time on, as war became inevitable, Keller began to spend more and more time with nonautomotive production challenges.

As Keller became more involved in defense work it is perhaps important to recite the litany of engineering developments credited to his years with Chrysler before the war. The list is impressive: one-piece curved glass windshields, automatic overdrive, built-in defroster vents, fluid couplings, rubber-insulated steering gears, power-operated convertible tops, safety rim wheels, rotor type oil pumps, powdered metal gasoline filters in fuel tanks, full-hydraulic disc brakes, key-operated combination ignition and starter switches, pressure-vent radiator caps, resistor spark plugs, the safety-cushion dash, splash-proof ignition systems, internal-expanding transmission parking brakes, the hemispherical combustion chamber in engines, full-time power steering, forced air-cooled brakes, the water-jacketed carburetor throttle body, one-piece molded plastic headliners on station wagons, mechanical actuation of automatic transmissions, transistorized car radios, four dual headlamp sealed-beam lighting systems, electronic fuel injection, swivel front seats, alternating current generators, canted 6-cylinder engine installation, airfoil windshield wiper blades, the addition of elemental tin to cast iron in V-8 engine blocks, a fusible link to protect electrical wiring systems, the safety shoulder harness, and many other developments. Of course Keller did not personally develop all these engineering innovations, but his decisions to incorporate these developments into products led to Chrysler's position of engineering leadership.

Following the British defeat at Dunkirk on June 1, 1940, when the army had been forced to abandon most of its tanks, the British Purchasing Commission sought to purchase replacement tanks from the United States. The U.S. Army's Rock Island Arsenal had built only a few light tanks, which were known as the M2A1. But the Arsenal had on its drawing boards the blueprints for a larger tank, the M-3, which weighed about 56,000 pounds. This was the tank the British eventually sought. Reportedly the U.S. government requested that GM tool up for production immediately, but

since the United States had not declared war, the army was told by Alfred Sloan that GM was too busy building passenger cars to take on an assignment that big. Keller was contacted instead, and two days after a conference between Keller and William S. Knudsen, ranking member of the U.S. Defense Commission, Keller, Hutchinson, and Zeder traveled to the Rock Island Arsenal near Washington to examine the tank. Sixty-five days later, after Keller and his engineering department had studied the project, Keller signed a contract to erect a $20-million plant for the army (for a nominal fee of $2) to handle the tank order. In order to avoid the problem of a marketless plant once the war was over, Keller devised a unique arrangement with the government. The actual title to the new tank plant and property rested in the War Department, which had supplied the money. Chrysler then leased the facility for $1 a year. The government was happy to be assured of a permanent tank arsenal while Chrysler was freed from potentially unneeded plant facilities at war's end.

Keller made the tank project his own personal assignment. In addition to handling initial negotiations with Knudsen, Keller accompanied Hutchinson and Zeder to Rock Island to study the tank, and after Chrysler engineers returned with the blueprints, he and his staff studied the prints, decided what tools were necessary, laid out plans for the factory, and carved a complete set of wooden tank parts. The preliminary work took only four weeks and cost nearly $100,000. In record time a plant was being erected on a 113-acre site outside Detroit in Warren, a few miles north of the Dodge truck plant on Mound Road. By late 1940 some of the badly needed tanks had already reached the British in North Africa, where General Rommel was forcing the British forces across the desert toward Cairo.

At the time Chrysler was gearing up for production of the M-3, no gasoline or diesel engine that could be mass-produced was powerful enough to propel a tank of the M-3's weight. Keller and his staff devised what was called the "eggbeater," which consisted of five Plymouth engines mounted on a frame to drive a central drive shaft and propel the tank's drive sprockets through a special transmission. The Ordnance Corps referred to this arrangement as the "multibank engine." Later, air-cooled Wright aircraft radial engines of 400 horsepower were adapted to drive the M-3 Chrysler tanks.

Following the passage of the Selective Service Act in September 1940 the U.S. Army wanted to move as rapidly as possible to build up its depleted supply of men and arms. The rest of the automobile industry eventually followed Chrysler's lead in concentrating on arms production in order to meet military demands. Chrysler eventually built 25,000 tanks for the army. In addition they also manufactured Wright B-29 engines, Bofors guns, B-29 fuselage assemblies, marine engines, Corsair landing gear, fire pumpers, rockets, bomb shackles, duraluminum forgings, army trucks, tank engines, Curtiss Helldiver center wings, radar antenna mounts, Sperry gyro compasses, small-arms ammunition, submarine nets, and searchlight reflectors. Chrysler, in concert with the rest of American industry, is justly credited with the rapid development of productive capacity for arms and war equipment, which permitted U.S. forces first to catch up and then surpass the enemy in World War II.

During the war Keller, as a matter of great personal satisfaction, was intimately involved with Chrysler's defense production. In recognition of his knowledge and production genius, he was invited to head the government's War Production Board but was forced to decline due to his worsening health, which was the result of overwork. He did, however, write reports and make a number of studies and recommendations which made significant contributions to the war effort. For this work and for his direction of Chrysler's war program, Keller was awarded the Medal of Merit, the Distinguished Service Certificate of the Army Ordnance Department, and a citation for distinguished services on behalf of the war finance program.

At war's end Keller's skill at directing production was again pivotal as Chrysler Corporation announced plans to spend $75 million in reconversion to peacetime automotive manufacturing. And true to Keller's reputation, two months after the end of World War II 300 Dodge trucks were daily rolling off the assembly line. Passenger cars were late in making their postwar debut at Chrysler, but the delay enabled the company to use accumulated stocks while most manufacturers were compelled by shortages of vital materials to slacken production at some point after introduction of the new models. As a result of Keller's approach to production, by the end of the 1947 model year the *Magazine of Wall Street* reported that Chrysler ranked second among domestic producers of motor vehicles.

But Chrysler's success during the resumption of production of automobiles did not last. Chrysler's leadership, centered in Keller's office, failed to take account of the changes in the automobile-buying public. Engineering distinction became less important to the public and a new element—styling—took on new importance. Eager car customers, suddenly released from wartime shortages and scarcities, at first gobbled up anything they could buy but soon looked for comfort, styling, and luxury. Keller and his engineers continued their prewar emphasis on performance. But even here they failed to come up with the magnitude of innovations that had created the Chrysler empire. Chrysler divisions had only one order from Keller—to build and sell as many cars as possible. The insignificance of Chrysler's immediate postwar "innovation" record is perhaps typified by the introduction in 1949 of the industry's first all-steel station wagon and the establishment of a standard of measurement that allowed the rear floor of its station wagons to accommodate a 4-foot x 8-foot piece of plywood. Neither of these minor changes excited the least bit of broad-based consumer interest.

Other industry analysts concluded that the consumer would rank styling first, automatic transmissions second, and high-compression engines third. Keller continued to maintain that "practicality" should outweigh all other considerations. Keller himself would often visit the company's styling studios and regale the staff with sketches, plans, and ideas inflexibly drawn from the decade of the 1930s. In 1949, when the auto industry unveiled its first all-new line of cars since 1941, Ford and GM introduced strikingly elongated and sleek cars whose sight appeal was immediate. The 1949 Plymouth was designed according to Keller's dictum that extra height had to be added because millions of people, he said, "are in the habit of getting behind the wheel, or on the back seat, wearing hats." Chrysler would continue for years to fly in the face of styling. One journalist quipped that "although the new [1949] Chrysler cars would not knock your hat off, they would not knock your eye out either."

Everyone had taken Keller at his word when he announced to the postwar public that Chrysler products would avoid fads in favor of practicality. The 1949 models proved it. As other manufacturers introduced their first fully redesigned cars of the era, Chrysler's models remained boxy and unattractive to the anxious consumer. The era of the sleek, elongated, stylish car had arrived in Detroit but not in Highland Park, the home of Chrysler. The reason for the failure to join the trend, say most historians, was Keller. In this matter Keller was solidly backed by conservative Fred Breer, still in charge of engineering, who bluntly told all that Chrysler would not rush pell-mell into streamlining at the expense of comfort. And so, lacking any major distinguishing features for their 1949 products, Chrysler's various makes were set apart only by minute differences in wheelbases and width and under-the-hood embellishments that no one except mechanics could see. By some miracle Chrysler Corporation managed to have a good year as it celebrated its silver anniversary. Sales were up for all divisions except DeSoto. The corporate model year total was close to 1 million units, some 110,000 more than in 1948.

Chrysler production for the 1950 model year continued to grow, eventually reaching 1.27 million units despite a three-month strike by the UAW. The boxy design initiated in 1949 was modified only slightly. It would appear on the surface that Keller's decision to stick to "practicality" had been correct, and in late 1950, with sales soaring and Chrysler's finances healthy, Keller began the process of choosing a successor. Additionally, Keller had been appointed to head the U.S. missile program shortly after the outbreak of the Korean War. This added responsibility made the need to relinquish operational management of Chrysler all the more pressing. The formal changing of the guard came in fall 1950 when Keller moved up to chairman of the board and Lester L. Colbert was elected to the presidency.

Colbert was forced to work under the dominating influence of men like Keller, Zeder, Skelton, Breer, and Hutchinson. Even after their retirements men trained in the philosophy of the 1930s continued to thwart Colbert in his task of leading the corporation to meet the challenges of the 1960s and to regain the reputation and the record the corporation had achieved prior to World War II.

Keller's decision to accept the invitation of the president of the United States to head the guided-missile program was not entirely unselfishly motivated. Chrysler's later share of defense work easily justified Keller's "volunteer work" for the government. At one time or another Keller also served on numerous advisory committees and commissions,

mainly dealing with military matters. The contacts he made were valuable to Chrysler Corporation when they later competed for lucrative defense contracts.

Keller also had interests in professional, civic, and cultural affairs. He was a fellow of the American Society of Mechanical Engineers and a member of the Society of Automotive Engineers and the Newcomen Society. He was a trustee of the Detroit Industrial Safety Council, a member of the Detroit Council on Foreign Relations, and a member of the Detroit Arts Commission. He also served as a director of the Automobile Manufacturers Association. Numerous memberships in golf and social clubs, plus his interests in chess and bridge, rounded out his life away from the Chrysler plants. Keller died on January 21, 1966.

Publication:

"Leadership and Labor Are The Twin Problems of Industry," *SAE Journal* (March 1933): 7ff.

References:

Walter P. Chrysler, *Life of an American Workman* (New York: Dodd, Mead, 1937);

"Chrysler," *Fortune* (August 1935): 30-37;

Chrysler Corporation, *A Pictorial History of Chrysler Corporation Cars* (Detroit, 1975);

B. C. Forbes, "Keller of Chrysler Motors," *Fortune* (October 1, 1939): 37ff;

Beverly Rae Kimes, "Chrysler: From the Airflow," *Automobile Quarterly*, 7 (Fall 1968): 206-221;

Richard M. Langworth, "Town and Country: Chrysler's Beautiful Land Yacht," *Automobile Quarterly*, 11 (Third Quarter 1973): 298-309;

Langworth and Jan P. Norbye, *The Complete History of Chrysler Corporation, 1924-1985* (New York: Beekman House, 1985);

Michael Moritz and Barrett Seaman, *Going for Broke: the Chrysler Story* (Garden City, N.Y.: Doubleday, 1981);

"Of Arms and Automobiles," *Fortune* (December 1940): 57ff;

John B. Rae, *American Automobile Manufacturers* (Philadelphia: Chilton, 1959);

Rae, *The American Automobile: a Brief History* (Chicago: University of Chicago Press, 1965);

Lawrence J. White, *The Automobile Industry Since 1945* (Cambridge, Mass.: Harvard University Press, 1971).

Archives:

No Keller papers or other primary source materials are known to be extant. The Chrysler Archives in Highland Park contain files and photographs and are available to the public by appointment.

Charles Franklin Kettering

(August 29, 1876-November 25, 1958)

by Stuart W. Leslie

Johns Hopkins University

CAREER: Electrical inventor, National Cash Register Company (1904-1909); vice-president, Delco (1909-1919); vice-president, Dayton Wright Airplane Company (1916-1919); vice-president, Domestic Engineering Company (1916-1919); research director and vice-president, General Motors Corporation (1920-1947); president, Ethyl Corporation (1924-1926).

Charles F. Kettering, inventor and automotive engineer, was born on August 29, 1876, in Loudonville, Ohio, and died November 25, 1958, in Dayton, Ohio. His life perfectly spanned America's automotive age. He was born the same year Nicholas Otto patented the 4-stroke engine (the direct ancestor of the modern automobile power plant) and died at the zenith of the car culture, in the year of tail fins and chrome. While his name was never immortalized in a familiar automotive marque, he nevertheless contributed more to the technical development of the automobile than any other American engineer, first as an independent inventor and later as director of research for General Motors (GM). His ideas, including battery ignition, the electric self-starter, leaded gasoline, high-compression engines, durable and fast-drying colored paints, among many others, remade the American automobile into a convenient necessity of everyday life.

Like so many other automotive engineers and executives of his generation, Kettering grew up on a midwestern family farm. He was the fourth child (of five) and third son of Jacob and Martha Kettering, third-generation emigrants from Alsace-Lorraine and Scotland who had settled in the hill country of central Ohio. As a boy Kettering displayed an inclination for tinkering and the precocious ingenuity expected of every great American inventor, but perhaps more important to his future success, he also showed an early interest in schol-

Charles Franklin Kettering

arly matters. His most vivid childhood memories were not about fixing things around the farm, but rather lessons learned from his teachers at the one-room schoolhouse down the road. Tall, awkward, and very nearsighted, with a habit of stooping forward to compensate for his poor eyesight, Kettering was shy and withdrawn as a youngster and had little social life. Instead, he found satisfaction in his studies, excelling at science and mathematics and graduating at the top of his high school class in 1895. For a time Kettering seriously considered a career in education and spent a couple of years teaching in local schools for $250 a year. He continued his formal education, attending summer classes at

Wooster College, and on his own he began reading scientific periodicals and performing chemical and electrical experiments.

Glimpsing in his reading and course work a world far more exciting than country teaching, he applied to and was accepted by the Ohio State University College of Engineering in 1898. A chronic eye inflammation forced him to withdraw at the beginning of his sophomore year. He spent the next two years working for the Star Telephone Company, a small local company in Ashland, Ohio, rising rapidly from wire stringer to foreman, learning a good deal about practical electrical technology. His experiences at Star gave him the knowledge and the self-confidence he needed to return to Ohio State in fall 1901. His academic performance was outstanding, and he graduated three years later with honors in electrical engineering. Even before graduation he was offered a job as an electrical inventor with the National Cash Register Company in Dayton, Ohio, at the remarkably high salary of $50 a week.

Kettering arrived in Dayton to take up his new position at the end of June 1904. His supervisor was John H. Patterson, then president of National Cash Register (NCR), who had virtually invented modern marketing and made a name for the company with a variety of creative schemes, from direct-mail advertising and "canned" sales pitches to statistically calculated sales quotas and annual sales conventions. Patterson was a bona fide eccentric. For a time he insisted that all of his executives drink only bottled water, and he sometimes gauged their executive potential by their equestrian skills, under the theory that only men who could manage horses could properly manage men. Idiosyncrasies aside, Patterson, like few businessmen of his day, appreciated the importance of marketing for the modern corporation and drilled that lesson into his employees, including Kettering. Under Patterson, NCR served as a business school for a generation of young executives who would take what they learned there about marketing and apply it very successfully in other companies and in other industries. Among NCR's illustrious graduates were Thomas Watson, the founder of IBM, and Richard H. Grant, the strategist behind Chevrolet's fabulously successful dealer network.

Patterson taught Kettering that the only inventions worth working on were those which had a good chance of making it out the laboratory door and into the market. Patterson and his sales committee took one look at Kettering's first invention, an elegant solenoid arrangement for depressing cash register keys, promptly dismissed it as too complex, heavy, and expensive, and sent its inventor to school with the company's sales force. In the weekly roundtable discussions of the "Owls Course" Kettering gained a new appreciation for the economic dimensions of invention and discovered that the dollar sign was often the most significant variable in any engineering equation. Recalling the most important lesson of his years with NCR, Kettering observed, "I didn't hang around much with the other inventors or the executive fellows. I lived with the sales gang. They had some real notion of what people wanted."

What Kettering learned from the marketing men helped him transform the cash register from a protective measure against weak-willed cashiers into a powerful tool for management planning. When Richard Grant, then sales manager in charge of cash register sales to department stores, explained how clumsy credit-approval systems—typically complicated arrangements of pneumatic tubes or wire baskets on wires—were hampering business, Kettering immediately set to work on improvements. Within just a few weeks he came back with a novel combination telephone/solenoid-actuated stamping device which allowed store credit managers to give approval automatically from a central location. To complete a credit sale the cashier simply lifted a telephone receiver at his station and alerted the credit manager, who could then approve the sale by tripping the solenoid.

Following this strategy of letting market needs dictate his choice of projects, Kettering developed several other important inventions for NCR, including the first electric cash register and automated accounting and banking machines. He also began to look beyond how his inventions fit into the existing market, to how they could come together into systems of innovation. For instance, he recognized that his electric cash registers, accounting machines, and credit-approval devices were simply parts of a potentially bigger system that could collect and tabulate data from an entire store. By tying together its various components Kettering came up with a system that could give a merchant an up-to-the-minute record of all store transactions. Although the inherent limitations of electromechanical processing kept Kettering from fully exploiting his idea, he clearly recognized its potential: "A complete balance of the store could be obtained in about twenty minutes after active business had ceased, and this would require the services of not more than two or three people." Kettering's innovation strikingly anticipated much later developments in computerized scanning and inventory-control systems, which are actually just refinements of his conceptual breakthrough, and prepared the way for the revolution in retailing in the 1970s.

Kettering spent five years as an electrical inventor at NCR, working his way up the corporate ladder to head of the inventions department at a salary of $346.67 a month. Kettering's coworkers from those days, including many who would later join him in his automotive enterprises, recalled how he bubbled over with ideas and energy. He got to work by 6:30 A.M. and often worked late into the night. He barely had time to outline one idea to his assistants before he was on to another.

Important as they were, however, Kettering's specific inventions were overshadowed by the more general changes in outlook and orientation he introduced to the NCR inventions departments, particularly his insistence that trial-and-error invention give way to more formally organized industrial research. He hired engineering graduates instead of ingenious tinkerers and set them working on fundamental studies of electricity and mechanics rather than simply on one kind of register or another. At the same time he understood the importance of hands-on experience. One assistant, a recent engineering school graduate, returned from an assignment on the angular deflection of a certain register shaft with a complexly argued and mathematically intricate answer that Kettering immediately recognized as wrong. Rather than rework the problem on paper, Kettering took the engineer into the shop, fastened one end of the shaft in a vise and the other to a dial indicator for measuring deflection. In a few minutes the young assistant had a lifetime lesson in commonsense engineering.

Kettering finally found time as well for a family and social life. On August 1, 1905, he married Olive Williams, whom he had met while working for the telephone company some years before. Their only child, Eugene Williams Kettering, was born on April 20, 1908. Olive brought a measure of stability to the life of a harried and somewhat absent-minded inventor. She managed the household finances, put up with Kettering's unusual moods and hours, and reminded him of a life beyond business and invention. She played the organ in local churches and occasionally dragged her husband to the symphony and the opera. He usually dozed off or doodled during the performances, but his boredom occasionally paid unexpected dividends in the form of patent sketches on the backs of the programs.

Kettering left NCR in 1909 to enter business for himself. He later liked to say that he did not want a man to have a job, he wanted the job to have a man, and over the last year or so at NCR he had become increasingly absorbed in technical problems unrelated to cash registers. Despite a grueling schedule at NCR, he managed to squeeze in several outside projects, including a farsighted (though ultimately unsuccessful) idea for talking motion pictures. In summer 1908, at the urging of Edward A. Deeds, the NCR executive who had hired him out of Ohio State, he turned his attention to electrical inventions for automobiles.

At the time most foreign cars employed some variation of the magneto ignition invented by German engineer Robert Bosch. American builders preferred dry cell battery ignitions, but these systems generally lasted only a few hundred miles. Kettering had a better idea, a magnetic relay arrangement borrowed from one of his cash register designs which would release the battery charge at precisely the right instant and significantly prolong battery life. When initial trials on one of Deeds's cars proved encouraging, Kettering borrowed $1,500 from his wife's savings account to get the project going. He recruited several assistants from NCR, including his closest associate, William Chryst, to work with him in the evenings and on weekends. Through Deeds's NCR connections, Henry Leland, president of the Cadillac Motor Car Company, heard about Kettering's work and sent his top engineer to investigate. Leland liked what he heard, especially about the new battery ignition giving the kind of slow, steady idle that luxury car buyers appreciated, and ordered 8,000 units.

The order caught Kettering completely off guard. He had no manufacturing facilities, no capital, and no full-time workers. With Deeds's help, Kettering hurriedly arranged a loan of $150,000 (splitting the liability with Deeds), hired a few NCR engineers, and incorporated the Dayton Engineering Laboratories Company (Delco). He and Deeds then subcontracted most of the Cadillac order to an electrical supplier they knew through

The first shipment of Delco electric self-starters in August 1911 (courtesy of the General Motors Institute Alumni Foundation Collection of Industrial History)

NCR. Kettering took out a patent on his ignition improvements on September 15, 1909, and quit NCR three days later. His friends, less certain of the company's prospects, kept their day jobs at NCR.

As he set out on his own, Kettering did not forget the lessons he had learned at NCR. Like Thomas Edison, he invented for the market, and what set his company apart from its competitors was less its engineering than its imaginative marketing. He promoted his battery ignition tirelessly, in advertisements (which he wrote himself) and in competitions from local hill climbs to the Indianapolis Speedway. Within a couple of years Delco ignition systems were standard equipment on a half-dozen car brands, including Cadillac.

Meanwhile, Kettering looked for ways of expanding his limited product line. He considered, and patented, several interesting ideas until hitting upon the one that would earn him automotive immortality, the electric self-starter. Many other engineers had thought up self-starting systems to replace cumbersome, wearying, and sometimes dangerous hand-cranking. Some had tried springs, others acetylene gas, still others compressed air. A few, including the engineering staff at Cadillac, had experimented with electrical systems. Only Kettering, however, envisioned not simply a starter, but an integrated system of starting, lighting, and ignition that would be simple and reliable and could be installed in existing cars with only minor modifications. Kettering was convinced that the solution to the self-starting puzzle could only be found by considering the entire system and the ways in which its components fit together.

For instance, within just a few weeks of beginning the project Kettering decided that one key to a successful electric self-starting system would be to use the starting motor not only for cranking the engine but for generating power for ignition and lighting. Making that decision in turn set the technical parameters for the rest of the components. To run the ignition and the lights (which used more rugged 6-volt filaments in those days) off the generator, Kettering had to develop a way of shifting from 12 volts for sufficient starting torque to 6 volts for head-lamp and ignition operation. To regulate the genera-tor output over the variable speed range of the engine and at the same time prevent it from over-charging the storage battery, he had to develop a new voltage regulator. To make the system small enough to fit under the hood, he had to reduce the size of each of the components substantially.

The Delco team that translated Kettering's in-spiration into practical hardware included seven NCR expatriates and a few part-timers like Chryst. They labored away in a makeshift workshop in Deeds's barn, machining their own parts, winding their own armatures, and testing and retesting the components. Kettering himself spent so many hours in the barn that the Dayton City Directory mistak-enly listed it as his official address. The men called Kettering the "Boss," a nickname that stuck, though Kettering often observed that the only rank in the group was when one man was ranker than the next. By February 1911 they had a prototype in-stalled and working in a Cadillac test car which they sent to Leland for inspection.

Leland immediately recognized the revolution-ary implications of Kettering's invention. He had the prototype carefully tested, invited Kettering up to Detroit for detailed technical consultations over the summer, and ordered 12,000 starting, lighting, and ignition systems from Delco in the late fall. Again, the scale of the contract came as a complete surprise and forced Kettering out of his accustomed role as inventor and consultant and into the broader roles of manufacturer and entrepreneur. Be-cause none of Delco's suppliers was willing to take a chance on such a large order, Kettering and Deeds had to take out additional loans, rent shop space, and make the units themselves.

Delco grew rapidly. By fall 1912 the firm counted Cadillac, Oakland, Oldsmobile, Jackson, Auburn, and other companies among its customers, and employed 1,200 workers. A year later, despite being shut down in spring 1913 by the disastrous Dayton flood, Delco was producing 600 starting, lighting, and ignition units a day. Two years later it built a new seven-story plant across the street from the original factory, reported profits of $1.5 mil-lion, and controlled 25 percent of the automotive starting, lighting, and ignition market. Delco also ex-panded into nonautomotive markets with the de-velopment of a portable, gasoline-powered electric generating and lighting system for farms which Ket-tering called the Delco-Light. Kettering hired Rich-ard Grant away from NCR to head the effort, and within a few years Grant was selling 60,000 units an-nually and employing 2,370 workers.

The electric self-starter was without question one of the true milestones of automotive history. Making it possible to start an automobile with a flip of a switch and the push of a button, it made the car accessible to nearly everyone. The claims of contemporary journalists that the self-starter did as much for the emancipation of women as universal suffrage may have been sexist and exaggerated, but the self-starter certainly helped put many more women comfortably behind the wheel. Like the auto-matic transmission later on, the self-starter opened up an enormous market among people who saw the automobile primarily as a means for traveling with minimum fuss and maximum convenience.

Though Kettering's official title at Delco was vice-president (Deeds was president), he invariably preferred technical puzzles to management. Busi-ness associates looking for the "Boss" frequently found him in overalls hunched over some experi-mental apparatus. Delco's astonishing success, and Kettering's lack of interest in management affairs, made the company particularly attractive as a take-over target, and in 1916 it caught the eye of the irre-pressible William Crapo Durant. Durant had founded GM in 1908 and in just a few years built it into Henry Ford's only real competition. His ca-reer with the company had been a series of spectac-ular rises followed by equally spectacular falls. He was a superb promoter and a terrible administra-tor. Durant had a sharp eye for the future of the auto-mobile industry, and looked forward to a time when it would be dominated by integrated compa-nies with full model lines. Yet he acquired compa-nies with only passing attention to their real worth or value and so burdened his enterprises with crush-ing debts. He built an automotive empire, watched it fall into the hands of the bankers, and then fought his way back into the presidency.

Bringing together a group of independent acces-sories manufacturers and combining it with GM was one of Durant's best ideas. In fall 1915 Durant began negotiating with five accessories companies—Hyatt Roller Bearing Company, Remy Electric Com-pany, New Departure Ball Bearing Company, Perlman Rim Corporation, and Delco. Although the companies were scattered across the country, and in some cases competed with one another,

The Dayton, Ohio, filling station which in 1923 was the first to sell Ethyl gasoline (courtesy of General Motors Institute Alumni Foundation Collection of Industrial History)

Durant had an easy time convincing their managements to join him. For one thing, Durant tended to be overly generous in his offers, and for another, the prospective members faced a common dilemma: they all depended on either Ford or GM for most of their business. As Alfred P. Sloan, Jr., then the forty-year-old president of Hyatt, explained to Kettering and Deeds during the negotiations, if one or both of the automotive giants chose to make their own starting, lighting, and ignition systems, Delco would likely go under. So Kettering, who had little taste for day-to-day management anyway, agreed to Durant's offer. On May 11, 1916, he and Deeds sold out for $2.5 million in cash and 15,000 shares of stock each in a new company, United Motors. After World War I, when Durant got around to merging United Motors into GM, those shares made Kettering one of the automotive giant's largest stockholders, and one of the nation's wealthiest men.

Along with the rest of the automotive industry, Kettering spent the war trying to apply the lessons of mass production to the military. Like some of the other automotive engineers of his generation,

he was confident (overconfident as it turned out) that techniques borrowed from automotive assembly lines could give a quick shot in the arm to aviation. To show the military how things should be done, and looking to earn himself a tidy profit in the bargain, he joined with Deeds, Orville Wright (another famous Dayton inventor), and several local businessmen in 1916 to form the Dayton Wright Airplane Company. They won several important contracts, constructed an enormous factory, and then learned the hard way that building combat airplanes was not at all like building automobile starters. Dayton Wright fell so far behind on its contract that the army and Congress sent an investigating team to Dayton to discover what had gone wrong. Kettering did better on an ignition systems contract for the famed Liberty aircraft engine. Airplane engines were still enough like car engines that the same assembly techniques could be used for both.

Kettering's most intriguing wartime assignment from the army was to develop a self-guided aerial torpedo. The original idea for the torpedo came from Elmer Sperry, already famous for his naval gyroscopic navigation and stabilization systems. Kettering's contribution was to make it simple and cheap. With a design team that included Orville Wright he designed a small biplane with a 15-foot wing span, a small gasoline engine, and automatic controls. The top secret project was decades ahead of its time, but its designers had a difficult time getting it to work reliably.

If Durant was not always the best of managers himself, he had a knack for spotting others with the talent. One of his best picks was Sloan, who rose rapidly from president of Hyatt Roller Bearings Company to president of United Motors to vice-president of GM, and ultimately to corporate president and chairman of the board. Unlike Durant, Sloan recognized the importance of formal corporate organization and management, and in 1919 he laid out a blueprint for restructuring GM which included an important new role for Kettering.

Sloan's plan called for, among other things, a central research laboratory devoted to "intensive study of the problems ahead of the Automotive industry ... examination and report upon engineering and research problems of a broad character, which are beyond the limitations of the equipment and personnel of the individual operations." At a time in the automobile's history when "development consisted of working on next year's model and research was thinking of what to do for the year after that," Sloan's proposal was unique and farsighted. It also offered an ideal post for someone of Kettering's long-range vision and unfettered imagination. His assignment was to look beyond the immediate needs of Chevrolet and Buick and the other divisions and plan a technical strategy for the entire corporation. It was exactly the kind of challenge Kettering relished. "I could see his eyes glitter with desire," said Walter Chrysler (then in charge of Buick) of Kettering's reaction to the negotiations. Tired of running his own business, Kettering was eager to devote himself full-time to research. His only real condition, to which Sloan agreed, was that the laboratory stay in Dayton, where he and Olive kept a lovely estate south of town. In 1920 Kettering sold his Dayton companies for GM stock and took up his new position as vice-president for research and director of the GM Research Corporation.

Despite a corporate charter that sounded open-ended and appeared to allow him great freedom in his choice of projects, Kettering realized that his laboratory had a direct responsibility for GM's long-term bottom line. Early in the negotiations Sloan reminded him, "Although it [the research laboratory] is not a productive unit and a unit that is supposed to make a profit, nevertheless the more tangible result we get from it the stronger its position will be.... It may be inferred at some future time ... that we are spending too much money down there and being in a position to show what benefits had accrued to the Corporation would strengthen our position materially." Kettering soon learned that it would take more than just a measure of autonomy and practical orientation to turn the laboratory into a corporate asset. A few hard lessons in the art of management came first.

"Industries are like some watches," Kettering often observed. "They have to be shaken hard every so often to keep them going." For his debut as research director, Kettering proposed to shake up GM with a radical innovation he had been interested in for some years, an air-cooled engine (called the "copper-cooled" for its copper cooling fins) that he thought would offer greater simplicity, lower cost, and better fuel economy than contemporary automobile engines.

GM's top managers believed that Kettering's idea could challenge Ford's Model T in the low-price market and turn around GM's slumping sales position in the wake of the postwar automotive recession. They gave Kettering a virtually unlimited budget and the assignment of developing not simply a new engine but a completely new automobile to be sold through the Chevrolet, Oakland, and Oldsmobile dealer networks. Instead of revitalizing the corporation, however, Kettering's project nearly bankrupted it, creating in the process a whole new set of management headaches that led many GM executives to question the value of the research laboratory itself.

What Kettering seemed to forget was that the laboratory could only develop the car. The divisions would have to manufacture and sell it. From the beginning there was little coordination or cooperation between the research laboratory and the production divisions. Rather than working together to develop a promising innovation, the research and production engineers worked at cross-purposes. The production engineers, assigned to a project they did not ask for and had not been consulted on, gave a halfhearted effort at best and spent most of their time finding fault with Kettering's ideas. For his part, Kettering, with the typical myopia of a research engineer, completely failed to appreciate the difficulties of moving from a carefully tuned prototype to an assembly-line automobile, and dismissed divisional complaints as further evidence of the limited imagination of manufacturing engineers.

The tension between the laboratory and the divisions escalated into an all-out corporate feud over the next few years, with politics only thinly disguised as engineering disagreements. Kettering privately urged Sloan to sack the divisional engineers he thought were getting in the way of his innovation, while the divisional engineers protested that Kettering was pushing a pet project detrimental to the best interests of GM. Things got so bad at one point that the general manager of Chevrolet had a nervous breakdown, and Kettering threatened to quit and take the project with him.

Finally, after three years of losing money (millions of dollars), momentum, and managerial control, Sloan had had enough. In late 1923 he ordered the entire venture scrapped and recalled the few hundred copper-cooled cars which had actually been sold. Fortunately, by that time the automotive market had recovered sufficiently so that GM no longer needed the copper-cooled as a weapon against the Model T.

It took a complete rethinking of the relationship between the research laboratory and the operating divisions to turn the laboratory into an asset. To coordinate research with other corporate activities, Sloan (who became GM's president in 1923) organized a special committee with members representing both the laboratory and the divisions. By opening more formal channels of communication between the technical staffs, and by integrating research with production and marketing, this committee helped eliminate much of the tension that had plagued the copper-cooled car and threatened the prospects of success for Kettering's later innovations.

Sloan ultimately concluded that GM had no real chance against Ford at the bottom end of the market. He conceded that segment and instead devised a new plan for the corporation. Rather than compete directly, GM would offer cars for buyers no longer satisfied with the spartan Model T. They would open up an escalator of style and status that could take American car buyers as far as their aspirations (and their wallets) allowed, from the practical

Chevrolet through the increasingly expensive Oakland (later Pontiac), Oldsmobile, Buick, and Cadillac. A car for every purse and purpose, Sloan liked to say. To help people onto the first step, Sloan introduced consumer credit, through the General Motors Acceptance Corporation (GMAC), and to keep them moving, even if only in the same place, he made effective use of the annual model change by stressing change in the cars' outer appearance.

Sloan's strategy depended in large measure on Kettering's ability to deliver the right kind of automobiles. For only when this year's model was significantly more convenient, comfortable, and appealing than last year's could GM entice American car buyers into falling for the annual model change and the full model line. Kettering called it keeping the customer dissatisfied, the incremental innovations that kept the buyers coming back year after year, and his laboratory mastered it. He once explained the strategy in one of his typically homespun but insightful stories. Select the best example of the automotive art and seal it in a glass case, he suggested. Then put the price in gold letters on the front. Check each year and see if the posted price isn't too high. "And what do you think you can get for that car at the end of fifteen years?" he asked. "It will be just as good as it was when we put it in the case, but the only man who will buy it is the junk dealer. Why? Because the car depreciated? No . . . because through the appreciation of new car designs, the eyes on the outside looking in have changed. . . . What we did do was appreciate your mind. We simply elevated your mental idea of what an automobile should be."

Keeping the customer dissatisfied became GM's secret weapon in the fight with Ford. In 1920, when Kettering became research director, Ford was selling more than half the automobiles in the country, and GM less than a quarter. Before the end of the decade those figures were reversed. On May 31, 1927, the last Model T rolled off Henry Ford's assembly line, a victim not only of Sloan's organizational and marketing strategies but of changing American tastes so brilliantly stimulated by Kettering's unceasing campaign to upgrade the comfort and convenience of the automobile in a cost-efficient way. When Ford finally came out with a new car some months later, the Model A, it was the ultimate compliment to Kettering's success when it was jokingly referred to as a Chevrolet with a different radiator cap.

Kettering as the head of GM Research Corporation in 1924

Perhaps symbolic of the relocation of the industry, Kettering's innovations came out of Detroit and not Dayton. Despite the original agreement with Sloan, the distance between the two cities began to be viewed by top management as a problem. Kettering spent hours driving or riding the train between conferences, and lines of communications (as in the copper-cooled episode) were frequently strained. Consequently, Sloan moved the research laboratory to Detroit in 1925. Kettering took a suite of rooms at the luxurious Book-Cadillac Hotel in downtown Detroit, but he kept the house in Dayton. He often joked that his home was in Dayton but since he could not find a job there, he had to work in Detroit.

The laboratory was housed in a new eleven-story downtown office building. Kettering had his office on the tenth floor. In the corner, to remind him of his commitment to practicality more than anything else, he kept a workbench with a vise, calipers, pliers, and other tools. On the wall he had a plaque reading, "Any problem, thoroughly understood, is fairly simple." A new headquarters, a bigger staff (260 in 1925, 400 by 1930, 500 a decade later), and more formal organization did little to change Kettering's informal style of running his laboratory. It was still "900 percent Charles Franklin Kettering," said a visiting journalist from *Fortune*. For Kettering management was a personal affair. He arrived at the reseach center at about nine o'clock in the morning, spent an hour or so answering the mail and taking care of administrative details, and then set off for the laboratory for his favorite part of the day. Unlike later research directors, Kettering was no armchair engineer. A favorite Kettering maxim was, "Anything more than two feet away from the job you are working on is too far." What he meant was that a good research administrator should be intimately acquainted with the work going on under him. While he did read technical literature, often in condensed reports prepared by his associates, he liked to pick up most of his information firsthand, from chats with the researchers and from the instruments themselves. Startled section heads and young assistants often looked up to see Kettering unexpectedly looming in the doorway. He would ask a few pointed questions about the work, sit down at a bench to look at the data, tinker with an engine, or record an observation or two. Sometimes his questions seemed superficially simple, occasionally outrageously so. He might ask what a catalyst was, or what sort of fuel a particular engine might like. Yet in re-examining the obvious, the researchers often stumbled onto surprising new insights and ideas. As one young chemical engineer recalled, "He could bring out things in an individual just by his talking. He looked at the total picture and we were so intense on our specific little spot that we were working on . . . that there was a tendency for us to become a little narrow."

Kettering kept things informal because he hated overspecialization. The problem had to be the boss, he said, and the person who was going to solve it had to "run errands for it." Any researcher who worked for him, he said, "has to be whatever he has to be to solve the problem, because the problems are not specialized, they are what they are." Consequently, Kettering looked for a grasp of fundamentals and a freedom from orthodoxy, not merely specialized training. Nor was he reluctant, when the occasion demanded, to suggest that a mechanical engineer investigate a chemical problem, or ask a physicist to do a bit of chemistry.

Kettering's style had its price, though. At any one time he usually had one or two pet projects to which he devoted himself. The rest he virtually ignored until another idea caught his fancy. The result was that his whims frequently determined which research would have top priority at GM. His department heads could do little to change this. They had an opportunity to express their opinions every Saturday at a weekly meeting in Kettering's office, but the meetings were far more like lectures than seminars. "Well, he was the meeting," one department head complained. "Because he did most of the talking and partly because we didn't find out exactly what was on his mind until the meeting had lasted as long as most of us wanted to stay there." Even Kettering could not possibly keep up with the details of all the research going on under him, though he tried anyway. When he fell behind on some of the details, "his solution was to go back to a phase that he understood so we sometimes found after we got a distance from our beginning experiments, we were suddenly urged back to doing them all over again," one staffer recalled.

Sometimes for better, and sometimes for worse, Kettering left his mark on his "boys," as he called them. "You can't help noticing how the department heads fall unconsciously into his ways of speech and constantly quote his aphorisms," noted one amused visitor. "It is doubtful if even the strongest-minded engineer could work for him without showing it." Because Kettering dominated research as he dominated conversations, his "boys" unfortunately got a somewhat undeserved reputation as yes-men.

When asked about his chief responsibility at GM, Kettering once replied, "Well, it is supposed to be running the laboratories, but the main problem we have, of course, is the selection of the proper research problems. That is really the most important thing we have to do." To make those choices effectively, Kettering had to keep an eye on innovation throughout the automotive industry, both at home and abroad.

As historian John B. Rae has pointed out, the automobile was European by birth and American by adoption. In the 1920s Europeans were working on a number of important ideas that Kettering thought might be useful for GM. To keep track of them, he stationed a network of correspondents abroad and attended the annual European automobile shows himself. Among the most important innovations which he borrowed from European practice and incorporated into GM designs were 4-wheel brakes and torsion dampers for crankshafts, which significantly diminished engine vibration.

Kettering also picked up new ideas from GM's suppliers. He learned about permanent molding techniques, which dramatically cut production time and cost on cast metal parts, from a visit to Holley Carburetor. His friend Willis Whitney, head of research at General Electric, told him about a new permanent bearing material being developed for electric motors. Kettering promptly set his metallurgists to work improving it and came up with Durex oilless bearings for automotive applications. From his friends at Goodyear he discovered the advantages of low-pressure, or balloon tires and introduced them on GM cars in 1925. While these and other incremental innovations were never widely appreciated outside the industry, they significantly lowered production costs and improved automotive performance. They joined the growing list of "invisible" improvements produced annually by Kettering's laboratory.

Some good ideas (and many not so good) came to the laboratory from independent inventors. The automobile was still young in the 1920s and a popular field for backyard mechanics. Kettering was a well-known advocate of untutored ingenuity, and many inventors took him at his word. His morning mail often brought several letters from hopeful amateurs with ideas. The more persistent waited outside the office door. Kettering could easily have dismissed these enthusiasts as cranks and crackpots, and in most cases he would have been right. For every useful idea there were dozens of fuel extenders and miracle carburetors. But instead, he set up a New Devices Committee to consider outside inventions. His effort was amply rewarded with a number of practical improvements. Occasionally, even the Boss let a good one get away. The New Devices Committee initially rejected the quarter window for the front door, and then had a hard time tracking down the inventor when they decided they wanted it after all. Another time someone suggested the first electrical signaling device, a neon sign in the shape of a hand to signal turns, but Kettering failed to follow up on it. More often, though, Kettering saw what the amateur inventors who brought him ideas could not see, and at least one commented after an interview with the committee that it seemed "a place where sheep were sheared."

Kettering liked to say he kept his customers dissatisfied by improving each year's model. Some customers, of course, were dissatisfied for other reasons. Kettering gathered suggestions on how to upgrade his product from this source too. For instance, he received many letters complaining about crankcase dilution, that is, gasoline diluting the oil and causing excessive engine wear. He went to work immediately on a crankcase ventilator which ended dilution and extended engine life.

One of the most dramatic, and visible, improvements Kettering introduced was Duco, a fast-drying and durable colored lacquer. Automotive paint was a vital issue not only from the standpoint of quality but time as well. Contemporary paints took so long to dry, required such expensive and time-consuming hand rubbing (up to three weeks worth), and tied up so much floor space in inventory, that finishing was a major cost in making cars. The introduction in the early 1920s of closed body designs (pioneered by Hudson) with even more area to paint made matters worse. The short-term solution was a black baking enamel that could be oven dried, thus saving time and lowering the cost. It was this economic reality, and not some concession to the sober tastes of the common man, that had inspired Henry Ford's famous quip about giving the customer any color he wants, so long as it was black. Only black baking enamel was cheap enough for the Model T. For GM, however, which depended on its hierarchy of styling to distinguish models that were assembled in exactly the same way and with essentially the same materials, basic black would not do. It desperately needed a fast-drying colored paint.

Du Pont had one, a pyroxylin lacquer that it had just developed and was looking to market. Moreover, through a complicated series of financial transactions dating from the Durant era, Du Pont owned a controlling share of GM and so had something of a ready-made outlet. But the finish was not perfected for automotive application. Kettering had to improve its composition, "build," stability, and its compatibility with various undercoatings. Then he had to convince the operating divisions to use it. As Cadillac's general manager told Kettering, "I think one of the most dangerous things the Corporation could do would be to adopt, generally, the new method of painting before it had been tried and in every conceivable fashion. I can conceive of a bad engine or other mechanical fault in a car which would do less damage, from an advertising standpoint, than poor paint."

The GM Research Laboratory in Detroit in 1929 (courtesy of the General Motors Institute Alumni Foundation Collection of Industrial History)

Once he had most of the bugs worked out, Kettering introduced Duco in 1925 through Oakland, a division in such poor shape at the time that nothing could have hurt it. There were still a few problems. The paint came in only one color, light blue, and left a dull, eggshell, finish. Kettering argued resourcefully that these apparent liabilities should be converted into assets by advertising the distinctive appearance and long life of the paint. His strategy worked, and customers, lured by the novelty and expected durability of Duco, waited in long lines for the "True Blue" Oaklands rather than accept a standard finish. Gradually Kettering's chemists did come up with other colors and a better sheen, and Duco was extended to the rest of the GM lineup.

Besides eliminating an expensive bottleneck in the manufacturing of automobiles, Duco helped transform the low-priced car from a strictly utilitarian vehicle into something more. The new durable finish was just one more advantage of the increasingly carefree, convenient, and comfortable automobile Kettering was creating for the American consumer. Henry Ford made the mass-produced automobile possible because instead of tooling up to make a cheap car, he designed a car suited for the mass market and then figured out how to manufacture it cheaply. In a similar way Kettering democratized automotive luxury. While addressing the problems of convenience and comfort on more costly GM cars first, he always found a way to refine his ideas for the less expensive models later. The result was a generally egalitarian technology within the system of status and style crucial to Sloan's overall strategy.

Of course, all this upgrading dramatically increased the cost of car ownership. Even Sloan was shocked to learn the cost of owning and operating a 1927 Chevrolet. Relaying his surprise to Kettering, he exclaimed, "The thing that strikes me is the average cost per car including depreciation. When you consider the millions of people who operate cars in this country on the income they must have, it is hard to see how they could set aside this relatively large amount of money to maintain a car." Kettering, on the other hand, was not at all surprised. He, better than Sloan, appreciated how attached to their automobiles Americans had become, and how important further technological innovations would be in extending the affair.

Kettering liked to define industrial research as a kind of corporate life insurance policy, as a way, he said, of finding out what you are going to do when you can no longer do what you are doing now. Consequently, he tried not only to keep pace with the market, but to stay a step or two ahead. "You are always too late with a development if you are so slow that people demand it before you yourself recognize it," he observed. "The research department should have foreseen what was necessary and had it ready to a point where people never knew they wanted it until it was made available to them." So while Kettering the businessman appreciated how the marketplace could influence next year's models, Kettering the engineer was more inspired by the long-range possibilities for efficient and technically sophisticated automotive design.

Long before other automotive engineers were worrying about petroleum shortages and miles per gallon, Kettering was devoting a large share of his time and energy–and a large chunk of his corporate budget–to improving the fuel economy and efficiency of the automobile. Although Kettering had been tinkering with the fuel problem since his Delco days, it was a post-World War I fuel crisis that convinced him to make fuel economy a top

GM research priority. A study of America's future oil supplies which Kettering completed in 1920 concluded that "this year will see the maximum production of petroleum that this country will ever know," an assessment corroborated by both the U. S. Geological Survey and the American Institute of Petroleum Geologists.

As Kettering and every other automotive engineer knew, the cheapest and easiest way of improving the efficiency and economy of a gasoline engine was by raising its compression ratio. Unfortunately, that route was blocked by knock, a perplexing malfunction characterized by a loud pounding that was often violent enough to crack pistons.

Kettering recognized that nothing could be done about knock until he understood what it really was. His attack on the problem was informed by two original assumptions: that knock was a failing of the fuel rather than of the engine (most automotive engineers believed the opposite), and that fuel behavior could be altered chemically, with some sort of additive. Relying on these assumptions, Kettering laid out a number of original theories about why fuels knock and how knock might be cured, and assembled a team of assistants, led by chemist Thomas Midgley, to test them. Kettering was no chemist, but if he sometimes got lost in the technical details, he contributed much of the vision and inspiration for the project.

Although most of Kettering's early theories proved to be wrong in some detail, they helped him focus the antiknock additive search. He had a knack for isolating the significant elements in an experimental failure and discarding the rest. For instance, he deduced that iodine reduced knock not because of its color, as he had originally suspected, but because it somehow acted as a catalyst. Consequently, he told his researchers to stop testing dyes and look into catalysts instead. So began the hunt for an antiknock additive. At times it could be discouraging–"a succession of failures with just enough successes to keep us going," Kettering recalled. After months of discouragement, he called his chemists together for his version of a pep talk: "By God, if you don't come up with something within the next six months you're all fired." And, as one staff member recalled, "He meant it!"

The breakthrough came in late 1921, when one of the trials revealed that an obscure lead compound, tetraethyllead (TEL), suppressed knock completely, even at dilutions of 1:1300. On February 1,

1923, "Ethyl" gasoline (a name Kettering coined himself) was first sold to the public at a Dayton filling station.

Though the commercial potential of TEL looked staggering–Americans were then using about 4 billion gallons of gasoline a year and increasing their consumption by 20 percent annually–GM was in no position to exploit its discovery directly. Instead it went into partnership with Standard Oil of New Jersey, buying rather than developing chemical production know-how. Kettering was appointed the first president of the joint venture, the Ethyl Corporation.

A national health scare in 1924 almost kept leaded gasoline off the market. Dozens of workers were killed and scores injured in an industrial accident at a TEL blending plant in New Jersey. Leaded gasoline was withdrawn from public sale while a surgeon general's panel looked into the health risks. Kettering already knew something about those risks. Several of his researchers had been forced to take extended vacations to throw off the effects of lead poisoning, and a couple of his workers had died in a spill in Dayton. But he firmly believed that TEL was only dangerous in the blending plant, not the fuel tank. The surgeon general's report agreed and recommended only better industrial safety standards. Unfortunately, neither Kettering nor the health investigators considered the long-term effects of low concentration exposure. Only in the 1960s, when more sophisticated measuring techniques became available and when the accumulated effects of lead in the environment became apparent, did leaded gasoline once again became a public health concern.

Over the years Ethyl grew into a multi-million-dollar company and one of GM's most profitable investments. To avoid some of the mounting criticism against the environmental impact of leaded gasoline, Ethyl was sold to the Albemarle Paper Manufacturing Company in 1962, in what the business press dubbed a unique example of Jonah swallowing the whale.

Kettering never considered TEL the final word on fuel performance. Throughout the 1920s and 1930s he kept a team of bright young chemists and physicists busy studying combustion fundamentals with spectroscopic and high-speed photographic techniques. Kettering asked two basic questions: how does TEL work, and what are the differences in chemical and physical properties between knocking and nonknocking fuels. His researchers did not come up with any definitive answers (no one has yet), but they did learn a great deal about how knock is related to chemical structure and how the right fuel structures can prevent it. They developed the modern octane rating of fuel performance. They also learned how to make nonleaded gasolines as knock resistant as leaded ones, without the polluting additives. Because these gasolines are more expensive to manufacture, gasoline without the lead paradoxically costs more than gasoline with it.

Kettering simultaneously looked into the diesel engine as a way of anticipating future fuel shortages. The diesel's extremely high compression meant that it could achieve higher efficiency and also use cheaper grades of fuel. However, in order to withstand those compression ratios, diesels had to be heavier and slower than their gasoline counterparts.

Kettering borrowed from many sources in his quest to improve diesel performance. From one he learned the advantages of the 2-stroke cycle. From another he found out how alloy construction could help. Better scavenging systems, solid fuel injection, and advances in electrical transmission came from others. When he decided he needed more know-how he bought out two small diesel engine firms to acquire it quickly. He then challenged his engineers to improve each of the ideas he had found. In the process they created a diesel of far less weight per horsepower than anyone had previously imagined.

Beginning in the 1930s Kettering's 2-stroke diesels revolutionized the power field in ships, locomotives, and trucks. By applying the same marketing techniques which had worked so effectively for automobiles–long-term financing, standard designs using common parts and technology, factory-trained maintenance men, and skilled advertising–GM ran traditional locomotive builders literally off the rails. The Burlington Zephyr was the first in a fleet of GM diesels that changed the way Americans powered their railroads.

Strangely, Kettering was also largely responsible for GM's failure in the automotive diesel field. Completely committed to his 2-stroke design, Kettering consistently killed off 4-stroke diesel programs at GM until his retirement in the late 1940s. Consequently GM found itself at a considerable disadvantage when 4-stroke automotive diesels proved to be the better bet. When GM did finally bring out a 4-stroke design in the 1970s, it was far inferior to the competition and was quickly withdrawn. Kettering's 2-stroke engines have remained an important part of the GM truck line, however.

Long after improved thermal cracking techniques, new oil strikes, and the success of TEL made the oil crisis of the 1920s a distant memory, Kettering continued his quest for fuel efficiency. He studied alcohol fuels seriously. And in the mid 1930s he developed a "light car" design which averaged 25 percent better fuel economy than contemporary cars and could still have passed for a "car of the future" decades later.

In the post-World War II years Kettering's fuel and engine innovations were put to quite a different use than he had originally intended—increasing performance rather than mileage. In 1949 both Oldsmobile and Cadillac introduced high-compression V-8 engines based on Kettering's designs (Oldsmobile called theirs the Kettering Engine), and the horsepower race was on. Power and top speed became the new watchwords of automotive marketing, not economy and efficiency. Ironically, Kettering's innovations were used not so much to conserve fuel as to increase performance, leading to more rapid depletion of petroleum resources and the gradual disappearance of his original vision of conservation until a decade and a half after his death. Yet if the fuel-saving innovations and improvements that Kettering presided over failed to inspire most of his contemporaries, they had a crucial role in creating the body of knowledge that ultimately produced the modern, fuel-efficient automobile.

Sloan often said that GM was in the business of making money, not making cars. Over the years Kettering's inventions helped GM diversify into new markets as well as strengthen its hold on traditional ones. His discovery of freon (a nontoxic and nonflammable refrigerant) in 1930, again with the assistance of Thomas Midgley, put GM into the home refrigerator market and shored up the sagging fortunes of its Frigidaire subsidiary. As with leaded gasoline, GM exploited its chemical discovery by going into partnership with an established chemical firm, this time Du Pont, with which it formed a joint-stock venture, the Kinetic Chemical Company, to manufacture and market freon. Once again Kettering's chemistry would have some long-term environmental implications, but none that would be known within his lifetime.

Kettering directed GM research from 1920 until his retirement in 1947 and served as a valu-

able consultant even after the laboratory moved to its new home at the Technical Center in Warren, Michigan, in 1956. He never rode the elevators (too slow) and never stayed in the office (too isolated). He poked around the laboratories as in the old days and surprised nervous young scientists with his tall presence and probing questions. Yet he did not fit very well into this new world of white-coated technicians and Ph.D.'s. The academic scientists he had brought into GM had transformed the place, made it their own, and left little room for a "screwdrivers and pliers man," as Kettering once described himself.

In his later years Kettering increasingly devoted himself to research questions outside the automotive field. He cofounded the Sloan-Kettering Institute for cancer research in New York. He established the Kettering Foundation for the support of photosynthesis and solar energy research. And he set up a series of private laboratories for fundamental studies of magnetism, hoping in the process to cap his career with an important theoretical contribution to science.

Kettering also found time to support innovative education. Like Edison, whom he greatly admired, he publicly downplayed the value of advanced study. "You can't do a job with educated people," he said. "They want to do it the way they were educated." Even at commencement addresses he could rarely resist poking a little fun at academic pretensions. At the same time he sponsored the progressive Moraine Park School in Dayton (and sent his son Eugene there), donated a library, a student union, and a science building to Antioch College, and gave generously to a variety of educational institutions and enterprises. What bothered him about contemporary education was its narrowness and its disregard for practical problems. Understandably, he became an enthusiastic proponent of cooperative education and other programs that might bring together education and business.

Retirement also gave Kettering a chance to reflect on the broader meaning of his career and to share those reflections with students, businessmen, and engineers. His dry wit and colorful style endeared him to nearly every audience, and his eloquence and quotability made him the best-known engineer of his generation. Conservatives particularly appreciated his amusing, if occasionally fanatical, defense of free enterprise. "If there is as great a gulf between practice and theory in Russian scientific education as there is in some other aspects of Russian life," he once said, "the more engineers they turn out, the safer we will be."

Well into his seventies, Kettering continued to view the world as a challenge, earning patents, making discoveries, and generally disproving his friend Midgley's declaration that scientists and engineers should retire at age forty, before their creativity evaporated. Only a few days before his death on November 25, 1958, at the age of eighty-two, he was working in one of his magnet laboratories trying to prove one of his pet theories.

Kettering's years with GM saw the company climb from a poor second in the automobile industry to the largest manufacturing corporation in the world. His innovations played a significant role in the process. Leaded gasoline and high-compression engines, quick-drying and durable paints in attractive colors, and a host of less obvious innovations transformed the utilitarian car of 1920 into a fixture of American aspiration in the 1950s. The American automobile, like the American consumer, was forever changed.

Like Henry Ford, Kettering had little use for history. You never get anywhere looking in your rear-view mirror, he often said. He looked to the future because, as he explained, "we will have to spend the rest of our lives there." Undoubtedly Kettering would have been troubled by how that future reshaped his industry. He would be shocked to see how hard GM was struggling against a new and tougher group of foreign competitors; to learn how far federal safety, emissions, and mileage regulations had set limits on automotive engineering; and to discover that Detroit had failed to take the lead in creating more fuel-conserving, affordable, and safe cars. He would have hated the 55 mph limit–85 mph was more his speed. And yet he would unquestionably offer his counterparts today some words of encouragement. As he liked to say, "The price of progress is trouble and I don't think the price is too high."

Publications:

"Some Points in Electric Lighting for Automobiles," *SAE Bulletin,* 3 (October 1912): 13;

"Engine Temperature Control," *SAE Bulletin,* 10 (September 1916): 685;

"Engineer's View of the Liberty Engine and the Airplane Program," *Scientific American* (June 8, 1918): 538;

"Tractor Engineering Possibilities," *SAE Journal,* 3 (July 1918): 5;

"The Future of the Airplane Business," *SAE Journal,* 3 (December 1918): 358;

"Automotive Power Plant," *Journal, Western Society of Engineers,* 24 (January 1919): 31;

"More Efficient Utilization of Fuels," *SAE Quarterly Transactions,* 1 (April 1919): 263;

"Statement on the Fuel Problem," *SAE Journal,* 5 (September 1919): 195;

"Studying the Knocks," *Scientific American* (October 11, 1919): 364;

"Engineering Possibilities as Indicated by the Progress of Science," *SAE Journal,* 7 (July 1920): 56;

"Combustion of Fuels in Internal Combustion Engines," *SAE Journal,* 7 (September 1920): 224;

"Consumption–The Automotive Industry," *American Petroleum Institute Bulletin* (December 10, 1920): 35;

"Cooperation of Automotive and Oil Industries," *SAE Journal* (January 1921);

"The Spirit of Adventure in Education," Bulletin No. 9, *Progressive Education* (September 1921);

"Fuel Research Developments," *SAE Journal,* 9 (November 1921): 291;

"Expect Great Things in the Automobile Industry," *Forbes* (October 13, 1923);

"The Car You'll Drive 10 Years From Now," *Motor* (January 1924): 84;

"Motor Design and Fuel Economy," *Industrial and Engineering Chemistry,* 17 (November 1925): 1115;

"The Engineer's Part in Increasing Highway Safety," *SAE Journal,* 17 (December 1925): 578;

"Research as Related to Banking," *Cleveland Trust Monthly* (December 1926): 4;

"Applying New 'Yardsticks' to Automobiles," *Scientific American* (January 1927);

"The Functions of Research," *Industrial and Engineering Chemistry,* 10 (November 1927): 1212;

"Research, Horse-Sense and Profits," *Factory and Industrial Management,* 75 (April 1928): 735;

"The Engineer and His Opportunity," *SAE Journal,* 23 (October 1928): 350;

"General Motors Budgets for Change," *Magazine of Business,* 54 (October 1928);

"Hurdles to Jump for Inventors," *Popular Mechanics* (December 1929): 954;

"Big Changes Ahead," *American Magazine* (January 1930);

"Research Made Your Motor Car," *Scientific American* (January 1930): 9;

"Automotive Developments Held Back by Lack of True Anti-Knock Fuels," *National Petroleum News,* 22 (April 30, 1930): 27;

"A Representation of the Dynamic Properties of Molecules by Mechanical Models," with L. W. Shutts and D. H. Andrews, *Physical Review,* 36 (August 1, 1930): 531;

"Fundamentals of Engineering Research," *Agricultural Engineering,* 11 (August 1930): 263;

"Research, Radio, Automobiles," *Electronics* (October 1930): 329;

"Unemployment and the Industrial System," *Saturday Evening Post* (December 13, 1930): 16;

"We Need New Things," *Country Gentleman* (March 1931): 19;

"Business Needs a New Broom," *Rotarian* (May 1931): 6;

"Coax Business Back," *Daily News Record* (June 18, 1931);

"Industry at the Crossroads," *Saturday Evening Post* (September 26, 1931): 8;

"Electrical Synchronization of Marine Diesels," *Motorship* (March 1932): 114;

"The World Isn't Finished Yet," *Saturday Evening Post* (April 25, 1932): 23;

"The Role of Invention in Industry," *Journal of the Patent Office Society*, 14 (June 1932): 500;

"Some New Engineering Problems," *Industrial Record* (October 1932): 13;

The New Necessity, with Allen Orth (Baltimore: Williams & Wilkins, 1932);

"Infrared Absorption Spectra of Certain Organic Compounds, Including the Principal Types in Gasoline," *Physics*, 4 (February 1933): 39;

"Tomorrow We Move," *American Magazine* (March 1933): 24;

"Will the Goblins Get Us?," *Good Housekeeping* (April 1933): 43;

"Relation of Chemistry to the Individual," *Industrial and Engineering Chemistry*, 25 (May 1933): 484;

"America Comes Through a Crisis," *Saturday Evening Post* (May 13, 1933): 3;

"Ignorance Sires Argument," *SAE Journal*, 33 (November 1933): 13;

"Do We Need Birth Control of Ideas? No!," *Rotarian* (April 1934): 8;

"Industry—Research," *Scientific American* (May 1934): 242;

"Science and Industry in the Coming Century," *Scientific Monthly* (July 1934);

"The Scientist in an Unscientific Society," *Scientific American* (August 1934): 79;

"The Motor Car of the Future," *Automobile Topics* (January 26, 1935): 762;

"It's Man's Turn Now," *Good Housekeeping* (January 1935): 16;

"Looking Ahead With Boss Ket," *Popular Mechanics* (February 1935): 202;

"Industrial Prospecting," *National Research Council, Cir. Series*, no. 107 (December 1935);

"Research and Social Progress," *Journal, Western Society of Engineers* (April 1936): 58;

"How to Create a Labor Shortage," *Saturday Evening Post* (May 30, 1936);

"Idea to Industry," *Journal of the Franklin Institute*, 222 (August 1936): 127;

"Looking Forward in Research, Science, and Industry," *Vital Speeches of the Day* (December 1, 1936): 101;

"Research and Industry," *Scientific American* (May 1937);

"Research Makes Jobs," *Review of Reviews* (May 1937): 38;

"Diesel Development," *G.M.A.C. News and Views* (November 1937): 24;

"Ten Paths to Fame and Fortune," *American Magazine* (December 1937);

"Engineering Principles of Diesel Design," *Official Proceedings, The Western Railway Club*, 50 (January 1938): 13;

"What Kettering Said," *SAE Journal* (February 1938): 15;

"Joint Responsibility of Automotive and Civil Engineers," *Proceedings, American Society of Civil Engineers*, 64 (June 1938): 1116;

"Scientific Training and Its Relation to Industrial Problems," *Journal of Applied Physics*, 9 (July 1938): 427;

"More Music, Please, Composers," *Saturday Evening Post* (September 10, 1938): 23;

"Research and Progress," *Armour Engineer and Alumnus* (December 1938): 6;

"We've Only Just Begun," *America's Future* (January 1939): 13;

"Industry's New Horizons," *Vital Speeches of the Day* (September 1, 1939): 686;

"Effect of Emergency on Scientific and Industrial Progress," *Vital Speeches of the Day* (September 1, 1939);

"Unfinished Business," *Industrial Business* (February 1940): 69;

"Opportunities for Youth," *Vital Speeches of the Day* (June 1, 1940): 504;

"The Age of Opportunity," *Popular Mechanics* (October 1940);

"Application of Modern Science to the Plating Industry," *Monthly Review of the American Electroplater's Society* (January 1941): 15;

"Guns Aren't Windshield Wipers," *Saturday Evening Post* (January 18, 1941): 12;

"The World Ahead," *Printer's Ink Monthly* (February 1941): 12;

"The Future Is Anything You Want It To Be," *Think* (August 1941): 30;

"New Vistas for Mankind After the War," *Liberty* (February 21, 1942): 10;

"There Is Only One Mistake; To Do Nothing," *Saturday Evening Post* (March 28, 1942);

"Horsepower Is War Power," *Scientific American* (July 1942): 4;

"The Role of Patents in the Automobile Industry's Growth," *Journal of Commerce* (March 11, 1943): 11;

"Chemistry and the Motor Car Industry," *Chemical and Engineering News*, 21 (June 10, 1943): 841;

"Looking Forward," *Vital Speeches of the Day* (June 1943): 532;

"Looking at the Future Through the Eyes of Research," *SAE Journal*, 51 (July 1943): 33;

"How to Plan for Victory," *American Magazine* (December 1943): 19;

"Education Begins at Home," *School and Society* (January 1, 1944): 10;

"How Can We Develop Inventors?," *Mechanical Engineering*, 66 (April 1944): 231;

"Catching Up With Nature," *Vital Speeches of the Day* (September 15, 1944): 736;

"Inertia of the Carrier of Electricity in Copper and Aluminum," with G. G. Scott, *Physical Review* (November 1 and November 15, 1944): 257;

"The Effect of the Molecular Structure of Fuels on the Power and Efficiency of Internal Combustion Engines," *Industrial and Engineering Chemistry*, 36 (December 1944): 1079;

"Research Opens the Door," *Scientific American* (January 1945): 7;

"Relationship of Research to Management," *Manufacturers' News* (April 1945): 3;

"Fuels and Engines for Higher Power and Greater Efficiency," *SAE Journal*, 53 (June 1945): 352;

"Within Yourself," *Boy's Life* (August 1945): 3;

"The Farm—A Mode of Life," *News and Views* (January 1946): 7;

"Get Out of That Rut!," *Rotarian* (February 1946): 8;

"War Sidetracks Science," *Nation's Business* (April 1946): 37;

"Muscles and Machines," *Vital Speeches of the Day* (July 1946): 575;

"Medicine and Industrial Research," *Journal, Michigan State Medical Society* (August 1946): 1063;

"The Future of Science," *Science*, 104 (December 27, 1946): 609;

"What is Our Competition?," *Diesel Power and Diesel Transportation* (January 1947): 92;

"Thomas Alva Edison," *Scientific Monthly*, 64 (February 1947): 109;

"Chemistry and the Automobile Industry," *Record of Chemical Progress*, 8 (July-October 1947): 58;

"More Efficient Utilization of Fuels," *SAE Quarterly Transactions*, 1 (October 1947): 669;

America's Battle for Abundance, with Orth (Detroit, 1947);

"Biographical Memoir of Leo Hendrick Baekeland," *National Academy of Sciences, Biographical Memoirs*, 24 (1947);

"Biographical Memoir of Thomas Midgley, Jr.," *National Academy of Sciences, Biographical Memoirs*, 24 (1947);

"Technical Education," *Air Affairs* (Winter 1948): 223;

"Age of Mechanical Power from Liquid Fuel," *Oil Forum* (November 1949): 479;

"Get Off Route 25, Young Man," *Collier's* (December 3, 1949): 13;

"Future Developments in Transportation," *Journal of the Franklin Institute*, 25 (January 1951): 109;

"Education is the Guardian of the American Heritage," *Vital Speeches of the Day* (March 15, 1951): 346;

"And Then Came the Horseless Carriage," *Popular Mechanics* (January 1952): 137;

"Don't Be Afraid to Stumble," *Rotarian* (January 1952): 8;

"An Engineer's Report on the Future," *American Engineer* (October 1952);

A Short History of Technology, with Harold G. Bowen (West Orange, N.J., 1952);

"The Engineer's Responsibility in Educating the Public," *Mechanical Engineering*, 75 (December 1953): 953;

"A Review of the Century," *Centennial of Engineering, History and Proceedings of Symposis* (Chicago, 1953): 46;

"You Haven't Seen Anything Yet," *Foundation* (June 1955);

"A Tribute to Automobile Old Timers," *Old Timers' News* (Winter 1955): 17;

"An Inventor Looks at Education," *Proceedings of the Sixth Thomas A. Edison Foundation Institute* (1955): 52;

"I Am Interested in the Future," *Sales Management* (March 1, 1956): 88;

"Engineering," *Journal of the American Medical Association*, 167 (July 12, 1958): 1360;

"Future Unlimited," *Saturday Evening Post* (May 17, 1958): 126.

References:

Thomas A. Boyd, *Professional Amateur: The Biography of Charles Franklin Kettering* (New York: Dutton, 1957);

Boyd, *Prophet of Progress: Selection from the Speeches of Charles F. Kettering* (New York: Dutton, 1961);

Alfred Chandler, *Pierre S. DuPont and the Making of the Modern Corporation* (New York, 1971);

Chandler, *Strategy and Structure: Chapters in the History of the Business Enterprise* (New York, 1963);

James J. Flink, *America Adopts the Automobile* (Cambridge, Mass.: MIT Press, 1971);

Flink, *The Automobile Age* (Cambridge, Mass.: MIT Press, 1988);

Flink, *The Car Culture* (Cambridge, Mass.: MIT Press, 1975);

Stuart W. Leslie, *Boss Kettering: Wizard of General Motors* (New York: Columbia University Press, 1983);

John B. Rae, *The American Automobile* (Chicago: University of Chicago Press, 1965);

Rae, *The American Automobile Industry* (Boston: Twayne, 1984);

Rae, *American Automobile Manufacturers* (Philadelphia: Chilton, 1959);

Rae, *The Road and Car in American Life* (Cambridge, Mass.: MIT Press, 1971);

Alfred P. Sloan, Jr., *Adventures of a White Collar Man* (New York: Doubleday, Doran, 1941);

Sloan, *My Years With General Motors* (Garden City, N.Y.: Doubleday, 1964);

Bernard Weisberger, *The Dream Maker: William C. Durant, Founder of General Motors* (Boston: Little, Brown, 1979);

Brock Yates, *The Decline and Fall of the American Automobile Industry* (New York: Empire, 1983).

Archives:

Most of Kettering's business papers are held by the Records Retention Unit of the General Motors Research Laboratories in Warren, Michigan. While I was given permission to use that material in preparing my biography of Kettering, and to quote extensively from it, the papers remain company property and are not yet open to scholars. The General Motors Institute Alumni Foundation Collection of Industrial History in Flint, Michigan, has an extensive collection of Kettering material, including valuable correspondence about the self-starter, an unpublished history of Ethyl gasoline by Thomas A. Boyd, and a massive oral history archives assembled by Boyd. This collection is open. Wright Patterson Air Force Base in Dayton, Ohio, has important holdings on Kettering's aviation interests. NCR (formerly the National Cash Register Company) has a substantial amount of correspondence, patent drawings, and artifacts relating to Kettering's days as an electrical inventor there. Unfortunately, this material is also closed to outsiders. The Pierre S. du Pont Papers, held by the Hagley Museum and Library in Wilmington, Delaware, contain a significant amount of correspondence between Kettering and du Pont from the period in the early 1920s when du Pont was chairman of the board of General Motors.

Semon Emil Knudsen

(October 2, 1912-   )

by James J. Flink

University of California, Irvine

CAREER: Engineer, Cross Gear & Machine Company (1936-1937); engineer, Bower Roller Bearing Company (1937-1939); special assignment, Pontiac Motor Division (1939-1941), assistant chief inspector, Pontiac (1941-1942), superintendent of inspection, Pontiac (1942-1943), supervisor of inspection, Pontiac (1943-1946), assistant plant superintendent, Pontiac (1946), assistant general master mechanic and general master mechanic, Pontiac (1946-1949), director, Process Development Section (1949-1953), assistant manufacturing manager, Allison Division (1953-1954), manufacturing manager, Allison (1954-1955), general manager, Detroit Diesel Division (1955-1956), general manager, Pontiac (1956-1961), vice-president, General Motors Corporation (1956-1965), general manager, Chevrolet Motor Division (1961-1965), group vice-president, Overseas and Canadian Group (1965-1966), executive vice-president, Overseas and Canadian Operations and Non-Automotive and Defense, General Motors (1967-1968); president, Ford Motor Company (1968-1969); chairman of the board and chief executive officer, Rectrans Corporation (1970-1971); chairman of the board and chief executive officer, White Motor Corporation (1971-1980).

Semon Emil Knudsen was born in Buffalo, New York, on October 2, 1912, the first of four children and only son of William Signius Knudsen and Clara Euler Knudsen. With the acquisition by the Ford Motor Company of Buffalo's John R. Keim Mills, a leading maker of pressed and drawn steel components, the Knudsen family relocated in Detroit shortly after Semon's birth. William S. Knudsen was charged with setting up the Ford branch assembly plants to produce the Model T. The Knudsens rented a small, two-bedroom house in Detroit. To ensure that William got his needed night's rest, for a time Clara and a baby sister shared one bedroom, while year-old Semon slept in the other with his father, who nicknamed him "Bunkie," pre-World War I army slang for "bunkmate."

William S. Knudsen was among the top production engineers in automotive history. After leaving Ford over disagreements about the company's arbitrary and repressive treatment of its employees and Henry Ford's intransigent commitment to the outmoded Model T, Knudsen joined Chevrolet in 1922. Under his leadership Chevrolet came to surpass Ford in sales in 1927. At Chevrolet he innovated modern "flexible" mass production. By reverting to more general purpose machine tools, outsourcing more components, and decentralizing operations, he made mass production compatible with the annual model change and individualization of product called for by General Motors (GM) presi-

Semon Emil Knudsen, left, with Henry Ford II (courtesy of Ford Motor Company)

dent Alfred P. Sloan, Jr. "Big Bill" Knudsen became GM president in May 1937 with Sloan's move up to chairman of the board. Then in May 1940 he left GM, at President Roosevelt's request, to accept an appointment at no salary as chairman of the advisory committee of the Council for National Defense. In January 1941 he became codirector, with Sidney Hillman, of the Office of Production Management (OPM) to coordinate defense production, purchasing, and priorities. When the OPM's functions were taken over by the War Production Board in January 1942, he became a lieutenant general and director of war production in the War Department. At the war's end in 1945 he returned to GM as a member of its board of directors for a few years before his death from a cerebral hemorrhage on April 27, 1948.

S. E. Knudsen was extremely close to his father and followed in his footsteps. They met for lunch together virtually every Saturday and took drives together Sunday mornings while his mother and three sisters got dressed to go to church.

Knudsen usually accompanied his father and GM vice-president for design Harley Earl on their trips to the annual London and Paris automobile shows. He was also his father's companion on important 1936 and 1938 missions to inspect the GM Opel facilities in Hitler's Germany. He shared both his father's passion for cars and mechanical aptitude. It took the fourteen-year-old Knudsen only a month to put into running order the parts of a completely disassembled Chevrolet that his father had given him as a gift on the condition that he assemble it. He received his bachelor's degree in engineering from the Massachusetts Institute of Technology in 1936.

Knudsen gained practical experience in two Detroit machine shops before beginning his automotive career at GM. After graduating from college he went to work at the Cross Gear & Machine Company, which made ring gears and pinions for Ford. Ralph Cross, his employer, had developed a machine for chamfering gear teeth that was generally used in the industry, and he was an expert at setting up the machinery for cutting gears. Knudsen was invited by Ralph Cross, Jr., a fraternity brother at MIT, to help set up an engineering department at Cross at the starting pay of 75¢ an hour. The young men modernized the Cross gear-cutting machine. They then became intrigued with the problem of moving work from one work station to another and developed some motorized conveyors to do the job, which Knudsen recalls as an early example of a transfer machine. He left Cross after a short time for a job at the Bower Roller Bearing Company, which made tapered roller bearings. He took the job at Bower, where 100,000 bearings a day were turned out, to gain experience in high-volume production.

At GM Knudsen learned automobile manufacturing from the ground up, even spending time as a laborer on the assembly line and as a foreman. His father, whose own training in a Danish government technical school was roughly the equivalent of an American college education, stressed the importance of practical experience on the shop floor. And Knudsen was expected to rise within GM on his own merits. "I busted my pick to gain the respect of people," he recalled. Knudsen began working on special assignment at Pontiac on January 9, 1939, and during his decade there he held the titles of assistant chief inspector, superintendent of inspection, supervisor of inspection, assistant plant superintendent, assistant general master mechanic, and general master mechanic. He was transferred to the GM Central Office on August 7, 1949, where he worked as director of the Process Development Section until January 31, 1953. From February 1, 1953, until February 15, 1955, he served first as assistant manufacturing manager, then as the manufacturing manager of GM's Allison Division, which made aircraft engines at Indianapolis, Indiana. Only after this long apprenticeship was Knudsen promoted on February 16, 1955, to a top GM management post as general manager of its Detroit Diesel Division.

Knudsen was appointed general manager of the Pontiac Division and a vice-president of GM on July 1, 1956. At forty-four he was the youngest executive ever appointed to head one of GM's five automobile divisions. In his five years as Pontiac general manager Knudsen gained widespread recognition for changing the stodgy Pontiac image and for innovating "widetrack" styling. He recalls that "we had to do something to get out of the old woman's category." He got rid of the traditional Pontiac Indianhead logo, believing that the six-foot-high wooden Indians that dealers placed in front of their showrooms made Pontiac agencies "look like cigar stores." "Forget the Indian," he said. "It's a dead race." Always a racing enthusiast, Knudsen moved Pontiac heavily into racing activities, despite a 1957 Automobile Manufacturers Association ban on factory participation in speed contests. For the 1961 stock car season, for example, Pontiac scored an unprecedented thirty-one wins, versus eleven for Chevrolet, and only seven for Ford. As Pontiac emphasized performance and appealed to younger buyers, who were becoming a more important segment of the automobile market, sales increased in 1961 and boosted Pontiac from sixth to third place in sales behind Chevrolet and Ford.

Under Knudsen's leadership Pontiac stylists and engineers were encouraged to innovate. Widetrack styling resulted from increasing the tread of 1959 models over 1958 models from about 60 inches to 64 inches. The all new 1959 bodies mounted on 1957-1958 chassis had looked like "a spindly operation" to Knudsen and stylist Earl. Moving the wheels out four inches on a clay model made the car, in Knudsen's words, look like "a real gutsy machine," while only adding about $5 to its unit cost. Chief engineer Elliott M. "Pete" Estes and the advance planning staff of assistant chief engineer John Z. DeLorean added popular new models to the Pontiac line. The Tempest compact, powered by an innovative overhead cam, 225-horsepower engine, was introduced in 1959 and voted *Motor Trend* car of the year for 1961. "The 1960-model year was Knudsen's year of triumph at Pontiac," observed Ivan Fallon and James Srodes. "Not only did the Tempest catch on among the new generation of economy-minded buyers, but the Estes-DeLorean engineers also unveiled the Grand Prix sports car as well as the luxury-market Le Mans, an important addition to the Pontiac arsenal."

On November 6, 1961, Knudsen was reassigned to the post of general manager of the troubled Chevrolet Division. Fallon and Srodes note that the basic design of the full-size Chevrolet "had not been changed since the classic 1956 model, which had become stale and boring." As sales slipped Ford was beginning to run neck and neck with number one Chevrolet. During Knudsen's tenure as general manager, Chevrolet sales increased from 1,604,805 units for the 1961 calendar year to 2,587,487 units for 1965.

An even more serious problem was the radically designed Corvair compact. Introduced in 1959, the Corvair featured unitary construction, four-wheel independent suspension, and a flat-six, aluminum, air-cooled, rear-mounted engine. The car had been championed within GM especially by Chevrolet general manager Edward N. Cole. As Ralph Nader was to point out in his crusading *Unsafe At Any Speed*, the 1960-1963 Corvair oversteered badly in the hands of the average driver. A $15 stabilizing bar that would have corrected the problem had been omitted, except as an option in the Monza sports package, by the cost-conscious accountants that held power at GM. Patrick Wright reports that after Knudsen's niece was brutally injured in a Corvair, he approached the GM Executive Committee and threatened to resign unless he was given permission to redesign the car's suspension, which he did for the 1964 model year. Knudsen confirmed his action but denies that it was because the car was unsafe.

On July 1, 1965, Knudsen was made group vice-president for the GM Overseas and Canadian Group and elected to the GM board of directors. He was promoted to vice-president for Overseas and Canadian Operations on February 7, 1966, then to executive vice-president for Overseas and Canadian Operations and Non-Automotive and Defense on November 1, 1967. This was as high as Knudsen would rise at GM. He was narrowly passed over for GM president that November in favor of Cole, the executive vice-president in charge of research, engineering, marketing, and public relations, as James Roche moved up to the GM chairmanship.

Knudsen resigned from GM on January 1, 1968, ending almost a half century of family identification with management of the giant corporation. He explains that his resignation was not disappointment over losing the presidency to Cole, but rather reflected his increasing disaffection over the lack of product development at GM and the increasing centralization of the corporation, which took power away from the managers of the product divisions. He correctly foresaw that these trends would be exacerbated under the presidency of Cole and the chairmanship of Roche.

The automotive world was stunned when, following secret negotiations with Henry Ford II,

Knudsen became president of the Ford Motor Company on February 5, 1968, and Arjay Miller, who had held the job for five years, was reassigned to a newly created vice-chairmanship. Ford explained to Lee Iacocca, the general manager of the Ford Division, who had expected to replace Miller, that "the addition of a high level GM man to our team at Ford would make a big difference." He assured Iacocca, "You're still my boy. But you're young. There are things you have to learn." It is clear that in 1968 Iacocca was outmatched by Knudsen's experience. Henry Ford II could not have hoped to hire an auto executive with a more rounded background or a more impressive record of accomplishments. Knudsen had been making $182,000 per year at GM, but Ford guaranteed him a base annual salary of $200,000 for five years and paid him stock bonuses valued at $750,000 to offset his losses in GM benefits.

Knudsen believes that he was hired because Ford expected to be awarded an ambassadorship, preferably to England, by President Lyndon B. Johnson, of whom Ford was a friend and great admirer. He even searched out the serial number of the Model T in which Johnson had learned to drive and presented the President with a restored replica. In Knudsen's opinion Ford in early 1968 was looking for someone that he could trust to take over the company during his anticipated ambassadorship, because he thought that Iacocca was still too young and inexperienced. Knudsen recalled the "look of shock" on Ford's face when Johnson announced that he would not be a candidate for reelection in November. "Any thought of an ambassadorship must then have gone out of his head," Knudsen related. "He must have realized that he was going to have to run the company himself and that there was no room for the two of us."

In any event Knudsen's tenure as Ford president lasted only eighteen months. He was fired by Henry Ford II on September 12, 1969. Knudsen was given no reason for the firing other than the vague statement, "Things just didn't work out." Whatever reasons there may have been, Knudsen's job had been made impossible by Iacocca's daily undercutting of his position. Designer Lawrence Shinoda, who followed Knudsen from GM to Ford, believes that Knudsen "did not bring enough troops" from GM and "failed to use the big hammer" to put Iacocca in his place. Knudsen pointed out that "Mr. Ford would not have allowed that."

After leaving Ford, Knudsen formed Rectrans on February 1, 1970, to manufacture motor homes. During the two years Rectrans was in business, only 638 units of its Discoverer were turned out at Brighton, Michigan. Rectrans was acquired by the White Motor Corporation when Knudsen joined White as chairman of the board and chief executive officer on May 1, 1971. He remained with White as chief executive officer until July 31, 1979, as chairman until April 23, 1980, and as a director until December 3, 1980. White was near bankruptcy when Knudsen took over, and under his leadership the entire White truck line was redone, plant facilities were modernized, and losing operations were sold off. Although sales of White trucks and tractors increased substantially, the firm never completely recovered, began to falter again in the 1975 recession, and filed for bankruptcy in 1980. It survives as White-Volvo.

Since leaving White, Knudsen has been in semi-retirement. His main business venture has been as chairman and chief executive officer of Knusaga, which makes seating modules that convert into beds and which are used in Dodge vans. He is also a director of the Michigan National Corporation and the First National Bank of Palm Beach, Florida.

Knudsen served as chairman of the Motor Vehicle Manufacturers Association (MVMA) in 1977-1978. Since 1978 he has been National Commissioner for the National Association for Stock Car Racing (NASCAR). He is also a member of the Society of Automotive Engineers and the American Society of Tool Engineers.

Among his civic and charitable activities, Knudsen is a member of the Massachusetts Institute of Technology Corporation, a trustee of both the Oakland University Foundation and the Cleveland Clinic Foundation, and a director of the Boys' Clubs of America. In 1972 he received the Freedom Award of the Boys' Clubs of America and the Human Relations Award of the American Jewish Committee.

Fallon and Srodes note that "Semon Emil Knudsen is not the retired elder statesman that he is entitled to be." He undoubtedly deserves more recognition by automotive historians than he thus far has been accorded. Knudsen himself says that he has had "a wonderful time" and that he has "ended up with no regrets." He takes particular pride and pleasure in his marriage of fifty years to Florence Anne McConnell and in their four children, thirteen grandchildren, and two great-grandchildren.

References:

Ivan Fallon and James Srodes, *Dream Maker: The Rise and Fall of John Z. DeLorean* (London: Hamish Hamilton, 1983);

James J. Flink, *The Automobile Age* (Cambridge, Mass,: MIT Press, 1988);

Lee Iacocca, with William Novak, *Iacocca: An Autobiography* (New York: Bantam Books, 1984);

Lawrence K. Shinoda, taped interviews with David R. Crippen, October 29, 1985, March 12, 1986, and June 10, 1986. Edsel B. Ford Design Center, Henry Ford Museum and Greenfield Village;

J. Patrick Wright, *On a Clear Day You Can See General Motors: John Z. DeLorean's Look Inside the Automotive Giant* (Grosse Pointe, Mich.: Wright Enterprises, 1979).

William Signius Knudsen

(March 25, 1879-April 27, 1948)

by James J. Flink

University of California, Irvine

CAREER: Apprentice wholesaler, Fritz Henningsen, Copenhagen, Denmark (1894-1898); junior clerk and bicycle assembler, Christian Achen, Copenhagen, Denmark (1898-1900); reamer and bucker-up, Seabury Shipyards, Morris Heights, New York (1900); boiler repairman, Erie Railroad, Salamanca, New York (1900-1902); various supervisory positions (1902-1909), general superintendent, John R. Keim Mills, Buffalo, New York (1909-1913); manager, Ford branch assembly plants (1913-1918), production manager, Ford Motor Company (1918-1921); general manager, Ireland and Mathews Company, Detroit, Michigan (1921-1922); vice-president, manufacturing (1922-1924), general manager, Chevrolet (1924-1933) vice-president and director (1924-1933), executive vice-president (1933-1937), president General Motors Corporation (1937-1940); member, National Defense Advisory Council, Washington, D.C. (1940-1941); codirector, Office of Production Management, Washington, D.C. (1941-1942); lieutenant general, United States Army, and director of war production, United States Department of War, Washington, D.C. (1942-1945); director and consultant, General Motors Corporation (1945-1948).

William Signius Knudsen (courtesy of General Motors Institute Alumni Foundation Collection of Industrial History)

Henry Ford, the man best qualified to know, called William Signius Knudsen "a wizard of mass production" and "the best production man in the United States." Knudsen's rise to the presidency of General Motors and director of war production during World War II exemplifies the American ideal of the self-made man's climb from rags to riches. He was asked late in life by his son, Semon, what had driven him to work so hard to succeed. He responded that as a poor, lanky, always-hungry youth in Denmark, he had vowed to be able one day to purchase all the pastries in a shop window that he passed each night on his way home from work. Later in his life Knudsen expressed another

reason for working hard to succeed: "whether a man is building a great fortune or working for a daily wage in a factory, he is usually doing it for a wife and children." He thought that it was a "poor man" who could not leave his desk for home by 5:30 P.M. As his obituary in the *Flint Journal* pointed out, "William S. Knudsen has been hailed as 'the greatest production genius of modern times.' But he was other things as well—a devoted husband and father, a loyal friend, a considerate boss, a patriot who gave unstintingly of himself to his adopted country in its hour of greatest crisis even though his age and physical condition provided him adequate reason for 'begging off.' "

He was born Signius Wilhelm Poul Knudsen on March 25, 1879, in Copenhagen, Denmark, the first of six children and the only son of Knud Peter Knudsen and Augusta Zollner Knudsen. Knud Peter had three sons and a daughter by a previous marriage. A cooper by trade, he had lost his cooperage business in 1873 and became a customs inspector. Augusta came from a family of artisans and carriage makers. The family shared four rooms in a two-and-one-half-story brick house and struggled to survive on Knud Peter's salary of 1,400 kroner (about $350) a year. At age six Knudsen was put to work from 1:30 P.M. until after 5 P.M. pushing a cart of window glass for a glazier named Andersen, who paid the boy 2 kroner ($.50) a week. During mornings, however, Knudsen attended public school.

By the standards of the time Knudsen received an above average education, and he was an outstanding student. Norman Beasley points out that his nine years in public school, including two years of night school at the Danish Government Technical School, "gave him a schooling comparable to high school and parts of an undergraduate college education in the United States." He won a silver watch for his high grades in mathematics in high school, but he excelled as well in history and literature, and graduated from the technical training school with honors. He took classes in German and informally studied English and French. Throughout his life he remained a serious reader of great books and amassed an immense library. He also developed at an early age a lifelong love of music. His mother wanted him to become a musician, and he took violin lessons at age seven and learned to play the piano by ear at fifteen. Later in life he picked up the xylophone and delighted in pounding out spirited marches on it for relaxation. John Philip Sousa's "The Stars and Stripes Forever" was a particular favorite. He enjoyed attending concerts.

Knudsen first had wanted to become a merchant seaman, but his father forbade this because he had already lost two sons at sea. Knudsen's next choice was to work with his eldest half brother, Semon Emil, at an importing firm, but there was no opening. So at fifteen he was apprenticed for four years to Fritz Henningsen, a wholesaler in crockery, hardware, and toys. His contract provided for 2 kroner a week the first year, 4 kroner the second, 6 kroner the third, and 8 kroner the fourth. At the ex-piration of his apprenticeship he joined his half brother at the importing firm of Christian Achen as a junior clerk and bicycle assembler for 100-kroner a month. He was soon placed in charge of the warehouse.

Achen imported bicycle parts and tubing from Germany and England. With Axel Klingenberg, a salesman, Knudsen built a tandem bicycle, one of the first in Denmark. Tandem bicycles were used by professional pacemakers in long-distance bicycle races. Knudsen and Klingenberg became pacemakers and participated in road races in Denmark, Sweden, and northern Germany. The pacemakers received 25 percent of the winner's usual 100-kroner prize. In his job with his half brother Knudsen became acquainted with various manufacturers who were importing machine tools from the United States. This exposure aroused his interest in machine tools and in the country where they were made.

Twenty years old, six feet 2 inches tall, and 152 pounds, Knudsen was rejected by a military board for induction into the Danish navy but told to report again in two years. After discussing the matter with his parents that night, he went back to the board and obtained an exit permit for two years of travel in the United States. On a clear, cold February day in 1900 he landed in New York from Copenhagen along with some 500 other immigrants aboard the *Norge* as a steerage passenger with $30 in his pocket. Years later he recalled that immigration officials had yelled at him as he loitered on the ship's gangplank, "Hurry," and that he had been in a hurry ever since.

Knudsen paid $1 a night to lodge at a Lutheran mission in the Battery and discovered that free lunch could be had for buying a nickel glass of beer at the saloons on lower Broadway. He tried to find work as a bicycle mechanic, but there were no bicycle factories in the city. After ten days of searching, Knudsen responded to an ad in an evening newspaper for a janitor. Harry Hansen, a Norwegian who was superintendent of an eight-story apartment building at Eighth Avenue and 152nd Street, offered him the job for $15 a month plus room and board. After only a week, however, Hansen announced, "This is no job for you. I heard today that they are putting on help at the Seabury shipyards." The next day Knudsen boarded a train for the fifteen-minute ride to the shipyards at Morris Heights. He was hired as a reamer at 17.5¢ an hour, ten hours a day, five and a half days a week to ream holes in ship plate for torpedo boats. When he gave his name to the timekeeper, he was reprimanded, "Give me something I can write!" So "Wilhelm Knudsen" was recorded as "William Knudsen," and the timekeeper dismissed him with "O. K., Bill, you've got a job. Get to work!"

Knudsen was soon known as "Big Bill." He returned to the boardinghouse from his second day of work at the shipyards with welts on his face and an eye nearly swollen shut from a fistfight with "a little fellow." Hansen took him to the Manhattan Athletic Club, at 125th Street and Eleventh Avenue, where he learned to box from an instructor named Carlson. He progressed so rapidly that within a few weeks he was appearing in amateur bouts.

Although Knudsen could read English, he had difficulty expressing himself so that he was understood. He had noticed that the immigrant workers who got promoted were those with the best command of English. To improve his fluency Knudsen made a practice of sitting evenings on the stoop of his boardinghouse and talking to the children of the neighborhood. Thus, as Beasley says, "He learned the simple language of children—direct, forceful, plain speech." "Kids haven't a big vocabulary," Knudsen recalled, "small words, nickel words. But I didn't need two dollar words."

He was soon promoted to "bucker-up," the worker who held an iron bar against the hot rivets while they were hammered into place by a riveter. Each riveting gang consisted of two riveters, a bucker-up, and a heater boy. The gang was paid on a piecework basis, with the two riveters and the bucker-up each receiving a third, and the heater boy receiving a third of the bucker-up's share and five cents on each dollar the riveters made. Knudsen was made treasurer of the gang by the Irish riveters and Irish heater boy. On Saturdays he collected the gang's pay from the paymaster and brought it back. Until he began to divide the money using simple arithmetic, it had been counted out into the workers' caps, and there had always been an argument.

Knudsen was making $21 and sometimes $22 a week by fall 1900, when the shipyards closed. He found another job repairing locomotive boilers in the Erie railroad roundhouse at Salamanca, New York. He worked seven nights a week and lived at a boardinghouse owned by a fellow Dane named Rasmussen who had married a German woman.

"He was on his way to being 'a bull of the woods,' as tough foremen were called," Beasley relates, "and he looked forward to the day when he would be able to distribute some of the indignities that had been his lot."

Knudsen learned "one of the most important production lessons of his life," according to Beasley, from a veteran boilermaker named Murphy, who, "although never seeming to hurry, invariably completed a job in less time than did his younger boilermakers. Knudsen watched and saw that Murphy always figured out the job on paper first and then followed each planned step." Murphy had been with the railroad thirty years and was making $100 a month, the same pay that Knudsen was making after only two years. Murphy pointed out that it was a steady job, but this had no attraction for twenty-two-year-old Knudsen. In spring 1902 he took a thirty-day leave from the railroad and returned to Denmark to see his family. He stayed only nine days, as he had taken out his first citizenship papers in the United States and was anxious to seek new prospects in his adopted land.

Shortly after Knudsen returned to Salamanca from his visit home, he received a letter from his step-brother, Semon Emil, who had become a partner in the Achen importing firm. Achen was interested in representing the John R. Keim Mills, a Buffalo, New York, bicycle manufacturer, in Denmark and was sending over their head salesman, a man named Tursleff. Semon Emil wanted Knudsen to accompany Tursleff as an interpreter on his visit to Keim.

At the Keim plant Tursleff and Knudsen were interviewed by William H. Smith, the plant superintendent, who was impressed by Knudsen's knowledge of bicycles and offered him a job at $10.50 a week. "The railroad's paying me $100 a month," Knudsen laughed. But he took the job after Smith countered, "Here you'll have a chance to work up. You won't get that there."

John R. Keim was a jeweler who left the operation of his bicycle business to general manager John R. Lee and superintendent Smith. The Keim plant employed some 500 to 600 workers and turned out about 200 bicycles a day in addition to various other products. Knudsen's first job at Keim was working on a contract to produce 1,000 engines for an English steam car, the Foster wagon. This was Knudsen's first experience with an automobile engine. Within a few months he was made foreman of the pedal department, which consisted of forty-four women, and told that he must turn out 2,000 bicycle pedals a day. He met the quota by turning the running of the department over to one of the women, Florence Shear, and spending his own time hustling material. In three months time he was ordered to cut back pedal production and given a raise to $20 a week.

Hard times came to the Keim mills with the saturation of the market for bicycles; by 1904 the company was continuously borrowing money to meet its weekly payrolls. To replace the lost bicycle business, Keim made switch boxes, telephone stands, washing machines, and a variety of stamped steel parts. Smith in particular saw that survival depended upon being able to switch over to the manufacture of automobile parts, and he tried without much success to solicit business from Buffalo's Pierce-Arrow Company and several other automobile manufacturers. Keim did fill an order for 4,000 brake drums, which were similar to ball bearing races for bicycles, for the Olds Motor Works, but Smith and Knudsen ruined the largest press in the shop turning them out.

To learn how to make steel components lighter and stronger, Knudsen took a course in steel making at the Lackawanna Steel Company plant. He and Smith then developed a new method for forming and drawing steel that they hoped to apply to automobile parts. Knudsen also was instrumental in establishing the first acetylene welding plant in the United States at Keim in 1906. Early in 1906 Smith and Knudsen conceived the idea for a rear axle housing from putting together two telephone bases. Hearing that Henry Ford was in the market for axle housings, they went to see him at his Piquette Avenue plant in Detroit. They left with a $75,000 order, the largest order in Keim's history. The order was for crankcases as well as for the axle housings. It took Knudsen eleven months to solve production problems for the crankcases that Ford had not been able to solve.

Beasley reports that "so satisfied was the Detroit manufacturer that the financial difficulties of the Keim company were ended. It was the beginning of a very close relationship between the two companies. Work poured into the Keim company in such volume that some six years later [on June 22, 1911] Keim was purchased by the Ford Motor Company." In their definitive history of the Ford Motor Company, Allan Nevins and Frank E. Hill note the main reason for the purchase: "Even more important than the Keim products were the Keim executives." Lee, Smith, tool and die maker John Findlater, and especially Knudsen "were to play important roles in the Ford Company."

His years at Keim were years of great personal growth and fulfillment as well as advancement in his career. He brought over from Denmark his sister Louise to keep house for him. Then on November 1, 1911, he married Clara Elizabeth Euler of Buffalo in a Lutheran ceremony in nearby LaSalle. Although Keim's business was making components for the Model T, the couple took a streetcar to their wedding and honeymoon. On October 2, 1912, the first of their four children, and only son, was born. He was named Semon Emil in honor of Knudsen's stepbrother.

Smith was a great influence in smoothing Knudsen's rough edges, which included the habits of cursing at his workers and settling differences with them with his fists. When he became general superintendent, Smith reprimanded him: "You can pretty well handle any four men here–but, here, there are 1,500 men. If you start something, they will make mincemeat out of you. Now I want you to learn one thing, and that is never to raise your hand to a man who is working for you, because if you do, you will lose his respect." The lesson was driven home a few days later by a druggist friend, whom Knudsen highly respected. The druggist related to Knudsen a denunciation of him by a Keim worker who had bought some salve for a hurt hand. "I'm not going to tell you who it was, Bill," the druggist said, "but its a hell of a way to have people talk about you."

Knudsen took the reprimand to heart and learned to control his tongue as well as his fists. He became the gentlest of bosses. "Big physically, and with the reputation of being a fighter, he [had] inspired fear in some, a challenge in others–[but] the fear and challenge disappeared as did his own fear and pugnaciousness," Beasley reports. "His direct manner of speaking often was blunt, causing resentment–[so] he learned to be careful with words because, as he afterward expressed it, 'a blunt man is like a blunt knife–wherever he cuts he hurts twice as much.' "

Smith also talked Knudsen out of leaving Keim to pursue an engineering degree at Cornell. "We need you here," Smith argued. "We've got 1,500 people here, and most of them are here because you've worked out ways to make things. This is a lot different business than it was when you came. You've had a hell of a lot to do with making it different. Practically all we're doing, we're doing for Ford. He trusts you. You've got to stay. If you don't, it's good-by Keim company. Then what about all these people? Where are they going to get jobs?"

Smith's plea was accompanied by an offer to raise Knudsen's salary from $150 to $195 a month. Knudsen agreed to stay on at Keim, and the next day he bought his first car—a Model T, which he and Smith promptly took apart and put together again. "He stayed up most of the night studying first one part of the car and then another, principally the transmission," Beasley writes. "When he went to bed, he had a good working knowledge of that particular automobile."

Ford was moving rapidly away from being an assembler of jobbed-out components toward integrated manufacturing. Complete independence from the Dodge Brothers, Ford's early supplier of engines and completed chassis, came in 1913. The acquisition of Keim in 1911 had given Ford the capacity to make many of its own parts, including crankcases, axles, and housings. A visit to the Briggs Manufacturing Company, which was supplying Ford bodies, convinced Knudsen that Keim also could make bodies and assemble cars and resulted in a contract with Ford to do so in Buffalo.

Knudsen was forced to rearrange the Keim plant to coordinate production. One of his first acts was to confiscate every hammer and file so that there could be no hand fitting of parts. He innovated a varnish flow system from a sprinkling can that did a better job than could skilled finishers by hand: cars moved on runners in which waste varnish was caught while being sprinkled with varnish from overhead.

The movement of the Keim machinery to Highland Park in late 1912 and its key executives to Detroit in 1913 was especially ironic in view of Smith's earlier plea to Knudsen that Ford's business must be maintained to provide jobs for Keim's Buffalo workers. Nevins and Hill report what occurred. Knudsen and Smith informed Ford by phone just before Labor Day in 1912 that the Keim workers had declared a wildcat strike to protest the piece-work rates on some outside contracts. "That suits me," declared Ford. "If the men don't want to work, get some flat cars and move the presses and

machinery to Highland Park." "Knudsen, much distressed, tried to talk to the strikers, who jeered him," relate Nevins and Hill. "So loyal machinists tore down the presses and other machinery; they were loaded on freight cars; and Knudsen, Smith, and Lee, followed by a gang of mechanics, set off to install them in the Ford plant. Three days after this gang and some Ford millwrights began work, the familiar machines were turning out the familiar crank cases." The Keim plant was reduced to an assembly operation.

In late 1913 Knudsen arranged for moving the families of sixty-two key Keim personnel to Detroit. His own family was not among them. Knudsen wanted to stay in Buffalo, where he was settled and happy, and he had received a job offer from the Seneca Steel Company in nearby Lackawanna of $750 a month and a bonus of a dollar for every ton of steel that he could produce over 1,500 tons a month. However, Smith talked him into going to Detroit to talk with Henry Ford before making up his mind.

Ford proposed that Knudsen's first job would be setting up branch assembly plants across the country. Beasley relates that Knudsen became "so excited over the magnitude of the projected operation that he was on his way back to Buffalo before he remembered that Ford had not mentioned what his pay would be—nor, had he, himself, thought about it." For the time being, Clara and the children were to remain in Buffalo.

Because cars could be shipped cheaper by rail in knocked-down form, Ford branch assembly plants were built beginning in 1909 at Kansas City, Missouri. As noted, Model T's began to be assembled at Keim in 1911. By summer 1912 assembly sites had been bought at St. Louis, Long Island City, Los Angeles, San Francisco, Portland, and Seattle, and, outside the United States, in Canada and at Trafford Park, Manchester, England. Knudsen was placed in charge of all Ford branch assembly plants. In 1913 and 1914 he set up additional plants at freight-rate breaking points in Atlanta, Boston, Chicago, Indianapolis, Memphis, Denver, Dallas, and Houston. By 1916 he was in charge of twenty-eight Ford branch assembly plants in the United States. Henry Ford had informed Knudsen on his first day in Detroit that he wanted him "to install in these plants the same sort of system you put into operation in Buffalo." Ford told him to "draw on us for whatever you need and hire local contractors wherever you have to make changes. Pay them on the spot for what they do." Knudsen soon learned that "there had been a splendid engineer on the buildings, but there had been no attempt to co-ordinate the layout that I was supposed to put in the building itself. . . . I spent about six months cutting holes in concrete floors." He spent some $400,000 breaking up and reconstructing newly constructed buildings.

Only a few minutes after he arrived back at his desk in Detroit in May 1914, Knudsen was called into the office of James Couzens, the Ford vice-president and treasurer, handed an envelope containing a bonus check for $5,000, and informed that his pay was being raised from $600 to $1,000 a month. He returned immediately to Buffalo to pack up and move his family to Detroit. He bought a new white, wire-wheeled Model T and a lot on Moss Avenue, a few blocks from the Highland Park plant. On the lot he constructed a California-style bungalow, the first home of his own, with $3,000 in borrowed money that was paid back in ninety days from another bonus check. He became a citizen of the United States in 1914.

The unprecedented demand for the Model T created at Ford an unprecedented demand for raw materials, particularly steel. In the spring of 1915 Henry Ford began buying up huge tracts of land along the Rouge River southwest of Detroit and announced plans for developing a great industrial complex there, including a steel plant, so that he would not be "at the mercy of suppliers." Knudsen was drawn into the project both because of his experience with setting up factories and his experience with steel. He disagreed strongly with Ford that steel could be made cheaper than it could be bought from outside suppliers, but he confined his objections to the need to build the blast furnaces fifteen miles further downstream at Trenton, where there were large deposits of limestone, needed to produce steel. He also advised Ford that the Rouge would have "too many people working in one place. I think we have too many people here at Highland Park, I think we ought to spread out more. I think the ideal manufacturing unit consists of anywhere from 5,000 to 10,000 people." But Ford was intransigent: "No, William, no," he interrupted, "I want the Ford business all behind one fence so I can see it. We are shipping out parts to the assembly plants anyway. That's spreading it enough."

The outbreak of the war in Europe resulted by early 1916 in a steel shortage that threatened to halt production of the Model T. Ford gave Knudsen, who had become experienced in large-scale purchasing, the job of obtaining adequate supplies of sheet steel. That very night Knudsen sent out a crew of handpicked young men to the leading steel-producing centers with instructions to order and ship to Detroit at once sheet steel in the proper lengths until told to stop. Before the yard at Highland Park was filled, the price of steel had been run up from 6¢ to 11¢ a pound by the Ford orders. Three months later Ford came to Knudsen's office to invite him to "come upstairs and start handling the shop" at a salary of $25,000 a year, plus a 15 percent bonus.

Until American entry into the war Henry Ford took an outspoken stand against conscription and preparedness. "I don't believe in preparedness," he said. "Its like a man carrying a gun. Men and nations who carry guns get into trouble." Once diplomatic ties between the United States and Germany were severed on February 3, 1917, however, Ford abruptly reversed himself, stating that "we must stand behind the President" and that "in the event of war [I] will place our factory at the disposal of the United States government and will operate without one cent of profit." After Congress declared war on April 6, 1917, Ford rationalized that "perhaps militarism can be crushed only with militarism. In that case I am in on it to the finish."

Ford's war production was the most diversified of any American manufacturer. With the receipt of an order from General Pershing for 2,500 ambulances on May 30, Knudsen was made superintendent over all war production at Ford in addition to his other duties. Early in the war Knudsen became convinced that private industry could do a better job at less cost in producing war materials if it were not held to drawings and specifications dictated by the military. He demonstrated that this was true. For example, Knudsen, who had experience working with bicycle tubing, developed a way to mass-produce cylinders for the Liberty aircraft engine by closing the end of a piece of vanadium steel tubing to form the head of the cylinder. And he used his knowledge of shipbuilding, acquired at Seabury, to work out a way to mass-produce the Eagle Boat submarine chasers without experienced shipyard workers. Knudsen accomplished this by eliminating the use of form plates; by detailing and numbering each of the Eagle Boat's parts; by punching the boat's plates on machinery; and by supervising the construction of a special assembly plant with three production lines, each capable of carrying seven boats. The result was that a 200-ton, 200-foot-long boat with a 20-foot beam could be turned out in only sixty-three shifts.

The war brought to the surface the jealousy of fellow-Dane Charles E. Sorensen, who was in charge of tractor production at Dearborn. Sorensen, who had traveled overseas to confer with British authorities on the Fordson farm tractor, called the emergency plant built by Knudsen to produce the tractor at the Rouge, "the damndest looking thing I ever saw." When Sorensen's criticism became personal, Knudsen lost his temper for the first time in years: "Shut up, Sorensen!" he threatened. "If you don't, I'll smash in your face, right here!" Sorensen backed down and left, only to return in a few minutes with Henry Ford, who said that he could not understand "why you two fellows can't get along together." Knudsen replied, "We can, Mr. Ford, if Sorensen will mind his own business." This marked the beginning of deteriorating relationships with both Sorensen and Ford that would culminate in Knudsen's resignation.

In 1918 Knudsen was named Ford production manager, under Sorensen and P. E. "Pete" Martin. Knudsen supervised the conversion of the Ford plants back to civilian production of the Model T. It took only two months, and Ford produced a record 820,400 units in 1919. In February of that year Knudsen was sent to Europe to audit Ford's British operations and to set up branch plants at Copenhagen and Cadiz. Then the bubble burst with the onset of the postwar recession: Ford production was almost halved to 419,500 units in 1920.

The recession hit Henry Ford in the midst of carrying out his plans to develop the Rouge, and, he was deeply in debt from a successful drive to buy out his minority stockholders. Ford discussed his pressing financial obligation with Knudsen: "We've got to do something," Ford announced. "William, we've got to begin cutting. I am going to reduce prices to see if that will improve sales; but to reduce prices we've got to cut costs." Knudsen was ordered to cut costs in materials and in labor by $100 per unit, cuts made necessary by Ford's announcement on September 21, 1920, of price cuts on the Model T averaging $148. The reduction theoretically meant a short-term loss on every car sold,

but the loss was covered by the profit on the $40 worth of parts and accessories sold with every new Model T.

Large savings could not be squeezed out of the labor and shipping costs, which accounted for only 24 percent of the total unit cost of a Model T. So Knudsen turned to material costs, the largest of which was for tires. He held meetings with the tire manufacturers. The lowest bid, $9 a set below the average bid, was submitted by a large manufacturer anxious not to lose the Ford business, but it was rejected by Knudsen as too low. Instead the manufacturer was given a share of the Ford tire business at the average bid. Beasley reports that Knudsen cut all material costs "in the same way—calling in the suppliers, getting in new prices, setting an average, and offering contracts."

Ford asked Knudsen to find out the cost of the Rouge River blast furnaces that Knudsen had advised would not be competitive with outside suppliers. Iron prices had dropped to about half of their wartime high in the recession, making the Rouge operation even more expensive than Knudsen had foreseen. Ford expected that the blast furnaces had cost $12 million. Knudsen found that they had already cost $19 million and that $5 million more was committed to them.

The price reductions had not increased sales sufficiently, the end of the year was approaching, and Ford was worried. "Following his custom when heavily worried," Beasley relates, "Ford remained away from the plant and went on a diet. He had the belief that the less work his stomach had to do, the clearer his thinking. He was absent from the plant several days when he sent for Knudsen, requesting him to come to the Ford home, in Dearborn. Knudsen arrived to find Ford lying on a davenport, a blanket half thrown over him." They discussed alternatives. Another price cut was rejected because Knudsen did not think that it would generate money fast enough. Ford rejected Knudsen's proposals that he sell "baby bonds" to Ford employees and dealers and that he send out trade acceptances (promissory notes) in lieu of cash to his suppliers. Knudsen then proposed that the Ford plants be closed "to get rid of all parts, and finished cars, and to make an inventory." He explained to Ford that "what you could do would be to ship out all these cars and parts to Ford dealers, and draw on them for the money."

The Ford Motor Company closed its plants "for inventory" on December 24, 1920, and remained closed until February 1, 1921, while the company disposed of "stocks on hand." Ford maintained full production up to the shutdown, curtailing only the purchase of raw materials. His strategy was first to turn the huge inventory of raw materials that had been bought at inflated prices into a reservoir of finished cars, then to stop production until those cars were disposed of and raw material prices had declined. In a turnaround from his objection to Knudsen that it would damage his credit standing, Ford's principal suppliers were paid with ninety-day trade acceptances. Consignments of unordered cars were forced on over 6,300 hardpressed Ford dealers, who had the choice of borrowing heavily from local banks to pay cash on delivery for them or forfeiting their Ford franchises.

The shutdown at Ford was accompanied by stringent austerity measures that went well beyond what was essential for survival and which jeopardized the future well-being of the firm. Under Knudsen's supervision the Ford plants were stripped of every nonessential tool and fixture—including every pencil sharpener, most desks and typewriters, and 600 extension telephones. The sale of this equipment alone netted $7 million. The company also benefited from replacing some of it with improved machinery and methods that increased output per man-hour of labor. Beasley reports that Knudsen "made further improvements in tools and machines, and in the conveyor system. With these improvements, there came a better arrangement of work, with the result that the number of men needed to assemble a car was reduced from fifteen to nine. Foremen were reduced in numbers from one foreman to every five men to one foreman to every twenty men. The inventory was reduced–and the most important improvement he worked out was a new flow system that cut the manufacturing cycle from twenty-two days to fifteen."

These innovations in the long run saved millions of dollars. The gain was canceled out, however, by a ruthless halving of the office force from 1,074 to 528 persons as most departments, including such critical ones as auditing, were overly simplified, merged, or eliminated. Many capable executives were lost to the company. Even more important the development of the organized bureaucracy essential to a mature corporation was stultified. "It is not necessary for any one department to know what any other department is doing," Ford foolishly boasted in 1922. "The Ford factories and enterprises have no organization, no specific duties attaching to any position, no line of succession or authority, very few titles, and no conferences. We have only the clerical help that is absolutely required; we have no elaborate records of any kind, and consequently no red tape."

The lack of "red tape" amounted to what an increasing number of ex-Ford executives called "Prussianization" as the entrepreneurial team responsible for the success of the mass-produced Model T disintegrated in the early 1920s. Although this critical loss of executive talent defies adequate summarizing, the 1919 departures to build the Wills-Sainte Claire car of C. Harold Wills, the chief designer of the Model T, and of John Lee, who had administered Ford's progressive labor policies, were of most symbolic significance. The departure of Knudsen was of far more practical significance: under his leadership Chevrolet surpassed Ford in sales in 1927.

Knudsen's differences with Sorensen and Ford became irreconcilable. Nevins and Hill observe that Sorensen combined "a complete belief in and devotion to Ford with a burning passion for advancement." Knudsen, in contrast, "while a great admirer of Henry Ford . . . tended to use more independence of judgement in serving him than did his fellow Dane. . . . He was quieter, pleasanter, and less aggressive than Sorensen, winning rather than forcing the cooperation of his subordinates." Knudsen was known to be tough but fair, Sorensen just tough. A Ford worker recalled that "Sorensen was a wild man, and Knudsen was a mild man." More than one Ford worker found out that "Bill's hand didn't get stuck in his pocket when the kid came and the wife was in the hospital." He knew many of the thousands of Ford workers by their first names and took a personal interest in their welfare.

At a testimonial dinner in 1938 on the occasion of Henry Ford's seventy-fifth birthday, Knudsen praised Ford especially for inaugurating the $5 day in 1914. But Beasley noted that Knudsen had argued against "checking into and reporting on the home life of the participating employees. To Knudsen, that was all wrong. As he saw it, the men were entitled to the money and, having earned it, it was theirs to spend without having to answer the snooping questions of investigators." Knudsen was a lifelong opponent of corporate paternalism.

According to his son Semon there were two major reasons for Knudsen's resignation. The callous treatment of employees by Sorensen and Martin appalled him. And he was disturbed by Ford's intransigent commitment to the Model T. According to Semon, Knudsen had a "tremendous admiration" for Edsel Ford, whom he felt was "a forward-thinking manager." Edsel alone in the top Ford management did not use "the hammer and tongs approach" in dealing with employees. Edsel and Knudsen worked together on a number of ideas to upgrade the Model T that ended up being vetoed by Henry Ford.

Ford had an irrational fixation on the Model T. He returned from a trip to Europe in 1912 to find that during his absence Wills, Sorensen, and Martin had developed a new model to replace the T. When shown the car Ford tore it apart with his bare hands and smashed it into a pile of junk. Again in 1919, at the time of reconversion to civilian production, Knudsen presented Ford with sketches of a new model to replace the T. When Knudsen told Ford that it would take six months to get the new model into production, versus only sixty to resume Model T production, Ford responded obliquely, "There's your answer." The subject was never mentioned again.

Nevins and Hill explain that Knudsen's resignation "reflected dissatisfaction on both sides. Ford objected to some of Knudsen's personal habits [he smoked cigars]; Knudsen found that Ford was countermanding his orders or telling Ford employees and officials to ignore him. He had no objection to Ford controlling his own company, but resented the method and felt that he must protest or quit." There can be no doubt that Sorensen sparked the resignation: "The precipitating incident involved Sorensen," Nevins and Hill write. "Edsel directed Knudsen to go to Europe, apparently to oversee Ford activities there. Sorensen felt that European affairs should be under his direction, appealed to [Henry] Ford, who spoke to Knudsen, and the latter left." Knudsen told William Smith, who was sent by Ford to talk him into staying, that he did not want to quarrel with Ford: "I can't avoid it if I stay, and I can't stay and keep my self respect." On February 28, 1921, Knudsen sent his letter of resignation to Edsel, the titular president of the Ford Motor Company. He went off the Ford payroll on April 1. His salary at the time was $50,000 a year plus a 15 percent bonus.

Knudsen was offered a job by Frank L. Klingensmith, who after leaving Ford had joined forces with John Kelsey, a Detroit parts manufacturer, and John S. Gray, who had been a minority Ford stockholder, to organize the Gray Motor Car Company. Klingensmith showed Knudsen an experimental car intended to compete with the Model T in the low-priced field. Although he thought that the car had possibilities, Knudsen declined the offer because in his opinion the Gray firm did not have sufficient capital to succeed. "The day when a man could start, like Mr. Ford started, on a little money, and build a big business in a few years is over," he told Klingensmith. "I think the automobile business is a good business. I think it has gone through the experimental stage.... [U]nless you have money—enough money!—to put real speed into the production of the Gray car, you will not have a successful company.... I don't want to go into the automobile business unless the company has enough money to see it through, and it can get enough money at a price it can afford to pay." Knudsen instead accepted a job as general manager of Ireland & Mathews, a Detroit manufacturer of stove trimmings, plumbers' supplies, and automobile parts. He was hired primarily to dispose of a large inventory, which he accomplished in ten months.

Anxious to get back into the automobile business, Knudsen asked Ireland to introduce him to General Motors (GM) vice-president Charles S. Mott, who in turn arranged an interview with GM executive vice-president Alfred P. Sloan, Jr. Sloan knew Knudsen from having done business with him at Ford while Sloan was the president of Hyatt, a supplier of roller bearings. Sloan was impressed that Knudsen was "a man who could do things and, if he had the opportunity, could do bigger things." He informed Knudsen that "at the moment, there was no particular job in General Motors but that there was need for someone to serve on the staff— someone who could help the operating units do a better job." Knudsen agreed to take the staff position beginning February 23, 1922.

While at Ireland & Mathews Knudsen had worked out an idea for a muffler, which he was particularly anxious to sell to Chevrolet. Although he considered himself "the world's worst salesman," he presented the muffler himself to Ormond K. Hunt, Chevrolet's chief engineer, and Donald O'Keefe, the Chevrolet purchasing agent. Knudsen startled them by slamming the muffler on the floor instead of giving a sales pitch: "See," he said, "it's strong." It was also low-priced, and Knudsen had designed the tools for manufacturing it. The day before he went to work for GM, Knudsen delivered an order for the muffler from Chevrolet to Ireland & Mathews.

Knudsen served on the GM staff for only three weeks before GM president Pierre S. du Pont asked for his help at Chevrolet. In addition to his duties as president, du Pont had taken over the management of Chevrolet because of the illness of its president, Karl M. Zimmerchied. Knudsen was made Chevrolet vice-president in charge of operations at an annual salary of $50,000. "As you know, Mr. Knudsen," du Pont understated, "operations at Chevrolet are somewhat confused." In fact the abolition of the Chevrolet Division had been recommended by a team of outside consultants called in to evaluate all GM units. "What do you think of the future of Chevrolet, Mr. Knudsen?" asked du Pont. "It will·be all right," Knudsen responded. "If we work hard enough we will get some business." As GM's model in the high-volume low-priced range, the Chevrolet was the corporation's main hope of competing with the Model T. In 1921 Ford outsold Chevrolet thirteen to one, and Chevrolet lost over $8 million.

Knudsen's first assignment was to work with GM vice-president Charles E. Kettering on development of a proposed "revolutionary car" of Kettering's design powered by a radical "copper-cooled" engine. Under du Pont's leadership the GM executive committee in early 1921 had endorsed this project as GM's entering wedge into competition with Ford. The car was being developed by Kettering at his Dayton, Ohio, Delco laboratories. Kettering sought to utilize the superior thermal properties of copper to design an air-cooled engine with a higher compression ratio and therefore better fuel economy and more power for a given displacement. His "copper-cooled" engine featured copper fins that were brazed to the cylinders in a specially designed oven, and a front mounted fan that turned at faster than engine speed. Du Pont saw the engine as a promising replacement for the conventional water-cooled engines on all GM cars.

Sloan was skeptical and had reservations about the corporation's strong commitment to the project. It was in trouble from the beginning because of a lack of communication and poor coordina-

Knudsen in 1913 (courtesy of Ford Motor Company)

tion between Kettering's laboratories at Dayton, where the car was designed, and the Chevrolet manufacturing units at Flint and Pontiac, Michigan, where the car was to be built. "Production engineers remained blind to the problems of perfecting a relatively new and radical technology," Stuart W. Leslie observes, "while design men failed to appreciate the difficulties in moving from a carefully tuned prototype to a trouble-free assembly-line automobile ready for mass production." Knudsen told Kettering, "This car isn't any good. You and the people you have working on it down in Dayton, and principally the people working on it in Dayton, aren't automobile people. This car isn't strong enough, the rear axle isn't any good, and even if you get things worked out so they are good, the car will cost too much for Chevrolet to make." After working with Kettering on the car for eighteen months Knudsen informed Sloan: "This copper-cooled car isn't any good. It won't stand the gaff. We've got seven or eight million dollars tied up in it, but it is my decision to abandon this car altogether." Sloan supported Knudsen's decision.

After a sensational debut at the January 1923 New York Automobile Show, the copper-cooled

Chevrolet flopped. It cost $200 more than the standard water-cooled Chevrolet. Only 759 copper-cooled Chevrolets were manufactured and 239 were scrapped in production. A mere 100 were sold to retail customers. "After initial sales," Leslie reports, "Kettering and the divisions were swamped with complaints about noise, wear on cylinders, carburetor malfunctions, axle breakdowns, and fan belt trouble." In addition to manufacturing difficulties and careless assembly, numerous components had to be redesigned to accommodate the car's light weight. Perhaps most important, "Chevrolet was [now] holding its own against Ford without the new engine or lightweight design," Leslie writes. "Tastes were changing. Buyers no longer seemed to want a light-weight and inexpensive automobile, but looked instead to the style and comfort that water-cooled Chevrolets provided quite adequately."

The copper-cooled debacle convinced Sloan that "it was not necessary to lead in design or run the risk of untried experiments," only that GM cars be "at least equal in design to the best of our competitors in a grade." Even earlier, in 1921, he had recognized "The very great importance of style in selling." In contrast with Henry Ford's disdain for styling and his intransigent commitment to the Model T as a single static model, in 1923 GM instituted the annual model change, which called for major stylistic changes every three years with minor faceliftings in between. The changes involved were overwhelmingly cosmetic. And the three-year cycle was predicated on the prohibitive cost of retooling for bringing out an entirely new model every year.

The annual model change and the new emphasis on styling in GM cars were Sloan's responses to stagnation in automotive technology and to market saturation. By the late 1920s most basic improvements separating the Model T from post-World War II models had been incorporated in production cars, and the need for basic transportation that the Model T had filled had largely been met. By 1927, when the Model T was withdrawn from the market, an annually restyled, mechanically superior, and far better equipped Chevrolet could be bought for only a few hundred dollars more; that year Chevrolet began to outsell Ford. While the annual model change was Sloan's idea, Knudsen deserves credit for Chevrolet's success in implementing the strategy.

On May 10, 1923, Sloan moved up to the GM presidency. Eight months later, January 15, 1924, Knudsen was named president and general manager of the Chevrolet Division and a vice-president and director of GM. In 1922, when Knudsen took charge of Chevrolet operations, sales were 243,621 units and net income from operations $11,288,603, a substantial rise from 1921 figures of 72,806 unit sales and a net operating loss of $8,692,142. In 1923 Chevrolet sales and net income from operations almost doubled over 1922 to 480,123 units and $19,084,876. In addition Chevrolet had acquired by merger the Detroit Gear & Axle Company, the Detroit Forging Company, and the Saginaw Foundry.

Knudsen's first step at Chevrolet had been to assure O'Keefe that his job as purchasing agent was secure and to ask O'Keefe to "tell the boys that I am not going to bring in any Ford men. Go back and tell them that I need them a damn sight more than they need me. If they don't want me here, I don't care how smart I am, I am not going to last very long; but if they will stick with me and work with me, then perhaps we can make something out of this buggy, before we get through."

Knudsen had become an expert on purchasing materials at Ford, and he asked O'Keefe to reorganize his department. Scales were installed to weigh materials so that the conversion cost from base material to finished material could be determined. Purchasing was decentralized so that each of the Chevrolet manufacturing plants became responsible for purchasing its own raw materials. O'Keefe's department was charged only with ensuring that the material reaching the plants was uniform. Knudsen explained that this was his "fundamental thought for all our operations. I do not want the Chevrolet company to become so unwieldy that we cannot make changes to keep in step with the possible demand. I want to get the base materials as close as possible to the source where they are being used. . . . The widest possible latitude should be given to the shop management. I feel that the buyer in each unit should, as far as possible, work with the shop manager so as to get the best result, and, on top of that, maintain a contact with the central purchasing department so that they are informed of any changes in prices and specifications which might affect another plant. In other words, let us have a coordinating office in the central office, and let each buyer do his job."

Knudsen similarly informed chief engineer Hunt that "The first thing we must do is to decentralize our operations. I do not want our organization to be so unwieldy that when we have to make a change we will not be able to make them quickly. That is what is happening to Mr. Ford, although he doesn't see it. His plant at River Rouge is too big, and when the day comes that he has to make a change in his Model T, so as to keep up with public demand, he is not going to be able to do it. I don't want to get stuck like that because, before very long, I think we are going to have to change our models every year." Hunt was to decentralize the engineering department "as much as possible. Let the people in the five assembly plants . . . be as close to self-supporting as they can be, and here in the central office you coordinate their work." The gear and axle plant, forging plant, and foundry were acquired to give Chevrolet "a more complete setup." Knudsen recognized that "Mr. Ford had a good idea when he set out to manufacture his own parts," and he thought that at Chevrolet "there are some things we ought to make for ourselves that we are not making." Still, he believed that Ford had "carried it too far. He wanted to get into everything and there are a lot of things he is manufacturing that he could buy for less than what it is costing him to make them."

Knudsen told Colin Campbell, the Chevrolet general sales manager, that "so far as sales are concerned, we have to get rid of the mechanical defects in the car, and while we are doing that, we will be working on a more attractive design. I am going to talk with Fred Fisher [of Fisher Body] about fixing up the body so that the car will be more attractive. . . . That won't happen right away of course, but we will get to it."

When Campbell resigned in 1924, Sloan was instrumental in transferring Richard H. Grant, the general manager of Delco Light Company, to Chevrolet to replace him. "In Grant," Beasley reports, "Knudsen found a kindred spirit in hard work. As Knudsen was never satisfied with the car, so was Grant never satisfied with sales." To find out what was the matter with the car, and to improve sales and service, Knudsen accompanied Grant on a tour of over 100 Chevrolet dealerships across the country. Grant persuaded Knudsen to attend sales meetings and make speeches. At a sales meeting in Chicago's Palmer House, Knudsen rose to address the 2,000 dealers assembled in the ballroom, pointed upward with the index fingers of both hands, and shouted in a thick Danish accent, "I vant vun for vun." When the salesmen figured out after a few minutes that he meant one Chevrolet sold for every Ford, they rose to their feet laughing and cheering. The challenge spread throughout the Chevrolet Division.

Beginning at Flint, Knudsen also visited the Chevrolet assembly plants to examine at firsthand the production process. In Beasley's words, "He called for blueprints of the factories, studied the rotation of the tools and machines, studied the flow of materials. . . . He rearranged some tools and machines, improved the flow of materials, reduced the cycle of manufacturing, and thereby greatly reduced the cost of production." Knudsen explained that he had visited the assembly plants and made the changes "to get all noses pointed in the same direction."

In his definitive history of mass production David A. Hounshell dates modern "flexible" mass production from Knudsen's innovations at Chevrolet. Flexible mass production, explains Gerald Bloomfield, "allows a wider range of options of body styles, colors, trim, power train, but within permissible standardized limits. The products of this type of mass production have a greater appearance of diversity. Flexible mass production involved a high degree of planning, and became more capital intensive than the earlier stages of rigid mass production." Instituting the annual model change was dependent upon the development of flexible mass production by Knudsen at Chevrolet.

GM production was far more decentralized and far less vertically integrated than Ford production. Sloan had reasoned that GM would have to make the same profit on capital invested in plants and equipment for the manufacture of its various components as outside suppliers charging reasonable prices for those components. So GM depended more on outside suppliers. This alone gave GM far more flexibility than Ford. Additionally Knudsen decentralized Chevrolet components manufacture among specialized plants at Toledo, Ohio, and at Flint, Detroit, and Bay City, Michigan, and bought still other components from other GM divisions and from outside suppliers. Assembly, too, was decentralized "At four assembly plants (Tarrytown, New York, Flint, Michigan, St. Louis, Missouri, and Oakland, California). . . . Subassemblies and thousands of parts purchased from vendors were brought together to make the Chevrolet," Hounshell writes. "Knudsen also had convinced GM executives that a Fisher body plant should be attached to each assembly plant so that body production could be coordinated precisely with the daily output of each assembly plant." The major innovation at Chevrolet, however, according to Hounshell, was that Knudsen replaced single-purpose machine tools with standard general-purpose machine tools, "For this reason, Chevrolet could accommodate change far more easily than could the Ford Motor Company."

The annual model change and diversity of product within model runs were incompatible with Fordist production methods. At the Ford Highland Park plant, in Hounshell's words, "every machine tool and fixture was fitted for the production of a single product whose every part had been standardized to the minutest detail." Even small changes in the design of the Model T bottlenecked its production. The switchover to Model A production at the Rouge was chaotic. More than half of the 32,000 machine tools used to produce the Model T had to be redesigned and rebuilt, and half of the remaining ones had to be scrapped. That the plant layout optimal for Model T production was not well suited to production of the Model A is evidenced by the change to a final assembly line at the Rouge that was only half as long as the Model T final assembly line at Highland Park. The switchover involved closing down the Ford assembly lines from late May to November 1927. For some time after that the expansion of Model A production was hampered by the Ford practice of extremely close spacing of machine tools, which exacerbated problems of rearranging plant layout. Hounshell estimates the total cost of the changeover to the Model A, "including experimental and design work, tooling and loss of profits," at about $250 million. Such a disruption of production and the consequent inordinate expense were irreconcilable with bringing out the essentially new model every three years that Sloanist marketing strategy envisioned. It is no wonder that at the Rouge, as a consequence of this costly initial lesson, "Sorensen aimed for greater flexibility in assembly rather than cost advantages through a single-purpose [machine tool] approach." There was an almost complete turnover of supervisory personnel at the Rouge as production-head Sorensen tried, in his own words, "to get rid of all the Model T sons-of-bitches . . . get away from the

Model T ways of doing things." In brief Sorensen was forced to adopt at the Rouge the "ways of doing things" worked out at Chevrolet by his old archrival Knudsen.

With the shutdown of the Ford assembly lines in 1927 Chevrolet for the first time came to outsell Ford, making "vun for vun" a reality. The ratio of Ford to Chevrolet sales had been cut from thirteen to one in 1921 to slightly more than two to one in 1926. Ford regained the lead in sales with the Model A in 1929 and 1930. But between 1931 and 1970 Chevrolet outsold Ford in every year except 1935 and 1945, and the latter year was an exception only because Ford was the first automobile manufacturer to restart production following World War II.

As Knudsen had promised Campbell in 1922, the Chevrolet was greatly improved and made more attractive. In 1924 the car's main fault, a bad rear axle, was corrected, and the Chevrolet was given semi-elliptic springs, a new clutch, and a new 4-cylinder engine. In the 1928 model the wheelbase was lengthened 4 inches to accommodate the introduction of a 6-cylinder engine in the 1929 model. The changeover was phased in over two years so as to divide the retooling time. Chevrolet advertised, "A Six for the price of a Four." Called the "cast iron wonder," with only minor modifications the engine served as the basic Chevrolet power plant until 1953. Henry Ford at first dismissed the 1929 Chevrolet with the quip, "I have no use for a car with more cylinders than a cow has teats." But to compete Ford had to one-up it by bringing out the first low-priced V-8 in 1932. With annual restyling of the V-8, he also came to emulate the annual model change innovated by Sloan.

GM led the industry in making styling an institutionalized activity carried out by professional designers, rather than a haphazard activity of engineers and salesmen, with the 1927 formation of its Art and Colour Section, headed by Hollywood stylist Harley J. Earl. The 1927 La Salle, Earl's first design for GM, in Sloan's words, was "the first stylist's car to achieve success in mass production." At Knudsen's request Earl next gave attention to restyling the bottom-of-the-GM-line Chevrolet.

Earl and Knudsen became close friends and during the 1930s attended the annual Paris and London automobile shows together accompanied by Knudsen's son. Semon relates how his father was smitten in 1936 at both the Paris and London shows with a particular Maybury custom body on a Rolls-Royce chassis. Earl became provoked when Knudsen questioned the Maybury people about the possibility of designing such a car for GM. Back at the hotel Earl told Semon, "If that's what he wants, I'll make one like it that really looks good. I don't think that that's as good as it can be done." After a few months back in Detroit, Earl called Semon down to the GM styling studios to view a clay model of his design. It became the 1938 Cadillac 60-Special, the first car to eliminate running boards and the first "standard size" American car to hold six passengers. It was a hardtop designed as a convertible, hence the forerunner of the "hardtop convertible" introduced in the 1949 Cadillac, Buick, and Oldsmobile models. The 60-Special, according to Sloan, was also "the first 'special' car, designed to introduce new features and to be sold at a higher price." The car convinced Sloan of "the dollars-and-cents value of styling, for consumers were willing to take smaller trade-ins on old cars to acquire it."

On October 16, 1933, Knudsen was made executive vice-president of GM in charge of coordinating production for all of the corporation's car manufacturing divisions. He moved up to the GM presidency when Sloan replaced Lammot du Pont as chairman of the board on May 3, 1937. Christy Borth claims that Sloan's 1920 organizational plan notwithstanding, it was in fact under Knudsen's guidance after 1933 that "the corporation's character changed; from an industrial empire with all the power concentrated at the top, it gradually reshaped itself into something resembling a federation in which the component divisions retained certain rights and powers as jealously guarded as the rights of states in a federal union."

Knudsen moved up to executive vice-president in the trough of the Great Depression and became president just as the general recovery of the economy was becoming apparent. Sloan had managed to pull in the giant corporation's horns well before the disaster. On October 4, 1929, shortly before the stock market crash, Sloan had "addressed a general letter to the organization noting the end of expansion and promulgating a new policy of economy for the corporation." He later understated that "in no year did the corporation fail to earn a profit." In fact, while the GM payroll was cut by two-thirds, working capital increased by a third and record dividends were paid in 1936 and 1937.

Aware that the recovery of the automobile industry was important to restoring prosperity, President Franklin Delano Roosevelt took a personal interest in the National Recovery Administration (NRA) code drafted for that industry. Under Section 7(a) of the National Industrial Recovery Act (NIRA), workers ostensibly were given the right to organize and engage in collective bargaining with management through a representative of their choice. Yet Roosevelt overrode his own Labor Advisory Board and permitted an affirmation of the automobile industry's open-shop policy to stand in the code. The National Automobile Chamber of Commerce (NACC), the industry trade association, was made the code authority and was entrusted with its administration, while neither organized labor nor the consumer was represented. After NIRA was declared unconstitutional by a unanimous decision of the United States Supreme Court on May 27, 1935, the pathetic ineffectiveness of the automobile industry code was summarized by Alfred Reeves, who spoke for the Automobile Manufacturers Association (AMA), the successor to the NACC: "Neither the industry nor its employees," said Reeves, "benefitted from the code while it existed and neither have [sic] suffered any loss from its termination."

The main impact of the NIRA was that it stimulated labor organization and gave an impetus for management to pay more attention to labor relations. Section 7(a) encouraged the American Federation of Labor (AFL) to establish a network of "United Automobile Workers Federal Unions," open to automobile workers whose skills did not fit other AFL unions. The automobile manufacturers, in turn, tried to neutralize Section 7(a) by setting up espionage systems to rout union sympathizers from their plants and by trying to organize company unions. "Labor spies were everywhere," Ed Cray reports. "The world's largest industrial corporation was also the world's largest employer of detective agencies; between the end of 1933 and July 1936, General Motors paid $1 million for the services of no less than fifteen agencies."

Sidney Fine describes workers in the pre-New Deal automobile industry as "almost entirely innocent of trade unionism in so far as their personal work experience was concerned." And John B. Rae describes the halfhearted attempts of the AFL to unionize them in the late 1920s and early 1930s as "monumental ineptitude. . . . The leadership of the AFL was obviously more concerned with protecting the jurisdictional rights of existing craft unions than with developing an organizational structure that would meet the needs of the automobile workers." AFL president William Green was derided by his own union members as "Sitting Bill"; and at the 1935 AFL convention Green revealed that Knudsen had "laughed at our efforts to organize the automobile industry."

The National Labor Relations (Wagner) Act (NLRA) of July 5, 1935, replaced Section 7(a) after the NIRA was declared unconstitutional. The Wagner Act, as the bill was known, set up a National Labor Relations Board (NLRB) empowered to conduct elections to determine workers' bargaining agents and to restrain employers from "unfair labor practices," including the discharging of workers for union membership and the setting up of employer-dominated company unions. Roosevelt at first opposed the Wagner bill but soon reversed himself to declare it "must" legislation.

Coincident with the passage of the Wagner Act by overwhelming margins in Congress, the AFL issued a charter to the international union, United Automobile Workers of America (UAW). And within the AFL, in November 1935, a group headed by John L. Lewis, Sidney Hillman, and David Dubinsky set up the Committee for Industrial Organization (CIO) with the intention of abandoning the craft union principle of the AFL and of organizing industrial unions in the mass-production industries that had resisted unionization. The CIO separated from the AFL and became the Congress of Industrial Organizations in August 1936, taking along the UAW, headed by Homer Martin and the aggressive young Reuther brothers, Walter and Victor.

Although at this time only about 15 percent of American automobile workers were organized, conditions were propitious for the UAW. Labor unrest in the automobile industry had spread with massive unemployment and the deterioration of working conditions as the depression deepened. There had even been violent encounters. The Wagner Act emboldened the UAW-CIO leaders to forceful action.

In retrospect, Sloan's response to the gathering crisis appears obtuse, Knudsen's naive. Neither GM leader was prepared to cope with the events that were unfolding. With uncharacteristic illogic and irrationality, Sloan played the tragic hero, contributing to bringing about what he most feared. With unusual lack of perception, Knudsen re-

marked on a September 1936 visit to a small French automobile plant experiencing a sit-down strike, "In America we could never have anything like this happen."

Sloan's behavior belied his image as a calculating business strategist, sensitive to the opinions of others, and guided by objective criteria and evidence. His irrational hatred of Roosevelt resulted in a personal vendetta against the president that invited retaliation against GM. Despite the fact that the NIRA was pro-big-business legislation that permitted the cartelization of major industries by the largest firms, that the automobile industry code simply maintained the status quo, that the NRA was derided by the automobile workers as the "National Run Around," Sloan publicly ranted and raved that "industry, if it has any appreciation of its obligations to future generations, will fight this proposal to the very last." Cray relates that "the president's 'experiments in economics' morally offended Sloan. He opposed the Social Security Act of 1935, which established unemployment insurance and old age pensions, for its 'dangers are manifest.' . . . Sloan's personal outrage was that of the pilgrim confronted with sacrilege. The New Deal, he asserted, sought to repeal natural economic laws."

Knudsen did not share Sloan's views. To be sure, he was nominally a Republican, and he objected to a number of New Deal policies and programs, especially to FDR's soak-the-rich taxes, which he considered confiscatory. Yet Semon relates that his father voted for Roosevelt in all four presidential elections in which FDR ran. The reservations that Knudsen had about the New Deal were outweighed in his judgment by FDR's personal qualities. Knudsen had great admiration for Roosevelt for having surmounted a crippling illness and severe physical handicap and for his ability to exude optimism and even buoyancy in the face of adversity during the depths of the depression.

Unlike Sloan, too, Knudsen was far from doctrinaire in his opposition to unionization. He was committed, as were all business leaders of the day, to the open shop, believing that although workers had a right to join a union, they had an equal right to refuse to join one. He favored company unions, dominated by management. And, failing to see the handwriting on the wall, he thought that skilled and unskilled workers had too little in common to be organized into the same union: "It is my personal opinion from my own experience," Knudsen informed NRA head Hugh S. Johnson, "you are not going to get very far with a vertical union. A craftsman will always be a craftsman, unless you appeal to the sociological instinct, and that is going to get you close to communism, and certainly to socialism." He preferred craft unions because they accorded with his view that "men are individuals and tend to express their individuality through pride in their craftsmanship." Borth further observes that "disliking mass discipline of any kind, his resistance to the organizing drive of the United Automobile Workers was based as much on his genuine respect for the sanctity of the individual as on his active regard for the sanctity of production schedules." The most important point, however, was that, as Borth relates, "among those who had occasion to listen to Knudsen fairly frequently in that period it was no secret that he believed unionization of the automobile industry inevitable. He may not have welcomed it, but it did not shock him. He was realist enough to recognize a trend and intelligent enough not to let it panic him."

Knudsen may not have panicked, but his disingenuous response to the UAW-CIO's December 21, 1936, request to negotiate differences at an "immediate general conference" undoubtedly triggered the sit-down strikes at key GM plants that he naively thought could never happen. A sit-down strike at the Atlanta Fisher Body plant already had begun on November 18 over the layoff of workers for wearing union buttons in the factory. This had forced the UAW to devise a strike strategy that would paralyze GM production by shutting down key Fisher Body plants in Cleveland, Detroit, and Flint. The UAW's hand was strengthened by a strike that began at Libby-Owens-Ford on December 15 and threatened to end automobile production by a shortage of plate glass in two to four weeks. The president of the Federation of Flat Glass Workers promised to help the UAW force its demands on GM. Then on December 16 a sit-down strike of Fisher Body workers began at the Kansas City Chevrolet plant over the dismissal of a union employee who had violated a minor company rule.

Knudsen made a speech on December 18 that collective bargaining was "here to stay" but should occur "before a shutdown rather than after." The December 21 union request for immediate negotiations was in response to this apparent overture. The union wished to put on the agenda a number of grievances; most importantly, flagrant discrimination

against union workers, the speedup of assembly lines, seniority rules, job security, and piecework methods of pay. The next day Knudsen met with Homer Martin in the GM Building in Detroit and advised the UAW leader disingenuously that these grievances should be taken up with the appropriate local plant managers. This was a reiteration of the position that the corporation had taken in the Atlanta strike, where the local management, in Fine's words, "would agree to nothing but a return to work on a status quo ante basis." The result was that on December 24 CIO president Lewis attacked Knudsen's position as "an evasion of General Motors' responsibility to bargain collectively." As Martin pointed out in his December 24 letter requesting another conference, the issues were "national in scope." Indeed, Knudsen's intransigence constituted nothing less than open defiance of the provisions of the Wagner Act. "In view of what had occurred at Atlanta and elsewhere and the limited authority of plant managers to alter GM policy in matters of substance," Fine concludes, "the UAW position on this question was altogether realistic. By the time Knudsen replied to Martin's [December 24] letter, the sit-down strike had spread to the vital center of the GM domain."

Workers sat down on December 28 in the Cleveland Fisher Body plant, which made all of the body stampings for two-door Chevrolets and some of the stampings for all Chevrolet bodies. On December 30 the sit-down spread to the two Flint Fisher Body plants, which produced all Buick bodies, some parts for all Pontiac and Oldsmobile bodies, and some Chevrolet bodies. Fine estimates that "three-fourths of GM's production was dependent" on the output of these Cleveland and Flint plants. "Within a week," Cray concludes, "the General Motors Corporation had been paralyzed." The strike quickly spread to other GM plants in other cities, and still other GM plants were closed by the corporation because of the strike. By January 10, 1937, the lion's share of GM workers, some 106,000 of them, were idle.

In the sit-down, workers stopped work but remained in the plant so that strikebreakers could not be brought in. It was, in Fine's words, "a formidable weapon and one ideally suited to the automobile industry. It seemed more sensible, moreover, to sit down inside the plant in the cold of winter than to march in a picket line outside. In Flint, in addition, union leaders thought that the police might attempt to break up an outside picket line ... but were less likely to storm a large plant to dislodge strikers sitting on the inside."

The tactic clearly constituted illegal trespass and was declared so by the United States Supreme Court in 1939. GM took the position that it would not negotiate with the UAW until the workers evacuated the plants, and a Gallup poll showed that the public supported the corporation's position by two to one. However, President Roosevelt piously considered the corporation's refusal to negotiate while the workers remained in the plants as "stuffy." And Sloan was outraged that Roosevelt, Secretary of Labor Frances Perkins, and Michigan governor Frank Murphy maintained "a steady pressure upon the corporation, and upon me personally, to negotiate with the strikers who had seized our property, until we finally felt obliged to do so." Sloan, Knudsen, Donaldson Brown, and GM counsel John Thomas Smith traveled to Washington, D.C., in Sloan's private railroad car to negotiate with Secretary Perkins. But the negotiations ended on January 19 when Sloan lost his temper and broke into a tirade against Lewis and the UAW-CIO.

The refusal of Governor Murphy to call out the Michigan National Guard to enforce a court order to evict the strikers from the Flint plants led to the capitulation of GM to the UAW-CIO on February 11, 1937. Although he knew the sit-down was illegal, Murphy was impressed both by the workers' grievances and by GM's defiance of the Wagner Act; and he did not want to go down in history as "Bloody Murphy." In this he was supported by GM director Lawrence P. Fisher, a close friend, who pleaded with Murphy, "Frank, for God's sake, if the Fisher brothers never make another nickel, don't have any bloodshed in that plant. We don't want blood on our hands."

Knudsen, too, stated publicly that GM wanted the strike settled through negotiations rather than violence, and his view prevailed against Sloan's harder stance. In the negotiations to end the strike GM was represented by the team of Knudsen, Brown, and Smith. Fine relates that, unlike the others, "Knudsen was far less interested in stubbornly defending the principles regarding representation and collective bargaining to which GM was committed than in resuming production in the company's idle plants. 'It was just hurting him,' Lee Pressman later recalled, 'that his machinery was idle.'" Knudsen took the position that President

Roosevelt had asked GM to negotiate and that "besides, this strike has gone on so long that women and children are hungry and cold, and when this happens, there is no issue but to get their men back to work." He wanted "to settle now and let the public decide later who was right and who was wrong." The important things to him were "to get people back to work, to get them some income, and to get the public some cars."

The UAW-CIO won a complete victory—an agreement that the grievances raised would be negotiated through collective bargaining, exclusive representation for six months in seventeen key GM plants, and no retaliation for the strike against the strikers or the union. Sloan fumed in a letter of April 1 to the GM stockholders that "the strike against General Motors Corporation was not actuated by any fundamental causes that affected, in any important degree, the welfare of the workers" and expressed his opinion that the unionization of GM "means the economic and political slavery of the worker, and an important step toward an economic and political dictatorship." In sharp contrast, Knudsen said, "Let us have peace and make automobiles," and informed a group of Flint executives, "I think there will be a very great improvement in labor relations because all of us are getting more experience. A little patience and the thing will square away."

Knudsen traveled to Germany with Fisher and Earl in September 1938 on one of his biennial inspection trips of the GM Opel facilities, a $38-million investment. He was impressed with the industrial activity and the improvement in living conditions since 1932. During a three-hour conference Air Marshal Hermann Goering informed Knudsen that GM would not be able to take any money out of Germany, speculated about the possibilities of war, and inquired, "If war does come, will you operate your plants under control of the German government?" Goering wanted to know about the Allison aircraft engine that GM was developing in Indianapolis for the U.S. Army Air Corps, then showed Knudsen drawings of a close copy of the Allison and asked: "Can you build that? We will build the plant. We will furnish all the money you need, in American dollars. We will pay you a fee, besides." Knudsen was evasive and informed Goering that he would have to take up the matter with the GM Board of Directors, and, regarding the Allison engine, GM would do anything that the United States government directed.

Goering's strong hints of war were strengthened by the comments of the Nazi political officer on the *Bremen* and by a "sad woman" in the cable office at Bremerhaven, who informed Knudsen that "there is threat of war everywhere, and one cannot speak one's mind anymore." Still Knudsen remained optimistic. "Knudsen returned from Europe in October 1938, convinced war was not imminent," Beasley writes. "In an interview in New York, he dismissed the Munich conference with a pointed reference to Hitler. 'Somebody drew to an inside straight and nobody called him.'" Nevertheless, he came back convinced that the United States should begin building "the strongest air force in the world."

On September 3, 1939, a Nazi-appointed board of managers took control of Opel and the German government prohibited the further transmittal of financial or operational reports to GM. Knudsen announced: "I have to report with regret that Mr. Hitler is the boss of our German factory." Knudsen still had family, including four sisters, living in Denmark, and its invasion on April 9, 1940, was a hard blow.

On May 24, 1940, President Roosevelt phoned Knudsen, asking him to come to Washington, D.C. "to work on some production matters." The following day, in New York City, Knudsen and Sloan had, according to Beasley, "an acrimonious debate" over Knudsen taking leave from GM to aid Roosevelt. Sloan did not think that the United States would go to war, but if it did, he told Knudsen, "we have a good setup here and can make parts. Your duty is here." Knudsen responded, "My duty lies in what the President of the United States asks me to do." Semon believes that Sloan's motivation had nothing to do with his assessment of Knudsen's value to the firm, everything to do with Sloan's hatred of Roosevelt.

Knudsen left GM on May 28, 1940, to assume his new duties as chairman of the National Defense Advisory Council (NADC). On September 3 he resigned his $459,000 position at GM to work for the government at no salary, not even the customary dollar a year, so that there would be no suspicion of favoritism in the awarding of government contracts. In late November, at a secret meeting in New York with over one hundred auto industry executives, he called on American automobile manufac-

turers to give their full cooperation to U.S. defense plans. With arms makers already working to capacity on British orders, contracts to produce arms were given to automobile manufacturers. Tank manufacturing capacity was created at Chrysler and at Detroit's Continental Motors Corporation. Knudsen's greatest production concern, "one big bottleneck" he called it, was aircraft production, which was resolved by calling upon the automobile manufacturers to help produce aircraft engines and a projected 35,000 planes. "To get things done," Borth relates, "Knudsen relied most on those whom he called 'my people,' the masters of mass production who were never farther from his desk phone. His power to command them was his prestige among them, but it was power enough."

In January 1941 Knudsen was made codirector—with Sidney Hillman, president of the Amalgamated Clothing Workers—of the Office of Production Management (OPM), the task of which was to coordinate defense production, purchasing, and priorities in consultation with Secretary of War Stimson and Secretary of the Navy Frank Knox. The OPM was under the Supply, Priority, and Allocations Board (SPAB), chaired by Vice-President Henry Wallace. When the SPAB was abolished in early 1942 its functions were taken over by the War Production Board (WPB), chaired by Donald M. Nelson. Knudsen was "demoted" to lieutenant general and director of war production in the War Department and served in this capacity for the duration of the war. This was the first time in history that a civilian was directly appointed as a general officer in the American military. During his first six months as director of war production Knudsen flew 55,000 miles to inspect 350 plants producing war materials.

After initial surprise attacks and lightning-paced advances by the Axis powers, World War II developed as a war of logistics. American superiority in mass-production techniques—techniques developed in the automobile industry—was the main reason for the Allied victory. The contributions of Knudsen both to the development of those techniques and to their effective employment in the Allied cause was unparalleled. Near the end of the war Secretary of War Stimson declared that "General Knudsen has been dealing with problems of industry that would have staggered most men. One by one he has solved them by becoming the master trouble shooter on the biggest job the world has ever seen." This was partially recognized by his adopted country with the award of two Distinguished Service Medals—our nation's highest non-combat-earned award. Years earlier, in 1932, the king of Knudsen's native Denmark had recognized his accomplishments by knighting him in the Order of Danneborg.

Upon his separation from the army in June 1945, Knudsen returned to GM as a member of its board of directors and consultant. Charles E. Wilson had replaced him as president. Knudsen was angered and hurt because it seemed that there was no longer a meaningful place for him in the corporation and that he had been put out to pasture. His son tried to reason with him to accept the situation, but, after a lifetime of hard work and responsibility, he was restless and bored in retirement.

After an illness of some sixteen months Knudsen succumbed to a cerebral hemorrhage at 4:55 A. M. on Tuesday, April 27, 1948. His family had been summoned to his bedside at midnight, and he died surrounded by his wife Clara and his four children. The Detroit Common Council passed a resolution of sorrow on behalf of the city and eulogized Knudsen as "a war casualty entitled to the acclaim of every citizen of the United States." The *Detroit Free Press* reported that "there were many who said that the war, when he gave unstintingly of his vitality and genius to inspire and guide America's amazing wartime output, aged him rapidly and that he never did regain his vigor." George T. Christopher, an associate at GM for sixteen years who had become president of Packard, said that "his passing is a great loss to our city and nation, to his native land and to all people everywhere who believe in the principle of free, individual enterprise which his life and work symbolized so well."

People above all remembered that despite his fame Knudsen had remained a simple, decent man. He wore a derby while at work because he claimed that he thought better with a hat on. He had a single secretary—always a male, for the reason that he did not wish to give up using profanity but would not swear in the presence of a woman. He answered his own phone and placed his own phone calls with "This is Knudsen speaking." His door was always open, and subordinates could walk in without making an appointment.

Knudsen was known as a "soft touch" and gave unstintingly and almost always anonymously to numerous charitable causes. Among those that received publicity were a new church he had built for his Lutheran congregation, and a fund that he founded in honor of his wife to improve the prenatal and postnatal care of mothers and infants in Flint. But perhaps nothing reveals as much about Knudsen as an incident first reported after his death by Henry T. Ewald, a close friend and one of his pallbearers. At the height of the bitterly divisive 1936-1937 sit-down strike, Knudsen called the Salvation Army, of which Ewald was vice-president, and said, "There must be a lot of strikers' kids who will have to go without milk while their fathers are on strike. . . . It will be bad for their health, so I want you to get a list of all GM strikers who have kids who need milk, buy the milk and send the bill to me." The milk was sent, and Knudsen paid the bill.

References:

Norman Beasley, *Knudsen: A Biography* (New York: Whittlesey House, 1947);

Gerald Bloomfield, *The World Automotive Industry* (Newton Abbott, London & North Pomfret, Vt.: David & Charles, 1978);

Christy Borth, *Masters of Mass Production* (Indianapolis: Bobbs-Merrill, 1945);

Ed Cray, *Chrome Colossus: General Motors and Its Times* (New York: McGraw-Hill, 1980);

Sidney Fine, *The Automobile Under the Blue Eagle* (Ann Arbor: University of Michigan Press, 1963);

Fine, *Sit-Down: The General Motors Strike of 1936-1937* (Ann Arbor: University of Michigan Press, 1969);

James J. Flink, *The Automobile Age* (Cambridge, Mass.: MIT Press, 1988);

Henry Ford, in collaboration with Samuel Crowther, *My Life and Work* (Garden City, N.Y.: Doubleday, Page, 1922);

David A. Hounshell, *From the American System to Mass Production: The Development of Manufacturing Technology in the United States, 1800-1932* (Baltimore: Johns Hopkins University Press, 1984);

Stuart W. Leslie, *Boss Kettering* (New York: Columbia University Press, 1983);

Allan Nevins and Frank E. Hill, *Ford: Expansion and Challenge, 1915-1933* (New York: Scribners, 1957);

Nevins and Hill, *Ford: The Times, The Man, The Company* (New York: Scribners, 1954);

John B. Rae, *The Automobile In America* (Chicago: University of Chicago Press, 1965);

Alfred P. Sloan, Jr., *My Years With General Motors* (Garden City, N.Y.: Doubleday, 1964).

Labor Relations in the Automobile Industry

by Gilbert J. Gall

Pennsylvania State University

Since the end of World War II, labor relations in the United States automobile industry have been on the cutting edge of change. During the last four decades the collective bargaining innovations pioneered between the United Auto Workers (UAW) union and the three largest automobile manufacturers (General Motors, Ford, and Chrysler) have been the models for labor relations throughout the country, in both good economic times and bad. If recent events are an indication, they will continue to provide direction for some time.

To a great degree the companies and the union have been able to set the labor relations standards because of the high centralization in the industry, both in terms of oligarchic, economic concentration and domination by one large industrial union. While all of the automobile manufacturers have collective bargaining agreements with numerous unions, the UAW represents the majority of automobile production workers and has done so since the 1940s. Although today the relationship is relatively stable it was born of considerable turmoil.

Initial efforts at unionization in the automobile industry are almost as old as the industry itself. Craft unions always had a presence and the automobile companies seemed willing to deal with them up to a point, perhaps because the skilled work component was continually decreasing. The first major attempt to organize nonskilled autoworkers came in June 1913 when the radical Industrial Workers of the World (IWW) led 6,000 Studebaker workers in three plants on a strike. The Detroit IWW local had previously had little success in attracting the relatively content autoworker. Pay and benefits in the industry compared favorably to similar manufacturing jobs before the depression, and while working conditions were often odious, on balance workers seemed to be able to tolerate them due to the financial compensation. Thus the IWW had only attracted about 200 autoworkers as members prior to the Studebaker conflict. The strike, however, dissipated quickly because of its poor timing, employer opposition, and an availability of replacements. The conflict did cause managers to take note, though. It proved that large numbers of unskilled workers could be moved to mass action under the right conditions.

After the IWW episodes unionism did not make significant progress again until World War I changed the balance of power. The Carriage, Wagon & Automobile Workers (CWAW), an American Federation of Labor (AFL)-affiliated body, had been organizing skilled painters, trimmers, sheet-metal workers, woodworkers, and upholsterers since 1913. Unlike other American Federation of Labor AFL unions, though, it was organized on an all-inclusive industrial union basis, which ultimately led to its expulsion from the AFL in 1918. Other skilled craft unions refused to allow the CWAW to organize any craft workers who came under their jurisdiction, even though those other unions were not organizing those workers. After the AFL expulsion the union reorganized as the United Automobile, Aircraft and Vehicle Workers of America (UAAVW) and prospered in war conditions; its membership rose to 45,000 by 1920, with a presence in Detroit paint shops, but primarily finding its strength in eastern U.S. plants. In a postwar antiunion employer offensive known as the second openshop drive, the UAAVW declined due to a severe strike defeat at Fisher Body in Detroit in 1921. Afterward it fell under communist influence, and transformed itself once again into the Auto Workers Union (AWU). The AWU continued to propagandize its radical anticapitalist message throughout the 1920s. In total membership it never amounted to much; it peaked at 3,000 in 1926 and gradually declined until an upturn occurred in 1933. It did, however, help create a cadre of important and militant shop floor commu-

Children of strikers picket during the GM sit-down strike in Flint, Michigan, in 1937 (courtesy of Labor History Archives of Wayne State University)

nists and radicals. Many of these same workers were ready to move into positions of union leadership when conditions for renewed labor militancy ripened.

The arrival of the Great Depression, however, fundamentally altered the power relationships between autoworkers and their employers, as it did in so many other industries. Though the grievances of autoworkers were great—periodic unemployment, favoritism, and the hated production line speedup—the prime catalyst to unionization was the National Industrial Recovery Act (NIRA) of 1933. The centerpiece of depression recovery legislation of the new administration of President Franklin D. Roosevelt, the NIRA aimed to revitalize the economy by allowing American business exemption from federal anti-trust laws. Government administrators were to assist industries in formulating codes of fair competition which included the setting of price levels. In order to garner the support of organized labor for the recovery legislation, the law contained a provision, section 7(a), which asserted that employees

would have the right to organize and bargain collectively through representatives of their own choosing. As the automobile industry set about to establish its own code of fair competition, unskilled and semiskilled auto operatives began to exhibit interest in union organization. Incipient efforts at industrial organization led to a strike threat and a mediated settlement by President Roosevelt himself in March 1934. The presidential settlement proved disheartening to the unionists, however, for in its application it adopted the principal of "proportional" worker representation in the application of section 7(a). This meant that employer-dominated company unions, company employee representation plans, and craft unions, as well as nascent industrial unions, were all on an equal footing so far as government was concerned. Industrial union adherents insisted the automobile industry could only be organized on an industrial—not craft—basis and that this meant arranging exclusive rights of recognition for the organization representing the majority of the workers. This had been the trend in applying section 7(a) elsewhere. The frustrating decision touched off increased worker militancy and convinced Sen. Robert Wagner of New York, chair of the National Labor Board, which administered disputes regarding section 7(a), that less amorphous federal labor relations legislation was needed.

Widespread industrial unrest continued to plague the New Deal's efforts to revive the economy during 1934. Senator Wagner, observing that the current legislation did not have enough power to force business leaders to recognize and collectively bargain with unions, proposed additional labor relations legislation. After the Supreme Court decision declaring the NIRA unconstitutional in spring 1935, Wagner's bill gained support within the Roosevelt administration and Congress as being the only readily available alternative to deal with industrial unrest. In July 1935 the president signed the National Labor Relations Act (NLRA). This law essentially took the philosophy of section 7(a) and transformed it into several "unfair labor practices" which henceforth would be illegal in labor-management relations. Arguing that workers should be free to decide if they want union representation, the legislation outlawed employer discrimination against unions and union supporters, and insisted companies bargain in good faith with representatives chosen collectively by their workers. Additionally it created a quasi-judicial board (the National Labor Relations Board [NLRB]) to investigate unfair labor practice charges and also to determine when a union represented a majority of the workers.

For decades American business leaders—and in this the automotive industry was no exception—had been accustomed to determining their own labor relations policies. For most of the twentieth century, the preferred mode of operation, especially in the mass production industries, was the "open shop." This term supposedly meant a workplace that would not discriminate between union sympathizers and nonunion workers. In actuality it meant a nonunion shop maintained by discrimination, industrial espionage, blacklisting, and strikebreaking. Thus in the early years of the NLRA employers basically ignored its provisions, hoping the Supreme Court would declare the statute unconstitutional.

With the law having little effect at first, workers had to force recognition on their own and they were willing to do so at some risk. In spring 1935 an autoworkers' federal local union—one of a num-

ber of AFL-sponsored efforts to organize the industry—struck a Chevrolet transmission plant; the critical nature of that plant resulted in a settlement granting recognition but no contract. This victory of sorts lent prestige to renewed militancy and persuaded AFL president William Green to hold a convention to establish an international union of autoworkers that would combine all the AFL-sponsored local unions then in existence into one organization, the United Auto Workers (UAW). He did so, but the organization only stayed affiliated with the AFL for a short time. Soon after the 1935 founding of the Committee for Industrial Organization (CIO) by United Mine Workers president John L. Lewis, autoworker unionists rejected the craft-oriented AFL and tied their fate to the CIO and the industrial union movement.

Shortly after this critical event in labor relations, Lewis sent CIO emissaries to Detroit to assist autoworkers in the establishment of an effective industrial union. CIO operatives unified various facets of growing autoworker unionization by striving to combine independent local unions, whose membership lay in Detroit, and the troubled AFL-initiated organizations, which covered many of the outlying areas of automobile production. The task of organizing the automotive industry in earnest began in summer 1936.

Strategically the UAW had to confront the Big Three automakers if it hoped to survive, and some among the fledgling union's leadership realized that General Motors (GM) must be first, for it set the standards for the automotive industry at the time. This was certainly no easy task; GM was the world's largest manufacturing enterprise. Its labor relations policy, controlled by its majority owners, the du Pont family, and implemented by its top manager, Alfred Sloan, Jr., was resolutely anti-union. Unions threatened the prerogatives of management and were rivals for power, Sloan thought, and management, especially in the decentralized business environment constructed by GM, must have unchallenged power to set the speed of the assembly line and decide who could work for the corporation. Unlike Ford, which often relied on violence to forestall unionism, GM preferred the more reserved approach of constructing an immense network of industrial espionage. The UAW was soon riddled with corporation spies who fed union sympathizers' names back to the corporation, which then laid off

Violence at the Chevrolet number 9 factory in Flint, Michigan, on February 1, 1937, ten days before the end of the GM sit-down strike (courtesy of Labor History Archives of Wayne State University)

those workers—an effective way to dampen union sentiment in times of economic hardship.

To challenge GM the union began organizing in Flint, Michigan, the heart of corporate operations and a classic company town. The UAW began an underground campaign there in summer 1936, primarily to avoid retribution for those brave enough to support the union, and met with startling success. Leaders of the organization knew recognition would come only from a strike, knew where the highly synchronized production of the corporation was vulnerable, and knew that timing would be critical. The hope was that a strike would not come before January 1937, after the holidays and the installation of a new governor, Frank Murphy, a liberal believed to be sympathetic to labor's cause. By the fall the campaign was out in the open, the UAW was publishing a paper, and the corporation was experiencing frequent "quickie" strikes, short job actions designed to disrupt production, often appearing in response to increases in the speed of the production line.

The strike was called at the very end of December 1936, inaugurating the most monumental labor conflict of the twentieth century, the Flint Sit-Down Strike. The traditional account of its inception contended that UAW strategists and shop-floor leaders decided to sit-down during the night shift in Fisher Body plant number 1 to prevent the corporation from moving critical stamping dies to another location if a conflict erupted. Earlier that day, December 30, a sit-in had occurred in the much less important plant number 2 after the company discharged three union adherents. Later, some participants stated that the controversy over the removal of the dies was only a pretext; union tacticians believed a strike would be necessary and were concerned that the plants were running out of raw materials and were near shutdown, an event that would take the steam out of the organizing and recognition drive. In any event, if the removal of the dies was not the immediate cause, it was certain that the grievances of the workers and the belief of their leaders, that a recognition strike was necessary, would have resulted in a strike on other grounds very near the time at which it actually occurred.

In the initial phases UAW militants within GM's Flint complex were able to occupy two of the corporation's factories. During the next six weeks Flint workers and the UAW leadership confronted GM at the heart of its power. With the critical help of Lewis and the CIO, the union and corporation sparred in the political arena, in the courts, and at times in the streets. The UAW and CIO succeeded for a time in delaying a GM plea for an injunction by revealing the judge granting it owned large amounts of GM stock. Moreover, the labor organization's legal counsel argued that GM could not plead trespass because the corporation itself had unclean hands; it denied the legal rights of workers to organize, protected under the NLRA. The union also succeeded in keeping both the Roosevelt administration and Gov. Frank Murphy, who mediated throughout the conflict, neutral and reluctant to use force to remove the strikers. In this it was assisted by the concurrent and widely publicized Senate La Follette Committee investigation into the antiunion labor relations policies of GM. The adverse publicity gave politicians the maneuvering room they needed to forestall company demands to forcibly remove the sit-down strikers. When necessary, the union's leadership and members in the plants defeated local police attempts to remove them (an aspect of government in which the corporation had controlling influence) in street fighting adjacent to the factories and within several of the plants themselves. The corporation's position was that it would refuse to negotiate while the union trespassed; the union's position was that it would not leave without a grant of recognition.

The critical point came when, in a brilliant tactical move, unionists leaked the information that they intended to occupy an additional adjacent Chevrolet plant not named in an impending injunction that GM ultimately won through the courts. Militant sit-downers feinted an occupation of one plant while a smaller group seized a different, more central (to production) plant. Soon afterward the corporation conceded defeat. It agreed to recognize the UAW for the members it represented throughout the company, and in those seventeen plants currently under strike, agreed not to bargain with any other labor organization for a set time. Negotiations on further collective bargaining were scheduled for shortly after the end of the strike on

February 11, 1937, and in the agreements stemming from those meetings, GM adopted a hard-bargaining approach, granting nothing more than it had to and zealously guarding its managerial prerogatives over production.

Though the UAW had emerged victorious against the largest and most powerful automobile company, its victory would have been hollow had it not been able also to organize Chrysler and Ford. Any unorganized company would have a competitive advantage and therefore put downward economic wage pressures on those already represented, a threat to the long-term survival of the union. Predictably, therefore, the UAW began campaigns in the wake of the Flint victory. Chrysler, in some ways mirroring GM in both business operations and labor relations policy, had most of its plants in the Detroit area. Although Walter Chrysler did not have the conservative reputation of Sloan or Henry Ford, the company's top managers still pursued antiunion espionage and discrimination to undercut union sentiment. After the events of Flint, the Chrysler corporation agreed to a meeting with the UAW (it had taken note that many of its workers had been streaming into the union). In March 1937 the UAW overconfidently called a sit-down strike over the corporation's refusal to grant exclusive recognition. Production effectively stopped, but public opinion had begun to turn against the sit-down tactic and Governor Murphy clearly informed the union he would remove sit-downers forcibly if they did not leave voluntarily. More importantly Murphy arranged a conference between Walter Chrysler and Lewis, who apparently liked each other. That meeting resulted in a negotiated settlement of limited recognition and voluntary evacuation. In April the Chrysler Corporation and the UAW concluded an agreement similar in many respects to the GM contract.

The final victory in the establishment of unionism in the automobile industry would not come so quickly. Idiosyncratic Henry Ford was above all determined to avoid unionism and threatened to close his company rather than accede to union demands for collective representation. Under Harry Bennett, a man with an unsavory reputation acting as Ford's personnel director and second-in-command, the company's Service Department became a haven for toughs and thugs, as UAW organizers Richard Frankensteen and Walter Reuther found out in May 1937 when the union began its Ford drive.

Workers of Fisher Body number 1 plant celebrate the end of the GM sit-down strike on February 11, 1937 (courtesy of Labor History Archives of Wayne State University)

Leafleting the sprawling center of Ford operations at the River Rouge complex in Dearborn, Michigan, Frankensteen and Reuther were attacked by Bennett's hirelings and brutally beaten in front of newspaper photographers in the famed "Battle of the Overpass." With the willingness to use force so openly, Ford signaled that the UAW's last major objective would not give up easily. In addition to building a quasi-military force Bennett also founded a company union and ordered discharges of UAW sympathizers throughout Ford plants nationwide. For several years the union was forced to pursue organization through the NLRB and court system. It was not until fall 1940 that the UAW could finally put together a meaningful Ford organizing campaign, and in this it again received help from Lewis and the CIO. A membership drive attracted numerous workers and after a period of tactical tolerance of an open UAW presence in Dearborn plants, Bennett fired the grievance committees that had been informally functioning over less important shop issues.

This touched off a traditional strike in April 1941. The union barricaded entrances to the complex with cars and thousands of picketing UAW members and sympathizers. Soon it appeared that the strike had been totally effective in shutting down Ford operations. Henry Ford, pressured by his wife and his son Edsel, finally relented and entered into negotiations with the union, government mediators, and CIO leaders. The parties reached an agreement to end the strike pending a NLRB representation election, which the UAW won decisively in May 1941. Ford, who had previously considered the UAW an "outside" force and could not believe his "loyal" workers would support the union, apparently experienced an abrupt personality shift. He instructed Bennett to accede to the UAW's demands without hard negotiating. The agreement reached gave the UAW the most attractive contract of all the Big Three automakers: a mandatory union membership (union shop) and dues checkoff. The Ford contract stunned the nation for it represented the succumbing of the most antiunion corporation of the Big Three and a symbol of the UAW's new power.

Thus in four years the UAW transformed from an underground organization to one of the most powerful industrial unions in the nation. In tandem with the unionization of the steel industry by the Steel Workers' Organizing Committee (SWOC), it formed the power base for the organization of other mass production industries of the country by the CIO. For thousands of autoworkers, who had chosen to be represented collectively by a labor organization, their wages and working conditions would henceforth be jointly determined between their representatives and their employers.

It was in the working out of that collective representation that the automotive companies and the union continued to be at the forefront of labor relations developments in the United States over the next four decades. During World War II the automotive industry was governed by the terms and mandates set by the National War Labor Board. As in other industries wage levels were frozen to dampen inflation. In exchange for a "no-strike" pledge from American labor during wartime, unions were granted "maintenance of membership" clauses in their contracts which made workers keep union membership for the length of the union contract once they had joined. This device greatly increased the portion of dues-paying members in all mass production industries. The increasing intensity of wartime production pressures frequently led to wildcat strike activity. At many points during the war the youthful UAW experienced a considerable degree of restiveness among the rank and file, a militancy often undesired by the leadership of the international union which at times cooperated with government authorities in squelching unauthorized labor actions. It was immediately after the war, however, when the broad outlines of automobile labor relations for the next thirty years took shape.

It began with the GM strike of 1945 to 1946. UAW leaders realized that the combination of wage controls, inflated corporate wartime profit levels, a high level of production grievances, and the specter of inflation had led to frustrations within membership that had to be vented. Reuther, then a UAW vice-president and a rising star in the union, developed a strike plan against GM which challenged the company's treasured sense of management prerogatives. Essentially GM was struck under Reuther's demand of a substantial wage increase

The beginning of the Battle of the Overpass, as Ford security men beat labor organizer Richard Frankensteen (back to camera) on May 26, 1937 (courtesy of Archives of Labor History and Urban Affairs, Wayne State University)

(30 percent) without an increase in the cost of cars, arguing that GM profits were so abundant that the company could easily afford to do so. More importantly Reuther challenged management to open the books if it chose to claim that it could not afford to raise wages to that level. For 113 days GM workers struck with the corporation's top management angrily denouncing Reuther's demands as socialistic and a fundamental challenge to sole management control of the enterprise. When a fact-finding board appointed by President Truman intimated that an open books policy was not out of the question, GM management began to bring financial offers in line with government price-control guidelines of 18.5¢ per hour. Still Reuther continued to hold out, but in the end, with other automotive companies and UAW departments concluding agreements falling within the guidelines without having to strike and make demands regarding prices, he lost the strike. The final settlement in March 1946 provided for an 18.5¢ increase in salary with no provisions on prices.

The significance of the 1946 GM strike was enormous for postwar labor relations in the automobile industry. In essence the corporation put down a challenge to link its labor relations policies with its other business concerns. The message to Reuther, who became president of the UAW in 1946, was clear: the automobile companies reluctantly accepted union demands in the areas of wages, benefits, and working conditions as the legitimate sphere of collective bargaining, but stridently rejected any labor demand which might lead to a joint union-management sharing of enterprise decisions. From this point onward the UAW made tremendous strides in negotiating pattern-setting contracts in the automotive industry under Reuther and his successors, but those victories would be limited chiefly to economic concerns.

But even so the victories were of impressive proportions. The UAW operated in an oligopolistic industry between 1946 and 1970, but one in which it could play one major automobile corporation off the other by choosing one strike target at a time. The company on strike would be threatened with a loss of its market share to its competitors. In combination these factors removed downward competitive price pressures on wages and benefits and made obtaining attractive settlements easier. In the 1948 GM settlement the UAW gained a Cost of Living Adjustment (COLA) clause to protect wages from inflationary pressures as well as an agreement to peg wage increases to a portion of the rise in productivity, to be granted periodically in an Annual Improvement Factor (AIF). Curiously enough both of these concepts were advanced by GM executive chief Charles E. Wilson, who agreed to expand upon them in 1950 and grant a union shop in exchange for a five-year contract to stabilize GM's labor cost calculations. In the 1949 Ford negotiations the UAW won the first fully funded pension plan in the automotive industry. In the 1955 Ford negotiations the UAW made collective bargaining history once more by securing a Supplemental Unemployment Benefit (SUB), designed to function as a form of guaranteed annual wage for autoworkers in an industry where periodic layoffs were endemic. All of these innovations spread from one company to the other through pattern bargaining, and more generally but with less replication, from one major unionized industry to another. In these developments labor relations in the automotive industry were the prime exemplar of the post-World War II labor-management consensus of constantly improving the economic standard of living for American workers based upon U.S. dominance of world manufacturing.

As other countries began to revive their export manufacturing potential in the late 1960s, though, the labor relations consensus in American manufacturing came under increasing strain. Beginning in the early 1970s foreign automobile manufacturers, first Germany and then Japan, made increasing inroads into the American automobile markets and captured greater and greater shares as their fuel efficient cars became more desirable to American consumers concerned about rapidly rising gas prices. Major Japanese automakers even built assembly plants in the United States—the Nissan plant in Smyrna, Tennessee, for example—which had no intention of operating under a UAW contract if it could be avoided. Younger, better-educated autoworkers occasionally rebelled through wildcat strikes and chronic absenteeism against the intense and deadening routines of the automated assemblyline, contributing to a steady decline in productivity rates. Reuther's successors in the UAW (he died in an airplane crash in 1970) struggled to deal with these events; eventually, the union and automotive companies began to explore new avenues of labor relations that differed from the dominant patterns of the postwar era. One area of experimentation was shop floor labor-management cooperation in the form of discussion work groups, often called Quality of Worklife or Employee Involvement. With the recession of the early 1980s the American automobile industry experienced severe hard times once again—the Chrysler corporation nearly went bankrupt and would have done so had not the union granted large concessions in already negotiated wages and work rules (as it was also later forced to do with GM and Ford). In response to the combination of these events GM, Ford, Chrysler, and the UAW negotiated unprecedented contracts during the 1980s that exchanged management decision-making power heretofore zealously guarded by industry executives (UAW President Douglas Fraser even gained a seat on the Chrysler board of directors as a result of the crisis negotiations) in return for modest wage raises, contingent compensation (profit sharing), and flexibility in work processes at the plant level. For the UAW a prime collective bargaining objective in recent years has been to increase job security for its members. How all of these changes will progress, and whether they will become institutionalized, is yet to be determined. The union has perhaps gone farthest in the projected Saturn automotive plant to be built in Spring Hill, Tennessee, which will serve as a flagship for the changing labor relations of worker participation and job security. Whatever the outcome, though, no one can deny that automotive labor relations still remains a prime bellwether of labor relations in the United States.

References:

John Barnard, *Walter Reuther and the Rise of the Auto Workers* (Boston: Little, Brown, 1983);

Harry C. Katz, *Shifting Gears: Changing Labor Relations in the U.S. Automobile Industry* (Cambridge, Mass.: MIT Press, 1987);

Nelson Lictenstein, "UAW Bargaining Strategy and Shop-Floor Conflict, 1946-1970," *Industrial Relations*, 24 (Fall 1985): 360;

Joyce Shaw Peterson, *American Automobile Workers, 1900-1930* (Albany: State University of New York Press, 1987).

Lincoln Motor Company

by George S. May

Eastern Michigan University

The Lincoln Motor Company was organized in August 1917 by Henry M. Leland a few months after his departure from General Motors (GM), where he had been in charge of Cadillac. (Many years later, Charles S. Mott, a member of the GM board, claimed that the story that Leland left GM voluntarily was not correct. "He didn't resign," Mott declared. "He was fired!") During World War I the Lincoln company built Liberty airplane engines, but in 1919, with the cancellation of their war contract, Leland and his son Wilfred turned to automobiles. This change in product to automobiles was probably planned from the outset, taking into account their earlier association with Cadillac dating back to the origins of that car in 1902.

The Lelands' reputation, held over from their Cadillac association, helped their $6.5-million stock issue for Lincoln to be oversubscribed in three hours. By the end of 1919 two prototypes of the Lincoln car, so named because of Henry Leland's devotion to the memory of the martyred president, had been completed. However, problems with suppliers and Henry Leland's fanatical insistence on the highest standards of precision work at all levels of production delayed the introduction of the car until September 1920, when all car sales were beginning to be affected by the onset of the postwar depression. First-year production was only half of the projected figure of 6,000 cars. Economic conditions no doubt dampened sales of a car selling in the $5,000 price range, but in addition the car was not what

many expected for that kind of money in the 1920s. Mechanically the 8-cylinder car surpassed what the Lelands had achieved earlier with the Cadillac, but the styling was uninspired and outdated. The resulting anemic sales, when combined with a federal tax claim of $4.5 million, caused the company's directors on November 8, 1921, over the protests of the Lelands, to ask that the company be placed in the hands of a receiver. The tax claim, which later was doubled, was subsequently shown to have been grossly overstated in terms of the amount of money owed, but this admission by the government came too late to save the company from filing for bankruptcy and from being sold under a court order. On the day of the sale, February 4, 1922, the sole bid came from Henry Ford, whose initial offer to pay $5 million for the company's assets was rejected by the bankruptcy judge, who set $8 million as an acceptable figure. This was the amount Ford paid, and although some have asserted that this figure represented only half of the assets' appraised value, others declared that $8 million was generous and considerably more than others would have been willing to bid.

Much controversy surrounds the relationship between Ford and the Lelands and what each understood to have been the nature of the arrangements worked out between them. The Lelands are said to have asked Ford for help prior to the time the company went into receivership. An influx of Ford money at the time, either in the form of a loan or

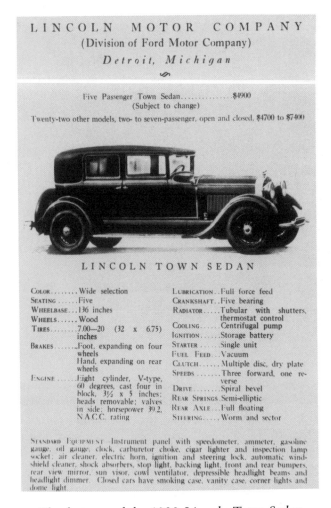

LINCOLN MOTOR COMPANY
(Division of Ford Motor Company)
Detroit, Michigan

Five Passenger Town Sedan..............$4900
(Subject to change)
Twenty-two other models, two- to seven-passenger, open and closed, $4700 to $7400

LINCOLN TOWN SEDAN

COLOR........Wide selection	LUBRICATION..Full force feed
SEATING......Five	CRANKSHAFT..Five bearing
WHEELBASE..136 inches	RADIATOR.....Tubular with shutters, thermostat control
WHEELS......Wood	COOLING.....Centrifugal pump
TIRES........7.00—20 (32 x 6.75) inches	IGNITION......Storage battery
BRAKES......Foot, expanding on four wheels	STARTER......Single unit
	FUEL FEED...Vacuum
Hand, expanding on rear wheels	CLUTCH......Multiple disc, dry plate
ENGINE.....Eight cylinder, V-type, 60 degrees, cast four in block, 3¼ x 5 inches; heads removable; valves in side; horsepower 39.2, N.A.C.C. rating	SPEEDS.......Three forward, one reverse
	DRIVE........Spiral bevel
	REAR SPRINGS.Semi-elliptic
	REAR AXLE...Full floating
	STEERING.....Worm and sector

STANDARD EQUIPMENT—Instrument panel with speedometer, ammeter, gasoline gauge, oil gauge, clock, carburetor choke, cigar lighter and inspection lamp socket; air cleaner, electric horn, ignition and steering lock, automatic windshield cleaner, shock absorbers, stop light, backing light, front and rear bumpers, rear view mirror, sun visor, cowl ventilator, depressible headlight beams and headlight dimmer. Closed cars have smoking case, vanity case, corner lights and dome light.

The features of the 1929 Lincoln Town Sedan

an investment in the company, might have staved off bankruptcy. But, if such a request actually was made, Ford took no action. However, when the company declared bankruptcy, Ford and Edsel Ford and even Clara Ford, who was a friend of Wilfred Leland's wife, expressed the view that Detroit and the automobile industry owed too much to the Lelands to allow them and their company to fail. The early indications that Ford intended to buy the company at the receiver's sale may have discouraged others who might have been considering a bid.

Henry Ford promised the Lelands that they would continue to run the company, and at the first meeting of the reorganized Lincoln Motor Company of Michigan, Henry Leland was elected president and Wilfred Leland vice-president and general manager. Edsel Ford's appointment as second vice-president was the only easily recognizable indication to the public that the company was wholly owned by the Ford Motor Company. The Lelands

soon complained, however, that their freedom to run the operations was being undermined by the interference of Ford production men. When the Lelands finally complained to Henry Ford, he is said to have promised to see that this harassment was stopped. Instead, on June 10, 1922, Ford officials appeared at the Lelands' office and told them they had been directed by Ford to leave the plant at once.

In the following years the Lelands claimed not only that Ford reneged on his promise to keep them in charge of the Lincoln company but that he had also failed to keep his promise to reimburse the stockholders in the Lelands' company for the money they had invested. Ford paid off the company's creditors, but nothing was done for the shareholders, and in 1931, after several years of legal wrangling, Henry Leland was forced to admit that nothing further could be done in the matter. Although there is some indication that Henry Ford may have expressed a desire to help the shareholders during the weeks in which he was negotiating to gain control of the company, the Lelands had made the mistake of not having such an expression, if it was made, written down in the form of a contract.

Henry Ford has usually been portrayed as a villain and the Lelands as the victims of injustice in accounts written about these events. In Ford's defense it should be pointed out that Henry Leland had always been a difficult man to work with, and in 1921 and 1922, when he was nearly eighty years old, age may have made him even less likely to accept any of the cost-cutting techniques the Ford staff had perfected. As for the Lincoln shareholders, the claim that Ford had made an oral commitment to reimburse them is based almost entirely on the word of the Lelands, and there is no strong reason to accept their word and reject the statements of the Fords.

In any event, no one can deny that the Lincoln car became a success only after the Fords took it over. It is not really clear why Henry Ford, with his love of the plain and inexpensive Model T, was interested in the Lincoln in the first place, but it is a different matter with his son. Control of the Lincoln company provided Edsel Ford with the opportunity to express his artistic interests. With the departure of the Lelands, the younger Ford became the new president of the Lincoln Motor Company. Under his direction significant improvements in produc-

The 1921 Lincoln 112 Phaeton

tion were made. Changes in some of the materials used in the cars enabled the price of the cars to be reduced without in any way compromising the original goal of the Lelands to produce a car of the highest quality. Not only was the mechanical excellence of the Lelands' car maintained, but the appearance of the car was improved greatly. Ford employed the services of the country's leading coach-building firms and ultimately built up a staff of stylists who created two of the classics of the 1930s, the Lincoln Zephyr and the Lincoln Continental. Initially the Lincoln was sold through Ford dealers, but in later years, as Lincoln was fully absorbed into the Ford organization as a division of the company, a separate dealer organization was set up. The company did not make a profit from the car until 1968. Although Lincoln sales have never approached those of Cadillac, it has always given

Ford a high-visibility presence in the luxury-car field, which helped to offset the long-standing association of the company name with the lowest-priced end of the market.

References:

Nick Baldwin and others, *The World Guide to Automobile Manufacturers* (New York: Facts on File, 1987);

Beverly Rae Kimes and Henry Austin Clark, *Standard Catalog of American Cars, 1805-1942* (Iola, Wis.: Krause, 1985);

Robert Lacey, *Ford: The Men and the Machine* (Boston: Little, Brown, 1986);

Mrs. Wilfred C. Leland, with Minnie Dubbs Millbrook, *Master of Precision: Henry M. Leland* (Detroit: Wayne State University Press, 1966);

Allan Nevins and Frank Ernest Hill, *Ford: Expansion and Challenge, 1915-1933* (New York: Scribners, 1957).

James Alvan Macauley

(January 17, 1872-January 16, 1952)

by Robert J. Kothe

Atlanta, Georgia

CAREER: Patent lawyer, Church & Church (1892-1895); patent lawyer, National Cash Register Company (1895-1901); general manager, American Arithmometer Company (1901-1910); general manager and vice-president (1910-1916), president (1916-1939), chairman of the board, Packard Motor Car Company (1939-1948).

James Alvan Macauley was born in Wheeling, West Virginia, on January 17, 1872. Although given the first name James, he was always referred to as Alvan. He was the son of James Alexander Macauley and Rebecca Jane Mills Macauley. James Alexander Macauley had come from Ireland in 1850 at the age of twelve. He served in the Union Army during the Civil War, was wounded, lost an arm, and was imprisoned for nine months in a Confederate prison.

After the war Macauley served as state treasurer of West Virginia and later worked for the Pension Office in Washington, D.C., where Alvan Macauley spent most of his youth. Macauley was educated in the public schools of Washington, D.C. In 1888 he entered Lehigh University, where he continued his studies through 1890. Macauley then enrolled at Columbian College (now called George Washington University), where he was awarded an LL.B. in 1892.

Macauley was first employed as a patent attorney at Church & Church, a law firm. In 1895 he joined the National Cash Register Company in Dayton, Ohio, where he also served as a patent attorney. That same year he married Beverly Littlepage of Virginia; they had three children: Alvan, Jr., Edward and Mary.

In 1901 Macauley was named general manager of the American Arithmometer Company of St. Louis, Missouri. In that position he headed up one of the most extraordinary relocations of an industrial organization in American history. The com-

James Alvan Macauley

pany had a dispute with the city government in St. Louis over its plans for expansion and the use of city land. Detroit courted the firm, and the entire company, including machinery and key personnel, was literally loaded on a train and moved to Detroit overnight. American Arithmometer was a predecessor to the Burroughs Corporation, which has been merged into the Unisys Corporation.

In 1910 Macauley joined the automobile industry when he was named vice-president and general manager of Packard. That company, like American Arithmometer, was transplanted to Detroit from another state, in this case, Ohio. Packard had been purchased and moved by a group that was made up of representatives of old, moneyed Detroit families including Henry B. Joy, Truman Newberry, Philip McMillan, and Russell A. Alger, Jr.

One important side effect of Macauley's move to Packard was the fact that Jesse Vincent, an engineer, came with Macauley to Packard from the Arithmometer Company. Vincent was a legendary industrial designer, who was the principal architect of the famed Liberty aircraft engine and a number of other Packard engineering milestones.

Henry Joy, who had been an important factor in the group that moved Packard to Detroit and was still a major stockholder, retired as president of the firm in 1916. He was replaced by Macauley. For the next thirty years, first as president and later as chairman of the board, Macauley was the leading figure in the operation of Packard. However, while Macauley headed Packard, the firm was a widely held public corporation, and he answered to a board of directors. As a result he never enjoyed the almost-total control of Packard that he desired.

Packard enjoyed a reputation in several diverse fields in the early part of its history. Although the early products of the company were small cars, after a few years production shifted to large, luxurious cars. The big Packard automobiles enjoyed a worldwide reputation for quality and were marketed internationally. Packard trucks were also among the most successful on the market. They were especially popular with the military after their performance during World War I.

The company was primarily responsible for the design and production of the Liberty engine, a mainstay for aircraft use during the war and for some time afterward. Packard researched advanced aircraft engines under Macauley's leadership, including a novel diesel aircraft engine. After World War I Packard, under Macauley's leadership, made the decision to stop the production of trucks, a move that was widely criticized at the time. Packard trucks were popular, and that part of the company was successful. However, by discontinuing that highly competitive business, Packard was free to concentrate on the production of luxury cars, a market it came close to dominating in the following twenty years.

Packard prospered in the years just before the 1929 depression. In 1928, the company's best year yet, the firm earned $25 million on sales of 47,178 cars. In 1929 the firm outsold Cadillac 3 to 1, and Packards were shipped all over the world as the vehicle of choice for the wealthy. Packards were quality-built vehicles and required far more skilled labor for production than most other cars built in the 1920s. Macauley, realizing the value of the company's work force, was a generous and humane employer. When possible he avoided the long lay-offs that were common in most of the industry. One worker said, "Even during the dark days of the Depression, they did their best to see we got some work." Managers and workers ate in the same cafeteria. In 1937 nearly 700 members of its relatively small work force had been with the company for twenty years or more. It was one of the more integrated plants, with a large number of Poles, Italians, and blacks among its work force. The company also observed an informal seniority system.

The depression threatened the company, as Packard sales dropped dramatically. The market for luxury cars was decimated by economic conditions in the early 1930s. Even customers with the funds needed to buy large expensive cars were often reluctant to display their wealth, when so much of the population was out of work. Other former customers, with their incomes reduced, moved down to less-expensive cars. Macauley was also hurt personally by the depression. In 1929 his total compensation from Packard had been over $250,000. By comparison Alfred P. Sloan, Jr., at General Motors (GM) was earning more than $3 million per year. By 1933 Macauley's salary and bonus had fallen to $30,000. He also suffered from the drop in the company's stock price, as he owned 339,245 shares of Packard stock.

In 1931 the company stopped paying dividends. Prior to that Packard had been profitable for many years and had paid excellent dividends. In 1933 sales dropped below 10,000 units, and Packard stock was selling for less than $2, down from a peak value of well over $100 a share. It was in this context that Macauley, as leader of the firm, made perhaps his most important decision. Macauley decided that the company would introduce a modestly priced, mass-produced car while continuing to build its luxury models. An earlier attempt to increase sales by reducing the price of its large cars had not been very successful. The new car was to be a truly new model, not a stripped-down luxury car. A new production facility was set up in the existing Packard plant. The new car was assembled, for the most part, using a different work force and much less hand finishing than the big Packards.

This decision was controversial. As late as 1929 Macauley had said that Packard would never enter the low-price market. The company's slogan had for years been, "Ask the man that owns one," and their marketing emphasized elitism. Profits per unit were extremely high, but so were expenses, which left very little room to reduce price on the big Packards.

What Macauley did was to take what *Fortune* magazine called "next to Ford, the most valuable name in the industry" and use it to sell a middle-class product. The new car, called the 120, was introduced and was an instant success. Employment increased, and the company returned to modest profitability. However, critics of the move argued that Packard's reputation, as perhaps the world's most successful luxury carmaker, was tarnished forever.

General economic conditions, while still grim, were improving by the time the new small Packards were introduced, and this helped company profits as well. Because of his position in the industry, Macauley, who was president of the Automotive Chamber of Commerce, took a leadership role in an effort to help in the overall recovery of the economy. This was mostly a public relations effort to persuade the public to buy more automobiles. An example of his efforts is the line "An hour of work is better for America than a dollar for dole." The phrase became closely associated with Macauley and was often quoted in articles written about him.

In 1939 Macauley became chairman of the board of Packard, a position he held until retirement in 1948. As chairman he led the company through World War II. Like most American firms during this time, Packard converted completely its manufacturing capacity to war production, turning out a myriad of products for the effort, including the legendary Rolls-Royce aircraft engine. War profits obscured its financial condition and the long-range impact of its move into the mass market.

After the war Packard's small size and its dependence on outside suppliers began to damage its prospects. The luxury end of the line was discontinued, and the smaller profit margins on lower priced cars made it more difficult for Packard to compete technologically with bigger firms. Although sales reached a postwar high of more than 104,000 in 1949, Packard's fortunes were on the decline. Macauley retired in 1948.

Macauley was an avid sportsman, especially fond of duck hunting and fishing. He played golf, collected guns, and was an accomplished woodworker. He was fond of making reproductions of English period furniture in his completely equipped shop. During much of his career Macauley lived on Lakeshore Drive just outside of Detroit in an English Tudor-style home designed by Albert Kahn, the architect who pioneered reinforced concrete design for industrial plants and had designed much of Packard's Detroit complex. Macauley also had a winter home in Florida, which he used every year beginning in the 1930s.

He was also active in the leadership of the automotive industry. Macauley was first elected as president of the National Automotive Chamber of Commerce, an organization that became the Automobile Manufacturers Association, in 1928. He served in that post until 1946. He died of uremic poisoning and pneumonia at his vacation home in Clearwater, Florida, on January 16, 1952.

Macauley's career is difficult to summarize. Under his leadership Packard grew rapidly and was, until the Great Depression, extremely profitable. Most of its large cars, produced while he ran the company, are unquestionably accepted as classics. Under Macauley's leadership Packard survived dramatic changes in the automobile market and the greatest economic crisis of the twentieth century.

But after Macauley's retirement Packard did not survive long. Whether its demise was the result of poor planning, poor leadership in the years after Macauley left, or just the inevitable result for a relatively small company in an industry that was increasingly dominated by a few extremely large companies, is unclear. Although management mistakes were made, it seems probable that Packard would have failed sooner if not for Macauley.

Reference:

Martin H. Jaffe, *Alvan Macauley, Automotive Leader and Pioneer: A Memorial Biography* (N. p., 1957).

Robert Strange McNamara

(June 9, 1916-   )

by Michael L. Berger

St. Mary's College of Maryland

CAREER: Instructor and assistant professor of accounting, Harvard University Graduate School of Business Administration (1940-1943); captain and lieutenant colonel, U. S. Army Air Corps (1943-1946); manager of the office of planning and financial analysis (1946-1949), controller (1949-1953), assistant general manager of the Ford automotive division (1953-1955), general manager and vice-president of the Ford automotive division (1955-1957), vice-president and group executive of all car and truck divisions (1957-1960), president, Ford Motor Company (1960-1961); U. S. Secretary of Defense (1961-1968); president, World Bank (1968-1981).

Robert Strange McNamara was one of a group of systems analysts who revamped the operational and financial management of the Ford Motor Company in the years following World War II. Joining the company in 1946, he worked his way through the administrative hierarchy, emerging as president of Ford in 1960, the first non-member of the Ford family to hold that position since 1906. He is generally recognized as one of the key people responsible for the revitalization of the Ford Motor Company. He left Ford in 1961 to serve in the cabinet of President John F. Kennedy.

Born on June 9, 1916, in San Francisco to Claranel Strange and Robert James McNamara, Robert Strange McNamara was the first of two children. (A sister, Margaret, was born three years later.) His father was of Irish Catholic ancestry and was the sales manager for a wholesale shoe company. By all accounts, the McNamara family lived a typical middle-class existence for a Bay Area family of the time.

Although reportedly a frail child, McNamara early on evidenced a keen intellect and an excellent memory. He learned to read at home and was advanced in this skill when he entered elementary

Robert Strange McNamara (courtesy of Henry Ford Museum and Greenfield Village)

school, which contributed to his success there. His secondary school record was an impressive one, with McNamara averaging an A- throughout his years at Piedmont High School. He subsequently entered the University of California, Berkeley, where he majored in economics. McNamara's academic excellence there allowed him to be elected to the Phi Beta Kappa honor society at the end of his sophomore year. He graduated from Berkeley with honors in 1937 and then went on to Harvard University, where he continued to excel academically, receiving his M.B.A. from the Graduate School of Business in 1939.

McNamara's first full-time position was with the San Francisco branch of the accounting firm of Price, Waterhouse & Company, but his tenure there was brief. In fall 1940, at the age of twenty-four, he accepted an offer to become an accounting instructor at the Harvard Business School. The choice between a career in the business world or in academia/public service would be one that McNamara would need to make several times in his life.

McNamara brought with him to Cambridge, Massachusetts, his new wife, the former Margaret McKinstry Craig, who had been a student with him at Berkeley and who was a high school biology and physical education teacher in San Rafael, California. (They eventually had three children: Margaret Elizabeth, Kathleen, and Robert Craig. His wife died in 1981.)

With America's entrance into World War II, McNamara attempted to enlist, but he was deemed unacceptable due to his nearsightedness. Determined to contribute to the war effort, he volunteered to teach young Army Air Corps officers who were enrolled in a program at Harvard designed to teach the principles of systematic management, especially as it applied to controlling the allocation of personnel, materiel, and money. The excellence of his work impressed his superiors and led McNamara, with a leave of absence from Harvard, to England to establish a statistical control system for the American air forces based there. His nearsightedness now deemed unimportant, McNamara was granted a captain's commission in the Air Corps, which proved useful in his dealings with the military. He served with distinction in England, as well as in India, China, the Pacific, and in several stateside assignments, winning the Legion of Merit and achieving the rank of lieutenant colonel before his discharge in April 1946. (He subsequently was promoted to colonel in the Air Force Reserve.)

While in the Army Air Corps, McNamara had been part of a hand-picked special unit–the Office of Statistical Control (OSC). Under the leadership of Colonel Charles B. "Tex" Thornton, a group of college-educated men–some, like McNamara, with graduate-school training–had been assembled to accumulate and analyze military data to provide logistical support for American bombers.

The management efforts of the OSC group had been so successful that Thornton believed he could sell its expertise to private industry in the postwar world. He selected what he believed were the ten best men from the group, of which McNamara was one, and attempted to solicit potential employers. (McNamara had intended to return to Harvard to teach following the war. However, his wife had contracted polio in the meantime, and Thornton convinced him that the costs of treating her illness would be better met by a position in the business world.) An initial offer to the Thornton group from the Allegheny Corporation was rejected in favor of pursuing other, more interesting prospects, chief of which was the Ford Motor Company.

Ford had been experiencing declining fortunes in the late 1930s and early 1940s. Although wartime contracts temporarily eased the situation, with peace the company's financial problems returned. Various estimates placed Ford's losses at between $9 million and $10 million per month. Henry Ford II, the grandson and namesake of the founder, was the company's president. A young, inexperienced executive with the reputation of being something of a playboy, Ford did have the wisdom and courage to realize that conditions would worsen if he did not seek outside help. Fortunately, the company possessed sufficient cash reserves, despite its monthly operating losses, to afford the best new management available.

It was at this juncture that Ford received a telegram from Thornton, requesting an interview to discuss "a matter of management importance," as Thornton worded it. Ford was intrigued, especially since Thornton listed the secretary of the Air Force as a reference. The telegram could not have come at a better time. The Thornton group was summoned immediately to Detroit for interviews with Henry Ford II and his assistants. Both sides liked what they saw and heard, and the group of ten was hired–en masse–to begin work in February 1946.

Realizing that Thornton and his men would not be experienced enough to run the company by themselves, Ford complemented those hirings with the appointment of Ernest R. Breech as executive vice-president, a position second only to Ford in authority. Breech had been president of Bendix Aviation, where he had developed a reputation as a brilliant administrator, and prior to that had been in management at General Motors for over twenty years. It was under Breech's assistant, Lewis D. Crusoe, that the Thornton group worked.

Thornton and his men brought with them personal qualities and professional skills that were destined to change forever the management of the

McNamara with the Whiz Kids (front row), from left: Arjay Miller, F. "Jack" Reith, George Moore, James Wright, Charles "Tex" Thornton, Wilbur Andreson, Charles Bosworth, Ben Mills, J. Edward Lundy, and McNamara (courtesy of Henry Ford Museum, The Edison Institute, Dearborn, Michigan)

Ford Motor Company. Their statistical and managerial expertise was of primary importance. Also significant, especially in light of the conservative history of Ford, was the youth of the group members, whose ages ranged from twenty-six to thirty-four. (McNamara was just shy of his thirtieth birthday at the time.) Their major weakness was their lack of knowledge of the automotive industry. As a result the group spent much of its early time at Ford asking questions, thus earning for themselves the opprobrium of "Quiz Kids," after a popular radio show of the time. When they stopped asking questions and began to provide answers, the opprobrium was dropped in favor of the laudatory "Whiz Kids" an appellation that has remained to this day.

What the Thornton group found at Ford was a company that had advanced little from the managerial and organizational beliefs of its founder. In consequence, records of current revenues and expenditures were ill-kept, future financial projections were almost unknown, and a general economic confusion pervaded the company. In addition, morale and effectiveness of both workers and management were low, partially as a result of years of autocratic

and financially inefficient management overseen by the elder Henry Ford.

With Henry Ford II's blessing the Whiz Kids set to work to bring Ford in line with mid-century managerial expertise. Major organizational changes were implemented, designed to make the planning and production processes more systematic and cost-efficient. For the first time, profit and loss figures for each area of the company were available, thus managers and workers in that area could be held accountable for their level of productivity.

Thornton, McNamara, and the other "kids" represented a new era in management for the automotive industry. These were men who had not been involved with the industry during its developmental years. In addition, they were not especially enamored of automobiles. Rather, they were financial experts, "bean counters" as they were pejoratively called, who welcomed the challenge of making a sick company well again. Although Thornton departed after only a year (moving on to Hughes Aircraft), the other Whiz Kids remained. Six of them would eventually become vice-presidents and two, McNamara and Arjay Miller, would be presidents of the Ford Motor Company.

With Thornton gone, McNamara was generally acknowledged as the group's new leader. No one questioned that he was the brightest, and when this was combined with his strong ambition, unbridled energy, and mastery of statistical argumentation, McNamara had the ability to control almost any decision-making process. McNamara's intellect and administrative skills allowed him to be an intimidating person when the occasion warranted, even with as strong-willed a person as Henry Ford II.

McNamara began as manager of the newly created office of planning and financial analysis. He became controller in 1949. It was in these initial positions that he built his reputation for attention to even the smallest detail. In 1953 he was promoted to assistant general manager of the Ford division, and two years later he became general manager and vice-president of that division.

Once in a position to make policy decisions regarding the type of car Ford should manufacture, McNamara broadened his belief in statistical management to include the systematic sampling of public opinion. "Market research" became the operating principle, and early decisions resulting therefrom enhanced McNamara's prestige. For instance, he supported the transformation of the Thunderbird model from a two- to a four-seater, a change which tripled sales of the car.

Nonetheless, McNamara was much more than a facts-and-figures man. He believed that automobile manufacturers also had social obligations, and for the 1956 model year he began to emphasize safety. Naturally, he also thought a safer Ford car would appeal to the consumer as well. In consequence, a national advertising campaign was undertaken, stressing new Ford standard features, such as a "deep-dish" steering wheel and dashboard padding, and how effective they would be in protecting the car's occupants in the event of a crash. Unfortunately for McNamara he had misjudged public opinion. Prospective buyers reacted negatively to the campaign, apparently associating Fords with death and mayhem on the highway, and sales slumped nationwide.

The only exception was in Philadelphia, where the district sales manager, Lee Iacocca, had side stepped the national efforts and introduced his own imaginative and highly successful sales campaign highlighting the affordability of the new cars. When McNamara found out who was responsible, he brought Iacocca to Dearborn to head up market-

McNamara with Henry Ford II in November 1960 (courtesy of the Associated Press, Inc.)

ing for Ford trucks. This was the beginning of Iacocca's meteoric climb within Ford management.

McNamara and Ford rebounded the following year with the introduction of the enormously popular Ford Fairlane, a car that consumers instantly recognized as providing extraordinary value for the money. However, that success was overshadowed by the fact that 1957 also was the fateful year in which the new Edsel line was introduced.

While neither McNamara nor any of the other Whiz Kids were directly responsible for the Edsel, there can be little doubt that the faith in statistical management, which they helped introduce, misled the company organization into thinking that the market was right for a new medium-priced car. As automotive writer Brock Yates has noted, the Edsel was a "monumental disaster created for tomorrow's markets based on yesterday's statistical inputs." An unexpected downturn in the economy, combined with unpopular design characteristics (especially the Edsel's "horse collar" grill), and quality-control problems doomed the new car. As the newly appointed (1957) vice-president and group executive of all car and truck divisions, it fell to McNamara to try to salvage the Edsel by improving its construction and appearance. When that failed to improve sales, production of the car ended, less than three years after its introduction and at a loss of $250 million.

As several of his biographers have noted, the Edsel was not the type of car Robert McNamara would have favored. In fact, once he achieved a leadership position, McNamara worked hard to convince Henry Ford II and others of the logic of building small cars that provided inexpensive, efficient transportation. In that regard, it could be said that McNamara was echoing the beliefs of the elder Henry Ford during the Model T years of 1908 to 1927. Predicting renewed public acceptance of such vehicles, McNamara engineered the introduction of the Falcon model in 1959. The first American "compact" car manufactured by one of the Big Three companies, the Falcon was an alternative to the gas-guzzling, tail-finned behemoths that had increasingly come to dominate the nation's highways in the 1950s.

The Falcon's lack of expressive styling and general utilitarianism never made it popular with automotive writers or "buffs." These sentiments were best expressed by one critic who observed that McNamara "wore granny glasses and he put out a granny car." Nonetheless, the Falcon met with overwhelming public acceptance, establishing a sales record of some 417,000 units in its first year. The car was able to compete in terms of price and fuel economy with the small imports that were beginning to make inroads into the American market. Just as importantly, it could seat six (which the imports then did not), and soon acquired a reputation for mechanical soundness and ease of repair.

The success of the Falcon further enhanced McNamara's reputation and the financial principles he espoused, even though the Falcon profit-margin was a slim one and Ford did not really begin to make money off it until "luxury" options were added (at the suggestion of Iacocca). Still, McNamara had once again produced a winner, and on November 9, 1960, at the age of forty-four, he was chosen to be president of the Ford Motor Company. McNamara was the first person outside the Ford family to hold that position since John S. Gray, a Detroit banker who served as president from the company's founding in 1903 until his death in 1906, when he was succeeded by Henry Ford.

McNamara never really functioned as a Ford president, for two months later he agreed to serve as secretary of defense in the cabinet of recently-elected president John F. Kennedy. (McNamara reportedly had been offered his choice of either the defense position or that of secretary of the treasury.) Although a registered Republican at the time, McNamara could best be described as being in the liberal camp of that party and had supported Kennedy in the 1960 election. His belief that people have an obligation to accept public service, combined with a personal admiration for President Kennedy and a recognition of the opportunities and challenges of a new administration, led to his decision to leave the automotive industry, despite the personal financial sacrifices it entailed.

Thus, in 1961 McNamara entered a period of long and distinguished service in the public sector. At the Defense Department, he attempted to apply systems analysis to streamline and cut costs of the multitudinous, often duplicative, and expensive military programs then in existence. At the same time he wanted to improve the defense posture of the United States by introducing efficient new weapons systems. In this respect he was following goals and strategies similar to those he had successfully introduced at Ford. He remained secretary of defense until 1968, a period which coincided with increasing American involvement in Vietnam under Presidents Kennedy and Johnson. McNamara initially supported that war and helped shape policy regarding it. However, he became increasingly skeptical regarding its merits and the possibility of victory, and these attitudes eventually led to his resignation.

Shortly thereafter he accepted the leadership of the World Bank, a post he held until 1981. Since then, McNamara has used his experience in foreign affairs and his position as elder statesman to lobby, both individually and with private foundations, for ideas that he thinks will enhance the prospects of world peace, especially a nuclear freeze.

In recognition of his achievements, McNamara has been awarded the United States Medal of Freedom and the Albert Einstein Peace Prize. He also has received approximately twenty honorary degrees from colleges and universities, beginning with an LL.D. from the University of Alabama in 1955, and including such prestigious institutions as Harvard, Princeton, Columbia, and the University of California.

Harking back to his academic roots, McNamara has remained an avid reader throughout his life, especially in the fields of sociology, history, and philosophy. (At Ford, he had a reputation for always wanting to discuss whatever book he had just read.) He also has continued his interest in outdoor pursuits, especially skiing and mountain climbing, activities he began during his boyhood. Other interests reportedly include art, music, and playing chess.

References:

David Halberstam, *The Reckoning* (New York: William Morrow, 1986);

Booton Herndon, *Ford: An Unconventional Biography of the Men and Their Times* (New York: Weybright & Talley, 1969);

Robert Lacey, *Ford: The Men and the Machine* (Boston: Little, Brown, 1986);

Henry L. Trewhitt, *McNamara* (New York: Harper & Row, 1971);

Brock Yates, *The Decline and Fall of the American Automobile Industry* (New York: Empire, 1983).

Archives:

McNamara's business papers can be found in the Executive Files of Robert S. McNamara, 1956-1960, Ford Motor Company Industrial Archives, Redford, Michigan.

Management

by John B. Rae

Harvey Mudd College

Management methods in the American automobile industry have been a developing art, changing as the industry expanded and becoming more complicated. In the early days management problems appeared to be reasonably simple; companies were small, so that there was no elaborate organization to control. In general, since all cars were assembled from parts made elsewhere, financing was accomplished by buying from suppliers on credit and selling to dealers for cash. The main problem was, therefore, to build and sell operational vehicles before the suppliers' bills came due. The process may sound easy in theory; in practice the early automobile business had a horrifyingly high attrition rate: almost 2,000 separate firms are on record as having produced motor vehicles commercially in the United States since 1896.

The entrepreneurs who went into motor vehicle manufacturing had critical choices to make. First and most important was what kind of car to build: gasoline, steam, or electric. In the period between 1896 and about 1920, this choice was far from obvious. Electric automobiles were very popular for local travel in cities and towns; and both electric and steam cars were easier to operate than the early gasoline-powered vehicles. Even when the gasoline engine became dominant, there were still technical choices: transmission systems, for instance, and some claims for two- rather than four-cycle engines. The successful firms were most likely to be those in which technical and managerial skills were combined. Conspicuously, the Ford Motor Company benefited from the fact that Henry Ford's mechanical abilities were supplemented by the ability of his business manager, James S. Couzens. Couzens handled the company's finances and, with Norval A. Hawkins, built the Ford dealer organization.

Alfred P. Sloan, Jr., has observed that in those pioneering years of the automobile industry, selling the cars was easy; the big problem was producing them. Consequently, managerial effort in those days concentrated on building the vehicles as promptly and economically as possible. Good production men were the most valued members of an executive staff, such as P. E. Martin, factory manager at Ford, or Walter Flanders, who began at Ford, went to his own company, Everitt-Metzger-Flanders (EMF), and then to Maxwell. They arranged the placement of machine tools for maximum efficiency, organized work gangs for chassis assembly, and in due course paved the way to the moving assembly line.

However, even then production was not the whole story. Ransom E. Olds achieved the first real production miracle in the American automobile industry with the curved-dash, one-cylinder buggy that became the "Merry Oldsmobile." By skillful plant organization, Olds was able to increase output of his runabout to a phenomenal 5,000 in

1904, but then he and his backers, Samuel and Frederick Smith, had a dispute over policy. They wanted to concentrate more on building heavy touring cars instead of the lightweight buggies, and since they controlled most of the stock in the Olds Motor Works, Olds was forced out. Henry Ford had a similar dispute with his principal backer, Alexander Malcolmson, but Ford was able to buy Malcolmson's interest, a purchase which gave him a majority of the stock in the Ford Motor Company. The Smiths have been criticized for shortsightedness, but in retrospect it appears more likely that they were right. The Olds buggy was far too light to stand up to the poor American roads of that day; when Olds returned to the automobile industry under the name Reo, he emphasized a heavier touring model rather than a lightweight runabout.

In 1905 the United States overtook France as the world's leading producer of motor vehicles. The rapid growth of the American automobile industry opened the way for, and in fact required, more sophisticated managerial techniques. It is an oversimplification to say that the era of the individual technician-entrepreneur came to an end; it had never actually existed. There were such figures, conspicuously Henry Ford, but for the most part American automobile companies were offshoots of manufacturers of bicycles, carriages and wagons, sewing machines, stationary gas engines, and such odds and ends as electrical equipment (Packard) and plumbing supplies (Buick). As the vehicle manufacturers grew and competition intensified, attempts at combining automobile firms developed. This first decade of the twentieth century was the era of the great trusts; the idea of forming an automobile monopoly or something close to it grew naturally in that atmosphere.

The activities of William C. Durant, Benjamin Briscoe, and John North Willys in this direction are described elsewhere. It is sufficient to say here that the combinations they formed all suffered from being loose assortments of motor vehicle and supplier firms, put together largely from what happened to be available in the industry and with no planned or orderly relationship to each other. Nor was there any effective central management structure. In each case whatever coordination and control existed lay entirely in the hands of the organizers: Durant or Briscoe or Willys. Of these efforts only General Motors (GM) survived in approximately its original form. Briscoe's United States

Motor Company lasted only two years from 1910 to 1912 before collapsing. It was reorganized as the Maxwell Motor Car Company with Walter Flanders in charge. Flanders reduced the sprawling organization to some measure of efficiency in production but did nothing with the financial structure. Maxwell went bankrupt in the early 1920s, was reorganized by Walter Chrysler, and soon afterward became the Chrysler Corporation. The various corporate reincarnations in this process have the interesting effect that Albert A. Pope's Columbia car of 1897 can be regarded as a remote ancestor of the Chrysler.

The Willys empire also collapsed in the 1920 recession. Willys was able to salvage the Willys-Overland Company, only to see it go into receivership in 1933. It was revived and after World War II became part of Kaiser-Frazer. Its one asset by then was the manufacture of the Jeep, and that was sold to American Motors and since to Chrysler.

The survival of GM after its collapse in 1910 has to be credited to the much-abused "bankers trust" that took charge of the company under the leadership of James Jackson Storrow. The trust promoted Charles W. Nash to be president of GM and undertook a thorough housecleaning. The automobile lines were cut to four (Buick, Cadillac, Oakland, and Oldsmobile), and truck manufacture was concentrated in the GM Truck division. Some of the plants of the discarded companies were converted to making parts; the remainder were abandoned. An engineering department was created to do research (the ancestor of the GM Technical Center). Rigorous financial discipline restored GM to solvency but also opened the way for Durant's return to power through exchanging stock of his Chevrolet Motor Car Company for GM stock on which the Storrow-Nash regime was not paying dividends.

Throughout this period the Ford Motor Company was a monolithic organization, totally controlled by its founder. Henry Ford professed to have no use for formal organization. He boasted that none of his executives had titles or specified functions; a man simply came into the company, found a niche that he could fill, and worked there. It is doubtful if this administrative anarchy was ever as complete as Ford professed, but it did foster rivalries among Ford executives, which Ford evidently considered to be desirable. His autocracy was solidified when he bought out all his stockholders in 1919, following a court case in which the Dodge brothers successfully compelled the Ford Motor Company to distribute a larger share of its enormous profits as dividends. To Henry Ford shareholders were parasites who contributed nothing to the functioning of his company.

For a time the Ford system, or lack of it, appeared to be a brilliant success. The Ford achievements in production astonished the world. They were studied and written about exhaustively, almost always in laudatory terms. Little attention was given to the persistent attrition among the ablest Ford executives: Couzens, Hawkins, C. H. Wills, Flanders, Knudsen, all gone by the beginning of the 1920s. In 1919 Edsel Ford officially became president of the Ford Motor Company, but he was never allowed to exercise real authority. The weakness of the Ford system soon became evident, and managers began to look for alternatives.

The 1920s brought a new era to management in the automobile industry and to industry in general, in the form of the organizational structure worked out for GM by Alfred P. Sloan, Jr. Sloan's rise to the presidency of GM has been recounted elsewhere, along with an outline of his reforms in management. His system has been described as following the staff-and-line pattern of a military organization. To some extent it did, but it went farther. Sloan's basic premises were: there should be a central authority with power to establish policy and coordinate the activities of the corporation; there should be a clear definition of the functions of the central authority and the separate divisions; and the corporation was too big to be run by one man. The structure that he designed was intended to provide the necessary central authority while giving the separate divisions a maximum of responsibility for their own affairs.

The reorganization plan became fully effective in 1924. Authority flowed from the board of directors through two committees, executive and finance, the former responsible for operating policy and the latter for financial policy. Active management was in the hands of the president, who was also chairman of the executive committee. The implementing of financial policy was the function of the vice-president, who was chairman of the finance committee. The corporation had three major subdivisions: finance, operations, and advisory services. The decentralizing feature of the plan appears most clearly under operations, where each division was to be as far as possible self-contained and at least semi-autonomous. Finally, there were the interdivisional relations committees, designed to promote coordination among the divisions.

Judged by results, the GM organization was a conspicuous success. The company grew rapidly to become the country's, and in fact the world's, largest manufacturer of motor vehicles. There was little immediate imitation, simply because only one other automobile company was big enough to be able to use such a system, and Henry Ford continued to reject the concept of formal organization. When the Chrysler Corporation emerged in the latter part of the 1920s as the third member of the Big Three, it adopted an organizational plan partially modeled on GM's.

The depression of the 1930s brought a major change to the automobile industry. Most of the smaller firms vanished, leaving for practical purposes the Big Three and five independents: Hudson, Nash, Packard, Studebaker, and Willys-Overland. There were also some separate truck manufacturers. The depression and the New Deal brought some new problems to automobile management but little change in structure. As the market for cars shrank, complaints from dealers became an important issue. The dealers protested against arbitrary cancellation of franchises, failure of the manufacturers to protect territorial rights, and forced acceptance of unordered cars. No solution was found, but GM and Chrysler led the way in establishing means for improving relations with dealers.

The New Deal brought vigorous union activity, resisted at first by the previously open-shop industry. After much conflict GM accepted the United Automobile Workers (UAW) as the bargaining agent for its employees in 1937, and the rest of the industry followed soon afterward, except for Ford, which held out until 1941 and then yielded reluctantly under the threat of government intervention to prevent stoppage of the production of war materials.

The quality of Ford management was in a prolonged decline. In the 1930s the aging and ailing Henry Ford came under the influence of Harry Bennett, head of the Ford Service Department. In the name of security Bennett cut Henry Ford off from the rest of the company and issued orders in his name. Edsel Ford was ignored, and management became a contest for power between Bennett and

Charles E. Sorensen, who managed production. By the mid 1930s the Ford Motor Company had fallen behind Chrysler in total sales.

World War II brought a major challenge to automotive management. Passenger car manufacturing was halted, but the companies found themselves with greatly expanded demands on their capacity to produce, and the available managerial talent had to be spread out to operate both existing facilities with vastly increased output and the new plants built by the government to make war materials. To complicate matters most of what had to be built were items that automobile companies had never made before, and which most of their executives had never even seen before. This challenge was met brilliantly. The motor vehicle industry was the nation's largest single reservoir of manufacturing capacity, and between 1940 and 1945 it produced 20 percent of America's entire output of war materials.

During the immediate postwar years automobile management was concerned with the adjustments of returning to peacetime operation and coping with a pent-up desire for cars. Labor relations were a major complication but were resolved without undue difficulty. GM broke new ground in 1948 with contract provisions linking wage increases to the Department of Labor's Cost of Living Index and an "improvement factor" providing for increases in response to technical advances that raised productivity. Both ideas originated with Charles E. Wilson. Then in 1955 the Ford Motor Company introduced a plan for supplemental unemployment benefits. Meanwhile the remaining independent firms were seeking survival through combination. In 1954 Hudson and Nash united as American Motors and Studebaker and Packard as Studebaker-Packard. The results were mixed; Studebaker-Packard ceased automobile production by 1965, while American Motors struggled into the 1970s before coming under the control of France's Renault and eventually being bought by Chrysler in 1987.

The most interesting managerial change occurred at the Ford Motor Company. Edsel Ford's sudden death in 1943 created an acute managerial crisis, because his father was no longer able to run the company. Edsel's oldest son, Henry Ford II, had to be brought back from the Navy to take charge, and even then he had to face a fight for power with Harry Bennett. The hostility of the women of the Ford family doomed Bennett, making sure that the stock owned by the elder Henry Ford and by Edsel's family (the only voting stock) was voted to make young Henry president. Bennett left soon afterward, and Charles E. Sorensen was made the scapegoat for the disappointing performance of the giant Willow Run aircraft factory, so that the new president had no challenger in the company.

Henry Ford II was aware that the Ford Motor Company was in poor condition, but he was appalled at what he actually found. He was acutely aware of his own inexperience and decided first that he had to have help, and second that Ford ought to have a GM type of organization. To this end he recruited Ernest Breech, at the time president of GM's Bendix Corporation, as executive vice-president of the Ford Motor Company. Breech then reorganized Ford much as his mentor Alfred P. Sloan had reorganized GM.

The Ford Motor Company was also strongly influenced by a group of ex-Air Force officers who had worked on financial controls for the Air Force during the war and then offered their services to Ford. They became known as the "Whiz Kids," and two of them, Robert McNamara and Arjay Miller, eventually rose to the presidency of the company. Their influence was very strong for a style of management based on elaborate and rigorous mathematical calculation of financial control and projections.

In 1955 the American automobile industry was in a seemingly enviable position. It dominated its domestic market and much of the world market, the United States producing two-thirds of the world's motor vehicles. It was to be expected that this happy situation would not last. Other industrial nations saw their own motor vehicle output expand as they recovered from World War II, and automobile ownership and use rose to levels comparable with the United States. Yet the question of the quality of American management in meeting changed conditions had to be faced. Admittedly managing a mature, established industry calls for different skills and techniques than are required to build that industry from scratch, but in the second half of the century American management of the automobile industry was hardly inspiring. Few outstanding figures emerged: Breech at Ford; George Romney, who introduced the first American compacts at American Motors but then left for a political career; and Lee Iacocca, one-time Ford president who can be credited with saving Chrysler from bankruptcy.

Part of the problem was a change in the character of top management. The technical people of the earlier years—Ford, Chrysler, Sloan, who was trained as an engineer—were replaced by executives whose backgrounds were in finance or sales. The atmosphere in which they worked invited complacency and caution. With the American companies so dominant, there was little incentive to innovate, because innovation was expensive and risky. Price competition was negligible. The rest of the industry followed GM's pricing policies. However, GM was not completely free to set prices, because the threat of the antitrust laws compelled it to set prices that would enable its competitors to stay in business. One result was that new techniques, like front-wheel drive and disk brakes, came from Europe.

The American companies preferred to make big cars because they were more profitable and were what American buyers seemed to want. Here a word has to be said for American management on this issue. Americans do have a preference for larger cars with accessories like power steering, power brakes, and air conditioning. There were panic swings to small cars during the oil shortages of the 1970s, but once the shortages ended there was a noticeable return to at least medium-sized cars, but not to the absurd behemoths of the 1950s and 1960s. Nevertheless there was unwarranted complacency about the rising popularity of smaller cars, especially imports. The attitude was that whenever the American companies chose to build compacts, they would "drive the imports into the sea." The American companies did make compacts, but import sales continued to rise.

The difficulty was that the finance and sales executives had no great interest in or understanding of the technical side of the automobile business (the technical people referred to them contemptuously as "bean counters"). The emphasis was on pushing out cars as rapidly as possible and relying on style and glamour to sell them. Yet the manufacture of motor vehicles is first and foremost an engineering operation. Neglect of this elementary fact had the unfortunate consequence that in time American cars came to be regarded as inferior in quality to European and particularly to Japanese cars.

Nor was American automotive management any happier in its response to new problems that emerged in the 1960s and 1970s and brought governmental pressure, problems such as atmospheric pollution, safety, and fuel economy. The industry's usual response was first to deny that the problem existed, then to admit that it did but that it had no solution, and finally to say that there was a solution but that it would be time-consuming and expensive—which was usually correct.

The oil shortage of 1979 again swung buyers to compact cars and precipitated a severe crisis in the American automobile industry, as imports captured up to one-third of total sales. This oil shortage was too slight and too brief to have been more than a catalyst. The causes of the crisis had been growing over the past thirty years. They include the complacency in management and the unwillingness to innovate that have been mentioned. In addition the industry was burdened with high labor costs. During the years since World War II the UAW had adopted a strategy of singling out one of the Big Three to negotiate with when contract renewals came due. The victim was then faced with the prospect of being closed down by a strike while its competitors were still in business. In an inflationary economy it was easier to make concessions to the union and add the cost to the price of the cars, knowing that the rest of the industry was going to have to make the same concessions.

Chrysler was hit particularly hard. It was the smallest of the Big Three to start with, and it had suffered from periodic poor judgment in the models it produced. It had also engaged during the 1960s in an ill-advised and expensive venture into the European market by buying control of two weak companies, Rootes in Britain and Simca in France. As a result, by 1978 the Chrysler Corporation was faced with bankruptcy, and there was a lively debate over whether the United States government should intervene to salvage it or simply let it go out of business. In the end concern over the adverse effects of a Chrysler bankruptcy prevailed. The government guaranteed $1.5 billion in loans and Lee Iacocca, former Ford president, was brought in to rehabilitate the company, which he did with striking success. Within five years Chrysler was restored to profitability, and the loans were paid off.

The Ford Motor Company was fortunate in that its foreign business remained profitable, but it had its own variety of managerial problems. Henry Ford II increasingly displayed his grandfather's trait of getting rid of executives who appeared to threaten his primacy in the company. Breech left in 1961, when Ford became board chairman. No president stayed long, although McNamara might have done so if he had not gone to Washington to be secretary of defense. The company did well enough until the crisis years, even though its venture in 1957 with the Edsel, a car in the range between the Lincoln and the Mercury, was a highly publicized failure.

The GM situation is more difficult to describe. The company seemed in good condition until the 1980 crisis, but no really outstanding executive appeared after Charles E. Wilson, and there were no really outstanding achievements. On the contrary, when a crusading attorney named Ralph Nader attacked the GM Corvair as inherently unsafe, the company's management responded so ineptly that GM had to make a substantial out-of-court settlement with Nader. There were some changes in structure, notably the creation of an assembly division with overall responsibility for manufacturing the lower-priced models. Even without structural change, there was obviously a greater degree of centralized control than Alfred P. Sloan had originally contemplated.

In the 1980s the management of the American automobile industry was faced with critical decisions. For the American producers to be effectively competitive in their own domestic market, let alone the world market, they needed to reduce costs, bring their production techniques up to the level achieved by the Japanese and the Germans, and above all convince the American public that domestically built cars were as well made as the foreign models. In the face of mounting layoffs the UAW agreed to some limited wage concessions, and experiments were undertaken with methods of industrial relations tested in Japan and Sweden, in which work teams were organized to break away from the rigid-ity of the assembly line and give the workers more responsibility in the production process. There was expanded use of robots and computers in production, again following Japanese and European experience, and there was association with the competition in the form of agreements between American and foreign firms for joint production. Beyond that there was widespread recourse by the American manufacturers to "outsourcing," having parts and components made in countries where labor costs were lower than in the United States.

The United States share of the world market for motor vehicles fell from the two-thirds of the 1950s to one-fifth in 1980. This was not in itself a sign of American decline; it was rather the consequence of growth in automobile ownership and use in the rest of the world. However, it was assuredly an indication that the automobile industry was facing radically different conditions from those to which it had been accustomed. This was the challenge that management had to meet.

References:

Alfred D. Chandler, *Strategy and Structure, Chapters in the History of the Industrial Enterprise* (Cambridge, Mass.: MIT Press, 1962);

Peter F. Drucker, *The Concept of the Corporation* (New York: John Day, 1946);

Henry Ford, with Samuel Crowther, *My Life and Work* (Garden City, N.Y.: Doubleday, 1922);

David Halberstam, *The Reckoning* (New York: William Morrow, 1986);

Alfred P. Sloan, Jr., *My Years with General Motors* (Garden City, N.Y.: Doubleday, 1964);

Lawrence J. White, *The Automobile Industry Since 1945* (Cambridge, Mass.: Harvard University Press, 1971).

Marketing

by George S. May

Eastern Michigan University

The techniques and strategies used to market automobiles changed drastically during the 1920s. Prior to that decade automobiles were still something of a novelty, and those who purchased them were, in the great majority of cases, people who had never owned a car before. It was a seller's market, and the major concern of the automakers was to try to produce enough cars to satisfy the demand. Automobiles were advertised extensively, but, in a period in which there were hundreds of automobile companies, the ads were designed more to make the public aware of a company's existence than to sell cars. As long as an automobile performed reasonably well, its manufacturer could be assured that a buyer would not be hard to find. Henry Ford demonstrated this for years by spending nothing on advertising while his Model T was setting new sales records each year.

Already in 1911 Hugh Chalmers was warning his fellow automobile manufacturers against producing too many cars because, he said, "there is only a certain percentage of men of enough means to buy motor cars." Another industry observer in 1912 declared that demand no longer exceeded supply, and the future of the industry now depended "on our ability to intensify retail sales." But claims that the market was saturated do not seem to have been justified until the mid 1920s. In 1927 an industry trade association declared that for the first time the majority of sales were made not to people who were buying their first car but to those who were seeking a replacement for a car they already owned. The national dealers' association argued that 1924 was the year in which replacement sales exceeded those of first-time car buyers. Regardless of the disagreement over when, it was clear the seller's market that had favored the manufacturers since the beginnings of car production in 1896 had ended after some thirty years. Nevertheless, around 40 percent of the country's households still did not own a car.

In the early 1920s automobile advertisements began to focus on expanding the market to women

In some cases the individuals or families involved did not want a car or could not use one, but in the majority of cases they could not afford an automobile. A quarter of a century would pass before economic prosperity would begin to reduce the percentage of households without automobiles. By the 1980s this figure had fallen to less than 15 percent.

Thus in the 1920s the industry had to adjust to the fact that the majority of potential automobile buyers already possessed vehicles. The major reason General Motors (GM) in the 1920s took the leadership in sales and earnings from Ford was because it was far quicker than its competitor in realizing the need to change its approach. While Henry Ford remained confident that he could continue to produce more and more Model T's, which would then be absorbed by a market which he felt was far from the saturation point, GM's Alfred P. Sloan, Jr., recognized that the focus of his company's efforts had to be shifted from the production of cars to their selling.

There were a number of approaches that the companies used to stimulate interest among customers who were now familiar with the concept of the automobile. The basic approach of the early advertisements, which had been intended to arouse the curiosity of and stimulate discussion among potential customers unfamiliar with automobiles, gave way to one that stressed the pleasures of driving and the satisfaction that would come with owning a particular make of car. At a time when there were few new mechanical features that could be used to distinguish one car from another, the styling of a car began to receive more attention as a means of drawing the attention of buyers. The practice of introducing new models each year dated back to the annual automobile shows at the start of the century, but GM in the 1920s helped to institutionalize the marketing concept of introducing new models each year, models which were generally distinguishable from the previous year's models only by their outer appearances. GM, under Sloan, also encouraged those who might own one of the company's less expensive cars to trade up and purchase a model in the next price range, a step up not only in expense but also in prestige. In the mid 1920s GM introduced the Pontiac and the LaSalle to fill slots in their lineup of cars where the gap in the price range was too great. This was all part of the corporation's announced goal of providing a car "for every purse and purpose." Another approach that became widely used sought to encourage people to buy a second car. The slogan "A car for her" played upon the need of the wife and mother to have a car for her own use when the husband and father used the family car to drive to work. By the end of the 1920s the two-car family, which had been a rarity ten years earlier, was much more common, as reflected in the number of new homes being built with double garages.

Important as these and other advertising and promotional approaches may have been in stimulating sales, by far the most important stimulus came from the adoption of installment sales plans. Selling cars for cash had worked in the early days when demand exceeded supply, and it continued to work for producers of low-priced cars, particularly Ford, who attracted cash customers through the use of mass-production techniques that enabled them to turn out ever larger numbers of cars at ever lower prices. Luxury car manufacturers, too, could continue to sell for cash since they were selling to customers for whom the price of the car was less important. Producers of medium-priced cars first felt the need to provide alternative means of payment to their customers by offering an arrangement that allowed the buyer to make a down payment upon receipt of the car and then to pay off the remainder of the price over a series of months. The establishment in 1915 of the Guaranty Securities Company by John North Willys to finance time sales of his Overland and Willys-Knight cars was the first major step in this direction, and by the 1920s there were hundreds of companies offering similar financing. GM was again in the forefront, creating the General Motors Acceptance Corporation (GMAC) in 1919 as its credit subsidiary. For nearly ten years Ford resisted the trend before it too established a similar credit subsidiary in the face of sales figures showing an overwhelming majority of cars being sold through such credit plans. The percentage of sales financed in this way has varied considerably through the years from over 70 percent in the early 1920s to as low as 50 percent in the immediate post-World War II era, but it eventually stabilized at around two-thirds of annual sales.

No matter what the automobile companies did to promote sales, the actual job of selling the cars rested with the dealers. By the 1920s relatively few cars were purchased directly from the factory, a practice that had been common in earlier years but accounted for only 4 percent of GM's sales at that time. The practice of wholesaling cars to distributors, who served as middlemen between the manufacturer and dealers operating in the area assigned to the distributor, was also largely a thing of the past, as manufacturers now dealt directly with franchised agents who sold the manufacturer's car in a particular locality.

Automobile dealers had always played an important role in the marketing of cars, but the market-saturated conditions of the 1920s called for dealers who did more than simply take orders but who

1928

World's Largest Selling "6"
—and Women by *Thousands* are Swelling These Sales

In the way women by thousands are turning to Essex is a story of the great and dynamic "man's Super-Six" made beautiful for women.

In all 6-cylinder history there has never been such spectacular acceptance of any car as that which everywhere greets the new Essex Super-Six. It is outselling all other "Sixes", and its own previous records, by such outstanding margins as to leave no doubt of its leadership.

In some places its sales excel its former mark by 100%, 200% and 300%. In Detroit, for instance, where automobile values are understood better than anywhere in the world, Essex sales have been greater than the *next three* "Sixes" combined.

Such success can only reflect an accurate and unmistakable public appreciation that Essex is the World's Greatest Value—Altogether or Part by Part—Please Compare.

Simple, Compact and Convenient

1. Light control   2. Horn button   3. Throttle
4. Radiator shutter control   5. Starter   6. Electro-lock
7. Gasoline gauge   8. Choke

COUPE $745 (Rumble Seat $20 extra). COACH $735. SEDAN (4 door) $795.
All prices f. o. b. Detroit, plus war excise tax

HUDSON MOTOR CAR COMPANY, DETROIT, MICHIGAN

ESSEX SUPER SIX

By 1928 women were an increasingly significant part of the automobile market, as this advertisement attests

were also capable of actively selling. A major reason for Walter Chrysler's purchase of Dodge in 1928 was to obtain the Dodge network of dealers, which was generally considered one of the two or three best in the country. Such dealers, Chrysler recognized, were necessary to assure the survival of his new corporation. The inability of other entrepreneurs attempting to enter the industry to acquire or to create effective dealer networks was one of the main causes of their failures.

Despite their importance in the marketing of the cars, however, the relationship between the dealers and the companies has often been strained. This results largely from the very nature of the business in which the dealers are involved. Traditionally, many automobile dealers have been among the leading businessmen in their communities and have been among the most influential shapers of local business and civic policies. But except for some metropolitan dealers they have rarely grown large enough to exert any great influence on the policies of the companies with which they are associated.

That association stems from the franchise they have been granted; and to them, as writer Peter Drucker observes, the term "carries with it the implication of a vested right which can be taken away only under 'due process' and 'just compensation.'. . . To the dealer, the 'franchise' is capital, 'his' capital," but to the manufacturer the franchise is simply a selling agreement, "freely made for a limited period, revocable under conditions laid down by the manufacturer, and renewable only at the manufacturer's pleasure." The manufacturer, Drucker declares, "cannot admit that the dealer has any right to the 'selling agreement' nor can he allow the dealer to sell or transfer this agreement as if it were his property. In other words, to stay in business the dealer must succeed in holding on to his 'franchise' while the manufacturer in order to stay in business must be able to cancel his 'selling agreement.' "

The abuses that could result when the manufacturer used his power to cancel the selling agreement to force products on the dealer was illustrated in 1921 when Henry Ford forced his dealers to accept and pay for Model T's they had not ordered as a means of raising the money he needed to repay loans that were coming due later that year. Faced with the threat of having their franchises revoked if they did not accept the shipment, most dealers went to their local banks and borrowed the money needed to pay for the cars. Sales of cars were down from their normal levels because of economic conditions, but the Ford dealers knew that when the economy picked up, their franchise would again be profitable. Later in the decade, however, when Model T sales began lagging, Ford undercut these loyal dealers by setting up many new Ford dealerships down the street or across the road from existing agencies, in the belief that the competition would force the older dealers to be more aggressive. In the 1930s Ford again dumped cars on his dealers as a means of reducing inventories at the factory. In rural areas Ford sales managers often forced dealers to take a shipment of Ford tractors in the winter, a season when few farmers were in the market for a tractor. During the depression, when many farmers could not afford to buy a new tractor, this practice became even more absurd.

GM, on the other hand, followed a more conciliatory policy toward its dealers. Although recognizing that at times the dealers should make sacrifices to aid the company in reducing its inventories, it sought to adjust its production schedules to control inventories. By carefully analyzing orders and sales figures received every ten days from all dealers and adding these to other data on factors affecting the market, the buildup of excessive inventories was avoided. GM also provided assistance to its dealers handling the sale of used cars taken in trade and offered some financial assistance beyond that provided through the GMAC support for credit sales of cars. In 1934 the General Motors Dealer Council was established, providing representatives of the dealers the opportunity to meet with top-level corporation officials to discuss distribution policies. A Dealer Relations Board was established in 1938 as a review body to which a dealer who had a complaint could file an appeal. Sloan, the corporation's chief executive officer, served as the first chairman of this review board. He felt that the principal benefit served by the board "was a preventive one. Divisions made very sure they had a sound case and were observing all the equities in taking action against any dealer, for it was the division itself, as well as the dealer, that came up for executive review."

Complaints regarding dealer-company relationships and the policies of dealers toward their customers were investigated by the Federal Trade Commission and by Congress in the late 1930s, but no action was taken until after World War II. In the 1950s, when the booming sales of the postwar period began to sag, there were widespread complaints from consumers' groups regarding the tactics used by dealers to sell their cars. These complaints resulted in the passage in 1958 of the Automotive Information Disclosure Act, sponsored by Senator Mike Monroney, and requiring every new car offered for sale to have a price sticker, which is still called the "Monroney sticker," that lists all items included in that particular vehicle and the manufacturer's suggested retail price for the car and for any optional equipment included. This was designed to make it impossible for dealers to engage in the kinds of misleading sales tactics with which they were charged. The dealers, however, re-

sponded that these tactics were the result of pressure put on them by the manufacturer. This led to the passage in 1956 of the Automobile Dealers' Day in Court Act which was designed to protect the dealers from some of the more flagrant sales pressures put on them. Nevertheless, the possibility for abuse remained, and in slow-selling periods dealers were still asked to help out, willingly or unwillingly, by adding to their inventory cars that might sit on their lots for a long period. Every day they remained unsold cost the dealer interest on the money he borrowed to purchase the cars.

By the 1980s the trend was toward fewer and bigger dealerships. In contrast to earlier days, many now sold more than one manufacturer's cars, some of them offering a veritable supermarket of cars, not only imports, which dealers had begun selling as a sideline in the 1950s, but sometimes cars of competing American automakers. In addition to selling cars on the installment plan, with payments by the late 1980s commonly spread out over a five-year period, the domestic manufacturers, beginning with Chrysler in 1974, sought to move slow-selling models by offering "incentives," rebating a certain amount of the price of the car to those who signed up to buy one. By the 1980s this practice was followed by all of the companies, and when a reporter asked Ford's Don Petersen why did they not simply cut the price of the car he replied that the customers had become accustomed to the incentives and that without them, cars did not sell. Such a response shows that good marketing does not always parallel good logic.

References:

Peter F. Drucker, *Concept of the Corporation* (New York: John Day, 1972);

James J. Flink, *The Automobile Age* (Cambridge, Mass.: MIT Press, 1988);

George S. May, *The Automobile in American Life* (Forthcoming, 1990);

Alfred P. Sloan, Jr., *My Years With General Motors* (Garden City, N.Y.: Doubleday, 1964).

Homer Martin

(August 15, 1901-January 22, 1968)

by John Barnard

Oakland University

CAREER: Vice-president (1935-1936), president, United Automobile Workers-American Federation of Labor (1936); president, United Automobile Workers-Congress of Industrial Organizations (1936-1939); president, United Automobile Workers-American Federation of Labor (1939-1940).

Warren Homer Martin, the first elected president of the United Automobile Workers (UAW), was born on August 15, 1901, in Goreville, Illinois, in the southernmost part of the state. He was the son of W. H. Martin, a farmer, and Sidney F. Smith Martin. The family was poor. Martin received his early education in Goreville and finished high school at Southern Illinois Normal College in nearby Carbondale in 1920. While a student he supported himself by working on local farms, with a railroad section gang, and as a preacher. In 1922 Martin was ordained and appointed pastor of the Goreville Baptist Church. He also taught school and attended Ewing College in Ewing, Illinois. A talented athlete, in 1924 and 1925 he was Amateur Athletic Union champion in the hop, skip, and jump competition, an achievement that led to the nickname, "The Leaping Parson."

Married in 1922 to Norma May Graves, Martin moved to Liberty, Missouri, northeast of Kansas City, in 1926, where he became pastor of a local Baptist church and attended William Jewell College, graduating in 1928. In 1932 he received a call from the Baptist church in the Leeds district of Kansas City, Missouri, and took postgraduate work at the Kansas City Baptist Theological Seminary in Kansas City, Kansas. While preaching in Kansas City, the site of a Chevrolet assembly plant, Martin came into contact with autoworkers, many of whom attended his church. Their economic insecurity and the harsh conditions of their labor moved him to compassion. Expressing his sentiments in his sermons, he criticized the management of the plant and urged the formation of a union. Although these views were popular with the workers in his congregation, the church's officers objected, and Martin was dismissed. He found employment at the Chevrolet factory as a trimmer on the truck cab line, where, putting precept into practice, he became an active union organizer. He was chosen president of the American Federation of Labor (AFL) Federal Labor Union No. 19320, which he had helped to establish, and in June 1934 went to Detroit, Michigan, as a delegate to the first national, AFL-sponsored conference of autoworkers. As a member of the national council established at this conference, an advisory body to the AFL, Martin emerged as a potential leader in an autoworkers union. Soon after the conference, however, he was fired from his job at Chevrolet. Thereafter, he devoted all of his time to union matters.

In August 1935 the AFL, trying to keep pace with the upsurge of prounion sentiment in the automotive plants, issued a charter to the UAW and convoked its first national convention. Over the objections of nearly all of the delegates, the AFL kept the UAW on a probationary tether by appointing its officers. Francis J. Dillon, an AFL stalwart but without experience as an autoworker, was named president. Martin, whose martyr's halo, autoworker experience, and rousing oratory had already brought him fame, was appointed vice-president. Soon he was devoting all of his time to organizing campaigns in midwestern automobile cities; early in 1936 he moved to Detroit, the industry's center. Displeased both with the AFL's refusal to endorse wholeheartedly industrial unions and with Dillon's inactivity, the autoworkers demanded their independence. At the UAW's South Bend, Indiana, convention in April 1936, the AFL quietly withdrew its control, and Martin, the only nominee for the post, was elected president on April 29, 1936, by a unanimous vote. Two months later the UAW formally aligned itself with the Committee (later Congress) of Industrial Organizations (CIO), the emerging giant in industrial unionism.

The time for automobile unionism had arrived. Since the launching of the New Deal, stirrings of revolt had coursed through the automotive plants, leading to strikes and workers' organizations. The passage of the National Labor Relations (Wagner) Act in 1935 bestowed the endorsement of the national government upon the industrial workers' quest for independent unions. The UAW, which claimed a membership of only 32,000 in 1936 and was virtually without open support among the employees of General Motors, Ford, and Chrysler, was about to explode. By 1941, after a series of massive strikes, it had negotiated contracts with all the important firms in the industry and grown to a membership of more than 600,000. No other major labor organization expanded so rapidly or came so quickly to represent the work force of its industry. By 1941, however, Martin had been driven out of office in disgrace after a prolonged, bitter, and, at times, violent struggle within the union.

Martin's strength lay in his mastery of the word, a skill much needed and in demand in the early days of the UAW. His medium, the oratorical style of border-state Baptists, perfectly suited a message of compassion, justice, and salvation for the downtrodden. The union had replaced the church, but the biblical imagery and cadences marched on. "Homer," one autoworker later recalled, "could lead you down the sawdust trail." Naturally, Martin's secular sermons most appealed to the many border-state and southern-born workers who had poured into the automotive factories since the 1920s. First in Kansas City and later in automobile cities throughout the Midwest, Martin's speeches at organizing meetings struck a chord in the hearts of thousands who thereupon made their decision, this time not for Jesus, but for the UAW. In the union's early days, when commitment entailed such risks as losing one's job, an emotional appeal was a necessity. As time passed and the union became more securely established, it was less important.

Difficulties of many kinds surfaced soon after Martin became president. With the potential of becoming one of the most powerful organizations in industrial America, the UAW quickly attracted a swarm of young, eager, ambitious, and talented leaders, many of whom, despite their youth, had more experience and training in union activities and in politics than did Martin. Several of the early leaders of the UAW were "progressives" in their political leanings, including some Communists, and they were well represented on the executive board. Distrust soon appeared, and Martin began to form an alliance with conservative board members, including former Dillon supporters. The political breach steadily widened. Martin, furthermore, was never able to establish administrative control of the union. Initiative remained with the locals with little central direction, a situation that defeated effective strategic planning. In fall 1936 a sit-down strike at the South Bend plant of Bendix Corporation revealed Martin's many shortcomings as a negotiator. He unaccountably disappeared at crucial moments, took inconsistent positions, and generally followed an erratic, unpredictable course. Once off the speaker's platform his inadequacies became apparent.

The major challenge for the UAW was to force one of the industry's giants, General Motors, Ford, or Chrysler, to accept a contract recognizing the union. Although Martin favored an early showdown, he played only a minor part in the preparations for the sit-down strike at GM's Chevrolet and Fisher Body plants in Flint, Michigan, that began on December 30, 1936, and lasted until February 11, 1937. His role in the conduct of the strike was largely confined to statements to reporters and speechmaking. Although he was initially involved in the discussions with management, his unpredictability, irresponsible behavior, and failure to construct and implement a rational strategy cost him the confidence of the rest of the union leadership. Nor did Martin devise the tactical moves that tipped the balance in the strikers' favor. He was finally removed from the scene at the insistence of John L. Lewis, who had taken over negotiations for the union, and sent on a speaking tour of GM locals. Consequently Martin was changing trains in Chicago when news of the settlement arrived. His remonstrance, "They can't do that!," was unavailing. His signature was not on the GM agreement, and he could claim little credit for the fledgling union's greatest victory, one that was quickly followed by securing contracts with the industry's other important automobile and parts manufacturers, with the exception of Ford.

For the remaining two years of his presidency of the UAW-CIO from 1937 to 1939, Martin was embroiled in steadily worsening controversy. The union was so seriously divided between rival factions that its very existence came into question. Martin tried to establish and consolidate a position by forming an alliance with Richard Frankensteen, a union vice-president and effective organizer in Chrysler Corporation's plants. The Martin-Frankensteen combination came to be called the Progressive caucus, a misleading designation because it was, in most respects, the more conservative group. Opposing it was the Unity caucus, which included the union's Communist element and its sympathizers; the Socialists, such as the Reuther brothers; and others more vaguely on the left. Martin became convinced, with reason, that the Unity caucus intended to depose him as president. The contest between the two factions erupted publicly at the UAW's disorderly Milwaukee convention in August 1937, where Martin, who was reelected president, could maintain only a semblance of control through resort to high-handed methods.

In need of advice and direction, Martin established a tie with Jay Lovestone and his followers. Lovestone had been expelled from the American Communist party in 1929 for "right wing deviationism." In response he founded his own organization and became a zealous anticommunist. Several Lovestoneites were appointed to important UAW staff positions, and anticommunism increasingly became the rallying cry of the Martinites. Martin's position was damaged by failure to gain better contracts with the automobile manufacturers and the dissolution of the Progressive caucus when Frankensteen deserted him. Defeated in a vote on the executive board, Martin struck back by suspending four vice-presidents and the union's secretary-treasurer. In protest six more members of the board refused to attend its sessions. Only one board member, R. J. Thomas, remained loyal to Martin.

Blaming the Communist party for all of his troubles, Martin insisted that the suspended officers be put on trial, with their expulsion the possible outcome. With the union publicly disintegrating, John L. Lewis of the CIO intervened to force the reinstatement of the officers. Martin, though still president, was shorn of control. He mounted a desperate attempt to recoup by reaching an agreement, through secret negotiations, with the Ford Motor Company, the only holdout among the Big Three manufacturers. Whatever his motives, his actions could be, and were, interpreted as a plot to carry the UAW out of the CIO and back into the AFL, an organization despised by most autoworkers, in return for limited rec-

ognition from Ford. The unsuccessful approach to Ford further damaged Martin's credibility.

In 1939 Martin, in a new dispute, suspended fifteen of twenty-four board members, who thereupon announced that they were nonetheless the official board and named R. J. Thomas acting president. The two factions battled for control of the union. Martin called a special convention for March 24; the CIO group announced theirs for March 27. Each side campaigned strenuously in the locals for their support. Although Martin had backing in some of the big Flint locals, his convention clearly drew only a minority of the delegates. Martin insisted that the convention authorize him to reaffiliate with the AFL. Because the AFL had little respect or following among autoworkers, this decision sealed Martin's fate.

Because GM refused to recognize either the UAW-CIO or the UAW-AFL as possessing a binding agreement, the two rivals tried to force recognition. Martin moved first with a strike in GM plants in Flint and Saginaw, but CIO workers refused to honor his picket lines, and the strike quickly collapsed. The UAW-CIO made a better showing in a strike of GM tool and die makers, winning recognition from the corporation as their bargaining agent.

The struggle now shifted to representation elections under the auspices of the National Labor Relations Board. In these the UAW-CIO racked up a series of decisive victories culminating in a large majority at GM plants on April 17, 1940. The UAW-CIO received 84,024 votes to 25,911 for Martin's UAW-AFL. This defeat marked the end for both Martin and his organization. He soon resigned as president and left the labor movement.

Martin's career reflects the rapid passage of the UAW from birth to maturity. A gifted and energetic speaker, he flourished when the task was to arouse workers to commitment to the union cause. But lacking even elementary administrative, political, and negotiating skills, he was intellectually and temperamentally ill-suited for the subsequent activities of organizing, sustaining, and leading an established union.

After his departure from the union, Martin held various positions. In 1942 he formed United Investors of America, an organization of small investors, and worked with the United States government for a time in World War II. He later operated a storm window and awning business and became organizational director of the Michigan

Dairy Farmers Cooperative Association, where he led an unsuccessful milk producers' strike in 1957. At times he returned to the ministry. In 1958 he lost the nomination for the U.S. Senate to Philip Hart in the Michigan Democratic primary. In 1961 Martin and his second wife, Vivian, moved to Visalia, California, where he became labor counselor for the Tulare and Kings County Employers Council. He died in Los Angeles after a heart attack on January 22, 1968. He was the father of three sons and one daughter.

References:

Sidney Fine, *Sit-Down: The General Motors Strike of 1936-1937* (Ann Arbor: University of Michigan Press, 1969);

Walter Galenson, *The CIO Challenge to the AFL: A History of the American Labor Movement, 1935-1941* (Cambridge, Mass.: Harvard University Press, 1960).

Archives:

Numerous collections at the Reuther Library of Labor and Urban Affairs, Wayne State University, contain material on Martin's activities. The most important are the Homer Martin and Henry Kraus collections. Oral histories of important UAW participants and observers are also available there.

George Walter Mason

(March 12, 1891-October 8, 1954)

by George S. May

Eastern Michigan University

CAREER: Line worker, Studebaker Corporation (1913-1914); layout and production worker, Dodge Brothers (1914-1915); purchasing agent, American Auto Trimming Company (1915-1916); purchasing agent, Wilder Tanning Company (1916-1917); supervisor of production, U.S. Army Ordnance Department, Rock Island Arsenal (1917-1918); business extension coordinator, Irving National Bank (1919-1921); assistant to vice-president, manufacturing (1921), general works manager, Maxwell-Chalmers Corporation (1922-1924); general works manager, Chrysler Corporation (1925-1926); vice-president and general manager (1926), president, Copeland Products, Inc. (1927-1928); president and chairman of the board, Kelvinator Corporation (1928-1936); president (1936-1948), president and chairman of the board, Nash-Kelvinator Corporation (1948-1954); president and chairman of the board, American Motors Corporation (1954).

George Walter Mason, creator of American Motors (AMC), the last of the smaller American automobile companies to fail in competition with the Big Three, was born on March 12, 1891, in Valley City, North Dakota. He was the son of Annie Simons Mason and Simon Mason, a farmer whose father had come to the United States from Norway in 1845. Growing up at the onset of the automobile

age, Mason was swept up in the enthusiasm for this new means of transportation. By the time he was a teenager the workers at the local Maxwell dealer had taught him both the mechanics of the car and how to drive. Shortly he was teaching customers to drive and selling cars. When he was seventeen he went to work for the Buick dealer for $50 a month; he also opened a shop to vulcanize tires and was selling and racing motorcycles. (His business associates in later years were said to be "wide-eyed" in their admiration of Mason's abilities to drive a car, "for here he is both demon and expert.")

With the money he had saved, Mason, when he was nineteen, enrolled at the University of Michigan where he obtained a bachelor of science degree in engineering, while also taking courses in business administration. While he was in college he and his father opened a Briggs-Detroiter car dealership in Valley City, but when he graduated in 1913 he went to Detroit to launch a career in the manufacturing of cars, rather than returning to North Dakota to be a car dealer. He attained a job at Studebaker's Detroit factory and so impressed William R. Wilson, assistant to the plant's general manager, that when Wilson joined the new Dodge Brothers company in 1914 he took Mason with him to work in a factory-layout and design engineering job. In 1915 Mason

George Walter Mason

moved on to become purchasing agent for Detroit's American Auto Trimming Company. In 1916 he moved to Waukegan, Illinois, to take a job with the Wilder Tanning Company, a Dodge affiliate. During World War I he supervised war production at the Rock Island Arsenal for the United States Army Ordnance Department.

After the war he went to New York and added to what was already an impressive and diversified résumé by taking a job at the Irving National Bank, where William Wilson was serving as vice-president in charge of business extension. In 1921 Wilson became involved with Walter Chrysler's effort to salvage the failing Maxwell and Chalmers companies, and Mason moved once again, this time back to Detroit, the city which would remain his base for the rest of his life. Wilson and Chrysler gave him increasingly responsible positions supervising manufacturing activities, ending with his appointment as general works manager at the new Chrysler Corporation in 1925. In 1926 he left Chrysler when Wilson, who had become chairman of the board at Copeland Products, hired Mason to be general manager of that Detroit manufacturer of electric refrigerators. Mason was promoted to president

in 1927, and he did such a good job that Copeland sales began to be a threat to the bigger and better-known Detroit refrigerator manufacturer, Kelvinator.

The Kelvinator Corporation was founded in 1941 by Arnold H. Goss, a onetime close associate of William C. Durant at Buick. In the mid 1920s Goss, following one of Durant's favorite practices, had moved too hastily in acquiring two other manufacturers of refrigeration equipment and in carrying through a huge expansion of Kelvinator's assembly facilities. These moves caused problems. Faced with pressure from banks to repay the loans used to implement the acquisitions and expansion, and also suffering from declining revenues caused by disappointing sales and corporate infighting, the Kelvinator board in 1928 fired Goss and hired Mason to be president. It was at Kelvinator that Mason made his reputation as an astute administrator, transforming a company that had been losing over $1 million per year in 1928 into a profitable one by the mid 1930s. He accomplished this by overhauling the firm's manufacturing and sales procedures, but, one observer declared, "without a single change in the executive organization, and . . . most of the improvement was done while the country was going through a depression."

In 1936 Charles W. Nash sought to lure Mason back to the automobile industry to become president of the Nash Motor Company. Nash was in his seventies and was interested in attracting someone with the same kind of practical experience in the manufacturing of automobiles to be his successor. Nash was one of the stronger independents and had pulled through the depths of the depression in good shape. But so had Kelvinator, and, although Nash was correct in believing that Mason yearned to return to the automobile industry, Mason had no desire to leave his job at Kelvinator, which brought him, with his salary and bonuses, $193,128 in 1936. He also frowned upon leaving Detroit for the Nash offices in Kenosha, Wisconsin. The result was that Nash, in order to hire Mason, had to agree to a merger of the two companies, with Mason becoming president. Nash continued as chairman of the board, but he became relatively inactive in terms of management matters after Mason arrived. He spent most of his time at his home in Beverly Hills, California, and at his death in 1948 Mason was named to succeed him as chairman while continuing to serve as president.

Nash-Kelvinator was, *Fortune* magazine declared, "the biggest merger of industrially disparate units since the beginning of the depression." Although acquisition of Frigidaire by General Motors (GM) two decades earlier provided a precedent for the manufacturers of cars and refrigerators being combined in one company, the merger of Nash and Kelvinator predictably spawned speculation that Nashes would now come equipped with ice cube trays while refrigerators would be fitted with 4-wheel brakes. However, with the extensive experience he had gained in both fields, Mason made the combination work. He combated the increasing competition Kelvinator faced in the late 1930s from Sears, General Electric, Frigidaire, and other producers with an aggressive sales campaign and by expanding the division's product lines into electric ranges, water heaters, home freezers, and other home and institutional appliances. Nash car sales, like those of the industry as a whole, slumped during the recession of 1937-1938 but recovered, and the company showed a profit by 1940.

At the end of that year the Nash Ambassador 600 was introduced, a car that reflected Mason's view that the independents should seek to provide cars that were different from, rather than imitative of, the models of the Big Three, with whom the smaller companies could not hope to compete in terms of manufacturing and marketing resources. The Ambassador 600 was economical to operate, the name resulting from its capability of being driven 600 miles on one 20-gallon tank of gas. Of greater importance to Mason, however, was the Ambassador 600's unit construction, a method that had been used earlier in Chrysler's 1934 Airflow models and in the Lincoln Zephyr, introduced in 1936. But Nash used an improved application of the monocoque construction techniques, resulting in a car that was 6 inches lower than previous Ambassador models and, because of its unit construction, was 500 to 600 pounds lighter than any other car in its class. The body was developed by the Budd company, and the engineer in charge declared that Mason "was vitally interested in every step. He stopped by my office every morning." The new car was a success with the public, and with the onset of World War II its excellent gas mileage was a bonus.

The war halted all civilian automobile production in February 1942, and Nash turned its attention to the production of aircraft engines and other war materiel. However, Mason was looking forward to the resumption of automobile production long before the war ended, and as a result Nash was better prepared than most of the competition when the war did end in summer 1945. Nash resumed production so quickly that it was the third-leading producer of cars that year. Once the industry as a whole made this conversion back to peacetime production, Nash quickly slipped to its prewar level, but nevertheless it enjoyed record sales up into the early 1950s.

As Mason had foreseen, Nash and the other independents benefited from the unusual conditions that prevailed after the war when the long absence of any new cars since 1942 created a seller's market such as the industry had not seen in a quarter of a century. Mason also realized that these conditions would not last and that once the pent-up demand for new cars had been resolved, the overwhelming superiority of the Big Three's resources would enable them once again to exercise their dominance. To survive, Mason believed the independents would first of all have to try to attract buyers by offering cars that were different from those found in the showrooms of GM, Ford, and Chrysler.

During the war Mason had ordered George W. Walker, an industrial designer who had begun working on the styling of the Nash in 1940, to prepare plans for a new postwar Nash model. Immediately after the war all automobile companies, Nash included, were forced to market warmed-over versions of their last prewar models because of the lead time involved in introducing entirely new models. In summer 1948 Mason previewed the new 1949-model-year Ford, the first new postwar car offered by that company. In anger he cried, "Walker has given the goddam Nash design to Ford." Walker admitted that the new slab-sided Ford was a close copy of the prototype Walker had developed for Nash. But Nash had done nothing with the prototype after the war. "Hell," Walker declared later, "I figured Nash wasn't going to use the design. It was a good one, so I had it modified a little and it became the 1949 Ford." However, Walker's prototype was used extensively in 1950 when Nash introduced the first compact car, the Rambler. The name of the car was one that had been used for the first cars produced by the Thomas B. Jeffery Company, the firm that Nash had taken over in 1916. The term *compact car* is said to have been suggested by George Romney, whom Mason had hired in 1948 as his heir apparent. But the car itself was very much a product of Mason's belief that it was necessary to offer the public an alternative to the products of the Big Three. In this case the Rambler, a small, economical car, was intended to counter the ever-bigger gas guzzlers. A two-seat sports car, the 1950 Nash-Healey, designed and built in Great Britain, and the Metropolitan, a subcompact long before that term was coined, that was also built in England and which began to be imported in 1954, were two other attempts by Mason to find a niche for Nash automobiles by exploiting a market that was being ignored by the big companies.

Innovative as the Rambler, Nash-Healey, and Metropolitan were, they experienced disappointing sales. These results reinforced Mason's belief that the only way the smaller companies could survive was through mergers. He alone, among the heads of the independents, seems to have recognized in the immediate postwar period that the circumstances that were doubling the market share of the independents would not last. Soon after the war Mason had discussed with A. E. Barit, Hudson's president, the possibility of a merger of their two companies. At the same time he had also broached the subject to James J. Nance, head of Packard. There is also some evidence that he talked with Studebaker officials. But given the difficulty of the independents in keeping up with demand, Mason's proposals do not seem to have received serious consideration.

By the early 1950s, with a sharp drop in the independents' market share, Mason's renewed interest in a merger received a different reception. In 1952 James Nance again turned down the idea of a merger with Nash and Packard. Apparently Nance opposed the merger not because he was opposed to a deal of any kind but because in Mason's proposal Packard would be viewed as the lesser of the two partners. But it was a different matter when Mason met with Hudson's Barit at Detroit's Book-Cadillac Hotel on June 16, 1953. Barit, who had begun his career at Hudson as a stenographer in 1910, a year after the company had been organized, was in no position to resist Mason's proposition. Hudson had fallen on hard times, and a merger with Nash was probably viewed by Barit as the only alternative to slow death for his once highly respected company.

On January 14, 1954, the directors of Nash and Hudson formally announced that they had agreed to consolidate the two companies, with the merger to take effect on May 1. Although there were some dissenters, the stockholders of the two companies approved the merger which formed the new American Motors Corporation. The fact that Nash-Kelvinator was the dominant partner was evident. Nash-Kelvinator stockholders received one share of the new AMC stock for every share they held while Hudson shareholders had to exchange three Hudson shares to receive two shares of AMC stock. In addition Mason became the president and chairman of the new corporation while Barit had to be satisfied with only a seat on the board of directors and a position as "consultant" to the new firm.

With his characteristic energy Mason applied himself to his new position of presiding over what was termed the biggest merger in automotive history. Hudson assets of some $60 million and 1,450 dealers were added to those in the Nash organization. Consolidating the operations of the two companies was a difficult task, but the announcement that summer that AMC would buy V-8 engines from Packard which in turn would purchase AMC products "suitable for use by Packard" was seen as evidence that a further merger of the independents was in the offing.

But then at the end of the summer Mason, who was, in spite of what was once described as his Falstaffian appearance, an ardent and active outdoorsman, went on a vacation trip to Wyoming. Upon his return he became ill on October 3 and died at Detroit's Harper Hospital on October 8 of pancreatic failure and pneumonia. Mason had been married twice, first to Hazel Bisbee in 1921, with whom he had two sons. They divorced in 1942, and Mason quickly married Florence Johnston Fead, with whom he had two daughters. He bequeathed to the state of Michigan $1 million worth of land along the Au Sable River, which he wished to be set aside as a wilderness area. He also left $25,000 to be used "to replace the trout I took out."

For the automobile industry the consequences of Mason's death, which occurred at a time when he was in the midst of potentially very important new developments, still are not clear. There are some who claim that the merger of Studebaker and Packard, which was officially consummated shortly after Mason's death, had been part of Mason's grand plan to complete the consolidation of Nash, Hudson, Packard, and Studebaker. Some maintain that if the large plan had been completed Mason would have created a small GM, with a full range of cars in all price levels, plus the "white goods," that is, the Kelvinator appliances. If anyone could have done it, Mason was probably the man. By the 1950s there were few, if any, automotive executives who had had such wide-ranging experience in all aspects of the business as Mason. The industry's respect for him had been shown in 1946 when he was elected to succeed Alvan Macauley of Packard as president of the Automobile Manufacturers Association, a job Mason still held at the time of his death.

However, whether even Mason could have made a success of the larger merger is doubtful. Aside from some executives, such as Roy D. Chapin, Jr., who presided capably as head of AMC during the late 1960s and 1970s, Hudson contributed little to the AMC merger, which owed its survival in its early years to the strength of the Nash organization, in particular the Rambler compact. It is not clear whether Mason still favored a merger with the Studebaker-Packard combine at the time of his death, but the dismal fate that befell that duo suggests that their addition would have created a larger burden that Nash, the strongest element in a combination of the four companies, would not have been able to carry. Because of his association with the developments that had led to the emergence of the Chrysler Corporation in the 1920s, Mason had been known as one of "Chrysler's boys," but the conditions that had developed by the 1950s made it unlikely that Walter Chrysler, let alone Mason, could have created a viable merger of the remaining independents that could have successfully challenged the Big Three.

References:

"Empty Chairmanship," *Newsweek*, 44 (October 18, 1954): 85;

Richard M. Langworth, *Hudson: The Postwar Years* (Osceola, Wis.: Motorbooks International, 1977);

Tom Mahoney, *The Story of George Romney: Builder, Statesman, Crusader* (New York: Harper, 1960);

George S. May, *The Automobile and American Life* (Forthcoming 1990);

Sam Medway, "Refrigerators and Two Georges—from Nash-Kelvinator to American Motors," *Automobile Quarterly*, 15 (Second Quarter 1977): 140-158;

"Nash-Kelvinator," *Fortune*, 15 (April 1937): 95-99, 140-152.

Mass Production

by James J. Flink

University of California, Irvine

The term "mass production" dates from an article by that title actually written by William J. Cameron, but attributed to Henry Ford, in the thirteenth edition (1926) of the *Encyclopaedia Britannica*. It is described there as "the focusing upon a manufacturing project of the principles of power, accuracy, economy, system, continuity, speed, and repetition." Prior to this description, the system of continuous-flow production techniques implemented at the Ford Highland Park plant in 1913-1914 to produce the Model T in ever greater numbers at an ever lower price was popularly known as "Fordism." Despite the earlier origin and use of the constituent elements of the Ford production system, their integration and refinement at Highland Park was unique. As David A. Hounshell concludes in his definitive history of the rise of mass production, "It is only with the rise of the Ford Motor Company and its Model T that there clearly appears an approach to manufacture capable of handling an output of multicomponent consumer durables ranging into the millions each year."

Up to the innovations at Highland Park, "artisanal" methods prevailed in the production of automobiles. Skilled machinists, capable of operating efficiently a large number of general-purpose machine tools, predominated in the work force and directed production in the workplace. They were aided by unskilled helpers, who performed the menial labor, such as carting and hauling material, at about half the pay of the skilled machinists. Increasingly semiskilled specialists, who could operate one or more specialized machines, were also employed, especially in the United States. The skilled machinist had wide latitude in determining the pace of work, in setting the standards of production, and in hiring and firing their unskilled and semiskilled helpers. Consequently there were few purely supervisory personnel, such as foremen, in the shops and small factories where components were made and/or assembled into completed automobiles.

General-purpose machine tools predominated over more specialized machines; there was a relative absence of specialized jigs and fixtures to position the work; and tool benches equipped with the machinists' personal hand tools were placed in close proximity to machine tools. Machine tools of the same or similar type were grouped together, and material was conveyed by hand from one group of machines to another to be processed. Final fitting and finishing to acceptable tolerances generally involved hand filing and/or grinding. The principal component remained stationary on the shop floor until assembly was completed, while other components were brought to it and affixed. Thus chassis stood in rows as assembly crews moved from one to another affixing bodies and wheels.

The initial capital as well as the managerial and technical expertise needed to enter automobile manufacturing was most commonly diverted from other closely related business activities, particularly from the manufacture of machine tools, bicycles, and carriages and wagons. The requirements for fixed and working capital were also met by shifting the burden to parts makers. The automobile was a unique combination of components already standardized and being produced for other uses—for example, stationary and marine gasoline engines, carriage bodies, and wheels. Consequently the manufacture of components was jobbed out to scores of independent suppliers, minimizing the capital requirements for wages, materials, expensive machinery, and a large factory. So once the basic design of his car was established, the early automobile manufacturer became merely an assembler of major components and a supplier of finished cars to his distributors and dealers. The modest assembly plant needed could be rented as easily as purchased, and

The first moving assembly line, installed at the Ford plant in 1914 (courtesy of Henry Ford Museum and Greenfield Village)

the process of assembling was shorter than the thirty- to ninety-day credit period that the parts makers allowed. Operating on this basis, for example, the Ford Motor Company was able to start in business in 1903 with paid-in capital of only $28,000, a dozen workmen, and an assembly plant just 250 feet by 50 feet. The chassis components (engines, transmissions, and axles) of the first Ford car were supplied by the Detroit machine shop of John F. and Horace E. Dodge, who became minority stockholders.

The era of artisanal production and freewheeling competition ended as, led by the Ford Motor Company, automobile manufacturing became capital intensive and economies of scale became essential for success. Capital investment in plant in relation to revenue at Ford increased from 11 percent in 1913 to 33 percent in 1926, even as Ford inventories shrank and the time to fabricate a Model T from scratch fell from fourteen days to four. The number of active producers in the American automobile industry concomitantly shrank from 253 in 1908 to 44 in 1929, with Ford, General Mo-

tors, and Chrysler responsible for about 75 percent of the output.

There was general agreement in the automobile industry that the 62-acre Highland Park plant designed by Albert Kahn that opened on January 1, 1910, possessed an unparalleled factory arrangement for the volume production of motorcars. Its well-lighted and well-ventilated buildings were a model of advanced industrial construction. However, it is clear from the fact that much of the plant was several stories high that it was not designed specifically for using moving assembly lines.

In a plant that employed fewer than 13,000 workers, by 1914 about 15,000 specialized machine tools had been installed at Highland Park at a cost of $2.8 million. "The policy of the company," relate Allan Nevins and Frank E. Hill, "was to scrap old machines ruthlessly in favor of better types—even if 'old' meant a month's use." After 1912 the 59 draftsmen and 472 skilled toolmakers in the tool department were constantly devising new specialized machine tools that would increase production. By 1915 they had turned out over 140 specialized machine tools and several thousand specialized dies, jigs, and fixtures. Jigs and fixtures to set up and/or position the work were called "farmers' tools" because with them green hands could turn out work as good as or better than skilled machinists. Machine tools became larger, more powerful, more specialized, and semiautomatic or automatic. A prime example was a special drilling machine supplied by the Foote-Burt Company. This machine drilled forty-five holes simultaneously in four sides of a Model T cylinder block and was equipped with an automatic stop and reverse. The cylinder block was positioned by a special jig, so all the operator had to do was pull the starting lever and remove the finished block.

Elementary time and motion studies begun at the Piquette Avenue plant were continued at Highland Park and in 1912 led to the installation of continuous conveyor belts to bring materials to the assembly lines. And with the move to Highland Park, manufacturing and assembling operations began to be arranged sequentially, so that components traveled to completion over the shortest route possible with no unnecessary handling. This entailed the abandonment of grouping machine tools together by type in plant layout.

Magnetos, motors, and transmissions were assembled on moving lines by summer 1913. After production from these subassembly lines threatened to flood the final assembly line, a moving chassis-assembly line was installed. It reduced the time of chassis assembly from twelve and a half hours in October to two hours and forty minutes by December 30, 1913. Moving lines were quickly established for assembling the dash, the front axle, and the body. The moving lines were at first pulled by rope and windlass, but on January 14, 1914, an endless chain was installed. That was in turn replaced on February 27 by a new line built on rails set at a convenient working height and timed at six feet a minute. By summer 1914 productivity in assembling magnetos had more than doubled, and chassis assembly took under two hours, about one-sixth the time required with artisanal production methods. "Every piece of work in the shop moves," boasted Henry Ford in 1922. "It may move on hooks or overhead chains going to assembly in the exact order in which the parts are required; it may travel on a moving platform, or it may go by gravity, but the point is that there is no lifting or trucking of anything other than materials."

At the industrial colossus that Ford began building on the River Rouge in 1916 Fordism was intensified. Nevins and Hill write that by the mid 1920s "in conveyors alone it was a wonderland of devices. Gravity, belt, buckle, spiral, pendulum gravity roller, overhead monorail, 'scenic railway' and 'merry-go-round,' elevating flight—the list was long both in range and in adaptation to special purpose." They recount that "at the entrance of the machining department, the various castings were routed mechanically to 32 different groups of machine tools, each unit then passing through a series of machine-tool operations—43 in the case of the Ford [Model T] cylinder block—before the finished shining element emerged, ready to be routed to assembly." By 1924 the River Rouge foundry cast over 10,000 Model T cylinder blocks a day, and by 1926 the 115-acre plant boasted some 43,000 machine tools and employed 8,000 tool and die makers. At the changeover to Model A production in 1927 the Ford Motor Company was estimated to have about 45,000 machine tools worth $45 million.

The mass-production techniques innovated at Highland Park were widely publicized and described in detail, most notably by Horace L. Arnold and Fay L. Faurote in their 1915 *The Ford Methods and the Ford Shops*. Within a few years moving assembly lines had been installed by all major American automobile manufacturers. Production reached peak efficiency at Hudson, where by 1926 assembling an automobile took only ninety minutes, and cars rolled off its four final assembly lines every thirty seconds.

As the need for basic transportation was met and rural roads were improved, the Model T's popularity waned. It remained in production long after it was technologically obsolete. By the time Ford withdrew the Model T from the market in 1927, a larger, more powerful, far better equipped, annually restyled Chevrolet was available, priced only $200 higher and able to be purchased on the installment plan. Henry Ford's marketing strategy of a single static model at an ever lower price lost out during the 1920s to Alfred P. Sloan, Jr.'s strategy at General Motors (GM) of the annual model change and "a car for every purse and purpose."

The annual model change and diversity of product were incompatible with Fordist production methods. At the Ford Highland Park plant "every machine tool and fixture was fitted for the production of a single product whose every part had been standardized to the minutest detail." Even small changes in the design of the Model T bottlenecked its production. The switchover to Model A production was chaotic. Machine tools highly specialized for Model T production could not be converted to Model A production, with the result that more than half of the 32,000 machine tools used to produce the Model T had to be redesigned and rebuilt and half of the remaining ones had to be scrapped. That the plant layout optimal for Model T production was not well suited to production of the Model A was evidenced by the change to a final assembly line at the Rouge that was only half as long as the Model T final assembly line at Highland Park. For some time the expansion of Model A production was hampered by the Ford practice of extremely close spacing of machine tools, which exacerbated problems of rearranging plant layout. Hounshell observes that "the changeover to Model A, including experimental and design work, tooling and loss of profits, totaled about $250 million." Such inordinate disruption of production and consequent phenomenal expense was irreconcilable with the Sloanist marketing strategy of bringing out the essentially new model every three years. It is no wonder that at the Rouge, as a consequence of this costly initial lesson, "Sorensen aimed for greater flexibility in assembly rather than cost advantages through a single-purpose [machine tool] approach." There was an almost complete turnover of supervisory personnel at the Rouge as production-head Sorensen tried, in his own words, "to get rid of all the Model T sons-of-bitches . . . get away from the Model T methods of doing things."

Sorensen adapted to the Model A production techniques that had been developed at Chevrolet by William S. Knudsen, who had been hired by Sloan on February 1, 1922, a few months after he had resigned from the Ford Motor Company over being constantly overridden by Sorensen and Henry Ford. Knudsen's first assignment at GM was to work out a long-range production plan for Chevrolet. GM production was far more decentralized and far less vertically integrated than Ford production. Sloan had reasoned that GM would have to make the same profit on capital invested in plant and equipment as outside suppliers charging reasonable prices for components. So GM depended more on outside suppliers. This alone gave GM far more flexibility than Ford. Additionally Knudsen decentralized Chevrolet

components manufacture among specialized plants at Toledo, Ohio, and Flint, Detroit, and Bay City, Michigan, and bought still more components from other GM divisions and from outside suppliers. Assembly, too, was decentralized. "At four assembly plants (Tarrytown, New York, Flint, Michigan, St. Louis, Missouri and Oakland, California) . . . subassemblies and thousands of parts purchased from vendors were brought together to make the Chevrolet. . . . Knudsen [also] had convinced GM executives that a Fisher body plant should be attached to each assembly plant so that body production could be coordinated precisely with the daily output of each assembly plant." However, the major innovation at Chevrolet, according to Hounshell, was that Knudsen replaced single-purpose machine tools with standard general-purpose machine tools. "It is important to emphasize that the entire Chevrolet production system . . . was based on standard or general-purpose, not single-purpose machine tools," he concludes. "For this reason, Chevrolet could accommodate change far more easily than could the Ford Motor Company."

Hounshell dates "flexible" as opposed to "rigid" mass production from these developments at Chevrolet. Perhaps so. Nevertheless, true flexible mass production came not so much with the annual model change, but with great individualization of product within model runs. And this in turn resulted not from a reversion to general-purpose machine tools, but from the automated automobile factory equipped with automatic transfer machines, other automatic highly specialized machinery, and the computer-controlled assembly line. The automated automobile factory did not become a reality until the 1950s.

Gerald R. Bloomfield describes this shift from "rigid" mass production, dictating strict standardization of product, to "flexible" mass production. He explains that "flexible mass production allows a wider range of options of body style, colors, trim, power train, but within permissible standardized limits. The products of this type of mass production have a greater appearance of diversity. Flexible mass production involved a high-degree of planning, and became more capital intensive than the earlier stages of rigid mass production." The result on individualization of product has been succinctly summarized by Brock Yates: "A Yale physicist whimsically calculated that a 1965 Chevrolet, offered in

A moving assembly line builds Cadillac engines during the 1950s (courtesy of Cadillac, division of General Motors)

46 models, 32 different engines, 20 transmissions, 30 colors, and 400 options, could be purchased in almost as many permutations as there are atoms in the universe." With the automated, computer-controlled assembly line, it became not only theoretically possible but likely that no two cars from the same model run were ever precisely identical.

Automatic production began with innovation of the transfer machine, described well by James R. Bright "as a number of machining stations mounted upon a base (or bases so closely integrated that the effect is the same), and having a work-feeding device integral with the machine and common to all stations." Bright believes that the first transfer machine in automobile manufacturing was used by Morris Motors in England about 1924 and that in the American automobile industry Graham-Paige installed the first true transfer machine in 1929 and the first transfer machine system, using automatic jibs and fixtures, in 1931. During the 1930s the use of transfer machines became commonplace in automobile manufacturing, where they proved to be "extremely important in cutting labor cost, increasing quality through uniformity and reduced tolerances, and in reducing manufacturing cycle time."

Because transfer machines alone perform only a part of the total operations required in assembly, however, a system of transfer machines would not

in itself constitute automation. Robert Bendiner defines automation as "the controlled operation of an entire factory or process in which the machines as linked units automatically perform their manipulations in specified sequences, with electronic judgement substituted for the perception of the machinist or foremen." For that to occur automatic controls had to be added to systems of transfer machines. Control was at first (1954-1955) by coded, punched, or magnetic tape, but after that by the computer.

Delmar S. Harder deserves the title "the father of automation." Under his leadership, in 1947 the Ford Motor Company became the first corporation in the world to establish an automation department. In 1949 Ford began work on the first factories built to make any notable use of automation–its Buffalo Stamping Plant and its Cleveland Engine Plant. In 1955 Peter Drucker hailed the application of automation to automobile manufacturing as "a major economic and technological change, a change as great as Henry Ford ushered in with the first mass production plant fifty years ago."

Until the very recent development of the microprocessor, which permits machine tools to be programmed for a large number of tasks, automation was only compatible with individualization of prod-

A modern assembly line with its large complement of industrial robots (courtesy of Motor Vehicle Manufacturers Association)

uct and the annual model change in the manufacture of components which remained basically unchanged from car to car and from model year to model year, such as engines and transmissions. Consequently automation was first and most fully applied to the production of large runs of standardized mechanical components. Heavy investment in specialized machinery in turn militated against technological innovation in mechanical components, so cars had to remain much the same under the hood. The MIT Report points out that "by contrast, large amounts of semi-skilled labor were used in the body plant and the final assembly line to accommodate the year-to-year changes in the product. . . . In the body plant the producer faced a choice between inflexible automation, with very high production volumes and long unchanged product runs to justify its cost, and flexible manual systems with higher labor content." Because high volume production of a single static model was essential to realizing economies from replacing workers with automated machinery, the full automation of body welding and final assembly was first instituted in stages between

1953 and 1966 at Volkswagen's Wolfsburg plant in the production of the Beetle, one of the most standardized cars of all time. "This meant low labor content, and it was suited to the labor shortage in postwar Germany," the MIT Report observes. "The alternative system, as developed by most of the other world producers, involved greater use of semiskilled labor for practically all operations and was suited to frequent model changes and simultaneous production of many body styles and accessory combinations."

Sloanism thus ironically intensified the amount and pace of dehumanizing work in automobile manufacturing at the same time that automation promised to shift it to the machine. In 1913 Henry Ford had created a new class of semiskilled workers. Substantial training, physical strength, education, and intelligence were no longer prerequisites for industrial employment. All that was needed on the assembly line was punctuality and the capacities to subordinate oneself to the pace of the machine and to withstand the boredom of repeating routine tasks hour after hour. In the mid 1970s about 75 percent of the jobs in automobile manufacturing remained semiskilled or unskilled, versus only about 10 percent for the rest of American industry.

Even where automation had displaced human operatives there was degradation of labor to lower skill levels and intensification of the production process. For example, the GM Lordstown, Ohio, plant was the most costly and technologically advanced factory in modern automotive history when it opened in June 1970 to produce the subcompact Vega—a design that was expected to remain fixed for several years to enable economies of scale to be realized. The major feature of the plant was twenty-six "Unimate" robots (programmable, multipurpose automatic machines), capable of welding Vega bodies more precisely and uniformly than could humans. Unskilled workers were still needed, however, to feed the robots materials. Thus despite (or because of) automation, rigid Taylorization (after Frederick Winslow Taylor) of the work force made Lordstown a hotbed of labor discontent.

Lordstown typified the growing alienation of automobile workers. Since World War II American mass-production methods have been universally adopted throughout the world. And as Sloanism intensified Fordism, high labor turnover, absenteeism, and industrial sabotage came to be formidable production problems in automobile plants worldwide.

In the 1980s automobile manufacturing is again being revolutionized. Traditional engineering "know how" and cut-and-try methods are being abandoned in favor of computer-aided engineering (CAE) and computer-aided design (CAD) to complement computer-aided manufacturing (CAM). "The product design, development and manufacturing process of the future will rely on the integration of a wide range of computer-based application programs," the Ford technical staff predicts. "Properly implemented the boundaries between CAE, CAD, and CAM will disappear and the term 'computer integrated manufacturing' (CIM) can properly be used to refer to this level of development."

Until very recently robots could be programmed to perform only a few repetitive operations. The microprocessor now gives robots the ability to handle complex materials, select and distribute parts, and discriminate in the performance of tasks in much the same way as can a human operator. For example, new robot welding systems can perform precise and uniform welds on a variety of models moving through the assembly process in random order, and parts can be moved from machine to machine as required by the model rather than following a fixed itinerary. The MIT Report observes that this new flexible robotics system at Volkswagen "takes the first steps along the path to automated final assembly, with robots installing the engine, brake lines, battery, and wheels. The system is able to produce not only Golfs in several body styles but also Jettas without changing tools or stopping production. In addition, Volkswagen and other producers are experimenting with more flexible tooling and automated material handling in engine and transmission plants to permit, for example, machining of a whole family of engines on the same transfer lines."

Flexible robotics thus has reconciled Fordism and Sloanism, with truly revolutionary implications for automobile manufacturing. It permits economies of scale to be realized on much smaller model runs. This means both increased diversity of product and that small specialized producers can remain competitive within the automobile industry. Manufacturing is more accurate, improving quality. Labor costs are significantly lowered, because flexible robotics can perform dehumanizing tasks much more cheaply than can human beings. This promises in the near future to erase the labor cost advantages of Japan and Third World countries. A far more technically skilled work force is required to program, monitor, and repair robots than to perform repetitive assembly-line tasks. "Significant gains in productivity are anticipated from this [flexible robotics] system," understates Jean-Pierre Bardoux. "But the salient point is that the introduction of electronic machine tools challenges the traditional sequential operation process, whether it is a line formed by human operatives or a line formed by a succession of machines. If the assembly line someday disappears, this will not only mark a page turned in the history of the automobile industry, but also in the history of labor." It is estimated that the general adoption of electronic machine tools will eliminate 37 percent of the jobs in automobile manufacturing, even as the number of motor vehicles in the world increases from 396.2 million in 1979 to 678.5 million by the year 2000.

Over half of all current sales of robots in the United States are to the automobile industry, and in 1987 some 26,000 robots were being used in final assembly plants in the United States alone. The most ambitious plan for a final assembly plant currently is the projected GM Saturn plant at Spring Hill, Tennessee, scheduled to go into production in 1990 building an advanced-design small car about 600 pounds lighter than current subcompacts. Initial production is slated to be some 250,000 units a year, turned out by 3,000 workers on a two-shift operation, an unprecedented labor productivity rate of 83 cars annually, versus current best practice at Toyota of 27 cars. A precedent-shattering contract with the UAW provides that Saturn workers will be paid annual salaries rather than hourly wages and that 80 percent of them will be guaranteed lifelong employment.

References:

Alan Altshuler and others, *The Future of the Automobile: The Report of MIT's International Program* (Cambridge, Mass.: MIT Press, 1984);

Horace L. Arnold and Fay L. Faurote, *The Ford Methods and the Ford Shops* (New York: Engineering Magazine, 1915);

Jean-Pierre Bardoux and others, *The Automobile Revolution: The Impact of an Industry* (Chapel Hill: University of North Carolina Press, 1982);

Robert Bendiner, "The Age of the Thinking Robot and What It Will Mean to Us," *Reporter,* 12 (April 7, 1955): 12-18;

Gerald R. Bloomfield, *The World Automotive Industry* (Newton Abbott, London, and North Pomfret, Vt.: David & Charles, 1978);

James R. Bright, "The Development of Automation," in *Technology in Western Civilization,* volume 2, edited by Melvin Kranzberg and Carroll W. Pursell, Jr. (New York: Oxford University Press, 1967), pp. 635-655;

Lynwood Bryant, "The Beginnings of the Internal Combustion Engine," in *Technology in Western Civilization,* volume 1, edited by Kranzberg and Pursell (New York: Oxford University Press, 1967), pp. 648-663;

Walter P. Chrysler, in collaboration with Boyden Sparkes, *Life of an American Workman* (New York: Dodd, Mead, 1937);

Hugh Dolnar, "The Ford 4-Cylinder Runabout," *Cycle and Automobile Trade Journal,* 11 (August 1, 1906): 108;

Peter Drucker, "The Promise of Automation," *Harper's,* 210 (April 1955): 41-47;

James J. Flink, *The Automobile Age* (Cambridge, Mass.: MIT Press, 1988);

Henry Ford, in collaboration with Samuel Crowther, *My Life and Work* (Garden City, N.Y.: Doubleday, Page, 1922);

Emmett J. Horton and W. Dale Compton, "Technology Trends in Automobiles," *Science,* 225 (August 1984): 587-593;

David A. Hounshell, *From the American System to Mass Production: The Development of Manufacturing Technology in the United States, 1800-1932* (Baltimore: Johns Hopkins University Press, 1984);

George S. May, *R. E. Olds: Auto Industry Pioneer* (Grand Rapids, Mich.: William B. Eerdman's, 1977);

Stephen Meyer III, *The Five Dollar Day: Labor Management and Social Control in the Ford Motor Company, 1908-1921* (Albany: State University of New York Press, 1981);

Allan Nevins and Frank E. Hill, *Ford: The Times, the Man, the Company, 1865-1915; Ford: Expansion and Challenge, 1915-1933;* and *Ford: Decline and Rebirth, 1933-1962* (New York: Scribners, 1954, 1957, 1963);

Emma Rothschild, *Paradise Lost: The Decline of the Auto-Industrial Age* (New York: Knopf, 1973);

Alfred P. Sloan, Jr., *My Years With General Motors* (Garden City, N.Y.: Doubleday, 1964);

Charles E. Sorensen, with Samuel T. Williamson, *My Forty Years with Ford* (New York: Norton, 1956);

Brock Yates, *The Decline and Fall of the American Automobile Industry* (New York: Empire Books, 1983).

Arjay Miller

(March 14, 1916-   )

by Michael L. Lazare

New Milford, Connecticut

CAREER: Economist, Federal Reserve Bank of San Francisco (1941-1943); U.S. Army Air Force (1943-1946); director of report analysis department (1946-1947), assistant treasurer (1947-1953), assistant controller (1953-1957), vice-president (1957-1961), vice-president of finance (1961-1962), vice-president of staff group (1962-1963), director (1962-1986), president (1963-1968), vice-chairman, Ford Motor Company (1968-1969); dean, Stanford University Graduate School of Business (1969-1979).

Arjay Miller was born on March 14, 1916, on a farm just outside of Shelby, Nebraska, about seventy-five miles west of Omaha. He was the youngest of eight children born to Rawley John and Mary Gertrude Schade Miller. His unusual first name derives from the initials of his father's first and middle names. When the boy was seven his father retired from farming and the family moved into Shelby, about two miles away. Miller's Uncle Ogal took over the farm, and the boy helped his uncle with farm chores and later cultivated corn and harvested wheat. His boyhood experiences remained with him. In an interview published in the *Omaha World Herald* on July 7, 1963, after Miller had been elected president of Ford, he said, "I believe as a boy I was able to get a greater appreciation of the free enterprise system. There was a direct association between effort and reward . . . the farmer probably more than anyone else sees the direct relationship between his work and his reward. In my day a big supply was equated with a drop in price. You didn't have to read a textbook to learn that. Sometimes we're apt to forget these elementary economic ideas in a sophisticated society." Whether or not he had developed these concepts of the market society as a young boy is not really relevant. The ideas, however, are a clear statement of his philosophy.

Miller's affinity with the automobile was evident early in life. When he was twelve years old he spent $10, a large sum of money at the time, for an old Model T Ford. He wanted to take it apart to see what made it run. Speaking of the experience later, he said, "I got full value in the fun of removing the electrical coils and hooking them up to a battery and the steel frame of a chair, which gave the unsuspecting occupant of the chair a harmless shock. It never ran again. I carried it, piece by piece, to the edge of town and dumped it in a ravine. If the scrapping of old cars stimulates the building of new cars, you might say I made my first contribution to the national economy in this way." He had no idea at the time that he would spend the better part of his life in the automobile business. His ambition as a youth was to be a college teacher. He was a brilliant student and all-around athlete in high school, being selected the valedictorian of the Shelby High School class of 1932. Shortly after his graduation his family moved to Long Beach, California. Miller attended Long Beach Junior College and later transferred to the University of California at Los Angeles to study banking and finance. During one of his college summers he worked in a gasoline station in Bakersfield, California, and two other summers he was an oil-field roustabout for Mohawk Oil, also in Bakersfield. As an undergraduate at UCLA he held a teaching assistantship and was a member of the national championship debating team. He continued his academic achievements and graduated in 1937 with highest honors.

He entered graduate school at the University of California at Berkeley to study economics. He stayed at the university for two and a half years as a student and teaching assistant, completing all the requirements for a doctorate except the dissertation. In 1941 he was a research technician with the California State Planning Board, and during the

Arjay Miller

same period he collaborated with Arthur G. Coons on a study entitled *An Economic and Industrial Survey of the Los Angeles and San Diego Areas.* He tried to enlist in the armed forces at the outbreak of World War II, but his eyesight was too poor and he was rejected. As he recalled later, "I couldn't read the big E on the eye chart." He spent the years from 1941 to 1943 as an economist with the Federal Reserve Bank of San Francisco. By 1943, however, the manpower shortage was acute, and he was drafted into the army air force. As a private he was an instructor for the Link trainer and later entered officers' candidate school. Because of his academic record and peacetime accomplishments, the army sent him to the Air Force Statistical Control School at Harvard University. Upon graduation he was assigned to Air Force Headquarters, Statistical Control Office, at the War Department. In this position he was involved in the procurement and supply of vital war material, a task to which he enthusiastically brought his systematic knowledge of procurement and disbursements. His major contribution was the articulation of a systematized planning sys-

tem for war material. He was discharged with the rank of captain in 1946. The economy was reverting to a peacetime footing, and many companies were having a difficult time adjusting. One of these was the Ford Motor Company, which desperately needed new talent as it tried to recover from the chaos of the last years of the Henry Ford era. Miller saw an article discussing Ford's difficulties, and he persuaded Charles B. "Tex" Thornton, leader of a group of ten ex-air force officers, including Miller and Robert McNamara, another future Ford president, to offer their services to Ford. All the officers were highly trained in the area of statistical control and analysis. Thornton wired Henry Ford II asking for an interview to discuss a "matter of management importance." The interview was granted, and Ford hired the ten men on the spot.

The men went to work with intense enthusiasm, roaming around the company's operations and asking so many questions they were called the "Quiz Kids," a term which may have carried more than a bit of derision. Later, however, when they had proven their talents and the soundness of their methods, the sobriquet was changed to the "Whiz Kids." Thornton stayed with Ford only a short time, but Miller remained to work his way through the ranks.

Miller and his colleagues brought an element that was new to much of the automobile industry: training and experience in economics and systems, as opposed to the more traditional engineering orientation of earlier automobile executives. Miller's first job was director of the report analysis department in the finance office. From there his rise was rapid: assistant treasurer in 1947, assistant controller in 1953, vice-president in 1957, vice-president of finance in 1961, and vice-president of staff group in 1962. In 1962 he was also elected to the company's board of directors, where he remained until he reached the age of seventy in 1986.

The job of vice-president of staff group was powerful because heads of all main divisions involved in planning and selling new products reported to Henry Ford through him. His experience, therefore, was broadened to include the planning and marketing functions. During this period Miller became a strong advocate of entering Ford products in racing competitions. Ford engines in British-built Lotus cars came in second and seventh in the 1963 Indianapolis 500 race. Miller said, "Racing demonstrates in dramatic fashion the total performance of our cars. We think we have the best car and can prove it–through open competition." He saw racing as demonstrating a company's total performance–safety, speed, and style.

The capstone to Miller's career at Ford came on April 10, 1963, when he was named president of the company. At the time he was virtually unknown outside Ford. Between the time he joined the company and his election as president he had made only two speeches to outside audiences–one dealing with cash management, the other with education. As president, Miller continued to direct the central staffs responsible for planning and marketing new Ford products. He also worked closely with Henry Ford II in the general management of the company. Miller's work with budgets over the years had contributed significantly to his broad understanding of all of Ford's operations. The *New York Times* of September 14, 1966, wrote, "His closest associates say that his chief contribution to the operations at Dearborn has been his ability–using his encyclopedic knowledge of the company–to weave together its diverse and intricate components." Henry Ford praised Miller in an address to the Detroit Economics Club in October 1965: "When he digs into a new problem he doesn't stop until he knows as much about it as the people whose specialty it is. His ability to master a problem both in detail and in broad perspective was put on public display recently when he went down to Washington to testify on highway safety." The safety issue had embarrassed most of the industry in 1965 because of charges that automakers were sacrificing safety to speed and styling. Miller arrived in Washington, D.C., fully equipped with details of Ford's safety program. He was frank about the industry's slow pace, called for a federal research program into highway safety, and pledged Ford's cooperation. His appearance was regarded as a coup for Ford, turning a potentially embarrassing appearance into a positive occasion.

Miller also demonstrated an understanding of the importance of styling. He backed the introduction of "1963 1/2" models to boost sagging sales and supported the introduction of the Mustang, which he called "a specific response to a felt need in the marketplace." He also persuaded Ford dealers to install diagnostic centers, where about one hundred performance tests were done for a cost of about $10.

Always a systems man, he was a strong believer in computers, cost analysis, and systems analysis. But he was quick to point out that "technical devices . . . are only a link in a chain of individual and social action. . . . Individuals must set up the requirements and ask the questions, and only individuals can decide what to do with the products and the answers."

In spite of Miller's statements in support of product programs, his role in the company had always been in the financial end of the business. Henry Ford II had great respect for the work that Miller had done, but he apparently looked upon his appointment as president as only a stopgap measure until a highly trained product man was available. Before appointing Miller as president in 1963, he had approached Semon E. Knudsen of General Motors (GM), who had won widespread recognition for his work in reviving the Pontiac division in the 1950s. Knudsen turned down Ford's offer of the presidency at that time, believing himself to be in line to become head of GM. But in 1968, after Knudsen had been passed over for the GM presidency, Ford was able to persuade him to take on the Ford job.

To break the news to Miller, Ford called the incumbent president back from South America, where Miller was touring various Ford facilities. Ford sought to temper the news of what had happened by telling Miller that he was being promoted to the new post of vice-chairman and that he would continue in charge of finance, corporate planning, and government and public relations, while Knudsen would be responsible for operations. However, Miller realized that he was politely being eased out, and within a year he had resigned to accept the position of dean of the Stanford University Graduate School of Business. Nevertheless, relations between Miller and Henry Ford II remained amicable. Miller continued in an active role as a director of Ford, and in later years, when he was also a member of the board of the *Washington Post,* he was always briefed on Washington gossip before coming to Detroit for a board meeting, knowing how much Ford liked to hear the latest inside news. After Ford died in 1987 it was revealed that in 1986 Ford, fearing that he might be in danger of being kidnapped, had a codicil attached to his will in which he directed that Miller would be given sole authority to deal with the kidnappers and to secure his release.

The years have brought Miller many honors. He was awarded honorary degrees from UCLA, Whitman College, the University of Nebraska, and Washington University of St. Louis. He was named UCLA alumnus of the year in 1964 and the following year won the Brotherhood award of the Detroit Round Table of Catholics, Jews, and Protestants. In his acceptance speech he said, "There is a need for businessmen to take an increasing lead in meeting industry-related problems before the pressures reach a boiling point and erupt in possible bad or ineffective legislation." In 1968 he won both the B'nai B'rith National Industry Leader Award and the Distinguished Nebraskan Award. He has served on the boards of the Urban Institute, the Brookings Institution, and the Commission for Economic Development. In 1967 he was named by President Lyndon B. Johnson to a panel to organize an independent research institute to study all aspects of urban problems. In 1979 he resigned the deanship at Stanford and was named dean emeritus. Miller married Frances Marion Fearing on August 18, 1940. They have a son and a daughter, Rawley John and Mary Gertrude.

Publication:

An Economic and Industrial Survey of the Los Angeles and San Diego Areas, with Arthur G. Coons (Sacramento: California State Planning Board, 1941).

References:

Peter Collier and David Horowitz, *The Fords: An American Epic* (New York: Summit Books, 1987);

Robert Lacey, *Ford: The Men and the Machine* (Boston: Little, Brown, 1986).

Motor Vehicle Manufacturers Association

by James Wren

Motor Vehicle Manufacturers Association

The Motor Vehicle Manufacturers Association (MVMA) is the principal trade association for motor vehicle manufacturers in the United States. MVMA member companies produce more than 98 percent of domestic motor vehicles. The criterion for membership is the manufacture of motor vehicles in the United States. But the interests of MVMA extend beyond manufacturing to involve the entire transportation industry and the personal mobility of every American. Interests in the areas of law, energy, materials, and environment and specifically vehicle safety, engineering research, environmental research, and other services also concern the MVMA. Member services also include patents and trademarks, statistics, public relations, international affairs, state relations, government liaison, education, and motor truck technical services, plus traffic and freight rates.

Among MVMA's nine member-manufacturers are some of the best-known and most familiar names in American industry. The members of the MVMA, listed alphabetically, are: Chrysler Corporation; Ford Motor Company; General Motors Corporation; Honda of America Manufacturing; LTV Aerospace & Defense Company, AM General Division; MAN Truck & Bus Corporation; Navistar International Corporation; Volkswagen of America; and Volvo North America Corporation.

The MVMA traces its origin to 1900 and the formation of the National Association of Automobile Manufacturers (NAAM). An additional ancestor was the Automobile Board of Trade, which was formed in 1911. These groups merged into the National Automobile Chamber of Commerce (NACC) in 1913, giving the industry a single trade association. The NACC changed its name to the Automobile Manufacturers Association in 1934. In 1972 it became known as the Motor Vehicle Manufacturers Association, in order to reflect representation of both car and truck manufacturers. The motivation behind operating the MVMA is to provide both a forum for collective problem solving and a means for undertaking the joint services and programs that the individual members would otherwise have to initiate.

Over the years the MVMA has undergone many changes—both in its role and in its staff and committee structure. For the most part these changes were evolutionary—gradually emerging to meet the technological and social challenges of the twentieth century. Engineering and scientific problems, which have faced the industry throughout its history, now are more complex because of environmental, safety, energy, and consumer issues. Also increasing the complexity has been the burgeoning list of legislative mandates.

In this climate the MVMA's members refocused their association to concentrate and expand its programs and activities in order to be an effective forum for mutual problem solving and a responsive service organization to meet the challenges facing the industry. This newly refined role is reflected in the MVMA's official objectives:

—To participate in the formation of and support for public policies that will support the U.S. democratic form of government, strengthen the free enterprise system, and promote national goals for individual freedom, mobility, and an improved standard of living.

—To meet its specific responsibilities to improve vehicle safety, reduce vehicle air pollution, and support long-term national objectives for energy and materials conservation.

—To improve the welfare of the motor vehicle industry, consistent with a balanced reconciliation of such national goals and industry responsibilities.

—To serve as a catalyst in identifying important issues and trends and to recommend and support appropriate actions for the association or its members.

—To promote a better public understanding of the role of the motor vehicle in society.

—To develop and perform services that are beneficial to the members and to advance the interests of the industry.

To achieve its objectives the MVMA maintains an administrative staff, a legal staff, and three primary operating divisions: Public Affairs, Technical Affairs, and Motor Truck Affairs. The divisions are comprised of specialized departments and personnel which provide expertise in motor vehicle affairs, including vehicle safety, environmental research, law, engineering, research, patents and trademarks, statistics, public relations, international affairs, state relations, motor trucks traffic, and educational and Federal liaison. The association, through its committees and staff, monitors all motor vehicle activities and coordinates research, information, studies, services, and programs which are beneficial to member companies and the motor vehicle industry. The MVMA also sponsors basic research projects in emissions, energy, noise, and vehicle and highway safety. Its expenditures for research average more than $3 million a year, the major part of which goes to independent researchers working under gifts, grants, or contracts at universities and other recognized research centers.

The association evaluates and responds to governmental regulations which it feels may be detrimental to the industry. It also coordinates lobbying on legislative issues pertaining to motor vehicles. In addition the MVMA makes available extensive collections of research, statistical data, engineering papers and studies, historical information, and vehicle regulation data to members, news media, community leaders, historians, and the public. As industry spokesman, the MVMA prepares numerous publications which are distributed to news media, trade associations, businesses, educators, community and governmental leaders, and the general public.

Over the years the association has extended its reach by providing financial support to many specialized organizations which carry out transportation-related activities beneficial to the industry. Among them are the Highway Users Federation for Safety and Mobility, the Society of Automotive Engineers, and the International Road Federation. The MVMA is also a member of national and international organizations seeking to harmonize motor vehicle standards worldwide, and to improve world commerce, transportation, safety, and industrial health.

The organizational staff is headed by Thomas H. Hanna, who is the president and chief executive officer. Four vice-presidents head the primary operating units with divisional directors and department managers. The MVMA's principal offices are in Detroit and in Washington, D.C. Eight regional offices are maintained throughout the country to monitor motor vehicle legislative and regulatory proposals at state and local levels of government and to provide local resource centers for information on the motor vehicle industry.

References:
Motor Vehicle Manufacturers Association, *MVMA* (Detroit, 1979);

Motor Vehicle Manufacturers Association, *MVMA* (Detroit, 1986).

Archives:
Material on the MVMA is located at the association's office in Detroit.

Thomas Aquinas Murphy

(December 10, 1915-   )

by George S. May

Eastern Michigan University

CAREER: Clerk and accountant, General Motors Corporation (1938-1943); officer, U.S. Naval Reserve (1943-1946); accountant and statistician (1946-1954), director, analysis of corporate and divisional pricing (1954-1956), director, financial analysis section, treasurer's office (1956-1959), assistant treasurer (1959-1967), comptroller (1967-1968), treasurer (1968-1970), vice-president and group executive, car and truck division (1970-1972), vicechairman (1972-1974), chairman and chief executive officer, General Motors Corporation (1974-1980).

Thomas Aquinas Murphy, the chairman of General Motors (GM) from 1974 to 1980, was born on December 10, 1915, the son of John Joseph and Alma O'Grady Murphy. Murphy did not fit the mold of the typical GM executive. He was a Catholic, for instance, in a corporate environment where Protestants were the norm. Similarly, although Murphy was born in Hornell, New York, sharing the small-town origins common to so many top industry executives, he spent his boyhood years from the age of six in the big cities of Buffalo and Chicago. Nevertheless, his subsequent career in business conformed to the standard norms to such an extent that he was later referred to, quite accurately, as "the quintessence of the modern corporate manager." However, as GM's chief executive he found himself grappling with problems quite different from those his predecessors had faced and with which he was sometimes ill-prepared to deal.

The Murphy family's move from Buffalo to Chicago resulted from the father being transferred by the company for which he worked, the City Products Company. In Chicago Thomas Murphy gradu-

Thomas Aquinas Murphy

ated from St. Leo High School in 1932. These years of the early 1930s marked the worst of the depression, and like so many people who lived through that era, including Murphy's immediate predecessor as GM chairman, Richard Gerstenberg, the experience was one that he never forgot. It made him realize the importance of a job and that a job "was something you had to get, and after you got it, you had to work to keep it." After he left high school, the only job Murphy could find was seasonal employment in the summers of 1932, 1933, and 1934 in a Cicero icehouse owned by the City Products Company. One day, Murphy later recalled, one of his fellow workers told him, "You know, you're going to be breaking your back for the rest of your life. You're going to find some smart little gal one of these days and get married, and you'll have family obligations. What you need is an education." When Murphy said he could not afford to go to college, the other worker told him he was using the money from his summer job to put himself through the University of Illinois. In fall 1934 Murphy took his summer earnings and, with his mother, who had also urged him to go to college, went to enroll at the University of Illinois. In part because he had been on the high-school basketball team and planned to play on the university's junior-varsity football team, Murphy had thought he might major in physical education, but as he was standing in line to register he told his mother, "I don't know as I'd want to be a coach—I think I'll go in business." Then, he said, "I was at the head of the line, and they said, 'What school do you want?' And I said, 'Commerce.'"

Four years later Murphy graduated with a bachelor of science degree in accounting, and within a short time he was hired as a clerk in the Detroit offices of the GM comptroller's staff. Within two weeks, however, he was transferred to the financial staff offices in New York; it would be nearly thirty years before his job would return him to the area where the corporation's production was centered. In 1941, with a secure job, Murphy married Catherine Rita Maguire, an Irish girl whose roots were similar to Murphy's, which were described as "nineteenth-century potato-famine Irish." They had three children, Catherine, Maureen, and Thomas Aquinas Murphy, Jr. But in 1943 Murphy was drafted, and he joined the United States Naval Reserve, from which he was discharged in 1946 with the rank of lieutenant junior grade. When he left for the service Murphy did not think he would return to GM, but as he talked with others of his age about the gripes they had concerning the jobs they had left, "my complaints in comparison with theirs were nothing. So when I got out, I went back to General Motors with the spirit that this was where I really wanted to be."

By the time Murphy returned to the financial staff in New York in 1946, the center of power in the corporation had been shifted from those offices to the production staff in Detroit with the naming of President Charles E. Wilson as chief executive officer. Murphy rose through the ranks of the financial staff, therefore, in a period in which its leadership was becoming increasingly unhappy at the way in which Wilson, and particularly Wilson's successor, Harlow Curtice, ignored the views of the financial officers. Murphy's appointment as assistant treasurer in 1959 came a few months after the financial staff's leader, Frederic C. Donner, had become chairman and had reestablished the ascendancy of the New York office by restoring to the holder of that office its earlier responsibilities of chief executive officer.

Donner was determined to assure the continued dominance of the financial staff over the production division and it was soon clear that he had his eye on Murphy as a future occupant of the chairman's job. Murphy was promoted to comptroller in 1967, a job that took him back to Detroit, and then in November 1968 he was named treasurer, climaxing a thirty-year move up the ladder in the financial staff. Murphy was thus understandably surprised in March 1970 when he was picked to be vice-president and group executive of the car and truck division, a job that would normally have gone to someone who had served in one of the motor vehicle divisions. Murphy went to James Roche, the corporation's chairman, and told him that while he had always gone along with the corporation's decisions, he had to question this assignment. "I'm a bookkeeper. I've been in the financial end all my life. I can count the plants I've been in. I don't know the first damn thing about running a plant." But Roche assured him that the directors knew he could do the job. A year and a half later, however, when Murphy was named to the new post of vice-chairman, it was apparent that his stint in manufacturing had been his final preparation for leading the corporation. When Gerstenberg reached the mandatory retirement age of sixty-five in 1974, Murphy, as everyone expected, succeeded him as chairman and chief executive officer, taking over on December 1. Murphy officially received his appointment from the outgoing chairman, James Roche, but insiders declared that Donner, who was still on the board, was responsible for the move.

The new head of the world's largest manufacturing company was described as a "tall, blue-eyed, and silver-haired" man who "wears large, dark-rimmed glasses and favors the traditional GM upper echelon attire—a dark, pinstriped suit." If there was anything that was untraditional about this GM executive it was his sense of humor and his ability to deal easily with the press, characteristics often lacking in previous chief executives. While earlier chairmen, such as Donner, had always projected an image of a highly disciplined businessman whose desk was always neat, Murphy met visitors in an office with what one writer declared was "one of the untidiest desks in American industry," on top of which Murphy had a plaque that read: "Bless this Mess." While others, when asked what they liked to read outside of business, would cite serious works in the areas of history or economics, Murphy said he loved to read detective stories and the comic strip *Peanuts,* from which, he claimed, "you can learn things . . . you can't get anywhere else." In one case Murphy's wit caused the corporation some embarrassment. Both Murphy and Elliott "Pete" Estes, who became president at the same time Murphy became chairman, were fifty-nine years old when they took over their new jobs. Murphy suggested to Estes that an appropriate way for them to observe their upcoming sixtieth birthdays would be to raise GM's market share to 60 percent and GM's stock back up to the same figure. For a short time "60-60-60" were the magic numbers among other GM executives, who thought Murphy had been serious in making this the company's goal for 1975. When it leaked to the press, however, the corporation had to deny hurriedly that Murphy had had anything in mind except a joke about the advancing age of GM's two top officers.

There was nothing very funny about the situation Murphy and Estes faced as they took office. Murphy proved to be an effective and quotable spokesman for the company, and like most heads of companies he tried to be as optimistic as possible in assessing the prospects for GM's products. But the sharp rise in gasoline prices that followed the oil embargo by Middle Eastern oil producers in fall 1973 had left GM, like the other American companies, overstocked with the big cars that had always been the corporation's biggest money-makers. Their heavy fuel consumption made them less popular with customers who wanted smaller, fuel-efficient cars. At the end of 1974 GM had little to offer in the latter category, and the sharp slowdown in its car sales, when combined with similar declines among the other domestic carmakers, helped

to trigger an economic recession which further exacerbated Murphy's problems. Soon the most optimistic thing he could say as he settled into his new job was that "We just know this thing is going to turn around."

Although Murphy and Estes have been credited with shifting the company's emphasis to smaller cars, Murphy's predecessor, Gerstenberg, apparently deserves more credit for having initiated the change. The fruits of Gerstenberg's initiative appeared in 1975 when several smaller car models were introduced. The most highly touted of these was the Chevrolet Chevette, an Americanized version of a car built by GM's German affiliate, Opel, that Chevrolet engineers had cobbled together in a mere eighteen months. Possessing features that were incorporated in versions of the car produced in other parts of the world, the Chevette was an early version of the "World Car," a term introduced six years later by Ford in reference to its Escort model. Murphy hailed the Chevette as "GM's first line of attack against the imports," which had been garnering an ever-larger share of car sales because of their higher gas mileage.

The Chevette was a disappointment, however. Although it was a subcompact, it was essentially a miniaturized version of a standard American car. It used rear-wheel drive instead of the front-wheel drive that some engineers were already beginning to recognize as vital if small American cars were going to truly compete with the imports. Although the Chevette's sales were less than had been projected, Murphy felt the car had played an important role in demonstrating that GM was capable of responding to the needs of the time. It also prepared the way for acceptance of a broader response for which Murphy and Estes can more rightfully be credited—the "downsizing" of GM's entire line of cars.

The need to produce smaller, lighter cars that had been triggered by the rise in gas prices in 1973 and 1974 took on a new urgency in 1975 when Congress passed the Energy Policy and Conservation Act, which mandated that the average efficiency of a company's cars must double within ten years. This projected an average rate of 26 miles per gallon in 1985 from a level of nearly 13 miles per gallon for all American cars in 1975. There were two ways the companies could reach the goal. They could concentrate on developing one or two models with very high mpg rates, which, when added into the performance of the company's other cars, would bring the overall average up to the required figure. Or they could try to improve the performance of all their models to achieve that figure. All three of the big American companies in the last half of the 1970s hesitated to abandon their big cars for fear of a backlash from their traditional clientele. (American Motors was not concerned since it no longer competed in the large-car market.) Chrysler and Ford made the decision to opt for the approach that would use one or two efficient models to achieve the necessary corporate average. Under Murphy, however, GM chose the other approach. A slimmed-down Cadillac, the Seville, had already appeared in spring 1975 and by fall 1976 downsized versions of other big GM cars were appearing for the 1977 model year. GM thus sought to maintain the full line of models that it had so carefully nurtured over the years, without sacrificing too much of the comfort and roominess that its customers had been accustomed to in earlier models.

The strategy seemed to work. As the country pulled out of the recession, automobile sales began to rebound and by the first quarter of 1976 GM could report staggering earnings of $800 million, fourteen times higher than 1975 first-quarter earnings. By 1977 GM's share of domestic car sales was approaching the 60-percent figure, two years after Murphy's sixtieth birthday but, late or not, obviously highly gratifying to the chairman. GM had moved ahead of its competitors with its lineup of smaller cars, and, with the public now accustomed to higher gas prices, the improved economic conditions led many to return to the bigger models that the corporation was still producing. Proposals to levy an extra tax on the full-size, "gas guzzling" cars were vigorously opposed by Murphy because, he said, such a tax would discriminate against the one out of every six American families that had three or more children and who had to have the space provided by the so-called "family cars."

But the good times were not to last long. Early in 1979 the Shah of Iran was deposed, fundamentalist Muslims took over control of that country, nationalized the oil fields, and halted sales to the United States, the Shah's leading supporter. Although Iranian oil was only a tiny percentage of America's oil imports, the action triggered a new gasoline panic that proved to have even greater economic consequences for automobile sales than the earlier crisis of 1973-1974. Domestic car sales slid from 8.3 million in 1979 to around 6 million in

1980 and although GM did not suffer the extensive losses at the start of the 1980s as did Ford and Chrysler, its downsizing strategy no longer appeared so successful. In far greater numbers than back in the mid 1970s buyers, seeing gas prices inch up to and over the $1 per gallon figure, now wanted cars that were far thriftier in their fuel consumption than GM's slimmed-down models. Chrysler, despite its near fatal financial condition, had introduced the first small front-wheel drive American models at the end of 1977 and by late 1980 had its slightly larger front-wheel drive K-cars on the market. Ford, which had been able to meet some of the demand for small cars by importing the Fiesta, a subcompact produced by its German subsidiary, in the early 1980s introduced its much-heralded Ford Escort subcompact. The Escort quickly became the top-selling car in the world and helped Ford generate earnings that by the mid 1980s topped GM's for the first time since 1924.

Thus, as a harried Murphy prepared to step down as chairman at the end of 1980, it was hard for him to be very optimistic. Some $40 billion was being budgeted in the next five years to enable GM to catch up in the building of fuel-efficient subcompacts. But in the meantime problems continued. GM's earlier efforts to save money by installing Chevrolet engines in Oldsmobile models without informing the public had led to a flood of suits that cost the company $40 million in 1979. There was actually very little difference between the engines used in the Chevrolet model and those normally used in the Oldsmobile model, and Murphy had remarked that he guessed that it had never occurred to them "that people were interested in where the engines were built." But the issue foreshadowed an increasing problem. Other actions, some of them part of the downsizing program, made the GM models look more and more alike, creating identity problems that seriously dampened sales of the higher-priced models by the mid 1980s.

Those were problems that had to be dealt with by Murphy's successor, Roger B. Smith, who was, like Murphy, a product of GM's financial staff. As did all GM chief executives, Murphy remained involved in the affairs of the corporation as a member of the board of directors for several years after he retired. The normal duration of such service was five years, but the bylaws provided that the time could be extended. Thus Murphy continued to be a director until 1988. By that time he had seen GM rebound in the years immediately after he retired, only to see it slip again in mid decade. By 1988, however, the drastic measures that Roger Smith had taken to slim down not only the products, but the corporation itself, were beginning to show results. As he severed his last official link with the corporation with which he had been associated for half a century, Murphy would have felt justi-

fied in saying, as he had at the end of his term as chairman, "The worst is over."

References:

"The Chairman of GM," *Newsweek*, 88 (July 4, 1976): 16;

Ed Cray, *Chrome Colossus: General Motors and Its Times* (New York: McGraw-Hill, 1980);

"Murphy's Law: Things Will Go Right," *Time*, 111 (March 27, 1978): 70;

Ralph Nader

(February 27, 1934-)

by Kevin M. Dwyer

George Washington University

CAREER: Attorney, Hartford, Connecticut (1961-1963); consultant, Department of Labor (1964-1965); consultant, Senate Sub-Committee on Executive Reorganization of Government Operations (1964-1966); consumer advocate (1967-); founder, Center for Responsive Law (1969); founder, Center for Auto Safety (1970); founder, Corporate Accountability Research Group (1970); founder, Public Citizen, Inc. (1971).

As America's foremost consumer advocate, Ralph Nader has trained his sights on a wide range of corporate targets, but his most indelible impression will likely remain upon the automotive industry. Nader's involvement in the debate over automotive safety, and the industry's reaction to it, catapulted him from relative obscurity in the mid 1960s to sixth place in a 1971 Harris poll of the most popular public figures in America. During his career Nader has remained well-known to many Americans.

Nader's choice of public policy as a career had much to do with his upbringing. The youngest of Nathra and Rose Bouziane Nader's four children, Nader was born on February 27, 1934, and raised in what David Halberstam calls "a completely politicized home." Nader's parents came to America from Lebanon; they settled in Winsted, Connecticut, where they operated a small but successful bakery-restaurant. They took seriously the American dream and imbued their children with their intense civic-mindedness. According to Nader's father, whom one of Nader's later associates likened to "an Old Testament prophet—

righteous," Nader was taught to "understand that working for justice is a safeguard to democracy."

Nader early began fulfilling his father's charge. He began bringing home copies of the *Congressional Record* from the local public library while still in elementary school. By age fourteen he had "read all the muckraker books . . . *The Jungle, America's 60 Families.*" While in college Nader wrote letters to the *Daily Princetonian* protesting the spraying of DDT on campus as an undergraduate, and although his letters were never published, he graduated from Princeton's Woodrow Wilson School of Public and International Affairs *magna cum laude* in 1955.

Automobile safety became a focus of Nader's concern after he entered Harvard Law School. His interest on the subject was piqued by a 1956 Harvard *Law Review* article by Harold Katz arguing that mechanical defects should factor into the determination of traffic accident liability. Through subsequent research Nader became familiar with the automobile safety studies conducted at the Cornell Aeronautics Laboratory and also with Congressional inquiries into the subject. His third-year thesis focused on vehicle design flaws and supplemented his 1958 *Harvard Law Record* article, "American Cars: Designed for Death."

Personal experiences helped sharpen Nader's focus on automobile safety. Without a car–he sold his 1949 Studebaker while at Harvard after concluding he did not need it–Nader hitchhiked extensively and witnessed several gruesome accidents. In one he saw a little girl nearly decapitated by a glove compartment door which had sprung open, and in

Ralph Nader

1961 a close friend was crippled for life in an automobile accident.

Nader served for six months in the United States Army after taking his L.L.B. from Harvard with distinction. As a cook at Fort Dix, New Jersey, he spent much of his spare time at the motor pool becoming better acquainted with the mechanical functioning of cars. Following his discharge in 1959, Nader established a law practice in Hartford, Connecticut, where he worked on consumer protection and automobile safety legislation and wrote articles on automobile safety. One of these, appearing in the *Nation*, brought Nader to the attention of Daniel Patrick Moynihan, who, as an aide to New York governor Averell Harriman, was concerned with highway safety. Moynihan himself had written an article on the subject for the *Reporter* in 1959. The following year the two met and began what would become an eventful relationship.

In 1961 Moynihan was appointed assistant secretary of labor for policy planning in the Kennedy administration. Moynihan retained his contact with Nader as well as his concern for automobile safety. Upon finding that no single federal agency was accountable for automobile safety, Moynihan commissioned a study on the subject. He asked Nader to conduct the study late in 1963, and Nader, dissatisfied with Hartford and still restless after traveling through the Soviet Union, Scandinavia, Africa,

and South America, gladly accepted. He moved to Washington in 1964.

Nader worked on the Department of Labor study for the next year. During this time he became well known to other Washington officials involved in the mounting inquiries into automobile safety. Nader assisted Wisconsin senator Gaylord Nelson in drafting a bill to make the safety features (most notably, seat belts) required on cars purchased by the Government Services Administration standard on all cars sold in the United States. He also shared the results of his research with Sen. Abraham Ribicoff of Connecticut, chair of the Executive Reorganization subcommittee of the Government Operations Committee, which had been investigating the subject. Also that year Grossman publishers contracted Nader to write a book on unsafe automobiles for the sum of $2,000.

Nader finished his study, "A Report on the Context, Condition and Recommended Direction of Federal Activity in Highway Safety" in May 1965. Although he then left the department to complete his manuscript, throughout the spring and summer he continued to advise the Ribicoff committee. Industry executives invited to testify before the committee in March 1965 were quite dismayed when they returned for July hearings to find senators asking tougher questions, many of them supplied by Nader. The executives' poor performance before

In October we will publish a book that tells why your car could kill you...and what must be done to make it safe.

UNSAFE AT ANY SPEED

The designed-in dangers of the American automobile
By Ralph Nader
$5.00 Order now from:

Advertisement for Nader's 1965 exposé of manufacturers' lack of concern with safety in American automobiles

the committee attracted the press and television cameras. Especially unsettling for both sides was the disclosure by General Motors (GM) executives that their company had spent only $1.25 million on safety research in 1964, when the company had earned a profit of more than $1.7 billion.

The Ribicoff hearings set the stage for the release of Nader's book, *Unsafe at Any Speed: The Designed-in Dangers of the American Automobile*, in November 1965. While indicting the entire industry for its long-running emphasis of style over safety, the book singled out GM's Chevrolet Corvair for special condemnation. Often compared with Upton Sinclair's 1906 classic, *The Jungle, Unsafe at Any Speed* details the Corvair's design flaws and the carnage they caused. Although it received favorable reviews and was featured on the front-page of the *New York Times*, the book did not have much commercial appeal until GM blundered into a public relations disaster.

In midsummer 1965, before the book's release, Nader had criticized the Corvair on television, radio, and in print. Already wary of the 103 lawsuits pending against the company, involving claims of over $40 million, the GM legal staff, without contacting top management, hired three private detective agencies to try and discredit Nader. When initial queries failed to link him with any of the lawsuits, investigators then focused on Nader's personal life. His phone was tapped, and detectives trailed him around Washington. He eventually began to suspect that he was being followed. Early in 1966 detectives, who thought they were trailing Nader, unknowingly alerted the *Washington Post* of their activities by following a reporter. A pair of detectives were arrested on February 11 by Washington, D.C., police while following Nader. In the following month the *Post*, the *New York Times*, and the *New Republic* all carried the story, and GM was forced to admit its involvement.

The episode made Nader an overnight celebrity. Sales of his book soared. GM president James M. Roche, appearing on national television before the Ribicoff committee, pleaded ignorance and publicly apologized to Nader. Although Roche said publicly, "I deplore this kind of harassment," and expressed his "shock" and "outrage" over the incident, he privately referred to Nader as "one of the bitter gypsies of dissent who plaque America."

The Johnson administration, meanwhile, wanting innovation in the field of transportation, included automotive safety in its 1966 legislative package. The Ribicoff hearings and the publication of Nader's book put the subject on the national agenda, and President Johnson mentioned automotive safety in his 1966 State of the Union Address. With support for highway safety legislation in Congress growing, a highway safety bill was proposed.

Throughout the spring and summer Nader spent sixteen to eighteen hours a day lobbying senators, congressmen, and their respective staffs. A constant presence on Capitol Hill that summer, he worked, unpaid, out of his DuPont Circle rooming house, living off savings and book and lecture royalties. Before the Ribicoff committee Nader criticized annual model changes and flashy advertising techniques that glossed over safety concerns. He also helped to draft Sen. Vance Hartke's amendments to strengthen the proposed automotive safety bill. To the Senate commerce committee's traffic and safety hearings, Nader declared: "Any automotive industry that requires the piling up of corpses and bloody limbs as evidence for them to eliminate . . . obvious and non-functional features, is not displaying sufficient responsibility in my judgment."

To offset Nader's efforts, the industry hired Lloyd Cutler, a prominent Washington lobbyist. Cutler attempted to water down the proposed Senate legislation but met with little success, removing only the criminal penalties for non-compliance. On the day of its final drafting, both Nader and Cutler, sitting in separate rooms, were invited to check and approve the bill, which was reported favorably out of the Commerce Committee on June 24, 1966, and breezed through the Senate. On August 17 it passed the House 371-0. President Johnson signed the National Traffic and Motor Vehicle Safety Act into law on September 9. The law required the industry by 1968 to install as standard equipment, in all American-made cars, seventeen safety features including seat belts. These features were the same as those adopted by government vechicles earlier that decade. The law also established the National Traffic Safety Agency to oversee enforcement. Although Nader was not invited to the signing ceremony, the act would have been a much weaker piece of legislation without his involvement.

Nader continued to lobby on Capitol Hill for increased automotive safety throughout the late 1960s, with GM remaining his primary target. In 1967 Nader urged the Senate Commerce Committee to reinstate criminal non-compliance penalties deleted from the original 1966 safety act. To improve competitiveness in the automobile industry, in 1968 Nader urged the Senate Select Committee on Small Business to break up GM. In 1970 he accused GM of keeping unfavorable test results from a Senate subcommittee and from the courts in the early 1960s for fear that their disclosure would have hurt sales.

In 1967 Nader filed a $26 million invasion of privacy suit against GM. The case was settled out-of-court in 1970 with Nader receiving $425,000. He used the money to found a host of consumer advocacy groups, including the Center for Auto Safety, the Corporate Accountability Research Group, and Public Citizen, Inc., all located in Washington, D.C. Nader eventually helped to found over two dozen groups; he is no longer affiliated with most of them, the Center for Auto Safety included.

The automotive safety movement that Nader championed became institutionalized by the early 1970s. Due in large part to his efforts, federal regulation had come to Detroit. Nader's efforts were similarly effective in the establishment of the Environmental Protection Agency in 1970, the passage of the 1974 Freedom of Information Act, and the creation of the Occupational Safety and Health Organization (OSHA) in 1976.

By the 1980s, however, Nader had become something of a national curiosity. Nader still owns no car and still dresses in the plain, usually grey, thin-lapelled suits and trenchcoat that have become his trademark. Nader, married to his causes, remains a bachelor.

Selected Publications:

Unsafe at Any Speed: The Designed-in Dangers of the American Automobile (New York: Grossman, 1965);

Beware (New York: Law-Arts, 1970);

What To Do With Your Bad Car (Washington, D.C.: Center for Study of Responsive Law, 1971);

Action For A Change with Donald Ross, (Washington, D.C.: Center For Study of Responsive Law, 1972);

You and Your Pension, with Kate Blackwell (Washington, D.C.: Center For Study of Responsive Law, 1973);

The Paper Plantation (New York: Viking, 1974);

Whistle Blowing (New York: Penguin, 1974);

Working on the System (New York: Basic Books, 1974);

The Commerce Committees (New York: Viking, 1975);

The Environment Committees (New York: Viking, 1975);

The Judiciary Committees (New York: Viking, 1975);

Ralph Nader Congress Project, six volumes (New York: Viking, 1975);

The Revenue Committees (New York: Viking, 1975);

Taming the Giant Corporation, with Mark Green and Joel Seligman (New York: Norton, 1976);

Verdicts on Lawyers, with Mark Green (New York: Thomas Y. Crowell, 1977);

The Menace of Atomic Energy, with John Abbotts (New York: Norton, 1979);

The Lemon Book, with Clarence Dittow and Joyce Kinnard (Ottawa, Ill.: Green Hill, 1980);

The Big Boys: Styles of Corporate Power (New York: Pantheon, 1986).

References:

James J. Flink, *The Automobile Age* (Cambridge, Mass.: MIT Press, 1988);

Robert D. Holsworth, *Public Interest Liberalism & The Crisis of Affluence* (Rochester, Vt.: Schenkman, 1981);

Charles McCarry, *Citizen Nader* (New York: Saturday Review Press, 1972);

Thomas Whiteside, *The Investigation of Ralph Nader* (New York: William Morrow, 1972).

PACCAR Incorporated

by George S. May

Eastern Michigan University

PACCAR Incorporated, which became one of the largest producers of Class 8 (over 33,000 pounds gross weight) trucks, had its beginnings with the Seattle Car Company, organized in 1905 by William Pigott, whose background was in the steel industry and who the previous year had been one of the organizers of the Seattle Steel Company. Seattle Car made railroad cars and eventually became the Pacific Car & Foundry Company, headquartered in Bellevue, Washington. By the 1980s the company's name had been shortened to PACCAR, and it was headed by the founder's grandson, Charles M. Pigott. It still sold a few rail cars and also manufactured underground mining equipment, industrial winches, and oilfield extraction pumps, but by far the major contributors to its over $3 billion in sales were its heavy-duty trucks.

PACCAR, then Pacific Car & Foundry, entered the truck manufacturing business in 1944 when it acquired the Kenworth Truck Company. This was followed in 1958 by its purchase of the Peterbilt Motors Company. Both companies had begun as manufacturers of heavy-duty trucks for logging purposes but had expanded into the production of both conventional and cab-over-engine trucks for long-distance hauling. Because the two were now subsidiaries of the same company, and because the type of trucks they produced were similar, they shared some components while still maintaining their separate identities. Both had come to be regarded by truckers, *Fortune* noted, "as works of art as well as hardworking tools." With them, PACCAR increased its share of the Class 8 market from 7 percent in the early 1960s to 20 percent by the 1980s. PACCAR was the marvel of the industry, being the only company in the industry to show a profit in the grim recession year of 1980. Unlike its major competitors, International Harvester and Mack, it was primarily an assembler, buying its major components from outside suppli-

William Pigott, founder of Seattle Car Company which became PACCAR

ers. It offered its customers a seemingly endless list of options, which enabled the trucker to obtain a custom truck that cost an average of $70,000 in 1984 and would last more than 500,000 miles. The cost of its trucks ran about 5 percent more than those of its competitors, but still they sold. Pigott believed that his company had an edge because the trucks were assembled in seven factories scattered over North America, none of them employing more than 750 to 1000 workers. "You lose the intimate touch" with a larger plant, Pigott asserted. "We don't think we could turn out as good a product under mass production."

In addition to its markets in the United States, PACCAR also expanded its sales into Canada, Mexico, Australia, and the United Kingdom, where, in the early 1980s, PACCAR bought up Foden, an old-line independent British truck manufacturer which had run into financial trouble and which PACCAR proceeded to convert to the same custom building approach that it had found so successful at Kenworth and Peterbilt.

References:
Andrew C. Brown, "Hard Times for Truck Makers," *Fortune*, 104 (September 7, 1981): 80-89;
Dero A. Saunders, "In the passing lane," *Forbes*, 134 (September 10, 1984): 50-51.

Paints and Finishes

by James Wren

Motor Vehicle Manufacturers Association

Before 1923, when Dupont introduced its Duco pyroxylin lacquer, painting was the single most time-consuming element in automobile production. During the early decades of the automobile, the painting process could last up to forty-five days for each car. At Ford, the venerable Model T could be purchased only in black after 1913, because only that color would dry quickly enough to comply with the company's mass-production processes. Pre-Duco methods used oleoresinous, varnish-based enamels, which were applied by brush in six to ten coats, each one hand-sanded and hand-rubbed. Besides the obvious labor-intensiveness of the technique, production time was lost because drying of the finish was accomplished through the slow process of oxidizing the oil in the varnish.

Still, slow progress was made in saving time and improving quality. Dust-free, heated rooms were developed, though high temperatures were prohibited because of potential damage to the wood body from charring, warping, or cracking. But drying time remained a point of inefficiency, in 1922 adding seventeen days to the time necessary to produce a car.

Duco, introduced on the 1924 Oakland, radically changed the situation. The pyroxylin lacquer, which dried not through oxidation but by the evaporation of its thinners, reduced drying time from weeks to hours. It also provided more durability and resistance to heat-induced cracking. The introduction of synthetic resin undercoats in the late 1920s magnified these positive properties of Duco.

Equally important to the improvement in drying time which Duco provided was the styling flexibility the paint offered. Bright and various colors were available on mass-production vehicles, marking the beginning of the ascendence of styling over engineering. The ability to offer colors was particularly crucial as the automobile industry neared the saturation point for the first-time buyer market. Such men as Alfred P. Sloan, Jr., of GM, where Duco made its debut, saw that continued prosperity for the industry depended on buyers replacing their cars. Sloan believed that style and fashion would play a large role in this strategy, and Duco was a very useful tool in persuading consumers.

But pyroxylin lacquer was not without its deficiencies. The major problem was that it did not weather well, losing its lustre over time. In fact this weathering problem led to the development of the next generation of automobile finishes. Introduced in the mid 1950s, acrylic lacquers possessed superior weathering characteristics and eliminated the need for rubbing between coats. The 1960s saw a further improvement, with the introduction of corrosion-resistant paints. These finishes are applied through electrodisposition, a process whereby paint is polarized and bonded to an oppositely charged surface. This system is extremely cost-effective, and the paint wears very well.

References:
"The Evolution of Automobile Finishes," *Automotive Industries* (September 15, 1957): 72, 115, 124;
"Goodbye to Rust and Corrosion," *Ward's Auto World* (April/May 1970): 39-40.

Donald Eugene Petersen

(September 4, 1926-   )

by James J. Flink

University of California, Irvine

CAREER: Various product planning assignments, Ford Division (1949-1953), programming-planning coordinator, Ford Division (1953-1955), assistant car planning manager, Ford Division (1955-1956), manager, Merchandising and Product Planning Office, Lincoln Division (1956-1958), car planning manager, Ford Division (1958-1962), product planning manager, Ford Division (1962-1963), forward marketing plans manager, Ford Division (1963-1965), director, Forward Marketing Plans Office, Marketing Staff (1965), assistant to the vice-president, Car and Truck Group (1965-1966), car product planning manager, Ford Division (1966-1967), car product planning manager, Product Development Group (1967-1969), executive director, Administration, Engineering, and Industrial Design, (1969), vice-president, Car Planning and Research, Product Development Group (1969-1971), vice-president and general manager, Truck Operations (1971-1973), vice-president and general manager, Truck and Recreational Products Operations (1973-1975), executive vice-president, Diversified Products Operations (1975-1977), executive vice-president, International Automotive Operations (1977-1980), president and chief operating officer (1980-1985), chairman of the board and chief executive officer, Ford Motor Company (1985-   ).

Donald Eugene Petersen is the youngest of three sons of William and Mae (Pederson) Petersen. He was born on a farm near Pipestone, Minnesota, on September 4, 1926. His father's asthma caused the family to relocate to Long Beach, California, when Donald was two years old. William Petersen, who only knew farming, tried a number of jobs in Southern California as a salesman, but in the depths of the Great Depression he never succeeded in finding stable employment. Despite the aggravation to his asthma, he moved his family in 1937 to Portland, Oregon, where he had found a job selling

Donald Eugene Petersen

service station and garage equipment at no salary, on consignment.

In the depression years, the family of the future Ford chairman was too poor to own a car, despite living in a society in which the automobile had become a middle-class necessity. But the family was brought closer by hard times, and Petersen recalls a warm and supportive family setting. His parents continually stressed the values of hard work and educational achievement. He was a gifted child with a determination to excel, and he dreamed of having a job someday that paid $200 a month. He skipped a grade, which enabled him in 1943 at the age of seventeen to enter the pre-engineering program at Oregon State University. There he met Jo Anne (Jody) Leonard, whom he married in 1948.

Petersen calls the Navy V-12 program "a godsend" that gave him the opportunity to obtain a first-rate technical education. In summer 1944 he entered the V-12 program and transferred to the University of Washington. There he became a member of Tau Beta Pi, Phi Beta Kappa, and Sigma Xi. He graduated magna cum laude in June 1946 with a B. S. degree in mechanical engineering, then served as an infantry officer in the United States Marine Corps until March 1947. The GI Bill and money he saved from a 1947 job as a catskinner on an Idaho grain farm permitted Petersen to continue his education at Stanford University, from which he received his M.B.A. in June 1949.

"I had a high priority as I started my work life that I wanted security," Petersen relates. "That was a very important Y in the road, because that led me into a large setting like the Ford Motor Company. I didn't even really consider what today we call 'start ups' or trying something on my own." During his second year at Stanford he acquired his first car, a Ford V-8 that he remembers ran well. During his last quarter at Stanford a Ford recruiter invited him back to Ford headquarters for an interview. After missing the bus at Dearborn, Petersen was dropped off, suitcase in hand, at the side of the highway in front of the Ford administration building. "I was dusty, but they liked me," he recalls. A month after graduating from Stanford, he was hired by Ford at $300 a month as "product planning analyst"–a job he himself had defined and created during his interview. Thus began a life career at Ford for Petersen interrupted only by his recall by the Marine Corps to active duty for eighteen months during the Korean War.

Petersen began his career at Ford at an auspicious point in the company's history. Ford had slipped from a near monopoly of 59 percent of the American market in 1921 to third place in sales behind General Motors (GM) and Chrysler by 1936. After a generation of gross mismanagement, Ford was losing about $10 million a month when Henry Ford II took over leadership of the family firm from his senile grandfather on September 21, 1945, and began a long overdue program of revitalization. The turnaround involved hiring a team of former Air Force Officers called the Whiz Kids, who came from the Office of Statistical Control and had been trained at the Harvard Business School. Ford also recruited an executive team from GM headed by Ernest R. Breech, former president of Bendix Aviation and GM assistant treasurer. The new management tried to emulate at Ford the GM committee structure, managerial bureaucracy, and financial controls. Ford sales doubled from 547,000 in 1948 to almost 1.2 million in 1950 with the introduction of the Model B-A, the first new postwar Ford car and one which set a styling trend still in evidence with its "envelope body." As a result, Ford surpassed Chrysler to regain second place in the industry. The sign identifying the Model B-A in the Henry Ford Museum claims, "It was visible evidence of the successful revitalization of the Ford Motor Company." Although retention of two-fifths of the Ford voting stock in the hands of the Ford family ensured continuing family control, in 1955 Ford went public as some 7 million shares of non-voting common were reclassified as voting shares and either distributed to key executives or put on the market. Petersen, who had never seriously considered "start ups," thus ironically had joined a recently moribund giant, now for the first time in decades on the move in new directions.

As a product planner during much of his early career, Petersen played a major role in establishing institutionalized product planning at Ford. After that his advancement was meteoric. Twelve promotions in sixteen years marked his advancement from programming-planning coordinator in the Ford Division in 1953 to vice-president for car planning and research of the Ford Motor Company Product Development Group in 1969. "For nearly two decades he helped refine and develop product planning at Ford," summarizes a corporate news department profile. "He played a substantial role in the development of cars such as the Ford LTD, Mustang, Fairlane, Maverick, and Mark III. He also served in the company's marketing and vehicle design activities. His time in the product planning area spanned the period from the revolutionary 1949 Ford, the first Thunderbird, the Mustang, and many other products introduced by the company in the 1950s and 1960s." By 1969 Petersen "already had made a significant impact on the company's products, although he has not claimed any particular model as his 'own.'" Moreover, as planning manager in the Ford Division, he had been responsible for a plan for future products that gave an excellent broad overview of the company. This demonstrated Petersen's ability to think in terms of the company as a whole—a sine qua non for further advancement.

A significant career shift from concentration on product planning and marketing, to making broader business decisions, came with promotion to vice-president and general manager of truck operations in 1971. "If that had not happened," says Petersen, "I could easily have become just the professional product developer and never done anything more." In addition to heavy development responsibilities for the Bronco, Econoline, Ford pickup, and CL-series trucks, Petersen was in charge of all aspects of Ford's North American truck business.

Petersen's success with the Ford line of trucks earned him a promotion to executive vice-president of Diversified Products Operations in 1975. This gave him, for the first time, personal exposure to Henry Ford II. Diversified Products in reality consisted of ten separate businesses, and Petersen relates that "Henry Ford seemed impressed that I knew as much about those businesses as quickly as I did. I had a concept of what I thought as a company we ought to do with each one of them." He developed "a semi-long term business plan. We really didn't have more than a two- to three-year look, and after the first year it was really pretty vague. In product planning we had gone to a ten-year cycle plan, and we were pretty firm about what we wanted to do ten years out. I was strong for a five-year business plan and tried to apply it to the business in general."

Petersen believes that it was the exposure to Henry Ford II as head of Diversified Products that resulted in promotion to executive vice-president, International Automotive Operations in April 1977, and that gained him a seat on the Ford board of directors in September 1977. These moves put Petersen in the group of legitimate candidates for the Ford presidency and chairmanship. The job not only gave Petersen an appreciation for the scope of the Ford business worldwide, it also put him into constant, intimate contact with Henry Ford II, who had begun to think seriously about the transition in leadership that would come with his retirement. "He and I traveled the world together," Petersen relates. "He was thinking through the transition of the company. One thing Mr. Ford had a strong feeling about was the people of the company, especially the overseas people, and he wanted to get to

as many locations as possible one more time. So he just started getting my calendar and hitchhiking."

The travel together gave Ford the opportunity to take Petersen's measure. However, explains Petersen, "I still don't think there was any sense of my becoming president and chairman. I personally think that happened primarily because of the major problems that the industry and Ford had starting in mid 1979. It happened that I had more years involved in what to do with our products than any of the top people in the company, and there was substantial concern about the clear lack of customer appeal in the American line of our cars."

Leadership of the Ford Motor Company passed out of the Ford family for the first time in its history with the retirement of Henry Ford II as chief executive officer (CEO) on October 1, 1979. Philip Caldwell, former chairman of Ford Europe, who in 1977 had been made vice-chairman and CEO in Ford's absence, took over as CEO. On March 13, 1980, Caldwell also succeeded Ford as chairman of the board, and Petersen became president and chief operating officer. When Caldwell retired on February 1, 1985, Petersen became chairman and chief executive officer. Henry Ford II continued to serve on the board of directors and as chairman of its finance committee until his death on September 29, 1987. He was succeeded as finance committee chairman by his brother, William Clay Ford.

The Caldwell-Petersen team took over at the nadir of the American automobile industry. In 1980 Japan passed the United States to become the leading automobile-producing nation in the world, and the U.S. share of the world market for cars had plunged from over 75 percent in 1950 to about 20 percent. With the shift to smaller cars following the oil shock of 1979 and Japanese competition making plant changeover and modernization mandatory, the U.S. auto industry in 1980 fell a record $10.7 billion short of meeting immediate capital needs from operating expenses. From 1980 to 1982 the Ford Motor Company lost $3.3 billion while investing $8 billion in new products and facilities. Some auto industry analysts even doubted whether the second-largest automobile manufacturer in the world could survive the crunch.

While the turnaround at Chrysler under the chairmanship of Lee Iacocca has received more public attention and approbation, the recovery of Ford under Caldwell and Petersen is both more impressive and more important in the history of the auto industry. Ford posted record after-tax profits of $1.87 billion in 1983 and $2.91 billion in 1984. In 1984 Ford's share of the U. S. passenger car market reached 19.2 percent, the highest level in five years and a 2-percent increase over 1983, while Ford led in European automobile sales with a record 13 percent of the market. From 1983 to 1986 Ford had net earnings of over $10.5 billion. With record profits of $3.3 billion in 1986 Ford surpassed GM in profits for the first time in sixty-one years and accomplished the feat on only about half of GM's sales. Ford again surpassed GM in profits in 1987 with after-tax net income of $4.6 billion, a record not only for Ford but for the entire automobile industry. At the end of 1987 Ford had $10 billion in cash on hand and a comfortable debt-to-equity ratio of 20 percent.

Led by Caldwell, Petersen and Harold A. Poling—a tough, aggressive manager who ran Ford North American Automotive Operations from 1980 to 1985 and then became company president—Ford became a far leaner and tougher company. Between 1980 and 1988 Ford closed fifteen plants and reduced its North American work force by 26 percent. As a consequence, operating costs were reduced $5 billion annually. Despite the cutbacks capacity was increased by 500,000 units through plant modernization and more efficient use of facilities. The Ford break-even point was reduced about 40 percent to 2.5 million units, and industry analysts estimated that operating profit margins were 11 percent at Ford, versus 9 percent at Chrysler and 6 percent at General Motors.

Petersen has been the driving force behind the main reason for the turnaround—new models with great customer appeal that have gained Ford market shares. A *New York Times* profile described him as "the first of a new wave of top auto executives who are more concerned about products and production systems than financial analysis." He was an early advocate of smaller cars, and as Ford car planning manager twenty years ago he predicted that people would one day "take their children to museums to show them the dinosaurs Americans used to drive." The 1981 subcompact Escort/Lynx was the first American-produced "world car," designed to be sold with minor variations throughout the world, and assembled in five countries with components sourced in seventeen. Since its introduction the Escort/Lynx has been the best-selling car in the world, and its design characteristics have become standard for state-of-the-art small cars.

Petersen attended the Bob Bondurant School of Performance Driving in Santa Rosa, California, so that he could do a better job of evaluating Ford cars on the test track. Training executives in performance driving has since become practice at Ford. At Ford, Petersen has pushed the concept of the "dynamic vehicle"–one which handles and performs well and in which form and function are closely integrated.

The story goes that shortly after becoming president Petersen confronted Jack Telnack, Ford's vice-president for design, with a query about a new model being developed: "Are you happy with it? Would you really like to drive that, Jack?" When Telnack responded, "No, sir" Petersen countered: "Why don't you design something you'd really like to drive, something you'd be proud to have in your driveway?" Early in his career at Ford, Telnack had worked in the studio of pioneer aerodynamic auto designer Alex Tremulis, and Telnack had become further convinced of the aesthetic and functional superiority of aerodynamic cars while design chief of Ford-Europe. Therefore he welcomed the opportunity to make a radical change in the new Ford models. "I'd heard top management tell us to reach as far as we could before," he says, "but when the moment of truth came, they backed down. This time they didn't. That's when I knew things had changed."

Petersen personally supervised the introduction of six new Ford models in twenty months at a development cost of $10 billion. The 1983 Ford Thunderbird/Mercury Cougar and the 1984 Ford Tempo/Mercury Topaz broke sharply with conventional design concepts. Their advanced aerodynamic designs made Ford the styling pacesetter in the automobile industry. At a development cost of $3 billion, the "Team Taurus" project attempted to develop the best possible intermediate-size car. Ford claimed that 80 percent of 400 of the "best in class" features of 50 comparable cars were matched or bettered by the 1986 Ford Taurus/Mercury Sable, which became the best-selling Ford models since the 1965 Mustang. *Motor Trend* named as its Car of the Year the Ford Taurus sedan for 1986 and the Ford Turbocharged Thunderbird coupe for 1987. Petersen also put a new emphasis on manufacturing quality at Ford, advertising it as "Job 1."

From 1980 to 1985 Ford claimed an average improvement, based on warranty claims and complaints, of more than 50 percent in its cars and light trucks, and *Consumer Reports* rated Ford cars the most improved. "We have taken a customer-driven approach to our products," Petersen explains. "We are absolutely committed to designing, manufacturing, and selling products that respond to the customer's needs and wants. A simple thing we learned: The customer is always right."

The change in the Ford corporate culture under Petersen has been as dramatic as the improvement in Ford products. Petersen came close to resigning twice over "some unfortunate experiences" with the people under whom he worked during his early years at Ford. He found their treatment of people "divisive, competitive, and brutal." A "Star" system prevailed that pitted against one another cliques loyal to one or another top executive; as a result the company was highly politicized. His early superiors "had patterns of how they managed that I simply didn't like and didn't want to be associated with," Petersen explains. "Therefore, I found myself trying to be seen as separate. It became a habit with me that I did not want to be seen as part of some one person's team. Back in those days 'team' meant a very different thing from 'team work.'" Consequently Petersen never hitched his star to anyone else's wagon, and he had a strong desire to see things work differently at Ford.

Robert S. McNamara, Ford president briefly in 1960 before becoming secretary of defense in the Kennedy administration, stands out in Petersen's mind as an exception to what he objected to in the Ford work environment. He remembers McNamara "as one man I learned a great deal from and was in some respects very influential on my life. I found him as intellectually stimulating as any man I've ever met. He had a lot of influence on how you deal with people." As spokesman for product planning, Petersen had "hours and hours of discussion about future products" with McNamara during the few months that McNamara served as the head of Ford's North American automotive activities prior to becoming president of the company. McNamara's open-mindedness and fairness left a lasting impression. "He gave me the opportunity to develop a rationale to convince him," Petersen says. "He even went so far as to let me make a presentation to the company's product planning committee, including Mr. [Ernest] Breech and Mr. Ford, even

though he didn't agree with me." From McNamara he learned the importance of respecting differences of opinion and of being "ready to be convinced if the facts are there or if a persuasive argument can be mounted."

Donald Frey was another role model. Frey received a Ph.D. in engineering from the University of Michigan and was known at Ford as "a car man," one who put the product first. He was the product manager behind the success of the Mustang. After beating Petersen out for the job of overall Ford product manager, Frey had the decency to drop by the Petersen home to inform him personally of the decision. The engineers and the product planners at Ford in those years "just didn't get along very well," Petersen explains. "Don Frey came along as a very positive personality–full of enthusiasm. And I saw what just one man could do to change the environment between a couple of warring factions. He held out the olive branch. And he was one of those people who made a point of coming to your office even if you were subordinate to him or at a lower level."

Petersen is a soft-spoken team player, who shuns personal credit for the Ford turnaround. "People are our most important resource and in teamwork is found their strength–and ours. This applies not only to employees but also to the way we treat and interact with our suppliers and dealers," Petersen informed the Ford stockholders on May 12, 1988. "We know that our survival and growth depend on satisfied customers. And there is no machine, no process, no business plan that can guarantee this goal. Only people can–involved people. We have sought to train, motivate and involve outside associates to the fullest extent. We ask them to contribute to, and share in, the pride of a job well done, to share in the spirit of teamwork, and to take pride in their contribution to the success of the company." Asked what he would like his epitaph to read, Petersen responded: "He helped Ford change the way its people work together."

Petersen has received a number of awards in recognition of his business leadership and community service. They include the University of Washington's Distinguished Alumnus Award (1981); the Stanford University Business School Alumni Association's Arbuckle Award for outstanding achievement in business management (1985); an honorary Doctor of Science degree from the University of Detroit (1986); an honorary Doctor of Humane Letters degree from the Art Center College of Design, Pasadena, Ca. (1986); the Business Statesman Award from the Harvard Business School Club of Detroit (1986); the Brookgreen Gardens (S. C.) American Achievement Award (1986); the Good Neighbor Award from the U. S.-Mexico Chamber of Commerce; the *Motor Trend* Man of the Year Award (1987); the B'nai B'rith Champion of Youth Award (1987); the Automotive Hall of Fame Distinguished Service Citation Award (1987); the National Humanitarian Award from the National Jewish Center for Immunology and Respiratory Medicine (1987); the Humanitarian Award from the Burden Center for the Aging (1987); the Automotive Hall of Fame Industry Leader of the Year Award (1987); the Freedom of the Human Spirit Award from the International Center for the Disabled (1987); the Columbia University Service to Democracy Award (1987); the *Business Month* magazine award for Ford as being one of the five best-managed companies in 1987 (1988); and the Good Scout Award from the Detroit Area Council of the Boy Scouts of America (1988). In October 1988 he was named the "most effective leader in U. S. business" by a Fortune magazine/CNN Moneyline poll of CEO's.

The Petersens have two children, Leslie Carolyn and Donald Leonard, and one granddaughter. He and his wife live in a condominium in Bloomfield Hills, Michigan, and have a second home in Rancho Mirage, California. They collect natural mineral specimens and gemstones, collect paintings and sculpture, play tennis, ski, like to travel, and are jazz enthusiasts.

The recovery at Ford has been largely a managerial turnaround involving operating economies, new products with great customer appeal, and improved human relations. Simultaneously, the worldwide automobile industry has been undergoing a massive transition toward computer-integrated, fully-automated manufacturing. At a conference of automotive historians and industry representatives sponsored by the Detroit Historical Society in 1982, Petersen spoke in his keynote address about "new realities," which represented "a major crossroads for our industry. They require that American industry—and its array of new magic machines—become competitive in every respect. . . . [T]he industry will have to change dramatically to survive. And change it will." To document his point, Petersen reported that "across-the-board retooling under way

in our industry is the most massive peacetime private-sector reconversion ever attempted, anywhere. At a cost of more than $80 billion it involves the retooling and reequipping by 1985, of forty-nine new engine and transmission lines and eighty-nine new or fully reequipped assembly lines. Few machine tools or parts will remain unchanged in the industry's 260 domestic plants and the plants of more than 5,000 suppliers of automotive parts and materials."

GM has outspent Ford about three-to-one since 1980 on acquisitions intended to improve manufacturing efficiency and on plant modernization, while continuing to lose market shares to Ford and see its profit margins dwindle. "Ford went into the transition more deliberately," Petersen explained in a May 26, 1988 interview. "It spent more time thinking about how to work toward the future paperless, automated manufacturing system, then proceeded in a deliberate and planned way. We've always had agreement from a broad base that we could undertake what we set out to do. And we now have confidence to undertake what we are setting out to do in the next five years." He told the Ford stockholders on May 12, 1988: "Our primary goal is that Ford remain strong in the automobile business. To this end we will spend substantially more in the next five years than the $16.6 billion we spent in the past five years. The spending will go for the development of new products as well as the application of new production processes and tooling."

"We've learned something very important about the competitive environment today—no advantage is permanent," said Petersen. "If we stand still, a competitor will most certainly catch us, and overtake us." He is determined that this will not occur. "Ford is well prepared to meet the challenges," he said. "And we have in place specific strategies to help assure our momentum in the years ahead."

Whatever the long-range future of the Ford Motor Company, it is clear that Petersen is writing a new chapter not only in its history but in the history of the American automobile industry.

Unpublished Documents:

Donald E. Petersen, "The Magic Machine at the Crossroads," address given at the national conference, "The Automobile and American Culture," sponsored by the Detroit Historical Society, Wayne State University, Detroit, Mich., October 1, 1982;

Petersen, address given to the Ford Motor Company Stockholders at the 33rd annual meeting, Henry and Edsel Ford Auditorium, Detroit, Mich., May 12, 1988.

References:
Robert Englund, "Ford Shifts Gears for Road to Riches," *Washington Times Insight,* June 13, 1987;
Anne B. Fisher, "Ford is on the Track," *Fortune,* December 23, 1985;
James J. Flink, *The Automobile Age* (Cambridge, Mass.: MIT Press, 1988);

Donald E. Petersen, taped interview with James J. Flink, May 26, 1988;
Richard Rescigno, "Spectacular Drive: What's Fueling Ford's Powerful Surge to the Top?," *Barron's,* June 15, 1987.

John Lee Pratt

(October 22, 1879-December 20, 1975)

by Richard P. Scharchburg

GMI Engineering & Management Institute

CAREER: Assistant engineer and various positions, E. I. du Pont de Nemours & Company (1905-1919); various positions, General Motors Corporation (1919-1975).

John Lee Pratt was born at Aspen Grove, near Passapatany, in King George County, Virginia, on October 22, 1879. He came from a Virginia family which had distinguished itself in many areas of public service, including serving the Revolutionary War, the War of 1812, and the Civil War. In his youth Pratt was a student in a rural school in King George County but received most of his preparatory education at Locust Dale Academy, a private school in Orange County, Virginia. After a year at Randolph-Macon College he transferred to the University of Virginia where he received a civil engineering degree in 1905.

Shortly after graduation he was hired by E. I. du Pont de Nemours & Company. He began as an assistant engineer, stationed at Rapauno, New Jersey, and occupied increasingly important positions. At the outbreak of World War I he was transferred to Chile, where the Du Pont company had extensive nitrate interests. He returned from the field in October 1914 to become resident engineer at Hopewell, Virginia, where the work of erecting the world's largest guncotton plant was just starting. In a short time he was called back to the home office in Wilmington, Delaware, to become head of Du Pont's Development and Civil Engineering Division. Pratt was actively engaged in the work of constructing war plants for the manufacture of munitions for the Allies. In October 1916 he was transferred to

John Lee Pratt

the American Nitrogen Company, a Du Pont subsidiary which was supervising the erection of plants for the production of nitrogen from the air. In connection with the project to develop the process for the fixation of atmospheric nitrogen, he made an intensive study of water power in the United States. When the country entered the war in February 1917, Pratt became an important figure in the selection of sites and the erection of plants for the manufacture of munitions. This work also included the supervision of important projects essential to all war production at these plants.

In early 1919 he was "loaned" to General Motors (GM) where he directed a number of housing studies in cities where there were large concentrations of GM employees and acute housing shortages. At the time GM, which was partially owned by Du Pont, often requested Du Pont's executive talent for special projects. Based on Pratt's initial housing studies, plans for GM employee housing were developed and implemented.

On December 1, 1919, Pratt officially joined GM as a member of president William C. Durant's staff. His earliest known assignment for the company was to go to Detroit to liquidate the Frigidaire operation which Durant had purchased in 1916. Fewer than 200 of the "iceless iceboxes" had been sold, and the operation was losing money. Furthermore the maintenance of the refrigeration units that had been sold was extensive, constant, and costly. Officials of Frigidaire, of course, protested the closing out of the endeavor on the ground that to do so would be a loss of a great opportunity. The product, they said, was sound, but more time was needed to correct the problems.

Before closing the plant Pratt was requested to talk to some of the owners of the refrigerators. Time and time again owners admitted they had had many service problems, but they insisted on keeping their units even when Pratt offered to take them back and return the purchase price. Pratt recalled that he visited one household in Grosse Point where the woman of the house told the following story when asked if she would like to have them take back her Frigidaire. "As a girl in the northern part of Michigan," Pratt related, "her mother had taught her to cook over an open fireplace. Now that she was able, she had gotten so far away from that drudgery as to have many labor-saving devices in her kitchen. But she would rather give them all up and go back to cooking over the fireplace than to let her Frigidaire go." In the face of what he had learned from owners of Frigidaire refrigerators—of how enthusiastic they were in spite of the very bad service experience they had had with the unit—Pratt reported back to Durant that it would be a mistake to give up the Frigidaire product. The company was not liquidated.

Pratt was next appointed director of the General Motors Development Department. The General Motors Housing Corporation was spun off, and he also assumed responsibility for the supervision of construction of housing developments in Flint and Pontiac. This included the Civic Park subdivision in Flint, which was the first totally planned housing development in the nation and is now listed on the National Register of Historic Sites.

After Durant's departure from GM in 1920, Pratt became a key figure in the restoration of GM to financial soundness by his chairmanship of the GM Inventory Committee, which reduced the tremendous overcommitments of the corporation under Durant's management to that which was dictated by sound business practice. On November 16, 1922, Pratt became a GM vice-president in charge of all of GM's nonautomotive divisions.

Following this assignment Pratt became the first executive vice-president of GM, acting for the president in his absences and being in effect the company's first chief of staff. Among his responsibilities was the selection and development of managerial talent at GM. Many people who later rose to prominent positions owed either their selection and/or some of their training to Pratt. One such man was Harlow H. Curtice, who rose from a bookkeeper at Champion Ignition to president of GM.

Speaking at the third GM "Greenbrier Conference" in 1934, Pratt told the corporation's high-potential executives that "There is a dual responsibility on each of us. First, to prepare ourselves for greater responsibilities in the Corporation, and second, to help those with whom we are associated to prepare themselves for greater advancement and responsibilities." He concluded his talk that day with a warning: "As an organization we must not become static. This means change. It would be very healthy for the Corporation if the younger men in the Corporation can be developed so rapidly that they will push some of us old fellows out. Too often executives fail to realize they have passed their period of usefulness, while their associates are too well aware of the fact. In my judgment General Motors has never carried much deadwood, and you must continue to see that dead limbs are removed as soon as they develop, in order that the younger branches can get their proper growth. We older fellows must not be allowed to hang on, if we should want to, beyond our days of usefulness—otherwise you will accumulate a lot of dead branches that will have to await some storm or reorganization for their removal. Reorganiza-

be produced by Chrysler at the former AMC plant in Bramalea, Ontario, as part of the agreement to honor the agreements that had been worked out between Renault and AMC, but the sale ended the most serious attempt ever made to convert an American automobile company into a subsidiary of a foreign firm.

References:
Nick Baldwin and others, *The World Guide to Automobile Manufacturers* (New York: Facts on File, 1987);
George S. May, *The Automobile in American Life* (Flint, Mich.: Henry Ford Museum, forthcoming 1989).

Replacement Parts and Components Manufacturers

by George S. May

Eastern Michigan University

By the 1920s the term "assembled car" was often used in a pejorative sense to describe an automobile whose manufacturer produced little or nothing that had gone into the vehicle but had instead simply assembled parts supplied by a variety of other companies. Because of the greater complexity and widely varying nature of motor trucks, particularly the heavy-duty models, truck manufacturers have usually been exempt from the criticism implied in the use of such a term, even though they have continued to rely on outside suppliers for many of their vehicles' most basic components. However, in the case of automobiles, a practice that had once been universally followed and condoned was no longer regarded as acceptable. Even though some "assembled cars," such as the Jordon, were among the better-known cars of the period, it was apparently felt by the 1920s that automobile manufacturers should actually be manufacturers, not simply assemblers. Nevertheless, although one industry observer in 1924 was predicting the demise of most of the independent manufacturers of parts and accessories, as the number of automobile companies declined and those that remained followed the example of the larger firms in producing many of the parts they used, such would not be the case. Instead, while the number of domestic automobile manufacturers with American beginnings had shrunk to three by the 1980s and the number of truck manufacturers had also been reduced to a handful, the number of companies producing motor vehicle parts and accessories has remained very large. To the general public they are little known, but in the industry the parts manufacturers as a group come close to equaling, if not exceeding, the economic impact of the vehicle manufacturers themselves.

Advertisement showing GM's role in the component business

The extent of that impact has never been easy to determine, however, because of the problems in defining who is or who is not a member of the automobile parts industry. Based on its 1919 census of manufactures, the Census Bureau listed 2,830 businesses as engaged in the manufacturing of automobiles and bodies and parts. Of these, only 315, or 11.1 percent of the total, were principally involved in the manufacture of the complete automobile, but they employed 61.4 percent of the workers in the entire automotive industry and accounted for 77.5 percent of the value of the industry's products. However, the bureau admitted that there was "considerable duplication" between the companies listed in the bodies and parts category and those in the automobile manufacturing category. The products of companies in the first group became the materials used by those in the second group, but at the same time "a number of establishments manufacturing chiefly complete automobiles reported considerable quantities of bodies and parts." Although Henry Ford's efforts to produce everything that went into his cars—even the steel and the glass that he needed—were the best publicized, General Motors (GM) from its founding had been acquiring control of firms that made a variety of parts. By 1920 it was already one of the major producers of parts as well as complete cars. It expanded its holdings in the following years, and the parts its divisions produced were used not only by GM's divisions but were also sold to other vehicle manufacturers. In 1970, during a two-month strike that shut down most of GM's plants, fifteen plants were kept open, by mutual agreement between labor and management, because these plants manufactured parts that GM sold to its competitors.

Not only was the division between vehicle manufacturers and parts manufacturers not clear cut, but the size of the parts segment of the automotive industry was also unclear because of problems with what should be included in that classification. The Census Bureau in 1919 excluded from its "bodies and parts" category companies that manufactured tires, engines, lamps, springs, electric motors, and starting and lighting systems. It admitted that their exclusion prevented it from indicating "the full extent and importance of the automobile industry," but the difficulty was in trying to determine how much of the resources of companies that were engaged in rubber manufacturing, for example, went into the production of motor vehicle tires and how much went into other rubber products. That the automotive component was substantial was indicated by data, admittedly incomplete, from manufacturers of internal-combustion engines that indicated

that about 35 percent of the engines, with a value of nearly $61 million, that these companies produced in 1919 were for automobiles.

The Census Bureau grappled with these problems over the years, but the result seemed to add only more confusion and uncertainty. Thus by the 1963 census of manufactures, the data under the heading "Motor Vehicles and Equipment" had been divided into three categories: Trucks and Bus Bodies, Truck Trailers, and Motor Vehicles and Parts. However, the bureau cautioned that "a considerable number of components, parts and accessories for motor vehicles" were classified under other industrial classifications, "based on the characteristics of the product itself rather than the Specific Application." Engines continued to be one of the motor vehicle components listed elsewhere, along with such things as automotive hardware, automotive stampings, sealed beam and other electric lamps, storage batteries, ignition equipment "such as spark plugs, distributors, switches, ignition coils, generators, cranking motors," and numerous other items. Obviously, the bureau failed to find any easy way of grouping all automotive parts activity under one single heading while at the same time succeeding in demonstrating how many industries were tied in to supplying parts for motor vehicles.

The changing nature of the automobile industry had an impact on both the companies that produced parts and on the kinds of parts that were required. The sharp reduction in the number of automobile manufacturers, a process that began in the 1920s, eventually drove nearly all the manufacturers of automobile bodies out of business. Most of them had made custom bodies for the producers of luxury cars, but that market collapsed in the 1930s. Several larger companies, such as Murray and Briggs, had prospered by providing production bodies to companies marketing cars in the lower price ranges. But the shakeout that occurred in the ranks of these assembling companies in the 1920s and 1930s caused more and more of the survivors to follow the example of GM. This company acquired complete control of the Fisher Body company in 1926, seeking to have a body-making subsidiary of its own instead of relying on an outside supplier. Engine manufacturers also saw their market shrink as more and more automakers developed their own in-house engine divisions. Thus in 1929, when motor vehicle production exceeded 5 million, only

279,611 of the engines used in those vehicles were from outside suppliers.

Changing styles also had an effect on the parts and accessories companies. Numerous small companies for years prospered by supplying owners of the Ford Model T with a variety of accessories that would dress up that bare-bones car and provide its users with some of the comforts found in more expensive cars. The end of Model T production in 1927 and its replacement by the Model A, which incorporated features previously found in only the costlier models, spelled disaster for these accessory manufacturers. The rapid growth in the popularity of the closed car in the 1920s adversely affected the business of firms that supplied fabric tops for the open cars that had predominated until the mid 1920s. The mid-1930s styling changes that made the trunk an integral part of the body "made some people unhappy," Alfred P. Sloan, Jr., recalled, "for these developments meant an apparent loss of accessory business in trunk racks, tire covers, and the like, at a time when accessories were very profitable items. But such is the price of progress." On the other hand, the closed car greatly increased the industry's needs for metal, while the introduction of car radios in the 1930s and new heating and air-conditioning features in later years provided an entry for industries previously represented to little or no extent among automotive suppliers. The government-mandated safety and emissions requirements imposed first in the 1960s opened up entirely new markets, with that for air bags, for example, estimated to be worth at least $2 billion annually by the early 1990s, a tenfold increase from 1987 sales of $200 million.

By the 1980s the number of companies officially classified as primarily supplying parts and accessories for motor vehicles was more than 2,500, a hefty increase over the figure of slightly more than 2,000 listed in the 1972 census of manufactures. Most of these companies were small, less than half of them employing more than twenty workers. In addition many other companies, numbering in the thousands, depended on sales to the automakers for part of their income. Total sales of new and replacement parts totaled $111 billion in 1986, a figure that, together with an estimated employment figure of 611,000, made the parts industry nearly as big as the automobile industry itself.

Fears that the automakers would take over more and more of the parts manufacturing activities ended. Instead, the three remaining American manufacturers, hard pressed to cut costs, were phasing out some of their existing parts divisions when cheaper sources of these parts could be found elsewhere. In 1988 GM was reportedly still supplying some 70 percent of its own automotive parts, Ford about 50 percent, and Chrysler only 30 percent. Domestic parts producers, however, were being affected by two threats of their continuing competitiveness. An increasing amount of parts was being purchased by the Big Three from producers in other countries, where labor costs were far lower than in the United States. At the same time a growing number of foreign companies, particularly Japanese firms, were locating plants in the United States. The arrival of Japanese car assembly plants in the 1980s raised hopes that these plants would buy many of their parts from American companies. But instead, the Japanese carmakers, who had always maintained a much closer relationship with their suppliers than had been true of their American counterparts, relied increasingly on parts supplied by Japanese companies that set up branch plants in the United States. Labor costs at these factories, which were generally nonunion, were often only half those at competing domestically owned companies. These transplanted parts companies, in addition to supplying Japanese assembly plants in the United States, also began competing for sales to the Big Three. By 1995, one survey forecasts, parts supplied by these firms, plus imported parts from foreign suppliers, will control 40 percent of the American parts market.

References:

Alan Altshuler and others, *The Future of the Automobile: The Report of MIT's International Automobile Program* (Cambridge, Mass.: MIT Press, 1984);

Standard & Poor's Industry Surveys (New York: Standard & Poor's, 1973-1989);

U.S. Department of Commerce, Bureau of the Census, *Fourteenth Census of the United States taken in the year 1920*, volume 10, *Manufactures: 1919, Reports for Selected Industries* (Washington, D.C.: GPO, 1923); *Fifteenth Census of the United States, Manufactures: 1929*, volume 2, part 2, *Reports by Industries* (Washington, D.C.: GPO, 1933); *Sixteenth Census of the United States: 1940, Manufactures, 1939*, volume 2, *Reports by Industries, Groups 11 to 20* (Washington, D.C.: GPO, 1942).

Walter Philip Reuther

(September 1, 1907-May 9, 1970)

by John Barnard

Oakland University

CAREER: Die maker, Ford Motor Company (1927-1932); president, Local 174 (1936-1939), general executive board (1936-1970), director, General Motors Department (1939-1946), vice-president (1942-1946), president, United Automobile Workers (1946-1970); vice-president (1946-1952), president, Congress of Industrial Organizations (1952-1955); vice-president, American Federation of Labor–Congress of Industrial Organizations (1955-1967).

Walter Philip Reuther was one of the pioneers in the establishment of the United Automobile Workers (UAW), president of that leading industrial union for twenty-four years, a key figure in the merger of the Congress of Industrial Organizations and the American Federation of Labor into the AFL-CIO, and a significant social and political liberal activist and reformer.

Reuther was born on September 1, 1907, in Wheeling, West Virginia, and died in Pellston, Michigan, on May 9, 1970. He was the second of the five children, four boys and one girl, of Valentine and Anna Stocker Reuther. Both of Reuther's parents were born and reared in German Rhineland villages. In the United States Valentine Reuther supported his growing family as a brewery workman until the adoption of prohibition in West Virginia eliminated his job. Thereafter the family struggled through several years of poverty until he developed an insurance business among friends and former fellow workmen. Throughout his youth Walter Reuther held part-time jobs.

Reuther received his formal education in the public schools of Wheeling. Beyond question, however, his most significant educational influence was his father. A tradition of dissent and nonconformity ran in the family. Jacob Reuther, Walter's grandfather, was a pacifist and critic of the Lutheran establishment who had left Germany to escape milita-

Walter Philip Reuther (courtesy of Chase Ltd.)

rism. Valentine Reuther, a fervent trade unionist and Socialist, was a founding member of a United Brewery Workers local, its delegate to the Ohio Valley Trades and Labor Assembly, and an officer in several other labor organizations. A member of the Socialist party of America, he campaigned actively for its presidential candidate, Eugene V. Debs, and unsuccessfully ran for office himself. His greatest achievement, perhaps, was to instill in three of his sons, Walter, Roy, and Victor, his philosophy of progressive, industrial unionism and his dedication to social, political, and economic reform. A self-taught student of trade union and Socialist literature, Valentine Reuther urged his sons to read and discuss the classics of the Socialist movement as well as studies of current economic, social, and political problems. During their youth the boys squared off in weekly Sunday afternoon debates on the controversial topics and causes of early-twentieth-century progressivism, such as trade unionism, the abolition of child labor, woman suffrage, government regulation of business, and public ownership of railroads. The boys prepared their cases at the public library or from their father's books. Father presided at the debates as timekeeper, referee, and judge. The easy mastery of trade union principles and practices, the skepticism toward unreformed capitalism, the belief in social progress, and the self-confidence and vigor in speaking that marked the Reuther brothers' maturity can be traced to this youthful preparation. Leaving high school at age sixteen, before graduation, Reuther went to work as an apprentice die maker at the Wheeling Steel Company. Although he did not complete the apprenticeship, Reuther mastered most of the skills of the die maker's craft during his three years at Wheeling Steel. In 1927, aware that the Ford Motor Company, after years of building the Model T, was preparing to introduce a new automobile, Reuther left Wheeling for Detroit, Michigan.

Although gaining a position at Ford was Reuther's objective, he had to settle for a drill press operator's job at Briggs Manufacturing Company, a major independent car body builder and parts supplier with a reputation for low wages, long hours, and unsafe working conditions. However, within a few weeks Ford advertised for die leaders, a foreman's position reserved for master die makers with years of experience. Undeterred by youth or inexperience, Reuther applied for the job and, when he encountered resistance, demanded a test of his die-making skills. His ability, self-confidence, and persistence paid off when he was hired as a die maker at the rate of $1.05 an hour, more than twice what he had made in Wheeling only a few weeks before. Reuther remained at Ford for five years, rising to a foreman's position. He completed high school, enrolling at Fordson High in Dearborn for a full schedule of classes, followed by a factory shift until midnight. In 1930 his youngest brother, Victor, joined him in Detroit, where they lived in a cooperative house with three friends. They attended classes at Detroit City College (later Wayne State University) in the morning and worked at night.

As the blight of the Great Depression settled over Detroit, with thousands laid off from the auto-

mobile plants and "Hooverville" shantytowns springing up throughout the city, the family heritage of social and political commitment reasserted itself. The Reuther brothers joined the Socialist party and frequented its Detroit headquarters, where they met like-minded young people and prominent Socialists such as Norman Thomas. At the college they organized a Social Problems Club, affiliated with the League for Industrial Democracy, a Socialist youth organization, for the study of society and the pursuit of reform. It successfully opposed the establishment of a campus ROTC unit and brought about the racial desegregation of a college swimming pool. In 1932 Reuther campaigned for Norman Thomas, the Socialist party candidate for president. He traveled and spoke in organizing Thomas for President clubs on midwestern college campuses. During the campaign Reuther was laid off at Ford, perhaps because of political activity, perhaps because of his membership in the small, left-wing Auto Workers Union, or perhaps because the hard times had caught up with him. In any event his industrial work was over for a time.

For months the Reuthers had discussed a sojourn in Europe. With both brothers out of work, and with Walter's savings for funds, they were free to leave. Their plan was to travel first to Germany, to visit relatives there and observe the conditions under the recently installed Nazi rule, and then proceed to France, England, and other countries of western Europe. Their ultimate destination was Gorki, in the Soviet Union, where they hoped to obtain work at the Molotov Auto Works, then under construction. Walter, a skilled machinist, would be a particularly valuable employee since the Russians had purchased Ford's production machinery for the Model A and were in need of experienced workmen to keep it in repair and to teach the Russian workers. Their experiences in Germany were terrifying. Contacts with Socialist and trade union youth groups, which were being rooted out and destroyed by the Nazis, exposed them to the suspicions of the authorities. At one point they became couriers in an underground network that was resisting Nazi tyranny. Their relatives were so badly divided between pro- and anti-Nazi sympathies that to meet with them was painful. With relief they left Germany for the Soviet Union and Gorki in November 1933. Their main task was to train Russian workers in the elements of tool and die making. The toolroom work force of 800 (the entire plant employed about

32,000 workers) included many unskilled workers ignorant of industrial techniques and machinery. Nevertheless, the Reuthers found the workers eager and responsive. The workers' progress, they believed, far outstripped the ability of the top-heavy, bureaucratized administrative apparatus to manage the factory. The spirit and morale of the workers were particularly impressive. "To a Ford worker especially," Reuther wrote in an article for an English-language paper published in Moscow, the social and cultural life of the Russian factory was "absorbing." Work, play, education, and discussion followed each other throughout the days and weeks so that, he continued, "I enjoy every moment here!" Before the Reuthers returned to the United States in 1935, the atmosphere in the Soviet Union had turned chilly and suspicious due to the opening of the first of the major purge trials. Although they admired and respected the monumental undertakings of Soviet industrialization and believed that most Russians' lives were improving in material respects, the mounting evidence of a brutal authoritarianism cast a dark shadow over all that had been achieved. Leaving their work, they traveled extensively in the Soviet Union, crossed Eurasia on the Trans-Siberian railway, paid brief visits to China and Japan, and returned to the United States across the Pacific.

The automotive industry that the Reuthers returned to was emerging from the worst of its Depression doldrums. The most spectacular American growth industry from 1900 until 1929, automobile manufacturing proved vulnerable to the Depression. Pre-Depression production peaked in 1929 when over 5 million units were built and sold, a figure not exceeded until 1949. By 1932 production had plummeted to 1.3 million vehicles. Gradually output edged up to 4 million in 1935, but demand fell off again sharply in 1937. Full employment and production returned only with the approach of war at the end of the decade.

By 1935 the autoworkers seemed ripe for unionization. In common with most semiskilled and unskilled American industrial workmen, it was not until the New Deal of the Roosevelt administration that autoworkers were in a position to take decisive steps toward forming independent unions to engage in collective bargaining and in settlement of their grievances. Although some attempts to establish autoworker unions had been made in the industry's early years, none had come close to success. Several factors contributed to this failure, including the

mixed immigrant and native composition of the work force, the relatively high wage rates paid, the absence of a clear and accepted philosophy of industrial unionism, and the implacable opposition of the employers. By 1935, however, the situation had changed. A new spirit of militancy among the workers themselves was evident in the massive marches of the unemployed that began in 1932 and in an outbreak of strikes in Detroit automotive parts plants in 1933. Also in 1933 Congress passed the National Industrial Recovery Act, which contained the first, though defective, federal guarantee of the right of collective bargaining. More effective legislation came in 1935 with the National Labor Relations (Wagner) Act, which guaranteed a right of collective bargaining through unions of their choice to workers in industries involved in interstate commerce and protected pro-union workers from discriminatory or punitive acts by employers. Led by John L. Lewis of the United Mine Workers, a group of union leaders pressed ahead to organize the unorganized. After considerable preliminary effort and delay, the American Federation of Labor (AFL) chartered a union of autoworkers in August 1935. Only two months later Lewis led a secession of industrial unions from the AFL and set up the Committee (later Congress) of Industrial Organizations (CIO). Just as Walter and Victor Reuther returned to the United States and Detroit, it appeared that the autoworkers were ready to take the decisive step toward unionization and that an appropriate instrument for industrial organization was at hand.

Reuther's work with the United Automobile Workers began on Detroit's West Side section in fall 1935. Unable to get a job in a parts plant or automobile factory, perhaps because of blacklisting, he became an unpaid organizer for UAW Local 86, a fledgling organization in the Ternstedt Division of General Motors (GM), a major West Side plant. In spring 1936 he attended the UAW's convention in South Bend, Indiana, where, despite a challenge to his credentials on the grounds that he had never been employed at the Ternstedt plant, he was elected to the general executive board. At this convention the UAW shed AFL influence and elected new officers consisting of men with autoworker experience. The convention's major decisions initiated a membership drive to carry the union into the entire industry. The West Side, which with the adjacent Ford River Rouge complex employed about 100,000 automobile workers in 1936, occupied a

Reuther, third from right, and other UAW organizers on the overpass as Ford security men approach, May 26, 1937, before the Battle of the Overpass (courtesy of the Archives of Labor and Urban Affairs, Wayne State University)

strategic position in the UAW's campaign. In September the union chartered Local 174, an amalgam of units in Ternstedt and independent parts plants, particularly Kelsey-Hayes, a maker of wheels and brakes. Reuther was elected president. For several years Local 174 was his principal base.

His first major success came through a sit-down strike at Kelsey-Hayes in December 1936, one of the earliest uses of the sit-down technique in the automobile industry, preceding the start of the far better known and more significant GM sit-down in Flint, Michigan, by about two weeks. The primary purpose of the sit-down was to demonstrate to the workers in the plant that the union was strong enough to force the company to recognize it. Once that happened the workers would join the union, something most of them had been reluctant to do for fear of losing their jobs. The start of the sit-down was carefully planned, built around an incident in which a woman assembly line worker would faint from "overwork." All went according to plan. On Christmas Eve a settlement was reached that included wage increases and the establishment of a grievance system. It was one of the

first UAW victories in Detroit and led immediately to a great surge in Local 174's membership.

The decisive struggle, the GM sit-down action in Flint, began on December 30, 1936, and lasted until February 11, 1937. Although Walter Reuther was not involved in important ways, his two younger brothers, Roy and Victor, played key parts. Thanks largely to the refusal of Michigan's Democratic governor, Frank Murphy, to employ force to eject the strikers from the plants, the UAW scored the most significant breakthrough in the history of American industrial unionism when GM agreed to recognize it as bargaining agent for the workers in the plants on strike. Although much organizing remained to be done in GM plants, attention now shifted to Ford, recognized as the most adamantly anti-union employer among the manufacturers. On May 26, 1937, Reuther and other UAW leaders and Ford workers organized a leaflet distribution outside the River Rouge plant as part of their Ford campaign. Set upon without warning by a gang of about forty Ford "servicemen," the UAW organizers were beaten, thrown down flights of steps on an elevated footbridge, and trampled underfoot. Reuther recalled that "the men . . . picked me up about eight different times and threw me down on my back on the concrete and while I was on the ground, they kicked me in the face, head and other parts of my body." Although the UAW's campaign at Ford was stalled until 1941, in the long run the attack greatly damaged Ford's reputation and helped the union. Pictures of the beaten victims, including Reuther, were carried by newspapers and magazines throughout the country and even the world.

Once established in the turmoil of the sit-downs, the UAW was racked by internal divisions. A young, boisterous organization, fresh from stirring victories and destined to become one of the largest and most influential of American industrial unions, it became the scene of maneuvering for power and position among rival leaders and factions. Homer Martin, its president, soon lost the confidence of most of those around him. A former preacher with an emotional oratorical style, Martin was ill-suited for most presidential duties. To shore up his eroding position he mounted a heavy-handed campaign against his rivals, particularly the Communists and others on the left, whom he blamed for his troubles. Those with Communist and many with Socialist connections were fired from union staff positions. Eventually, an organized left-wing opposition to Martin emerged, the Unity Caucus, which consisted of the Reuthers and other Socialists and independent leftists, the Communists, and a large nonideological element of the rank and file.

Like many other Socialists, Reuther moved toward the New Deal as the New Deal and President Roosevelt edged toward the left. With officeholders such as Michigan Governor Frank Murphy providing indispensable support for the UAW, and President Roosevelt gaining popularity with the union's rank and file, no aspiring automobile union leader could afford to withhold support from the Democratic party's candidates. In 1938 Reuther endorsed Murphy for reelection, in preference to the Socialist party candidate, and he later withdrew from the Socialist party. Though nominally thereafter politically independent, he regularly supported liberal Democrats in national and state elections. Although he ceased to belong to the Socialist party, many of his ideas about the role of unions bore witness to his democratic-socialist heritage. For example, in addition to the union's responsibility to advance the economic interests of its members, Reuther believed that it should take a progressive stand on political issues and actively support social and economic re-

forms to enhance equal opportunity. Furthermore, both unions and government should seek to enlarge the coverage of collective decision making at the expense of strictly private interests.

For a time Reuther's relation to the numerically small but politically influential and well-organized Communist faction within the UAW rested on the Popular Front principle: the unity of the left against common enemies. To many UAW non-Communists Reuther himself appeared to be at least a fellow traveler and perhaps a full-fledged Communist. In 1938 he was named, without supporting evidence, as a Communist in the first hearings of the Dies Committee, the predecessor of the House Un-American Activities Committee. Although Reuther cooperated with the Communists in the UAW for several years, there is no convincing evidence that he ever was or wished to be a party member. In 1938 his cooperation with them, already strained, came to an abrupt end over an election dispute. Henceforth, he and they were on opposite sides in nearly every union controversy.

Homer Martin, meanwhile, stumbled toward oblivion. By 1939 he was at odds with most of the union's officers, most of the members of the executive board, most of the rank and file, and with Lewis and the national CIO. Lewis engineered a reorganization of the UAW's leadership that set Martin adrift as the president of a rump UAW which soon affiliated with the AFL, brought in R. J. Thomas as the new UAW-CIO president, and promoted Reuther to the important post of director of the General Motors Department.

During the factional struggle the union's position in the plants deteriorated. Membership fell off sharply, and reduced car sales led to layoffs. GM, detecting the union's weakness, took the position that, faced with two rival UAW's, it would recognize neither. In order to secure the union's future, Reuther had somehow to devise a way to restore the UAW-CIO's position in GM. Since a sit-down strike, given the state of public opinion, was out of the question and a conventional strike of production workers risky and uncertain, Reuther turned to the skilled tool and die makers as the instrument for the union's revival. In summer 1939 he led a four-week strike that pressured the corporation by stalling preparations for manufacturing its 1940 models, dealt the Martin rump union in GM a fatal blow, and resulted in the acceptance of the UAW-CIO as exclusive bargaining agent for tool and die

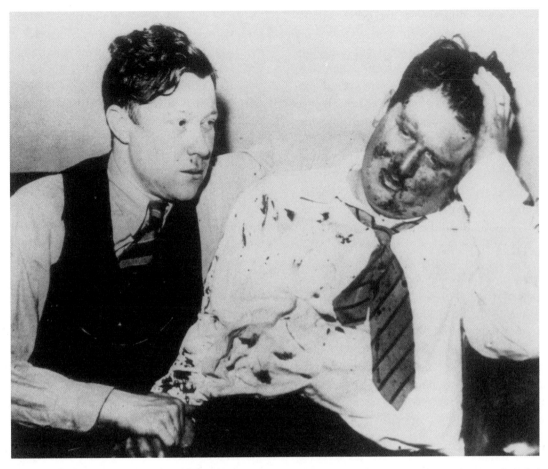

Reuther, left, and John Frankensteen after being beaten by Ford security men during the Battle of the Overpass (courtesy of Ford Motor Company)

makers in forty-two of GM's plants. Membership soared once again as the union demonstrated its clout and staying power. In April 1940 the result was confirmed when the National Labor Relations Board conducted a representation election in GM plants, five years after the passage of the Wagner Act, with the UAW-CIO winning a landslide victory over its Martinite rival. This victory constituted virtually a refounding of the UAW. Chrysler workers had already chosen UAW-CIO representation. In April 1941 a brief but bitter strike against Ford established the UAW in the last holdout among the major manufacturers, completing the task of building an independent industrial union in the nation's major manufacturing industry.

World War II's approach raised new issues for Reuther and the UAW. Controversy now focused on political issues of national defense and foreign policy. The revelation that Hitler and Stalin had agreed to a nonaggression treaty in August 1939, followed soon after by the Nazi invasion of western Poland and the Soviet seizure of Polish and other

lands on its western borders, forced the American Communists and their allies to oppose the military preparedness measures proposed by the Roosevelt administration. Pressure to curb Communist influence in the UAW mounted. At the union's 1940 convention Reuther launched an attack that isolated the Communists, exposed their lack of rank-and-file support, and embarrassed many of their usual friends. A resolution that condemned "the brutal dictatorships, and wars of aggression of the totalitarian governments of Germany, Italy, Russia and Japan" carried by a large majority, with many who commonly relied on the UAW's Communists for support voting in its favor. A resolution to endorse President Roosevelt for reelection passed by an overwhelming margin over Communist objections. In 1941 two strikes in defense industries, at Allis-Chalmers in Wisconsin and North American Aviation in California, both allegedly provoked by Communists in order to disrupt military production, further split the union's ranks. The North American strike, which was condemned by the

UAW's leadership, was broken by Roosevelt's use of troops. In its 1941 convention the UAW barred from office in the international union anyone who was "a member of or subservient to any political organization ... which owes its allegiance to any government other than the United States or Canada. ..." These political struggles were put in abeyance once Germany invaded the Soviet Union in June 1941, which quickly transformed the American Communists into champions of military preparedness and American intervention in the war. With the entry of the United States into the war following the Japanese attack on Pearl Harbor on December 7, 1941, the struggle for power in the UAW was postponed until the war's end.

In 1940 Reuther turned to the challenging problem of increasing defense production, advancing a daring plan to build "500 Planes a Day" for military purposes by utilizing the idle plants and machinery of the car industry and the mass-production methods the industry had perfected with automobiles. The plan produced a storm of controversy. William S. Knudsen, formerly GM president and now in charge of the government's Office of Production Management, refused to support the plan, thereby dooming it. Spokesmen for the aircraft industry denied that car manufacturing methods and equipment could be applied to aircraft, and the Army Air Corps criticized the plan on the ground that it would lock in production of a single model, precluding modifications suggested by testing and experience. Although the plan received considerable national publicity and the support of numerous writers and some cabinet members, President Roosevelt was unprepared to overrule Knudsen. One part of the proposal, Reuther's suggestion that labor receive an equal role in the management of aircraft production through its participation in an aircraft production board, received little attention but certainly did nothing to make the plan more acceptable to businessmen in and out of government. Reuther served on several wartime boards and committees, such as the Labor-Management Policy Committee of the War Manpower Commission, which was charged with coordinating the supply of available workers with production needs. He consulted with government agencies and was twice considered by President Roosevelt for important positions in the war production apparatus. Appointment to a prominent office encountered opposition from

other labor, particularly AFL, figures and from FBI director J. Edgar Hoover.

The war drastically altered the UAW's activities and its relations with management and government. Soon after the attack on Pearl Harbor the union pledged to forego strikes for the war's duration. No authorized strikes occurred during the war, but there were many unauthorized "wildcats." With wages and prices subject to government control and the unions denying themselves the right to strike, the question of why workers should join a union naturally arose. Contract enforcement through the grievance procedure was still necessary, but without bargaining over wages, unions had lost their major function. The Roosevelt administration, however, had no intention of undermining unions and their leadership in the midst of a war requiring national unity. Consequently, it wrote into its contracts a "maintenance of membership" clause, a modified union shop guarantee which assured that most workers in unionized plants would belong to their union. By the end of the war UAW membership had risen to 1.2 million, of whom about 350,000 were women, making it the largest free union in the world.

Although the union's wartime record was mostly a success story (the automotive industry produced over 20 percent of the nation's military output), economic and social strains within the work force were evident. Wildcat strikes over grievances and alleged mistreatment occurred frequently in some plants, provoking counteraction by management and government often with the cooperation of the union's leadership. Particularly troublesome were a series of wildcat walkouts and brief sitdowns over the transfer and upgrading of black employees, the so-called "hate strikes." In June 1943, 25,000 Packard workers walked out in the worst such incident, and later that month a race riot in Detroit raged for two days, leaving twenty-five blacks and nine whites dead. As Reuther had warned in a speech, "The UAW-CIO would tell any worker that refused to work with a colored worker that he could leave the plant because he did not belong there." With the combined support of the union's leadership and the government authorities, racial strife was eventually suppressed, and black workers were afforded a real, though still inequitable, share of the new job opportunities.

Among proposals made to improve the status of minorities within the UAW, it was suggested that

Reuther with his wife, May (courtesy of AFL-CIO News)

a seat designated for a black on the executive board be created. Black membership rose during the war to over 100,000, and a substantial representation of black delegates to union conventions, 8 percent, for example, in 1943, kept the issue before the union. Reuther favored establishment of a union Fair Practices Commission which would take the lead in urging racial justice and harmony within the union, but he opposed a designated black seat on the executive board as a Jim Crow device. That proposal was not adopted.

As the war's end approached, opposition to the no-strike pledge mounted. Workers had many grievances, including authorized pay raises lagging behind price increases, rising production standards, longer hours of work, health and safety concerns, transfer and promotion disputes, and a host of other issues. Short-lived but numerous and widespread wildcat strikes broke out in 1943 and 1944, reflecting dissatisfaction with the industry and the union's leadership. Soon a rank-and-file demand for repeal of the no-strike pledge was generated. Although Reuther's attempt to straddle the issue by proposing that the pledge be maintained in plants

producing war materiel but not in those manufacturing civilian goods was not fully satisfactory, his opposition on the left within the union lost much more ground by upholding the pledge without exception in all circumstances.

Reuther drew upon his Socialist heritage in thinking about the transition to a peacetime economy, emphasizing public coordination and planning and a broad distribution of income and goods to maintain production and prosperity. Although many feared a renewed depression, he was optimistic that a national planning effort, involving labor as an equal partner with management and government, could avert that disaster and lead to a secure, prosperous future. He proposed a complex economic program including establishment of a Peace Production Board with representatives of labor, management, consumers, agriculture, and government to allocate manpower, materials, and machines. The huge government wartime investments in plants and machinery should be converted to civilian goods, particularly the mass production of prefabricated, low-cost housing. Although these and other ideas were imaginative, they gained little public support.

The transition to peacetime production was anything but smooth. Within both the union and management the pent-up grievances of wartime created an explosive mood. From summer 1945 through the end of 1946 there were more strikes with more participants than in any similar period, with major disputes in the automotive, steel, electrical equipment, meat-packing, longshoring, and trucking industries. The longest and most bitterly contested strike was that of the GM workers, which began in November 1945 and lasted 113 days. Reuther, as director of the UAW's GM department, was the key figure. His novel proposals dealt not only with the workers' wages and working conditions but also with the price of the corporation's product. Reuther proposed a 30-percent wage increase, which would maintain but not exceed the workers' overtime-swollen wartime pay, and that GM pledge not to raise the prices of its cars. According to his reasoning, the mass purchasing power needed to sustain the nation's productive machinery would be maintained by the wage increase, while the inflationary surge that would come with price increases, eventuating perhaps in unemployment and depression, would be avoided. GM's earnings, he asserted, could meet a bigger wage bill and still supply funds for both reinvestment and a fair return in dividends. If GM disagreed with this assessment, he said, let it prove its case by allowing union accountants to review GM's books and, if the corporation's claims were correct, the union, he pledged, would scale down its demands.

These unconventional proposals angered management and upset some union leaders. GM vowed to resist any encroachment, such as setting prices, on the prerogatives of management and predicted that acceptance of Reuther's proposals would lead to "a Socialistic nation with all activities controlled and regimented, and with the people the servants of government." Within the labor movement Reuther also encountered some hostility. CIO president Philip Murray endorsed the strike but privately tried to talk Reuther out of his concern with prices. UAW president R. J. Thomas formally supported the strike but ridiculed Reuther's proposals, and Lewis, the head of the United Mine Workers, was harshly critical of the strike's strategy and tactics.

Although the strike of 320,000 GM workers challenged the status quo, provoked heated exchanges between the parties, and lasted much longer than any previous autoworker strike, it was nonetheless peaceful since the corporation made no effort to operate the plants. In a war of attrition, however, the union finally had to give way. The application of the federal excess profits tax minimized GM's reduced earnings from lost production. Settlements with Ford and Chrysler, achieved without strikes but at approximately half the sum demanded of GM, were demoralizing. The United Steel Workers settled for a similar amount, and the steel companies were promised a price increase by the government. A pattern of modest wage increases covered by inflationary price increases had been set for the first round of postwar collective bargaining. Reuther finally agreed to a comparable settlement, and the strike, the UAW's last against GM until 1970, following Reuther's death, was over. Never again did Reuther attempt so bold a challenge to management or so bold a departure from the aims of conventional "bread and butter" unionism.

While the strike demonstrated the limits of the union's power to restructure economic rights and responsibilities, it propelled Reuther into the UAW's presidency. The militant challenge to GM pleased many workers, and, since the strike's failure to gain its objectives resulted in part from half-hearted support by other labor leaders, Reuther glowed with the aura of a martyr for the cause. He challenged R. J. Thomas, the UAW's president since 1939, in a hard-fought campaign that culminated in Reuther's election at the union's Atlantic City convention in March 1946. Reuther attacked Thomas's dependence on the union's left-wing faction, including its Communists, charging that the price for its support was policies like wartime incentive pay that were against the workers' interests and a damaging perception that the union's positions on public issues were influenced by Soviet needs. Along with a core of Socialist and ex-Socialist followers, Reuther had the support of a large nonideological element that feared the factional struggles were weakening the union's impact and of many of the Catholic autoworkers, some organized in the Association of Catholic Trade Unionists, who opposed the left as a matter of principle. Although Reuther won the presidency by a very narrow margin, Thomas was elected a vice-president, and other opponents took the other vice-presidency and the secretary-treasurer's post and gained a two-to-one margin over Reuther's followers on the executive board.

Campaigning for the 1947 election began immediately, with the union engaged from top to bottom in a sustained, intense debate. Since Reuther's opponents controlled the union's newspaper, they did not lack an effective means of communication. Excesses on their side, however, turned votes against them. An attempt to pack the next convention with left-wing votes by absorbing the Farm Equipment Workers Union failed after Reuther rushed around the country speaking in opposition. A comic-book pamphlet entitled *The Bosses' Boy*, produced at union expense and aimed at Reuther, suffered from scurrilous excess. The outcome was a triumph for Reuther. A disheartened opposition put up no presidential candidate, and Reuther supporters captured all other positions. The new executive board had an eighteen-to-four Reuther majority. Although pockets of opposition to Reuther remained within the UAW, his position as president was thereafter secure.

The end of factional strife in the UAW coincided with the dawn of a golden age for the automotive industry and, to a lesser degree, its employees. In 1948 only half of American households owned automobiles; twenty years later the figure had increased to over 80 percent. From 1946 through 1972 American manufacturers built 170 million passenger cars and 35 million trucks and buses. As personal and household incomes rose, most Americans chose to spend a substantial portion of their new riches on cars.

Automobile manufacturing was the most prosperous of major industries. For nearly every year from 1947 to 1967 the annual rates of return (net profits after taxes divided by net worth) were at least twice as great in the automotive industry as in all other manufacturing corporations. For those twenty-one years the industry's average rate of return was 17 percent. According to a UAW calculation, the profits of the Big Three from 1947 to 1969 were $35 billion, fourteen times their invested capital. Since the companies constituted an oligopoly, with no price competition among themselves and, until the end of the period, little sustained foreign competition in major segments of the market, they simply passed rising labor and other costs through to consumers.

The American market, dominated by domestic manufacturers since its inception, began to be shared with foreign firms, with Volkswagen's successful entry in the late 1950s followed several years later by the appearance of Japanese products. American manufacturers showed little interest in the small, economical cars built by foreign companies as long as they could sell big cars with their higher profit margins. In 1949 Reuther urged the manufacturers to produce small cars affordable by the ordinary worker, and again in 1958, during negotiations, he asked whether the company's mix of products was best for the market. In 1959, facing the prospect of a mounting tide of imports, the companies introduced lines of small cars, but their commitment was temporary and halfhearted.

For two decades after 1947, exploiting the opportunities afforded by good times, the union, with Reuther's leadership, charted a pioneer's course in collective bargaining, emerging with pay and other benefit provisions that set a standard for workers everywhere. The objectives were traditional, but many of the means were novel. In addition to increases in straight-time wage rates workers received wage increases from advances in productivity brought about through more efficient organization and automation of production. Automatic cost-of-living increases provided protection against inflation. Retirement income security was guaranteed by pensions that supplemented Social Security benefits. Finally, in an agreement that was especially important in the seasonal and cyclical automobile industry, an income for workers approximating their normal wage was guaranteed throughout the year. Fringe benefits like medical and dental care were also part of the UAW's program, but the union was not so much a pathfinder in those kinds of compensation as it was in wage security and retirement income.

Beginning with negotiation of the 1948 contract with General Motors, the UAW achieved a series of notable advances. GM proposed that an annual improvement factor, based on general expectations of greater efficiency rather than GM's own performance, be built into the wage structure. Another major change proposed by the company was a cost-of-living allowance (COLA) that would raise or lower a worker's wage in accordance with price changes as measured by the consumer price index, the first such plan to be implemented in a mass-production industry. The improvement factor and COLA increases immediately added 11¢ per hour to the workers' pay. By 1980, 75 percent of the increase in wages, from an average of $1.50 an hour in 1948 to $10.77 in 1980, had come from COLA and the improvement factor.

Almost as pressing as wages was the question of workers' pensions. Security in old age had once been the individual's responsibility. With the passage of the Social Security Act in 1935 a system was inaugurated that would provide a minimal retirement benefit to covered workers, but the original benefit of $32 a month was too low in the inflationary postwar economy. Many companies took the position that they were not required to bargain on pensions since the immediate beneficiaries were no longer employees nor eligible for full membership in the union.

Reuther believed that pensions, as a form of compensation, were a legitimate subject for bargaining, and he contributed perhaps more than anyone else to gaining acceptance of that view. It was essential, he thought, for the union to share in the administration and operation of the pension funds. Employees had to be guarded against a scheme to raise capital disguised as a pension plan.

Reuther launched a strong campaign to build support in the union for pensions, popularizing, perhaps inventing, the telling phrase "too old to work and too young to die" to dramatize the plight of many retired workers. Ford agreed to a funded pension plan in 1949 without a strike, but Chrysler endured a strike of 104 days, the longest and most damaging in its history, before it agreed to the essentials of the UAW's plan. GM relented a few months later. In 1949, before the pensions, the typical monthly retirement income for an autoworker and his wife under Social Security was only $54. A decade later the sum available from Social Security had doubled to $108, but the addition of the negotiated pension brought the total to $245 a month. Later improvements included an early retirement program, with reduced benefits, negotiated in 1964, and the "thirty and out" provision of 1970.

The most daring innovation in compensation was the guaranteed annual wage. The idea was not entirely new, but few experiments had been tried. Automobile manufacturing was a challenging place to start since it was both a seasonal and cyclical business subject to sudden and drastic changes in the level of demand. By the same token the often laid-off autoworker was most in need of the protection a guaranteed annual wage could provide. From 1950 to 1955 Reuther worked to develop a plan

and commit the union to its implementation. The union's objectives were to give employers an incentive to plan year-round employment, provide income sufficient to maintain living standards for laid-off workers, protect against short workweeks, integrate the annual wage with unemployment compensation, and establish joint administration of a compensation fund.

The companies resisted. General Motors, viewing the annual wage as a challenge to management's control of policies, claimed that it was being asked to pay wages for work not performed and refused to discuss the issue. After much hard bargaining Ford accepted the union's position as the basis of a settlement and proposed a "supplemental unemployment benefits" (SUB) plan that would provide payments of $25 a week for up to twenty-six weeks for laid-off workers. When unemployment compensation was added, a worker would receive 65 percent of take-home pay for the first four weeks of layoff and 60 percent for the next twenty-two weeks. Thus the original plan was a semiannual rather than an annual guaranteed wage. Reuther made improvements in SUB benefits and coverage a high-priority bargaining item and in 1967, following a two-month strike at Ford, gained a settlement that provided 95 percent of take-home pay for up to fifty-two weeks. SUB provided a new degree of income security in an industry notorious for irregular earnings.

In the national bargaining with the companies, less attention was given to working conditions than to monetary issues, but supplementary agreements dealing with issues such as job classifications and descriptions, production standards, transfer and seniority rights, relief time, and a host of other matters were hammered out at each plant. Circumstances varied so much from plant to plant that entirely uniform rules were impossible, so a division of labor allotted the handling of monetary issues to the international and of working conditions issues to the locals.

The bargaining encounters between Reuther and the car companies captured public attention in the postwar decades. Skilled in publicity and mindful of the need for public and union support, Reuther began negotiations with a forceful presentation of the union's position to mobilize the rank and file, gain public approval, and put the companies on the defensive. Throughout most of this period the UAW followed a model of "pattern bargaining,"

Walter Reuther, center, with his brothers Victor, left, and Roy

selecting one company, usually Ford, as the target for sustained negotiations and a possible strike, then taking the settlement reached with the target firm as a pattern to the other companies. The procedure worked well as long as each of the Big Three was profitable. Once talks began Reuther took little direct part until the contract expiration date approached and a strike loomed. In the small group that came together as negotiations moved toward a conclusion, Reuther emerged as a tough and resourceful bargainer, often able to gain a favorable settlement without a strike but confident of the backing of the rank and file if a strike was necessary. One innovation of the 1950s that eased the membership's burden during a strike was the establishment of an adequate strike payments fund.

Although the gains that could be made through collective bargaining were at the core of the autoworkers' quest for equity, Reuther had never believed that collective bargaining alone should be relied upon to deal with all the problems of the workers. Many conditions that needed correction or improvement in order to establish adequate

living standards could be better dealt with through political and governmental action. In the postwar era most of his efforts were focused on housing and health, next to employment opportunities and income security the two most important needs, in Reuther's opinion, in a good society. He was never able to persuade the government to adopt a housing program featuring the mass production of prefabricated units, nor was the UAW able to get a national medical insurance plan as part of the Social Security system through Congress. Though never conceding that anything less than a national health insurance plan would suffice for autoworkers and other Americans, Reuther and the UAW could achieve medical care for the union's members through bargaining. Major steps forward came in 1948 when Kaiser-Frazer, a short-lived automobile manufacturer, agreed to a hospitalization and medical benefits program and in 1950 when General Motors consented to pay half the cost of hospital and surgical coverage for the worker and his family. Ford and Chrysler soon followed suit. Reuther also backed the option of a health maintenance plan as an alternative to the more restricted coverage available through Blue Cross/Blue Shield, which led to the establishment of the Community Health Association in 1957 with Reuther as president.

As measured by earnings, security of employment and income, medical care, and retirement pensions, autoworkers entered the middle class during Reuther's UAW presidency. In 1947 the annual wage in the automotive industry averaged $2998; by 1958 it had climbed to $5409. Detroit and Flint, the two major manufacturing and assembly centers, and the residences of many workers, had the highest proportion of owner-occupied homes of any American cities of their size. Instead of riding streetcars and buses to work, workers now usually drove their own cars or light trucks. New factories were placed more frequently in the outskirts of cities partly in order to secure adequate space for employees' parking lots. In personal life and habits, as well as in income and other material standards, the automotive work force became more and more middle class. Although Reuther knew that workers expected the union to produce a rising standard of living and judged the leadership by its ability to do so, he never failed to impress upon the membership the claims of broader goals of social and economic justice for all, union and nonunion members alike, that transcended the limits of business unionism.

In the spectrum of American politics Reuther's position was always on the left, but, in the tradition of the American left, some of his fiercest political struggles were with others in that position. Since 1938 he had been at odds with the UAW's Communists and their allies, administering the final blow to them with his reelection to the presidency in 1947. In the postwar world a Communist presence in the CIO, previously tolerated by John L. Lewis and Philip Murray, increasingly became a source of strain as the foreign policy conflict between the United States and the Soviet Union worsened. Reuther, who believed that war-torn economies must be rebuilt in order to bring their people prosperity, provide a secure place for free trade unions, and erect a barrier against the spread of communism in western Europe, supported the Marshall Plan and other economic aid and trade programs. Such measures were opposed by the Communists. Although opposed to communism, Reuther strongly favored liberal reform. American foreign policy, he feared, was falling into the trap of supporting reac-

tionary regimes because they were anti-Communist. As he said in a speech in 1948, "The chief weakness of American foreign policy is the predilection of our State Department for dealing with anybody who will promise to hate Communism. It is fatal to resist Communism by courting reaction."

When CIO president Philip Murray decided to seek expulsion from the CIO of eleven unions that had consistently supported the Communist position on a variety of political issues, Reuther supported the effort, which was completed by 1950. Largely deprived, as a result, of its lodgment in the American union movement, communism in America henceforth ceased to have any significant connection with the American working class. Earlier Reuther had participated in the founding of Americans for Democratic Action, a non-Communist political pressure group of liberal political activists, intellectuals, and labor figures that he hoped would mobilize the independent left to exert a liberal pressure on the Democratic and Republican parties. Americans for Democratic Action was Reuther's most comfortable and enduring political affiliation, and, with his support, the UAW became a major financial backer of the organization.

Like many controversial public figures, Reuther received threats to his life. In 1948 the threat almost became reality when he was shot by a concealed gunman firing a shotgun at close range. The charge nearly severed one arm. A long period of hospital recovery and surgical reconstruction followed. The identity of the assailant and the motive for the attack were never established. Reuther, by necessity, became more security conscious, changing his residence to more easily guarded premises and traveling with a bodyguard.

In 1952 Reuther succeeded Philip Murray as president of the CIO. The original issue that had divided the AFL and the CIO, the refusal of the AFL to accept industrial organizations, was long since resolved. The CIO's industrial unions were permanently established, and several large AFL affiliates, such as the teamsters, machinists, and ladies' garment workers, were primarily industrial in nature. The liabilities of dual unionism were apparent. Interunion rivalry diverted energies from more constructive tasks and made organizing more difficult. Public support and political influence were harmed by disunity within labor's ranks. The succession of new leadership in both organizations (in the AFL, George Meany, its secretary-treasurer, became president in 1952 following the death of William Green) cleared the way for a united labor federation. Both Meany and Reuther favored a merger, although Reuther conditioned his support on AFL progress in disciplining and, if necessary, expelling corrupt or gangster-ridden unions, and, he insisted, there must be a commitment to ending racial discrimination within the unions. Following protracted negotiations the merger agreement was announced in February 1955. Meany became president of the AFL-CIO, while Reuther was chosen vice-president and director of the new Industrial Union Department. The federation's program, which included mounting new organizing drives and campaigning against racketeering and racial discrimination, reflected Reuther's ideas, but its activities were more in line with Meany's moderate approach. An experienced and skillful politician who established a firm hold on the executive council and the bureaucracy, Meany was able to dominate the new organization.

The establishment of an Industrial Union Department, in a sense a continuation of the CIO, acknowledged the parity of industrial unions with craft unions in the new organization. Initially the department included over 7 million members, nearly half the AFL-CIO's total membership of 15 million. Although it soon became under Reuther's leadership the most active of the organization's departments, it fell short of attaining his ambitious goal of doubling the AFL-CIO's membership to 30 million in the next decade.

Meany and Reuther agreed on the need to cleanse labor of corruption. When Congress in 1957 established a special committee under Senator John McClellan, Democrat of Arkansas, to investigate criminal and other improper activities in the labor-management field, Reuther welcomed its efforts, pointing out that the righteous had nothing to fear and everything to gain if wrongdoers were exposed and driven out. He also urged the committee to give equal attention to management, advice it did not take. Although one high UAW official was eventually sentenced to a jail term on a tax evasion charge, the UAW was pronounced generally free of corruption.

Almost from the moment of the AFL-CIO merger Reuther and Meany differed over issues of foreign policy. Meany divided the world between anti-Communists and Communists, leaving no middle ground. Though unswerving in opposing Soviet totalitarianism and aggrandizement, Reuther did not believe that undeviating allegiance to American objectives was the sole test of international virtue, nor that military strength could be the solution to the problem of insecurity. It was necessary for the United States to acknowledge with sympathy the constructive role that nonaligned nations, such as India, could play, and to pledge its own resources, skills, and wealth to improving living standards in poorer nations. He proposed, for example, that the United States make available 2 percent of its gross national product for a period of twenty-five years to a United Nations-administered fund to assist less developed nations in raising their standards of living, health, and education. He also proposed the establishment of a United Nations task force of skilled young Americans to provide technical and educational assistance, an anticipation of President John F. Kennedy's celebrated Peace Corps.

Although Meany and Reuther agreed in principle on the necessity of progress in civil rights, Meany preferred a quiet, behind-the-scenes approach while Reuther thought that public activities, including demonstrations, were necessary. For Reuther—"the one white labor leader of national stature who was close to both the NAACP and Martin Luther King," in the words of two historians of civil rights—the great public event of the 1960s was King's massive demonstration in Washington, D.C., in August 1963. A longtime member of the board of directors of the National Association for the Advancement of Colored People, Reuther had responded to many appeals for help in civil rights causes, supplying, for example, $160,000 in UAW funds as bail for King and his followers when they were held in a Birmingham, Alabama, jail. Meany refused to endorse King's march or support it with AFL-CIO funds. The UAW, however, went ahead, supplying funds as well as many marchers, and Reuther was the most prominent white civil rights leader to be involved.

At bottom the disagreements between Reuther and Meany stemmed from different conceptions of the purpose of unions. Meany was a business unionist who stressed the workers' material interests. When asked what unions wanted, he repeated Samuel Gompers's famous reply to the same question: "More." An active politician who expected to be consulted on legislation and government appointments important to labor, Meany preferred to conduct business in private without trying directly to influence public opinion. To Reuther the union movement was a reform cause as well as the means for pursuing the workers' material interests, and shaping public opinion to pursue liberal goals was one of the movement's and the leadership's responsibilities.

Differences in personal behavior and taste reflected differences in values. Meany drew a large salary (in 1970 about three times Reuther's modest $31,000), had a gourmet's taste in food and wine, smoked expensive cigars, and thrived in the gaudy atmosphere of the AFL-CIO council's winter meeting, usually at a Miami Beach oceanfront hotel. Reuther, who believed that labor leaders should only slightly exceed the workers' standard of living, had little interest in food and none in drink, did not smoke, did not relish the masculine camaraderie of his AFL-CIO colleagues, and was offended by Miami Beach.

Interwoven in the estrangement between Meany and Reuther were conflicting ambitions. Each aspired to be the voice of the labor movement, and each believed he had earned that right. Reuther was experienced in all dimensions of union leadership: strikes, negotiations, contract administration, and public advocacy. Meany's experience, confined to labor bureaucracies and political contacts, struck Reuther as too narrow. Undoubtedly Reuther expected Meany, who was thirteen years his senior and turned sixty-five in 1959, to retire, but Meany remained in his position until his death in 1980.

Although many issues divided the two, the one that finally drove them apart publicly and irrevocably was the Vietnam War. Meany never wavered in his commitment to a military solution in Vietnam, and he carried the AFL-CIO's executive council with him in supporting President Lyndon B. Johnson's war policy. Reuther, a steadfast and influential supporter of the domestic programs of Johnson's Great Society, particularly the civil rights and antipoverty campaigns, refused to criticize Johnson publicly on Vietnam but betrayed a growing discontent. He pointed out the dangers of an escalation of American forces in Vietnam and advocated a negotiated settlement but refused to countenance the unconditional withdrawal of American forces. In August 1966 differences between Meany and Reuther over Vietnam broke into the open following issuance of a council position statement at variance with Reuther's views. Urging an end to the bombing of North Vietnam in order to get negotiations started and restating that "in the long pull,

there are no military solutions to the problems of Asia," he entered the antiwar camp though still declining to challenge President Johnson directly.

In July 1968 Reuther and the UAW board decided to disaffiliate from the AFL-CIO, the result of a long accumulation of grievances and frustrations. For nearly two years Reuther had openly discussed his "very fundamental trade union differences" with Meany, warning against the AFL-CIO's "sense of complacency," its lack of "social vision" and "crusading spirit." Henceforth the UAW would take independent positions on foreign policy, civil rights, organizational drives, and other issues. In a statement prepared for circulation among UAW locals, Reuther's most severe strictures against the Meany leadership had condemned the federation's "narrow and negative" anti-Communism, which, he charged, "had not strengthened but rather weakened the free world's efforts to resist Communism and all forms of tyranny." "The most effective way to fight Communism," he continued, "is to make democracy work. We believe that anticommunism in and of itself is not enough." When the UAW left the AFL-CIO, it went alone. Reuther's failure to enlist any of the other former CIO unions in a movement to revitalize the labor movement was a serious setback. Although the UAW's withdrawal from the AFL-CIO violated the principle of labor solidarity, Reuther felt it was necessary in order to break the united front of labor's support for a narrow anticommunist position and to begin the renewal of labor's fragmented ties with other liberal elements.

Although employment and profits in the domestic automobile industry remained at high levels while Reuther was alive, he recognized that foreign manufacturers were making serious and perhaps permanent inroads into the American market. As he had before, Reuther urged the manufacturers to meet foreign competition by offering an inexpensive, well-designed, and well-produced small car. In 1965 he proposed that the antitrust laws be suspended to allow the American manufacturers to establish jointly a new corporation to produce a small car, similar in price and quality to the Volkswagen and other imports. With cooperation, he argued, development costs could be reduced and a car quickly brought to market.

By the end of the decade the problem was worsening, and Reuther recognized that the autoworkers themselves would have to exercise restraint as a contribution to controlling costs. In 1970 he pointed out to a UAW skilled-trades conference that the loss of the monopoly of the domestic automobile labor market had reduced the American autoworkers' bargaining power. Although he was spared the traumas of the 1970s and 1980s, Reuther was sufficiently sensitive to conditions to anticipate that some changes in expectations were necessary.

Within the UAW the potential for class, racial, and generational conflict increased in the 1960s. The heightening of tensions coincided with, and in part reflected, a transformation of the union's composition. By 1970 one-third of the members had less than five years seniority. Among both the rank and file and the leadership in the locals, the generation that had built the union was rapidly passing out of the plants. Only in the upper reaches of the international union were there still familiar faces, which may have intensified the alienation from authority in the ranks.

The most explosive internal strain revolved around the union's growing black membership. For years black workers in automotive plants had been exposed to unfair and offensive instances and expressions of racism. Although the UAW had, since World War II, attacked racism within its ranks through policies and educational programs with as much determination as any major union, blacks had grounds for dissatisfaction. By 1968 they made up 19 percent of the blue-collar work force of the Big Three but furnished only 3 percent of skilled craftsmen. For years they had little representation in union leadership. Although locals with large numbers of black members, like Ford Local 600, had some black officers, in 1968 only 7 percent of the representatives and other staff officers in the international were black. In 1962 for the first time a black unionist was elected to the UAW board, and in 1968 one was chosen as a regional director. These and other steps toward a biracial leadership failed to avert the emergence of extremist black revolutionary groups within some of the plants in the late 1960s, the best known being the Dodge Revolutionary Union Movement (DRUM). In the face of a separatist challenge, Reuther and other UAW leaders adhered to the UAW's traditional integrationist position. In his last major speech to a UAW convention, he said: "There are no white answers to the problem. There are no black answers. There are only common answers that we must plan together in the solidarity of our common humanity."

As memories of the Depression and the union's early days dimmed, divisions within the work force became more apparent and significant. Although this resulted from several factors, in part it stemmed from the union's success. As union members gained the income security, status, and standard of living of the middle class, their bonds with all expressions and instruments of working-class culture weakened. Reuther, who had long recognized the need to "unionize the organized" as the work force renewed itself, sought to attack the problem through a new concept of worker education. The development of leaders and members to their full potential required the allegiance of both the worker and the worker's family. If the union was to flourish as a way of life, it had to be anchored in the family as well as in the workplace. Reuther committed the UAW to the purchase of a large and scenic tract of land on Black Lake in northern Michigan for the construction of a Family Education Center where diversified programs to train future union activists could be conducted. Through open communication and cooperative thought the ties between workers and union would be reknit.

Reuther's personal experience amply confirmed the importance of a family commitment. The influence of his father and of the two brothers, Roy and Victor, who were his close colleagues in the labor movement, remained with him for life. On March 13, 1936, he married May Wolf, a Detroit teacher and unionist, who fully shared his philosophical and political commitments and perspectives. For years she worked as his secretary because, she said, it was the only way they could spend much time together. A knowledgeable confidante and adviser, May Reuther was the ideal partner for her husband. The couple had two daughters, Linda Mae and Elizabeth Ann (Lisa) Reuther.

Reuther was warm and affectionate within a trusted circle of family, friends, and close union associates. His lively, well-stocked mind, abundant energy, and definite point of view made him a stimulating friend and companion. To those who did not fully share his values, including some other union leaders, his self-discipline and habit of tireless work made him seem stiff and austere.

Reuther did not live to see the completion of the Family Education Center. On the night of May 9, 1970, he left Detroit for Black Lake on an inspection trip, accompanied by May Reuther, a nephew, and the center's architect. As the chartered jet approached the airport at Pellston, Michigan, in a light rain under an 800-foot ceiling, it clipped the top of a tree and crashed in flames, killing all of those aboard. The subsequent investigation pointed to a faulty altimeter as the most likely cause of the crash.

Reuther was matched to the needs and opportunities of his time. Reared in a family committed to trade unions and social democracy, he was both motivated and trained to step forward during American capitalism's worst crisis to guide and assist in a reconstruction of the system that would give to industrial workers a greater voice in their future. Although the reconstruction fell short of what he originally hoped for and envisioned, significant changes were wrought in the distribution of power in the industrial workplace, in the standard of living of the automobile workers, and in the national climate for social, political, and economic reform.

Selected Publications:

500 Planes a Day: A Program for the Utilization of the Automobile Industry for Mass Production of Defense Planes (Washington, D.C.: American Council on Public Affairs, 1940);

Purchasing Power for Prosperity; The Case of the General Motors Workers for Maintaining Take-Home Pay (Detroit: International Union, UAW-CIO, General Motors Department, 1945);

Walter P. Reuther; Selected Papers, edited by Henry P. Christman (New York: Macmillan, 1961).

References:

John Barnard, *Walter Reuther and the Rise of the Auto Workers* (Boston: Little, Brown, 1983);

Frank Cormier and William J. Eaton, *Reuther* (Englewood Cliffs, N.J.: Prentice-Hall, 1970);

Sidney Fine, *Sit-Down: The General Motors Strike of 1936-37* (Ann Arbor: University of Michigan Press, 1969);

Jean Gould and Lorena Hickok, *Walter Reuther: Labor's Rugged Individualist* (New York: Dodd, Mead, 1972);

Irving Howe and B. J. Widick, *The UAW and Walter Reuther* (New York: Random House, 1949);

Murray Kempton, "Fathers and Sons (the Reuther Boys)," in his *Part of Our Time: Some Ruins and Monuments of the Thirties* (New York: Simon & Schuster, 1955), pp. 261-298;

Victor Reuther, *The Brothers Reuther and the Story of the UAW: A Memoir* (Boston: Houghton Mifflin, 1976).

Archives:

Reuther's papers are in the Archives of Labor and Urban Affairs, Walter P. Reuther Library, Wayne State University, Detroit.

John Joseph Riccardo

(July 2, 1924-   )

by George S. May

Eastern Michigan University

CAREER: Manager, Touche, Ross, Bailey & Smart (1950-1959); financial staff executive, International Operations (1959-1960), general manager, Export-Import Division (1960-1961), vice-president, operations manager, Chrysler Canada (1962-1963), executive vice-president, Chrysler Canada (1962-1963), general sales manager, Dodge division (1963-1964), assistant general manager, Dodge division (1964-1965), assistant general manager, Chrysler-Plymouth division (1965-1966), vice-president, marketing (1966), group vice-president domestic automotive (1967), group vice-president U.S. and Canada automotive (1967-1970), director (1967-   ), president (1970-1975), chairman, Chrysler Corporation (1975-1979).

John Joseph Riccardo was born on July 2, 1924, in Little Falls, New York, which was also the birthplace of Richard C. Gerstenberg, who retired as chairman at General Motors (GM) at the end of 1974, a few months before Riccardo took over the same job at Chrysler. Riccardo was the son of Peter Riccardo, a bicycle maker, and Mary Cirillo Riccardo. Riccardo was a student at New York College of Teachers in 1942 before entering the army in World War II and serving as a corporal in the Quartermaster's Corps in the China-Burma-India theater. After the war he attended the University of Michigan, the source of many chief executive officers in the automotive industry. A Phi Beta Kappa scholar, he was awarded his B.A. degree in business in 1949 and an M.A. in 1950.

With his university degrees and shortly his C.P.A., Riccardo in 1950 went to work for the large Detroit accounting firm of Touche, Ross, Bailey & Smart. Another University of Michigan business graduate, Lynn Townsend, was one of the top officials in that firm, and he soon assigned Riccardo to work with him on the annual audit of the Chrysler Corporation, one of Touche, Ross's larg-

est accounts. The knowledge that he gained of Chrysler's operations led to Townsend being hired by the company in 1957, and two years later Townsend hired Riccardo. As Townsend rose rapidly to the presidency at Chrysler in 1961 and the chairman's job in 1967, he carefully groomed Riccardo to follow in his footsteps. Although Riccardo began on the corporation's financial staff, he was quickly given exposure to a wide range of Chrysler operations by annual job shifts to posts in the Export-Import division, Chrysler Canada, the Dodge division, and the Chrysler-Plymouth division, leading finally to responsibilities at the vice-presidential level in the last half of the 1960s. In 1967 he became a member of the Chrysler board and, as the vice-president of North American automotive operations, was the third-ranking executive in the company.

Early in 1970 Chrysler's president, Virgil Boyd, was kicked upstairs to the largely meaningless new position of vice-chairman. He had been made the scapegoat for production and design mistakes that had caused Chrysler serious financial difficulties, the latest in a recurring series of crises the corporation had suffered during the 1950s and which would continue to plague it in the 1970s. Replacing Boyd as president was Riccardo, who now became the company's number two man behind Townsend, the chief executive officer.

Although Riccardo, appearing before the annual stockholders meeting later in 1970, was optimistic about the future of the industry, his immediate response to Chrysler's problems was to cut costs with a vengeance. Riccardo succeeded in reducing costs by $150 million, and these actions, together with an improvement in the nation's economy, helped Chrysler to weather the storms of 1970 and enjoy better times as the industry racked up record sales. However, as had often been the case in the past, Riccardo's austerity program forced the shelv-

John Joseph Riccardo (courtesy of Chuck Ternes)

ing of some important development programs, including one that had planned to introduce Chrysler's version of the subcompact that GM, Ford, and American Motors (AMC) introduced at the start of the decade to combat the rising tide of European and Japanese imports. Pointing to the booming sales of Chrysler's compact and full-size models, Riccardo early in 1973 declared that he thought "the day this company really turned around was the day we decided not to build that subcompact. Chrysler no longer operates by knee-jerk reaction. It does not imitate everything competitors do." The last remark reflected Riccardo's recognition that Chrysler did not have the resources to try to compete with all the lines that GM and Ford placed on the market, although such competition had always been Townsend's objective. But by the end of 1973 the Arab oil embargo sent gasoline prices soaring, and Chrysler soon found itself stuck with a growing inventory of cars the public did not want and without the fuel-efficient subcompact (or "minicar" as some were calling it) that was now in great demand.

Like the automobile industry as a whole Chrysler suffered staggering losses in 1974, but with a new wave of ruthless cost cutting a return to profitability seemed in sight by summer 1975. Townsend, declaring that Chrysler had once again turned the corner, made the surprise announcement that he was retiring as of October 1975. The board agreed with Townsend's recommendation that Riccardo be moved up to the chairmanship and that Eugene Cafiero, a veteran Chrysler executive whose experience was in production, replace Riccardo as president. One observer said that Townsend "tried to make it look as if he was passing the torch. . . . In reality he was tossing a hot potato.".

Although Riccardo had been a top Chrysler executive for nearly a decade, he now had to face the full glare of the limelight that had been centered on Townsend. Despite the fact that he had served in so many areas within the corporation, Riccardo, like Townsend, still faced the perception that he was primarily an accountant. Whereas Townsend had successfully fought the usual image of accountants by dressing flashily and effecting a commanding presence, Riccardo seemed to many to be the typical "cold bookkeeper," who, the *New York Times* reported, was "known as a methodical hard-nosed operator who speaks quietly but with rapid intensity; who does not flinch when it comes to hard decisions involving money, and who is fond of charts and figures." Although admitting that "his public manner tends to be somewhat starched and formal," those who knew Riccardo well declared that he was "more broad-gauged" than the bookkeeper image suggested. He was very well traveled, he knew several foreign languages, he was well read in literature and history, and he was active in cultural activities. Out of the office "his beetle-browed features relax and he becomes warm and congenial." He was a Catholic, rarely missing Mass, and a family man, spending most of his leisure time with his wife, Thelma L. Fife Riccardo, whom he had married in 1950, and their five children.

In the first quarter of 1976 Chrysler, which despite Townsend's rosy projections had continued to lose money in the last half of 1975, showed a profit of $72 million. Riccardo was hailed as the hero of the latest rescue of the company from the brink of disaster. "Mr. Riccardo stepped up to the plate and hit some home runs," a stock analyst declared. The change had been accompanied by another series of cost-cutting actions. In a move that presaged his later efforts to get help from the United States government, Riccardo's threat to shut down the unprofitable Chrysler operations in Great Britain forced the British government to contribute $300 million toward Chrysler's British losses and to guarantee loans that the British subsidiary negotiated. This strategy ushered in a period in which Riccardo reevaluated the empire of foreign subsidiaries that Townsend had created in the 1960s and which led the new chief executive officer to begin to sell these units. These foreign operations were virtually eliminated by summer 1978 when Peugeot took over Chrysler's British, French, and Spanish plants for a little more than $400 million in cash and stock. In the United States Riccardo cut losses by selling other parts of the corporation's diverse holdings, including its air-conditioning division, its stake in a Montana resort development, and an unfinished plant in New Stanton, Pennsylvania, which was sold to Volkswagen as the site for that company's first American assembly facility.

At the same time he was cutting costs in many areas, Riccardo was also trying to find the money needed to develop the new models that both he and

Eugene Cafiero agreed, despite the icy and strained relationship that had developed between them, were required to enable the corporation to survive in the market conditions that would prevail in the 1980s. The first of these new models to emerge were subcompacts that were begun in 1975 and were introduced in the 1978 model year. The cars, the Plymouth Horizon and its look-alike twin, the Dodge Omni, were the first small American front-wheel-drive cars. These were not slimmed-down versions of standard American cars, on the order of the Ford Pinto and Chevrolet Vega subcompacts, but were instead the first small American cars that were truly competitive in engineering, fuel-efficiency, and price with the small imports. As a good accountant should, Riccardo had done his best to hold down costs by shopping around for parts and, to speed up the cars' introduction, acquiring engines from Volkswagen, even though he boasted: "These are American vehicles built in Belvidere, Illinois." The cars were a critical success, with *Motor Trend* magazine awarding the two virtually identical models its "Car of the Year" award and naming John Riccardo its "Man of the Year." Riccardo, who had always seemed to be the typical bookkeeper executive whom the production men derided as a "bean counter," suddenly, *Fortune* magazine declared, had "become something of a hero to his engineers."

But Riccardo did not have long to savor the honors bestowed upon him for directing a development that had enabled Chrysler to get a jump on GM and Ford. In addition to the Omni and Horizon, he knew that the K-car, a more expensive front-wheel-drive car in the compact-car range, would reinforce the new image Chrysler was gaining for finally being up with the times. But the K-car was still several years away from the production stage, and in the meantime the Omni and the Horizon, although they sold well, were not enough to offset the losses the company was sustaining from the public's lack of enthusiasm for Chrysler's other models. In particular the massive series of recall notices for defects on the Aspens and Volarés, which by the end of 1977 had been received by about nine out of every ten owners of these Chrysler compacts, had raised grave questions concerning Chrysler's quality controls. These questions seriously damaged sales. The profits made in 1976 and 1977 suddenly disappeared, and in April 1978 Chrysler stunned the business community by announcing it had suffered a loss of $120 million in the first quarter of the year. A few days later Riccardo appeared before the stockholders to ask their approval of new stock issues that would be the first part of a new $7.5-billion modernization program. The request was finally approved but only by a rather small margin and after many shareholders, mindful of the losses when GM was reporting first-quarter earnings of nearly $900 million, voiced sharp criticism of Riccardo's management. Riccardo, who urged them to look at the long-term prospects for success, declared, "I can only tell you, we believe very seriously that we know how to run this company." The audience's response was "laughter and catcalls."

Second-quarter 1978 earnings showed a profit of over $30 million, but third-quarter earnings again showed a loss, this time a shocking $159 million, killing any hopes that the company would end the year on the plus side. In a desperate effort to keep the company on target to introduce new models each year Riccardo resorted to the approach he and Townsend had followed so often in the past—cutting costs, selling off what few saleable and disposable assets remained, and borrowing to the limit—but it was soon evident that the old approaches were not going to work. Bankers were increasingly skeptical of Chrysler's prospects, and when Moody's Investors Service and Standard & Poor's early in 1979 downgraded their appraisals of Chrysler's credit rating, the chances of securing additional money from private financial sources became increasingly limited. Recognizing this, Riccardo had already begun making a bid for federal help, bitterly charging that federally imposed safety and emissions requirements were largely responsible for Chrysler's predicament because meeting these standards had been proportionately a much heavier financial burden for Chrysler than it had been for Ford and GM. But the response he received was no more encouraging than that which he got in his efforts to drum up support from the bankers.

In summer 1978 Riccardo made the decision for which he is best remembered. Riccardo realized that Chrysler's main problem lay in the view that others had of the corporation's management. Although many industry analysts respected the changes that Riccardo had instituted and agreed with him that these would pay off in the long run, the more common view was that he represented a continuation of the same tired approach that Chrysler's management had been following for thirty years. This ap-

proach had resulted in a wild roller-coaster ride with short periods of prosperity always followed by steep declines, new crises, and pleas for help to enable Chrysler to "turn the corner" and return to a profitable condition that was never as long lasting as the management had promised it would be. Riccardo recognized that Chrysler needed a fresh face that would restore confidence in the company's ability to accomplish what it said it could accomplish. In summer 1978 the ideal choice suddenly became available when Lee Iacocca was fired from his post as president of Ford.

Since the sensational introduction of the Ford Mustang in 1964, for which Iacocca had taken full credit, no one in the industry had become as well-known to the public as Iacocca. Despite the problems Ford had suffered in the 1970s and the souring of his relationships with Henry Ford II, which had led to his dismissal on July 13, 1978, Iacocca's reputation with the public was not affected. Although a number of individuals were involved in persuading Iacocca to come to Chrysler, it was Riccardo who made the first approach in August, and it was Riccardo who was most responsible for the successful conclusion of the negotiations with the Ford ex-president. "It was John who did it all," one insider declared. "John perceived the need for change. If it wasn't for Iacocca, it would have been somebody else." At the start of November 1978 Iacocca became the president and chief operating officer of Chrysler. Cafiero, who had been kept in the dark about the negotiations, declined the offer of a vice-chairmanship and left the company, signing on a few months later as chief executive officer with John Z. DeLorean's ill-fated attempt to produce sports cars in Northern Ireland.

Riccardo stayed on only temporarily as chairman and chief executive officer of Chrysler. He realized that a man of Iacocca's stature and ego would not be content to remain subordinate. Originally Riccardo had proposed that he would stay on as chairman for two years, but when Iacocca insisted he would not wait that long to achieve his long-time ambition of being the top man in a major automotive company, it was agreed that Riccardo would step down on November 1, 1979. Riccardo thought this time frame would give him time to hammer out the details of a federal rescue program for Chrysler while Iacocca worked on boosting the morale of Chrysler's production forces. But by summer 1979 the Congress and the executive branch made it clear that government support would not be forthcoming until Iacocca was in complete control and the old management was out. "Congress wanted to hang somebody," Wendell Larsen, Chrysler's vice-president for public relations, declared. "They wanted an expression of guilt; they wanted contrition and punishment. So eventually, to get the loan guarantees, we did something that was very dramatic and very cynical: We helped John Riccardo see that the company would be better served if he resigned." Riccardo agreed. His doctors had warned him that the strain of the negotiations, which had already brought on heart problems, could have serious health consequences. But on September 18 he cited the need for a change at Chrysler as the main reason for his announcement he was retiring "effective immediately. . . . I am closely associated with the past management of a troubled company. . . . It would be most unfair to the new management and the employees of Chrysler if my continued presence should . . . in any way hinder our request for Federal loan guarantees."

Two days later the Chrysler board appointed Iacocca to be the new chairman. Succeeding Iacocca as president was J. Paul Bergmoser, one of a host of Ford executives whom Iacocca brought in as he dismissed virtually all of the remaining top Chrysler executives. Iacocca installed the kind of orderly management to which he had been accustomed at Ford and which he said he had been shocked to find did not exist at Chrysler. Under his direction and with his unmatched abilities as a salesman, Chrysler received the controversial federal aid it needed. But it was a legacy of the Riccardo administration, the K-car, which Iacocca introduced with great fanfare in September 1980, that provided the product that enabled the new management to "turn the corner" and begin to show a profit and meet its debt obligations. But while Iacocca was the man of the hour, Riccardo was the forgotten man, joining the two preceding Chrysler chief executive officers, Lem "Tex" Colbert and Townsend, in having departed the chairman's job long before the normal retirement age.

References:

"Chrysler Changes Its Driver," *Newsweek*, 94 (October 1, 1970): 55;

"In the News: 'We are out there with the first,' " *Fortune*, 97 (January 30, 1978): 15-16;

Michael Moritz and Barrett Seaman, *Going for Broke: The Chrysler Story* (Garden City, N.Y.: Doubleday, 1981);

Robert B. Reich and John D. Donahue, *New Deals: The Chrysler Revival and the American System* (New York: Times Books, 1985).

Rickenbacker Motor Company

by Beverly Rae Kimes

New York, New York

The Rickenbacker Motor Company represents one of the more compelling failure stories in the American automobile industry. Seemingly the venture had everything in its favor: a car with an advanced technical specification, a company carrying the name of a bona fide hero in an era when hero worship was a national pastime, and a management team brimming with industry expertise and heavily laden with automotive credits. Essentially the Rickenbacker saga concerns two men: America's "ace of aces" and the world's second largest automotive body builder.

Logic might have indicated that Edward V. Rickenbacker–or Captain Eddie, as he was known to millions–would follow his epic dogfight performances during World War I with work in the nascent aviation industry, but visits to Washington, D.C., had convinced him that "aviation was not yet ready for me." Becoming a matinee idol–which Hollywood producers suggested–did not appeal to him either, nor did a return to race car driving, in which he had made a name for himself prior to the war. But cars remained a passion, and becoming an automobile manufacturer seemed natural.

Meanwhile, in Detroit Byron Forbes "Barney" Everitt was entertaining notions of automobile manufacture himself. His Everitt Brothers body-building empire was prospering but did not provide the thrill that being a carmaker did. Prior to the war Everitt had produced an automobile–the E-M-F–which had languished because of quarreling among its partners and was ultimately taken over by the Studebaker brothers to form the basis for their automobile empire. But Everitt again became associated with his two former partners, William E. Metzger, the super salesman who had made Cadillac a household word, and Walter Flanders, the production genius who had helped move the Ford Motor Company toward assembly-line production. When Everitt and Rickenbacker agreed to collaborate on

Edward V. Rickenbacker, designer of the Rickenbacker car and a war hero, was the motor company's most effective spokesman.

a new automobile, both Metzger and Flanders agreed to help in every possible way.

Although Rickenbacker's name was on the company, Everitt's money was behind it, and he was responsible for recruiting the management team as well, which read like an E-M-F alumni reunion and included LeRoy Pelletier, the automobile industry's first great advertising man.

The new Rickenbacker automobile debuted at the New York Automobile Show in January 1922. A $1500 to $2000 model with a V-6 engine capable of 60 mph, it featured the novelty of a flywheel at both ends of the crankshaft, which Rickenbacker had first spotted on a German plane he had shot down. This feature eliminated the teeth-jarring vibration at high speed that medium-priced car buyers had tolerated for years. But bigger news followed in 1923: 4-wheel brakes. Rickenbacker was the third American automaker–after Duesenberg and Packard–to offer them, and the first in the medium-priced field. Orders reached 1,500 units on the day after the announcement. In less than two years the Rickenbacker Motor Company had climbed from 83rd place in the industry to 19th. In Detroit Everitt oversaw Rickenbacker fortunes at the factory as president and general manager. As vice-president and sales director, Rickenbacker spent most of his time on the road spreading the Rickenbacker gospel.

The "Car Worthy of the Name" sailed into 1925 with an 8-cylinder model added to the line and its "Hat in the Ring" emblem (from Rickenbacker's flying squadron) fitted to three times as many cars as in 1922. In January 1926 the show-stopping Super Sport was marketed as "America's Fastest and Most Beautiful Stock Car." In September Rickenbacker resigned. Four months later the Rickenbacker Motor Company was dead.

In his autobiography Rickenbacker blamed the company's demise on the early introduction of front-wheel brakes. While it was true that surprised competitors hastened to advise the American public that front brakes were unsafe, most of them adopted the same technology within months. The death of Walter Flanders in an automobile accident was more significant. And paramount was the character of the automobile industry itself. Everitt be-

lieved real success lay in offering a complete range of cars. An alliance with low-priced Gray of Detroit and high-priced Peerless of Cleveland would have nearly arranged that, but when Everitt's negotiations for merger with those two companies fell through, he decided to expand his own facilities. The immediate result was a draining of capital, and even worse were the price cuts. Rickenbacker was no different than other manufacturers in this regard. With demand for cars at an all-time high, and the firms providing them so many, price-slashing was common practice among those looking for a larger slice of the pie. Unfortunately the Rickenbacker company was too new to have developed a solid network of dealers willing to endure the price vagaries. They protested vigorously to the man spreading the Rickenbacker gospel. "You're a hero today and a bum tomorrow," Rickenbacker lamented. The criticism devastated him.

Without Rickenbacker, there was no Rickenbacker Motor Company. When he left, company assets were $7 million, liabilities less than $1.5 million, but working capital was negligible. At Everitt's request the firm was placed in receivership pending "a rigorous reorganization." The next news from Rickenbacker revealed that the company was heading for the auction block. Total production had been approximately 34,500 cars.

References:

Beverly Rae Kimes, "Hat in the Ring: The Rickenbacker," *Automobile Quarterly,* 13 (Fourth Quarter 1975): 418-435;

Kimes, "Salon: 1926 Rickenbacker Super Sport," *Road & Track,* 38 (January 1987): 76-85.

James Michael Roche

(December 16, 1906-   )

by George S. May

Eastern Michigan University

CAREER: Statistician, Western United Corporation (1923-1927); statistical researcher (1927-1928), assistant to branch manager (1928-1933), eastern regional manager, business management department (1933-1935), manager, national business department (1935-1943), director, personnel department (1943-1950), director, public relations (1949-1950), general sales manager (1950-1957), general manager, Cadillac Motor Car division (1957-1960), vice-president (1957-1960), vice-president, distribution (1960-1962), director (1962-), executive vice-president, overseas and Canadian operations (1962-1965), president and chairman of executive committee (1965-1967), chairman and chief executive officer, General Motors Corporation (1967-1971).

James Michael Roche was born on December 16, 1906, in Elgin, Illinois. His father, Thomas Edwin Roche, was an undertaker, and his mother, Gertrude Buel Roche, was a schoolteacher. When Roche was twelve his father died, and the boy took various jobs to help his mother support the family, which included two other sons. When he graduated from Elgin High School in 1923 Roche was hired as a statistician with a gas and electric utility company, Western United Corporation. He had neither the money nor the time to go to college, a fact that would be duly noted forty years later when he became one of the few noncollege graduates to rise to the top of a major corporation in the last half of the twentieth century. Roche did take correspondence courses in business administration, accounting, and economics from Chicago's LaSalle Extension Institute between 1923 and 1925.

In 1927 Roche left the utility company for what he felt would be a more interesting and promising future in the automobile business, taking a job with the Cadillac Motor Car division's Chicago retail branch. He started out at 60¢ an hour as a statis-

tical researcher, but his abilities so impressed his superiors that in 1928 he was named assistant to the branch manager. Before long Roche was in the corporation's "black book," which contained information on the 700 or so brightest prospects for top managerial posts.

Over the next thirty years Roche advanced steadily upward in the Cadillac organization, being promoted in 1933 to eastern regional manager in New York City of Cadillac's business management department and two years later being transferred to Detroit to be manager of the division's national business department. After sixteen years experience at various levels of sales activity, he was named director of Cadillac's personnel department in 1943, which he headed for seven years. This position gave Roche his first direct contact with the production side of the business, including labor relations and public relations, the last which he directed for one year.

In 1950 Roche became Cadillac's general sales manager, and he presided over a period when Cadillac sales boomed, topping the 100,000 figure for the first time in 1951. This was also the period in which Cadillac, under GM styling chief Harley Earl, led the industry in adopting features such as the tail fins for which the 1950s were notorious. It was while Roche was general manager of the division from 1957 to 1960 that this styling trend reached its extreme with the 1959 Cadillac Eldorado.

In June 1960 Roche, who had become a vice-president of GM three years earlier when he was named Cadillac's general manager, was promoted to vice-president of GM distribution. In September 1962 he was moved up to executive vice-president in charge of overseas and Canadian operations, including certain nonautomotive operations within the United States. Speculation that GM's chairman, Frederic Donner, was grooming Roche to succeed

James Michael Roche, right, with his attorney, Theodore Sorensen, testifying before the U.S. Senate on March 22, 1966 (courtesy of World Wide Photos)

President John F. Gordon when he retired was confirmed in June 1965, when, after nearly three years in charge of the corporation's increasingly important international operations, Roche moved into the president's office. Two years later, on October 20, 1967, he succeeded Donner as chairman and chief executive officer of GM.

Fifty-eight years old when he became president, the gray-haired Roche was a kindly, hardworking type who was well-liked in the company. Aside from his lack of a college education and the fact that he was a Catholic who was said rarely to miss daily mass, two things that served to set him somewhat apart from most of his fellow top executives, Roche seemed to fit the image of past GM leaders. He and his wife, Louise McMillan Roche, whom he had married in 1929, lived comfortably in the Detroit suburb of Bloomfield Hills. Their daughter was married to a Florida Chevrolet dealer, and their two sons both graduated from Harvard Law School. Roche belonged to all the right

clubs, played golf "when he had time," and drank "a little Scotch with a lot of water." He had long and varied experience in both the domestic and international side of the corporation's activities and impressed his colleagues with his ability to absorb and retain masses of information. John Z. DeLorean, when he was general manager of Pontiac, recalled visiting Roche to discuss a business matter. After awhile Roche interrupted to say, "Well now, wait a minute. We talked about that two years ago, and you said just the opposite of what you are saying now. Why has your position changed?" DeLorean, who could not recall the earlier discussion, was embarrassed, and he thought to himself, "Holy Moses! I'm talking with a goddamn genius here." Later DeLorean learned that it was Roche's practice to keep detailed notes on everything and to refer back to them to jog his memory. "He became mortal once again."

Although DeLorean liked Roche, he had definite reservations about Roche's elevation to the presidency. That job traditionally had been held by production men, and although Roche had headed the Cadillac division for three years, his main experience in the corporation had been on the sales side. To DeLorean and, he says, many of the other members of the production staff, Roche's rise to the top was further proof of the determination of Chairman Donner and the finance staff to retain control of GM. Instead, they promoted men like Roche, who were, DeLorean declared, the "unobvious choices" who would be, because of their surprise selection, all the more grateful to Donner for having been picked. In many respects Roche proved to be a leader of more than ordinary abilities, but he always labored under the reputation of being Donner's man, in part, perhaps, because he was one of the few men in GM who developed a warm, friendly relationship with the cold, forbidding chairman.

Roche was president for only a few days before he made the first of two appearances before a U.S. Senate subcommittee headed by Sen. Abraham Ribicoff of Connecticut. These two appearances were the two events in his career at GM for which he is best remembered. Ribicoff's subcommittee was holding hearings on the subject of highway safety, and Roche, together with Donner and Harry F. Barr, vice-president for engineering, was called to testify in July 1965 on what GM was doing to increase the safety of their cars. It was a subject the automobile industry had traditionally dismissed by placing the blame for traffic deaths primarily on the drivers and on road conditions. The three GM executives were obviously poorly prepared on the subject and taken aback by the manner in which they were treated by the committee members. In reading his prepared statement Roche appeared nervous, occasionally stuttering as he listed the various things GM had done to make its cars safer. He concluded, however, with what amounted to the usual contention of the industry, that no matter how safe the cars were made, it was the drivers that were ultimately responsible for nearly all accidents. But then in the question period committee members discovered a surprising lack of knowledge on the part of the witnesses on matters relating to the corporation's safety program, even the amount of money spent each year on safety research. In response to a question from Sen. Robert Kennedy, Donner, famous for his ability to rattle off precise figures on the corporation's finances, was unable to cite how

much profit GM had made the previous year. Roche, who had finally come up with an estimate that about $1.25 million was spent annually on safety research, came to Donner's rescue and said the corporation in 1964 had made $1.7 billion. This response gave Kennedy the opportunity to drive home the point that GM placed so little importance on the safety issue that it allocated less than a tenth of 1 percent of its profits to research.

The performance of the GM executives, which the *Wall Street Journal* labeled "dismal," helped assure support for legislation requiring automakers to include seat belts and certain other safety features in all their new cars. GM's image was further damaged by an incredible public relations blunder which led to Roche's second appearance before Ribicoff's subcommittee on March 22, 1966. That appearance grew out of the revelation that GM's legal staff had hired detectives to discredit Ralph Nader, author of *Unsafe at any Speed*, which had appeared in 1965 and had charged that American companies knowingly built cars that were unsafe, with Chevrolet's Corvair being cited as the worst example of such "designed-in dangers." Early in March newspapers broke the story that the detectives had been ordered not simply to check into Nader's background but to smear his credibility by proving that he was an anti-Semite or a homosexual.

Donner was out of the country, and it fell to Roche to deal with the public outcry. Roche, who had not been informed of the actions authorized by the corporation's legal staff, first released a statement on March 9 stating that the investigation had been confined only to an examination of Nader's qualifications as an attorney and as an expert on safety matters that might have a bearing on his status as a witness in cases in which GM might be involved. He denied that there had been "any of the alleged harassment or intimidation recently reported in the press." However, Roche subsequently learned this version was not true, and, as he prepared to appear before the Ribicoff committee, for which Nader had acted as a consultant, he came to the decision that he must apologize. Other corporation executives voiced strong opposition, declaring that an apology was beneath a corporation such as GM. Roche's response, as a reporter later learned it, was "Goddammit! What the hell do you want me to do? This is the only thing that can be done." Thus, when Roche appeared before the committee, with the television cameras grinding, he read a statement in which he started off immediately by deploring "the kind of harassment to which Mr. Nader has apparently been subjected. As president of General Motors, I hold myself fully responsible for any action authorized or initiated by any officer of the corporation which may have had any bearing on the incidents related to our investigation of Mr. Nader." Then, visibly sweating, whether from the strain or the heat of the lights, Roche declared: "To the extent that General Motors bears responsibility, I want to apologize here and now to the members of the sub-committee and Mr. Nader. I sincerely hope these apologies will be accepted."

Clips from the film coverage appeared on the evening news programs that day and invariably surfaced in television documentaries on Nader or highway safety in the years and decades that followed. Afterward Roche was widely admired for the courage he had shown accepting responsibility. But GM did not fare so well. Public support for its opposition to federally mandated automobile safety features was virtually destroyed. With the passage later in 1966 of the National Traffic and Motor Safety Act and the establishment of the National Highway Safety Bureau, Roche's tenure as president, and then chairman, was the first in which the head of GM had to adjust the company to the fact that it was no longer free to do as it wanted in designing and producing cars. Roche made no effort to hide the fact that he disliked such government interference, but he was realistic enough to recognize that the new conditions were permanent.

The main objection raised to the new requirements was not government intervention but cost, which would have to be passed along to the consumers and would affect sales. A decline in car sales was a matter of grave concern to Roche. He had taken over as president in 1965 when GM was experiencing extraordinary profits, but by 1969 the annual return on the stockholders' equity had dropped from 26 percent in 1964 to 18 percent while the return on sales had declined from a little over 10 percent to 7 percent. There is little evidence that the relatively small costs added to cars by seat belts and other required safety features had any serious effect on sales, but the impact from the sales of small imported cars was another matter. GM had returned to its usual emphasis on big cars after the ebbing of the compact-car fad of the early 1960s, but the rapid growth in import sales late in the decade led Roche in fall 1968 to announce that GM

planned a revolutionary small car designed to compete with the Volkswagen and other imports. Before he left office at the end of 1971 it was already evident that the car, introduced as the Chevrolet Vega in 1970, did not live up to the expectations raised by Roche in 1968. But it was only under Roche's successor, Richard Gerstenberg, that the truly disastrous nature of the Vega venture became apparent.

Initial Vega production had been halted by a strike in fall 1970 that closed nearly all GM operations for sixty-seven days and cost the corporation at least $1 billion in profits. It was the first time since 1945 that the UAW had struck GM rather than choosing Ford or Chrysler as the target firm for a labor agreement. The 1970 strike reflected in part the union leadership's unwillingness to accept Roche's assertion that the relative decline in corporate profits would make it impossible to meet the union's demands. In addition both Roche and his staff and the UAW leadership had to contend with the work attitudes of a new generation of workers in the 1960s, attitudes which made them increasingly unwilling to accept traditional contractual obligations and seriously undermined productivity and profits. This last problem threatened both the union and the corporation and led the two sides to negotiate an agreement designed to strengthen both parties. Both Roche and his union counterpart strongly defended the pact against government charges that it would have an inflationary effect.

The one area in which Roche had the most lasting impact, however, was not in the area of economic issues but in social change. Roche was convinced of the need to change long-standing attitudes toward minorities, especially blacks, and his beliefs often brought him into conflict with both corporate and union leadership. During World War II, when he was Cadillac's personnel director, Roche and Cadillac's general manager, Nicholas Dreystadt, caused much consternation by hiring 2,000 black prostitutes to fill a desperate need for workers on one war contract. The women were untrained in automotive work but proved to be fully up to the demands of the job. Despite Roche and Dreystadt's best efforts to keep them after the war GM insisted that they be dropped from the payroll. Reputedly, some of the women committed suicide rather than go back on the streets. Later, when he was general manager of Cadillac in the 1950s, Roche again clashed with the prevailing corporate and union racial sentiments by attacking plant segregation practices, and he succeeded in abolishing racially separate drinking fountains and eating facilities in the factory.

It was, however, the Detroit riots in July 1967 that fully aroused Roche's social consciousness. "I never thought I would see anything like that in the City of Detroit," Roche declared. From the executive suite in the GM building he could hear gunshots at night. As did Lynn Townsend, Chrysler's chairman, and other prominent Detroit businessmen, Roche became a member of the board of the New Detroit Committee, which was formed to deal with the problems that had brought on the tragedy. But Roche went beyond that general commitment to one that struck at the unofficial but very real GM policy of providing few opportunities for blacks in the organization. Within three months after the riots, GM had hired 5,000 blacks. Not all of them possessed the education or the self-discipline necessary to stay on the job, but by the time Roche retired at the end of 1971 the percentage of minority employees had risen to more than 15 percent and over 5,000 blacks were holding white-collar jobs. The last figure represented only 3 percent of all management and staff positions, but even that was a dramatic increase in a company in which only one of 5,346 white-collar employees in eleven assembly plants in 1958 had been black. In addition Roche instituted recruitment and training programs that increased the number of black-owned GM dealerships from two at the time of the riots to thirty-two by 1972. He also brought in the Reverend Leon H. Sullivan, minister of Philadelphia's largest black church and an outspoken advocate of black capitalism, as the first black member of the board of directors. In response to criticism that this was mere tokenism, Roche responded: "We think it's going to make a great difference and a great contribution to our understanding and our ability to cooperate in some of the affairs that have to do with our minority relationships." That Sullivan publicly disagreed with some GM policies was a healthy sign that he was not a mere token. In addition the fact that Roche's successors as chairmen continued his new initiatives was a further indication of Roche's impact in turning GM in new directions.

In December 1971, as he reached the mandatory retirement age of sixty-five and prepared to turn over the office of chairman to Richard C. Gerstenberg, Roche expressed no regrets on giving up the $800,000-a-year job. "No," he said, "I don't regret it because it's part of our normal system of operation, and I'm in complete agreement with our retirement policies." Nor did he have any regrets over the years he had headed GM, in spite of the problems the job had entailed. "I can sleep at night, regardless of the pressure. . . . That's the important thing, and I've been able to do that." Roche had led the company through a difficult period, but when he left the job the company was enjoying an upswing in the economy that promised record sales. As was true of all retiring GM chief executives, Roche stayed on the board of directors and continued to be involved in some decisions before becoming less a factor in corporate affairs. But at the end of 1971 Roche had the satisfaction of having done the best he could do—and that best was considerably better than many would have expected when he took over in 1965.

References:

Ed Cray, *Chrome Colossus: General Motors and Its Times* (New York: McGraw-Hill, 1980);

Forbes, 107 (May 15, 1971): 48;

Newsweek, 78 (December 6, 1971): 88;

Time, 87 (May 20, 1966): 100-106;

J. Patrick Wright, *On a Clear Day You Can See General Motors* (Grosse Point, Mich.: Wright Enterprises, 1979).

Rolls-Royce of America

by George S. May

Eastern Michigan University

Until Volkswagen launched its American assembly operation at New Stanton, Pennsylvania, in the late 1970s, Rolls-Royce of America had put forth the most determined and prolonged attempt of a foreign automobile company to establish an American manufacturing presence. Long before the Rolls-Royce American subsidiary was formed in November 1919, Claude Johnson, the chief executive officer of the British company, had been looking at the possibility of establishing such a branch as a means of fully capitalizing on the American market. The first American sale of a Rolls-Royce occurred in 1906 and a New York Cadillac dealer became the agent for the company in the United States. In 1913 Johnson, dissatisfied with the work of the Cadillac dealer, transferred American distribution rights to Robert Schuette, a New York agent for various coach building firms, including Brewster, the Long Island coach builder that had bought several dozen Rolls-Royce chassis on which it fitted custom bodies. However, by 1919 fewer than 500 Rolls-Royce cars had been imported during the thirteen years since the first sale was made. Although Charles S. Rolls had declared that the 45-percent tariff put on the imported Rolls-Royce did not deter sales, this high tax was seen by Johnson as a strong argument in favor of producing Rolls-Royce cars in the United States.

During World War I Johnson explored the possibility of linking up with Pierce-Arrow. Initially his plan called for Pierce-Arrow to produce Rolls-Royce aircraft engines, but he envisioned it producing Rolls-Royce cars in the United States after the war, while Rolls-Royce would serve as the agent in Europe for Pierce-Arrow trucks. Johnson could not persuade the Rolls-Royce board to support this arrangement, perhaps because it would have placed the control of American Rolls-Royce production in the hands of an American company.

No complete Rolls-Royce aircraft engines were built in the United States during the war. But engine components were produced, and the small staff Rolls-Royce had sent to the United States to direct this production was used by Johnson after the war as the nucleus around which he built Rolls-Royce of America. Johnson sought and obtained American investment funds in the company, which was capitalized at $15 million in 1919, but he served as chairman of the company. The common stock in the firm was held by a voting trust of three officers, two of whom were Johnson and Ernest Claremont, also of the British Rolls-Royce firm. Johnson's intent was to assure Americans that the company was controlled by the home office in Great Britain and the cars would be built by "British mechanics under British supervision," and would be identical to the imported Rolls-Royce. A factory in Springfield, Massachusetts, was purchased in December 1919. Springfield was chosen because of the abundance of highly trained workers available in the area and also because it was close to the potential clientele represented by the wealthy residents of Boston and New York and was far removed from the center of the American automobile industry in Detroit. "As in Britain," Edward Eves declares, "Rolls-Royce liked to remain apart from the run of the motor industry. It reinforced the company's elitist image."

By July 1920 the first engines were being produced at the Springfield plant, and by early 1921 the first cars had been assembled, although chassis and bodies had had to be imported from Great Britain until the American operations were fully underway. The American venture, however, never lived up to the expectations Johnson held for it. The insistence that the American-built Rolls-Royce be a replica of the British car caused financial difficulties for the company from which it never fully recovered. The expense of purchasing materials that had to be specially made to meet British standards narrowed profit margins greatly. Increased American investment in the firm brought changes in the management by the winter of 1921-1922, with the American H. J. Fuller succeeding Johnson as the chairman of the company. By 1923 the company had to confess that American mechanics were being employed along with British mechanics, and some changes were produced in the cars to conform to American practices, most notably the introduction of the left-hand drive by 1925. However, all changes had to be approved by the British home office, which often meant many months of delays before a change could be included on the American cars.

In 1926, when prospects for the American company seemed to be improving, Rolls-Royce of America acquired control of Brewster, greatly improving its ability to provide bodies for its cars. However, that same year the expense of retooling to produce the American version of what became known as the Rolls-Royce Phantom I was a heavy burden for the cash-poor company. It was just beginning to re-

cover its investment when the depression dealt a blow from which the company could not recover. A total of 2,944 American-made Rolls-Royces were produced between 1921 and 1931 but after 1931 only limited work was done. Reputedly the company's name was changed to the Springfield Manufacturing Corporation on August 24, 1934, to keep the Rolls-Royce name from being tainted by the failure that was by then clearly impending for the American firm. The corporation filed for bankruptcy in 1935, and the Springfield plant and all non-cash assets were sold to the Pierce-Arrow Sales Company of New York, while John S. Inskip, who had become president of Rolls-Royce of America in 1931, formed a company to handle the sales of imported Rolls-Royce cars in the United States.

References:

Edward Eves, *Rolls-Royce: 75 Years of Motoring Excellence* (Secaucus, N. J.: Chartwell Books, 1979);

Beverly Rae Kimes and Henry Austin Clark, *Standard Catalog of American Cars, 1805-1942* (Iola, Wis.: Krause, 1985).

George Wilcken Romney

(July 8, 1907-   )

by Michael L. Lazare

New Milford, Connecticut

CAREER: Clerk to Sen. David Walsh of Massachusetts (1929-1930); apprentice (1930), salesman, Aluminum Company of America (1931); lobbyist, Aluminum Company of America and Aluminum Wares Association (1932-1938); manager, Detroit office (1939), general manager, Automobile Manufacturers Association (1942-1948); special assistant (1948-1950), vice-president (1950-1953), executive vice-president and director, Nash-Kelvinator (1953-1954); chairman, president, and general manager, American Motors Corporation (1954-1962); governor of Michigan (1963-1969); secretary of housing and urban development (1969-1972).

George Wilcken Romney, lobbyist, pioneer in the postwar development of small cars, governor of Michigan, unsuccessful candidate for the Republi-

can nomination for president, and cabinet officer, was born on July 8, 1907, in a Mormon colony at Colonia Dublan, Chihuahua, Mexico, about 200 miles south of El Paso, Texas. (The fact that he was born in Mexico would later cause questions when he sought to be the Republican candidate for president as to whether he met the constitutional requirement that a president be a native-born American.) Romney was the son of Gaskell and Anna Amelia Pratt Romney. The name Wilcken was from his mother's family; Romney seldom used the name and later dropped it. His grandfather, Miles Park Romney, was born in 1843 in Nauvoo, Illinois, of English-born parents. A member of the Church of Jesus Christ of Latter-Day Saints (Mormons), Miles Romney had four wives and sired thirty children with the result that George Romney had 165 cousins. Gaskell Romney was born on September 22,

George Wilcken Romney, right, with George Mason, center, and A. E. Barit during the ceremonies in 1954 which marked the beginning of American Motors Corporation (courtesy of Chrysler Corporation)

1871, in St. George, Utah. In 1885, when the U.S. Congress outlawed polygamy, a number of Mormons obtained permission to buy land and establish colonies in Mexico. The Romneys moved to Chihuahua in 1886. Gaskell and Anna Romney were monogamists; neither of them applied for Mexican citizenship.

In 1912, when Pancho Villa led a revolution in Mexico, the Mormons feared they would be harmed, and returned to the United States. Gaskell Romney did not fare well. The family first lived on government relief in Texas, then moved to Los Angeles, where the elder Romney entered contracting. He lost everything in the recession of 1921 and moved to Idaho to begin afresh. The crash of 1929 and the resulting depression again wiped out the family. Gaskell Romney at various times worked as a farmer, carpenter, and building contractor, without much success.

Romney's childhood was impoverished and difficult. His first job, in Los Angeles, was as a sugar harvester. He later became a skilled plaster-and-lath workman. He returned to Utah to work his way

through a Mormon high school in Salt Lake City. Upon graduation he served his two years of missionary work in England and Scotland for his church, an experience he later credited for his skill in debating. He returned to Utah and entered the University of Utah in 1929, but he was soon forced to drop out. He moved to Washington, D.C., and became a typist in the office of Sen. David I. Walsh of Massachusetts. While in this job he became interested in tariff matters and took courses on taxes and tariffs at George Washington University, but he did not graduate. Throughout his life, however, Romney has never regretted his lack of a college degree. His faith has always been extremely strong; he once commented, "I do not think there is any college training that is a substitute for my religious training." Romney served as president of the Detroit Stake of the Church of Jesus Christ of Latter-Day Saints, a post equivalent to a bishopric in some Protestant denominations.

He began his business career in 1930 as an office apprentice with Aluminum Company of America (Alcoa) in Pittsburgh; the following year Alcoa sent him to Los Angeles as a salesman. His persuasive skills were considerable, and from 1932 to 1938 he worked in Washington as a lobbyist for his own company and for the Aluminum Wares Association. In 1937 and 1938 he served as president of the Washington Trade Association Executives. By now his reputation as a lobbyist was firmly established, and in 1939 he was asked to manage the Detroit office of the Automobile Manufacturers Association. In 1941 he was elected president of the Detroit Trade Association, and the following year he became general manager of the national association, a post he held until 1948. During that time he also served two terms (1944 and 1947) as a director of the American Trade Association Executives. As general manager of the Automobile Manufacturers Association, he gained prominence as the industry's chief wartime spokesman. He was often called on to testify before congressional committees about war production methods, as well as labor policies and management concepts. He helped organize the Automotive Council for War Production in 1941, became its managing director, and later helped create the Automotive Committee for Air Defense. Romney was one of the men who organized the Detroit Victory Council. He also served as employer-member of the labor-management committee of the War Manpower Commission for Detroit. By the end of World War II, his reputation as the automobile industry's leading spokesman was firmly established, and in 1946 he was made managing director of the National Automobile Golden Jubilee Committee.

Until this point, Romney had been on the periphery of the automobile industry. Impressed with what he had observed, George Mason, then chairman of Nash-Kelvinator, offered Romney a job as his special assistant, and on April 1, 1948, Romney took his first job with an automobile manufacturer. Romney later told the *Christian Science Monitor* that he could have had a job with a bigger title, but he chose the job with Mason because he wanted to "roam throughout the company, learning the ropes about every plant and visiting every department." He brought to Nash the same talents that had made him a successful trade association executive, and his rise was rapid: vice-president in 1950 and executive vice-president and member of the board of directors in 1953. The following year Nash-Kelvinator merged with Hudson Motor Car Company, forming the American Motors Corporation

(AMC). A few months after the merger George Mason died, and Romney was elected president, general manager, and chairman of the new corporation.

Romney had worked closely with Mason in formulating plans for the future of the new company. Mason had formulated a complete overhaul of production and administration in order to cut production costs and prepare for the future. Romney was imbued with the fundamental belief that the only way any automobile company could survive against the Big Three—Ford, General Motors, and Chrysler—was to make cars these companies did not have. Therefore AMC mortgaged its future and bet virtually its entire stake on the Rambler, a compact car first introduced by Nash in 1950. Romney is reputed to have coined the term "compact car," as well as the phrase "gas-guzzling dinosaur," the last in reference to the Big Three's large, heavily powered cars. Romney toured the country promoting the advantages of AMC's small car. There were skeptics. Romney, after all, had very little experience in producing automobiles. Indeed, the first few years of the Rambler were a struggle. In 1957 AMC had dropped its Nash and Hudson lines. But in the first quarter of the 1958 fiscal year, AMC turned a profit—its first since 1955—and increased its production of cars by 250 percent. The company was to remain profitable for the rest of Romney's tenure as chairman. *Business Week* commented on January 11, 1958, that "To auto industry observers too often tempted to believe that GM, Ford and Chrysler have a monopoly on brains, George Romney looks like the smartest or the luckiest man in Detroit."

His opposition to the Big Three went further than merely building cars that were different. He testified before a Senate committee in 1958 that there was not enough competition in the automobile industry. He opposed concentration of power, either in companies or in labor unions, and he proposed that the larger auto companies be split into smaller ones and that no company be allowed to control more than 35 percent of the market. He termed his business philosophy "competitive cooperative consumerism" and volubly preached an antimonopoly philosophy. *Business Week,* on February 15, 1958, quoted his "passionate conviction that monopoly, either by labor or industry, is bad for America." It was not an idea he had recently embraced. Eleven years earlier the *New York Times* of November 13, 1947, had quoted a speech in which he said, "Competition is the economic counterpart of individual liberty, and requires the banning of union monopoly just as we long since outlawed industrial monopoly."

Because of these beliefs, he opposed industry-wide bargaining with unions. He had told the *New York Sun* on March 14, 1947, that employees and management "form a team that competes with other teams supplying the same product." Therefore, employees should bargain only with their own companies, not with the entire industry. But Romney, as was vividly demonstrated during his presidential campaign, could be inconsistent. In 1957 he did a turnabout, and suggested that automobile management present a solid front to unions to fight inflation. His views about the United Automobile Workers (UAW) president Walter Reuther also changed startlingly. During the war, as director of the Automobile Manufacturers Association, Romney had termed Reuther "the most dangerous man in America." By 1959, however, he was praising Reuther's statesmanship, explaining that Reuther had changed. "The Walter Reuther of today is a different Walter Reuther," he noted. In 1961 AMC signed the industry's first profit-sharing contract with the UAW, a pact Reuther termed "the most significant and historic bargaining agreement ever written in the United States."

It was during his leadership of AMC that Romney began to take an active part in civic affairs, beginning with his leadership in 1956 of a citizens' committee to draft a $90-million, long-range program of improvement for the public schools of Detroit. Three years later, with Michigan's economic situation deteriorating, Romney helped organize a statewide committee to try to do something about the problem.

By 1959 the state treasury was virtually bankrupt. Government was deadlocked, with Democratic governor G. Mennen (Soapy) Williams constantly at odds with the Republican-controlled legislature. Factories were being moved to other states, new businesses were reluctant to come to Michigan, and unemployment was high. In that year, Romney held a private dinner for six people to form a nonpartisan civic campaign. Among those who attended was Robert McNamara, later the president of Ford and a controversial secretary of defense in the administrations of Presidents John F. Kennedy and Lyndon B. Johnson. That meeting led to the formation of a 300-member committee

called Citizens for Michigan. Among its directors were Leonard Woodcock, second only to Walter Reuther in the UAW; Jack Conway, assistant to Reuther; Daniel Gerber, head of the baby food company; and McNamara. Despite union participation on the committee, not all labor officials applauded Romney's leadership. The president of the state AFL-CIO, August Scholle, wrote to Reuther, "Mr. Romney has been a cog in the Republican Party machinery here. Needless to say, I have always found him to be fundamentally anti-labor."

Citizens for Michigan decided to solve the state's problems by rewriting its constitution. In 1961 it won a referendum calling for a constitutional convention. The new constitution, approved by voters in 1963, called for reorganization of the state's government, tax changes, and fiscal reforms.

The referendum was not Romney's first brush with partisan politics. He had wanted to run for the U.S. Senate in 1960 and had called a meeting of the Citizens for Michigan to tender his resignation. But at the meeting a member rose and accused Romney of having used the group to further his political ambitions. Stung by the charge, he left the room. When he returned a few minutes later he said he had decided not to run for the Senate.

Romney ran for, and won, a post in the 1961 Michigan constitutional convention. In 1962 President Dwight Eisenhower persuaded Romney and William Scanton of Pennsylvania to run for the governorships of their respective states, in order to strengthen the Republican party at the state level. Romney, in February 1962 after a day of fasting and prayer, announced his candidacy. His opponent was John B. Swainson, who had succeeded Williams as governor in 1961. Romney did not emphasize his party affiliation in the campaign but rather called himself "a citizen first, then a Republican." His campaign slogan was "Romney for Michigan." He won the election with 51.4 percent of the votes cast. None of the other six statewide offices on the ballot were won by Republicans. Romney's political philosophy was predictable: greater reliance on the private economy, less on government spending. He said on several occasions, "We must recognize that we cannot buy our way into universal prosperity and affluence on the strength of federal dollars." He consistently called for more citizen participation and greater cooperation with private agencies and encouraged individual initiative and family life.

As governor he faced a formidable task, but he turned out to be successful in many respects. He cut the state budget by 10 percent, balanced current books, and started on the arduous job of erasing previous years' deficits. He was helped along by a boom in the automobile industry, which helped raise the state's revenues. Because of this financial windfall, the urgency in dealing with fiscal problems seemed to be lessened, and he was unable to persuade the legislature to inaugurate a state income tax until 1967. One of his major accomplishments as governor was to oversee the streamlining of state government in accordance with the new constitution. Several elected offices were abolished, and 135 agencies were consolidated into nineteen principal departments. He also was given credit for raising the state's minimum wage, raising unemployment compensation benefits, providing bus transportation for students in nonpublic schools, instituting controls against air and water pollution, giving local governments permission to issue revenue bonds to equip industrial plants, and establishing a state crime commission with a computerized network of police information.

Romney was reelected in 1964 and 1966 with increasing margins. His third term was marred by violent riots in Detroit in 1967, but his policies were not held responsible. His appeal was not based on party affiliation. In fact he alienated Republican leadership nationally by refusing to endorse Barry Goldwater, the Republican candidate for president in 1964. Not only did he not endorse him, but he advocated ticket-splitting, persuading voters to support him but vote against Goldwater. His reputation was as a moderate, although in many circles he was termed a liberal Republican. He refused to accept any labels. He devised a statement, which he used repeatedly: "I'm trying to be as conservative as the Constitution, as liberal as Lincoln and as progressive as Teddy Roosevelt before the Bull Moose movement." But the *New York Times* on June 19, 1966, reported that "Liberal Republicans have made him the sole repository of their hopes for the 1968 campaign."

He had two major handicaps as he faced a possible run for the presidency in 1968. One was his lack of experience in foreign affairs. He tried to overcome this detriment by traveling to foreign countries and reading leading periodicals in the field, such as *Foreign Affairs,* but he was never able to convince voters of his expertise in foreign policy. The other stumbling block was his church's stand on blacks. The Church of Jesus Christ of Latter-Day Saints held that descendants of Cain, the murderer of his brother Abel, had been marked by God and became the ancestors of modern blacks. At the time of Romney's campaign for the presidency, blacks were not allowed to become priests in the church, although later the church revised its stands and admitted blacks to full membership and prerogatives. Romney, however, said he did not subscribe to that particular belief and repeatedly took every chance he could to state his belief in equal rights. A correspondent for the *Detroit News* wrote, "As if to compensate [for his church's teaching] Governor Romney has become one of the leading civil-rights advocates in the Republican Party. He personally walked in civil-rights marches in Detroit in 1963 and 1965. If Mr. Romney runs for the Presidency in 1968, he is prepared to wage the same kind of state-vs.-church campaign that served the late President Kennedy so well in 1960." In fact, Romney's percentage of the black vote in Michigan increased from 8 percent in 1962 to 19 percent in 1964 to more than 30 percent in 1966.

It became obvious that Romney was strongly inclined toward running for the Republican presidential nomination. In September 1967, however, he suffered a stinging setback over the war in Vietnam. Some observers had noted that Romney's greatest weakness was the inconsistency in his positions. Dramatic proof of the truth of that observation was provided by his views on the war. In 1965 he strongly supported the war. In November 1965 he and a group of other governors toured the war zone. On his return to the United States, Romney said United States involvement in Vietnam was "morally right and necessary." In 1967, however, he called the United States commitment a "tragic mistake."

As reported by *Time* magazine on September 15, 1967, during an interview on a Detroit television station on Labor Day, Romney was asked by commentator Lou Gordon why he had changed his mind. The transcript of the interview showed his response was:

"When I came back from Vietnam, I had just the greatest brainwashing that anybody can have when you go to Vietnam."

Gordon: "By the generals?"

Romney: "Not only by the generals but also by the diplomatic corps over there, and they do a very thorough job, and, since returning from Vietnam, I've gone into the history of Vietnam, all the way back into World War II and before that. And, as a result, I have changed my mind."

Reaction to his statement was immediate and strong. Gov. Philip Hoff of Vermont, a Democrat who had been on the same trip to Vietnam, called his statement "outrageous, kind of stinking. Either he's a most naive man or he lacks judgment." Other governors joined in the outcry. Two days later, in Washington, a reporter asked him if he had been misunderstood. Romney missed his chance to back out of an embarrassing situation. "I was not misunderstood," he said. He then compounded his troubles by accusing Secretary McNamara of having given the public inaccurate information when, before the 1966 midterm election, he said draft calls would be cut the following year. "That information was not accurate," Romney said. The Pentagon quickly pointed out that draft calls for the first ten months of 1967 were, in fact, 137,000 lower than in the same period of 1966.

Much of Romney's support evaporated. The *Chicago Daily News* asked whether the country could afford as its leader a man "who, whatever his positive virtues, is subject to being cozened, flim-flammed and taken into camp." The *Detroit News,* a longtime supporter of Romney's, said it could no longer back him for the nomination and suggested he drop out of the race in favor of New York governor Nelson Rockefeller, whom the *News* termed a man "who knows what he believes." In November 1967, however, Romney ended speculation about whether or not he would run. He called a news conference and announced, "I have decided to fight for and win the Republican nomination. I have made my decision with great earnestness."

By now he had too many burdens—lack of broad party support, inability of commentators to classify his ideas, the brainwashing fiasco. After the New Hampshire primary in March 1968, in which he trailed Richard Nixon by a significant margin, Romney dropped out of the race. He supported Nixon in the November election, in which Nixon narrowly defeated Democratic vice-president Hubert H. Humphrey.

Nixon appointed Romney to the cabinet as secretary of housing and urban development (HUD), a post he held with distinction for more than three years. HUD was not an easy department to lead. Its bureaucracy was staggering, and the national problems of housing were almost intractable. *Fortune*

magazine, in December 1970, commented, "As he did with American Motors during the Fifties and then with the State of Michigan in the Sixties, Romney has rejuvenated the department through a combination of evangelical enthusiasm and executive skill." He decentralized HUD's operations to the extent he could, tried valiantly to cut down on the bureaucratic red tape, and tried to give the country's mayors more control over model-cities projects. He fought hard to overcome white middle-income home-owners' reluctance to support housing for low-income blacks. But the job proved too much for him. Indeed, it is doubtful if anyone could have successfully dealt with the tensions of the late 1960s and early 1970s. Commented *Fortune:*

> According to an old political associate in Michigan, Romney's approach to any institution that he sets out to manage is "to pick it up and shake it." That, the friend says, is what he did with American Motors, with the Michigan Constitutional Convention, with the Republican Party in Michigan, finally with the state of Michigan itself. That is what he tried to do with the national Republican party. Now he is using the same method with the nation's urban crisis.
>
> As a style of management, picking up institutions and shaking them has its limitations. The collapse of Romney's presidential campaign was in part due to excessive reliance on enthusiasm and "the will to win" at the expense of hard analysis of problems. At HUD he sometimes seems to rise on clouds of rhetoric, designed to conceal the underlying difficulties even from himself. . . . So long as his relations with the President remain reasonably amiable, Romney should continue to provide a welcome beacon of moral generosity and high-spirited enthusiasm amid the prevailing gray of Richard Nixon's Washington.

Relations with Nixon were not to remain "reasonably amiable," however. Romney had never been considered a member of the inner circle, and he had been viewed with mistrust by many Republican politicians for his refusal to embrace all Republican tenets, as well as for the Goldwater incident in 1964. He espoused housing programs Nixon was not prepared to fund and became increasingly frustrated with the White House and the way it operated. In August 1972 matters came to a head over a flood caused by Hurricane Agnes. The flood left twenty-eight thousand families homeless in Wilkes-Barre, Pennsylvania, and the victims blamed the federal government for not setting up temporary housing. Nixon issued a memo ordering Romney to go to Pennsylvania immediately to "take personal charge" and cut through the red tape. The memo, which also instructed Romney to file a written report within three days, was released to the press before Romney knew about it. Romney went to Wilkes-Barre and got into a shouting match with Democratic governor Milton Shapp in the presence of a crowd of angry citizens. Romney blamed presidential assistant John D. Ehrlichman, as well as the president, for making him appear "an underling who failed to cope with a politically charged emergency," reported *Business Week* on August 19, 1972.

Romney resigned from the cabinet and from public life. He organized a group known as the Concerned Citizens Movement, a conservative citizens' lobby, but the movement was never very active. *Forbes* magazine of May 15, 1973, commented, "The feeling in Washington is that Romney left frustrated with the White House, and vice versa. . . . Romney was a star in business. He ultimately bombed in politics." Romney told the magazine's reporter, "In politics you can't be successful by selling ideas whose time is in the distant future. You know, elections are coming up all the time. You have to have ideas that win a majority of vot-

ers. . . . The Rambler, now. That took seven years just to develop the concept, and then another seven to sell it to the public. At the end of those 14 years we proved that 4 percent to 5 percent of the public was willing to buy the Rambler. And for the Rambler we didn't have to get special ordinances and go through local building codes as we had to do with housing."

Romney, a persuasive speaker, was brilliant as a lobbyist and a business executive. He did well as governor of Michigan, probably because the Michigan electorate shared common concerns about unemployment and the state economy, concerns that he parlayed into three electoral victories. But his attempts to become a player on the national political scene failed. Perhaps it was because he was not able to deal with the myriad constituencies that make up a national electorate or a federal bureaucracy. Hampered by a somewhat imperious personality and a tendency toward inconsistency of style and ideas, Romney was never able to fire the imagination of the public or of the chiefs of his own party. But his personal integrity and the strength of his character were invariably admired.

Reference:

Tom Mahoney, *The Story of George Romney: Builder, Salesman, Crusader* (New York: Harper, 1960).

Safety

by Kevin M. Dwyer

George Washington University

The automotive safety movement of the 1960s compelled the federal government to respond to the problems of automotive safety. These problems were apparent after sixty years of cultural and industrial development predicated largely on the proliferation of the automobile. Concurrent with, and related to, the growth of consumer and environmental activism, the automobile safety movement raised public awareness and concern about America's most popular and personal mode of transportation. The combination of increased public scrutiny, governmental activism, a sudden jump in the annual highway death rate, and several well-publicized cases of manufacturer neglect of product quality resulted in mandatory federal safety requirements for all motor vehicles sold in the United States. The passage of the National Traffic and Motor Vehicle Safety Act and the Highway Safety Act in 1966 marked a definite break from the traditional approaches which the federal government, the consumer/constituent, and American industry took toward matters of public and product safety and manufacturer accountability.

As Joel W. Eastman points out in his book *Style vs. Safety* (1984), automobile industrialists initially hoped for federal regulation of automobiles in order to set national standards for driver competence and rules of the road. But by 1910 the uniformity of state and local codes eased that concern. Federal nonintervention became the precedent during the sixty-year rise of what historian James J. Flink terms "the car culture." State and local governments would make laws to determine the rules of the road, and improving the safety of motor vehicles would be left largely to the industry.

Automobile regulations were first imposed in cities and states experiencing a high concentration of motor vehicle traffic and thereafter the rules spread haphazardly from state to state as automobile travel became more popular and problematic.

Around the turn of the century, Chicago and New York required the licensing of drivers, and Connecticut and New York State mandated motor vehicle registration and set speed limits (usually not in excess of 10 miles per hour). Yet by 1910 only twelve states required the licensing of drivers, and not until South Dakota imposed licensing requirements in 1954 did the practice become universal in all states.

The automobile makers, for their part, approached the question of safety with hesitation. From their perspective, adding safety features was tantamount to admitting that the automobile was inherently unsafe, or that their products had heretofore been dangerous. Either perception, they feared, would hurt sales. The industry instead focused buyer attention on the style of their cars. The age of the Model T, when, as the joke went, "You could get any color you wanted as long as it was black," quickly gave way to increasing variety of not only color but design. As automobiles became status symbols, style became a most important consideration for the buyer and, as such, a selling feature for the industry. The annual model change, an institutional brainchild of the legendary General Motors (GM) president Alfred P. Sloan, Jr., was intended to increase replacement sales. As car styles were updated, affluent consumers would buy new ones and sell their old ones to those less well-off. With the lion's share of engineering initiative and research budget allocations going in pursuit of superficial design changes, little remained for upgrading the safety of the automobile itself.

Lack of public demand for improved safety gave manufacturers little impetus to challenge their conventional ways of doing business. Warnings about the dangers of automobile travel had emerged virtually since its introduction–a New York real estate agent run over in Central Park in 1899 became the first recorded automobile-related

Tests such as this, conducted by the federal government, were mandated by the safety legislation of the 1960s

fatality–but Americans were undeterred. By the close of World War I, a cultural transformation prefaced on the development and proliferation of the automobile was clearly underway, and postwar prosperity encouraged the process. With consumer income rising and the price of the Model T falling to about $300 by 1925 (a comparable Chevrolet cost $700), 23 million automobiles traveled America's roads in 1930. That figure represented 75 percent of the world's total and was up from just 8 million in 1920. Although the highway fatalities climbed 150 percent in that time, little blame for the carnage was leveled either at the industry or its product. The dangers of driving, which the industry downplayed as much as possible, were, in the minds of the vast majority of the American traveling public, simply outweighed by the advantages.

Moreover, the common view was that accidents were unnatural conditions, having more to do with the work of fate than the design of the automobile. Manufacturers accepted and helped to reinforce this attitude, more likely for its convenience than for its intellectual merits. Such a view of accidents kept the onus for them on things other than the car, and manufacturers reasoned that if accidents were not the fault of the cars themselves then they need not be redesigned for improved safety. Furthermore, developing a safer design, if such were even possible, would cost money, which would increase costs for the producer and thus prices for the consumer. With the general acceptance of this rationale, responsibility for automobile safety would rest with the other components basic to driving.

Foremost among these was the driver, and automobile makers, insurance companies, and local authorities institutionalized the characteristic popular tendency to hold the driver, as the operator of his individual means of transportation, accountable for accidents. Given this assumption, manufacturers and safety organizations like the National Safety Council (which received substantial funding from automobile makers) launched campaigns aimed at accident prevention and emphasizing careful driving. Driver education was the answer to the safety problem, maintained the conventional industry wisdom, and carmakers allocated funding to ensure proper driver education and testing programs to impart the techniques of "defensive driving" nationwide. By 1980 driver education programs were a standard part of the curriculum in more than half the high schools in the United States.

Another focus of the industry-sponsored initiatives to promote safety was law enforcement. Here the responsibility for safety was with the state and local police, who concentrated on enforcing speed limits and catching drunk drivers. Punishing perpetrators with fines and threatening license suspensions and even incarceration for repeat offenders, law enforcement was stressed as a necessity to the safety of the highways. State establishment of periodic vehicle inspections also proved effective in lowering automobile fatalities.

Another aspect of improving motor vehicle safety focused on the highways themselves, as poor road condition was also stressed as a frequent contributor to car accidents. Since the industry's take-off period it lobbied continually for federal assistance in this regard. The government responded, beginning with the reluctant passing of the Federal Aid Road Act in 1916, which committed the government to pay 50 percent of the cost for construction of roads in rural areas. With that act, as Eastman writes, "the extent of major national involvement in the motorized highway transportation system was set for the next fifty years." The government's involvement would increase proportionately with the proliferation of the automobile, as indicated with the passage of the Federal Highway Act of 1921 and the establishment in 1923 of the Bureau of Public Roads to oversee the development of a national highway system. New Deal public works programs continued the federal development of the nation's automotive infrastructure, and federal funding for roads increased massively following World War II, from $79 million in 1947 to $429 million in 1950. In 1956 the Eisenhower administration's landmark Interstate Highway Act aimed at completing a national interstate highway system, a job nearly accomplished by 1970. Federal funding for the nation's roads had by 1960 increased to $2.9 billion and to $4.6 billion by 1970.

But despite adequate driver education, effective law enforcement, and the construction of better roads–from back road paving to superhighway construction–accidents continued, and highway deaths continued to mount. Industry spokespeople were, however, quick to point to the rather substantial improvement in rate of deaths per miles traveled, but as deaths continued to climb other parties concerned about safety took little solace from that

fact. Between 1945 and 1963, as the federal government funded the construction of more roads and economic prosperity allowed automobile sales to top 7 million units annually, the number of automobile-related deaths hovered between 28,000 and 43,000 a year. Such figures motivated several concerned parties, including the media, the medical community, and engineering professions, to act.

Periodicals and newspapers traditionally covered automobile safety in detail, in part because accidents traditionally had been found to make good copy. Local newspapers commonly carried motor vehicle accident columns, supplying intricate detail depending upon the severity, and early muckraking magazine articles with titles such as "Slaughter on the Highways" and "Menace of the Automobile," warned of the dangers. But in 1935 *Reader's Digest* printed an article by J.C. Furnas that had a tremendous national impact. The article, "–And Sudden Death," described in great detail the prospects facing drivers unfortunate enough to experience a severe crash, reporting that an "accident produces either a shattering dead stop or a crashing change of direction" which in either case sends the driver hurtling "at the original speed" making "every surface and angle of the car's interior . . . a tearing, battering projectile aimed squarely at you–inescapable. . . . It's like going over Niagara Falls in a bucket full of railroad spikes." Furnas correctly recounted the physics of a collision and concluded that "There is no bracing yourself against these imperative laws of momentum."

The Furnas article illustrated the gruesome concept later known as the second collision and the bodily damage resulting. The concept was a departure from the traditional view of automobile accidents for it showed that, in an accident, injury to the driver was actually inflicted by his own car. Although this logically leads to the conclusion that interior redesign, to recess steering wheel hubs, protruding knobs, and doorhandles, and to smooth and pad sharp edges and other potential points of impact, might reduce fatalities, even Furnas missed the point. The avowed purpose of his article was not to question design but to shock people into driving carefully.

Medical and engineering professionals, however, better grasped the concept of second collision and understood that design change could be of tremendous value to the motoring public. A Detroit plastic surgeon, Dr. Claire L. Straith, was among

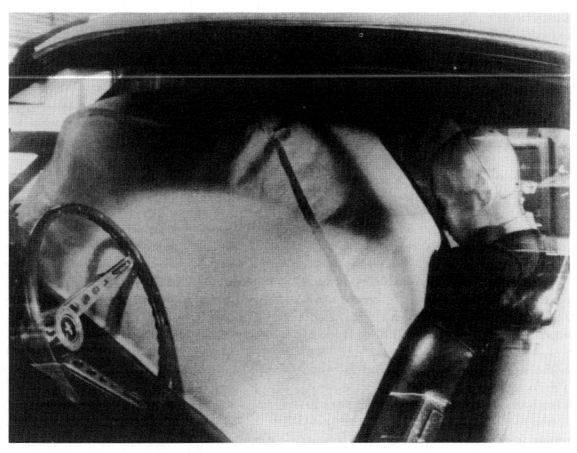

Safety test for the air bag, which inflates automatically upon impact

the first of a long line of agitators for improved interior design. Over the years Straith had seen scores of patients injured in automobile accidents, which prompted him to install seat belts and crash padding to his own family car. He also worked on shock-absorbing designs for dashboards and began appearing before engineering conventions to give lectures on his findings. Straith in 1935 met with Walter Chrysler, founder of the Chrysler Corporation, and Chrysler was impressed. By 1937 many of Straith's as well as other ideas were incorporated into the Dodge. Many of these improvements were adopted by other manufacturers.

Straith's work continued into the 1940s, when two new manufacturers, the Tucker Corporation and the Kaiser-Frazer Corporation, entered the industry. Straith's findings impressed tremendously the top executives at both, and their products were designed with the second collision in mind. Both companies refused to install seat belts, however, for fear of hurting sales. Installing seat belts would, after all, connote the possibility of an accident. As it had been for the rest of the industry, the negativism of that connotation was sufficient to dissuade both the Tucker and the Kaiser-Frazer Corporations from installing passenger restraints.

By the later 1940s Straith was no longer working alone. Organizations like the American Medical Association held presentations at their annual conferences, and the issue took hold throughout the medical community. The American College of Surgeons also took an interest in automobile safety, and throughout the 1950s both organizations sponsored research programs and lobbied the industry to improve interior design. The American Medical Association's journal was influential in spreading the word, particularly in 1955. Dr. Fletcher Woodward's editorial in the June 5 issue, "Wanted: Safety Devices for Automobile Passengers," made a powerful case for the installation of seat belts. In November, a detailed study by Dr. C. Hunter Sheldon titled "Prevention, The Only Cure For Head Injuries," addressed the flaws of automotive design and suggested improvements. The automobile, the wonders of which doctors frequently espoused as a means for making house calls fifty years before, was now coming under sharp and increasingly frequent attack by the medical community, and the message was gaining momentum.

Highway carnage had also caught the attention and concern of engineers and law enforcement personnel. Tests conducted by researchers like Hugh DeHaven, a self-taught engineer and pioneer in the field of crash protection, demonstrated the beneficence of automotive restraints and improved design. Studies he conducted in conjunction with the Civil Aeronautics Board, the Cornell Aeronautical Laboratory, and the Indiana State Police noted that automotive design flaws did indeed result in many injuries during crashes. DeHaven's research showed "forcible ejection," in which the passenger is thrown from the car when, as often happened, doors sprang open on impact, to be a common occurrence in many accidents. DeHaven recommended the installation of seat belts to prevent both passenger ejection and the "second collision" to industry engineers at meetings of trade organizations, most notably the Society of American Engineers.

The focus of the automobile safety question was at last by the 1950s coming around to the automobile, and the industry was, in the face of growing pressure from professional associations and the media, forced to respond. Corporate management, however, did so reluctantly, and improvement came slowly. Before the lobbying efforts of the medical/engineering coalition, in fact, none of the Big Three automakers had departments to oversee safety in their engineering divisions. They instead relied upon the traditional method of advertising campaigns by what later critics would call "the safety establishment," in which the industry had up to that point exercised tremendous muscle. Even the Committee on Traffic Safety, established by President Eisenhower, reflected the industry's dominance as Eisenhower appointed his friend Harlow H. Curtice, president of GM, to chair the federal board of inquiry.

When, in the early 1950s, corporations did appoint safety engineers, many were hostile to what they perceived to be undue interference by the "safety lobby." At the Ford Motor Company, however, that was not the case. Alex Haynes, formerly an aviation engineer, was appointed by Ford in 1952 to oversee product safety and was enthusiastic about the innovations being suggested in medical and engineering trade association journals. He lobbied his superiors at Ford to include them in the company's cars. He found a receptive audience in several executives, including Robert S. McNamara, assistant general manager. McNamara's receptivity to, and lobbying for, the concept of safety design prompted Ford to introduce a "safety package" for the 1956 model year, which featured increased padding, crash-proof door latches that would not spring open, and seat belts. The demand for seat belts surprised suppliers, who could not keep up with demand, and the competition, who feared losing customers to the "safer" Ford models and who could also make more money by adding the optional seat belt. Although Henry Ford II is said to have quipped that "McNamara's selling safety but Chevrolet is selling cars," Ford's "lifeguard design" was a breakthrough achievement on the road to safer automobiles because it represented an acknowledgment by the industry that cars could be made with safety "designed in." But because the sales ratio of Ford to Chevy remained unbalanced, top Ford executives remained convinced of the old industry adage that "safety doesn't sell." Although the features were still installed, the safety angle was dropped from Ford advertising for 1957.

Within the government, several legislators were by this time beginning to investigate the subject. The attention of medical and engineering professionals and local authorities had first drawn the concern of Alabama congressman Kenneth A. Roberts, himself a victim in a serious crash. Throughout the late 1950s and early 1960s Roberts held committee hearings on automobile safety and heard testimony from doctors and engineers that manufacturers were failing to design the safest cars possible. In 1964 Roberts succeeded in pushing legislation through Congress that required the installation of seventeen safety devices, most notably, seat belts, in all cars purchased by the Government Services Administration, the major buyer of cars for the federal government. He next planned to propose similar legislation for all cars sold in the United States but was defeated in 1964 by a Goldwater Republican. Roberts's legacy was carried on by Senators Warren G. Magnuson, Vance Hartke, and especially Abraham Ribicoff.

Other officials outside the Congress picked up the safety issue as well. One was Daniel Patrick Moynihan, assistant secretary of labor for the Kennedy administration. Moynihan had first become concerned with automobile safety as an aide to New York governor Averell Harriman and had in 1958 published a critique of current industry practices in the *Reporter*. Moynihan commissioned a Hartford lawyer named Ralph Nader to study the problem for his department in 1964, and Nader, in turn, transformed the study into one of the best-selling books of 1966. The appearance of both Nader's *Unsafe at Any Speed: The Designed-In Dangers of the American Automobile* and Random House's *Safety Last: An Indictment of the American Automobile Industry* late in 1965 put the subject high on the national political agenda of 1966. That January, President Lyndon Johnson received commendation for addressing the problem in his State of the Union Address, and he assigned aide Joseph Califano the task of preparing a legislative package to address the felt need to improve the safety of cars and car travel.

The traditional manufacturers' emphasis on comfort and style over safety were by this time working against them. By 1965 the number of deaths jumped to 49,000 and was projected to reach 56,000 by 1972. Investigations by Congressional committees, Senator Ribicoff's Government Operations Committee in particular, heard evidence that cars were by 1965 overpowered, underbraked, undertired, and that their weight was poorly distributed.

The testimony of corporate executives revealing the proportionately small sums spent on motor vehicle safety improvements, and their generally poor performance in the face of charges leveled about the safety of their products ensured the passage of the National Traffic and Motor Vehicle Act and the Highway Safety Act of 1966. These pieces of legislation mandated the inclusion of seventeen safety features from safety doorlocks and padded seats and dashes to seat belt installation. By 1977 the number of required safety features had nearly doubled to include dual braking systems, collapsible steering columns, seat headrests, emergency flashers, and automatic passenger restraint. Federal safety legislation also forced the automobile makers to conduct public recall campaigns, presuming that having to admit to poor product quality would deter the industry from allowing it. Such has not been so, however, as there have been more than 86 million units recalled since the 1966 regulations took effect.

But automobile travel has indeed become progressively safer. By 1985 the death rate per 100,000 miles traveled had dropped to 19. The death rate per 100 million vehicle miles traveled was reduced to 2.48, one-fourth the rate of the 1940s. Still, automobile accidents constitute one-half of all accidental deaths in the United States each year, affecting particularly those between the ages of fifteen and forty-four.

References

Joel W. Eastman, *Style vs. Safety: The American Automobile Industry and the Development of Auto Safety, 1900-1966* (Lanham, Md.: University Press of America, 1984);

James J. Flink, *The Car Culture* (Cambridge Mass.: MIT Press, 1970);

"Traffic Safety '87" (Washington, D.C.: Department of Transportation, 1988): 1-11, 45-53.

Sears, Roebuck & Company

by George S. May

Eastern Michigan University

Late in 1951, nearly forty years after it had stopped production and mail-order sales of its Sears high-wheeler automobiles, Sears announced that it would again sell automobiles. This time, however, the cars would not be sold through its catalog, but through some of its retail stores. Ironically, these stores had begun to open in the 1920s when farmers began doing less shopping through the catalog and more by driving their cars to shop in nearby towns and cities. During the interim, Sears had concentrated on selling tires, batteries, and automobile parts, including parts for the Model T many years after Ford had ceased producing that car. In 1926 Sears began to sell a new line of tires under the trade name Allstate, a name selected in a nation-wide contest. Sears also adopted the Allstate name for the automobile insurance company it established in 1931 and eventually applied the name to its batteries and other automotive parts. Obviously Allstate was the logical name for the automobile Sears began selling at selected retail outlets in the South and Southwest.

Unlike its earlier automobile, which Sears had manufactured at a factory in Chicago, the Allstate automobile was manufactured by another company, the Kaiser-Frazer Corporation. For several years a Kaiser subsidiary had been making bathtubs and other enamelware for Sears, which had purchased a large amount of stock in the company. The Allstate was essentially the Henry J compact that Kaiser had introduced in 1950. The only difference between the two models was several cosmetic design changes provided by Alex Tremulis, the stylist who had earlier designed the ill-fated Tucker. The Allstate suffered a similar fate. After tallying sales of only 2,363 at its test markets in seventeen states Sears announced in November 1953 that it was abandoning the car. The company said that it might get back into the automobile business "at some future time," but as it turned out, this would mark the last attempt to sell an automobile through a department store.

References:

Nick Baldwin and others, *The World Guide to Automobile Manufacturers* (New York: Facts on File, 1987);

Boris Emmet and John E. Jeuck, *Catalogues and Counters: A History of Sears, Roebuck and Company* (Chicago: University of Chicago Press, 1950);

John A. Gunnell, ed., *Standard Catalog of American Cars, 1946-1975* (Iola, Wis.: Krause, 1983);

"H. J.'s Allstate," *Time*, 58 (December 3, 1951): 95;

"Week in Business," *Newsweek*, 42 (November 9, 1953): 75.

Seat Belts

by Kevin M. Dwyer

George Washington University

Although the seat belt has become a required feature in American motor vehicles, such has not always been the case. The installation of seat belts in all cars sold in the United States became standard manufacturing practice only with the passage of traffic safety legislation in 1966. Since then, many states have passed mandatory seat belt legislation, but their use—being difficult to impose and enforce—has been largely a question of individual choice.

Not until 1955, however, did the consumer even have that choice to make. The Ford Motor Company first offered consumers seat belts as optional equipment as a part of its "lifeguard design" campaign of the 1956 model year. Consumer demand outpaced the capacity of Ford's parts suppliers, and other manufacturers soon followed the practice of offering seat belts. But the adaptation of the seat belt to the automobile was a development with which manufacturers had little to do. Not since the earliest production models had the seat belt been employed, and then only as a strap to keep the driver stationary. Corporate management, particularly at General Motors (GM) but throughout the industry as well, resisted the trend toward seat belt installation. Rather than seek to change the design of the automobile to protect motorists in the event of an accident, the industry favored solutions involving the improvement of road quality and safe driving campaigns, many of which it sponsored through organizations like the National Safety Council. But in the late 1940s others, mostly medical professionals, suggested the idea and later compelled the industry to offer the device in its cars.

By the early 1950s medical professionals and engineers had compiled sufficient evidence to convince industry professionals of the value of the passenger/driver restraint. The objective, they argued, was to prevent the "second collision," that of the driver/passenger being thrown against interior surfaces. Hugh DeHaven, an independent pathologist and engineer and a pioneer in the field of crash protection, adapted the idea of passenger restraint from his experience as an aviator. Having once crashed during his World War I training, he saw the benefit of the seat belt. His research in the late 1940s, much of it self-financed, and that of others at the Indiana Crash Research Project and the Cornell Aeronautics Lab, demonstrated that passenger restraints would protect the human body from the violent effects of the "second collision." "Packaging the driver" for protection in the event of an accident, similar in concept to packaging cargo to be shipped, was commonly stressed by proponents of restraining devices.

A coalition of engineering and medical associations led the efforts to lobby the industry, efforts which by the 1956 model year had met with partial success. Since Congress passed the National Traffic and Motor Vehicle Safety Act in 1966, seat belts have been required equipment on all cars sold in the United States, although many people choose not to employ them. By 1973 government estimates recorded as many as 10,000 fatalities a year traceable to the failure to use seat belts. In an effort to stop such needless fatalities, prior seat belt requirements have been surpassed by recent federal regulations. U.S. Department of Transportation requirements in 1984 stipulated that automobile makers must install either automatic seat belts (with a shoulder harness which fastens automatically around the driver or passenger when the car door closes) or safety airbags in all cars sold in America by October 1, 1989.

Reference:

Joel W. Eastman, *Styling vs. Safety: The American Automobile Industry and the Development of Automotive Safety, 1900-1966* (Lanham, Md: University Press of America, 1984).

Alfred Pritchard Sloan, Jr.

(May 23, 1875-February 17, 1966)

by John B. Rae

Harvey Mudd College

CAREER: Draftsman (1895), president, Hyatt Roller Bearing Company (1898-1916); president, United Motors Corporation (1916-1919); vice-president and director (1919-1923), president (1923-1937), chairman (1937-1956), honorary chairman, GM Corporation (1956-1966).

Alfred Pritchard Sloan, Jr., automobile executive, was born on May 23, 1875, in New Haven, Connecticut, and died in New York City on February 17, 1966. He was the oldest of five children of Alfred Pritchard and Katharine Mead Sloan. His father was in the wholesale tea, coffee, and cigar business, under the name Bennett-Sloan & Company; his mother was the daughter of a Methodist minister. In 1885 his father's business moved to New York City, and Alfred grew up in Brooklyn, acquiring an accent that he retained for the rest of his life.

Sloan graduated from the Massachusetts Institute of Technology in 1895 with a bachelor's degree in electrical engineering. He was the youngest member of his class and completed the normal four-year program in three years. He had distinguished company in college. One classmate was Gerard Swope, future head of General Electric; a year later came Paul W. Litchfield, future head of Goodyear; and a year after that Irénée du Pont. Roger Babson, the economist, was in the class of 1898. After graduation Sloan went to work as a draftsman in Harrison, New Jersey, for the Hyatt Roller Bearing Company, which made a tapered roller bearing designed by John Wesley Hyatt, an eccentric genius who was also the inventor of celluloid. Sloan left shortly afterward to work on a project for making a mechanical refrigerator, but it failed and he returned to Hyatt. About this time, in 1898, he married Irene Jackson, of Roxbury, Massachusetts. They had no children.

Alfred Pritchard Sloan, Jr.

Sloan found the Hyatt company in difficulties; its founder was a brilliant inventor but a poor businessman. Sloan's father and a business associate invested $5,000, with which Sloan was able to buy into the business and manage it; he was given six months to show what he could do. This investment was Sloan's introduction to management, and he promptly demonstrated his talent. He was undoubtedly fortunate that the rapid growth of automobile manufacturing after 1900 created a booming market for his product, but nevertheless stabilized the firm and built it into the largest single manufacturer of roller bearings in the country. Early in his career Sloan traveled to Detroit to deal with a complaint from the Cadillac Motor Car Company about his bearings (actually the bearings were sold to the Weston Mott Axle Company, which sold axles to Cadillac). Sloan was greeted by Henry M. Leland, the founder and then president of Cadillac and a fanatical precisionist, with: "Mr. Sloan, Cadillacs are made to run, not just to sell." He was then shown a large pile of discarded axles and told that he must grind his bearings so that no matter how many thousand he made, the last would be exactly like the first. Sloan stated that this experience gave him an appreciation of what mass production really meant.

After this incident, he had another valuable learning experience, this time with Ford Motor Company. C. H. Wills of Ford told him that because of the size of Ford orders, Hyatt should offer the Ford Motor Company a reduced price on its bearings. It was a common Ford tactic to encourage and even assist supplier firms to expand their facilities in order to keep pace with the rapid growth of Ford production and then require those firms to make price concessions on the threat of having Ford's business withdrawn. Although Sloan and Wills came to an amicable agreement, the incident must have given Sloan cause to think about the dependence of his company on the large motor vehicle producers and probably on the strong possibility that Henry Ford, who wanted the Ford Motor Company completely integrated, might well decide at any moment to manufacture his own roller bearings. Sloan's immediate reaction to the incident was a realization that successful large-scale production called for a constant search for better methods and lower costs and that these had to be achieved by systematic planning, research, and accurate accounting.

The next stage in Sloan's career began in 1916 with an invitation to lunch from William C. Durant. Durant, a flamboyant and aggressive promoter and salesman, founded the General Motors (GM) Company in 1908, only to lose control of it two years later when injudicious expansion brought a threat of receivership. The company was managed for the next five years by a bankers' syndicate headed by James J. Storrow of Lee, Higginson & Company. Now Durant was back in control, with the support of Du Pont money and the profits from his Chevrolet Motor Car Company, founded in 1911. The Du Pont interest originated because John J. Raskob, the treasurer of the Du Pont Company, saw in GM a promising investment for his company's large World War I profits. Durant had been very successful in convincing GM stockholders to exchange their holdings for Chevrolet stock because the bankers' trust, as one of its steps to restore GM to solvency, had paid no dividends.

Durant embarked on another program of expansion, part of which was to create a great combination of supplier companies as part of the GM structure. This was the reason he approached Sloan. The keystone of this combination was to be the Hyatt Roller Bearing Company, and Durant proposed to Sloan that he sell his company to a new organization called the United Motors Corporation.

Sloan was understandably startled. He was proud of his company and what he had done with it, and at first he could see no advantage in Durant's offer. But as he reflected on the proposal, he came to accept that Hyatt had become too big to remain independent. Hyatt was organized for mass production, which meant that it had to have a mass market in order to operate profitably, and the only such markets in sight were the Ford Motor Company and GM. Hyatt had to be assured of one or the other. Durant's offer, $13.5 million in United Motors stock and cash, was reasonable, and Sloan accepted it.

Thus, the United Motors Corporation was born, and Alfred P. Sloan, Jr., entered the GM family. In addition to Hyatt the combination consisted of: the Dayton Engineering Laboratories Company (Delco), which brought Charles F. Kettering into the GM fold; the Harrison Radiator Company; the Klaxon Company; the New Departure Manufacturing Company (ball bearings); the Perlman Rim Corporation; and the Remy Electric Company. Sloan became president. It is quite possible that Durant's eagerness to buy Hyatt without long negotiations was because he wanted Sloan in the GM organization, just as Kettering was undoubtedly the principal attraction in Delco.

This arrangement lasted two years. Durant's use of Chevrolet stock to assist in recovering control of GM had created the anomalous situation that the whole was owned by one of its parts; in other words, the Chevrolet Motor Car Company owned GM. This organizational confusion was cleared up in 1918, when a new GM Corporation was created which by exchanges of stock became the owner of the GM Company, Chevrolet, and United Motors. Sloan was made a vice-president and director of the GM Corporation. United Motors was dissolved two years later.

It should have been predictable that Sloan and Durant would not work well together. Two more contrasting personalities would be difficult to find. Durant, the promoter, who had left school at sixteen to begin a successful sales career, was impulsive, mercurial, given to following his hunches; Sloan, the engineer, was a methodical planner and organizer who would study a situation thoroughly before arriving at a decision. Conceivably their management styles could have complemented each other, but they did not, primarily because Durant was not interested in management.

The GM that Sloan joined was in a vigorous but unplanned and uncoordinated expansion. Sloan became directly involved in the construction of the GM headquarters complex in Detroit. Durant's intention was to erect the building in the downtown area, but Sloan proposed constructing it farther out, in an area on West Grand Boulevard. When he was president of the Hyatt Roller Bearing Company, Sloan established an office there because of Hyatt's business with the automobile industry. That office subsequently became the headquarters of United Motors. Sloan argued that land in the downtown area was very expensive and the Grand Boulevard site would be more accessible and have less traffic congestion. Durant accepted the suggestion and put Sloan in charge of acquiring the necessary land.

Some of the acquisitions Durant made for GM at this time were valuable, such as Fisher Body, Frigidaire, and the GM Acceptance Corporation (GMAC); others were not, including a venture into farm equipment that Durant undertook against the advice of Walter Chrysler, then president of Buick. The corporation was a loose conglomerate of separate companies with no central financial or other controls. Whatever central authority existed was vested in Durant himself, and he was preoccupied with ideas for further expansion and increasingly with speculation in the stock market.

Such a situation was anathema to Sloan's orderly mind. It was also personally distressing. He liked Durant; Sloan later stated that Durant was brilliant, a man of unquestioned integrity, and totally devoted to GM (to Sloan, writing about these events many years later, this last may well have appeared as Durant's greatest virtue). But Durant was an individualist, operating by intuition, sometimes bril-

liantly, paying little attention to assessment of facts or to systematic planning, and careless about the use of his own and others' time. Sloan also later recounted how he and other GM vice-presidents, including Walter Chrysler, were summoned on short notice to Detroit for a conference with Durant and waited all day because Durant had become distracted by other matters. Early in 1920 Chrysler could stand it no longer and quit. He was annoyed by Durant's periodic and erratic interference in the affairs of Buick and complained that Buick accounted for the greater part of GM profits, but Durant spent the money faster than Buick could make it.

The less volatile Sloan stayed on, but with increasing misgivings. He was convinced that GM was too big to be run by one man, even a genius. His response, early in 1920, was to submit to Durant a plan for the reorganization of the company, the plan that he later put into effect. Durant looked at it, approved it, and did nothing more.

The climax came with the financial panic that struck in September 1920. Sloan saw it as a normal transition from a wartime to a peacetime economy and urged Durant to reduce expenditures and cut the prices of GM cars. Durant refused because he felt that such steps would hamper his efforts to maintain the price of GM stock and he believed that the panic would be short-lived. It was, but not short enough to save Durant. Sloan decided that he must take time to think about his position. He and his wife went on a trip to Europe in the course of which he determined to return to the United States and resign. However, when he returned home, he found that the GM situation had completely changed. Durant was gone.

During the crisis the du Ponts became alarmed about the security of their GM holdings. Durant was speculating heavily in GM stock, in part from the quite creditable motive of trying to protect the people who had bought it on his recommendation. But the market continued to fall until Durant was faced with bankruptcy, in which event GM might well have gone down with him. Consequently, Pierre S. du Pont and John J. Raskob intervened. Durant's affairs were badly entangled, but they arranged for the Du Pont Company and J. P. Morgan & Company to buy his 2.5 million shares of GM and pay off his obligations. By this transaction the Du Pont holding in GM was increased to 36 percent.

Sloan, second from right, with Charles E. Wilson, right, William S. Knudsen, at microphone, and M. E. Coyle, leaning on car, taking part in ceremonies on January 11, 1940, marking the production of GM's 25-millionth car (courtesy of GM)

When Durant gave up the presidency of GM late in 1920, Pierre S. du Pont took his place. He did not particularly want the post, but he was urged to take it by Sloan, Raskob, and others on the ground that his own reputation in business and the du Pont name were needed to restore public confidence in GM. Sloan became executive vice-president and with du Pont's approval began to implement his plan for reorganization. The fact that the Du Pont Company, under the leadership of Irénée du Pont, adopted an almost identical system of organization at this same time has led to an assumption that du Pont influence was responsible for the structure that Sloan gave GM. Sloan always maintained that this was not so, that the two schemes were formulated quite independently of each other. He pointed out that Du Pont was seeking to diversify instead of being exclusively a manufacturer of explosives, while GM needed a central structure that would bring order out of the administrative chaos of the Durant years.

During his term as executive vice-president, Sloan was further impressed with the defects of the existing GM structure by a controversy that arose over an air-cooled engine designed by Charles F. Kettering known as the "copper-cooled" engine because of the copper fins used in the cooling system. Kettering was thoroughly convinced of the superiority of his engine, and Sloan and Pierre du Pont were interested, but the operating divisions that were going to have to put the engine into their cars lacked in enthusiasm. The project was abandoned, and for a time Kettering threatened to resign from GM. To Sloan the incident underlined the company's urgent need for an administrative structure that would establish clear lines of authority and provide for adequate communications among its various parts.

Sloan's plan was officially adopted at the end of December 1920, but it was several years before it was fully implemented. In the meantime, with the panic over and GM in a secure position, Pierre du Pont turned the presidency over to Sloan early in

1923, so that Sloan became fully responsible for the implementation of his own ideas.

The fundamental concept was analogous to the staff-and-line system of military organizations. It was desirable that the company's operating divisions should be reasonably free to manage their own affairs, while at the same time there should be adequate central authority to insure smooth coordination and clear definition of the corporation's overall policies. Sloan acknowledged the comparison with military structures but pointed out that in his system the distinction was between the central office and the divisions. This is a more accurate description because the central office at GM engaged in some line activities, and it had the final power of decision on which activities should be dealt with by the central authority and which by the divisions.

In brief the new organization had at its top the board of directors, functioning primarily through two committees, executive and financial, which formulated the corporation's basic policies. Implementation of these policies was the role of the president. Under him were the operating divisions, organized into groups—car and truck, accessories, parts, export, each with a vice-president in charge. Then there was a financial staff and an advisory staff, each with its vice-president also. The advisory staff handled such matters as real estate, patents, research, sales, and advertising and as its name indicated was there primarily to advise the operating divisions and also to administer functions that belonged to the corporation as a whole rather than to any individual division. Finally, there were several interdivisional relations committees: general purchasing, general technical, operations, institutional advertising, and general sales, their responsibilities identified by their names.

It took some years to complete this organization. In this work Sloan was materially assisted by two Du Pont men who came over to GM, Donaldson Brown and John Lee Pratt. Like Sloan they were engineers by training, but their principal contribution to the GM organization was to work out an elaborate system of financial controls which established general corporate standards for expected return on capital, budgeting, inventory, purchasing, and so on.

As part of the reorganization process there was a careful pruning of the acquisitions made during the second Durant regime. Frigidaire was retained as it was an outstanding success; in fact, it so dominated its market that for a number of years any electric refrigerator was referred to simply as a "Frigidaire." Fisher Body and the GM Acceptance Corporation were likewise retained as valuable parts of the corporate structure. On the other side, two car companies that Durant had acquired, Sheridan and Scripps-Booth, were dissolved and their lines discontinued, and what remained of the ill-advised venture into tractors and farm equipment was liquidated. GM as it emerged consisted of the operations that were then profitable or that in Sloan's judgment (which time would show to be correct) could be made profitable.

This reorganization was an outstanding achievement in management, attested to not only by the subsequent rise of GM to become the world's largest privately owned manufacturing enterprise but still more by the tribute of widespread imitation. Most large motor vehicle manufacturing companies and many other big business concerns throughout the free world have chosen to follow the GM pattern of management in one form or another. Yet, except among business executives and students of management, Sloan himself has received little recognition. He was a reserved, serious individual with none of the glamour that Henry Ford acquired, and sought. The art of management does not provide the kind of news that attracts public interest. At the time Sloan was creating this model of management organization, Henry Ford was practically a demigod whose every word and action attracted acute public interest. Figures such as Durant and John North Willys were definitely more colorful than Sloan, although events proved that neither one was in Sloan's class as an administrator.

One other comment should be made. No organization chart can provide for the human personalities who will actually run the system. Any large organization has within it both centripetal and centrifugal forces. With GM, careful management was going to be needed to keep the balance between the two; the evidence is that Sloan did so successfully, although he never left any doubt about who was in charge. There remained the future possibility that a strong-willed president would dominate the executive and finance committees and concentrate authority in his own hands, or that a weak president would be dominated by one or the other of those committees. The possibility of such problems remained a contingency that could not be provided for in even the most carefully planned organizational structure. Sloan recognized the risk, but he also recognized that managerial technique and structure would have to be adapted to changing conditions.

When Sloan took charge of GM, corporate reorganization was just one of the major problems he had to face. Only two of the motor vehicle divisions, Cadillac and Buick, were showing a profit, and the company as a whole was second in the American automobile market. Ford was securely in the lead with 50 percent of the market while GM commanded only about 20 percent. Chevrolet, which was supposed to have challenged Ford in the low-price class, had floundered after a good start, so badly indeed that a number of GM directors believed it should be discontinued.

Sloan was not willing to give up a GM car (evidently he regarded Sheridan and Scripps-Booth as intruders that should not be considered as genuine members of the club), and he found a remedy. In 1921 Charles S. Mott brought William S. Knudsen into Sloan's office to meet him. Knudsen was already well known in the automobile industry as one of the Ford Motor Company's abler production men—he had installed the system of regional assembly plants which saved Ford millions of dollars in transportation costs—but he had now joined the long line of Ford executives who became dissatisfied and left. Sloan made him a special consultant in the president's office and soon afterward made him head of the Chevrolet division, with the mission of rehabilitating it and making the Chevrolet an effective competitor in the market for low-priced cars. Knudsen overhauled Chevrolet production methods and, with a good car and a competitive price, conducted an aggressive sales campaign. At meetings of Chevrolet dealers he would exhort them in his strong Danish accent: "I want vun for vun"—one Chevrolet sold for each Ford. In 1926 Chevrolet cut severely into Model T sales, and in the following year Henry Ford was finally persuaded that the Model T was obsolete, something his son Edsel and others in the Ford Motor Company had been trying to tell him for several years. Chevrolet stepped into the lead among low-priced cars and retained it with only occasional interruptions from Ford.

The Oakland division, producing a medium-priced car, was also sluggish. A market survey showed that there was an opening in the GM line between the Oldsmobile and the Chevrolet. The trans-

formation here was not as spectacular as at Chevrolet, but it was important. Sloan's objective was defensive; the purpose was not to dislodge an established competitor but to prevent any prospective competitor from preempting this segment of the market before GM had an entry. The outcome was that the Oakland division was to build a 6-cylinder car to be called the Pontiac (Pontiac, Michigan, where the factory was located, is the county seat of Oakland County) sufficiently like the Chevrolet so that it could share some of Chevrolet's economies of scale. This was possible because Knudsen, in rehabilitating Chevrolet production, had introduced the basic Ford methods but had also provided for greater flexibility than existed then at Ford.

The Pontiac went into production in 1926; the Oakland was later dropped and with that the GM passenger-car line was complete: from top to bottom, Cadillac, Buick, Oldsmobile, Pontiac, Chevrolet. This fulfilled Sloan's principle that GM should offer a car "for every purse and every purpose." The divisions overlapped and to some extent competed with each other, but that was all right with Sloan; it kept the division managers alert, and if one GM division lost sales to another, that was better than losing them to an outside competitor.

By this time GM was rising to undisputed first place among American and, indeed, world motor vehicle manufacturers. It can be argued that in achieving this position Sloan had a stroke of luck; namely, the closing down of the Ford Motor Company for nearly six months between the termination of Model T production in May 1927 and the introduction of the Model A late in that year. It can also be argued that this was not luck at all, that the competitive pressure from Sloan's efficiently organized and well-managed company compelled Henry Ford, reluctantly and belatedly, to abandon the Model T and stop production until a new and more up-to-date design could be developed. What is certain is that the GM leadership continued and was never seriously threatened when Ford returned to the market. Ford outsold Chevrolet during the first year of the Model A in 1928, but Chevrolet immediately came back.

This result must be credited to Sloan's system and his management. He had able assistants, like Knudsen and Brown, but that too was evidence of managerial ability. The Ford Motor Company had a long line of able assistants, virtually all of whom were forced out by Henry Ford's jealousy and suspicion of any possible competitor. In Sloan's system, recruiting and encouraging the best talent available was one of the attributes of good management.

By 1926 Sloan's reorganization of GM was substantially complete, and the corporation was ready to proceed with Sloan at its head and his system of management in full-scale operation. There were still things to set right, as there always are in a large organization, and there were plans for expansion as GM grew and prospered. The policies adopted by Sloan have been termed "Sloanism" by the automotive writer Emma Rothschild, as a counterpart to "Fordism," for the purpose of demonstrating that Sloan's influence on the management and operation of the motor vehicle and other industries worldwide was just as great as Henry Ford's influence on the technology of production. Both terms can be used pejoratively, and have been, but "Sloanism" does testify that Sloan, a relatively obscure and unknown figure except in high industrial circles, exercised every bit as much influence on industrial management and practice as the highly publicized Henry Ford. Indeed, from the time he became president of GM, Sloan's influence on the motor vehicle industry as a whole was arguably greater than that of the aging and declining Henry Ford.

Sloan was as fully aware of the marketing side of the industry as of the production and financial aspects. Throughout his presidency he made a point of visiting every GM dealer at frequent intervals. The dealer, after all, was the intermediary between the manufacturer and the customer; it was with him that market penetration took place. By the early 1920s the restricted franchise dealership had become standard in the automobile industry, and problems of manufacturer-dealer relationships were beginning to develop. As could have been expected, Sloan had studies made of GM marketing problems and dealer relations. Out of these, and from continuing experience with the situation, came two organizations: Motors Accounting Company in 1927, which developed a standard accounting system for GM dealers, and Motors Holding Corporation (later Motors Holding Division) in 1929, to provide capital to dealers, a function which led it to develop management techniques and training for dealers. In 1934 came the GM Dealers Council, formed for the purpose of improving communications with and among dealers. Some practices had to be modified in the light of experience, especially during the depression years, and during those years dealer complaints increased throughout the industry. Nevertheless the GM record in dealer relations remained good, certainly better than that of the Ford Motor Company.

One major marketing problem which arose during the 1920s was the used car, a direct product of the American automobile industry's success. Constantly increasing purchases of new cars, particularly with buyers "trading up" as the boom period of the 1920s developed, meant a rising influx of serviceable used cars on the market. By 1927 it was calculated that most new cars were being bought as replacements. Yet, if the automobile industry was to grow, new car sales must increase. Sloan's solution was to institutionalize the already common practice of bringing out a new model each year. Sufficient change was to be made each year so a new car was distinguishable from its predecessors; the automobile as a "status symbol" was emerging. At the same time the yearly changes should not be so great as to give the buyer concern about his vehicle's future trade-in value. This required a careful planning of design and greater flexibility in production technique than had been possible with the Ford Motor Company's original assembly line. Whether or not this practice has been a desirable one has been the subject of much discussion. European and Japanese automobile manufacturers—conspicuously Volkswagen—have done quite well without the annual model, but most have chosen to follow the American practice.

As GM's business expanded, the question of developing markets in other countries became increasingly important. When Sloan became president there was already a GM of Canada, but otherwise foreign markets were served through export. However, after World War I there was an upsurge of economic nationalism which resulted in discrimination against American cars through tariffs and other regulations. Even before this situation developed the Ford Motor Company had established assembly plants in Great Britain in 1911 and in France in 1913. Ford's subsequent practice was to establish manufacturing subsidiaries in other countries. When the economic nationalism of the 1920s became a problem for GM, the question Sloan had to resolve was whether to follow this example or to acquire existing companies in the countries where GM wanted to develop markets. Sloan himself preferred the latter solution. As early as 1919, while Durant was still head of the company, Sloan was ac-

Sloan late in his career at GM (courtesy of Motor Vehicle Manufacturers Association of the United States, Inc.)

tively involved in negotiations for GM to buy a half interest in the Citroën Company of France. André Citroën was willing to sell, but the French government disapproved, and the GM negotiators had misgivings about Citroën management and the investment that would be required to renovate Citroën's production facilities. There was a suggestion that either Sloan or Walter Chrysler should move to France and run Citroën, a step that undoubtedly would have changed the course of automotive history. Sloan was not interested, neither presumably was Chrysler, and in the end, the whole idea was dropped.

After Sloan took charge of GM, attention turned to Great Britain, where a horsepower tax that favored vehicles with narrow-bore, long-stroke engines made the selling of American-built cars especially difficult, since Americans and most others preferred engines in which bore and stroke were approximately equal. At first, consideration was given to buying the Austin Motor Car company, but the same objections arose as had developed

with Citroën, except that there was no opposition from the government. These negotiations were terminated early in 1925, and before the year was out GM had bought Vauxhall Motors, Ltd., a small company that built a high-priced car. Vauxhall then took over the Bedford truck, which GM had been building in Britain since 1913, using a Buick chassis. In the 1930s Vauxhall's passenger-car line was successfully changed to smaller cars.

The same policy was followed in Germany, where after intensive study and discussion typical of Sloan management, GM bought the Adam Opel A. G., one of Germany's principal automobile manufacturers. In Australia GM bought Holden's Motor Body Builders in 1932 and merged it with a previously organized General Motors assembly operation to build the Holden car. Elsewhere GM adopted the Ford policy of establishing manufacturing or assembly plants. It is of historical interest that in the 1920s and 1930s GM of Japan and Ford of Japan, both assembly operations, were the principal producers of motor vehicles in that country.

The wisdom of undertaking these overseas operations is demonstrated by the fact that exports of GM cars from the United States and Canada reached a peak of 290,000 units in 1929. The coming of the Great Depression naturally had its effect, but even in later prosperous years the American automobile companies found it advisable to manufacture abroad rather than rely on direct exports. In actual practice, there seems to have been no great difference in results between the GM and the Ford systems; in fact, there were more similarities than differences. Yet the policies of GM during these years represented a triumph for Sloan's leadership and his system. He knew what he wanted, but he never tried to impose his ideas on others autocratically. He felt at the time that Austin would not be a desirable acquisition, but he left the final decision to the group that was conducting the negotiations. There were some GM executives who wanted to follow the Ford method of establishing foreign subsidiaries under the company's name, and some who wanted to rely on direct exports for foreign business, perhaps with assembly plants in the market areas. Sloan worked to achieve a reasonable consensus, so that no one would appear to have been arbitrarily overruled.

Along with laying the foundation for its overseas expansion, the Sloan regime also took GM into two new fields, aviation and diesel engines. For aviation the incentives were the anticipated boom in air transport stimulated by the Kelly Air Mail Act of 1925 and still more by the public excitement generated by Charles A. Lindbergh's New York-to-Paris flight in 1927. Since automotive and aeronautical technology were still somewhat closely related, it was natural for the automobile producers to take a strong interest in the possibilities of aviation. The Ford Motor Company was already building the famous Ford Trimotor, the "Tin Goose," and there was talk of a "flying flivver." Understandably, GM felt that it should have a foothold in aviation also.

Its activity began in 1929 when GM purchased a 24-percent stock interest in the Bendix Aviation Corporation, a manufacturer of aircraft parts and components; a 40-percent interest in the Fokker Aircraft Corporation of America; and bought the Allison Engineering Company of Indianapolis. Allison was previously a service operation for racing cars at the Indianapolis Speedway but had also developed a business working on Liberty aircraft engines. As part of GM it became a major manufacturer of water-cooled aircraft engines. Bendix also became a prosperous adjunct to GM. Fokker was founded by the great Dutch aeronautical engineer, Anthony Fokker, but shortly after the GM investment there was a dispute about management; Fokker left and returned to Holland.

The company then became involved in a complex merger of aircraft manufacturing and air transport companies named North American Aviation. Following an alleged scandal over the award of air mail contracts, a new Air Mail Act in 1934 required the separation of manufacturing and transport companies. As a result North American emerged as an airframe manufacturer, still with a strong GM interest. This relationship was terminated in 1948 because GM decided that as a producer of aircraft engines and parts, it should not be in the airframe business, where it would compete with its own customers.

Sloan's role in the aviation business is difficult to identify, largely because his own management style kept him in the background. He definitely believed that commercial aviation had a great future in which he would certainly want GM to share, but it is not possible to determine from available evidence how much of the initiative came from him. What can be said with assurance is that none of

these steps could have been taken without his approval and that if the aviation ventures had proved unsuccessful the blame would have been put on Sloan's shoulders.

With the diesel engine the decision-making process is clearer. The central figure was Charles F. Kettering. The diesel of the 1920s was bulky and heavy, mostly restricted to use as a marine or stationary engine. Yet its potential merits were clear enough so that Kettering, with encouragement from Sloan, was studying it at the GM Research Laboratories as early as 1921. Kettering became more heavily involved when he bought a diesel-powered yacht in 1928. At that time Sloan assured him that he would provide the necessary manufacturing facilities if Kettering could improve the diesel engine by reducing its weight-power ratio. Kettering did this, largely by making it a 2-cycle rather than a 4-cycle mechanism and by providing for much greater precision in the fuel injection system.

Sloan carried out his part of the bargain in 1930 by having GM purchase the Winton Engine Company and the Electro-Motive Engineering Company, both of Cleveland, Ohio. Both had built gas-electric rail cars, and both were exploring the more attractive potential of diesel power. Consequently GM was in a commanding position when American railroads became interested in diesel power during the 1930s. The 78-hour test run of the Burlington Zephyr from Denver to Chicago in 1934 attracted much attention and touched off widespread interest by the railroads in streamlined, diesel-powered passenger trains. However, by the end of the decade the improvements to the diesel were not yet sufficient for it to replace steam power. The principal market for diesel locomotives was switching engines, for which weight was an advantage rather than a handicap. Yet in his lifetime Sloan would see diesel locomotives replace steam power on all American railroads and GM attain a near monopoly of diesel locomotive manufacturing. He would also see diesel engines widely used in buses and trucks and to a lesser extent in passenger cars, although these categories were not dominated by GM.

The coming of the depression and the New Deal presented Sloan and GM with an entirely new set of problems. During Sloan's career with the company there had been a steadily rising market for motor vehicles, except for the brief slump in 1920-1921. Now there was deep and long-term decline in demand. Between 1929 and 1932 annual output dropped by 80 percent; the level of 5 million vehicles produced in 1929 would not be reached again until 1948, although it probably would have been attained a few years earlier if not for World War II. This situation required painful contraction, but it was the smaller automobile companies that suffered most. The "Big Three" (GM, Ford, Chrysler) suffered from declining sales but actually increased their share of the market because many of the independents went out of business altogether.

Sales began to recover slowly after 1933, but then the automobile industry was faced with the regulations of the New Deal and with aggressive unionism promoted by the depression conditions and a sympathetic national administration. The Automobile Code formulated under the National Industrial Recovery Act of 1933 did not present any great problems. It was drafted by the National Automobile Chamber of Commerce, predecessor of the Motor Vehicle Manufacturers Association, and it was not in effect long enough to have any important impact on the industry.

The labor situation was a radically different matter. The automobile industry had been rigorously open-shop and had easily defeated activity by the Industrial Workers of the World in the union's early years and some half-hearted efforts later by the American Federation of Labor. Now, however, it was faced with federal legislation (Section 7a of the National Industrial Recovery Act) guaranteeing labor the right to organize and bargain collectively. When the Supreme Court invalidated the NIRA, the labor provisions were renewed and strengthened in the National Labor Relations Act (1936), better known as the Wagner Act. With this encouragement vigorous union activities emerged in the automobile industry under the aegis of the newly formed United Automobile Workers (UAW).

Sloan opposed unionization, as did the rest of the automobile industry. He saw it as an infringement of the proper prerogatives of management, and he honestly believed that various welfare and benefit programs established by GM for its workers made unions unnecessary. He was particularly incensed by the novel technique of the "sit-down" strike that the UAW introduced. He saw this as a clear violation of his company's property rights and was deeply embittered by the refusal of either federal or state authorities to evict the strikers from the plants they had occupied. The verdict of history undoubtedly favors Gov. Frank Murphy of Michigan, who saw that attempts at forcible eviction would inevitably lead to bloodshed and chose to deal with the situation by negotiation.

However strong his feelings were, Sloan could accept reality. Early in 1937, GM production was at a standstill because of acrimonious labor disputes, and Sloan realized that this was a battle he could not win. Continued governmental support of the unions was assured by the overwhelming victory of Franklin D. Roosevelt in the presidential election of 1936, and it was reasonably certain that the Supreme Court would uphold the constitutionality of the Wagner Act, as in fact it did. Sloan opted for industrial peace. In February 1937 he announced that GM would accept the UAW as the bargaining agent for all its work force. This must have been a painful decision for Sloan. By training and temperament he disapproved of labor unions, and he had previously expressed his opposition to the idea of requiring all workers in a company to belong to the same union whether they wished it or not. But for the sake of industrial peace, the step had to be taken.

This act of industrial statesmanship was a fitting close to Sloan's term as president of GM. In 1937 he became chairman of the board and chief executive officer. William S. Knudsen succeeded him as president, but he had little opportunity to make a further impression on GM because he was called to Washington in 1940 to help to organize military production. His place was taken by Charles E. "Engine Charlie" Wilson. Wilson had his hands full directing GM wartime operations, so full in fact that at one point his health failed and he had to take a three-month leave of absence.

Thus Sloan remained in a policy-making role throughout the crucial years of World War II. The policy objective was quite straightforward: to meet an ever-increasing, insatiable demand for materiel, some of which GM normally manufactured but most of which were items that GM had never made before. As early as June 1940 Sloan decided that since GM possessed 10 percent of the nation's manufacturing capacity, it should undertake to meet the same proportion of the nation's armament needs. During the war GM produced $12 billion of wartime materiel, about 8 percent of the nation's $150 billion total. Sloan argued that GM costs were lower than most others so that the actual materiel delivered could well have come to 10 percent. In 1942, when the United States was actually in the war, GM adopted a policy of restricting its profits to 10 percent on sales instead of the 20 percent that previously had been its target. The result was that its average net income for the years 1942-1945 was less than it had been for the depression years of 1936-1939.

In 1946 Sloan gave up the post of chief executive officer, although he continued as chairman. The immediate postwar years were a period of acute labor unrest not only for GM but for industry in general. GM dealt with this situation by two imaginative proposals, which after some discussion were accepted by the UAW. One was an "improvement factor" providing for wage increases based on an assumed gain in productivity resulting from technological advances. The other was an "escalator clause" which tied wage increases to the consumer price index. These ideas originated with Wilson, who had given much thought to the problem and who enjoyed good relations with the work force and the UAW. Sloan went along, although he had some misgivings. He felt that there was no accurate way to measure productivity and that the escalator clause tended to pull all wage rates toward an average. He would have preferred outright merit increases, but he accepted the agreement that was achieved.

Sloan's remaining active years as board chairman saw a steady improvement in GM labor relationships and a complete justification of his policy of undertaking the manufacture of diesel-electric railroad locomotives. In addition GM retained and even strengthened its domination of the American automobile industry. Sloan's functions, at this time, appear to have been predominantly advisory. There were no innovations in management or for that matter in product, other than to have American cars become bigger and higher-powered.

Sloan became honorary chairman of GM in 1956 at the age of eighty-one. In other words he retired. For part of his remaining years, he devoted himself to writing his autobiography, *My Years with General Motors*. The title is significant. If Sloan had a life outside GM, it does not appear in anything written by or about him. Perhaps this was because he never received the kind of publicity that Henry Ford did. There was no comparable public curiosity about his personality or his private life. At any rate, any discussion of Sloan's career has virtually to be a history of GM during the same period; the two are inseparable.

Yet he did have outside interests. He established the Alfred P. Sloan Foundation in 1934 with an initial endowment of $10 million. Its initial purpose was to promote education in economic principles and economic problems. Later it expanded its objectives to include fostering the study of science and technology and their relationship to economic and social concerns. He also joined with Charles F. Kettering to create the Sloan-Kettering Foundation for Cancer Research. He was a devoted alumnus of MIT and a generous donor. Shortly before his retirement he founded the Sloan School of Industrial Management at MIT, a gift which included buying the former Lever Brothers headquarters building on Memorial Drive in Cambridge and presenting it to the school.

His true monument was the GM Corporation, at least as it was in the days when it dominated the automotive world, when it had close to 60 percent of all motor vehicle sales in the United States and had to control its pricing policies to enable its competitors to remain in business. Durant had founded GM and had twice almost destroyed it. Sloan took charge of the company, made it highly profitable, and kept it that way. More important, GM under his hand became a model of management organization for large industrial concerns. He initiated business practices that became the accepted standards for the entire automobile industry, and he made GM a power in the world automotive industry.

Yet through it all Sloan remained, if not unknown, at least obscure. His personality did not lend itself to publicity, and there is no indication that he ever sought it. He was serious-minded and methodical, with nothing in any public statement to suggest that he possessed much humor or even human warmth. Charles E. Wilson was erroneously credited with saying, "What's good for General Motors is good for the country" while he was being questioned on his qualifications to become President Eisenhower's secretary of defense. What he actually said was, "What's good for the country is good for General Motors, and vice versa." Sloan could have made the first of these statements in all seriousness.

An assessment of his place in the history of the American automobile industry inevitably invites comparison with Henry Ford. They were completely contrasting personalities: Sloan, the MIT-educated engineer, content to stay out of the limelight as long as he held the controls; Ford, a sketchily educated, bench-trained machinist, eager for publicity. Their managerial styles were equally contrasting: Sloan seeking rationally planned organization, Ford claiming to despise formal organization. Sloan surrounded himself with able lieutenants, like Brown, Knudsen, and Pratt, and gave them a free hand; Ford got rid of every able executive who threatened to rival him in prominence or who opposed his policies.

It would be a pointless exercise to try to establish which of these two had the greater impact on American industry in general and the motor vehicle industry in particular. Their contributions were so different as to be impossible to compare. It can be argued that Henry Ford ended his career in decline and with his company in disarray while Sloan retired with his company still growing and prospering. When it is considered that when Henry Ford II took charge of the Ford Motor Company, he decided that it must have a Sloan-type organization and went to GM for the people to do the reorganizing, it could be argued that in the long run Sloanism absorbed Fordism.

A good measure of Sloan's lifetime achievement can be found in the British motor industry. Twice since 1950 the British government has encouraged mergers in the avowed hope of creating a British counterpart of GM: Austin and Morris as the British Motor Corporation, and later the British Motor Corporation and Leyland as British Leyland Motors. Neither achieved the goal. The reasons are complex, but one factor that was made clear was that a GM organization is not created simply by putting companies together. The same was true of GM itself under Durant. It helps to have an Alfred P. Sloan, Jr.

Selected Publications:

Adventures of a White Collar Man (with Boyden Sparks) (Garden City, N.Y.: Doubleday, Doran, 1941);

My Years with General Motors (Garden City, N.Y.: Doubleday, 1964).

References:

Alfred D. Chandler, Jr., *Giant Enterprise: Ford, General Motors and the Automobile Industry* (New York: Harcourt Brace & World, 1964);

Chandler, *Strategy and Structure, Chapters in the History of the Industrial Enterprise* (Cambridge, Mass.: MIT Press, 1962);

Ed Cray, *Chrome Colossus: General Motors and Its Times* (New York: McGraw-Hill, 1980);

E. D. Kennedy, *The Automobile Industry* (New York: Reynal & Hitchcock, 1941);

Arthur Pound, *The Turning Wheel: The Story of General Motors through Twenty-Five Years, 1908-1933* (Garden City, N.Y.: Doubleday, Doran, 1934);

John B. Rae, *The American Automobile Industry* (Boston: Twayne, 1984);

Rae, *American Automobile Manufacturers, The First Forty Years* (Philadelphia: Chilton, 1959).

Sloanism

by James J. Flink

University of California, Irvine

The term "Sloanism" was coined by Emma Rothschild in her 1973 volume *Paradise Lost* to refer to the product policy and marketing strategy innovated at General Motors (GM) in the 1920s under the leadership of Alfred P. Sloan, Jr. She claimed that the diversity and increasing complexity of product called for by Sloanism was incompatible with Fordist manufacturing methods, which were intended to mass-produce the Model T as a single, static model at an ever-decreasing unit price.

The GM marketing strategy of diversity of product did not in fact originate with Sloan. Diversity was the main reason that William C. Durant put together the GM combination of automakers in 1908. Whereas Henry Ford was certain by then that his Model T was the universal car for the masses, Durant at Buick continued to offer several models rather than concentrate on the popular Buick Model 10, the T's chief competitor in the moderately priced field. Durant was bewildered by the rapidly developing state of automotive technology and sought security through diversity of product in the GM combination. "How could I tell what these engineers would say next?" he later lamented. "I was for getting every kind of car in sight, for playing it safe all along the line." The indiscriminate expansion that this strategy entailed led in 1910 to a five-year period of banker control of GM, then a financial crisis in the 1920 recession that resulted in Durant's ouster by the du Ponts and the Morgan banks and in Sloan's consequent rise to power as the GM president in 1923.

One of Sloan's significant contributions to GM was the rationalization of its product policy. He recalled in his 1964 autobiography, *My Years With General Motors,* that "there was then [in 1920] in General Motors no established policy for the car lines as a whole. We had no position in the low-price area, Chevrolet at that time being competitive with Ford in neither price nor quality." GM of-

fered ten models in seven car lines–Chevrolet, Oakland, Oldsmobile, Scripps-Booth, Sheridan, Buick, and Cadillac–with prices ranging from $795 for a Chevrolet "490" to $5,690 for the top-of-the-line 8-cylinder Cadillac. "Superficially this was an imposing car line," Sloan observed. GM's net sales in 1920 totaled $567,320,603, while Ford's were only moderately higher at $644,830,550. Nevertheless, in Sloan's opinion, "From the inside the picture was not quite so good. Not only were we not competitive with Ford in the low-price field–where the big volume and substantial future growth lay–but in the middle, where we were concentrated with duplication, we did not know what we were trying to do except to sell cars which, in a sense, took volume from each other. Some kind of rational policy was called for. . . . Each division in the absence of a corporation policy operated independently, making its own price and production policies, which landed some cars in identical price positions without relationship to the interest of the enterprise as a whole."

"The primary object of the corporation," Sloan declared, "was to make money, not just motorcars. . . . The problem was to design a product line that would make money." On April 6, 1921, the GM Executive Committee set up a special committee of the GM advisory staff to look into product policy. Its members were Sloan, then GM executive vice-president; Charles S. Mott, group executive for car, truck, and parts operations; Norval A. Hawkins, head of sales at Ford before joining GM; Charles F. Kettering, head of research; Harry H. Bassett, general manager of Buick; and K. W. Zimmerschied, general manager of Chevrolet. "To raise the utility and lower the cost of our cars, one of our first conclusions was that the number of models and the duplication that then existed within the corporation should be limited," Sloan recalled. "The product policy we proposed is the one for which General Motors has now long been known. We said first that the corporation should produce a line of cars in each price area, from the lowest price up to one for a strictly high-grade quantity-production car, but we would not get into the fancy-price field with small production; second, that the price steps should not be such as to leave wide gaps in the line, and yet should be great enough to keep their number within reason, so that the greatest advantage of quantity production could be secured; and third, that there should be no duplication by the corporation in the price fields or steps."

This product policy resulted in a hypothetical price structure for only six standard models: (a) $450-$600; (b) $600-$900; (c) $900-$1,200; (d) $1,200-$1,700; (e) $1,700-$2,500; and (f) $2,500-$3,500. "The new set of price classes meant that the General Motors car line should be integral, that each car in the line should properly be conceived in its relationship to the line as a whole," Sloan explained. "Having thus separated out a set of related price classes, we set forth an intricate strategy which can be summarized as follows: we proposed in general that General Motors should place its cars at the top of each price range and make them of such a quality that they would attract sales from below that price, selling to those customers who might be willing to pay a little more for the additional quality, and attract sales also from above that price, selling to those customers who would see the price advantage in a car of close to the quality of higher-priced competition. This amounted to quality competition against cars below a given price tag, and price competition against cars above that price tag." Sloan further explained that "the core of the product policy lies in its concept of mass-producing a full line of cars graded upward in quality and price."

In 1921 the Sheridan and Scripps-Booth lines were dropped and a product line marketed consisting from bottom to top of Chevrolet, a new Buick 4, the Buick 6, Oldsmobile, and Cadillac. "Only the price-class positions of Chevrolet and Cadillac, as it turned out, were to be permanent," Sloan observed. The GM car lines evolved by the 1930s into Chevrolet, Pontiac (which replaced Oakland), Oldsmobile, Buick, and Cadillac, each producing and marketing several models.

The GM marketing strategy of "a car for every purse and purpose" was, according to Sloan, "formulated before its time. It took a number of

events in the automobile market to give full substance to its principles. Also, a number of events in General Motors, particularly with respect to research and development—that is, the revolutionary car—were to hold up application of the concept."

The so-called revolutionary car was to be powered by an improved air-cooled engine designed by Kettering. Theoretically, air cooling promised several advantages over water cooling: an engine that did not freeze in winter or overheat in summer, that dispensed with a radiator and hoses, and that weighed less per horsepower and therefore gave better fuel economy. In practice, however, the air-cooled engines of the day overheated badly, causing burned valves, sticking pistons, and loss of power. Kettering attempted to utilize the superior thermal properties of copper to design an air-cooled engine with a higher compression ratio and therefore better fuel economy and more power for a given displacement. His "copper-cooled" engine featured copper fins that were brazed to the cylinders in a specially designed oven and a front-mounted fan that turned at faster than engine speed. A few weeks before the formation of the special committee on product policy, the GM Executive Committee, under the leadership of GM president Pierre S. du Pont, had endorsed the copper-cooled Chevrolet as GM's entering wedge into competition with the Ford Model T in the low-priced field. Du Pont saw the copper-cooled engine as a promising replacement for the conventional water-cooled engines on all GM cars. While Sloan recognized the potential of the copper-cooled engine, he had reservations, which proved to be well founded, about the corporation's strong commitment to the project.

The copper-cooled project was in trouble from the start because of a lack of communication and poor coordination between the Delco laboratories in Dayton, Ohio, where the car was designed, and the Chevrolet manufacturing units at Flint and Pontiac, Michigan, where the car was to be built. Stuart Leslie writes that "all during the project, poor coordination and lack of effective dialogue between design and production engineers resulted in crippling disputes and delays.... Production engineers remained blind to the problems of perfecting a relatively new and radical technology, while design men failed to appreciate the difficulties in moving from a carefully tuned prototype to a trouble-free assembly-line automobile ready for mass production." The copper-cooled Chevrolet made a sensational debut at the January 1923 New York Automobile Show. It cost $200 more than the standard water-cooled Chevrolet. Only 759 copper-cooled Chevrolets were manufactured and 239 were scrapped in production. A mere 100 were sold to retail customers. "After initial sales," Leslie reports, "Kettering and the divisions were swamped with complaints about noise, wear on cylinders, carburetor malfunctions, axle breakdowns, and fan belt trouble." In addition to manufacturing difficulties and careless assembly, numerous components had to be redesigned to accommodate to the car's light weight. Perhaps most important, "Chevrolet was [now] holding its own against Ford without the new engine or lightweight design. . . . Tastes were changing. Buyers no longer seemed to want a lightweight and inexpensive automobile, but looked instead to the style and comfort that water-cooled Chevrolets provided quite adequately."

The failure of the copper-cooled car resulted in the formation by Sloan in September 1923 of a General Technical Committee to facilitate communication and cooperation between the operating divisions and research and development within General Motors. Even more important, Sloan was convinced that "it was not necessary to lead in design or run the risk of untried experiments," only that GM cars be "at least equal in design to the best of our competitors in a grade." Similarly, Sloan thought that "it was not essential that, for any particular car, production be more efficient than that of its best competitors, or for that matter that the advertising, selling and servicing methods in any particular product be better than its competitors." Sloanism thus eschewed both technological leadership and competition based upon manufacturing quality. The business success of General Motors under Sloan's leadership was ensured instead by an elaborate system of financial controls worked out by Albert Bradley and Donaldson Brown combined with a new emphasis on styling and innovation of the annual model change.

By the late 1920s the automobile industry was a technologically mature industry in both product and manufacturing methods. The automatic transmission, introduced in the 1941 Oldsmobile, was the only innovation under the hood separating the obsolete Model T from post-World War II production cars not yet incorporated by 1929. Indeed, the 1929 Chevrolet 6-cylinder engine, called "the cast iron wonder," remained the basic Chevrolet power

plant until 1953. Under William S. Knudsen, at Chevrolet there had been a reversion from the highly specialized machine tools used at the Ford Highland Park plant to produce the Model T to more general machine tools to accommodate the annual model change required by Sloanism. But the result was to intensify rather than change basically Fordist assembly line production techniques.

The need for basic transportation that the Model T had filled had largely been met by 1927, when Ford's model was belatedly withdrawn from production. And the T's hard springing and high clearance turned from assets into liabilities as rural America got out of the mud with the building of improved roads in the 1920s. Model T owners tended to trade up to faster, more comfortable, more stylish cars. Also 1927 was the first year in which National Automobile Chamber of Commerce statistics revealed more new car sales for replacement demand than sales to first-car owners and multiple-car purchasers combined.

Sloan responded to the onset of technological stagnation and market saturation with the annual model change. He considered installment selling, the used-car trade-in, the closed car, and the annual model change "a complex of elements [that in the 1920s] came into existence to transform the market . . . and create the watershed which divides the present from the past." The annual model change "was not a declared policy of General Motors" in the 1920s, despite the fact that GM came out with annual models every year after 1923. "We had not in 1925 formulated the concept in the way it is known today," Sloan recalled in 1964. "When we did formulate it I cannot say. It was a matter of evolution. Eventually the fact that we made yearly changes, and the recognition of the necessity of change, forced us into regularizing change. When change became regularized, some time in the 1930s, we began to speak of annual models."

What Sloan euphemistically called "constant upgrading of product" has become known as "planned obsolescence." The annual model change induced owners to trade in cars long before their useful lives were over. It came to call for major stylistic changes every three years with minor face-liftings in between. Sloan related this three-year cycle to the demands of the new model program, in which styling dominated the first year and engineering design and retooling the second and third years. A more substantial reason for the three-year cycle was that the cost of retooling would have been prohibitive for bringing out an entirely new model every year. The changes involved in the annual model were overwhelmingly cosmetic. Sloan understated, for example, that the time involved in bringing out a new model was "determined principally by the requirements of body production. Body changes, of course, are usually substantial from one year to the next and the body work takes the most time. . . . Only occasionally in any one year do we introduce changes in all the chassis units—the frame, engine, transmission, front and rear suspensions."

The annual model change thus was intimately related to a new emphasis on styling, which was first undertaken as an organized activity in the automobile industry at General Motors in the late 1920s. "The very great importance of style in selling" was recognized by the special committee on product policy in 1921. "But it was not until 1926, when closed bodies were becoming dominant, that I first turned to the problem of styling in a practical way," Sloan recounted. In early 1926 Harley Earl was hired under special contract as a consultant to the Cadillac Division of Lawrence P. Fisher. Earl had been chief designer at the custom body shop of Don Lee in Hollywood. Earl's first design for GM was the 1927 LaSalle, in Sloan's words, "the first stylist's car to achieve success in mass production." In June 1927 an Art and Colour Section was formed with Earl as its head "to direct general production body design and to conduct research and development programs in special car designs." This became the GM Styling Section in the 1930s, and Earl rose to the rank of GM vice-president. The Styling Section under Earl gave GM "a long lead" in styling over its competitors. The 1938 Cadillac 60-Special, "the first 'special' car, designed to introduce new features and to be sold at a higher price," convinced Sloan of "the dollars-and-cents value of styling, for consumers were willing to take smaller trade-ins on old cars to acquire it."

Sloanism remained the predominant marketing strategy of the American automobile industry until very recently. It was carried to its illogical extremes in the 1950s and 1960s. The Big Three under GM's leadership engaged in an orgy of nonfunctional and dysfunctional styling that made cars each year bigger, more powerful, and more expensive to buy and operate, while manufacturing quality, handling, and safety deteriorated.

The era of automotive history dominated by Sloanism evaporated with the imposition of federal standards on automotive safety (1966), emissions (1965 and 1970), and fuel consumption (1975), and with the oil shocks of 1973 and 1979. The federal standards put severe limitations on automotive design, raised production costs, and necessitated an overdue emphasis on the development of advanced automotive technology and on manufacturing quality. The oil shocks dramatically changed the nature of the automobile market in the direction of small, fuel-efficient, technologically advanced cars. EEC and Japanese producers, who had eschewed Sloanism, were far better able to adjust to these new market conditions. The American share of the world market for cars consequently plunged from 75 percent in 1950 to a mere 19.3 percent in 1982, and Japan passed the United States in 1980 as the leading producer of motor vehicles, a position it continues to hold. The MIT report on the future of the automobile concluded in 1984 that the Japanese approach to manufacturing and marketing motor vehicles had surpassed both Fordism and Sloanism to become "best practice" in the world automobile industry.

References:
Alan Altshuler and others, *The Future of the Automobile: The Report of M.I.T.'s International Program* (Cambridge, Mass.: MIT Press, 1984);

James J. Flink, *The Automobile Age* (Cambridge, Mass.: MIT Press, 1988);

Stuart W. Leslie, *Boss Kettering* (New York: Columbia University Press, 1983);

Emma Rothschild, *Paradise Lost: The Decline of the Auto-Industrial Age* (New York: Random House, 1973);

Alfred P. Sloan, Jr., *My Years With General Motors* (Garden City, N.Y.: Doubleday, 1964);

Bernard Weisberger, *The Dream Maker: William C. Durant, Founder of General Motors* (Boston: Little, Brown, 1979).

Roger Bonham Smith

(July 12, 1925-   )

by James J. Flink

University of California, Irvine

CAREER: Senior clerk, General Accounting (1949-1950), accountant, General Accounting (1950-1953), statistician and analyst, Cost Analysis (1953-1955), assistant to the director, General Accounting (1955-1957), staff assistant, Treasurer's Office (1957-1958), director, General Accounting (1958-1960), director of financial analysis, Treasurer's Office (1960-1967), assistant treasurer, Treasurer's Office (1967-1968), general assistant comptroller (1968), general assistant treasurer (1968-1970), treasurer (1970-1971), vice-president, Financial Staff (1971), vice-president and group executive, Non-Automotive and Defense Group (1972-1974), executive vice-president, Finance (1974-1975), executive vice-president, Finance, Public Relations, and Industry-Government Relations (1975-1978), executive vice-president, Operations Staffs and Financial Operations (1978-1980), chairman of the board and chief executive officer, (1981-   ) General Motors.

Roger Bonham Smith was born on July 12, 1925, in Columbus, Ohio, the third of four children of Emmet Quimby and Bess Belle Obetz Smith. Until she married, Bess had been assistant superintendent of schools in Columbus. When no local bank would exchange the French francs that World War I veteran Quimby Smith had brought home, he entered banking with a foreign-exchange window and was soon president of his own bank. But like other small-town bankers, Quimby Smith was wiped out in the banking collapse that followed the 1929 stock market crash. So when Roger was five, the Smith family moved to the Detroit area, where Quimby Smith joined the Bundy Tubing Company, an auto industry supplier, as comptroller.

Quimby Smith was an energetic and creative entrepreneur, rising during the depths of the Great Depression to vice-president of Bundy. He later es-

Roger Bonham Smith

tablished his own company, Allagoy Metal Tubing, which made a variety of items for the military during World War II. He had a mechanical bent and patented several inventions. "Dad invented systems and methods and even invented some parts on machines," Roger Smith proudly observes. "He didn't believe you couldn't do things better."

Quimby Smith was the greatest influence on Roger Smith's career and personal life. Quimby and Bess Smith were model parents who instilled the values of educational achievement, creativity, self-discipline, and work in Quimby, Jr., Marilyn,

Roger, and J. Walter. The children were expected to take schoolbooks to read in the car when traveling and were paid for good grades—5¢ for an A, 2¢ for a B, and nothing for grades below that. All the children were outstanding students and skipped grades in elementary school. Quimby Smith would present problems to the children and expect each to come up with a creative solution. He was extremely conscious of using time wisely, even for leisure, and impressed upon the children the importance of not wasting time. Despite the fact that the Smiths were moderately wealthy and hired household help, the children were assigned chores and were expected to earn their own spending money. Roger Smith, for example, delivered the final edition of the *Detroit News* after dark on his bicycle. The Smith family was close and supportive of one another. Togetherness was fostered especially by an agenda of family excursions of camping, boating, fishing, and hunting. Not surprisingly Roger Smith developed a lifelong passion for these outdoor activities.

Roger Smith graduated from Detroit University School, an excellent Grosse Pointe prep school, in 1942 and at age seventeen entered the University of Michigan at Ann Arbor. While in college he worked as night superintendent of his father's plant at nearby Ypsilanti, Michigan, which made ammunition boxes for the military. But he was fired when his father discovered that he was neglecting his studies. Roger's college education was interrupted when he served as a radar technician in the United States Navy from 1944 to 1946. He saw sea duty in the South Pacific aboard the light cruiser USS *Montpelier*. Upon his discharge Smith worked for a summer installing insulation in the roofs of De Sotos at the Chrysler assembly plant in Detroit. The University of Michigan awarded Smith his bachelor's degree in accounting in 1947 and a master's degree in business administration in 1949.

The future chairman of GM shared his father's mechanical aptitude, and at age sixteen he dismantled and put back together his first car. He also had great natural talent for mathematics and enrolled in a course in differential calculus at Michigan just to improve his grade point average. He chose his courses and teachers carefully. Smith was especially influenced by accounting professor William A. Paton, whom he credits with teaching "a hell of a lot more than just accounting. He really taught entrepreneurship and looking around the next corner. He would rarely give you an answer but would walk you through a problem until you came up with the answer. He would never do your thinking for you." Paton's previous students had included GM chairmen Albert Bradley, Frederic Donner, and Richard Gerstenberg and vice-chairman Oscar Lundin. Yet, as Albert Lee observes, "Roger didn't know that he was following the traditional route to the chairmanship of General Motors." Indeed, he did not even make an appointment with the GM interviewer who visited the campus because he intended to relocate to southern California and seek a job in the aviation industry.

Once again his father's influence became critical. "General Motors is one of the best managed companies in the world, and it's right here in your own back yard," his father advised him. "You'd better go and see what it's like." So Smith went down to the General Motors Building on Detroit's West Grand Boulevard, parked his car at a thirty-minute meter, and walked into the employment office in the lobby without an appointment. Several hours and a $2 parking ticket later, he walked out with a job as senior clerk in General Accounting in the GM Central Office.

Smith's rise to the GM chairmanship by age fifty-five has been described by Albert Lee as "meteoric, marked by a major promotion every two years until he reached executive vice president of finance, in 1974, one step from the top." By 1958 he was director of General Accounting in the GM Detroit Central Office. He was moved up to the GM New York financial headquarters in 1960 as director of financial analysis in the Treasurer's Office and became assistant treasurer in 1967. He returned to Detroit as general assistant comptroller in 1968, then moved up to become GM treasurer in 1970 and vice-president of the GM Financial Staff in 1971. Promotion to vice-president and group executive of the Non-Automotive and Defense Group in 1972 removed him from finance for the first time and gave him experience in the manufacturing operations of the corporation. The crucial promotion to executive vice-president of Finance in 1974 was followed by moves to executive vice-president of Finance, Public Relations, and Industry-Government Relations in 1975, then to executive vice-president of Operations Staffs and Financial Operations in 1978. Smith says, "I always loved the work that I was doing and plowed ahead and did the best that I could. Most of my promotions surprised me."

Smith's dedication and creativity soon attracted attention from top management, including GM chairmen Frederic G. Donner, Richard C. Gerstenberg, James M. Roche, and Thomas A. Murphy. He stated as the most important reason for his early advancement that he was fortunate enough to have assignments that attracted the attention of the chairmen, especially the attention generated by the reports that he worked on for testimony at congressional hearings. From Detroit he worked closely with Murphy in the New York Treasurer's Office on several projects, most importantly on the 1958 testimony of GM president Harlow Curtice before the Subcommittee on Antitrust and Monopoly chaired by Sen. Estes Kefauver. "When I'd come to Detroit," Murphy recalls, "I found that if I needed anything in a hurry, Roger was the one to go to. He knew just where to go to find the right facts, no matter whose department it might be in." Albert Lee goes further to credit that "Roger didn't just come up with the facts for Curtice; he developed a brilliant rationale justifying GM's existence in terms of jobs and economic stability for the entire nation. That one event was enough to gain attention from top management for the young accountant. He jumped on the fast track."

Murphy thought that Smith "had more good ideas in a day than most people have in a lifetime." While in the New York Treasurer's Office he developed a computer program that yielded instant information on the current status of the securities in GM's government portfolios. Back in Detroit he headed a small highly motivated group that, in addition to its regular work, took on special projects. Among the more important was development of GM's first truck financing program. He recalls: "it got so that when somebody wanted something done they'd say, 'Hey, let's get Roger Smith and his gang.' " He is a firm believer that "those who do not plan end up by working for those who do." And even his harshest critic, Albert Lee, credits as "one of Roger's greatest innovations," in a corporation then obsessed with short-term reporting and results, his introduction of strategic, long-term planning, despite the resistance of higher management. His ability to make tough major decisions was demonstrated when, shortly after becoming vice-president and group executive for the Non-Automotive and Defense Group, he recommended to GM president Edward N. Cole that the Frigidaire Division (household appliances) and the Terex Division (earth-moving equipment) should be sold because they were not competitive. Finalization of these sales fortuitously coincided with the contraction of the U.S. auto industry as a result of the oil shock following the 1979 Iranian revolution. Lee thinks that this "clinched Roger's nomination as chairman—ironically for the wrong reason." Whereas Smith was in fact a risk-taking entrepreneur enthralled with technological innovation, an unidentified GM director involved in the nomination process is quoted as explaining that "Smith looked like a traditional finance guy, a conservative who could hold the line on costs and raise capital should we need it."

With the retirement of Murphy, who had hand-picked Smith as his successor, Smith became chairman and chief executive officer of GM on January 1, 1981. The task before him was formidable. In 1980 Japan had passed the United States to become the leading automobile-producing nation in the world, and the U.S. share of the world market for cars had plunged from more than 75 percent in 1950 to about 20 percent. With the shift to smaller cars following the oil shock of 1979 and Japanese competition making plant changeover and modernization mandatory, the U.S. auto industry in 1980 fell a record $10.7 billion short of meeting immediate capital needs from operating expenses. GM's products and production processes belonged to a bygone era, and the corporation faced a crisis even greater than that of 1921, which had seen the ouster of its freewheeling founder, William C. Durant, and its subsequent transformation under the du Ponts and Alfred P. Sloan, Jr. GM's total motor vehicle sales for 1980 were 7.1 million units and its total revenues $57.7 billion, a sharp decline from almost 9 million units and $66.3 billion in 1979. Net losses for 1980 were $762.5 million, GM's first losing year since the 1921 du Pont-Sloan takeover. Clearly, if GM were to survive into the twenty-first century as the world's number one auto manufacturer and industrial corporation, the GM team under Roger Smith's leadership would have to accomplish, in his own words, "the biggest turnaround in General Motors history. That's what's driving us all."

Sloanism, the management design and philosophy developed by Alfred Sloan, had been carried to an illogical extreme and had become increasingly dysfunctional in the developing post-World War II international market for cars. The centralization of strategic decision-making and system of financial controls worked out by Sloan, Albert Bradley, and Donaldson Brown to curb the anarchy of GM's divisions in the 1920s had become, during the 1958-1967 tenure of Donner as chairman, a tyranny of cost-cutting accountants in GM's New York City financial headquarters over the engineers in the operating divisions. As Brock Yates said, the "numbers oriented executives" who "came to dominate industry thinking on all levels . . . were obsessed by the financial structure of the car business and viewed the product mainly as an abstraction out of which profit or loss could be generated." Sloan explained in his 1964 autobiography that "the primary object of the corporation . . . was to make money, not just to make motor cars. . . . The policy . . . was valid if our cars were at least equal in design to the best of our competitors in a grade, so that it was not necessary to lead in design or to run the risk of untried experiments." Thus, in Sloan's GM technological innovation was discouraged and technological leadership eschewed. Sloanism instead emphasized cosmetic changes and styling over engineering. Yates observes that in the 1950-1980 period "Stylists and engineers were becoming little more than gadget builders, slaving compulsively over such problems as the creation of opera lights or automatic headlight dimmers while the essentials of the automobile–the brakes, suspension, steering–were left virtually unimproved." Manufacturing quality deteriorated to the point that by the mid 1960s American-made cars were being delivered to retail buyers with an average of twenty-four defects per unit. Also, a shift to larger, more powerful cars that generated higher unit profits was inaugurated in the mid 1950s and was especially evident in the low-priced makes. One result was that American cars became more and more expensive to own and to operate, especially relative to imports such as the Volkswagen Beetle at the bottom of the market and the Mercedes-Benz 250 at the top. Another result was that Sloan's rationalization of the GM line into "a car for every purse and purpose" evaporated as the "full size" Chevrolet came more and more to resemble a Cadillac in size, power, and appearance.

The era of the gas-guzzling, technologically stagnant, shoddily built, annually restyled, all-purpose road cruiser came to an end with federal safety regulations in 1966; emission of pollutants in 1965 and 1970; fuel economy in 1975; escalating fuel prices due to the oil shocks of 1973 and 1979; and mounting competition after 1968 from fuel- and space-efficient, low-priced, well-built Japanese models. As a result, by the mid 1970s Sloanism was clearly outmoded.

"The conditions were different," Smith replied to critics who contrasted his corporate strategy with Sloan's. "We've gone from regional to national to international markets, and technological progress is going to be the key. Who gets there first with those technological developments is going to lead. I think that Mr. Sloan, were he in my job today, would be doing exactly what I'm doing." Be that as it may, the differences between Sloan's and Smith's corporate strategies are striking. Sloan emphasized the security of invested capital and the primacy of short-range returns; for example, he opposed the introduction of safety glass in the 1928 Cadillac as an unnecessary cost at the GM stockholders' expense. In contrast, on October 13, 1987, Smith gave a speech to the Economic Club of Chicago titled "The Competitive Paradox: There's No Security Without Risk," in which he said that "if you turn from risk and seek security, it's not security you'll find–but disaster. . . . The fundamental truth is that there is no security without risk. . . . Short term reality sometimes gets too short, and people get too consecrated to it," he said. "That's part of our immediate gratification society." Characteristically, he informed *Automotive News* in October 1981 that "we may have to take some current setbacks to accomplish long-term goals, but that's the way to do it." He did not expect that the unprecedented $40 billion capital expenditure program to modernize GM's plants and products, approved in late 1980, would come to fruition for at least a decade; and he has remained willing to sacrifice possibly higher short-term returns for potential industry leadership in the long run. As a consequence, by the time of Roger Smith's mandatory retirement from GM at age sixty-five in 1990, he will have transformed General Motors into a corporation that Alfred Sloan would not recognize but one which he might well approve of. After all, Sloan observed in his autobiography that "any rigidity for an automobile manufacturer, no matter how large or how well established, is severely penalized in the market."

Smith's first priority was restoring profitability. By the end of 1982 some 23,000 white collar and 153,000 blue collar jobs had been trimmed from the GM payroll. Fixed expenditures had been reduced by nearly $3 billion and another $3 billion pared from operating expenses. More than $1 billion was raised through the sale of nonearning assets, including the New York City General Motors Building that housed its financial headquarters. These moves resulted in record profits of over $3.7 billion in 1983 and $4.5 billion in 1984.

In early 1984 the most extensive organizational change in GM history was announced. GM's North American operations were restructured into two car groups. One car group included Chevrolet, Pontiac, and GM of Canada. The other included Oldsmobile, Buick, and Cadillac. Previously GM had consolidated its worldwide truck and bus engineering and its assembly operations into the corporate Worldwide Truck and Bus Group. And subsequently the Body and Assembly Group–consisting of Fisher Body, General Motors Assembly Division, and Guide–was phased out, with the result that body engineering and assembly responsibilities were integrated into the two car groups.

The new structure reversed Donner's centralization of GM into the hands of the bean counters. Decentralizing decisions down to the engineers and sales experts in the operating divisions improved GM's ability to respond to changing markets. It was also intended to lead to greater diversity in GM's line of passenger cars. "Badge engineering," which centralized design and many components and led to look-alike cars from the divisions that took sales from one another, was virtually eliminated. The divisions began to produce distinctive products, albeit on common chassis platforms.

The most ambitious program of plant modernization in American corporate history was undertaken by GM. By 1987 eight of the corporation's thirty-three North American assembly plants were completed and eighteen others were thoroughly modernized, as were twelve metal stamping plants, six major die rooms, and virtually all of GM's paint systems. Between 1980 and 1987 GM invested in plant and equipment in the United States alone more than $41.5 billion, about 75 percent of its worldwide capital investment during that period. This led GM to claim that its "commitment to reindustrializing the nation and maintaining American jobs is larger than that of anyone else in the auto industry, if not in all of American industry."

One of the most extensive single-plant modernizations has been GM's construction of Buick City

from the sixty-year-old Buick assembly plant at Flint, Michigan, which was scheduled to be shut down in 1986. GM planned Buick City jointly with the United Automobile Workers as a "totally integrated facility" with "total employee involvement." Buick City employs the "just-in-time" inventory system, popularized recently by the Japanese but actually innovated in the 1920s at the Ford River Rouge plant. Some 90 percent of the parts used at Buick City are manufactured within a 300-mile radius of Buick City, and several major suppliers have located near the complex. The plant's approximately 250 flexible robots perform a variety of assembly operations, including windshield and back glass setting and wheel and tire installation. A guided vehicle system replaces the traditional conveyor in engine and chassis assembly. More modular components, such as fully assembled dashboards, are utilized. No provision has been made for inspection because none is needed. Between four thousand and five thousand employees are needed to operate the entire assembly complex. The corporation reports that "The realization of the 'Buick City' concept will bring GM closer to the goal of establishing a totally automated and integrated automotive manufacturing facility."

GM has assumed leadership in the revolution in auto manufacturing that began because of the computer-controlled electronic machine tool. Until the mid 1980s robots could be programmed to perform only a few repetitive operations and were largely used in welding and paint spraying in final assembly. In the late 1980s, however, the microprocessor allowed robots to handle complex materials, select and distribute parts, and discriminate in the performance of tasks in much the same way as can a human operator. Flexible robotics permitted economies of scale to be realized on much smaller model runs, hence more diversity of product and faster retooling to meet changing patterns of consumer demand. Manufacturing techniques were more precise, improving quality, and labor costs were significantly lowered as flexible robots performed routine tasks much more cheaply than human beings. The implementation of robotics was specifically intended to counteract the labor cost advantage enjoyed by Japan and Third World countries. Half of all current sales of robots in the United States in the 1980s were to the automobile industry, and in 1987 some 26,000 robots were being used in final assembly plants in the American automobile industry.

GM assumed leadership in robotics in 1982 with the formation of GMFanuc Robotics Corporation, a joint venture, headquartered in Troy, Michigan, with Fanuc, Ltd. of Japan, a major robot and computer control manufacturer. GMFanuc was the largest manufacturer of robots in the United States, and GM expected by 1990 to employ about half the robots in the worldwide automobile industry. GMFanuc was the first of several GM affiliations with high-tech partners arranged under Roger Smith's leadership.

By 1988 GM had completed a program of strategic diversification into electronics and aerospace to increase its high-technology capabilities. While the main benefits were expected to accrue to the manufacture of truly advanced passenger cars and trucks, nonautomotive products increased from 5 percent to 10 percent of GM's business and were expected to account for 20 percent by the year 2000. Paralleling this product diversification, General Motors Acceptance Corporation (GMAC) diversified from auto financing into home mortgages and homeowners' insurance, and GMAC became the nation's second-largest mortgage servicing firm.

In October 1984 GM purchased for $2.55 billion H. Ross Perot's Electronic Data Systems Corporation, a leading advanced computer-services company based in Dallas, Texas. In June 1985 GM outbid both Ford and Boeing Aircraft to acquire Hughes Aircraft Company, a leading defense electronics supplier, for $5 billion. "These two companies are major 'building blocks' in GM's long-term competitive strategy," the corporation's 1987 *Public Interest Report* relates. "They are providing the corporation with leading edge technology in addition to expertise and impetus for the transfer of new technology throughout GM."

The report explains that "EDS is working to integrate all of GM's computer and data processing systems and develop an information-sharing network for employees, suppliers, plants, dealerships, and staffs that will be unique in the industry." Prior to the EDS acquisition GM owned at least thirty different types of computers and corporate thinking about computer use was even more diverse. GM units typically had several noncompatible computers in service, each only partially utilized. The potential economies from integrating a system in which internal data processing and office automation alone cost over $2 billion in 1984 are enormous. It is estimated, for example, that integration since the

EDS acquisition saved GM $200 million annually in health-care benefit costs.

Roger Smith explained that the Hughes acquisition would help GM to "redefine" the automobile "from a mechanical product with a few electrical subsystems to one with major electromechanical and electronic elements." The *Wall Street Journal* reported that GM expected the Hughes acquisition to result in "a marketing edge over competitors. It sees lasers one day helping guide vehicles under poor visibility conditions; microelectronics and sensors under the hood improving engine performance; cockpit-like computerized dashboards, and space age materials in a range of uses. And on the factory floor, Hughes's advanced computer science—especially artificial intelligence capabilities—could offer far more efficient ways to assemble a car."

EDS and Hughes have played significant roles in implementing "a complex and sophisticated automation compatibility and standardization program." In 1980 GM began to develop Manufacturing Automation Protocol (MAP), which permits computers and robots on the factory floor to exchange information with one another. MAP is fast becoming an international software standard for full-scale computer-integrated production. It is being tested at GM's Factory of the Future project at Saginaw Vanguard, a fully automated plant in which about thirty-five computer-controlled manufacturing cells, manned by more than fifty robots, turn out a variety of front-wheel drive axles. It is anticipated that after 1990 all new automation installed at GM plants will use MAP.

The most ambitious attempt "to leapfrog the foreign competition" is GM's Project Saturn, launched in 1982 after a study revealed that the Japanese built small cars for about $2,000 less per unit than GM. Saturn was given the largest commitment of resources—$3.5 million approved for Phase 1—of any GM experimental project in the corporation's history. From its outset Saturn was intended "to be an advanced manufacturing process for an automobile employing new tools, new facilities, new management systems, and new forms of employee participation never before realized in General Motors. . . . [I]mprovements that flow from Saturn in product design, manufacturing, and assembly will be applied throughout the corporation."

In early 1985 GM announced the creation of a separate, wholly owned subsidiary to build the Saturn car, the first new GM car line in the United

States since the 1920s. The prototype, Saturn, was some 600 pounds lighter than current GM subcompacts but has since been upscaled in size and price. Saturn Corporation will operate its own manufacturing and assembly complex at Spring Hill, Tennessee, and set up its own distribution system. Initial production is now slated at 250,000 units a year, turned out by three thousand workers on a two-shift operation, an unprecedented labor productivity rate of eighty-three cars annually per worker. Extensive use will be made of modular assembly of the car's subsystem by teams of workers in an environment designed for optimal work-place ergonomics. Computer-integrated manufacturing will result, for example, in a computer-designed fender being stamped out by a computer-designed die. GM's innovation of "lost foam" casting will reduce engine machining to a mere 7 percent to 9 percent of that required with regular casting methods. Altogether some fifty-eight new technologies involved in Saturn are already being tested in other GM plants and will be brought together at Spring Hill in 1990. Sophisticated new data systems will permit the Saturn plant to operate with a minimum of paperwork, foreshadowing Roger Smith's goal of a paperless corporation.

The setbacks anticipated by Smith have occurred. To his credit, he has been among the first to acknowledge his mistakes and to take steps to rectify them. The integration of EDS into GM proved particularly troublesome. EDS was supposed to maintain its own corporate culture, which differed markedly from GM's. Whereas GM had a well-developed committee system, Perot was what Sloan described as a "personal entrepreneur." EDS was not unionized, and its benefits, which were standard for the computer services industry, were less than the auto-industry benefits at GM. EDS employees are rewarded based solely upon their contribution to the success of the company and not on formulas or pay scales. Some friction was bound to occur in 1984 when seven thousand GM data processors and managers were transferred from the environment they knew at GM to a very different one at EDS. While more than 90 percent of these GM transferees decided to stay with EDS, some six hundred or so elected to take an early retirement option offered by GM. Some of those who stayed with EDS attempted to organize under the United Auto Workers union, which later withdrew its peti-

tions for the thirteen sites in question due to lack of interest on the part of the employee population.

Perot himself posed an even larger problem. With the acquisition of EDS he had become GM's largest individual stockholder and a member of its board of directors. Although he had no experience in automobile manufacturing, Perot repeatedly engaged in public criticism of GM and Smith. This not only made the integration of EDS into GM more difficult but also damaged GM's public image. Conflict and confrontation became inevitable. On December 1, 1986, Perot accepted a buyout offer of $33 per share for his 11 million shares of GM class E (EDS) stock in return for his resignation as a member of the GM board and as chairman and CEO of EDS. "We had a tough time with Ross Perot," Roger Smith admits, "but we handled it. He is a great guy, but there is a hell of a lot of difference between running a computer service firm and making automobiles, and that's the heart of the matter." In May 1988 Smith estimated that the increase in market value of the stocks bought back from Perot thus far had yielded GM a $55 million paper profit.

A far more serious setback than the Perot affair was that GM's profits slipped to $3.99 billion in 1985 and to $2.94 billion in 1986, as GM's market share dipped to a low of only 37 percent, from 55 percent in early 1984. In 1986, for the first time in sixty-two years, Ford surpassed GM in profits on only about half of GM's sales. GM's break-even point had risen an estimated 30 percent from 1981 to 1986 and despite much higher volume was about $250 per unit over the break-even points of Ford and Chrysler. Industry analysts estimated that it was costing GM $11,500 to produce a car, versus $9,800 for Ford and $9,300 for Chrysler, and that operating profits were 11 percent at Ford, 9 percent at Chrysler, and 6 percent at GM.

The 1981-1982 cutbacks, criticized at the time as "Draconian," turned out to be not nearly Draconian enough. Given new aggressive competition from Ford and Chrysler, not to mention the Japanese, GM had excess plant capacity. And acquisitions and putting the new organizational structure into place had increased the total number of GM employees from 691,000 in 1983 to 876,000 in 1986. Far more drastic cutbacks were clearly necessary. In late 1986 decisions were made to cut back on capital spending, close eleven assembly and stamping plants, shift some 10 percent of components production to outside sources, and trim the salaried work force 25 percent. These measures are expected to result in an annual saving of $10 billion by 1990. The market share goal for this much leaner and tougher GM has been downsized to 40 percent.

Putting the new technology into place involved unanticipated snags. *Business Week* reported in March 1987, for example, that the model Buick City plant "has had one of the slowest startups of any auto plant on record and is still not making its rated capacity of 75 Buick Le Sabres and Oldsmobile 88s per hour. For weeks, the robot arms that glue and set windshields dropped the glass on the front seat. GM pulled out an entire roboted welding line and let people do the work." *Barron's* similarly reported in June 1986 that the Hamtramck plant turning out Cadillac, Buick, and Oldsmobile luxury models was operating "at about half to two-thirds of the 60-car-an-hour rate for which the highly automated plant was designed. . . . Its 260 industrial robots haven't always behaved as they were supposed to, causing, among other things, some cars to be painted so badly that the work had to be redone elsewhere. And 50 automated guided vehicles that were to have ferried parts to the assembly line were nowhere to be seen during a visit to the plant several weeks ago; technicians were attempting to come up with reliable guidance software."

These problems have been largely overcome. Yet there was a lesson to be learned from New United Motor Manufacturing, Inc. (NUMMI), a GM-Toyota joint venture launched in late 1985 to build the Toyota-designed Nova compact at a reopened Chevrolet plant. *Fortune* observed in November 1986 that "although NUMMI's humble Fremont, California factory hasn't been stuffed with fancy robotics or other high-tech marvels, its productivity is about twice that of most GM plants, and its Novas have earned the highest customer-satisfaction ratings and lowest warranty costs of any GM car. The reason was Japanese-style management and a labor agreement that made it possible. Hoping to replicate NUMMI's performance on a wider scale, GM has been dispatching hundreds of managers from Detroit and elsewhere around the country to Fremont. Many have come back convinced that NUMMI's way of managing workers can do more good for GM than all the world's lasers and robots." The big gains in efficiency at Fremont have come from reducing union work rules

from several hundred to four, from eliminating jobs, and from increased employee involvement in decision-making and teamwork. Applied at GM stamping plants, the NUMMI way of organizing workers into teams has reduced a typical die change from twelve hours to a mere fifteen minutes.

"We found that automation isn't the be-all end-all," Smith concedes. "It's the skills of the people that are still your limiting factor." Nevertheless, he stands firm in his conviction that the high-tech road is the key to the future and that GM's competitors will be forced to emulate its massive program of plant modernization at much higher tooling costs and without the benefit of the investment tax credit. "We've crossed the muddy river and now we're on high ground on the other side," he confidently asserts, "while our competitors are on the far bank just getting their feet wet."

In retrospect, the critical error made in turning GM around was not huge capital investment in plant modernization and acquisitions but false economies realized from the delay in bringing out a new line of technologically advanced, aerodynamically designed cars and trucks. Sticking too long with badge-engineered, rear-engine drive mid-size models led to the loss to a revitalized Ford not only of market shares, but of the styling leadership that GM had held since the 1920s.

GM began making a dramatic bid to regain market shares and leadership in design with its 1987 models. GM's first aerodynamically designed cars, the Chevrolet Corsica and Beretta models, were introduced in March, and the aerodynamic yet distinctively designed mid-size GM10 Oldsmobile Cutlass Supreme, Buick Regal, and Pontiac Grand Prix models were brought out in mid year. An unprecedented $7 billion had been invested in the GM10 program, compared, for example, with a $3 billion Ford investment in its Taurus-Sable program. In late 1987, too, GM announced the revolutionary Quad 4 engine, called by *Business Week* "one of the most sophisticated mass-production engines ever . . . lean, mean, and clean." The port fuel-injected, 4-valve-per-cylinder Quad 4, rated at 150 horsepower and 26.5 miles per gallon in city driving, offers V-8 horsepower with 4-cylinder economy. Ford is not expected to have a comparable new engine until 1993. The 1988 model year line of aerodynamic Chevrolet and GMC full-size pickups is the first completely redesigned small truck line to appear in a decade. Manufacturing quality has improved to the point that in August 1988 GM announced a change in its warranty coverage to a "Bumper to Bumper Plus" program that will cover everything except routine maintenance and tires for three years or 50,000 miles on most of its 1989 cars and trucks. In August 1988 GM also announced that a new four-phase process developed with the aid of Hughes Aircraft now permitted design time in bringing out new models to be cut from the usual five years to three, permitting the corporation to respond more swiftly to changes in consumer demand and to lower development costs significantly.

The Automotive Hall of Fame has twice selected Smith as Industry Leader of the Year, in 1983 and 1986. Other business leadership awards include: the *Automobile Industries* Man of the Year Award (1984); the Northwood Institute Outstanding Business Leader Award (1984); the *Wall Street Transcript* Best Chief Executive, Automobile Industry Award (1984); the University of Michigan School of Business Administration Business Leadership Award (1984); the *Business Times* Businessman of the Year Award (1984); the *Financial World Magazine* 11th Annual Gold Award for Chief Executive Officer of the Year (1985); the International Association of Business Communicators Excellence in Communication Leadership Award (1985); the *Advertising Age* Adman of the Year Award (1985); the University of Arizona Executive of the Year Award (1986); the Columbia University Graduate School of Business Leadership in Business Award (1986); the National Management Association American Manager of the Year Award (1986); the Brazilian-American Chamber of Commerce Man of the Year Award (1986); and the *Chief Executive Magazine* Chief Executive of the Year Award (1986).

Additionally, he has received numerous awards in recognition of his outstanding record of community service. These include: the Better Business Bureau's Annual Service Award (1983), the B'nai B'rith International Great American Traditions Award (1983), the Pontifical Institute for Foreign Missions Knights of Charity Award (1984), the National Council on Alcoholism Meany-Roche Award (1984), the American Assembly's Service to Democracy Award (1984), the Work in America Institute Award (1985), the Salvation Army Citizen of the Year Award (1986), the New York Navy League Admiral Jack Award (1986), and the Advertising Council Public Service Award (1986).

His interest in cancer research is particularly noteworthy. In 1978, with the support of Thomas Murphy, who was then the GM chairman, he sold the GM board of directors on his idea to establish the General Motors Cancer Research Awards. Since 1979 three awards have been presented each year to scientists throughout the world for their accomplishments in research on the causes, prevention, and treatment of cancer. Recipients are chosen by a panel of thirty-five of their peers, and along with the prestige of this peer recognition is a $100,000 cash award. Smith is chairman of the General Motors Cancer Research Foundation, which administers the awards. In the mid 1960s he successfully fought a personal battle against melanoma.

Smith serves as a trustee on the boards of several educational institutions: the California Institute of Technology, the Cranbrook Educational Community, and the Michigan Colleges Foundation. He has received honorary doctor of law degrees from DePauw University (1979), Albion College (1982), and Western Michigan University (1983); an honorary doctor of science degree from the University of Detroit (1985); an honorary degree in business administration from the University of Dayton (1986); and an honorary doctor of management degree from the GMI Engineering and Management Institute (1986). He has been an outspoken advocate of broad liberal education over narrow specialization.

In addition to his responsibilities as GM chairman and CEO, Smith is a member of the boards of directors of Johnson & Johnson and Citicorp, chairman of the Business Roundtable and a member of the Business Council, chairman of Detroit Renaissance, and a director of the Detroit Economic Growth Corporation, New Detroit, Inc., and the Detroit United Foundations. He also is a member of the Advertising Council's Industries Advisory Committee, the Society of Automotive Engineers, the Economic Club of Detroit, the Detroit Club, the Detroit Athletic Club, and the Links Club in New York.

"I don't see my family as much as I like," Smith complains. "Maybe that's the toughest sacrifice of all." He married Barbara Ann Rasch, a clerk in the GM Public Relations Office, in 1954. They have four children—Roger, Jr., Jennifer, Victoria, and Drew. The years the Smiths spent in New York were particularly difficult ones because of a long commute and frequent trips away from home on corporate business. Smith gives his wife great credit for the successful rearing of their three older children. He tries now to spend time hunting and fishing with Drew, his youngest son.

Probably no business leader in American history has had a more vacillating or controversial public image. A New York-based executive newsletter, the *Gallagher Report,* for example, rated Roger Smith one of the ten worst executives in 1983, one of the ten best in 1986, and one of the worst again in 1987. Media opinion has ranged from denigration, for being a bumbler, to praise, for being a communicator on a par with President Ronald Reagan.

What will be Roger Smith's long-term reputation? That will be determined by the long-range outcome of his attempt to turn around giant General Motors. "If he pulls this off," concludes University of Michigan business professor Eugene Jennings, "he's going to be looked upon as the rebuilder. He's going to take his place beside Alfred Sloan in the pantheon of GM gods." Smith himself says, "If they judge me by the results, then I'll be satisfied." Asked in May 1988 what he would like his epitaph to read, he did not hesitate to respond: "He got General Motors ready for the twenty-first century."

Unpublished Documents:

Roger B. Smith, "The Competitiveness Paradox: There's No Security Without Risk," address given at the Economic Club of Chicago, Chicago, Illinois, October 13, 1987;

Smith, taped interview with James J. Flink, May 9, 1988.

References:

Ed Cray, *Chrome Colossus: General Motors and Its Times* (New York: McGraw-Hill, 1980);

Anne B. Fischer, "GM is Tougher Than You Think," *Fortune* (November 10, 1986);

James J. Flink, *The Automobile Age* (Cambridge, Mass.: MIT Press, 1988);

"General Motors: What Went Wrong?," *Business Week* (March 16, 1987);

"GM Moves into a New Era," *Business Week* (July 16, 1984);

John Holusha, "General Motors: A Giant in Transition," *New York Times Magazine,* November 14, 1982;

Albert Lee, *Call Me Roger* (Chicago: Contemporary Books, 1988);

Cary Reich, "The Innovator: The Creative Mind of GM Chairman Roger Smith," *New York Times Magazine,* April 21, 1985;

Richard Rescigno, "Race to the Future: Can Billions and Mr. Smith Make GM a Winner?," *Barron's* (June 30, 1986);

Alfred P. Sloan, Jr., *My Years With General Motors* (Garden City, N.Y.: Doubleday, 1964).

Charles E. Sorensen

(September 7, 1881-August 13, 1968)

by George S. May

Eastern Michigan University

CAREER: Apprentice pattern-maker and pattern-maker, Jewett Stove Works, Art Stove Works, Michigan Stove Works, and Bryant & Berry (1895-1904); pattern-maker, assistant superintendent, general superintendent (1904-1941), vice-president and director Ford Motor Company (1941-1944); president (1944-1946), vice-chairman, Willys-Overland Motors, Inc. (1946-1950).

Charles E. Sorensen, who had the distinction of serving as one of Henry Ford's executives longer than anyone else, was born in Copenhagen, Denmark, on September 7, 1881, the son of Soren and Eva Christian Sorensen. The family moved to the United States in 1885, where Sorensen was educated in the public schools of Buffalo, New York. When he was fourteen, he went to work as an apprentice in the pattern department at the Jewett Stove Works, where his father was employed. The family later moved to Detroit, which was at the time the main center of the stove industry, and Sorensen, now an experienced pattern-maker, worked at the Art Stove Works, then at the Michigan Stove Works, one of the largest stove companies in the world, and finally at Bryant & Berry, machinists and foundrymen.

Sorensen was a tall, handsome, athletic man with a physique and profile that *Fortune* magazine would later observe "might have earned him a smashing salary in Hollywood." An enthusiastic bicyclist, Sorensen became acquainted in Detroit with Tom Cooper, a champion on the bicycle racing circuit, and it was through Cooper that Sorensen first met Henry Ford. By 1902 Cooper had turned to the new sport of automobile racing, and he had joined with Ford to build two racing cars that would be the most powerful of any yet built. Cooper asked Sorensen to use his pattern-making skills to construct wooden models of some of the components they planned to use in the racers. Ford, who always

Charles E. Sorensen (courtesy of Ford Motor Company)

found it much easier to visualize an object if he saw it in a three-dimensional representation, rather than on a blueprint, was impressed with Sorensen's work. Sorensen shared Ford's preference for models, telling a reporter in 1942, "Unless you can see a thing you cannot simplify it. And unless you can simplify it, it's a good sign you cannot make it."

The success of Ford's "999" racing car in fall 1902 helped bring about the formation of the Ford Motor Company in 1903. Ford shortly hired

Sorensen as a pattern-maker at Ford with a skilled worker's wage of three dollars per day. Some records indicate Sorensen was hired in spring 1905, but Sorensen later claimed that he went to work for Ford in 1904.

He would remain with the company until March 1944. Throughout much of that time it is difficult to determine precisely what position and responsibilities Sorensen had with the company. In his autobiography, published in 1956, he succumbed to the normal human desire to present himself in the best possible light, and in so doing he almost certainly at times exaggerated the importance of his role. The problem of assessing the role he actually played is compounded by Henry Ford's utter disdain for the normal practice of assigning definite titles and carefully prescribed duties to his employees. Not until 1941, when Sorensen was named a vice-president and director, did he have an official title. Until then he had served in various capacities, but his use of the term general superintendent to describe his company position when he first appeared in *Who's Who* in 1940 got him into trouble. Newsmen interpreted this to mean that he was the company's general manager. The announcement in 1943 that the company had "never created a general managership," but that Henry Ford was assuming the duties of such a position as well as taking over the job of president, was one of the signs of Ford's growing displeasure with his long-time employee and an indication that Sorensen's days with Ford were numbered.

Nevertheless, it is clear that Ford relied on Sorensen because of his skills as a workman and because of his toughness and his unquestioning willingness to do whatever Ford asked him to do. Sorensen's pattern-making abilities were used to help solve some of the problems in the development of the Ford cars, including the Model T. Logically, Sorensen then progressed to the foundry, where he was involved in creating molds from his wooden models and where he earned the nickname of "Cast-iron Charlie." Sorensen's preliminary work led him to assist in the production of the cars, in which he contributed to the development of the mass production techniques for which Ford became famous. Sorensen later disputed the idea that mass production was a conscious development and that Ford was its primary architect: "Henry Ford had no idea of mass production. Far from it; he just grew into it like the rest of us. The essential tools and the

Sorensen near the beginning of his career at Ford (courtesy of Detroit Public Library)

final assembly line with its integrated feeders resulted from an organization which was continually experimenting and improvising to get better production."

Sorensen was part of that organization, one of many highly talented individuals who had contributed to the enormous success of the Ford Motor Company by the beginning of World War I. But the war period marked the beginning of the breakup of that organization as Henry Ford showed an increasing unwillingness to tolerate employees that did not agree with him. Sorensen survived, not because he did not realize that Ford was not always right, but because he saw that Ford would not tolerate being told that he was wrong. By the early 1920s the ranks of former Ford employees included the likes of James Couzens, the business brains of the early years, C. Harold Wills, a mechanical genius who had been with Ford before there was a Ford Motor Company, Norval Hawkins, the master salesman, and John Lee, creator of the personnel policies for which Ford had been praised. But for Sorensen the most important of the executives who had departed had been William S. Knudsen, a fellow Dane who had become a Ford employee when Ford acquired the Buffalo firm for which Knudsen worked. Although Sorensen had recommended that acquisition, he soon recognized in Knudsen the most serious challenge to his own emergence as Ford's top production man. Knudsen left in 1921, in part because Ford, as he later implied, found it difficult to work with someone smarter than he was, and in part because Knudsen would no longer put up with Sorensen's interference.

With Knudsen gone, Sorensen became Ford's undisputed production chief. More than that, however, he was for a time the second most powerful man in the company. Ford's son Edsel was officially company president from 1919 to his death in 1943, but, lacking the strength to stand up to his father, he possessed only as much authority as his father allowed him to exercise. It was Sorensen to whom Henry Ford turned if he wanted something done, and thus there was some real basis for Sorensen's claim that the years from the mid 1920s to 1944 should be called the Sorensen period.

That period, however, was one of decline for the company. During World War II there were those who seriously doubted that Ford could survive in the postwar years. The completion of the great Ford Rouge complex in the mid 1920s was the last of the creative actions that had astounded the industrial world during the company's first two decades, and Sorensen presided brilliantly over that huge manufacturing facility. When Ford finally abandoned the Model T in 1927, it was Sorensen who geared up the Rouge to produce the new Model A. Sorensen recognized that Ford could no longer rely on one standard, unchanging model to carry them along, year after year, as the Model T had. In order to achieve the flexibility in the assembly operations that would be needed to adapt to constantly changing models, he adopted the techniques that his old rival, Knudsen, had installed with such success at General Motors (GM). Sorensen, who was ruthless in dealing with any worker who he did not think was doing his job or who he felt was no longer needed, proceeded to overhaul the entire supervisory staff "to get rid of all the Model T sons-of-bitches," as he put it, and to "get away from the Model T methods of doing things." The Model A was successful and its replacement, the 1932 Ford V-8, was a happy throwback to the kind of mechanical innovation that the public had come to expect

Sorensen, after his retirement, with his grandson Charles II in Florida

of Ford in earlier years. But without the wide-ranging talent which had been able to exercise a restraining influence on Henry Ford's unorthodox and sometimes irrational approaches to management during those earlier years, the company under its aging founder was no match for the smoothly functioning GM and the newcomer Chrysler. Ford slipped to third place in the industry.

By the 1930s Sorensen's influence was also slipping, as Harry Bennett replaced him as the man closest to Henry Ford. Bennett, a rough and ambitious ex-sailor who had come to work at Ford during World War I, had correctly sized up Sorensen as the man who was going to emerge on top in the fight to be Ford's top assistant. For sometime Bennett was known as Sorensen's man, and Sorensen, who physically towered over Bennett, took pleasure in having him do some of his dirty work. But by the latter part of the 1920s Bennett was using the position he had acquired to win the confidence of Henry Ford. Sorensen remained the man Ford depended on to handle production matters, but Bennett deftly played on Ford's emotions and fears to become the man Ford relied on to deal with a host of other concerns, not all of them connected with the company.

But although Sorensen's status declined in the 1930s, his greatest moments at Ford still lay ahead as the outbreak of World War II presented the Ford Motor Company with the challenge of meeting the need for war materiel. Sorensen had visited Europe regularly in the 1930s to inspect Ford's overseas plants, and he possessed firsthand knowledge of Hitler's efforts to rearm Germany. Whatever his feelings on that subject may have been before 1940, the German invasion and occupation of Denmark in April 1940 settled the matter. As a child he had become an American citizen when his father completed the naturalization process, but Sorensen retained a love for his native land, and he was now determined to do all he could to see that the Germans were defeated. Henry Ford's feelings were quite different. He rejected a contract in 1940 to build aircraft engines when he learned they were to be used by the British, but later in the year he agreed to begin to take on such work if it was intended to strengthen American defense forces.

Ford produced a vast amount of war materiel over the next five years, but it was most famous for producing over 8,000 B-24 bombers. In December 1940 Ford was asked if it would become involved in the production of this plane, which had been developed by Consolidated Aircraft. Henry Ford agreed to look into it, and the following month Sorensen, along with Edsel Ford and his sons Henry II and Benson, went to San Diego to look over the bomber. Consolidated was hoping to raise production to one per day, but Sorensen that night in his hotel room sketched out plans for a production layout that he said could produce one B-24 every hour. His ideas were accepted, and a huge new plant, built by the government, began to rise at Willow Run, some 20 miles west of the Rouge plant. Over the next two years innumerable problems had to be overcome, many due to the Air Corps making constant design changes in the bomber. These changes forced Sorensen to alter his assembly plans, but by 1943 the bombers were coming out of the factory, and Sorensen's production goal of a bomber an hour was being met and exceeded.

It was the most dramatic production story of the war. Central casting could not have found anyone better suited than Sorensen to play the leading role in the drama, and the press loved him. Until this time Sorensen had received scarcely any na-

tional publicity. Henry Ford had always been the focus of attention, but now the attention shifted to Sorensen. Sixty years old and still a striking figure of a man, "Cast-iron Charlie," as the reporters liked to call him, had the commanding presence that was reassuring in this time of emergency. So the newsmen pulled out all stops, starting with an article in *Time* in November 1940 that referred to Sorensen as "a wizard," and as Ford's "tough, brilliant Production Manager." This was soon followed by similar praise in *Newsweek*, in stories over the Associated Press wires, and finally a long and adulatory profile treatment in *Fortune* in 1942. Entitled "Sorensen of the Rouge," the article included a full-page photograph of Sorensen.

Sorensen's sudden emergence as a celebrity may have been his downfall. As Sorensen wrote in his autobiography, Ford did not like anybody taking the spotlight away from him: "My ability to keep out of the public eye was one reason I stayed as long as I did at Ford while others left." But he obviously forgot that in the early 1940s, and Bennett, now his archrival, undoubtedly saw that Henry Ford was kept aware of every story that featured "Cast-iron Charlie."

Edsel Ford's death in May 1943 ended any chance Sorensen might have had of remaining at Ford. As long as the younger Ford lived, he provided at least a semblance of balance in the company, but his death allowed Bennett to gain the upper hand in the struggle to be the real power in a company whose octogenarian founder was no longer capable of administering. The Ford family was able to block Henry Ford's effort to make Bennett the new president, by persuading Ford himself to return to that job. But Bennett did convince Ford to name him to a new position that in effect made him Sorensen's superior.

Realizing that the battle had been lost, Sorensen said that he asked Ford in November 1943 to be relieved of his responsibilities so that he could retire to Florida, where Sorensen had a home in Miami Beach. Ford, however, did not seem to understand what Sorensen was asking. Later, in what must be one of the most poignant scenes in business history, Sorensen, as he was about to leave for Florida, ran into Ford. He said good-bye to the man he had served so faithfully for some forty years. "I guess there's something in life besides work," was all Ford had to say. It was the last time Sorensen ever saw him.

From his Florida home Sorensen kept asking Ford for his release. Perhaps he may have been hoping he would be asked to stay on, but in March Ford's personal secretary informed Sorensen that Ford wanted him to resign because Ford believed he was conspiring to take over the presidency of the company. A furious Sorensen called in reporters and announced that he was "resigning from the Ford Motor Company after 39 years of continuous service. . . . I am compelled to take a much-needed rest." Noting that Sorensen looked as fit as ever, the reporters decided that the need for a rest was not due to any health problems. The *Detroit Free Press* flatly declared that Sorensen had been fired by Henry Ford himself.

The exact cause of Sorensen's forced departure is still not clear. It was no doubt a combination of factors–the publicity Sorensen had been receiving, the machinations of Bennett, and even, as Sorensen believed, the intervention of Clara Ford who blamed Sorensen, as well as Bennett, for Edsel Ford's problems. She was powerless to effect Bennett's removal, but when Sorensen became vulnerable she used her influence to get him out.

For Sorensen it was a crushing blow for his years of service. When asked how he felt, he tapped his chest and said, "It hurts here." But Sorensen was not idle. He accepted the presidency of Willys-Overland Motors in June 1944. The Toledo company had been the major producer of the Jeep during the war, and it was Sorensen who persuaded the company to produce a civilian version of the vehicle in 1945. The popularity of the rugged little Jeep kept the Toledo factory busy during the following decades and under four different owners. Sorensen resigned as Willys's president in 1946 and served as vice-chairman until retiring in 1950. He spent his remaining years at his home in Miami Beach, where he served as a director of the First National Bank, at another home in St. Croix in the Virgin Islands, and at a home in Bethesda, Maryland, which he used in the summer and where he died after a long ill-

ness on August 13, 1968. He was married twice, the first time to Helen E. Mitchell, whom he married in 1904. They had one son. After her death he married Edith Thompson Montgomery in 1960, and she survived him.

"Of all the men who served Henry Ford after he acquired complete control of the company, Sorensen was the most powerful, and stands alone as the most dynamically ruthless." That judgment of Sorensen by Allan Nevins and Frank Ernest Hill seems fair. "Nobody ever questioned his grasp, drive, or vision. These qualities, edged with harshness, had been knit into every element of Ford activity, but most of all into factory production, a field in which he stood with Knudsen, Flanders, and Zeder of the Chrysler company as master."

Publication:
My Forty Years With Ford with Samuel T. Williamson (New York: Norton, 1956).

References:
"Fact & Fancy," *Time*, 36 (November 18, 1940): 23;

James J. Flink, *The Automobile Age* (Cambridge, Mass.: MIT Press, 1988);

Robert Lacey, *Ford: The Men and The Machine* (Boston: Little, Brown, 1986);

David L. Lewis, *The Public Image of Henry Ford* (Detroit: Wayne State University Press, 1976);

Allan Nevins and Frank Ernest Hill, *Ford: Decline and Rebirth, 1933-1962* (New York: Scribners, 1963);

Nevins and Hill, *Ford: Expansion and Challenge, 1915-1933* (New York: Scribners, 1957);

Nevins and Hill, *Ford: The Times, the Man, the Company* (New York: Scribners, 1954);

"Sorensen of the Rouge," *Fortune*, 25 (April 1942): 78-81, 114-120;

"The Winner," *Time*, 43 (March 13, 1944): 85.

Archives:
The papers of Charles E. Sorensen are in the National Automotive History Collection in the Detroit Public Library. There are, in addition, extensive materials dealing with Sorensen's activities in the Ford Archives at the Henry Ford Museum in Dearborn, Michigan.

Styling

by George S. May

Eastern Michigan University

Industrial design, a profession devoted to improving the look of machine-made products and thereby stimulating their sales, first attracted attention in the 1920s, and it was in that same decade that an emphasis on the physical appearance of automobiles became increasingly evident. However, while those who designed refrigerators, toasters, radios, and a host of other consumer products were referred to as industrial designers, those who dealt with the exterior and interior look and feel of cars were most commonly referred to in the United States as "stylists." But not all automotive stylists were comfortable with the term, which served to set them apart from their fellow industrial designers. In the 1980s, in fact, a trend seemed to be underway to drop the use of "stylist" and replace it with the broader "designer." The earlier usage was no doubt related to the fact that there was a need to distinguish this work from that of men such as Henry Ford, Ransom Olds, and Howard Coffin who had been responsible for the mechanical features of a car and had been touted by their companies as the foremost "automotive designers."

The excitement generated by early automobiles stemmed chiefly from the fact that they actually worked. "Built to run and Does it!" was the slogan, for example, of the curved-dash Oldsmobile at the start of the century. Under these circumstances it was natural that the engineers and mechanics had the upper hand in determining what could be used to sell the new models and that the framework that housed the car's mechanisms and occupants was of secondary concern. Similarly, when the problem of basic design and technological innovation was solved by the 1920s and few significant mechanical improvements remained that could be used to distinguish one make from another, companies turned to the "stylist" to provide the cosmetic changes that would be a highly visible means of con-vincing consumers that one year's car was better than that of the previous year.

That does not mean that no attention had been paid to a car's looks prior to the 1920s. One automotive journal in 1901 felt it necessary to caution buyers "not ... to be influenced by the exterior of the carriage or by the more or less happy arrangement of parts. . . . What is of greater moment is the motor and co-acting mechanism. . . ; everything else is of secondary importance." Nevertheless, *Scientific American* in 1899 hoped that "some gifted genius" would arrive on the scene who would take the automobile and "whip it into shape and make it presentable. All things are possible," the magazine stated, "even a good-looking horseless carriage."

The term "horseless carriage" is the clue as to why so many of the early motor vehicles were unattractive. The automobile manufacturers concentrated on putting together the chassis and were satisfied to have carriage manufacturers and their designers provide the bodies. As early as 1891 the French had created the basic automobile profile by placing the motive power out front, under a hood, but American automotive engineers until about 1905 continued to place the engine beneath the body, creating an awkward-looking carriage that lacked the balancing effect of the accompanying horses for which it was originally designed.

By 1905 in the American market the era of horseless carriage styling began to be replaced by one in which the vehicles were recognizably automobiles. The design of the front portion of the car was added to the responsibility of the chassis engineers, while the body, that portion of the car's upper structure from the cowl back, was still left to the carriage companies or the body manufacturers that were offshoots of these carriage and wagon firms. Aesthetically the resulting collaborative efforts left a great deal to be desired, with the great industrial de-

Before computer modeling, wood and clay mock-ups were used by stylists.

signer Raymond Loewy, who would later be responsible for some classic automotive styling, declaring that in this period "The automobile was an invention and it looked like one."

By the second decade of the century a growing number of body designers were emerging who were more attuned to the needs of the new form of transportation and less wedded to those of the old horse-and-buggy age. At first their work was most apparent in those companies that specialized in providing custom bodies for purchasers of luxury cars. Examples of their advanced, sometimes exotic, styling were exhibited at the annual Salon shows held in New York's Commodore and Chicago's Drake hotels. On the other hand, those who could not afford custom-made vehicles found that the manufacturers of mass-produced bodies for the less expensive cars had, for economic reasons, stayed with more traditional lines. As a result, one observer in 1920 declared that the difference between the Salon car and the standard stock factory model was like that between "the priceless peachblow vase" and "the humble earthenware bowl we employ in our kitchens." The latter "is essential; an accepted part of our life. So is the average standard automobile.

The stock car no longer represents luxury, except by contrast with the past. It is merely modern, efficient, comfortable, economical personal transportation."

However, these differences were beginning to become less apparent. Attributing part of the change to the increasing number of women car owners and drivers, *Vogue* in 1921 found that most American stock cars had improved dramatically in appearance as the manufacturers deferred to "feminine taste through the entire design" of the new models, "most notably in a certain attention to details and finish, such as could be obtained ten years ago only from the great makers on the Continent." The adoption of the all-steel, welded body in the early 1920s allowed designers to move away from the sharp, square outlines to which they had been limited by wood-frame construction. The development in the early 1920s of fast-drying Duco lacquer finishes not only eliminated the last important bottleneck in the mass production of cars but it freed designers from the use of only a few colors, mostly black, and allowed them to experiment with the use of the far greater variety of shades and colors that were now available. Most important, however, was the sudden growth in the popularity of the closed car, which had constituted only 10 percent of the output in 1919 but by 1925 for the first time exceeded the number of open cars. By requiring the body designer to take into account its roof line, the windows, and the full-length doors, the closed car, as Alfred P. Sloan, Jr., maintained, brought about "styling as we know it."

These developments came at the very time that manufacturers were realizing that the bulk of their sales was no longer being made to people who were buying their first car, but instead to people who already owned one. Cars that exhibited a bright new look were seen as having the greatest appeal in this new replacement market. To meet the demand, the body companies that mass-produced bodies for the large-volume car producers began in the mid 1920s to hire experienced designers from custom body companies in order to make their production bodies more attractive. Custom bodywork, too, changed, with Edsel Ford and Allan Sheldon, president of the Murray Body Corporation, one of Detroit's largest body companies, bringing to Detroit the veteran custom body designer, Raymond Dietrich, to establish the Motor City's first major custom body company, Dietrich, Inc. However, rather than producing custom bodies, Dietrich developed a catalog of bodies, each of which could be produced in quantities that were, although limited in size, enough to reduce their cost and then could be individualized to meet the buyer's tastes. By 1928 Dietrich was said to be the largest producer of bodies for luxury cars, and his Lincoln and Packard convertible sedans were the hits of the New York and Chicago Salon shows in the winter of 1928-1929.

The era in which body manufacturers dominated the styling of American cars came to an end by the late 1920s. For the luxury car manufacturers, there were sound economic reasons why they should take over much of the work previously handled by custom body firms. They sold the customizer the chassis, at dealer's cost, and the custom house then pocketed the profits from selling the completed car to the customer. As early as 1914 Locomobile had established its own custom body shop and had begun collecting the full amount by selling in-house-designed custom cars. The decision of Packard, which accounted for about half of the sales of the luxury cars, to establish its own custom division in 1928 had a disastrous effect on many companies that supplied custom bodies for the Pack-

ard chassis. Most of the luxury car manufacturers went bankrupt during the 1930s, and their demise doomed to failure most of the remaining custom body businesses by the end of that decade. Meanwhile, GM's decision in 1926 to make Fisher Body a wholly owned subsidiary was the beginning of the end for the big production body companies as more automotive firms set up their own body divisions.

Sloan acquired Fisher Body in order that its body designers could work more closely with the engineers who designed the GM chassis. Instead styling was placed in the hands of a separate department, called the "Art & Colour Section," in 1927 under the direction of Harley Earl. The previous year Earl, who had attracted the attention of Sloan and Lawrence Fisher, head of the Cadillac division, through his custom bodywork for a California Cadillac distributor, had been commissioned to design the LaSalle, a new car that was to be produced by the Cadillac division. Inspired by the great European luxury car, the Hispano-Suiza, Earl's LaSalle is an automotive classic, with rounded, graceful lines that gave the resulting production car a look that had been found only in custom cars. The LaSalle convinced Sloan that Earl should be put in charge of the styling of all the corporation's cars.

For over thirty years Earl was the best known of the automotive stylists, but his emergence at GM in the late 1920s was simply confirmation of a general realization by the automobile companies that styling demanded more attention than it had previously received. GM's two largest competitors, Ford and Chrysler, quickly followed suit by setting up their own styling staffs. For a good many years neither rivaled in size GM's section. In the case of Chrysler, a quarter of a century elapsed before its stylists emerged from the shadow of the engineers, who kept a tight control over that company's car designs. At Ford, however, Edsel Ford's personal interest in styling helped to guarantee that this work was on firmer ground in that company. As a result the Ford Model A, which debuted at the end of 1927, was the first example of this new approach to styling in a low-priced, high-volume production car.

For the most part the smaller companies did not set up their own styling divisions but instead relied on outside designers. Several turned to Norman Bel Geddes or Walter Dorwin Teague or Raymond Loewy, heads of three of the four large industrial design firms that opened offices in New York City between 1926 and 1928 and offered their services to any manufacturer who wanted help in designing industrial products. Other automotive companies turned to such designers as Amos Northrup of the Murray Body Company or Alexis de Sakhnoffsky of the Hayes Body Company, who specialized in automotive design. But no matter where the ideas came from, the late 1920s and the 1930s saw an explosion of creative energy that made this the golden age of American car design. Following the 1927 LaSalle and Ford Model A came such cars as Sakhnoffsky's 1928 Auburn boat-tailed Speedster, Teague's 1931 Marmon Sixteen, Northrup's Reo Royale of the same year and his 1932 Graham Blue Streak, and Chrysler's engineer-designed 1934 streamlined Chrysler and DeSoto Airflow models.

Also notable were Ford's 1936 Lincoln Zephyr, Gordon Buehrig's famed "coffin-nose" Cord, also introduced in the 1936 model year, the 1938 Cadillac Sixty-Special, primarily the work of William Mitchell of Harley Earl's staff, and the 1939 Continental, designed by Edsel Ford and his chief stylist, Eugene T. "Bob" Gregorie. The Continental would later appear on many lists as one of the most beautiful cars ever designed. But no other period saw so many cars of such generally recognized design significance as those that appeared in the dozen or so years before World War II. Each had its own unique features, but as a whole they reflected certain ideas and approaches that influenced all of their designers. There was a common desire to get away from the high, square, boxy look that was characteristic of cars prior to this time. "Why?" Harley Earl asked. "Because," he said, "my sense of proportion tells me that oblongs are more attractive than squares, . . . or a greyhound is more graceful than an English bulldog." Sometimes the change was actual, and in other cases the change was an illusion, as when Earl sought to reduce the viewers' perception of the height of his 1927 LaSalle by adding a decorative strip to the beltline. Such decorative features could also accentuate the length of the car, which had long been regarded as a symbol of power and prestige. But decorations were scarcely needed to accent the visual impression created by the awesome hoodline of the Duesenberg, which, together with the Auburn and the Cord, was part of the design-rich automotive empire built up by Erret L. Cord in this period.

The Duesenberg hood, a part of the car that had been a responsibility of the engineers, was de-signed by Cord's stylist, Gordon Buehrig, who, along with other stylists, now took over the design of the car's entire outer shell. This unitary approach did away with the conflicts between engineers and body designers that had sometimes detracted from the look of the final product. It also freed the stylist to cover up or disguise aesthetically unattractive mechanical features.

However, what probably struck most people as the newest styling trend was the attention given to the use of streamlining in an attempt to achieve the supposed benefits of an aerodynamically designed vehicle. Norman Bel Geddes in the late 1920s had included streamlining in a series of automotive designs commissioned by the Graham-Paige company. The onset of the depression forced the company to scrap plans to put the designs into production and efforts to sell them to other companies failed. Aerodynamic features were also part of Walter Dorwin Teague's and Amos Northrup's designs in the early 1930s, but it was not a stylist but an engineer, Chrysler's Carl Breer, who was responsible for the period's most famous effort along these lines. Breer's pioneering use of the wind tunnel, a use which grew out of his interest in airplanes, demonstrated that the wind resistance of cars as they had been designed was less when they were driven backward than forward. The result was his designs for the Chrysler and DeSoto Airflow models. Their low, sloping front profile attempted to create the teardrop configuration that was the streamliners' ideal, and it made the prototypes a sensation when they were displayed in New York early in 1934. Although the cars were a critical success they were a commercial failure, for reasons that are unclear. On the assumption that the public found the cars unattractive from a stylistic standpoint, Norman Bel Geddes and then Raymond Dietrich were brought in to make some cosmetic changes. They met with limited success, as measured by sales. It remained for Ford's Lincoln Zephyr, which looked much like the Airflow models from the cowl back but whose sharply pointed front end, encompassing a 12-cylinder engine, had a more pleasing look, to be the first streamlined car to sell well.

World War II interrupted automotive developments for some four years, and the creative impulses that characterized the prewar years were never fully regained in the years after the war. There were exceptions, of course, as a number of the stylists of the earlier period continued to be ac-

The 1949 Ford, the first new design for the company since the end of World War II, marked the company's acceptance of the importance of styling.

tive. Raymond Loewy, who with his design staff had begun a long association with Studebaker in the 1930s, was responsible for two famous postwar models: the 1947 Studebaker with front and rear ends so much alike that some people professed not to know whether the car was coming or going; and the stunning, aerodynamic classic, the Avanti, which could not save Studebaker when it was put into production in 1962 but which, in modified forms, has been kept in production by others since Studebaker went out of business in the mid 1960s. William Clay Ford, who inherited some of his father's bent for styling, brought in Gordon Buehrig, among others, to create the 1957 Continental Mark II, which recalled the timeless elegance of the original Continental.

But for every Avanti and Mark II and a few others, such as the original Ford Thunderbird and the Chevrolet Corvette, there were far more cars in the late 1940s and 1950s whose designers exhibited a tendency toward the extravagant or the bizarre. As a result, this period has been called the Baroque Age of American car design. The graceful look of the prewar period gave way to styles that often had a big, heavy, clumsy look. The first new postwar

Packard, for example, introduced what was immediately called the "inverted bathtub" style which, although it won top honors in a number of design competitions, gave the car a full-bodied look that saddled the latest entry of this distinguished marque with the nickname of the "pregnant elephant."

By incorporating the fenders into side panels that seemed to flow along the car's entire length, Ed Macauley, the Packard stylist, helped establish a postwar trend designed to create a smoother look to the car's outer shell. Buehrig had earlier started this trend by disposing of the running boards and recessing the door handles in his 1936 Cord. The slab-sided 1949 Ford continued the trend with clean lines that compensated for its rather chunky look. Its success pushed Ford ahead of Chrysler into second place in sales. Chrysler, which had been the most conservative in its styling practices, brought in Virgil Exner, formerly part of Loewy's design staff, and gave him final authority over styling decisions. By the mid 1950s Exner was giving the Chrysler products a longer, lower, flashier look than the higher, boxier models which the company's management had previously preferred.

Although Chrysler sought to depict Exner's work as having made the corporation the styling leader, he was simply following the lead of Harley Earl, who was unquestionably the most influential trendsetter of the postwar era. Unfortunately his influence led to the stylistic excesses that fell under critical attack during the 1950s. Earl's longtime emphasis on longer, lower, and wider cars was carried to an extreme. The average height of cars dropped 10 inches between 1949 and 1959, while the length of the cars, which already had caused consumers to object by the late 1940s that they were becoming difficult to park, was increased until by 1959 the Series 75 Cadillac had an overall length of just over 20 feet, longer than the average garage, while many other models, although not quite that long, could be put in a garage or a parking space only with great difficulty. Length was accentuated through the use of trim, which again was carried to garish extremes, with the 1958 Buicks carrying some 44 pounds of chrome, the so-called "bright work" which many stylists claimed to dislike but which dealers claimed aided sales. Earl's most famous postwar innovation was his adaptation of the twin tail fins of the World War II P-38 fighter plane. Introduced on the 1949 Cadillac, these tail fins, which were at first of modest size, quickly grew in dimensions and were soon adopted by stylists throughout the industry as a feature that could readily identify one year's model from the next. Although the 1959 Cadillac Eldorado probably set the record for having the tallest fins, Chrysler's models under Virgil Exner's direction were a close second, with "fins so outlandish," the automotive writer Brock Yates declared, "that they appeared to have been stolen from the drawing boards of Boeing Aircraft."

Although there is a good deal of evidence that would support the companies' contention that the public really liked these cars, the growing volume of negative comments led to a pullback in the 1960s to cars of somewhat more modest dimensions and more restrained styling. Cars such as the 1963 Buick Riviera marked a definite move away from the lavish use of chrome, the "ventiports," and the buck-toothed grilles of the Buicks of the 1950s, which may have increased the division's sales but had diminished the image of excellence established by some of its earlier models.

But it was not simply public opinion that was changing the character of automotive design. Beginning in the mid 1960s government requirements regarding safety features, emission controls, and fuel efficiency restricted the freedom of both the stylists and the automotive engineers. The rising costs of producing cars were a factor in causing the American companies to give less emphasis to the radical yearly changes in appearance that had fueled some of the excesses of the 1950s. The principle that "form follows function" that had still guided much of the design work in the 1930s but had been largely forgotten in the 1950s became fashionable once more. "We're not in the 50's anymore," Charles Jordan, head of Harley Earl's old styling section at GM, declared in the late 1980s. "We no longer are styling cars. What we do is work with engineers now to design a car where concept is woven into technology."

In the 1970s and 1980s the smaller, saner cars that were the first products resulting from the new constraints under which the designers had to operate were greeted with some derision by veteran stylists. William Mitchell, Earl's old right-hand man and successor as chief GM stylist, referred to the new cars as "those little cracker boxes." There was no excitement to these cars, he said: "you've got to have a car go down the road and you turn your head and say: 'God, what is that?' and you don't have it today." Mitchell was also upset at the increasing tendency of American companies to look to European designers for their inspiration. The day of the great American individual stylists seemed to have passed. In their place were huge styling departments made up of people to whom names like Earl and Northrup and Buehrig and Mitchell were part of history and names like the Italian designers Pininfarina, Ghia, Bertone, and Giugiaro represented the present.

William Mitchell died in 1988, just about the time that some observers were seeing the excitement that he missed coming back. The Ford Taurus in 1985 demonstrated that a fuel-efficient, aerodynamically designed car could be attractive. The competition soon followed suit, and by the end of 1988 William Jeanes, editor in chief of the car enthusiasts' magazine *Car and Driver,* expressed the belief that "there are more exciting cars on the market today than probably at any time in the history of this country or the world, without question."

References:

Stephen Bayley, *Harley Earl and the Dream Machine* (New York: Knopf, 1983);

Gordon M. Buehrig, with William S. Jackson, *Rolling Sculpture: A Designer and His Work* (Newfoundland, N.J.: Haessner Publishing, 1975);

James J. Flink, *The Automobile Age* (Cambridge, Mass.: MIT Press, 1988);

Raymond Loewy, "Jukebox on Wheels," *Atlantic Monthly*, 195 (April 1955): 36-38;

George S. May, *The Automobile in American Life* (Forthcoming 1990);

Brock Yates, *The Decline and Fall of the American Automobile Industry* (New York: Empire Books, 1983).

Roland Jay Thomas

(June 9, 1900-April 18, 1967)

by John Barnard

Oakland University

CAREER: Vice-president, Automotive Industrial Workers Association (1935-1936); president, Local 7, United Automobile Workers (1936-1937); vice-president (1937-1939), president, United Automobile Workers-Congress of Industrial Organizations (1939-1946); vice-president, Congress of Industrial Organizations (1939-1947); first vice-president, United Automobile Workers-Congress of Industrial Organizations (1946-1947); assistant director of organization, Congress of Industrial Organizations (1947-1955); administrative assistant to the president, American Federation of Labor-Congress of Industrial Organizations (1955-1964).

Roland Jay Thomas, known as "R. J." or "Tommy," was one of the pioneer organizers of the autoworkers union and its president during the challenging days of World War II. In 1946 he lost the post in a close contest to Walter P. Reuther. Thomas attempted to regain the presidency in 1947 but failed following a bitter campaign.

Thomas was born in East Palestine, Ohio, on June 9, 1900, the son of Jacob William Thomas, a railroad worker, and his wife, Mary Alice Jackson Thomas. He was the eldest of seven children, five brothers and two sisters. His father was brought to the United States from Germany as a boy in order to escape military service. His mother, of Scotch-Irish ancestry, had been raised on a farm in nearby Enon Valley, Pennsylvania. The family was poor and religious, and Thomas was raised as a Presbyterian. When he was fourteen years old, the family moved to New Waterford, Ohio. During World War I his father obtained work in the booming steel mills of Youngstown. The family lived in

Roland Jay Thomas

nearby Hubbard, Ohio, where Thomas, after taking a year out to work in a steel mill, completed high school in 1918.

For a year and a half, from 1919 until 1921, Thomas attended Wooster College in Wooster, Ohio. Lacking financial assistance from his family, he supported himself by cleaning furnaces and dormitory rooms and waiting on tables. With jobs and sports absorbing much of his time, his grades suffered. Discouraged, he left college at the end of the first semester of his second year and returned home to go to work.

As a young man Thomas worked for Ohio Bell Telephone, Western Electric, and in a Youngstown steel mill, where he learned welding. In 1923 expanding automobile production drew him, as well as many other young midwesterners, to Detroit. For a few weeks he worked as a metal finisher, a trade he was not trained for, at the Fleetwood plant of Fisher Body. He later found a job as a welder at Cadillac. The pay for his work on rear axle housings was nearly double his most recent wage in Youngstown (over $10 a day versus $5.50), but he was laid off several times because of slow sales. On one occasion he attempted, without success, to organize welders for a protest against wage cuts. In 1929, before the stock market crash, he left Cadillac for a welding job at the Kercheval Road factory of the Chrysler Corporation on Detroit's east side. Referring to the wage cuts, layoffs, and speedups that arrived with the Great Depression, Thomas said that the Chrysler Corporation made him a union man.

In 1924 Thomas married Eletha Lutes, but the marriage was not a success. Their work took them apart, they developed different sets of friends, and they had no children. In 1933 Thomas obtained a divorce.

Thomas was caught up in the organizing fervor that swept the auto plants following the election of President Franklin D. Roosevelt in 1932. The passage of the National Industrial Recovery Act of 1933, which contained the first federal collective bargaining guarantee, encouraged workers to launch organizing drives. Unlike the other major auto manufacturers, the Chrysler Corporation opted for the formation of company unions, known as "employee representation plans" or "works councils," as the best way to head off independent unions. In 1934 President Roosevelt proposed proportional representation for autoworkers and set up the Automobile Labor Board to apply it. This permitted different unions, including company unions, to compete for workers' support and gain seats on a works council, an arrangement that guaranteed workers would remain divided and weak. At the Chrysler Kercheval plant in 1934 Thomas ran as an unaffiliated candidate for a seat on the twelve-member works council. Popular with his fellow workers and already convinced of the need for an in-

dependent union, he was easily elected and was chosen as secretary of the council.

The works council afforded Thomas his first opportunity to engage in bargaining, although the practical results were minimal. When the council met with Chrysler officials, the workers' representatives proposed steady work and higher pay as suitable subjects for discussion. Under no compulsion to bargain, the corporation's representatives refused to talk about wages and work but ultimately agreed to have the drinking fountains cleaned and the dirty windows washed. In frustration Thomas wished to resign as a protest, but his fellow workers—he was now widely known throughout the Kercheval plant—talked him out of it. Since the workers were already acting in many ways as union members, an independent local was formed with Thomas elected as its chairman. He was authorized to meet with workers' leaders in other Chrysler Corporation plants where similar movements were taking place.

At the Dodge Main plant in nearby Hamtramck, Michigan, a young organizer named Richard Frankensteen had already succeeded in establishing the Automotive Industrial Workers Association (AIWA), an independent, unaffiliated industrial autoworkers union. Although the American Federation of Labor (AFL) maintained that organized autoworkers should ultimately be absorbed in its trades affiliates, Frankensteen and Thomas recognized that craft-based organization was impractical in modern auto plants with their many semiskilled workers and assembly-line method of production. The Chrysler Kercheval plant local affiliated with the AIWA, and Thomas was elected vice-president of the parent organization. Although the AIWA locals were not officially recognized as bargaining agents by Chrysler, their membership grew rapidly. Much of Thomas's energy went into recruitment. One of the first new members he signed up was his future wife, Mildred Wettergren, who was employed in the Trim Department, and whom he married on August 7, 1937. By fall 1935 the AIWA claimed a membership of about 25,000, nearly all in Chrysler Corporation plants in Detroit.

In 1936 the AIWA, assured that the recently chartered United Automobile Workers (UAW) favored an industrial rather than craft-based organization, and that it was free of control by the parent AFL, affiliated with the larger union at the UAW's convention in South Bend, Indiana. Later in the year the UAW affiliated with the Committee on Industrial Organization (CIO), a move that led to its expulsion by the AFL. The AIWA local at the Kercheval plant merged into UAW Local 7. Thomas, issued card number one in the local, was elected its president. Henceforth, he worked full-time for the union as organizer, bargainer, and administrator. As president of Local 7 he received $50 a week, about what he had been averaging in pay as a welder. Since Chrysler refused to grant him a leave of absence to serve as union president, he had to surrender his seniority and whatever job security it afforded.

In 1937 the UAW made its first major, permanent gains with successful sit-down strikes at General Motors (GM) factories in Flint in January and February and then in the Chrysler plants in Detroit from March 8, 1937 to April 6, 1937. As president of one of the largest Chrysler locals Thomas participated in planning and executing that key strike. Although the National Labor Relations (Wagner) Act, containing a stronger and more comprehensive guarantee of collective bargaining rights, had been enacted in 1935, its constitutionality was contested by many employers, and the Supreme Court rendered no decision until the Jones & Laughlin Steel Company case of May 1937. The Chrysler Corporation held that, because it believed the Wagner Act was unconstitutional, it was not obliged to recognize or bargain with a union of its employees. The major objective of the Chrysler sit-down was to force the company to grant recognition as the first step to a bargaining relationship and agreement. Of nearly equal importance, the sit-down was intended to demonstrate to the Chrysler workers, many still fearful from years of blacklists, discriminatory firing of union members, and company use of spies on workers' organizations, that the new UAW was a militant organization that could confront the employer and protect its members against retaliation.

Once the strike began, the reservoirs of union support were apparent, and workers rushed to join. More workers wanted to sit down inside the plants than the union could sustain, and many had to be sent home. Negotiations were carried on throughout the five-week strike. With auto sales relatively strong and the example of GM's recent accord with the UAW before it, Chrysler was eager to avoid a long strike, but it gave ground grudgingly and only under pressure. Most of Thomas's activities consisted of visits to the plants and speeches to work-

ers to boost morale or to persuade them to join the union and support the strike. He estimated that he averaged less than three hours of sleep a night during the strike. A major event was the massive rally in Cadillac Square in downtown Detroit on March 23, 1937, which drew a crowd of more than 100,000. The largest union rally in the nation's history, it solidly demonstrated the support for the strike among the city's work force, both automotive and otherwise. As in the GM strike, an active role in negotiations was taken by John L. Lewis, head of the United Mine Workers and the CIO, on behalf of the autoworkers, and, as a mediator, by Michigan governor Frank Murphy. Walter P. Chrysler and K. T. Keller were the principals involved for the corporation. Thomas, present at some of the meetings, was not a major participant in the talks. He did, on one occasion, assure Walter P. Chrysler that the strikers were not Communists, contrary to what Chrysler had been told. Under pressure from Governor Murphy to settle, the union ultimately compromised on an agreement to bargain only on behalf of its own members, while the corporation agreed not to support any other union or to engage in any acts harmful to the UAW. Although the agreement drew some criticism from within union ranks for the concessions that were made, the pact laid the foundation for future growth and power.

Success in the Chrysler strike brought Thomas notice throughout the UAW, but he was not yet among its outstanding leaders, nor was he identified with any of the factions that were already forming within it and which would soon be locked in struggle. On the contrary, Thomas was always somewhat aloof from the political and ideological rivalries that marked the UAW's early years. Much of the controversy swirled around Homer Martin, a former preacher and sometime autoworker, who had become the UAW's president on the strength of a fiery oratorical style. Lacking administrative and bargaining experience and skill, Martin, whose erratic ways finally led Thomas to consider him mentally ill, was steadily losing credibility and influence among those taking a more active and effective part in building the UAW. Despite his weakening position Martin was determined to cling to it to the bitter end. From 1937 to 1939 the UAW was wracked by the problem of what to do with Homer Martin. His rivals included Wyndham Mortimer, the UAW vice-president who laid much of the groundwork for the successful sit-down strike against GM;

George Addes, the union's secretary-treasurer; and Frankensteen, another vice-president and Thomas's associate in building the organization in Chrysler.

During spring and summer 1937 two broad, rival coalitions emerged within the UAW. The group that supported Martin, called the Progressive Caucus, gained the support of Frankensteen and Thomas. Martin soon made anticommunism its leading rhetorical thrust. In opposition to Martin the Unity Caucus was formed, consisting of Mortimer, Addes, the Reuther brothers, and others. The Unity Caucus, more ideological and left-wing in its orientation, included the union's small but active and influential bands of Communists and Socialists.

The first major clash came at the UAW's Milwaukee convention in August 1937. For Thomas the convention was a novel experience, as it was for most of the other delegates in the new and growing union. He had little previous experience with formal organizations and parliamentary procedure and later confessed that he had not had the slightest idea how large meetings were organized and conducted. The convention was one of the most tumultuous in union history: disorderly, raucous, and wracked by bitter disputes over a host of issues that challenged Martin's power. Finally, behind the scenes, CIO president John L. Lewis arranged a compromise between Progressive and Unity Caucuses that kept the organization from falling apart but accomplished little more. Martin was reelected president and the number of vice-presidencies was expanded to five to accommodate more of the leaders. Thomas, with support from both caucuses, was chosen as one of them. Although he was recognized as still a supporter of Martin's, he was acceptable to the other side. Added responsibilities came with the new position as Thomas was placed in charge of the union's dealings with Chrysler. He was also named president of the Auto Council, a coordinating body for all locals in the Detroit area.

In fall 1937 Thomas made his one foray into politics. A "labor slate," drawn almost entirely from the UAW, was put together to run in the municipal elections for mayor and for the Detroit Common Council. Heading the ticket as candidate for mayor was Patrick H. O'Brien, a former Michigan attorney general. Four UAW officers were candidates for Common Council seats: Thomas, Richard Frankensteen, Walter P. Reuther, and Tracy Doll. The fifth UAW candidate was Maurice Sugar, the union's legal counsel. Although the election was offi-

cially nonpartisan, the labor slate was backed by the local branch of the Socialist party, and the candidates talked of forming a permanent labor-socialist political organization if they were successful. In their campaign they attacked Detroit's mayor for corruption, called for the removal of the antiunion police commissioner, and pledged themselves to a host of reforms including public housing, cheaper milk, medical and hospital care, municipal ownership of utilities, and full civil rights for blacks. Despite heated attacks by the city's newspapers, which denounced union domination of politics and warned of municipal bankruptcy if the "reds" came to power, the labor slate survived the October primary. In the general election on November 2 Thomas received 126,238 votes and finished in fourteenth place. None of the labor candidates was elected. Thomas was never tempted again to run for public office.

Thomas became UAW president as a result of the failure of Homer Martin. Between 1937 and 1939 Martin's incapacity for leadership alienated one important UAW leader and group after another. The union, which had been launched with such promise with its victories over GM and Chrysler in 1937, was virtually paralyzed by the struggle within its ranks. Contract gains were few. Where limited recognition had been won, as at Chrysler and GM, it was in jeopardy. The union was incapable of mounting an offensive against the holdout Ford Motor Company, which was not organized until 1941. In summer 1938 the struggle moved toward a climax when Martin, whose presidential powers were formally strong, suspended and put on trial four of the vice-presidents plus Secretary-Treasurer Addes. Thomas alone among the officers managed for a time to steer clear of openly antagonizing Martin. CIO president John L. Lewis, apprehensive that the UAW would collapse if Martin continued as president, intervened. Although Thomas had only reluctantly and recently broken with Martin, had conducted no campaign for the presidency, and professed to be shocked by the selection, Lewis recommended that Thomas be chosen by the executive board as acting president while a convention was called to make the change permanent. Thomas became acting president of the UAW-CIO in January 1939. Martin, of course, disputed Thomas's selection, maintaining that he was the union's legitimate head.

The drama in the struggle focused on the union's officers. Although Thomas was the last of the officers to break with Martin, once in opposition he was an energetic opponent. In speeches to union and radio audiences he belittled Martin's administrative ability, attacked him for reckless and irresponsible expenditure of union funds, and, most damaging, criticized Martin's unauthorized contacts with Harry Bennett, the labor boss of the Ford Motor Company, which raised suspicions about Martin's loyalty. Violence was an ever present possibility. All of the officers carried guns; Thomas packed a Colt .22 automatic in his hip pocket which, happily, he never had to fire. Before some especially tense meetings UAW officers checked their weapons at the door in order to clear the atmosphere. Even so, at times Thomas's life was in danger. An angry band of Martin supporters from the Packard plant threatened to throw him out of an upper window of the UAW's headquarters in the Griswold Building in downtown Detroit before they were backed off by another UAW vice-president, Ed Hall, armed with a pistol.

Much of the heat of the struggle was generated in the locals, which were sharply divided by crosscurrents of faction, ideology, or simple lack of confidence in one or another leader. Martin, although discredited in the eyes of most, still had a following in some of the big GM locals in Flint and other Michigan cities. Thomas's designation as acting president reflected Lewis's view that Thomas, as the last of the major leaders to abandon Martin and the one least personally involved in his overthrow, stood the best chance of winning back the Martin locals to the UAW-CIO.

In spring 1939 two special UAW conventions were held. The first, under the auspices of the Martin forces, met in Detroit to confirm Martin as president and rally his troops. It was poorly attended and revealed the weaknesses of its backers. The second convention, under the auspices of the CIO (Lewis sent lieutenants Philip Murray and Sidney Hillman to manage the affair), met in April in Cleveland, Ohio, to choose Thomas as UAW president and to rearrange the union's affairs. Most UAW locals, demonstrating their loyalty to the CIO and their distrust of Martin, sent their delegates to Cleveland.

Although he had the powerful and crucial backing of the CIO hierarchy, Thomas's choice was not a foregone conclusion. Some questioned his ability to lead the union, as he was neither a powerful orator nor a proven administrator. He had not built, and never would, a personal machine to generate votes and other support in his behalf. Even his standing among Chrysler Corporation employees, with whom his early union experiences were shared, was overshadowed by that of Richard Frankensteen, a tough organizer, strong speaker, and nimble politician. Nor was Thomas, who was utterly without pretensions to theoretical knowledge, allied with any of the union's factional or ideological groups. One of them, the Communist party and its element of close allies, reached the zenith of its UAW strength at this convention. Unimpressed by Thomas, the Communists hoped to put forth their own candidate. Their preference was for Wyndham Mortimer, an unavowed party member, experienced organizer, and vice-president of the union, but a candidate who was too much of an easy target of Martin's red-baiting attacks. They would have been content with Secretary-Treasurer George Addes, who was no Communist but was a close friend and saw eye-to-eye on most substantive and factional issues. Neither was acceptable to Lewis and his agents at the convention. To them, Thomas was the safe, "available" candidate, a down-to-earth, likeable man, reasonably popular with the rank and file, still on friendly terms with some of Martin's supporters and therefore able to bring them along, and, hopefully but less certainly, capable of managing and leading the union. He looked like the best all-around choice.

Thomas was overwhelmingly elected, facing only token opposition from Carl Shipley of South Bend and Frank B. Tuttle of Detroit, neither a prominent figure. As a result of the election the new executive board was strongly tilted to the left by nearly a three-to-one margin with Frankensteen the leading figure on the left and Reuther on the right. Thomas had no personal following among the board members. As Irving Bernstein writes, Thomas "had no intellectual or leadership qualifications for the presidency of the UAW. But he was loyal, honest, big-hearted, stable, and colorless, all wildly attractive characteristics after Homer Martin."

Other important issues at the convention included the writing and adoption of a new constitution. Martin had attempted to centralize power in the president's hands at the expense of both the locals and the other officers. In reaction the 1939 constitution protected the autonomy of the locals, built up the departments which dealt with each of the major automobile manufacturers, and gave the executive board greater independence in its relationship with the president. Board members, for example, could no longer be suspended by the president, a device that Martin had abused. Since Thomas lacked Martin's autocratic temper and ambition, these changes did not constrict his conduct of the office.

Another important change was Thomas's selection of Walter P. Reuther as director of the GM Department, the largest and most important of its internal divisions. Reuther, though barely thirty years old, was already tagged as an ambitious, able union leader whose destiny encompassed the UAW presidency and perhaps more. Thomas needed the support that the well-organized Reuther following could provide, and he needed the gifted Reuther's administrative skills and shrewd mind. The threat in Reuther's selection was pointed out to Thomas shortly after his election by Sidney Hillman, who warned that Reuther would probably succeed, sooner or later, to the presidency.

It was Thomas's fate to be overshadowed by more daring and abler men. The most important was Reuther, who, despite support for Thomas, did not conceal his opinion that Thomas did not measure up as the UAW's chief officer. Thomas also suffered, though to a lesser degree, in comparison to other leading UAW figures: Addes, Frankensteen, Mortimer, whose star was fading, and Richard Leonard, a rising force. Thomas was a mediator among these more dynamic, and rival, chieftains, rather than an initiator or decision maker. On several of the contentious issues that swirled through the UAW in these years, Thomas was strangely detached, often above the battle, while his putative lieutenants struggled in the trenches. This tactic let him escape the blame when things went wrong, but, by the same token, he received little credit when things went right. Although capable of taking firm and even courageous stands once an issue was defined and presented, he had neither the temperament, intellect, nor organizational capacity to shape events. Consequently, although he was UAW president through seven tumultuous years and was regularly re-elected, there always hung around the edges of his rule the air of a caretaker.

Thomas's lack of presence was revealed within days after he became president, when Reuther, as director of the GM Department, planned, executed, and won a brilliant and decisive strike of GM tool and die makers in summer 1939. Commonly called the "strategy strike" in tribute to its shrewd assessment of both GM's and the UAW's current situations, the strike drove another nail in Homer Martin's coffin, restored morale among the rank and file, and was the prelude to an overwhelming UAW-CIO victory in a National Labor Relations Board representation election among GM workers in the following year. Nor did Thomas play a prominent role in some of the other significant confrontations and issues of the time, such as the strike against the Ford Motor Company in April 1941, which brought the last holdout into the UAW fold, and the 1940-1941 strikes at the North American Aviation and Allis-Chalmers companies.

In an intensely political union, Thomas failed to build a political organization. His power rested on the support given him by rival leaders, such as Reuther and Frankensteen, who had powerful organizations of their own. The executive board was ordinarily divided about equally between Frankensteen and Reuther allies. Personally, Thomas had some qualities that endeared him to rank and file unionists. A large, ruddy-faced man, Thomas was unassuming and possessed no pretensions to intellectual distinction. He spoke, from long familiarity, the rough language of the shop. He always carried and used chewing tobacco. (At the outset of a wartime trip to the Soviet Union, Thomas received a gift from some union admirers: a suitcase full of chewing tobacco for his trip to this tobacco-short country.) A hearty man, he enjoyed a drink and a joke, and his devotion to poker became legendary throughout the labor movement. All in all, Thomas was a man with whom many workers felt comfortable and on more or less equal terms. Ironically, that positive characteristic was one of his problems. Among the secondary ranks of leadership, as well as among the rank and file, many expected more in a leader than a reflection of themselves.

Within months of Thomas's election to the presidency it became clear that the UAW, like the union movement as a whole, faced entirely new opportunities and challenges as an impending war thrust aside old problems and preoccupations. Even before World War II erupted in September 1939, the nation had to confront the question of rearmament. With the German advances of 1940 and 1941, including the air assault on Great Britain and the invasion of the Soviet Union, the question of American aid to the Allies became urgent. With the attack on Pearl Harbor in December 1941 the

Thomas, right, watches as Harry Bennett, center, and Philip Murray sign in 1941 the first Ford-UAW contract (courtesy of Ford Motor Company)

United States officially entered the war. The approach of war had a profound effect on the auto industry and on the aircraft industry, where the UAW was also engaged in organizing workers. Detroit, in a popular phrase, became the "arsenal of democracy" as its production capabilities turned from making cars to making the weapons of war.

The changes in the union were manifold. Most important, perhaps, was sheer growth. In spring 1939, when Thomas became president, paid-up UAW membership stood at 152,000. When the war ended in August 1945, membership had skyrocketed to 1.2 million, making the UAW the largest independent labor union in the world. Hundreds of thousands of workers, including women and minorities, many without experience as union members, entered the industrial work force in factories organized by the UAW. To represent adequately and fairly this far more heterogeneous work force was a formidable challenge.

Since the government became the sole consumer of the automotive industry's product (civilian car production halted early in 1942 and was not resumed until the summer of 1945), the union's relationship with Washington shaped its actions and set limits to its achievements. Shortly after Pearl Har-

bor virtually all American unions, including the UAW, voluntarily offered a wartime "no-strike" pledge. Unions foreswore the use of what was, in normal times, their most effective weapon. Officially the no-strike pledge, which Thomas wholeheartedly supported, was adhered to, but unauthorized wildcat strikes were a plague. To combat inflation the government imposed price controls and set wage ceilings. Although the worst excesses of price and wage inflation were avoided, the system fell short of perfection. Much of the UAW officers' wartime activity, since there were no authorized strikes for improvements, went into trying to persuade the bureaucracy to grant wage increases to keep pace with rising prices. The union also was very active in representations before government agencies dealing with manpower, materiels allocations, and related production questions. Ultimately, owing to rank and file criticism, there was a reexamination of the commitment to the no-strike pledge. The issue came to a head at the 1944 Grand Rapids convention. Thomas, who had recently returned from a speaking tour of armed services bases in England, reported that American soldiers were distressed by the thought that unions would waver over or even abandon the pledge. He urged its reaffirmation in the strongest terms and threatened withdrawal as a candidate for reelection if the pledge was rescinded. Although his position was rejected by the convention delegates, it was upheld by the membership in a mail referendum. As a sign of the seriousness of the issue Thomas, for the first time at an annual convention, encountered opposition in his bid for reelection.

Another wage-related wartime issue involved the establishment of an incentive pay system. Ordinarily incentive pay schemes, such as piece rates, were an anathema to unions, and the UAW had fought a largely successful battle against their use in the auto industry prior to the war. But some, particularly the union's Communist element and its sympathizers, who were prepared to support any sacrifice to increase production as long as the Soviet Union was an American ally and the recipient of American military aid, sought to reestablish incentive pay. The proposal, unpopular with the rank and file, badly divided the organization. Thomas, perhaps exploring the possibilities for an alliance with the left, at first skirted the issue and then took a vague position.

One of the most explosive issues in the wartime union was race relations. Changes in the composition of the work force provided much of the fuel. The white work force, which included both large numbers of southern-born migrants and immigrants from abroad and their descendants, was susceptible to racial suspicion and hatred. In some of the auto plants, north as well as south, the Ku Klux Klan had, at times, attained substantial support. The war stimulated black migration, with 80,000 blacks coming into the Detroit area alone between 1940 and 1945. As labor shortages developed in the plants, more blacks were hired, and as workers left for the armed services, opportunities for promotion to better paying and more interesting jobs increased. Hostility between the races was aggravated by competition for scarce housing, crowded schools and other public services, inadequate transportation, and many other inconveniences in a city at war. In June 1943 a savage race riot in the streets of Detroit left twenty-five blacks and nine whites dead. The riot was kept out of the plants, an achievement for which the UAW claimed credit, but a series of wildcat "hate strikes" occurred in the plants before and after the riot. These were usually sparked by the hiring of additional black workers and particularly by the upgrading of black workers to better

jobs from which they previously had been excluded. The most serious strike came at the Packard plant on Detroit's east side when 25,000 angry workers from three shifts walked out over the upgrading of three blacks to assembly-line jobs. Thomas and several other union officers responded quickly and decisively to uphold the union's commitment to equal treatment of its members. In cooperation with the military authorities who were responsible for maintaining war production, Thomas threatened to expel union members who participated in the strike and, if necessary, shut down the plant. Thomas courageously strode on to a platform before an angry crowd and bluntly told the rebellious white workers that they must work with "our colored brothers." Nearly thirty of the ringleaders were suspended, and ultimately several lost their jobs. Over the next few months negotiations between union, management, and government representatives resulted in promotion for significant numbers of black workers.

A second issue revolved around the union's response to racism in its own practices. Officially, of course, the union was committed to a position of nondiscrimination and equal treatment. There were never any racial stipulations for membership or office-holding although some southern locals had violated these rules. But until the successful Ford strike in 1941 brought about 10,000 black Ford workers into the UAW, there was no large black contingent in the union. As a result there had been little pressure to choose blacks for staff positions or as officers. As black membership increased, and particularly as the giant Ford Local 600, the union's largest, exerted its influence, this began to change. A focus of controversy during the war years was a proposal to designate an executive board seat for a black unionist. This proposal was supported by most of the active black members and by the left wing, including the Communists. Thomas, among others, attacked the proposal on the grounds that a designated seat was a demeaning "Jim Crow" device. It would be better, he argued, to elect a black to one of the regular board seats. The proposal was not adopted. Greater consensus was evident on the need to tackle racism through educational activities aimed at the membership. Thomas supported the establishment of a Minorities Department charged with studying racial problems in the work place, preparing educational programs to combat them, and with mediating and resolving racial disputes when they arose. During Thomas's presidency, with his active leadership and backing, the union began to awaken to its responsibilities as a multiracial organization.

Like many Americans, both military and civilian, Thomas spent much of wartime in travel on public missions. He established close ties with President Roosevelt and other high government officials, particularly Secretary of War Robert Patterson, during numerous visits to Washington, D.C. In 1942 he was appointed by Roosevelt to the Labor Advisory Committee of the War Labor Board, the government agency that was chiefly concerned with resolving the many wage and working conditions disputes that arose. Under government sponsorship he made five trips to Europe during the war. The main object was to assure American soldiers of labor's support for the war effort, particularly the no-strike pledge, an effort made necessary by the great publicity given to wildcat strikes in some industries. Thomas also made many contacts with European trade unionists and headed the American delegation to the World Trade Union Conference in London in 1945, which resulted in the formation of the International Confederation of Free Trade Unions.

An occurrence on one of his trips produced so much international notoriety that a reporter tagged Thomas as "labor's undiplomatic diplomat." While in England he was invited to Buckingham Palace for tea with King George VI and Elizabeth. The visit went pleasantly enough. But the inept Thomas got into hot water, after returning to the United States, when he disclosed to two inquiring Detroit newspaper cronies that "the queen wears the royal britches," a quote that was picked up by newspapers here and abroad and caused a critical stir among some of the UAW's Canadian members. Thomas avoided contact with the State Department and reporters until the heat subsided.

As the war's end approached, it became evident that Thomas's leadership would be challenged. Reuther's wartime activities had enhanced his reputation and solidified his standing, and his following was deep and well organized, particularly in the mammoth GM locals. Thomas, though personally popular, had still neglected to create a large, cohesive organization. As the war came to an end, he drew closer to Addes, Frankensteen, and Richard Leonard, the union's other major figures, to create a countervailing force to the Reuther organization and to muster rank and file support.

Reuther seized the initiative when he insisted that the GM workers should take the lead in defining and pursuing the union's postwar objectives. With civilian car production resuming and an uncertain outlook on the maintenance of price controls, Reuther argued that the workers' wartime income should be maintained, despite the loss of premium overtime pay rates. The car makers, he claimed, could afford to pay 30 percent higher wages without raising the prices of cars. Not surprisingly, GM declared that it could not afford the increase and that in any case the prices the company charged for its cars were none of the union's business. Reuther responded with the demand that the company "open the books" to union accountants to determine its ability to pay. If the GM claim was upheld, Reuther pledged to reduce the union's wage proposal. Reuther launched a massive public relations campaign to generate support for his controversial and complex proposal.

Thomas, although the UAW president, was little more than a spectator in this major postwar confrontation. He endorsed the strike that began on November 21, 1945, but gave it little active leadership and privately believed that Reuther's proposals, which he dismissed as "fancy economics," were wrongheaded and unnecessarily provocative. He ridiculed them as offering food for thought for intellectuals but little bread for workers.

Thomas's relations with Reuther were tense since Reuther always acted, and sometimes spoke, as though he was destined for the UAW's presidency. Reuther's family heritage of unionism and leftist politics—his father was a Debsian socialist and union activist and two younger brothers, Roy and Victor, were close UAW associates—excited Thomas's envy. More than once he confessed that Reuther's mastery of words and his ease with ideas were formidable assets for union leadership which he did not possess. On many occasions he had let his hostile feelings show. He often referred to Reuther, with friends, as "the comet." In early 1946 while the strike was on, returning to Detroit on a train from Washington, D.C., where Reuther had presented the union's wage case to a presidential fact-finding board headed by William Davis, Thomas, as a reporter recounted the story, revealed his opinion of his rival:

"Multiple correlations, multiple correlations," [Thomas] mumbled over a drink in the club car. "That's all he talked about, multiple correlations."

"I didn't know what he was talking about. I don't think Will Davis knew what he was talking about."

Then, in an emotional crescendo full of hate and jealousy, R. J. concluded: "And I don't think the red-headed little s.o.b. HISSELF knew what he was talking about."

As the strike dragged on—it did not end until March 13, 1946–Thomas became more critical. At Ford and Chrysler the union obtained, without strikes, settlements that almost matched what it ultimately accepted from GM.

Thomas, an ordinary union leader with a conventional mind, was overmatched in a contest with the intellectually nimble and creative Reuther. Furthermore he failed to sense the postwar mood of the autoworkers. After the frustrations and fears of World War II, generated by the no-strike pledge and the prospect of postwar unemployment, workers were ready for a militant, progressive advance. Even though the results of the GM strike fell far short of what Reuther had pursued, his aggressive attack on the giant of the industry (the strike was the longest the union has ever conducted against GM) struck a responsive chord in the minds and spirits of many autoworkers and provided a platform on which to challenge Thomas for the presidency.

Reuther's presidential campaign was launched early in March 1946, when presidents of seventeen locals, representing a combined membership of 250,000, announced their support. It came as Thomas's usual allies were having second thoughts. Thomas sought to strengthen his hand by attending the Addes caucus before the convention, a move he later regretted as having compromised his independence and laying him open to criticism by Reuther. Reuther tried to divide the opposition by letting Secretary-Treasurer George Addes know that he could continue in office in a Reuther administration. Although Addes was unhappy with Thomas's uninspired leadership, he decided against abandoning an old ally. Thomas's other principal backer, Richard Frankensteen, in the final stages of winding down his union career, was unable to deliver to Thomas all of the support he previously had controlled.

The convention in Atlantic City, New Jersey, was passionate and boisterous. Heckling and rowdiness marred caucus meetings. Philip Murray, the CIO president, concluded a speech to the delegates with an oblique but unmistakable endorsement of Thomas, "this great big guy for whom I have a distinct fondness, the President of your Union." Seven years earlier, in 1939, national CIO backing had been crucial in Thomas's selection as president. By 1946, however, the UAW was a much changed organization—far more self-confident and mature. Murray, who had always felt uncomfortable with Reuther, could not risk an open endorsement of Thomas, let alone issue an order that he should be reelected, a testimony to the independence the UAW had achieved.

The Reuther forces followed a two-pronged strategy. While avoiding personal attacks on Thomas, the Reuther following stressed their leader's skills and abilities. The candidate rushed from one meeting to the next borne onward by an endless flow of political oratory. In order to display Reuther's talents to the best advantage, Thomas was challenged to an off-the-record, wide open debate before all the delegates in a closed session. George Addes, chairing the convention, blocked the call for a debate by a parliamentary maneuver, saving Thomas the embarrassment of having to face his quick-witted rival. But the vote taken on the convention floor to uphold Addes's ruling revealed that the Reuther forces were gaining the edge.

The other Reuther thrust was an attack on the Thomas-Addes combination for its alliance with the union's Communist faction which had led, it was asserted, to pro-Soviet policies harmful to the union's interests. Although Thomas had distanced himself from Communist positions on many issues, the views of numerous supporters were close to or identical with the party line, and on some questions such as the incentive pay and no-strike pledge issues of wartime he had been either equivocal or vague. This remote connection, as the memory of wartime cooperation with the Soviet Union rapidly faded to be replaced by the unremitting suspicion and hostility of the cold war, became politically damaging. Both within the union and in the country at large, where a swelling antiunion chorus was demanding the restrictive legislation that would, in the following year, produce the Taft-Hartley Act, a strong shift away from the left was discernible. Thomas, although certainly no leftist himself, was dragged down by his dependence on those who were.

During the voting, which took place on March 27, 1946, tension mounted as the clerk read for more than four hours through the list of hundreds of locals in the only closely contested presidential election in the UAW's history. Reuther won by a mere 124 votes (each vote represented approximately 100 members) out of a total of 8,764 (4,444 to 4,320). Although Addes could not keep all of his allies in line behind Thomas, most of Thomas's support came from Ford and Chrysler locals and, to some degree, from the aircraft locals which were a legacy from his alliance with Frankensteen. When it became clear that Thomas was headed for defeat, "he stood there in a daze, with tears trickling down his cheeks."

Immediately following his defeat for reelection Thomas was persuaded to run for first vice-president against Melvin Bishop, the candidate of the Reuther caucus. CIO officials Sidney Hillman and Allan Haywood gave further encouragement. The somewhat surprising result of this counterattack by the anti-Reuther forces was that Thomas was elected vice-president by a vote of 4,474 to 3,913, and Thomas-Addes candidates swept to victory in races for the union's other major offices, including a majority of the contests for the executive board. Far from vanquished, the anti-Reuther group was in position to compete for control of the union. The next convention was scheduled for November 1947, a year and a half away, and the union was kept in an almost constant electoral uproar during the interim.

By the time of the 1947 convention, Reuther's reelection was assured. Indeed, the Thomas-Addes forces decided not to run a candidate against Reuther (presumably it would have been Thomas) because it seemed hopeless. They focused their energy on reelecting their leaders to the lesser positions they currently occupied, but here too they fell short. Thomas was defeated for first vice-president by the Reuther candidate, Richard Gosser, by a vote of more than two to one (5,084 to 2,091). Addes was defeated for reelection as secretary-treasurer by only a slightly smaller margin, and the Reuther forces gained fourteen of eighteen seats on the executive board.

The electoral campaign was unedifying, as both sides engaged in personal abuse and unscrupulous maneuvers. The Reutherites attacked their opponents indiscriminately as followers of the Communist line while Reuther in turn was attacked as "the bosses' boy," a creature of the auto manufacturers. The Thomas-Addes group attempted to bring the left-wing Farm Equipment workers union into

the UAW as a way of strengthening their hand in the approaching election. Over this issue Thomas lost the support of Local 7, his home local in the Chrysler Corporation plant, an ominous and disheartening development. Thomas played a relatively minor role in this last struggle. The major strategic decisions were made by others, particularly Addes and the UAW's counsel, Maurice Sugar.

Thomas was in many ways a capable and attractive leader who perhaps in another union than the UAW could have had a longer and conventionally more successful career. Unassuming, approachable, and forthright, he rated well with the rank and file. He stood in the Samuel Gompers tradition of labor leadership, uninterested in broad ideological questions and social activism, focused on immediate gains for the workers. As he once told a reporter, "I don't know much about the class struggle. I'm interested in wages, hours, and working conditions." Normally, this has been a formula for successful leadership in American organized labor, but the UAW during these years had an unusually high level of intellectual and ideological sophistication, which was a disadvantage for Thomas. Nevertheless he worked well with those of differing perspectives. He was without bigotry and tolerant, perhaps too accepting, of those with opposing views. Under his aegis the UAW was an unusually open organization, with free debate and lively interchanges on a wide range of subjects. His leadership was ultimately undermined by his failure to grasp the political character of his position and to take the necessary steps to put it on a firm political foundation. This required more than merely building a loyal political following within the union; it required a moving vision of the force for betterment in the lives of its members and even of society at large that the union could become.

Only forty-seven years old when his UAW service ended, Thomas became assistant director of organization for the national CIO. He was appointed by president Philip Murray and worked under director Allan Haywood. As a "trouble shooter" he took on a variety of tasks; much of his effort went into arranging amalgamations of competing unions. He also headed up a number of organizing committees in areas where the CIO sought to establish new unions. When Reuther succeeded Murray as CIO president in 1952, he asked Thomas to remain on the job despite the fact that Thomas had supported Haywood as the new CIO president. Although the rivalry between Thomas and Reuther had deteriorated into enmity in their final years in the UAW, Reuther did not allow that to lower his opinion of one he knew was a loyal, competent unionist. Following the CIO merger with the AFL Thomas became, on Reuther's recommendation, an administrative assistant to president George Meany, serving as the highest CIO contact in the president's office. Thomas and Meany, who had much in common, worked well together. Thomas was particularly involved in ironing out jurisdictional disputes between unions, and he often represented Meany at state conventions, local councils, and before other labor bodies. In 1962 Thomas suffered a stroke that forced him to restrict his activities. On January 1, 1964, he retired from the AFL-CIO and moved to Muskegon, Michigan, where he died on April 18, 1967.

Unpublished Document:

George D. Blackwood, "The United Automobile Workers of America, 1935-1951," Ph.D. dissertation, University of Chicago, 1952.

References:

John Barnard, *Walter Reuther and the Rise of the Auto Workers* (Boston: Little, Brown, 1983);

Frank Cormier and William J. Eaton, *Reuther* (Englewood Cliffs, N.J.: Prentice-Hall, 1970);

Christopher H. Johnson, *Maurice Sugar: Law, Labor, and the Left in Detroit, 1912-1950* (Detroit: Wayne State University Press, 1988);

UAW Convention *Proceedings,* 1936-1947;

UAW *Report of the President,* 1939-1946;

United Auto Worker, 1936-1947.

Archives:

The most valuable body of papers includes the official records of the United Automobile Workers of America in the Walter P. Reuther Library of Labor and Urban Affairs, Wayne State University, Detroit. Other collections there include the R. J. Thomas Biographical File and the R. J. Thomas Papers. Thomas's reminiscences are

Lynn Alfred Townsend

(May 12, 1919-   )

by George S. May

Eastern Michigan University

CAREER: Clerk, National City Bank (1935-1936); accountant, Briggs & Iceman (1939-1941); accountant, Ernst & Ernst (1941-1944, 1946-1947); disbursing officer, U.S. Navy (1944-1946); supervising accountant, George Bailey & Company (1947); supervising accountant (1947-1951), partner, Touche, Ross, Bailey & Smart (1952-1957); comptroller (1957-1958), vice-president, international operations (1958-1960), director (1959-1975), administrative vice-president (1960-1961), president and chief operating and administrative officer (1961-1966), chairman and chief executive officer, Chrysler Corporation (1967-1975).

Lynn Alfred Townsend took over as president of Chrysler in 1961 at one of the corporation's lowest points and ran it for fourteen years. Because of his background as an accountant, he seemed to many the embodiment of what is derisively referred to as the "bean counter." This was because his actions often supported the implication that he was more interested in making a good profit than in the company's products. But Townsend's knowledge of automobiles was much greater than the critics have asserted. That was the result of his upbringing in Flint, Michigan, the center of automobile manufacturing. It was here that Lynn Townsend was born on May 12, 1919.

His father, Lynn A. Townsend, Sr., an autoworker, managed his wages wisely by investing in rental properties in Flint, where housing had been in short supply since the start of the automotive boom early in the century. In 1923, however, Townsend moved his family to Los Angeles where the climate was more suitable for his wife, Georgia E. Crandall Townsend, who suffered from asthma. The Townsends and their two children, Lynn, Jr., and a daughter, drove to California in a Dort, a Flint-made car that was not produced after 1924, a fact that may have influenced the senior Townsend to

open a service shop for obsolete cars. The family lived in Beverly Hills, and Mrs. Townsend dreamed of her children becoming actors. Townsend and his sister for several years attended the Hollywood Conservatory of Music and Arts, where the boy took elocution lessons and learned to play the violin. Although he did not become an actor, the handsome Chrysler executive of later years looked the part, with his nontraditional business suits and jewelry and unusually bright blue eyes.

The course of Townsend's life began to change in 1929 when his mother died. Four years later Townsend's father, whose business suffered as a result of the depression, died of a heart attack. Orphaned at fourteen, Townsend went to live with an uncle, North I. Townsend, who was the controller of a company in Evansville, Indiana. The uncle's position may have stimulated Townsend's interest in accounting, but he had also helped his father with his bookkeeping. When he graduated from high school shortly after turning sixteen (his mother, a teacher, had tutored her son at home so he could begin public school at the second grade level), Townsend took a job as clerk in Evansville's National City Bank at a salary of $62.50 a month. In 1936 he enrolled in the University of Michigan, where he majored in business administration. The money he had earned as a bank clerk, together with a small income he received from his parents' estate, was not enough to support him so he peeled potatoes, washed dishes, and performed other odd jobs before gaining a part-time position in 1939 with the Ann Arbor accounting firm of Briggs & Iceman. Townsend credited his struggle to stay in school with having instilled in him "a great drive to achieve" and having made him "a very competitive person."

Shortly after receiving his undergraduate degree in 1940, Townsend married Ruth M. Laing, daughter of a University of Michigan economics pro-

Lynn Alfred Townsend, center, announcing the transfer of management of Chrysler to John Riccardo, left, and Eugene Cafiero (courtesy of Chuck Ternes)

fessor. The couple had three sons. When Townsend became head of Chrysler in the 1960s, the family lived in what was described as a relatively modest ranch house in Bloomfield Township, a part of metropolitan Detroit that was a favorite of the newer generation of automotive executives. It was close to the Oakland Hills Country Club, of which Townsend was a member, but he rarely was seen there. Instead he preferred to be at home with his family or waterskiing with his sons. He insisted that he was not married to his job and very rarely took work home with him. "I work from 8:30 in the morning until 5:15 at night, and I go home. . . . I've said many times that I have 234,000 people helping me here. And if I've got to work an extra two hours, there's something wrong."

The fact that Townsend did not take work home reflected in part his ability to identify and quickly resolve problems, an ability that had been noted by his accounting professor at Michigan, William A. Paton. Among the thousands of students Paton taught during a long career at Michigan were Albert Bradley, Frederic Donner, Richard Gerstenberg, and Roger Smith, all of whom were

later chairmen at General Motors (GM); but none of his students, Paton declared, had "a greater flair for financial analysis than Lynn Townsend." "As a student," Paton said, "he had a knack for getting down to essentials and going to work on them. . . . In less than 50 minutes he would complete and get a top grade on a test that took most students two hours."

It was Paton who convinced Townsend, after he received his M.B.A. in 1941, not to waste his talents by opening an accounting office in a small town, as Townsend had planned. Townsend instead went to Detroit and was hired as an accountant by a major firm, Ernst & Ernst. He left the firm in 1944 to serve as a disbursing officer on the aircraft carrier *Hornet* in the Pacific. In 1946 he returned to Ernst & Ernst but left the next year when one of the firm's partners, George Bailey, set up his own accounting company and hired Townsend to be the supervising accountant. A few months later Bailey's firm was acquired by Touche, Niven, Bailey & Smart. Townsend continued as supervising accountant and four years later, at age thirty-two, became a partner in the business, then known as Touche, Ross, Bailey & Smart.

The accounting firm's major client was the Chrysler Corporation, and thus for a decade, beginning in 1947, Townsend became thoroughly acquainted with the Chrysler financial operations through his work on the annual audit of the company's books. "Lynn learned so much about Chrysler," Bailey declared, "that I was not really surprised when Tex Colbert [Chrysler's president] hired him away as controller in 1957." When Townsend was asked years later why he had taken the job, he replied that as he had thought about the work he was doing in one of the country's largest accounting firms, he could not picture himself doing that until he was sixty-five. He realized that the Chrysler job represented a risk since "Chrysler was having difficulty, and I didn't know how I'd fit or anything else. But it was a whole new avenue, and I just decided, let's take it and see what happens."

When he came to Chrysler, Townsend said he "never intended to get into operations," but as comptroller he was continuing in his financial career. "I think I'm a very, very good finance man—number one," Townsend, who never lacked self-confidence, declared. He hired some members of Ford's financial staff to help him install at least a semblance of the financial controls that his fellow Michigan alumni Albert Bradley and Frederic Donner had set up at GM thirty years before and that Ford had belatedly adopted in the late 1940s.

But then in 1958 Townsend, whose "grasp of things [was] phenomenal," one of the other Chrysler executives observed, was transferred into operations by being named group vice-president in charge of international operations. Once again Townsend, who in his first year with the company had tried to bring Chrysler's financial activities closer to those of GM and Ford, had to play catch-up with the other big automobile companies whose foreign branches and subsidiaries had for decades contributed in a major way to their profits. Colbert had been seeking unsuccessfully to establish an overseas operation where none existed. In August 1958 Townsend persuaded Chrysler to acquire 25 percent of Simca, a French car company. Within a few years Townsend expanded Chrysler's foreign operations into Latin America, Australia, Asia, and into other parts of Europe, including Spain, where Chrysler bought into Barreiros Diesel, and Great Britain, where Chrysler acquired a stake in Rootes Motors.

These later acquisitions came after Townsend had gone on to higher positions in the company.

Ever more impressed with Townsend, the Chrysler board in 1959 made him a director. Then in 1960 William C. Newberg, Colbert's handpicked successor as president, was forced to resign after only a few weeks in office over conflict-of-interest charges. Although Colbert resumed the presidency, his involvement in the Newberg case virtually destroyed his ability to run the company. In December 1960 Townsend was named administrative vice-president and assumed responsibility for day-to-day Chrysler operations.

During the seven months preceding Colbert's resignation in 1961, George Love, a Pittsburgh businessman and member of the Chrysler board, directed the effort to find a new president. After failing to persuade such GM notables as Edward Cole and Semon Knudsen to take the job, he turned to Townsend, who reportedly had boasted when he came to Chrysler that he would be president in two years. It took him four, not two years, but on July 27, 1961, two months after celebrating his forty-second birthday, Townsend was named president to succeed Colbert. Townsend said at the time that he had been chosen because of the confidence he had expressed in Chrysler's future. Within a short time Love, who in September assumed the post of chairman in order to monitor Townsend's actions, declared that the directors realized they had picked the right man "more by fortune than deliberation."

Within a year after taking office, Townsend was being hailed for revitalizing Chrysler; by the end of 1962 he was on the cover of *Time* magazine. The actions for which he would probably be best remembered had been initiated while he was administrative vice-president and stemmed from what George Love termed his ability to see "figures as living things to base decisions upon and fit all the pieces together." Looking at the Chrysler puzzle, Townsend concluded that not all the pieces were needed, and he launched a cost-cutting program that reduced annual production and operating costs by $100 million. A fourth of the white-collar staff was fired, old plants and buildings were closed, and the corporation's executive planes were sold. As a result Chrysler, which had sustained net losses of $5 million on sales of $2.6 billion in 1960, showed a net profit of $11 million in 1961 on reduced sales of $2.1 billion.

Although Townsend's background was in accounting, not production, he recognized that without a good product no amount of cost-cutting was going to maintain a healthy company. Cost-cutting had reduced Chrysler's break-even point, but Chrysler's market share, which had constituted more than 23 percent in 1951, dipped to a low of only 8.3 percent in February 1962. Obviously, increasing sales had to be the next priority in Townsend's campaign to restore Chrysler to its former strong position.

In late 1960 Townsend wisely rejected a proposal to merge Studebaker with Chrysler. The Studebaker name was an honored one, but acquiring a company that was terminally ill and whose cars basically competed with Chrysler's lower priced models did not interest Townsend. Instead he sought to improve the public's perception of Chrysler's cars. An effort was made to upgrade the quality of the vehicles, which had suffered badly during Colbert's 1950s crash program to introduce new models. After several years of Townsend's quality program a difference was noticeable. In previous years a Chicago dealer said, "the doors didn't fit, the moldings didn't jibe, and the upholstery wasn't straight. This year everything fits perfectly." To show his confidence in the company's products, Townsend in 1962 introduced a warranty that covered the engine, transmission, and rear axle for five years or 50,000 miles, far more generous than Ford's one year or 12,000-mile warranty that had led the industry. Townsend estimated that one of every ten Chrysler sales was attributed to this extended warranty. As Chrysler's market share rebounded, Ford and GM, which had been willing to extend their warranty only to two years or 24,000 miles, finally matched Chrysler in 1965, which led Chrysler to expand its coverage to several other components on its 1967 models.

Late in 1961 Townsend hired one of Ford's top designers, Elwood Engel, to begin a move away from the extreme styling practices that Virgil Exner had adopted in the Chrysler models of the late 1950s. The 1962 models were too far along to change, but by spending $125 million, Townsend and Engel were able to incorporate some late changes in the 1963 models before they went into production. These models were more restrained in design than the often bizarre creations of the previous decade, and although such changes represented an industry-wide reaction to the styles of that period, Townsend was hailed for initiating an evolutionary approach to annual model changes in contrast to the revolutionary approach of the 1950s.

While Townsend drew attention to the styling of the Chrysler products, he did not overlook what had always been the strongest selling point of those cars–their engineering. He approved a campaign touting Chrysler's gas-turbine car. Work on such a car had been going on for years, but in 1963 fifty Italian-designed, $250,000 gas-turbine cars were turned over to fifty consumers in an unusual program to gauge the public's reactions to the turbines. The program revealed that people were not interested in paying more for a gas-turbine engine, and Chrysler quietly shelved the project. Still the company had gained an enormous amount of publicity as being on the cutting edge of experimentation.

To make Chrysler more competitive, Townsend in the early 1960s allocated nearly $400 million for new plant construction, four times the amount spent ten years earlier during the last major expansion of Chrysler's facilities. Townsend also increased the number of models Chrysler offered so that by the mid 1960s the company competed in about 90 percent of the markets covered by Ford and GM. In addition Dodge's share of the truck market increased from about 4 percent before Townsend took over to nearly 8 percent by 1965, although Townsend's hopes of grabbing a larger share of the heavy truck market were dashed when the federal government blocked his plan to acquire Mack Truck.

Selling Chrysler's vehicles was the responsibility of its dealers, and at the beginning of Townsend's tenure they were one of the weakest elements in the Chrysler organization. The corporation had provided little help to its dealers, in contrast to Ford and GM. This neglect, combined with the bad reputation Chrysler's cars had acquired in the late 1950s, resulted in mass defections, leaving the company by 1961 with a dealer network badly depleted in numbers and ability. In a move that spoke volumes about the confidence the company had in its own management teams, Townsend went outside the company, as he had when he had raided Ford to beef up Chrysler's financial and design staffs. Virgil Boyd was brought in from American Motors and Stewart Venn was lured away from Ford to revive the Chrysler dealer network. In 1964 Townsend set up the Chrysler Credit Corporation, shortly renamed Chrysler Financial, to provide wholesale and retail credit to Chrysler dealers as GM and Ford had been doing for years.

By 1965 the new policies had added 1,100 Chrysler outlets, with 200 to 300 new ones planned over each of the following three years. Chrysler still lagged well behind GM and Ford in the number of its dealers, but Townsend used a clever marketing technique to create the illusion that this was not so. All Chrysler dealers, no matter what cars they sold, were identified by the same large blue-and-white signs sporting the Pentastar. The idea originated with Howard Johnson's familiar orange roofs. "I said in my mind there's a million Howard Johnsons out there," declared Townsend. One day, however, when he checked, he "was surprised how few there were. I said, why do I think there're so many . . . ? Well, because of their orange roofs and because you immediately identify them. And I said, well, our problem is that our dealers don't have any identity. . . . Let's create an identity for them, so people will think we have a million dealers."

The Pentastar, which was displayed outside all Chrysler factories and offices, as well as at all dealerships, on all Chrysler vehicles, on the workers' hard hats, and on the lapels of company executives, symbolized Chrysler's rebirth under Townsend's direction. Sales rose to $5.3 billion in 1965, two and a half times the figures for 1961, Townsend's first year in office, and 23 percent above 1964's sales. Chrysler's market share was back up to 16 percent, double what it had been in the early months of Townsend's presidency, and earnings for 1965 exceeded $233 million, up 9.2 percent over the previous year. In addition to automobiles, Townsend aggressively pushed Chrysler's involvement with the space program, defense, chemicals, marine engines, and air conditioning, and in 1967 established a real estate division that was soon involved in a wide range of land developments.

Reviewing this record in 1965, *Forbes* magazine noted that this time, unlike in the 1950s when Chrysler was always making a comeback only to slip behind again, the response to the query " 'Is Chrysler's new strength a flash in the pan?' is almost certainly 'No.' " Wall Street obviously agreed, as it bid up the price of Chrysler stock by 1965 to five times its 1962 price. A year later, in December 1966, Chrysler's board of directors promoted Townsend to the chairman's office being vacated by George Love. But conditions at Chrysler began to worsen, and Townsend soon faced the same kinds of pressures that had forced Colbert to an early retirement.

To the outside world Chrysler's problems were not immediately apparent, and Townsend continued to be hailed as a miracle worker, as sales and market share continued to rise in the late 1960s. But that rise in market share was a problem. Chrysler's debt level, quite modest when Townsend took over, was increased enormously after 1966 in order to finance his expansion programs. Increased sales and market share were essential to maintaining the confidence of the banking community in Chrysler's ability to handle its debt. "We'd look at the numbers," one executive recalled, "and say, 'Last year we got twelve percent of this market segment, so this year we'll shoot for thirteen and a half.' " Production schedules were set according to such optimistic and often unrealistic projections, and in order to reach the required volume, more cars were built than were ordered. The inventory of unordered cars, called the "sales bank," was stored in lots all over Detroit and across the river at the Windsor Raceway. Plant managers were pressured at the end of a quarter to meet their quotas, and in the rush to comply, quality standards went out the window. District sales managers were under extreme pressure to force the cars on the dealers, who soon learned that the company was so desperate to reduce inventory that they simply had to wait, and they would be offered ever larger incentives to take the vehicles.

As long as consumer demand remained high, the risk involved with the high inventories could be minimized, and the bankers were impressed with the production figures and the number of cars shipped from the factory (even though they may have only been shipped to a storage lot). But the public did not like the 1969 models, and when the drop in sales was accelerated by a recession in 1970, Townsend was forced to cut back on production, curtail construction projects, and reduce staff. Improved economic conditions sent sales rebounding in 1972 and 1973, and Townsend was credited with engineering another Chrysler turnaround. The good times were short-lived as Chrysler faced new problems that were more easily met by Ford and GM. Government requirements regarding safety, and especially environmental protective, features were harder for Chrysler to absorb because of the smaller number of cars over which it could spread the cost. But the crippling blow came late in 1973 with the sudden rise in oil prices resulting from the developments in the Middle East and the demand that soon arose from the public and the government for smaller, more fuel-efficient cars.

At the end of the 1950s, when the industry had first been faced with a demand for small cars, Chrysler under Colbert had responded with the Plymouth Valiant and Dodge Dart, two of the more successful small cars. But under Townsend, Chrysler did not follow GM, Ford, and American Motors in the early 1970s by introducing subcompacts which competed with Volkswagen, Toyota, and other foreign producers. Like most Americans, Townsend liked big cars, and Chrysler's failure to introduce its own subcompact may have been in part because he believed the demand for such cars would be of short duration. He also claimed that Chrysler could not build a profitable subcompact, but others suspected that Chrysler did not have the resources in 1969 and 1970 to even begin such a development. Engineering and design had suffered some of the deepest cuts in Townsend's austerity programs, while his ambitious expansion programs left little money available to put a subcompact into production. Thus, although Chrysler still had its compact lines, its overall mix of cars was heavily weighted with big, full-size cars when the fuel crisis arrived in 1974. Save for the Colt, a "captive import" made in Japan by Mitsubishi, a company in which Chrysler had a minority interest, Chrysler dealers lacked the small cars that were suddenly in demand. In the last quarter of 1974 Chrysler sustained record losses of $74 million, and a *Business Week* cover pictured acres of big Chrysler models stored at the Michigan State Fairgrounds, part of an inventory of 360,000 such cars the company could not sell.

Townsend again resorted to drastic measures, firing more than 15,000 white-collar workers including 80 percent of the engineers, and over 30 percent of the hourly workers, halting new construction and restructuring Chrysler's complicated debt load. Then in February 1975 he inaugurated the practice of giving buyers rebates if they bought a car, a move that drew much criticism within the industry but which would become a standard selling technique in the 1980s. The losses continued to mount–$94.1 million in the first quarter of 1975–and at the annual meeting that spring Townsend came under heavy attack from the stockhold-

ers for his management practices. Townsend still had support on the board of directors, but when it met on July 3 he surprised everyone by announcing his retirement, as of October 1, 1975. Upon his recommendation the chairmanship was turned over to John Riccardo, whom Townsend had been grooming as his successor since the 1960s. Townsend, who expressed his confidence that Chrysler had turned the corner in this latest crisis, announced that he was also resigning as a director, declaring that he did not approve of retired executives staying around on the board and second-guessing the new administration.

Townsend in 1975 was only fifty-six years old, but he appeared to be older. The strain of the job had taken its toll on a man who had appeared younger than his age when he first took over fourteen years earlier. Now he was clearly exhausted, and two years after leaving Chrysler he suffered a heart attack. But he bounced back and by the end of the decade was described as much more relaxed, spending several months each year at his home in Hawaii and returning, tanned and fit, to his home in suburban Detroit.

In 1979 Townsend emerged briefly from the obscurity of business executives who have fallen from lofty positions of power. Chrysler had, as he predicted, recovered as the nation's economy rebounded, but in 1978 Chrysler was faced with the worst crisis in its history. The empire Townsend had built was dismantled as foreign and domestic divisions were sold off in a desperate effort to keep the creditors at bay. By 1979 extraordinary measures were being taken, and the corporation once again went outside the company to hire ex-Ford executive Lee Iacocca to head the company. When Iacocca fired nearly all the top Chrysler executives and replaced them with Ford recruits, it was natural to evaluate Townsend's administration to determine to what extent he was to blame for Chrysler's nearly fatal collapse.

Undeniably Townsend could not escape responsibility for much that had weakened the company in the 1970s. Although he was always clearly in charge and, unlike Colbert, did not back off when division heads objected to the changes he was making, he left in place an administrative structure top-heavy with highly paid vice-presidents who ran their divisions like little fiefdoms, without the controls found at GM and Ford. In addition the financial controls that Townsend had installed were inadequate, and Iacocca declared that he was aston-ished to find that "nobody in the whole place seemed to fully understand what was going on when it came to financial planning and projecting." In contrast with GM and Ford, Iacocca declared, Chrysler was being "run like a small grocery store."

Yet Townsend's record in the 1960s was an impressive one. He was, one longtime Chrysler official declared, "probably the most creative and energetic" leader the company had "ever had, Iacocca included." He had made Chrysler once again a strong number three automaker. Beginning in the late 1960s, however, Townsend's personality, associates felt, began to change. Always a hard-driving leader who was famous for goading executives with a "damned long needle," he became testier, and the needle was applied in a far less friendly way. He seemed to be losing interest in the job, and decisions which had once been based on an exhaustive study of the situation were now often made on the basis of only a casual acquaintance with the issues. He developed more outside interests. Rumors that he might go into politics never became reality, but he did become active in New Detroit, the civic organization formed after the 1967 Detroit riots that tried to deal with the problems that had caused them. These developments all may have made him

less able to cope with the unprecedented problems that the industry confronted in the 1970s, problems that proved almost as difficult for GM and Ford to handle as they were for Chrysler.

There were those, like Douglas Fraser of the United Auto Workers who became a member of the Chrysler board at the end of the 1970s, who dismissed Townsend as "a bad manager." In contrast, the well-respected industry observer Arvid Jouppi declared that he had been "a good manager," whose technique "was to swing for the fences each time. He was a long ball hitter who occasionally struck out, and when he did he looked bad." But Jouppi, although sympathetic to Townsend, did not think in 1979 that he was likely to end up in the history books as "a hero–because the pieces he put together were unable to stay together."

References:

"Can Chrysler Make It Stick?," *Forbes*, 96 (September 15, 1965): 19-26;

Michael Moritz and Barrett Seaman, *Going for Broke: The Chrysler Story* (New York: Doubleday, 1981);

"Out, but not down, Lynn Townsend tells how he built Chrysler and why he left it," *Detroit Free Press*, August 10, 1975;

Robert Reich and John D. Donahue, *New Deals: The Chrysler Revival and the American System* (New York: Times Books, 1985);

Time, 80 (December 28, 1962): 52-53;

Time, 106 (July 21, 1975): 46.

Trucks

by William R. Childs

Ohio State University

The modern truck, in contrast to its cousins the train and automobile, has been neglected by academic and popular writers alike. Unlike the train, which required a large number of employees to operate it, and unlike the automobile, which allowed American expressions of freedom and wanderlust, the truck reflected an age-old individualistic business endeavor—one man, one truck hauling goods from one point to another. The truck eventually followed the modern trend of collective action in the economic and political markets, which the railways had done so much to develop. The truck had evolved by the mid twentieth century to become an important force in the national transportation system.

Much as the steel rail and steam locomotive had solved the problem of hauling heavy loads over long distances, so too did the internal combustion engine of the late nineteenth century encourage the moving of small shipments more quickly and efficiently than did horses, railways, or steam wagons. The technology of the gasoline engine made possible the emergence of the modern truck, but not until the military during World War I demanded motorized vehicles to supply large-scale armies was that technology realized. At first, in the 1910s, the motorized truck supplanted local delivery wagons in urban areas and extended hauling of goods into areas not easily served by the railways. In the 1920s surplus war trucks supported the full emergence of the trucking business in the United States. The truck's low costs and flexibility suited well the shifting demands of the consumer culture; for short distances (local delivery to 250 miles), the truck simply outstripped the rigid railway's ability to deliver goods quickly on demand.

Once the truck's effectiveness had been recognized, manufacturers increased production and improved the technology. Financial investment topped $2 billion in 1926 and by the early 1930s medium-sized trucks outnumbered smaller delivery trucks. Improvements in tires (pneumatic), lighting (electric headlamps and stoplights), and refrigeration techniques increased the capabilities of trucking. The advent of the "fifth wheel" (originally used on intracity delivery wagons) enhanced the truck's flexibility, for with the fifth wheel the trucker could "drop" a trailer at a dock and, while that trailer was being loaded, the trucker could hook up his tractor to another trailer and haul it to another destination. Such innovations as the tractor-trailer made the truck even more competitive with the railroads as the distances trucks traveled expanded to include trips from the Midwest to the East Coast. Intercity truckers never hauled more ton-miles than the railroads, but they took from the railways highly valued freight (express shipments, household goods, and retail products). The variety of trucks underscored the atomistic nature of the business: trucks helped build highways (dump trucks), hauled farm and ranch products (refrigerated and cattle trucks), and transported dry goods and retail products (vans and flatbed trucks).

Such expansion, however, not only cut into the railway revenue, but also strained the existing highway system. As a result truckers faced more and more state regulation of their business. Entry into trucking was curtailed to protect the railways from competition and the highways from congestion and destruction. Most state laws in the 1920s and early 1930s restricted the size of trailers, which threatened the further expansion of trucking. In response truck manufacturers developed the "cabover" tractor, in which the driver's seat, steering wheel, clutch, gearshift, and dashboard rested directly over the engine. Such a shortened tractor, along with lighter trailers, allowed the trucker to haul more freight and still remain within legal limits.

The 1938 Dodge truck utilized a cab-over-engine design

Paradoxically, trucking grew during the depression of the 1930s. Even as total freight tonnage fell, trucks hauled more and the railroads less because the costs and flexibility inherent in trucking served the needs of shippers looking for the cheapest possible transport. Expansion of trucking, however, harmed truckers as well as railways. Unemployed workers found it fairly easy to buy a truck on time and to enter the business. Intense competition for diminishing freight ensued, and entries into and exits from the business increased in frequency. It was at this point that trucking was recognized in transportation circles as a viable industry.

By the 1930s trucking had expanded from an essentially one-man, one-truck ad hoc business to include an identifiable economic structure that included several kinds of trucking. This underlying economic structure would remain essentially intact into the late twentieth century. The largest number of truckers were the common carriers. These truck firms (following regulatory legacies dating to medieval England) were required to serve any and all shippers willing to pay; in return the states agreed to protect them from unfair competition. That proved difficult, for there had emerged two other kinds of trucking–private and contract–that were difficult to control. Private truckers (farmers for the most part, but also some manufacturers and retailers) were historically not subject to state control; trucking was really only incidental to their main business. Contract

truckers, however, were transport agents, yet they did not follow the rules of common carriage. Technically, but not always in reality, these contract truckers engaged in special hauling–oil field equipment, oversized loads, lumbering, household goods, and the like. Too often, however, they picked only those shipments that were convenient or paid the most and left to the common carriers the less desirable hauls. By 1932 leading common carriers recognized that they too would have to follow the modern trend toward organization if they were to protect their business.

Issues other than rate-cutting plagued all truckers, however. Many citizens (in some cases encouraged by railway lobbyists) complained that the trucks were too dangerous to the general motoring public because they blocked highways, moved too slowly, and were driven by unqualified drivers. Closely related was the issue of subsidies: were the trucks paying their "fair share" of the cost of constructing the highways?

Thus, trucking followed the twentieth-century trend of organized political response and increased government regulation of the economy. First on the local level, then on the state level, truckers joined in associations designed to exchange information on business practices and to defend the business before state legislators who wanted to curtail its expansion. In the late 1920s and early 1930s private efforts failed to make the associational movement

Since the introduction of this 1957 Hendrickson model, major developments in wind resistance, fuel economy, and engine power have taken place in truck design (courtesy of Hendrickson Manufacturing Company)

national in scope. When the Great Depression exacerbated the tensions, however, the New Deal's National Recovery Administration in 1933 forced truckers to combine into one national trade association. At first such an organization seemed doomed, for it included in its membership truckers who competed against one another for business (contract and common carriers), as well as truckers who had very little to do with one another (tank trucks and dump trucks, for example). Nonetheless the American Trucking Associations (ATA) worked with state and federal officials to design a regulatory system based on the economic structure of the industry. In 1935, through the Motor Carrier Act, Congress placed interstate trucking under the control of the Interstate Commerce Commission (ICC). Even though the ICC was associated with the railroads, it regulated trucking, with advice from the ATA, as a separate industry with its own particular problems. These private-public efforts stabilized the competitive business of trucking, but some unintended consequences emerged: individual initiative and innovation were curtailed, and the industry was not al-

lowed to integrate naturally with other transportation modes.

Trucks grew larger and more had diesel engines after the 1930s, but little innovation occurred in the fundamental nature of the truck. Factory sales of trucks with diesel engines (domestic) were only 3,684 in 1948; but increased to 22,883 in 1958; 91,801 in 1970; and 324,471 in 1985. Low fuel prices before the 1970s did not move the manufacturers to build lighter rigs, but rather to construct still larger tractors and trailers.

During World War II the truck fell under the control of the Office of Defense Transportation. Generally, along with other transportation modes, the truck contributed greatly to the American war effort, both at home and on the battlefield. During the late 1940s and the 1950s the major problem facing trucking was the lack of a national road system that could withstand and facilitate the use of heavier trucks. Joining urban planners and engineers, truckers lobbied for a national system, and in 1956 President Dwight D. Eisenhower signed the Inter-

The double trailer, introduced in 1960, increased the economy and efficiency of motor freight haulage

state Highway Act creating the 42,500-mile road system (97 percent complete in the 1980s).

Along with other regulated industries, trucking came under increasing attacks from reformers in the 1960s and 1970s. The stable system created in the 1930s and reaffirmed during and after the war (especially through antitrust immunity granted in the Reed-Bulwinkle Act of 1948), seemed too inflexible to economists. Not only was innovation lacking, but the rate system also seemed too rigid and too costly to American consumers. Despite lobbying by truckers and shippers alike, the economists won the argument and in the late 1970s and early 1980s, Congress engaged in a so-called "deregulation" movement that extended to trucks, rails, and airlines.

Trucks had not undergone the extensive innovative development that airplanes had after World War II. Despite futuristic designs available in the 1950s, truckers and truck manufacturers clung to the old models, adding only larger engines, some driver comforts, and, for the independent (contract) truckers, glittering chrome fittings, a nonservice-

able reflection of the individuality inherent in trucking from the beginning.

The decade of the 1970s promoted changes. With the energy shocks of 1973 and 1979, truckers sought ways in which to cut costs in order to pay the higher fuel bills (which had increased from about $.40 to more than $1.00 per gallon). At first regulated trucks were helped when the ICC allowed fuel surcharges on waybills, thus passing fuel costs on to the consumer. Aerodynamic innovations came forth, such as windscreens on top of the tractor to lessen wind resistance and thus improve fuel economy. Some headway was made in making engines more efficient, but still too many trucks coaxed only 4 to 6 miles per gallon. In the 1980s truck lobbyists found success in persuading lawmakers to authorize "doubles" and "triples" (one tractor hauling two or three trailers at one time) on some interstate highways.

The changes wrought in the 1970s had cultural consequences as well. For the first time the truck became a widely regarded symbol of Americana. Use of the Citizens Band radio (CB) by truckers to avoid weigh stations and police spread to other areas of society: auto enthusiasts bought CBs in order to listen to the "colorful" language over the airwaves, and Hollywood brought out several movies highlighting the trucker. Some equated the long-haul trucker with the cowboy of the late nineteenth century: a supposedly lonesome figure on the road not bothering anyone else and not wanting to be bothered, but willing to help people in distress. In fact, for both the old cowboy and the modern trucker, the image of a businessman competing in an atomistic market would be more appropriate.

Continuities rather than discontinuities mark the history of the truck in America. The problems plaguing first-generation truckers in the 1920s and 1930s haunt their children and grandchildren in the later decades of the century. Many are inherent in the industry: nontrucking citizens still complain about large trucks blocking the highways and the subsidy issue still occasions heated debates. Other problems have been resurrected as a result of deregulation. More entries—and exits—since 1980 have reminded old-time truckers of the early years of their industry. Nonetheless, most articles once hauled by the railroad are now hauled by truck.

References:

William R. Childs, *Trucking and the Public Interest: The*

Emergence of Federal Regulation, 1914-1940 (Knoxville: University of Tennessee Press, 1985);

Denis Miller, *The Illustrated Encyclopedia of Trucks and Buses* (New York: Mayflower Books, 1982);

Mark H. Rose, *Interstate: Express Highway Politics, 1941-1956* (Lawrence: Regents Press of Kansas, 1979).

Archives:

Material concerning trucking is located in Record Group 9, National Recovery Administration, National Archives, Washington, D.C., and in "Woods Highway Truck Library," New York Times Oral History Program (Glenn Rock, New Jersey: Microfilming Corporation of America, 1975).

Preston Thomas Tucker

(September 21, 1903-December 26, 1956)

by George S. May

Eastern Michigan University

CAREER: A variety of positions, primarily in the automotive industry (1916-1940); owner, Tucker Aviation Corporation (1940-1942); executive vice-president and general manager, Higgins-Tucker Motor Company (1942-1944); general manager, Ypsilanti Machine & Tool Company (1944-1946); president, Tucker Corporation (1946-1949).

For an automobile manufacturer whose company apparently produced only fifty-one automobiles, including prototypes, Preston Thomas Tucker has received an inordinate amount of attention, not only in print but also in a motion picture based on his life which opened in 1988. The best explanation for this interest would seem to be that in the immediate post-World War II period he represented a welcome throwback to the flamboyant promoter who had been so common in the early years of the automobile industry but who had been largely superseded by less colorful business leaders as the industry matured.

Tucker was born on September 21, 1903, in Capac, a small town in Michigan's Thumb district. His father, Shirl Tucker, died when Tucker was two years old. Tucker's mother, Lucille, supported herself and Preston and his younger brother by teaching, eventually moving her family to what became the Detroit suburb of Lincoln Park. Tucker quickly became intensely interested in automobiles, as did many boys who grew up in the heart of the industry. He helped to support himself while attending Cass Technical School in Detroit by working as an office boy at Cadillac. In that position he worked for D. McCall White, a Cadillac official whom Tucker,

with much fanfare, some thirty years later hired to work for him at his new company.

The job at Cadillac was the first of many positions that Tucker held in the following years, so many and so overlapping that even Tucker was unable to put them in order in his entry in *Who's Who in America*. However, aside from a short time when he served on the police force in Lincoln Park, the jobs were related to automobiles in one way or another. Although Tucker worked briefly for Ford, he soon demonstrated a showmanship that enabled him to make a name for himself selling Studebakers, Chryslers, Pierce-Arrows, and Packards. Tucker's main interest, however, was in racing, and in the mid 1930s he joined Harry A. Miller, famed builder of cars that dominated the annual Indianapolis 500 races, and worked with him intermittently until Miller's death in 1943.

Aside from this work on racing cars, Tucker's career as a manufacturer began in 1940 when he formed the Tucker Aviation Corporation to manufacture a combat vehicle that he had designed for use by the army. The company was located in Ypsilanti, Michigan, which became home base for Tucker, his wife, Vera Fuqua, whom he had married in 1923, and their five children for much of the time until his death in 1956. The combat vehicle was much too fast for the army's needs, but officials were interested in the powered gun turret that Tucker had designed for the car. Tucker received a contract to build the turrets and moved his facilities to a larger plant he acquired in Detroit, but when the war came, Tucker said the government took over his patents and his royalty rights. In later years he sued companies for royalties on turrets they had

The Tucker at its world premiere in Chicago on June 19, 1947

produced under his patent. In 1942 Tucker joined forces with Andrew J. Higgins, a New Orleans ship-builder, to produce these turrets and also engines for the torpedo boats Higgins was building for the government. Tucker was executive vice-president and general manager of the company, but the two men had conflicting personalities. Tucker shortly quit and returned to Ypsilanti, where he worked on various war contracts at the Ypsilanti Machine & Tool Company. Tucker listed himself as the firm's general manager but in actuality it was his company.

As the end of the war approached, Tucker gave more and more thought to plans for building an automobile. Because of the complete halt in civilian car production that followed America's entry into the war, demand for cars would be strong after the war. Tucker was only one of many who foresaw an opportunity for a newcomer for the first time since the early 1920s possibly to make a success of a new automobile venture. Only Henry Kaiser and Joseph Frazer came close to achieving that success with their Kaiser-Frazer company that began operating just east of Ypsilanti in the huge

plant at Willow Run where Ford had built bombers during the war. Tucker was one of the more spectacular failures.

Initial reports that came out in 1945 indicated that Tucker planned to build a sports car to be called the Tucker Torpedo. But the public soon learned that Tucker's plans were always subject to change. The sports car became a 4-door sedan, and the name was ultimately changed to the Tucker 48. But regardless of the type of car, it was the radical features that were to be included that drew attention. The engine was designed for the rear and would reportedly produce power equivalent to that of aircraft engines. A hydraulic torque converter would eliminate the need for a transmission and differential. In front, the streamlined car would have a cyclops headlight in the middle while the two outer headlights would be mounted in fenders that would turn with the wheels. The driver would steer from the center, not the left-hand side, and the driver and passengers would sit in a crash-proof interior compartment, one of a number of features designed to ensure passenger safety. Air-cooled brakes, air conditioning, and doors that opened into the roof

The 1948 Tucker, with Preston Tucker at the wheel

were other features listed by the early part of 1946. Through the use of aluminum and plastic construction, the Tucker would weigh only 2,000 pounds and would sell for the equivalent of fifty cents a pound.

Tucker first sought to gain support for the manufacture of his car at a meeting held in the Detroit Athletic Club, but it broke up because Tucker's publicity man and sympathetic biographer, Charles T. Pearson, declared the potential promoters "wanted too big a slice for their effort." The theory endorsed by Tucker supporters that the Detroit automobile establishment conspired to torpedo Tucker's plans probably had its origins with this meeting. Tucker then moved his promotional activities to Chicago, knowing, Pearson claims, that it "could be fatal" if he tried to continue in Detroit. A more likely reason for the move, however, was that Chicago was the site of a huge government-owned plant where Dodge had built airplane engines during the war and which Tucker in February 1946 announced he planned to acquire for the production of his car. Although nothing of the car had been seen except some fanciful artist's sketches, the fact

that the new Tucker Corporation included the names of men who had served in high executive positions with Ford, Plymouth, Dodge, Briggs, and other automotive producers added a much needed element of credibility to the venture and undoubtedly helped Tucker to reach an agreement with the War Assets Administration in September to lease the former Dodge plant. Tucker, who had earlier projected that he would have 25,000 workers turning out 1,000 cars a day on "the largest auto production line under one roof," now talked of peak production in 1,500 cars daily and a staff of 35,000 to 40,000 employees. In addition, however, the price of the car, which had been set at $1,000 a few months before, was now projected to be in the $1,600 to $1,800 range.

To raise money for his company, Tucker sold dealer franchises to individuals who put up $50 in cash for every car they expected to sell during their first two years as a Tucker agent. The deposit would be applied toward the purchase price of the car when the dealer took delivery. The Securities and Exchange Commission (SEC) objected that this arrangement amounted to the sale of a security as defined by the securities laws, and the SEC had not approved any such sale. After considerable legal wrangling, the SEC approved a new agreement whereby the dealer provided only $20 per car but on the understanding that this money "would not be refundable under any circumstances but would be used by the corporation forthwith for general corporate purposes." Although Pearson claims that this dispute hampered Tucker's efforts to raise much needed cash, he still raised $7,168,900 from nearly 2,000 individuals who thought they were going to be dealers or distributors.

Meanwhile, in fall 1946 Tucker signed an underwriting agreement with Floyd D. Cerf, a Chicago investment broker, to handle the sale of $20 million in Class A and Class B stock in the corporation contingent on the issue's approval by the SEC. The agreement with the War Assets Administration (WAA) called for Tucker to provide evidence by March 1, 1947, that he had a capital of $15 million before the lease arrangement became final. The WAA proved to be nothing if not accommodating. It stood by its agreement with Tucker in the latter part of 1946 when another federal agency sought to lease the Chicago plant to a manufacturer of prefabricated housing that did not need any time to prove that it was solvent enough to meet the lease payments. When on March 1, 1947, Tucker advised the WAA that he did not have the $15 million, the agency obligingly gave him a new deadline of July 1, and when he again missed that deadline, it did nothing. Finally on September 12, 1947, Tucker provided the evidence that he could take care of the lease payments, and he was officially granted the use of the war surplus factory.

The reason for the delay was that the SEC had held up the sale of the stock, claiming, for example, that the company's prospectus failed to meet the legal requirements for full disclosure. The problems were resolved, and the stock sale was allowed to proceed but only with a warning from the SEC that prospective stock buyers should be aware that Preston Tucker had put none of his own money into the company, that there had been no significant tests conducted of the car, and that Tucker held no patents on any of the unique features that were to be included on the car. Although the SEC may have cooled the enthusiasm of some potential investors, 54,000 people still came forward in summer 1947 to buy $15.7 million worth of Tucker stock certificates.

The sale, although falling short of the $20 million originally planned, was helped by the fact that in summer 1947 an actual Tucker automobile was displayed, first at a gala World Premiere in Chicago on June 19, 1947, and then at numerous points around the country. At the end of 1946 Tucker had commissioned Alec Tremulis, who had been a stylist for Erret Cord's automotive combine in the 1930s, to design the car. Tremulis had plans prepared within five days, and within one hundred days a full-size prototype of the production car was ready to be painted. The prototype and the production models that Tucker's engineers came up with by early 1948 differed in many ways from the concept that had been originally publicized. The front fenders and their attached headlights did not turn with the wheels, the driver sat on the left, not in the center, and the engine, although located in the rear, was not the monstrous 589-cubic-inch displacement design Tucker had talked about but a 6-cylinder Franklin air-cooled engine which Tucker's engineers converted to a water-cooled engine. Tucker's idea of using a double torque converter that would eliminate the need for a transmission and differential proved to be "a complete fiasco," even Charles Pearson admitted, and was scrapped and replaced by an automatic transmission system. Despite these and other changes the car was still strikingly designed, with the cyclops headlight at the front end being retained. And from the evidence of the fifty or so Tuckers that were actually produced and driven, the car was an exceptional value for its time, even at the price of $2,450 quoted by 1948. But real production never commenced.

What caused the collapse of the Tucker operation is much debated. It is clear that one major cause was friction between Tucker and his other executives. Shortly after the completion of the stock sale Harry A. Toulmin, Jr., a prominent business figure from Dayton, Ohio, resigned as chairman of the board, charging that Tucker would not agree with Toulmin's "written demands that any money raised from the public should be spent and administered under the strictest regulations and controls normal to legitimate business." Shortly afterward the executive vice-president and the treasurer and comptroller, along with several lesser officials, either resigned or were fired, with more bitter words and charges. The loss of most of the experienced automobile men that Tucker had brought into the company was particularly damaging. Pearson claims they left

Preston Tucker with his wife celebrating the first anniversary of the Tucker car

because they had been accustomed to working in established companies and could not adjust to the fact that with Tucker they did not have unlimited money and time in which to develop a new product.

Money was undoubtedly the major source of Tucker's problems by 1948. The $15 million raised from the sale of stock and the several millions coming in from dealer deposits would have sounded more than ample for a new automobile company in the earlier days of the industry, but in the postwar era it was too little for the large-scale operation Tucker planned. Ever resourceful, he approved an ingenious plan to sell car radios, seat covers, and other accessories that the buyers could use in their Tuckers when the cars were available. Incredibly, more than $2.5 million was raised by the sale of such items to buyers who were assured that the purchase gave them top priority when the cars went on sale. In a more traditional approach, Tucker, claiming he had 300,000 advance orders for the cars, applied for a $30-million loan from the Reconstruction Finance Corporation (RFC). Pearson felt that it was manifestly unfair for the RFC to turn down Tucker while granting loans to the Kaiser-Frazer Corporation. While it may be true, as Pearson declares, that Kaiser-Frazer was just as guilty as Tucker of not meeting preproduction claims, the RFC was undoubtedly more interested in the fact that Kaiser-Frazer had been producing and selling cars since 1946 while Tucker had not.

Any further hopes that funds could be found to keep the company afloat were ended in summer 1948 when word leaked out that the SEC was investigating Tucker's operations, contending that stockholders may have been fraudulently misled by Tucker's failure to develop a car with the unique features that had been promised. When the SEC petitioned to be allowed to look at his records, Tucker called it a "fishing expedition" and shortly shut down the plant. He then went off to try to find investors. "We hit every s.o.b. in the country for money," he declared, but no funds were found, and in March 1949 Tucker filed for bankruptcy.

Meanwhile, a federal grand jury probe had brought in an indictment charging Tucker and seven associates with mail fraud conspiracy and violation of securities laws. The case went to trial late in 1949 in Chicago, and the federal attorneys brought in seventy-three witnesses and a mass of documents to show that Tucker and his fellow defendants had used money raised from the sale of stock and dealer franchises for their own benefit, and that the advertising for the car was "a pack of lies" since none of the handful of cars that had been assembled contained any of the radical mechanical features promised. Tucker's attorneys presented no witnesses, contending that it was not necessary to defend something when there had been no offense. The judge instructed the jury that the question it had to decide was whether Tucker had intended to defraud the stockholders or whether he had acted in good faith. Despite the fact that the company had failed to produce cars, he said "good faith is a complete defense." The jury, after due deliberation, acquitted Tucker and his associates on all charges.

Tucker felt vindicated by the jury's decision, but he was out of business. Most of the remains of the defunct automobile operation were auctioned off in August 1950. Later in the 1950s there was talk of a new car, designed by Alexis de Sakhnoffsky, which would be produced in Brazil. But whatever hopes there were for the success of this project ended when it was discovered that Tucker had cancer. He returned home to Ypsilanti and died there on December 26, 1956.

Whatever may be the final verdict on Tucker, his experience illustrated the difficulties that a newcomer in the middle of the twentieth century faced in breaking into the automobile industry. This was true not only for someone like Tucker but also for the more solidly financed and managed Kaiser-Frazer Corporation. It did not take a conspiracy to put Tucker out of business. The market conditions took care of that.

References:

"New Car Makers?," *Business Week* (January 26, 1946): 18-19;

Charles T. Pearson, *The Indomitable Tin Goose: The True Story of Preston Tucker and His Car* (New York: Abelard-Schuman, 1960);

"A Question of Faith," *Time*, 55 (January 30, 1950): 77;

"Torpedo Torpedoed?" *Time*, 49 (June 23, 1947): 79-80;

"Tucker Advances," *Business Week* (September 28, 1946): 25-26;

"Tucker Remains Go on the Auction Block," *Business Week* (August 26, 1950): 22-23;

"Tucker Solidifies," *Business Week* (February 23, 1946): 28;

"Tucker Was Here," *Newsweek*, 33 (March 14, 1949): 62-63;

"Tucker's Troubles," *Time*, 52 (July 12, 1948): 75-76.

United Automobile, Aerospace, and Agricultural Implement Workers of America

by Gilbert J. Gall

Pennsylvania State University

The United Automobile, Aerospace, and Agricultural Implement Workers of America (UAW), an international union currently representing approximately 1 million workers in collective bargaining in a variety of settings, has for years been considered a model of progressive unionism by liberal admirers, and a quasi-socialistic force in American society by conservative detractors in the business world. Dating its beginnings from 1935 as an American Federation of Labor (AFL)-affiliated organization, and from 1936 as a Committee for Industrial Organization (CIO)-associated body, the UAW has celebrated its fiftieth anniversary as an international union. For most of that period it has been on the cutting edge of innovation in collective bargaining, in many ways serving as the model of large-scale industrial unionism in the private-sector economy. In politics it has consistently placed itself in alliance with the most liberal elements of the Democratic party, advocating social reform on a variety of fronts.

As with many of the other mass-production unions, in many ways the UAW owes its existence to the labor legislation established during the New Deal era. Since its beginnings at the turn of the century the automotive industry should have been fertile organizing ground for American unions: seasonal work leading to severely depressed annual earnings, generally unsafe working conditions, rampant favoritism by foremen, and the hated "speedup" of production lines were universal grievances among autoworkers. Nevertheless unions had little success in the industry, partly because the skilled craft unions dominating American labor could not organize it effectively along skill lines and *would* not organize it on an industrial, or all-inclusive basis, and partly because employer opposition to unionism was intensely discriminatory.

The Great Depression and the early New Deal labor provisions of the National Industrial Recovery Act (NIRA), which became effective in June 1933, acted as catalysts to change those unfavorable conditions. By this point American business lost considerable social prestige, and those American workers who were still employed, after four years of declining wages, turned to unionism to make demands for an end to their economic misery. Section 7(a) of the law provided generalized guarantees that workers should have the right to bargain collectively with their employers through representatives of their own choosing but did not have a way to enforce violations of that principle. In 1935, after the Supreme Court had declared the NIRA unconstitutional, Congress passed the National Labor Relations Act (NLRA), commonly called the Wagner Act after its author Senator Robert Wagner of New York, which took section 7(a) as its guiding philosophy, enumerated illegal employer unfair labor practices, added procedures for determining questions of union representation, and created an agency, the National Labor Relations Board (NLRB), as a quasi-judicial tribunal that could go into federal court for orders to enforce its decisions.

American unions had never had a guarantee of governmental protection of their constitutional rights to freedom of association before, and autoworkers responded enthusiastically. The AFL, though dominated by craft union leaders, launched into an ambivalent industrial union organizing drive by creating a number of directly chartered federal labor unions in the industry—106 in the year before June 1934 when they organized themselves into a National Council of Auto Workers' Unions in Detroit, Michigan. During the period from 1933 to 1935, however, membership in the federal locals declined precipitously in many areas due to company discrimination against union sympathizers—layoffs in the midst of the depression effectively

The UAW's women's auxiliary picketing in support of the 1937 sit-down strike of GM in Flint, Michigan (courtesy of William Cahn Collection)

chilled the desire to organize no matter how much one might have objected to working conditions. Though membership dropped from 100,000 in 1933 to 23,000 in 1935, the militancy of some of these federal locals during 1934 and 1935–striking successfully for recognition and resolution of shop-floor grievances in some instances–signified that autoworkers could win victories. But to be victorious industry-wide meant organizing on an industrial basis to prevent employers from shifting work from organized to unorganized plants. It was clear to rank-and-file activists that a craft structure in an industry dominated by semiskilled and unskilled mass-production work would never provide workers with the bargaining leverage they needed to confront their employers effectively.

Finally the AFL granted the autoworkers a national union charter, establishing the UAW at a convention in August 1935 in Detroit. Unfortunately, AFL President William Green had caved in to his federation's craft union leaders, making the charter of the national union granted by the AFL fatally flawed: it specified limitations on its organizing jurisdiction to protect future craft interests, and the automobile unionists could not even choose their own officers. Francis Dillon, the UAW president named by Green, in fact, had very little experience in the auto industry. After nine months of agitation auto unionists convened a second time at South Bend, Indiana, in spring 1936 and cast off AFL influence. Delegates elected Homer Martin, a Kansas City autoworker with a background as a Baptist preacher, as president and George Addes, an activist of the militant Toledo, Ohio, federal local union, as secretary-treasurer. Soon the newly independent UAW totally cut its formal AFL ties by affiliating with John L. Lewis's CIO, which Lewis, regarded as a renegade by the old guard of the AFL, founded to foster industrial union organization in all mass-production industries.

Autoworkers had thus established their own democratically controlled union, but as yet had no contracts with the auto companies and less than 30,000 members. Their great challenge was to orga-

The Battle of the Overpass, on March 26, 1937, when UAW organizers were severely beaten by Ford security personnel

nize the industry leader, General Motors (GM), for without that victory there would be no hope to organize other segments of automobile manufacture on a permanent basis. In summer 1936 the UAW began an organizing drive in Flint, Michigan, the center of GM power, under the direction of Wyndham Mortimer, a Cleveland autoworker who had been elected vice-president at the South Bend convention. Mortimer, reputedly a Communist, was an effective and committed organizer and the youthful UAW organization in Flint grew. Mortimer knew, however, that victory over GM would only ultimately come from a recognition strike. The union's leadership only hoped they would be able to build a strong enough organization by that time.

At the very end of December 1936, somewhat unpredictably, the UAW's chance came. A sit-down strike–where workers stayed in the plant and refused to leave or work–broke out in the Flint, Michigan, Fisher Body complex. For the better part of the next six weeks an epic struggle ensued. UAW militants held several plants, the corporation denounced the trespass, and liberal Democratic governor Frank Murphy of Michigan mediated the con-

flict. Unlike the labor struggles of the nineteenth century, however, Murphy refused to evict the strikers because of the revelations of the U.S. Senate's LaFollette Committee investigation into the antilabor practices of GM, which were held concurrently to the strike. Murphy contended that GM's hands were as unclean as the trespassing sit-downers for it was apparent that the mighty corporation had engaged in wholesale violation of the National Labor Relations Act. In mid February 1937, the UAW prevailed. GM recognized the union and signed a contract. Soon afterward the UAW won recognition at the Chrysler corporation after sit-down strikes in Detroit. By the end of 1937 it had 256 locals and had negotiated 400 contracts. It was not until 1941, though, that it defeated the last major holdout, the violently antiunion Ford Motor Company, through a traditional strike at the corporation's huge Rouge Complex in Dearborn, Michigan. By 1941 the UAW represented 461,000 autoworkers and by the end of World War II its membership had risen to 673,000 members.

That the union was able to do this was all the more remarkable for in the first decade of its exis-

Walter P. Reuther, raised, celebrates with supporters his election as UAW president in 1946 (courtesy of the Archives of Labor and Urban Affairs, Wayne State University)

tence it was rent with factionalism. Martin, a pyrotechnical speaker who had a following with autoworkers of southern descent, was a highly unstable personality. As a leader he was inconsistent, administratively incompetent, and viewed by his co-officers as likely to destroy the organization through his erratic behavior; he had, in fact, been sent off on a speaking tour, ostensibly to garner support but in reality as a ruse, during the critical Flint engagement for fear of his impact. Once the initial sit-down battles had been won, Martin, fearful of the growing reputations of other UAW leaders, organized what became called the Progressive Caucus, which generally represented the political right wing of the union. Opposed was the Unity Caucus, the left wing, containing the Socialists like Walter, Victor, and Roy Reuther and the union's Communist activists. Until 1939 the battle for control over the international union raged and almost destroyed it as a going concern for its leadership, consumed in its own power struggles (at one point Martin suspended the entire executive board), had less energy to devote to company confrontations. Finally, after

the Communists split with the Reuthers, who temporarily remained unaligned, John L. Lewis had influential CIO officials Philip Murray and Sidney Hillman work to reinstate the board and engineer the election of R. J. Thomas, an officer out of the Chrysler locals who was acceptable to the warring factions because he was relatively innocuous. Out of that 1939 convention Walter Reuther emerged as head of the GM Department and Martin, who had deserted the CIO with a UAW rump group in 1938, establishing, once again, a UAW-AFL, eventually faded into obscurity.

The presidency of R. J. Thomas likewise collapsed into factionalism. During the war years Walter Reuther marked himself as an ambitious and intelligent leader–good at positioning himself in the internal political battles, capable of leading strikes, equally persuasive in speaking at union conventions or before press and government forums. His wartime production proposals also marked him as an innovative thinker. Opposed to the growing Reuther caucus was the Addes caucus, led by secretary-treasurer George Addes and supported by the Communists and other left-wing elements in the union. Reuther, by this time, had abandoned the socialism of his younger days and moved ever closer to mainstream political liberalism, which in the context of the internal UAW politics of the time, was regarded as the right wing of the union. In 1946 he won election as president, and then consolidated his power in 1947 when enough Reutherites were elected to the executive board to give him control of the union.

For the next twenty-four years Reuther led the UAW as president and put his imprint on the union as no other leader has before or since. Reuther, a skilled tool-and-die worker, hailed from a family of German social-democratic immigrants and was born in West Virginia. He and two of his brothers, Victor and Roy, became imbued with their father Valentine's social-democratic vision and trade unionist commitments at an early age. Although Walter Reuther's sentiments always lay on the left of the political spectrum, this did not prevent him from stridently attacking Communist influence within the UAW. As early as 1940 it became evident that the Communist activists, who had in fact been some of the ablest organizers of the young union, would become enemies of the Reutherites. Reuther scored the far leftists for their subservience to the needs of the Soviet Union's wartime foreign policy at the expense of the needs of UAW members, and after assuming undisputed control in 1947 deposed what was left of his opposition. In the words of one of his slogans for the presidency of the union, which became an oft-repeated UAW leadership chant during the next quarter of a century, the union would finally end its years of infighting through "teamwork in the leadership and solidarity in the ranks."

With Reuther's accession, the UAW found itself in a somewhat unique position. The bitter internal factional battle was now over, the auto industry was almost completely organized, and the economy faced neither depression nor wartime regulation. Labor relations, that is, its relationship to the major auto employers, now loomed largely as the union's main order of business. The new union president's vision of the future was an amalgamation of European social-democratic sentiments, a proclivity for emphasizing the necessity of political involvement to stimulate Keynesian economic expansion, and traditional union collective bargaining objectives. The result, according to Nelson Lichtenstein, was that "Reutherism" as a union ideology meant

the "use of collective bargaining as a lever to shift the balance of forces in the political economy and open wide the welfare state."

While successful in some arenas, Reuther's "social unionism" approach did not achieve all he hoped. His first assault trying to establish his vision came during the GM strike of 1946 and met defeat. During that critical strike, which in retrospect seems to have set the parameters of post-World War II collective bargaining, Reuther sought to tie the union's collective bargaining objectives to the pricing policies of the corporation (and hence profit margins). The company's hard-line refusal to countenance any union priorities save those of increasing wages and benefits forced Reuther to back down. The pattern set was one in which management would control the enterprise as the union bargained for increasingly attractive wage and benefit packages.

Although Reuther never managed to achieve the social transformation he hoped for, the UAW made tremendous strides in collective bargaining during the 1950s. Innovations such as cost-of-living escalators, annual improvement factors, supplemental unemployment benefits, and the like elevated his reputation even during the conservative Eisenhower years. As the auto industry expanded and contracted, so did the union's membership; the UAW had 1.4 million members in 1953, but by 1962 it had dropped to approximately 1.1 million before going on the rise again. Nevertheless the UAW was always one of the largest, and at times *the* largest union in the country. Its headquarters—Solidarity House—remained in Detroit, Michigan, and housed a large technical and professional staff in a multitude of departments to service the locals in the various regions, the geographic midlevel administrative structures composing the union. It also maintained a Washington office, as did most other unions of influence.

While the UAW president never gave up the effort to push collective bargaining goals towards industrial democracy when he could, he understandably turned to politics to achieve those aims that apparently were not forthcoming from his direct engagements with the auto companies. He sought and achieved close ties with the liberal luminaries of the Democratic party and pushed all levels of his union into more active political involvement. Politicians also courted him for support, for not only was he the president of the UAW but, from

UAW members participating in the 1963 civil rights march on Washington, D.C. (courtesy of the Archives of Labor and Urban Affairs, Wayne State University)

1952 through 1955, also the president of the CIO as well. And, in 1955 he assisted in facilitating the merger of the AFL and CIO, taking a place as its widely regarded second-in-command after George Meany. Indeed, many expected him to succeed Meany upon the older man's retirement, an event which never occurred.

The decade of the 1960s brought the hope that American society was finally achieving some of the beneficial social welfare legislation the UAW under Reuther had been advocating for years, even as the liberal coalition that achieved those victories unraveled due to the war in Vietnam. Reuther and the UAW were one of the labor mainstays of President Lyndon Johnson's Great Society. The UAW threw its backing behind both the civil rights movement and the United Farm Workers struggles and began to publicly criticize the stodginess and inactivity of the AFL-CIO hierarchy under Meany. Finally Reuther's restiveness and personal disagreements with Meany caused the UAW's withdrawal from the unified federation in 1968. But even before that point the UAW had come to be generally regarded as one of the more progressive, noncomplacent unions in America. It was a reputation that the

union's successors would extend after Reuther and his wife May died in a plane crash in May 1970 on their way to Black Lake, the UAW's impressive multimillion-dollar labor education center in northern Michigan.

And under its last three presidents, Leonard Woodcock (1970-1977), Douglas Fraser (1977-1983), and Owen Bieber (1983-   ), the Reuther philosophy has remained dominant, though the collective bargaining and political environments have changed dramatically. Both Woodcock and Fraser (who led the UAW into reaffiliation with the AFL-CIO in the early 1980s), in fact, served as Reuther's administrative assistants and strongly shared his ideological commitments. Even Bieber, the first leader not of the founding generation, can be said to be cast in the Reuther mold. In the years following Reuther's death the union has had to cope with the fact of a rapidly transforming world auto industry and collateral decline of the United States' manufacturing industries. Membership has slipped from the high point of 1.6 million in 1978 to just under 1 million members currently. Employment levels in the auto industry have fallen sharply as both foreign competition took market share away from

Wendell W. Larsen, left, a Chrysler vice-president, confers with Howard G. Paster, a UAW official, on their lob-bying efforts to secure federal loans for Chrysler in 1979 (courtesy of George Tames/New York Times)

domestic producers and companies put more re-sources into automation to increase productivity. The UAW leadership's negotiation of concessionary contracts during the early 1980s–in return for guar-antees of job security and increased involvement in corporate decision-making–have been lauded by some observers but have also stirred internal turbu-lence.

The disturbing impact of these developments was clearly evident at the union's fiftieth anniver-sary (1935-1985) celebration during the twenty-eighth constitutional convention in June 1986. The theme of the gathering–"We make our own history"–was eloquent testimony to the tenacity of the re-form spirit still dominant in the UAW. Despite that, however, the convention had a good deal of inter-nal dissension. Delegates intensely debated the wisdom of the leadership's survival strategy of exper-imenting with advanced forms of labor-management cooperation, using the nonpattern agreement between GM and the UAW for the corpo-ration's new facility in Spring Hill, Tennessee, as an example. Also, the challenged election of the direc-tor of Region 5, where the incumbent barely sur-

vived the campaign of an insurgent assistant op-posed to the top leadership's directions, was further proof of internal opposition. Most significantly, per-haps, was the ratification of the de-parture of the Canadian autoworker UAW locals, who disaffiliated because of dismay over the strate-gic positions of the international union in tumultu-ous bargaining rounds of the 1980s.

These occurrences, though, belie the charge by critics, both within and outside of the union, that the motto of "teamwork in the leadership, solidar-ity in the ranks" has come to mean a one-party orga-nization with very little true democracy. The last generation of UAW leaders have tried to remain true to the union's progressive heritage, making the adjustments they have because they have been con-vinced that it was in the long-term interest of their members to do so. In so doing they have never adopted the parochial attitudes common to some other labor organizations. The UAW leadership from Reuther onward has always maintained that the union and its members could not advance un-less all of American society advanced. It has periodi-cally sought to serve as a voice or in other ways to assist those segments of our society seeking to become a part of the American dream of equality and opportunity. While through most of its history its membership has been centered in the three main industries reflected in its official name, in recent years it has tried, like many other unions, to broaden its representational base. It now services clerical, professional, and public employees, among others, though the automobile, aerospace, and agricultural implement sectors will remain the most powerful groupings in the union in the near future.

References:

"Automobile, Aerospace and Agricultural Implement

Workers of America; International Union, United (UAW)," in *Labor Unions,* edited by Gary M. Fink (Westport: Conn.: Greenwood Press, 1977);

John Barnard, *Walter Reuther and the Rise of the Auto Workers* (Boston: Little, Brown, 1983);

Henry Guzda, "Constitutional Convention Marks Golden Anniversary of the UAW," *Monthly Labor Review,* 109 (October 1986): 23;

Nelson Lichtenstein, "UAW Bargaining Strategy and Shop-Floor Conflict: 1946-1970," *Industrial Relations,* 24 (Fall 1985): 360;

A. H. Raskin, "Walter Reuther's Great Big Union," *Atlantic Monthly* (October 1963): 90;

Jack Stieber, *Governing the UAW* (New York: Wiley, 1962).

Harold Sines Vance

(August 22, 1890-August 31, 1959)

by Alan R. Raucher

Wayne State University

CAREER: Purchasing agent, Studebaker Corporation (1915-1918); production engineer, Bethlehem Steel Company (1918); assistant to president (1919-1922), general sales manager (1923-1926), vice-president (1926-1933), receiver (1933-1935), chairman of the board (1935-1948), chairman and president (1948-1953), president, Studebaker Corporation (1953-1954); chairman of the executive committee, Studebaker-Packard Corporation (1954-1955); member, Atomic Energy Commission (1955-1959).

Harold Sines Vance, Studebaker executive, was born in Port Huron, Michigan, on August 22, 1890. The son of Samuel W. Vance, a lawyer and circuit judge, and Carrie Sines Vance, he attended public schools. After reading law with the partner of his deceased father, he unsuccessfully sought appointment to the United States Military Academy. In 1910 he took a job at 15¢ an hour as a mechanic's apprentice in a local machine shop owned by Everitt-Metzger-Flanders (EMF), a Detroit manufacturer of cars and car parts. The twenty-year-old Vance never completed his apprenticeship. His superiors, impressed by his managerial as well as mechanical abilities, transferred him to the stores division.

Vance's career opportunities broadened in 1912 when the recently organized Studebaker Corporation of South Bend, Indiana, acquired EMF. With a talent for solving difficult problems and a willingness to assume responsibilities, Vance rose rapidly in the larger corporation. Within three years he was purchasing agent with managerial responsibilities for assigning other employees to suitable jobs. Except for eight months during World War I, when he worked as a production engineer for Bethlehem Steel, Vance spent the rest of his business career with Studebaker, rising to chairman of the board and, eventually to president.

Vance's career at Studebaker received a major boost from Albert Russel Erskine, the corporation's ambitious and powerful president. When Vance returned in 1919 from his wartime assignment with Bethlehem Steel, Erskine appointed him his personal assistant. Three years later Erskine placed him in charge of export sales, and the following year Vance became the general sales manager for the Studebaker Corporation. Also in 1923 Vance, then thirty-three, married Agnes M. Monaghan in the Episcopal church. They had four children.

Vance moved up the corporate ladder during the 1920s while Studebaker pursued bold expan-

Harold Sines Vance

sion efforts under Erskine's leadership. At its peak Studebaker ranked third in assets within the automotive industry behind only Ford and General Motors (GM). Although Erskine lost out to Walter P. Chrysler in a bid to take over the Maxwell Motor Company, he continued his plan to make Studebaker one of the true giants of the industry.

In the mid 1920s Erskine attempted to strengthen his top managerial team and to provide future leadership. In this attempt he appointed two new and young vice-presidents and placed them on the board of directors. Paul G. Hoffman, owner of a highly successful Studebaker dealership in Los Angeles, took charge of advertising, sales, and a wide range of external relations. Vance took charge of manufacturing and directed the modernization of facilities in South Bend, where Studebaker consolidated production. From 1931 to 1933 Vance also served as the president of the new Rockne Motor Company. A wholly owned subsidiary, Rockne manufactured a lightweight car at a newly acquired plant in Detroit. Launched during the worst years of the depression, the Rockne sold poorly and the firm went out of business in 1933.

The depression of the 1930s had a devastating impact on the automotive industry and especially on small firms like Studebaker. The rapid decline in car sales revealed fatal flaws in Erskine's policy of expansion and high dividends. By 1933 the corporation simply lacked the cash both to continue operations and meet immediate obligations. In March creditors sought protection in the U.S. District Court. Judge Thomas W. Slick responded by removing Erskine from the management and placing the corporation in receivership. As receivers Slick appointed vice-presidents Hoffman and Vance and also Ashton G. Bean, president of White Motors, a Cleveland-based truck manufacturer with which Erskine had sought a merger.

For two years Hoffman and Vance operated Studebaker under the receivership and tried to obtain the financial means to reorganize the corporation. They frequently traveled to New York to persuade investment bankers and other underwriters to refinance the corporation. Finally in January 1935 they convinced Judge Slick to approve their reorganization plan. Within the new Studebaker Corporation Vance became chairman of the board and Hoffman became president. Although they earned considerably less than they had while vice-presidents under Erskine, they had the opportunity to establish policies for Studebaker's recovery.

In personal temperament and life-style Hoffman and Vance were quite different. Known to many employees by his first name, Hoffman was an extrovert who traveled widely and gave Studebaker the kind of positive public exposure it needed to win over investors, car dealers, and customers. Vance had fewer interests outside the business and concentrated on the manufacturing operations in South Bend, where he was known to employees as Mr. V. Shunning the limelight, he preferred quiet relaxation at his nearby farm. Hoffman and Vance rarely socialized together but on the job got along well, and each possessed talents that complemented the other in ways that benefited Studebaker.

Both men firmly believed that Studebaker, despite its size, could compete successfully within an automotive industry dominated by the Big Three: GM, Ford, and Chrysler. As Vance explained in 1935, they rejected the widely held argument that small firms could not operate profitably. "Progressive, hard-hitting compact organizations," he insisted, could adjust more quickly to market changes than could the Big Three. Testifying before the Tem-

Vance early in his career at Studebaker

porary National Economic Committee in 1939, Hoffman and Vance admitted that the larger auto-makers did enjoy economies of scale. Nevertheless Studebaker managed to overcome such handicaps by giving better attention to personal relations that stimulated innovation, good workmanship, and superior service for customers. By offering customers better cars at comparable prices, Studebaker increased its sales and thus its profits.

By the time Hoffman and Vance made those claims, Studebaker had already demonstrated the efficacy of their managerial concept. Unencumbered by a large corporate bureaucracy, they had given free reign to Studebaker engineers. For the low price range that offered the potential of a mass market, they wanted a distinctive looking, lightweight car more fuel efficient and better equipped but not smaller than competitors' cars. What they got was the 1939 Champion. With a trim, conservative appearance provided by industrial designer Raymond Loewy, it won praise from Consumers Union and automotive experts. More important, it sold well. Until it ceased car production early in 1942,

Studebaker enjoyed an increase in car sales that outstripped the gains made throughout the industry.

To succeed with their strategy Hoffman and Vance also sought a cooperative relationship with Studebaker's workers. Even when those workers rallied behind a new union for protection against hardships created by the depression, they tried to run Studebaker according to its "Friendly Factory" slogan. Unlike other leaders in the industry, they did not resist unionization. In February 1934 they met directly with leaders of a newly formed local union and granted recognition. Their labor relations policies partly reflected Studebaker's economic vulnerability. But Hoffman and Vance also believed that workers had legitimate grievances and that unions could represent workers without hurting the profitability of employers.

Just when the strategy of Hoffman and Vance seemingly paid off, the outbreak of World War II interrupted Studebaker's recovery. In June 1940 William Knudsen, on leave from the presidency of GM to coordinate military production for the federal government, selected Vance to supervise production of machine tools, shells, and artillery. Vance's brief participation in the early stages of conversion to a war economy provided Studebaker with valuable information for its own planning. Once the United States entered the war and car production ceased, he and Hoffman traveled to Washington and obtained contracts for military production.

Overall, wartime production provided a magnificent record of what Studebaker could achieve. The company built tens of thousands of airplane engines and military vehicles at one of the lowest unit costs of any supplier. It delivered all orders on schedule and even found ways to cut shipping costs for the government. And in all its contractual relations with the government it avoided legal impasses and court action.

While Studebaker achieved that wartime record, Hoffman and Vance mapped out a bold strategy for a rapid reconversion to peacetime production. Correctly predicting a postwar boom economy with a strong demand for new cars, they wanted Studebaker to reenter the market quickly with a distinctive and modern model that would capture the fancy of car buyers. Toward that goal, in mid 1945 they refinanced Studebaker's debt, negotiated a new contract with the UAW, and began costly retooling. Thus Studebaker launched the first entirely new model car of the postwar era for only about $11 million.

The reconversion strategy implemented by Hoffman and Vance brought quick commercial success in the expanding postwar market. The 1947 Champion's modern engineering offered motorists ease of handling and fuel economy as well as improved safety. Its distinctive styling created by Raymond Loewy's studio emphasized efficient functionalism and driver visibility. With the Champion as its top seller, Studebaker captured more than a 4-percent market share for four straight years and reached record sales of 268,000 cars. Just in 1948 it earned $18 million in profit, enabling it to pay stockholders extra dividends. That postwar success gave Hoffman and Vance further confidence about Studebaker's future and their own economic philosophy.

In December 1948 Vance had the opportunity to expound on that economic philosophy when testifying before a Congressional committee in opposition to a proposed excess profits tax. Studebaker's miraculous recovery from bankruptcy, he declared, followed a "long, hard pull." Until 1943 it paid stockholders no dividends because it retained all profits to retire debts or to reinvest for expansion. Higher profits per car and increased volume then enabled it to reach a point where it could operate profitably even if its business fell 55 percent to 60 percent. According to Vance the excess profits tax proposed by some Democrats would stifle small firms like Studebaker which assumed risky ventures with the prospect of profits. Without incentives for such firms, the economy would be further dominated by giant corporations.

For five years, beginning in 1948 when Hoffman left to administer the Marshall Plan and continuing until 1953, Vance led Studebaker with the dual titles of chairman and president. During that period he tried to build upon the strategy Hoffman and he had applied with success. However, the Friendly Factory concept required breadth and dynamism which Vance lacked. No longer in tandem with Hoffman, he faced difficulties that proved beyond his abilities.

Central to Vance's difficulties may have been his overestimation of a compact form of management over elaborate corporate bureaucracy. That view too easily became an excuse for him to avoid committees and subordinates with contrary opinions. Unimaginative, overly cautious, yet also lax,

he fell behind a rapidly changing automotive industry.

Vance's labor relations policies illustrate that failing. First of all he continued Studebaker's practice of permitting workers to transfer to jobs for which they lacked sufficient training. Besides agreeing to overly generous union contracts, Vance personally intervened in labor disputes and undercut the efforts of subordinates to maintain adequate discipline. As a result of such leadership, Studebaker suffered from high labor costs while achieving low productivity and poor quality of workmanship. Vance seems to have bought labor peace at too high a price.

Production problems also stemmed from Vance's failure to keep pace technologically with Studebaker's competitors. What Vance dismissed as "tooling problems" on the new 1953 models illustrated that point. He permitted his top managers to cut corners by setting up the assembly line without investing in sufficient trials. They discovered too late that new sheet metal would not fit the old chassis. Dealers then had to refit brand-new factory-delivered cars in their own body shops.

Poor quality and noncompetitive retail prices due to excessive labor costs resulted in other problems. Studebaker's market share declined, and its dealers suffered and became demoralized. But because Vance rarely left South Bend, he lost touch with dealers and with consumer tastes. In some ways he seems to have resembled Henry Ford during the 1920s, stubbornly clinging to his own vision while falling behind competitors that kept in touch with market changes. Ford, of course, had saved enough for his company to survive his errors. Studebaker, lacking that huge cash reserve, had become overly dependent on military contracts and government loans. Cuts in defense spending after the Korean War ended left Studebaker especially vulnerable when the sellers' market ended for automakers.

Vance did not fully appreciate the gravity of Studebaker's condition in 1953 when he welcomed Hoffman back to its management. Serving as a consultant for the Office of Defense Mobilization in the new Eisenhower administration, he turned over the chairmanship of Studebaker to Hoffman to reduce his own responsibilities as president. When Hoffman quickly tried to revitalize Studebaker by hiring outside experts to help solve its many problems, he cooperated. But when Hoffman concluded that Studebaker was too small to survive on its own in the competitive market and started negotiating a merger with the Packard Motor Company, Vance strongly opposed. According to Vance, the new models would increase sales and thereby make merger unnecessary. Sales did not live up to his optimistic forecasts, however, and Vance reluctantly yielded to Hoffman's merger efforts.

When those merger efforts created the Studebaker-Packard Corporation, Vance's role in the automotive industry essentially ended. Within the new organization he became chairman of the executive committee and Hoffman the chairman of the board, but the real decision-making power lay with James Nance of Packard, who was president of the new company. Angry when he discovered Studebaker's real plight, Nance ignored Hoffman and Vance and reversed their policies regarding car design and labor relations. Instead of the Friendly Factory, Studebaker-Packard became a small and weak imitation of the automotive industry's Big Three.

Unwanted by Studebaker-Packard's president, Vance left in 1955 when President Eisenhower appointed him to the Atomic Energy Commission (AEC). On the AEC he gave strong support for the industrial application of nuclear power for generating electricity in the United States and abroad. A Republican but not an advocate of laissez-faire, he was untroubled by the close relationship between the government regulatory agency and the private power industry it fostered. Vance died in Washington, D.C., on August 31, 1959, while still a member of the AEC.

Reference:
Alan R. Raucher, *Paul G. Hoffman, Architect of Foreign Aid* (Lexington: University Press of Kentucky, 1986).

Archives:
Material on Vance is located in the Studebaker Papers, Discovery Hall Museum, South Bend, Indiana.

Volkswagen U. S.

by George S. May

Eastern Michigan University

Although the "people's car" that Ferdinand Porsche had developed with the full support of Adolf Hitler began to be produced in limited numbers in 1938, it was not until after World War II, in 1949, that the German manufacturer, Volkswagenwerk Ag, made the first attempt to export the Beetle to the United States. The association of the car with Nazi Germany caused it to catch on very slowly in the United States, but by 1955 interest had picked up sufficiently for the company to establish an American branch to handle sales of the imports.

In the last half of the 1950s and throughout the 1960s sales of the Volkswagen Beetle reached far beyond anything ever seen in the United States in the imported car market, but by the early 1970s interest in the oddly shaped car declined sharply. The German company suffered heavy losses, due in part to the escalating price of gasoline that caused problems for all automobile companies, but also due to Volkswagen's failure to forecast the need to find a re-

placement for the Beetle. Briefly in 1974 it appeared that the company might not survive, but a turnaround began in the mid 1970s with the introduction of new small car models.

In 1976 Volkswagen made the decision to strengthen its position in the United States by beginning to assemble some of its cars in the country. Chrysler, which had unsuccessfully approached Volkswagen in the 1950s and would do so again at the end of the 1970s over the prospects of a merger, in 1976 sold Volkswagen an uncompleted assembly plant in New Stanton, Pennsylvania, which the financially strapped American company was eager to sell. Volkswagen completed work on the facility and began operations in 1978, producing its Golf model that had been introduced in 1974 but which was sold in the United States as the Rabbit. By 1980 production at the plant had reached 1,050 cars a day, and the domestic Volkswagen manufacturing operation had moved ahead of American Motors Corporation to become the fourth leading American car producer. But despite this promising start, Volkswagen's hopes that this venture would lead to a continuing increase in its share of the American market were not fulfilled. The German company's once-proud reputation for product excellence was seriously damaged in the 1970s, turning away many customers who already had doubts about Volkswagens produced in America because of the poor reputation of American car manufacturers and workers. In addition the German cars could not compete with the Japanese imports that had come to dominate the foreign car market in the United States. As a result, at the end of 1987 Volkswagen an-

nounced that the New Stanton plant, which some analysts estimated was losing $120 million a year, would be shut down by the end of 1988 after which time the only Volkswagens available in the United States would once again be imports.

References:

Nick Baldwin and others, *The World Guide to Automobile Manufacturers* (New York: Facts on File, 1987);

Robert B. Reich and John D. Donahue, *New Deals: The Chrysler Revival and the American System* (New York: Times Books, 1985);

"What Ended VW's American Dream," *Business Week* (December 7, 1987): 63.

Volvo AB

by George S. May

Eastern Michigan University

Volvo AB, Sweden's largest manufacturer, was organized in 1926 and produced its first automobiles in 1927. In the years after World War II Volvo vehicles began to develop a following in the United States because of their reputation as extremely durable, well-built cars. As a result the United States became one of Volvo's major markets. Volvo opened an overseas car assembly plant in Canada in 1963 and announced plans for a similar plant in the United States in 1973, but this was subsequently dropped. Until 1949, however, Volvo had produced more trucks and other commercial vehicles than passenger cars, and it was in the former category that the Swedish firm appeared as a manufacturer in the United States in the 1980s.

Volvo had found an outlet for some of its trucks in 1977 when it reached an agreement with Consolidated Freightways to have imported light- and medium-weight trucks sold through Consolidated's Freightliner subsidiary dealers. Freightliner manufactured Class 8 heavy-duty trucks in the 33,000-pound gross weight and above classification, and because of differing European and American standards Volvo could not import their trucks in this weight category. In September 1980 White Motor Corporation filed for bankruptcy, and several European truck producers began scrambling to purchase White's heavy-duty truck operations as a

means of entering this more lucrative phase of the American truck market. On May 8, 1981, White announced that it had agreed to sell its heavy-truck operations to Volvo for a price that was "significantly below" book value. The sale was approved by the federal bankruptcy court and was completed at the end of August. The Volvo White Truck Corporation, with headquarters at Greensboro, North Carolina, was formed as a subsidiary of the Swedish company. Meanwhile, the selling arrangement with Consolidated Freightways ended after that company sold Freightliner to Daimler-Benz.

Although White's share of the heavy-truck market had fallen from 20 percent to only 6 percent by 1981, Volvo acquired two of the best-known and oldest names in the truck business, White and Autocar, which White had purchased in 1953. In addition to producing these trucks at several locations in the country, Volvo now also used the White plant at Dublin, Virginia, to assemble some of the lighter Volvo models. Volvo then increased its stake in the domestic truck manufacturing industry in 1986 when, on December 11, it signed an agreement with General Motors (GM) for a joint venture between the two automotive companies which transferred the responsibility for the production of GMC heavy-duty trucks from GM to Volvo. This was part of GM's effort to shed itself of some of its less profitable operations, while at the same time being part of moves that had seen foreign companies acquire an increasingly large share of the production of heavy-duty trucks in the United States in the 1980s.

References:
Nick Baldwin and others, *The World Guide to Automobile Manufacturers* (New York: Facts on File, 1987);
Andrew C. Brown, "Hard Times for Truck Makers," *Fortune*, 104 (September 7, 1981): 80-89;
Nick Georgano, *World Truck Handbook*, new edition (London: Jane's Publishing, 1986).

Charles Erwin Wilson

(July 18, 1890-September 26, 1961)

by E. Bruce Geelhoed

Ball State University

CAREER: Electrical engineer, Westinghouse Manufacturing & Electric Company (1909-1919); chief engineer and factory manager (1919-1925), president, Delco-Remy Company (1925-1929); vice-president (1929-1939), executive vice-president (1939-1941), president (1941-1953), chief executive officer, General Motors Corporation (1946-1953); United States secretary of defense (1953-1957).

Charles Erwin Wilson was born on July 18, 1890, and died on September 26, 1961. Wilson's parents, Thomas Erwin and Rosalind Unkefer Wilson, were schoolteachers in the family's hometown of Minerva, Ohio. Charles Wilson spent his boyhood in Minerva and the nearby community of Mineral City, Ohio, before his family moved to Pittsburgh when he was sixteen. Although Wilson went on to become the president of General Motors Corporation and, later, secretary of defense in the administration of President Dwight D. Eisenhower, he maintained throughout his life many of the small-town values, mores, and customs which he acquired during his youth. Wilson was always known for his friendly manner, his sense of humor, and his lack of ostentation.

Wilson was one of the most important businessmen and public figures in America during the middle decades of the twentieth century. An able engineer and business administrator, Wilson made important contributions to American industry during the 1940s, first when he guided the General Motors production effort in World War II and then as he advanced several lasting concepts in labor relations between 1946 and 1950. Between 1953 and 1957 Wilson served as secretary of defense, in

Charles Erwin Wilson

which capacity he implemented a cost-sensitive program of defense spending as well as a far-reaching reorganization of the Pentagon's management structure. During Wilson's career in the private and public sectors, he achieved the unique distinction of being the only individual ever to administer the world's largest corporation, General Motors, and the world's largest public agency, the United States Department of Defense.

Wilson's youth typified the experiences of millions of small-town American boys in the early twentieth century. While growing up, Wilson earned a reputation as a conscientious, hardworking student who was talented at mathematics. The Wilsons were neighbors of the Diebolt family in Mineral City, and the two Diebolt brothers, Bill and Charlie, were engineers for the Baltimore & Ohio (B&O) Railroad. The Diebolt brothers were fond of Wilson, who was fascinated by the power and intricate operations of the steam engine locomotive. Wilson often accompanied the Diebolt brothers in the cabs of the B&O locomotives on their numerous trips into Cleveland. Growing up in the shadow of the railroad fueled Wilson's fascination for the world of engineering, mechanics, and industry.

In 1906 the Wilson family moved to Pittsburgh, Pennsylvania. By that time, at age sixteen, Wilson had already graduated from high school, and, once in Pittsburgh, he enrolled in the local Carnegie Institute of Technology to pursue a degree in electrical engineering. Wilson completed Carnegie Tech's demanding engineering program in three years and graduated with honors in 1909—one month before he celebrated his nineteenth birthday. Following his graduation from Carnegie Tech, Wilson accepted his first electrical engineering position with the Westinghouse Manufacturing & Electric Company in Pittsburgh. Some confusion, however, exists about Wilson's work experience. In the mid 1940s, when he had become the president of General Motors, Wilson informed Peter F. Drucker, who was then conducting a management study for the corporation, that he had been a pattern maker and president of a union local in Pittsburgh during and immediately after his college years. In fact, Wilson said, he had been an ardent Socialist and actively campaigned for Eugene V. Debs, the candidate of the Socialist party, in the presidential campaign of 1912. Wilson also maintained that he had received his union sympathies from his father, a Welsh immigrant, and that Wilson was almost "kicked out of college in 1912 for agitating for Debs."

Wilson's official biography (assembled presumably from sources at General Motors), however, records that he went to work for Westinghouse shortly after graduation from Carnegie Tech. According to those sources, Wilson could not have been "almost kicked out of college in 1912" because he had graduated three years earlier, in 1909. Likewise,

Wilson's official biography claims that Wilson's mother and father came from old-line American stock; neither was an immigrant.

Regardless of the confusion on the point Wilson skillfully discharged his 13-cents-per-hour position at Westinghouse, and by 1915 he had become the junior assistant to B. G. Lamme, Westinghouse's chief engineer. While at Westinghouse Wilson made two significant contributions. First, he designed the company's first electrical ignition for automobiles, a device which was essential to the firms which functioned as suppliers to the expanding American automobile companies. Second, Westinghouse placed Wilson in Washington during World War I, where he worked on several special projects for the army and navy. These assignments included the design and development of radio generators and dynamometers, as well as new communications systems.

After the end of World War I, Wilson returned to Pittsburgh. Although his career had progressed steadily at Westinghouse, Wilson soon became attracted to the promising opportunities which existed for electrical engineers in the automotive industry. In 1919 he arranged for an interview with Alfred P. Sloan, Jr., who would later become the chief executive of General Motors (GM) and at this time headed its United Motors division. Wilson was immediately hired for a temporary post at GM in Detroit. Later that year he was reassigned as the chief engineer and factory manager for the Remy Electric Company, one of the United Motors subsidiaries.

The Remy Electric Company, located in Anderson, Indiana, supplied various types of electrical equipment (including ignitions and generator distributors) to GM. In 1919 Remy was well on its way to becoming one of the world's largest manufacturers of electrical equipment. This new assignment gave Wilson his first responsibility as a general manager, and he was determined to make the most of it. Wilson's wife, Jessie (whom he married in 1912 and with whom he had six children), had other ideas, however. She had quickly become enamored of Detroit, and she resisted the move to central Indiana. Wilson was unyielding, however, and his wife finally relented.

Wilson faced a number of difficult tasks in Anderson with the Remy Electric Company. First, many of the company's production methods needed modernizing. Using his skills as an engineer, Wilson managed to improve Remy's production operations in fairly short order. Second, Wilson helped to institute an improved safety program in the plants and also raised worker morale. In 1925 Wilson was named president of Remy, a post which he held for the next three years. In 1926 Wilson became the president of the Delco-Remy Company, which resulted from the merger of the Dayton Engineering Laboratory (Delco) with Remy.

Although Wilson's decade at Remy Electric Company between 1919 and 1929 was largely a triumph for him, there were occasions on which he necessarily showed his resolute determination. For example, in 1927 Wilson spearheaded a campaign to build a second electrical power facility in Anderson. At the time Anderson's electrical power needs were supplied by a municipally owned utility, and Wilson wanted an alternative source of power available for the company's plants in case of a temporary failure at the local utility. Wilson's plans provoked strong resistance from several vocal elements in the community who claimed that GM was attempting to take over the power company. Wilson denied these charges at a public hearing called to discuss the proposal, but the political leadership of the city refused to support his plan. The following morning Wilson drove to Muncie, located about 25 miles to the east, a community which was the location of several suppliers to the automotive industry, and purchased a vacant power plant. From that location Wilson developed an alternative production operation which ensured that Delco-Remy was firmly positioned to supply electrical equipment to the other GM plants.

During the 1920s Wilson was undoubtedly the most important individual in Anderson. Not only did he increase Delco-Remy's earnings to new levels, he also worked with the city government and business community to build housing for the ever-growing number of workers who came to Anderson to work in the GM plants. Early in the 1920s it had become obvious to Wilson that the company would be able to grow only to the extent that Anderson was able to support that growth.

Wilson returned to the headquarters of GM in Detroit in 1929 to accept a corporate vice-presidency with responsibility for GM's accessory companies, including firms such as Delco-Remy. Despite the onset of the Great Depression, Wilson's career progressed steadily at GM, and by the mid

1930s he was handling additional responsibilities in the corporate sales area.

The 1930s were a troubled time as the Great Depression stifled business and curtailed earnings. Especially hard hit, of course, were the vast numbers of unemployed autoworkers who lost their jobs when car sales fell dramatically. In 1935 Congress passed the Wagner Act, which gave workers the right to collective bargaining, legislation which ushered in a new era in labor-management relations within the automobile industry. GM became the target of a well-planned and well-timed organizing effort by the United Auto Workers (UAW)-CIO in late 1936 and early 1937. Through a series of sit-down strikes at GM factories in Flint, Michigan, and elsewhere throughout the Midwest, the blue-collar work force of General Motors held out for forty-four days until GM finally agreed to recognize the UAW-CIO as the bargaining agent in labor negotiations with the corporation.

Wilson was a member of the General Motors negotiating team during the sit-down strike period of 1936-1937. In that capacity he functioned as one of the principal assistants to William S. Knudsen, the GM vice-president in charge of production who became the president of the corporation later in 1937. Wilson was often the GM representative on the scene in Flint, where tensions between the workers and GM plant security ran especially high. The difficulty with organized labor was one of the low points of Knudsen's career at GM, and he finally gave Wilson the responsibility for the corporation's labor relations policy. "C. E., you handle this union business," Knudsen reportedly told Wilson during one of his fits of exasperation with the leadership of the UAW. "You have more patience than I do and you like to talk more."

Wilson's career at GM during the 1930s was also notable for the rapport which he established with the senior leadership of the company. Wilson became a trusted colleague not only of Sloan, GM's longtime president, chairman, and chief executive officer, and Knudsen but also with other important men on the fourteenth floor of the GM building in Detroit, including Donaldson Brown, who built the famous GM managerial system; Albert Bradley, GM's chief financial officer; Marvin Coyle, the powerful general manager of GM's Chevrolet division; and Harley Earl, GM's chief automobile designer. Unlike later GM executives, who became known more for their administrative and financial skills,

Wilson, center, with Ernest Breech, left, and Senator Robert Taft of Ohio

Wilson and many of his generation were "car men," managers who loved the automotive industry and developed a fierce pride and affection for GM as an employer and business enterprise.

The onset of World War II in 1939 and GM's role as a prime government contractor added to Wilson's importance at the corporation. In 1940 Knudsen accepted President Franklin D. Roosevelt's request (over the protestations of Alfred P. Sloan, Jr., one of Roosevelt's archenemies within the business community) to come to Washington at the salary of $1 per year to take charge of the nation's defense mobilization. Wilson succeeded Knudsen as GM's chief operating officer and held the title of acting president.

Wilson was both an obvious and responsible choice to succeed Knudsen. He had accumulated over two decades worth of experience and had worked in a variety of important areas within the corporation, including factory management, finance, production, and labor relations. An engineer, Wilson was also well qualified to handle not only the large-scale production effort which awaited GM as a war contractor but also the complex process of converting the GM factories to wartime production. Wilson began mobilizing the GM industrial capacity for the war effort with his customary blend of enthusiasm, energy, and efficiency. In winter 1941-1942, however, he was sidelined temporarily after suffering a broken hip in an ice-skating accident and was

confined to the hospital for a lengthy stay. He continued to work, however, at least to the extent that his physical condition allowed. GM executives made frequent visits to his hospital room, and Wilson's secretary conducted her daily work from the hospital.

Once he was discharged from the hospital, Wilson tackled his responsibilities at a grueling pace. His normal workweek consisted of a pattern where he worked at his office on Monday and returned home that evening. Then, from Tuesday to Friday, Wilson worked at his office and remained in downtown Detroit, sleeping in an apartment reserved for GM executives. Although Wilson spent the weekends at home, he also spent a good percentage of that time on GM business.

After he left GM in the early 1950s, Wilson often spoke with pride about his role as a manager of GM's war production record, which was impressive. During World War II, GM manufactured 25 percent of the tanks, armored cars, and airplane engines used by the military; almost 50 percent of the machine guns and carbines; 67 percent of the heavy trucks; thousands of carrier aircraft; and 75 percent of the diesel horsepower used by the navy. Under Wilson's leadership GM fulfilled over $12 billion of war contracts with the federal government.

According to Peter Drucker, the managerial responsibilities of World War II placed a heavy physical demand upon Wilson. Late in 1943 he collapsed from exhaustion and may have suffered a slight stroke. Officially the corporation referred to Wilson's temporary hospitalization in 1943 as the result of a "circulatory episode." As with the circumstances of Wilson's childhood experiences, however, some confusion exists about the degree to which Wilson may have been affected by this stroke. In an interview in March 1979 one of Wilson's sons, Charles E. Wilson, Jr., expressed doubt that his father suffered a stroke or that he had exhibited any post-stroke behavior.

In any event Wilson's performance at the helm of General Motors impressed Sloan and the GM board of directors sufficiently to make him in 1946 not only president but chief executive officer, a position previously held by Sloan. Sloan was rumored to have preferred Albert Bradley for the post but did not oppose the selection of Wilson. With that action Wilson received the responsibility of leading GM into the next phase of its history, that of meeting the projections for a huge explosion of consumer demand for GM products.

Wilson had three fundamental concerns about the managerial challenge of GM in the years immediately after World War II. The first concern obviously involved the conversion of the GM plants to peacetime production. Wilson recognized that the pent-up demand created by the absence of automobile production during the war would result in the placement of huge orders for new cars. To meet the anticipated demand GM needed the assurance of a continuous flow of production and the absence of labor strife and its attendant work stoppages.

The first concern inevitably led to the second: that of creating a more stable relationship between GM and the UAW. Wilson had no illusions about the potential difficulty of this task. The demands of the UAW promised to be considerably more ambitious in the postwar period, especially if the corporation returned to its anticipated level of profitability. The establishment of a workable relationship with Walter Reuther, who headed the UAW's GM division and became the leader of the union in March 1946, was absolutely imperative.

Wilson's third concern also dealt with labor relations, albeit in a different sense. After two decades of observing factory life and the hierarchical structure of the typical American industrial enterprise, Wilson understood that the commercial success of American industry held out the prospect of significant material gains for the blue-collar worker. "We have succeeded in this country in making manual work productive, well paid, and middle class," Wilson told Drucker in 1944. "And now we have to make the manual worker as effective a citizen as he has become a producer." Continuing in that vein, Wilson pointed out that designing the structure and constitutional principles "for the big business enterprise was the great achievement of the founding fathers of GM, the last generation. To develop citizenship and community is the task of the next generation. We are, so to speak, going to be the Jeffersonians to Mr. Sloan's Federalists."

World War II had scarcely ended before Wilson was thrust into the challenges of the postwar period. GM faced a new round of labor negotiations prior even to the formal surrender of Japan. On August 16, 1945, the UAW presented the Big Three automakers–GM, Ford, and Chrysler–with a demand for a 30 percent increase in wages. Wilson and the GM management waited six weeks before commenting on the demand, but then rejected it on October 2. Responding to Reuther, Wilson declared in a strongly worded public statement: "We shall resist the monopolistic power of your union to force this 30 percent increase in basic wages." Were GM to grant this increase, "automobiles would shortly cost 30 percent more to produce. Prices to consumers would have to be raised 30 percent. If wage raises in automobile plants forced such increases in car prices, the market for automobiles would be restricted. Fewer cars would be sold; fewer people would be able to afford and enjoy them; and fewer workers would be employed in making them."

On October 19, slightly over two weeks after Wilson delivered his response to Reuther, collective bargaining talks began between the UAW and the automakers. The negotiations between the GM bargainers and the UAW delegation were acrimonious and unproductive from their outset. In early November Reuther gave the order for the UAW to strike GM for the second time in less than a decade. In December, President Harry Truman brought the weight of his administration into the dispute, terming the strike injurious to the national economic recovery program. Truman appointed a three-member fact-finding board which recommended in January 1946 that GM provide the UAW membership with a pay increase of 17.5 percent (19.5 cents per hour) without an increase in car prices.

Wilson and the GM negotiators continued to hold out against a settlement, however, rejecting both the demands of Reuther and the recommendations of Truman. Reuther found his position deteriorating somewhat in early 1946 when Chrysler and Ford finalized contract negotiations with their UAW locals without a provision to hold down automobile prices. Meanwhile, the strike against GM continued.

Finally, in mid March 1946, after a 113-day strike, GM and the UAW came to terms. The UAW accepted an offer of a pay increase of 18.5 cents per hour, although the fringe benefits of the final package put the settlement above the 19.5 cents per hour recommended by the Truman pay board. Reuther argued that the final contract vindicated his efforts to secure higher wages for the UAW membership. Wilson and the GM delegation claimed that the final settlement represented a triumph for the corporation in resisting both the demands of the union and the administration.

Regardless of who won or lost the strike of 1945-1946, Wilson reckoned that the stoppage, even though it was peaceful, cost the corporation an estimated $1 billion in lost sales, unearned wages, and dealers' profits. Given the resumption of consumer demand for automobiles, Wilson clearly wanted to avoid any more lengthy work stoppages. His proposal to the UAW in 1948, one of the most far-reaching plans ever advanced by a major corporation in labor negotiations, reflected that desire. In the 1948 negotiations Wilson introduced three important concepts: the so-called "escalator" clause, which tied wage increases to the annual cost-of-living index; the annual productivity factor (known as the AIF: Annual Improvement Factor), giving workers additional income based on the profitability of the corporation; and finally, the agreement on a multiyear contract which eliminated the necessity for annual bargaining skirmishes between GM and the UAW. In truth Wilson had been planning to introduce the "escalator" clause, now frequently referred to as the cost-of-living adjustment (COLA), for many years prior to the 1948 negotiations. By his own account (and those of others), he had first given thought to the idea in 1941-1942 when he was hospitalized after his ice-skating accident. During the hospitalization Wilson assigned two junior GM executives to research the concept of the "escalator clause," as well as the "annual improvement factor," with the intention of introducing these concepts into a future bargaining process.

The Wilson proposals were incorporated into the 1948 agreement, with both GM and the UAW claiming victory over the outcome of the negotiations. Both sides could point to evidence in the contract to support their arguments. Wilson received an agreement for a multiyear contract, assuring the continuation of production and labor peace for at least the next two years. Reuther contended that the escalator clause provision, combined with the annual improvement factor benefit, gave the members of the UAW protection against inflation and a share in the future prosperity of the corporation. These were two specific demands which Reuther and the UAW had been making of the automakers since the end of World War II.

The GM-UAW agreement of 1948 provided a boost to the American automotive industry. By the end of 1949 industry production reached an all-time record of 6.2 million cars and trucks. GM sales for the year totaled almost $6 billion with profits also at record levels. GM's share of the market for new cars was 43 percent, and under Wilson's leadership the corporation continued on the road to becoming the largest business enterprise in the world.

In the next round of negotiations with the UAW in 1950, Wilson once again proposed a multiyear contract, this time for five years, which incorporated, updated, and even institutionalized the provisions of the 1948 agreement. One significant difference was the GM-UAW agreement to establish a corporation-wide pension plan for the UAW membership. The concept of the pension plan grew out of Wilson's longstanding interest in establishing some form of a permanent profit-sharing plan for GM workers. As he explained to Peter Drucker prior to the 1950 negotiations, "Profit sharing has to be applied where it can make an impact. What about employee pensions? There 4 or 5 percent can make a difference and social security isn't going to provide adequate employee pensions for individuals whose lifetime wages have been as high as those of automobile workers are going to be." Drucker asked Wilson how he proposed to invest the funds generated by the contributions from the employees and the corporation. The UAW obviously preferred that such funds be invested in public securities such as government bonds. Wilson replied that he intended to invest the funds "in the stock market. Altogether they should be invested the way a prudent financial manager would invest them." Drucker responded that

Wilson about 1941, when he was named president of GM

such an approach would make American workers, through their pension plans, the owners of American business within one generation. "Exactly what they should be and must be," Wilson said. "The income distribution in this country surely means that no one else can own American industry unless it be the government," he concluded.

Ironically, the pension plan proposal became part of the 1950 master contract between General Motors and the UAW as the result of a union demand instead of as a proposal originating from Wilson. Wilson accepted the reality of this circumstance, too. "If [the plan] is to be of any value to a union, it's got to be a hard-war gain. I'll plant the idea—I know enough UAW people; but will yield to them, and [only] after a show of great reluctance. The union leaders won't go along unless it's a demand we resist and they 'win.' "

The 1950 negotiations brought five years of further labor stability between GM and the UAW. Taken together, the 1948 and 1950 contracts represented Wilson's finest accomplishments during his career as the president of GM. Without question the corporation enjoyed the most prosperous period in its history, and Wilson deserved a major share of the credit for GM's successful conversion to peacetime production as well as its contributions to the Korean War effort between 1950 and 1953.

The nature of the relationship between GM and the UAW during the period of Wilson's presidency has become the subject of considerable study. Some observers, such as journalist Frank Cormier, see this period as the high point of Reuther's leadership of the UAW, a time when he won victories for the UAW membership which he found difficult to repeat in future bargaining rounds. Other writers, such as Peter Drucker and automotive industry historian Ed Cray, have claimed that Wilson was consistently ahead of Reuther in judging worker sentiment and in fashioning GM's proposals accordingly. What remains clear is that both GM and the UAW negotiated historic agreements between 1946 and 1953, despite the adversarial relationship which both Reuther and Wilson maintained for public consumption.

Privately, Wilson was more than willing to take credit for the success which GM enjoyed at the bargaining table in 1948 and 1950. "The test of labor relations isn't rhetoric," he once told Drucker. "The test is results. We lose fewer days to strikes than any other major company in this country or in any unionized country. We have greater continuity of union leadership. And both the union and we [GM] get the things the country and the company and the union need: high discipline, high productivity, high wages, and high employment security. A union is a political organization and needs adversary relations and victories in battle. And a company is an economic organization and needs productivity and discipline. At GM we get both—and to get both we need the union relations we have."

Wilson took an active interest in the 1952 presidential campaign and was an open, even ardent supporter of Dwight D. Eisenhower ("General Ike," he called him privately). Eisenhower and Wilson were acquainted prior to the election, and Wilson's personal papers reveal a correspondence with the general which dated to 1949. Wilson regularly sent Eisenhower copies of speeches which he declared on economic issues, and Eisenhower occasionally returned them to Wilson with his comments.

Eisenhower's victory in the 1952 election brought an end to two decades of rule by the Democratic party in the White House. It was hardly a surprise, therefore, when Eisenhower looked to the business community for potential cabinet members, and even less of a surprise when the president-elect asked Wilson to join the administration as the next secretary of defense. At the time of his appointment Wilson expressed astonishment that he would be considered for a post in the new administration. The private record shows, however, that Wilson had actively courted Eisenhower for at least three years and considered himself qualified for a number of cabinet positions including secretary of defense, secretary of commerce, or possibly secretary of the treasury.

Wilson accepted Eisenhower's request and relished the challenge of moving to Washington and becoming a key player in the first Republican administration since 1928. His associates at GM were not so pleased. Sloan particularly was known to be opposed to Wilson taking a prominent public position, even though he recognized that Wilson must accept Eisenhower's request. Sloan was no Eisenhower partisan and, just as importantly, did not relish the prospect of GM being drawn into national politics.

Despite Sloan's reservations Wilson went to Washington in January 1953, ready to tackle the immense job of bringing sound financial management to the Department of Defense, the largest agency in the federal government, then spending over $40 billion annually while fighting a war in Korea. Once in Washington, Wilson acquired the nickname of "Engine" Charlie, which distinguished him from "Electric" Charlie Wilson, the former head of General Electric, who had served as the head of the Truman administration's mobilization effort during the Korean War. Wilson expected that he would encounter little difficulty in winning Senate confirmation of his nomination, confiding to a friend that he felt he "was going to be pretty pleased and surprised at how easily these boys [the members of the Senate Armed Services Committee] can be handled." But Wilson's nomination encountered immediate opposition on Capitol Hill. The cause of Wilson's difficulties involved his unwillingness to sell his large holdings of GM stock and to forego the future benefits entitled him under the corporation's bonus and salary plan. Assuming that he did sell his shares of GM stock, Wilson stood to pay an enormous capital gains tax which he preferred to avoid if possible.

GM remained a large defense contractor, of course, and a number of senators were skeptical that Wilson could avoid a conflict of interest, even

if he did sell his stock. Asked at his confirmation hearing before the Senate Armed Services Committee if he could distinguish between the public welfare and the interests of GM, Wilson responded affirmatively to his questioner, Sen. Robert Hendrickson of New Jersey. But then Wilson added: "I cannot think of [such a conflict] because for years I thought that what was good for our country was good for General Motors, and vice versa."

This relatively off-handed comment linking the company's welfare with that of the country soon gave way to the notorious misinterpretation of Wilson's remark: "What's good for General Motors is good for the country." In making the remark Wilson suggested that the corporation's interests ran parallel to those of the nation: that GM could not be profitable if the country were not prosperous. The use of the two words *vice versa* in this context represented Wilson's belief that what was bad for the country was bad for GM.

To the end of his life Wilson never completely understood the public furor which resulted about his comment linking the interests of General Motors with the performance of the American economy. As was noted in James Truslow Adams's book *Big Business in a Democracy* (1946), GM management subscribed to the view that GM could not be profitable as a corporation if the entire national economy was not prosperous. Wilson was referring to that belief when he testified before the Senate Armed Services Committee in 1953. Furthermore Wilson had used identical language when responding to both House and Senate committees during World War II when he came to Washington to testify on GM's performance as a defense contractor. For those reasons, apparently, he saw no reason why anyone in Congress should object to such a statement.

Notwithstanding Wilson's assumptions, neither the members of the Senate Armed Services Committee nor the entire Congress were willing to accept Wilson's arguments. To win confirmation Wilson sold his stock and thereby made a material sacrifice of about $2 million over the next four years to serve as secretary of defense. More important to Wilson's credibility, he never recovered in the public's eye from the misinterpretation of his remark. He became the frequent target of administration critics in the Democratic party who charged the administration with being more concerned about the rich than the average working American.

Once in office at the Pentagon, Wilson tackled his new assignment with his customary zeal. Eisenhower chose Wilson because he believed that Wilson possessed the organizational, managerial, and administrative skills necessary for the position. Eisenhower intended to handle matters of strategy himself, or in consultation with his secretary of state, John Foster Dulles. Wilson was assigned the primary responsibility of enforcing financial discipline at the Pentagon. Since one of Eisenhower's major objectives was to balance the federal budget, and the Defense Department consumed over 50 percent of the total federal expenditure, the president expected Wilson to find a substantial amount of savings within the Pentagon. In that respect Wilson succeeded admirably, devising ways to reduce the level of defense spending substantially and then to restrain the escalation of military costs.

When Wilson took office in January 1953, total defense spending amounted to $40.5 billion. The end of the Korean War in mid July 1953 combined with the decision to "stretch out" the procurement program for the air force gave Wilson the latitude to trim $5 billion from total defense spending in his first year in office. These reductions were politically unpopular, of course, both within Congress and within the military services. Wilson's critics charged that he was more concerned "with dollars than security," but Eisenhower strongly supported his defense secretary's cost-cutting programs, and Wilson's policies were implemented.

Between February 1953 and April 1953 Wilson also carried out his own administrative reorganization of the Defense Department. Under his plan the Pentagon abolished a number of bureaus which had been created during the Korean War period and replaced them with a staff-and-line, decentralized management structure. It was no accident, of course, that the new Defense Department management hierarchy resembled the administrative chart of GM. In the Wilson design the secretary of defense functioned as the chief operating officer of a corporation and the civilian secretaries of the three military services (army, navy, air force) served as presidents (or general managers) of a corporation's subsidiary companies. To provide liaison between the secretary of defense and the service secretaries, Wilson created several new positions for assistant secretaries of defense who functioned as corporate staff vice-presidents. This reorganization went into effect in April 1953 and quickly became a permanent feature of the management program at the Defense Department.

Wilson served as secretary of defense until 1957, a tenure three times longer than any of his three predecessors, James Forrestal, Louis Johnson, and Robert Lovett. Wilson's tenure as secretary of defense still ranks as the third longest in history; only Robert McNamara (1961-1967) and Caspar Weinberger (1981-1987) have held the position for a longer period. In almost five years in office Wilson spent the majority of his efforts in helping the American military establishment make the transition from the defense policies of the post-World War II period to those of the new technological era. The scientific revolution in the field of warfare continued at a breathtaking pace while Wilson was secretary of defense. Under his leadership the Pentagon added new jet-engine aircraft to the air force, nuclear propulsion to the navy, and modernized the equipment of the army. Work also continued on the American guided-missile program as the Pentagon began research and development on, and eventually deployment of, the Atlas, Titan, and Polaris intercontinental ballistic missile (ICBM) programs as well as a number of intermediate range ballistic missiles (IRBMs) for the three services.

Wilson managed to engineer this transition through a massive reallocation of Pentagon resources, essentially by taking money from the manpower and conventional forces areas and redirecting them to the strategic area. For obvious reasons this policy was not popular within certain elements of the armed services. In 1953 and 1956 such prominent air force generals as Hoyt Vandenberg and Curtis LeMay publicly criticized Wilson's cost-cutting program as it related to the procurement of the B-52 long-range bomber. The leadership of the army, including generals Matthew Ridgway, Matthew Taylor, and James Gavin (all combat heroes of World War II), wrote books, after their retirements, where they vigorously criticized Wilson's reductions in army troop strength.

President Eisenhower publicly supported Wilson's management of the Defense Department repeatedly, however, and Eisenhower's support sustained Wilson while he was in office. By the end of Eisenhower's first term in 1956, however, Wilson clearly had reached the physical limits of his endurance for positions of great responsibility, stress, and pressure. After two decades at the top of the corporate world and in government, Wilson knew that the time had come for him to announce his retirement. Furthermore he was concerned about his wife's health. Wilson stayed at the Pentagon long enough to complete the preparation, presentation, and passage of the Pentagon budget for fiscal year 1958, which totaled $38 billion, almost $3 billion less than the budget he had inherited four years previously. Wilson resigned as secretary of defense in October 1957.

Any assessment of Wilson's career must take into account his achievements at GM and at the Pentagon. Wilson was truly a pioneer in labor relations, as his proposals for the "escalator" clause, profit sharing, and employee pensions demonstrated. Future generations of GM negotiators would become critical of Wilson, however, primarily because Wilson's proposals became so popular with the UAW that they were institutionalized within the GM-UAW collective bargaining framework. Admittedly, GM reached a time when it was unable to afford the amount of benefits which were contained in the 1948 and 1950 master contracts.

At the Defense Department Wilson's efforts to restrain the growth of Pentagon spending, while at the same time financing a necessary modernization of America's military capability, were largely successful. He was roundly criticized, however, for his reorganization of the Defense Department management structure in 1953. Critics of this plan argued (and subsequent events have largely vindicated their criticism) that Wilson's addition of more assistant secretaries of defense contributed to the growing bureaucratization of the Pentagon and tended to slow down the decision-making process.

After leaving the Pentagon, Wilson spent his retirement years in Michigan, occasionally visiting his various properties throughout the country. He suffered a heart attack in his sleep on September 26, 1961, while staying at his farm in Louisiana. He died that evening, just a few short weeks prior to his golden wedding anniversary. His death brought numerous expressions of sympathy from his many friends from his corporate and public life, including his associates at GM; Robert McNamara, his successor as secretary of defense; former president Eisenhower; and Walter Reuther.

References:

James Truslow Adams, *Big Business in a Democracy* (New York: Scribners, 1946);

Ed Cray, *Chrome Colossus: General Motors and Its Times* (New York: McGraw-Hill, 1980);

Peter F. Drucker, *Adventures of a Bystander* (New York: Harper & Row, 1979);

Drucker, *The Unseen Revolution* (New York: Harper & Row, 1976);

E. Bruce Geelhoed, *Charles E. Wilson and Controversy at the Pentagon* (Detroit: Wayne State University Press, 1979);

William Serrin, *The Company and the Union* (New York: Knopf, 1973);

Alfred P. Sloan, Jr., *My Years with General Motors* (Garden City, N.Y.: Doubleday, 1964).

Archives:

Charles E. Wilson's papers are housed at the Charles E. Wilson Archives at Anderson University, Anderson, Indiana. Other materials are available at the General Motors Archives in Detroit, Michigan.

Leonard Freel Woodcock

(February 15, 1911-   )

by Gilbert J. Gall

Pennsylvania State University

CAREER: Machine assembler, Borg-Warner Corporation (1933-1938); member, United Automobile Workers, AFL and United Automobile Workers, CIO (1934-1936); education director, Wayne County CIO Council (1938-1939); international staff, Region 1D, United Automobile, Aerospace, and Agricultural Implement Workers (UAW) (1940-1944); punch press operator, Continental Motors (1944-1946); administrative assistant to president, UAW (1946-1947); regional director, Region 1D and director, American Motors and Continental Motors departments, UAW (1947-1955); vice-president and director, General Motors and Aerospace departments, UAW (1955-1970); president, international union, UAW (1970-1977); president emeritus, UAW (1977); United States ambassador to the People's Republic of China (1978-1982); professor, University of Michigan (1982-   ).

Leonard Freel Woodcock, fifth international union president of the United Automobile, Aerospace, and Agricultural Implement Workers (UAW) union, assumed the office upon the unexpected death of longtime incumbent Walter P. Reuther in May 1970. For the next seven years Woodcock led one of the nation's largest industrial unions—an organization which he helped establish through a period marked by the rising rebellion of younger automobile workers against production pressures, as well as the first signs of the intense foreign competition which would hit the industry full force in the following decade. As president he furthered Reuther's traditional accomplishments: impressive collective bargaining gains, interest in the international labor movement, involvement in liberal Democratic party politics, and promotion of social-welfare legislation.

Woodcock was born in Providence, Rhode Island, on February 15, 1911, the son of skilled machinist Ernest Woodcock, a British citizen, and Mary Freel Woodcock. Sent by his employer to in-

Leonard Freel Woodcock

stall machinery in Germany in 1914, the elder Woodcock was imprisoned by the German government upon the outbreak of World War I. Mrs. Woodcock and the three-year-old Leonard returned to England where the boy received his early schooling in Northampton. After the war the Woodcocks reunited and spent the next eight years in England, where Leonard attended Chipsey, a prestigious preparatory school. In 1926 the family returned to the United States, but this time to Detroit, Michigan, where Leonard continued his education first at Detroit City College (which later became Wayne State University) and then at the Walsh Institute of Accountancy.

However, with the arrival of the depression he was forced to drop out of school, and he took a job at the Detroit Gear & Machine Company, a subsidiary of the Borg-Warner Corporation. There he worked for 35¢ an hour, twelve hours a day, seven days a week. While his father's Labour and Socialist party activities in Great Britain made Woodcock sympathetic to unions, the harsh working conditions at Detroit Gear reinforced his leanings. Woodcock joined the federal local union that sprang up at the plant, so called because its federal charter had been directly issued from the national office of the American Federation of Labor (AFL). He soon became increasingly active in organizing the nascent UAW after his local affiliated with the amalgamation of automobile workers' unions, formed in the wake of John L. Lewis's establishment of the Committee for Industrial Organization (CIO) in 1936. Shortly afterward tuberculosis forced Woodcock to spend time in warmer climes, but he returned to the labor movement as a Wayne County (Michigan) CIO official in the late 1930s.

In 1940 he came back to UAW work in Grand Rapids, Michigan, as a staff representative. Then, from 1944 through 1946 he worked at the Muskegon, Michigan, facility of Continental Motors as a punch press operator. During this time he abandoned his affiliation with the Socialist party and became part of the Reuther faction in the internal conflict for control of the international union. The Reutherites, generally regarded as the right wing of the union (such as it was since most had youthful socialist sympathies), engaged in an internecine factional battle with what was called the Addes faction (after secretary-treasurer George Addes). This latter grouping consisted of militant trade unionists without any political leanings (such as incumbent president R. J. Thomas, Addes, and vice-president Richard Frankensteen) along with the far-left Communist wing of the union. Years later Woodcock still remembered the turbulence of those days. "I lived through the great factional fight, and no union in this country was ever more torn by factionalism than the UAW," he once informed convention delegates. "All [through] the period from our beginning . . . until November 1947, this union was a great big cockpit" from the national level down to the individual local levels, where there would be contesting slates at each election.

Woodcock, though, had allied with the winning side. Reuther first captured the presidency at the 1946 convention and asked Woodcock, who had been a key member of his caucus, to become his first administrative assistant. He agreed to take the job, serving from 1946 to 1947. Woodcock knew, however, that to fulfill his aspirations within the union he would have to win an elective office, and constitutional provisions required a sufficient amount of plant time to hold union office. He thus went back to the plants in Grand Rapids, and, when Reuther won reelection and control of the executive board in fall 1947, Woodcock was elected regional director of Region 1D in western Michigan. His mentor then appointed him director of the American and Continental Motors departments, administrative positions he held until 1955.

In 1955 Woodcock successfully ran for one of the six vice-presidencies in the union and moved into the top leadership echelon. With little delay Reuther marked him as his potential successor by naming him to the most important post in the organization: director of the General Motors (GM) department, the largest in the union. It was not until 1958, though, that Woodcock had a chance to become the leading spokesperson during contract negotiations.

The negotiations of that year took place in the midst of a recession which created substantial unemployment in the automobile industry. Working against that difficulty Woodcock managed to produce a landmark contract for the UAW. He had stressed in internal union councils the need for local union bargaining supplements to the national automobile agreements. His prime objective was the obtaining of the legal right for locals to negotiate local supplements—supported by the right to strike with international union authorization. That he was able to achieve this concession from a reluctant GM management was evidence of his growing skill as a national negotiator.

That accomplishment also marked his emergence as Reuther's most likely successor. Through the rest of the 1950s UAW watchers thought Woodcock was the odds-on favorite to succeed Reuther should the latter succeed AFL-CIO president George Meany as the nation's top labor spokesman. However, he was only two years younger than Reuther, and if his mentor retired at sixty-five, the mandatory UAW retirement age, he would only have been able to serve for a brief period. Thus in the early 1960s—as Meany continued on as the AFL-CIO's top executive—it appeared as though Reuther would stay as head of the UAW. He began to groom the younger Douglas Fraser, who directed the union's Chrysler department and had been the president's administrative assistant for most of the 1950s, to replace him when he chose to step down.

This also became apparent to Woodcock, who grew restless at being cut off from further advancement. His active interest in international labor affairs garnered him an offer for an ambassadorship in the Kennedy administration, an offer he wanted to accept. Reuther asked Woodcock to stay, though, and out of loyalty he did. Again turning his attention to bargaining, internal union developments, and politics, the director of the GM and Aerospace departments negotiated the first contract prohibitions on employment discrimination and several patterns in aerospace that eventually spread to the automobile industry. He and Reuther also did their best to expand internal union support, among the rank and file, for bargaining objectives that would expand employment opportunities for younger workers who were locked out of jobs in affluent industries, rather than simply protect the jobs of current UAW members. They did so because they regarded the creation of a large, discontented younger work force as fertile organizing ground for conservative political reaction—reaction that would target the suppression of labor unions as one of its first objectives. "Whom did Hitler first mobilize?" Woodcock rhetorically asked delegates to a GM bargaining council meeting in 1964. "He mobilized the young men. The Storm Troopers, the Brown Shirts were made up of kids who had no hope in the German Republic in the late 1920s and early 1930s. Who is going to exploit this dissatisfaction against the labor movement?" he queried his audience. "It is going to be the extreme right, which is gathering political force in this country. . . . and if to them the labor movement stands as a group of selfish people concerned only with themselves and not with their plight, then we are really going to get the business."

Though there were reasons to believe an energized conservative movement was possible in 1964, a unique convergence of political forces caused the opposite. Organized labor became a part of the broad liberal coalition of the mid 1960s and strongly supported the advances of the civil rights movement and the social welfare programs of Lyndon Johnson's Great Society. Woodcock's career as top GM negotiator continued, and he suc-

ceeded in achieving incremental gains in each negotiation round. He and his wife, whom he had married in 1941, divorced, and in 1969 he suffered a second tuberculosis attack. By 1970 it appeared that the union executive was trapped and would retire from the organization at that post. He was, in the words of a close associate, "a fellow of tremendous abilities . . . acting as if things were at a dead end."

The fatal crash of Reuther's light aircraft in May 1970, however, changed all that. Suddenly, although greatly saddened by the death of Reuther, Woodcock became one of the two top candidates to succeed the longtime UAW president—his rival being Douglas Fraser, who had the support of Victor Reuther, Walter's brother. The UAW's executive board met twelve days after the May 9 accident to choose a new president to fulfill the remainder of Reuther's term. When a poll revealed that Woodcock had a one vote edge, 13 to 12, Fraser graciously withdrew from the race. Woodcock thus became the fifth international president of the UAW and its first since 1946.

Reuther's legacy, both as leader of the UAW and as an American labor leader, was substantial. His mentor's long record of accomplishment, however, did not seem to phase Woodcock. "I am always asked," he reflected in the early years of his presidency, " 'How does it feel to try to fill Walter Reuther's shoes?' I'm just not going to try to fill them. I'm just going to do the best I can. And when I made that determination, I felt very relaxed and at peace with myself and the world." And, perhaps reflecting a release of the stress he had felt at being shut off from further advancement: "The funny thing is I've been much more relaxed since I've been president than I was before."

Nevertheless, Woodcock faced great pressure to prove himself in the automotive contract negotiations of fall 1970. In appearance as well as personal proclivities he was quite a contrast to Reuther. Tall, lanky, and bespectacled, it was said that he could be mistaken for a management representative. Reuther loved the public spotlight and liked to make public pronouncements but was often distant in person, particularly in his later years. Woodcock, on the other hand, while cool to outsiders, in reality "is a very warm individual," according to Victor Reuther, and was considered approachable by other UAW officials. And, unlike Walter Reuther, he did not relish the spotlight.

Woodcock, left, presenting Victor Reuther with the UAW's Social Justice Award in 1972 (courtesy of UAW)

There were also differences in how each dealt with problems. Reuther operated on an intuitive level in his relationship with the automobile companies. Woodcock was much more of an intellectual; he preferred to analyze a situation coolly before speaking "thoughtfully and concisely," in the words of a labor reporter. Indeed, shortly after his ascent to the presidency both company and union functionaries realized that "Woodcock possessed a mind superior to Reuther's. . . ," wrote labor writer William Serrin.

While his bearing might be "professorial" and "princely," by some accounts, in bargaining sessions the more forceful aspects of his personality arose. Serrin characterized him as "rough, intense, forthright; he also possesses what an associate calls 'a magnificent temper.'" Moreover, he was totally honest in his dealings with GM executives; more than his predecessor, they believed, he meant what he said. As one of his fellow negotiators on the GM bargaining committee said of Woodcock: "He don't dilly around. He comes right to the point. . . . If he tells the General Motors bosses that he is going to do something, if he tells them he is going to jump

off the bridge, they can be waiting for him with the stretcher, because old Leonard, he is going to jump."

There were many factors that predicated that the 1970 negotiations would be more difficult than usual. For one thing, Ford UAW members pleaded that they should be exempted from being named as the strike target yet again–meaning that in all likelihood the union would have to choose hard-nosed bargainer GM (as Chrysler was in poor financial condition) as the pattern setter. As always, the economics seemed most salient; in this round it would be the restoration of an uncapped cost-of-living clause in the agreement. But that was only on the surface. Hidden resentments were perhaps more important.

On the union side, foremost among the hidden causes of what was to be the first strike against GM since it defeated the UAW's collective bargaining initiatives in 1946, was the spectacular increase in local union demands in supplementary bargaining–indicative of the restiveness of a rank and file operating under intensely frustrating factory working conditions. In 1958 the UAW GM locals put forth 11,000 of these local demands; twelve years later the corporation received 38,000. The size of the problem was enormous, for often the date of return to work at a given plant after a national strike depended on the successful resolution of these local demands. Oftentimes these demands centered on creating a more hospitable work atmosphere; just as often company executives considered them frivolous and without merit. However, *New York Times* labor reporter Serrin wrote that they "illustrate . . . the double standard that exists in American labor. Most of them represent benefits that are given to white-collar workers without thought, and become frivolous only when blue-collar workers seek them."

On the company side the 1970 negotiations were regarded as critical to the future. GM "wanted to teach a lesson to the UAW," according to Serrin, even if it took a long work stoppage. Specifically, the company would strive to obtain union assent to the imposition of penalties for excessive absenteeism, tardiness, and poor quality work. Executives wanted more than just these changes designed to increase productivity rates, though; they also made up their minds to contain labor costs. In many ways, according to Serrin, GM officials considered their corporation "as the defender of American business, of the American free enterprise system." Thus, given the demonstrated restiveness of UAW members at the shop-floor level, and those of the corporate management hierarchy, an agreement without a strike would have been almost impossible for Woodcock to achieve.

Facing these circumstances, Woodcock and the UAW struck GM. For the next eight weeks the adversaries combated with rhetoric and demonstrations of resolution. In the early period of the engagement, particularly, the new UAW president's temper flared; his denunciations of the corporation were strident. As the strike dragged on, however, cooler heads prevailed upon Woodcock to tone down his statements. He later admitted his mistake. "I had forgotten some of my early organizing experience," he commented. "And that is, when you indulge in inflammatory rhetoric, you delight the people who are with you in the first place; you don't do much to the people who are in the middle; the people who are against you anyway you offend, and you also tend to alienate some of those in the middle whom you have to convince in order to win."

As the strike continued, with little progress being made in local bargaining, GM also became more sympathetic to settlement. Its white-collar work force continued to draw its salary and the backlog of inventory dwindled. Thus, corporation executives decided to settle at the terms Woodcock needed to obtain ratification. While those terms imposed higher labor costs than the corporation wanted, it was a realistic economic settlement. Perhaps more important, top company officials realized that they had very little to gain from undercutting Woodcock's position in the union, which would be sure to happen with an interminable strike.

Although the agreement was consummated, and both sides believed they could live with the economics of it, critics such as Serrin charged that the entire episode revealed a good deal about the relationship between GM (and the automobile companies generally) and the international union. The relative inattention given to the local-level demands—which to Serrin represented the truly critical issues for UAW members—symbolized that the union and company had an "arrangement" of sorts. This state of affairs saw the union acceding to company productivity rationalizing plans—in the hopes of increasing members' standard of living and protecting their jobs from foreign competition—which at best did not deal with the major problem of worker alienation, and at worst intensified those types of problems. While occasionally the international union was forced by rank-and-file pressure to give authorization to job actions at the local level trying to deal with these frustrations, its leadership—now being perpetuated through the Woodcock presidency—did not seem to have an overall strategy with which to handle these issues.

In some ways the 1970 GM strike brought national attention to the problems of the "blue-collar blues"; work alienation, boredom, and assorted frustrations of a younger, more educated, modern manufacturing work force. Indeed, these subjects drew increasing public attention as the new GM Assembly Division, launched during Woodcock's tenure as president (he was reelected to a two-year term in 1972 and to a three-year term in 1974), began its automized intensification of work, provoking high-visibility strikes in both the Norwood and Lordstown, Ohio, assembly plants. While Serrin's study of the 1970 GM strike, *The Company and the Union* (1973), was critical of the UAW leadership under Woodcock, a good deal of that criticism was perhaps overstated, as the national leadership did coordinate work-load "mini-strike" actions afterward and made those problems an important topic in the 1973 negotiating rounds. Woodcock's administration made significant gains in the Chrysler negotiations (led by Douglas Fraser) that set the pattern after a nine-day national strike. The agreement abolished compulsory overtime, and the union achieved its historic "30 and out" pension program, allowing workers with sufficient seniority (30 years) to receive their company pension regardless of their chronological age. In addition, the union concentrated on winning improvements in health and safety by establishing joint inspection teams. Woodcock improved upon these accomplishments in the 1976 negotiations—his last as international union president—by emphasizing reductions in work time.

During his presidency, while Woodcock concentrated on collective bargaining, believing, as he once stated, "If we can't do that well . . . we can't unite our people on other questions," he maintained Reuther's support of liberal politics and the union's reputation as one of the most reform-oriented unions in the country. His active involvement in the liberal wing of the Democratic party at times brought him into conflict with the AFL-CIO (Reuther had disaffiliated the UAW from the umbrella organization in 1968) over foreign policy, especially regarding the continuing war in Vietnam. In contrast to George Meany, Woodcock endorsed the antiwar candidacy of Sen. George McGovern in 1972. And in the 1976 Michigan Democratic primaries, he was one of the first liberal activists to back the campaign of former Georgia governor Jimmy Carter for the presidency.

His ties to the Carter campaign, in fact, led to his appointment as an ambassador for the new administration upon his mandatory retirement from the UAW presidency in 1977. For years he had been exhorting his union to make stronger commitments in international affairs. The UAW's participation in the International Metalworkers' Federation (IMF) World Auto Council had been a forum from which unionized automobile workers from different countries could discuss common concerns. "Within 10 years, it is predicted 200 companies will dominate the economy of the whole world," he informed the 1974 UAW convention that elected him to his last term as president. "UAW prestige is high across the world," he further said, "and . . . working with our counterpart elements . . . and other democratic countries, can be a major force for peace and for the control of the multinational companies." It was this interest in foreign affairs, along with his political support, that brought him the appointment as the Carter administration's ambassador to the People's Republic of China. Woodcock served in that capacity for several years, leaving the post shortly after the start of the Reagan administration. He is now a professor of labor studies at the University of Michigan and carries on an active public life.

It was in his career as an official of the UAW, however, that Woodcock has made the most important impact on American life. In the main his accomplishments have been his steady continuance of the goals Reuther had pursued through the course of his much longer presidency: commitment to advancing UAW members' standard of living through collective bargaining, the promotion of active government involvement in the economy on behalf of community concerns, and repeated, if limited, attempts to broaden the traditional concerns of the labor movement in the United States.

Unpublished Documents:

"Keynote Speech, UAW President Leonard Woodcock, 24th UAW Constitutional Convention, Los Angeles, California, 2 June 1974" UAW, *Proceedings of the Constitutional Convention,* 1974 (Archives of Labor History and Urban Affairs, Walter P. Reuther Library, Wayne State University, Detroit, Mich.);

"Keynote Speech, UAW President Leonard Woodcock, 25th UAW Constitutional Convention, Los Angeles, California, 15 May 1977" UAW, *Proceedings of the Constitutional Convention,* 1977 (Archives of Labor History and Urban Affairs, Walter P. Reuther Library, Wayne State University, Detroit, Mich.).

References:

Gary M. Fink, "Leonard F. Woodcock," in *Biographical Dictionary of American Labor,* 2nd edition, edited by Fink (Westport, Conn.: Greenwood Press, 1984);

William Serrin, *The Company and the Union: the "Civilized" Relationship of the General Motors Corporation and the United Auto Workers* (New York: Knopf, 1973).

Archives:

Material on Woodcock is located in the records of the UAW President's Office: Leonard F. Woodcock Files, Archives of Labor History and Urban Affairs, Walter P. Reuther Library, Wayne State University, Detroit, Michigan.

Yellow Truck & Coach Manufacturing Company
by Robert J. Kothe

Atlanta, Georgia

One of the most complicated business stories in automotive history, involving various taxicab, automobile, bus, and truck operations, the activities bearing the Yellow name apparently had their origins in 1910 when John D. Hertz painted nine Thomas Flyer cars yellow and hired them out as cabs on the streets of Chicago. In *Chrome Colossus* (1980), a history of General Motors (GM), the company which eventually absorbed a number of Hertz's varied businesses, Ed Cray repeats a story that Hertz, a Chicago car salesman, acted in desperation when he found himself stuck with these nine cars which he could not sell. But in actuality, Hertz's involvement in the cab business resulted from his connection with the Walden W. Shaw Livery Company of Chicago, first as a salesman and then, by 1908, as a partner. In a period when cab service was enjoying increasing popularity in big cities, Hertz, a shrewd businessman, turned the Shaw company's emphasis from selling cars, at which it had not been very successful, to the use of cars as taxicabs. In the beginning he used secondhand cars, waiting until the Shaw company's finances were healthy enough for him to buy the nine Thomas Flyers, which he intended to use as taxis from the outset. He is said to have painted them a bright yellow after a "chance reading of a scientific journal detailing color tests" indicated that this was the most visible color he could use to attract attention to his cabs.

In the next several years Hertz's Yellow Cabs were operating throughout the country, and he reportedly became a millionaire. In 1915 the Yellow Cab, or Taxicab (the terms seem to have been used interchangeably) Manufacturing Company was organized, both to run Hertz's cab operations and also to manufacture the cabs. The actual manufacturing of the cabs took place in the Shaw company's factory; 150 were constructed in 1915 and thousands in the years that followed.

Features of the 1929 Yellow Cab

After World War I the Shaw company announced plans to produce passenger cars as well as cabs, and it introduced a car it called the Shaw at the Chicago Automobile Show in February 1920. To avoid confusion with the known connection of the Shaw name with taxicabs, the automobile's name was shortly changed to the Colonial, and in July the 4-cylinder engine, similar to the engine used in the cabs because of their economical operation, was replaced by a 12-cylinder design. The passenger car did not do well, and in 1921, when John

D. Hertz gained complete control of the Shaw company, he switched to a 6-cylinder Continental engine and marketed the former Shaw/Colonial cars under the Ambassador name. He sought to promote sales of the big Ambassador Six by declaring that it was backed by the years of experience he had had in "building motor vehicles for heavy duty service." The Ambassador came in two-, four-, and seven-passenger models and in 1923 was offered in prices ranging from $1,440 for the bare chassis to $2,340 for the top model. In 1924 Hertz, who had acquired a car rental company as well as a truck rental company, introduced a smaller 6-cylinder Ambassador designed for the rental business for which Hertz would become most famous. He changed the name of the car to Hertz in 1926 and continued to produce rental cars under this name until late 1927, when he decided it was more economical to use cars of other manufacturers for his Hertz Drive-Ur-Self operation.

Meanwhile Hertz had expanded into the bus business, gaining control of the Chicago Motor Coach Company in 1922, followed shortly by several other acquisitions, the most important of which was the Fifth Avenue Coach Company of New York, a bus manufacturer since 1915. He combined these into the Omnibus Corporation of America in 1924. To provide his bus companies with their buses he organized the Yellow Coach Manufacturing Company, headquartered in Chicago and headed by officials from the Fifth Avenue Coach Company. In addition to supplying buses to Hertz-owned bus companies, Yellow Coach in 1924 landed orders from two outside companies, agreeing to supply $5 million worth of coaches to Public Service of New Jersey and over $6 million worth to the Philadelphia Rapid Transit. Typical coaches cost about $10,000 each in the 1920s, so these orders represented more than 1,000 units.

The bus-building activities of Yellow Coach and the truck manufacturing activities of Yellow Cab attracted the attention of GM, which was producing trucks and commercial vehicles with limited success and was much interested in producing buses. GM's larger trucks, which were produced for the most part without bodies and sometimes without engines or transmissions, were usually sold to specialty companies that designed custom-made bodies for specific purposes and fit them to the bare trucks. These heavy commercial vehicles were manufactured by the GMC truck division. Smaller trucks, 1- and 1.5-ton models for the most part, were built by the automobile divisions. Competition was fierce in the large truck market, and profits were small for even the best producers. In Yellow Cab Manufacturing and Yellow Coach Manufacturing, Alfred P. Sloan, Jr., and other GM executives saw an opportunity to link up with an important truck and bus manufacturing operation and also the chance to add a large number of experienced truck and bus executives to its organization. This last purpose is clearly shown by the fact that former Yellow executives dominated the new firm for many years despite GM's majority interest in the business.

The proposal agreed to by GM and the Hertz organizations in 1925 mandated the creation of a new company to be called Yellow Truck & Coach Manufacturing Company. GM transferred its GMC truck division, valued at $11 million, plus $5 million in cash, to the new company in return for about 57 percent of the voting stock. The Yellow cab and bus manufacturing operations were transferred to the new company, along with some of Hertz's other enterprises, including the car rental business, but not including the Yellow Cab operating companies or the Omnibus Corporation of America. Hertz served as chairman of the board of Yellow Truck & Coach until 1929 when he resigned to devote himself to the Omnibus operations and other interests.

Yellow Truck & Coach consolidated its production in new facilities in Pontiac, Michigan, and it became the largest American bus producer and the fifth-largest truck manufacturer. It was also at one point the third-largest producer of taxicabs, behind the Checker Corporation and P. Moller, but the depression nearly destroyed that market and production dropped sharply in the 1930s. The varied nature of the company's background was reflected in the fact that the bus division continued to use the Yellow name on its products while the trucks and taxicabs used the GMC nameplate.

While the company enjoyed market success, Yellow rarely made money. However, its close relationship with GM makes it difficult to determine Yellow's true economic value to its primary owner, GM. Yellow, for example, purchased most of its accessories and parts from various units of GM and paid the larger company for assorted services. The bus business did well in the late 1920s and 1930s. Electric trolley and interurban lines were disappearing in many communities for a variety of reasons. Maintenance of their right of way was expensive, as was electric power for operations. There had been little improvement in the technology of the systems for a number of years while buses were rapidly improving in speed and comfort. There had been more than 800 companies operating streetcars in 1922, and about half that number remained in 1936. In contrast, even during the depression, buses did fairly well, since they were more flexible than rail systems and less expensive to operate under many conditions. As a result the market for buses was fairly strong even under the difficult conditions of the early 1930s.

Yellow was an innovator in bus design. Its city buses, with the early use of rear engines, were among the best selling and most progressive urban vehicles. The company was also a leader in the design of relatively high-speed buses for highway travel. The production of buses for large companies was, to a large extent, a custom business. The larger operating companies would practically design their own units by writing specifications that were best suited to local conditions. To satisfy these customers Yellow produced vehicles with a variety of power sources. In addition to gasoline-powered units, it built a few gas-electric hybrids, which used a gasoline motor to turn a generator that produced electricity to drive the vehicle. GM moved heavily into the production of diesels and diesel-electric buses in the 1930s.

Greyhound, the intercity bus line, was an important customer for Yellow Truck & Coach. In 1936 the models the company built for Greyhound ranged in price from $7,200 to $14,200. Hertz's Omnibus Corporation and the Public Service Corpora-tion of New Jersey were Yellow's other major customers. Yellow also invested in or acquired control of marginal bus and trolley companies as a means of gaining new outlets for its coaches. These actions preceded the larger and more famous step taken in 1936 by GM, together with Firestone and Standard Oil of California, to organize National City Lines, which bought up streetcar lines, converted them to bus systems, and then sold them on the condition that the new owners would use only equipment powered by gas. This practice insured a ready market for buses and, of course, benefited Yellow, the largest producer of buses. It also led to charges and court actions that contended that GM's only intention was to wreck electric transportation systems in order to build up sales of its coaches.

In 1943 GM purchased the rest of the voting shares in Yellow Truck & Coach and ended its existence as an independent company. It shortly was renamed the GMC Truck & Coach Division and would completely dominate the American urban bus market. It also continued to produce trucks but with less success. The Hertz car rental business continued to be owned by GM until it was sold in 1953, although a close link remained as Hertz for twenty years continued to use GM cars for its customers.

References:

Ed Cray, *Chrome Colossus: General Motors and Its Times* (New York: McGraw-Hill, 1980);

Beverly Rae Kimes and Henry Austin Clark, *Standard Catalog of American Cars, 1805-1942* (Iola, Wis.: Krause, 1985);

"Yellow Truck & Coach," *Fortune*, 4 (July 1936): 61-67, 106-115.

Zeder-Skelton-Breer Engineering

by Richard P. Scharchburg

GMI Engineering & Management Institute

In the early years of the horseless age—the last decade of the nineteenth century and the first decade of the twentieth century—automobiles were most frequently developed by those associated with manufacturing, especially machinists. Backyard sheds, barns, and carriage houses figured prominently as sites for tinkering with early gasoline-powered horseless carriages. As a result of this unsystematic approach to development of automotive technology, collective knowledge advanced sporadically.

However, by the second decade of the twentieth century the accumulated knowledge was being passed to college-educated and professionally trained engineers whose impact on automobile technology was soon to result in vastly more dependable and reliable vehicles. By the 1910s men like Charles Kettering had already established industrial research laboratories dedicated to engineering and research in regard to specific areas of automobile technology. Gradually spreading through the industry, engineering and research departments were established by progressive automobile manufacturers in efforts to adapt the new technologies to established product lines and for development of entirely new products.

In 1913 the Studebaker Corporation, which had begun the manufacture of gasoline-powered vehicles in 1904, established an engineering department headed by Fred M. Zeder, who had come into the organization when Studebaker purchased the facilities and assets of Everitt-Metzger-Flanders (EMF), an automotive company, in 1912. Three years later Zeder invited two young engineers, Owen Skelton and Carl Breer, to join him in Studebaker's engineering department. In 1920 Walter Chrysler persuaded the engineering team of Zeder, Skelton, and Breer to join him in helping to launch a newly designed Willys car in Elizabeth, New Jersey. Efforts to develop a quality auto progressed satisfactorily, but financial backing could

Fred M. Zeder

not be secured and the Willys Corporation's assets, plant, and car designs were sold at public auction in 1921.

After the Willys debacle Zeder formed his own engineering consulting firm, which was based in Newark, New Jersey, under the name of the Zeder-Skelton-Breer (ZSB) Engineering Company. Zeder personally financed most of the venture. The firm, its founding partners, and the small team of other engineers struggled to meet payrolls and operating expenses but continued to dream of building a new car embodying the highest possible level of engineering skill. Over the next four years they were responsible for the development of the Flint Six, manufactured by Durant Motors, and the 1924 Chrysler Six, the flagship of the Chrysler Corporation.

Zeder, Skelton, and Breer went on to form the nucleus of the Chrysler engineering and research departments, which were regarded as among the most innovative in the industry. Zeder, Skelton, and Breer's leadership continued to dominate Chrysler engineering until the late 1940s when age and changing consumer demands forced the replacement of ZSB.

The "front man" of the famous engineering triumvirate was Fred Morrell Zeder. Possessing a salesman's gift of persuasion and a wealth of engineering talent, Zeder, who brought the three men together, was usually their spokesman. As an engineer Zeder was conservative, always including a large margin of safety in his work. Throughout his career Zeder emphasized quality over fads and appearance. His conservatism, often a strength, eventually left Chrysler products technically and stylistically behind the rest of the industry in the late 1940s, and the corporation's sales suffered greatly.

Zeder was born in Bay City, Michigan, on March 19, 1886, the fourth of the five sons and one daughter of Rudolph Zeder and Matilda Jane McKendry Zeder. Zeder was educated in the Bay City public schools. During summer vacations and the summer following high school graduation he was employed as an apprentice machinist by the Industrial Works in Bay City. His first full-time job was as a mechanic with the Michigan Central Railroad in its Motive Power and Train Divisions. In 1905 he entered the University of Michigan, and he graduated in 1909 with a bachelor of science degree in mechanical engineering. Immediately after graduation from college, he was selected to serve as a graduate apprentice with the Allis-Chalmers Company and subsequently became erecting engineer in 1910. During his apprenticeship Zeder met Carl Breer, an association which warmed into a friendship and professional bond that were to last throughout Zeder's lifetime.

After completing a job erecting a power plant in Detroit, Zeder joined EMF late in 1910. He was placed in charge of the engineering laboratories and also headed a consulting firm specializing in power plant engineering. EMF was located in the center of Detroit's automotive district on Piquette Avenue east of Woodward, close to the Fisher Brothers, the Regal Car Company, the Ford Motor Company,

and General Motors Research. While at EMF Zeder was responsible for the design of a new 4-cylinder engine which was used in most production models. In 1913 Zeder was appointed consulting engineer for the Studebaker Corporation, which acquired EMF in 1912, and a year later he was promoted to the position of chief engineer. Zeder had some initial difficulty in organizing and directing the many temperamental designers already at Studebaker, but he prevailed and automobile production and sales climbed steadily until reaching a peak in 1916. However, accumulating car troubles and field problems started depleting Studebaker finances, threatening the company with bankruptcy.

Recognizing the deficiencies of his engineering organization, Zeder was successful in convincing Studebaker's general manager of production that the addition of qualified and proven engineering talent would solve many problems. He invited Owen Skelton, then working at Packard, to join him at Studebaker, and shortly thereafter he also enticed his friend and fellow engineer Carl Breer to make the same move to Studebaker. Thus, by late 1916 Zeder had brought together what was to become the most famous engineering team in the automotive industry. The new line of Studebaker cars was designed, tested, and introduced through concentrated efforts of the new engineering group. By 1918 Studebaker sales were rising again, as were its profits, a trend due in part to Zeder's engineering and organizational talents.

The second of the "Three Musketeers," as Zeder, Skelton, and Breer were affectionately called, Carl Breer was born in Los Angeles, California, on November 8, 1883, the son of German immigrants. His father, Louis Breer, was born in 1828 in the Black Forest region and was a blacksmith. He worked his way to the United States on a sailing ship about 1838. After living with an aunt in Indiana he traveled to California in 1849 and made his way to the goldfields. After quickly deciding his prospects at gold mining were poor, he took the same ship to Los Angeles where he again became a blacksmith. Breer's mother, Julia Buehn, was also born in the Black Forest area in 1840. While yet a teenager Julia and a sister left home and traveled to the United States where they settled with an uncle who operated a shipping line. After she moved to Los Angeles, Julia met and married Louis Breer in July 1863 at the San Gabriel Mission. Breer was the last

From left, Owen Skelton, Zeder, and Carl Breer (courtesy of Chrysler Corporation)

of nine children born in the family home on San Pedro Street.

Breer was educated in the Los Angeles public schools and attended the Commercial High School but upon graduation was unable to enter his chosen college, Stanford University. Breer later recalled that his father's carriage and blacksmith shop had provided an ideal early outlet for his mechanical interests, one which "proved of great value to my future activities." With the craftsmanship and machining learned in the blacksmith shop, he set to work to build a steam-driven car of his own design, which he subsequently drove to Pasadena. He demonstrated his steam car to the Tourist Automobile Company, at the time the major West Coast manufacturer of automobiles, a demonstration which garnered Breer his first job following graduation from high school. He later became associated with several makes of vehicles–Toledo Steam Cars, the Spalding, the Northern, the White–and a little later assisted in the design and building of the Duro car in Los Angeles. The Duro had a 2-cylinder opposed engine with the transmission set forward and a solid drive shaft to the rear axle, a most advanced concept for early automobiles.

Breer's real desire, however, was to continue his education, and he sought entry into the highly respected Throop Polytechnic Institute, at that time a preparatory school for Stanford. At the institute he was allotted one year to graduate and to meet the entrance requirements to Stanford. His year there was satisfactory, and he entered Stanford in 1905, graduating four years later with a degree in mechanical engineering.

After graduation Breer accepted a two-year graduate apprenticeship with the Allis-Chalmers Company in Allis, Wisconsin, near Milwaukee. While there he participated in research work on its portable electric generating units, work which took him all over the United States. While in the apprentice program Breer met Zeder, who was also in the apprentice program. Following the apprenticeship he and Zeder went their separate ways for a few years, but in 1916 they formed a lifelong association in automotive engineering and careers at Chrysler. In his engineering career Breer was a careful and thorough thinker. Not an inventor, his forte was the application of existing technology to solve perplexing problems. His expertise was engines, but he was interested in every aspect of a car's design

Zeder, right, with Walter P. Chrysler (courtesy of Chrysler Corporation)

from front-wheel drive to aerodynamics.

Owen R. Skelton was the least charismatic of the ZSB engineering team; he also left little information on himself. He was born in Edgerton, Ohio, on February 9, 1886, and served his early apprenticeship in his father's harness and saddlery shop. After completion of his high school education he attended Ohio State University. Following graduation he took his first job with the Pope-Toledo plant in Toledo, Ohio. At the time the Pope-Toledo was one of the most progressive of all gasoline motor cars, with engineering far advanced over its competition. There he gained a reputation for his knowledge of axles and transmissions. About 1907 he joined the design drafting department of the Packard Motor Car Company located in Detroit. Skelton remained at Packard for seven years. While at Packard he entered a partnership with a friend to build the Benham car in Detroit. Produced from 1914 to 1917, the Benham had a Continental engine and other standard components. Its novel feature, however, was streamlining—perhaps the Skelton touch—which was most unusual for the time. Skelton left Benham in 1916 when he found that his experience and talent were in demand elsewhere. He received what he considered an attractive offer to join the en-

gineering department at Studebaker under the direction of Zeder.

Skelton, characterized as thorough, studious, and quiescent, possessed the ample analytical skill and experience Zeder needed. His design background, especially with rear axles, drives, and transmissions, proved invaluable in the expedited design of the projected new car line to replace the obsolete, cumbersome Studebaker line.

Later in 1916 Breer arrived from California, and he completed the triumvirate of engineering diversification, background, and ability that eventually earned them a place in automotive history. The team setup avoided most of the costly mistakes that led to the failure of so many motor car manufacturing companies. Skelton's ability with his personalized leadership in organizing and directing design activity of other team members was superb. His spirit of cooperation in the design of engineering innovations was immense. During his many years in Chrysler engineering he was personally responsible for a mounting arrangement for a rear-engine car, 4-wheel hydraulic brakes, all-steel body construction, and fluid coupling. "Floating Power," a method for mounting the engine, was another Skelton innovation which was widely copied throughout the industry. Later he was cofounder of the Chrysler Institute of Engineering and was given a seat on the corporation's board of directors.

In 1920 Zeder was asked by Walter Chrysler, then the head of the Willys Corporation in Elizabeth, New Jersey, to join him in an effort to design and market a car that was a spin-off from the Willys-Overland operation in Toledo, Ohio.

Consequently Zeder, Skelton, and Breer, along with their organization of approximately fifteen men, left the Studebaker Corporation on July 14, 1920, to join the Willys Corporation. Chrysler hoped that the Willys Light Six, which had been developed in Toledo and shipped to Elizabeth, would require little engineering since it was the same car as the one being built at Willys-Overland except for the addition of two more cylinders and a longer wheelbase. His ultimate plan for the ZSB organization was to form an engineering department capable of designing an entirely new car. But Chrysler's plan for the new car had to be delayed by problems with the redesigned Willys-Overland car.

The car suffered from constant breakage of both frames and bodies, and tests by the ZSB organization confirmed the car's overall flimsiness. Their adverse report agreed with an earlier report given to Chrysler in spring 1920. After meeting with the bankers, and informing them of the engineering and testing reports on the car's poor performance, Chrysler announced that the car would not be built.

The engineering department began a frantic effort to develop what they referred to as a "hurried replacement car" to try to ease the tension and embarrassment of the whole situation. Working around the clock at the plant and at Skelton's rooms at the Beechwood Hotel in Summit, New Jersey, an entirely new car was ready for testing early in 1921. The car was tested for 30,000 miles, after which it was torn down and found to be in perfect condition. The engine design, a 7-bearing, high-compression configuration with interchangeable bearings, became the hallmark of initial Chrysler engineering.

Meanwhile, Chrysler had taken on the Maxwell and Chalmers motor car companies, and as the interest of the Willys Corporation in his car began to fade, Chrysler devised a plan whereby Maxwell-Chalmers would purchase the Willys plant in Elizabeth and manufacture the car ZSB had been working on. While Chrysler negotiated with Willys,

Zeder, Skelton, and Breer chafed at delays. In the midst of the talks, and to the surprise of Chrysler, on November 30, 1921, the Willys Corporation entered receivership.

As a result of the receivership, which scuttled Chrysler's plans, Zeder, Skelton, and Breer decided to form their own engineering consulting firm and leased space in the Willys plant in Elizabeth. While they took any job available to meet payrolls for their organization, at no time did they stop their engine research. During the early part of 1922 the engineers did not see much of Chrysler, who seemed no longer interested in their car. But unknown to ZSB, Chrysler had continued with plans to purchase the Elizabeth plant when it went up for public auction. When the sale finally took place on June 9, 1922, Chrysler was there, determined to obtain the property, but he had not anticipated the presence of Joseph P. Day representing William C. Durant. Durant wanted the plant in order to manufacture the Flint automobile for his nascent company, Durant Motor Corporation. Durant's final bid of $5.525 million was $525,000 over Chrysler's final offer.

After this reversal the ZSB Engineering Company moved to 26 Mechanic Street in Newark, New Jersey. Again they went to work on a new car design. On November 11, 1922, Skelton telephoned Chrysler from his room at the Robert Trent Hotel and asked if he would look over the latest plans for a new car. After seeing the drawings, an excited Chrysler signed a contract with ZSB Engineering, in effect approving specifications for the car that became the 1924 Chrysler Six.

About this same time Durant Motors was tooling up to manufacture the Flint car which was very nearly the same car that ZSB had designed and planned to manufacture in the Willys plant in Elizabeth. Several experimental Flint cars were built, but their performance was not equal to the original "Elizabeth" cars developed by ZSB. Durant asked ZSB to tune up the old experimental cars to improve their performance. As a result ZSB Engineering Company was given the job of redesigning and developing the Flint engine. This gave them access to the old dynamometer laboratory at Elizabeth and a splendid opportunity to test their new Chrysler engine. Their actions were perhaps not entirely ethical, but the actual development of the Chrysler engine took place in their Newark laboratory and only testing was carried out on the Durant company's dynamometer.

In April 1923 Chrysler was invited to see an operating version of the latest engine for the proposed Chrysler car. He was immediately impressed with the smoothness and performance and gave orders to proceed with the final design.

On June 6, 1923, the ZSB Engineering Company, with its cadre of engineers, arrived in Detroit and took space on the second floor of the old Chalmers plant on Jefferson Avenue. Before final designs were approved and production started, they redesigned the engine's conventional oil system, changed the cooling system to obtain higher efficiency, and dampened vibrations. For testing purposes they hid their experimental power plant under the hood of an aging Maxwell and drove it around the streets of Detroit, thereby attracting little attention. Rapid progress was achieved and the first experimental cars were completed by the September 1 deadline. At first they all were built with 2-wheel brakes, but Chrysler made the decision to incorporate hydraulic 4-wheel brakes, the first 4-wheel system in the automobile industry installed as standard equipment.

The new car caused so much interest that ZSB's old employer, Studebaker Corporation, made a determined effort to buy a controlling interest in Maxwell. This effort progressed so far that some of the Studebaker executives and financial backers came to Detroit and were given a demonstration of the car's performance. Chrysler, as president of Maxwell, was in a predicament. He had been dreaming for years of a new car that would bear his name but still retained a responsibility to Maxwell's stockholders. At what proved to be the final meeting with Studebaker interests, he imposed terms that he knew could not be met, and the negotiations were dropped. Chrysler meant to have his car, even to the point of outmaneuvering those in the way of his objective and resorting to somewhat devious methods.

The new Chrysler Six was America's first medium-priced, high-styled automobile. It had a high-compression engine, 4-wheel hydraulic brakes, aluminum pistons, full-pressure lubrication, air cleaner, oil filter, shock absorbers, tubular front axles, and many other features that never before had been combined in a mass-produced car. Only 160 inches overall, it nevertheless offered plenty of room for five adults. Weighing 2,650 pounds, it rode as steadily as heavier models because of its low center of gravity and its carefully engineered balance.

After his success in introducing the car in 1924, Chrysler moved to gain financial backing and a corporation under his own name. In 1924, under a voluntary plan and a mere flutter of legal papers, the Maxwell Motor Corporation transferred its business and property to a new company, the Chrysler Corporation. With little fanfare the Zeder-Skelton-Breer Engineering Company and its team of engineers merged into the Chrysler organization where they directed the corporation's engineering and design department until they left the company in the early 1950s. As the front man for the triumvirate, Zeder headed the engineering department as a corporate vice-president. He also was a director, the vice-chairman, and a member of the all-powerful operations committee. Skelton and Breer were also directors but were more interested in the daily operations of the engineering department than with management decisions.

It is significant that in the Chrysler organization the engineering function was the determining force behind all product innovation. Throughout ZSB's long tenure all new product designs began in engineering. Only when engineering was satisfied did any designs go to accounting for pricing or to the operations committee for final production decisions.

With the nearly instantaneous success of the ZSB-developed Chrysler Six and the new 1925 Chrysler Four the corporation began its steady sales climb within the automobile industry. By fall 1925 nearly 3,800 dealers were selling Chrysler cars, and by 1926 Chrysler had moved from twenty-seventh to fifth place. That year four new models emerged from the engineering department: a 4-cylinder Series 50; a 6-cylinder Series 60; the Series 70, which was a new version of the original Chrysler Six; and the Chrysler Imperial, Series 80. By 1927 the firm was fourth in the industry in new car sales with registrations of 192,000 vehicles. The year 1928 was the most spectacular in the early history of Chrysler Corporation. That year Chrysler launched two new cars—the Plymouth and the DeSoto, and purchased one of the industry's largest companies, Dodge Brothers. The "Dependable Dodge" was in third place with a strong product and a loyal dealer body. The introduction of two new models and the addition of a third car taxed to capacity the ZSB-directed engineering department. Not only had two entirely new car designs and developments taken place, but there were also changes in the Dodge line as production under Chrysler management quickly took place. By 1929 Chrysler had arrived as one of the Big Three automobile companies joining Ford and GM.

Chrysler cars of 1929, the year that ended with the start of the Great Depression, pioneered the downdraft carburetor and rust-proofed fenders and other sheet metal parts. In spite of a diminished demand for cars Chrysler continued investments in its new models, developed by the engineering department. The 1933 Plymouth was introduced late in 1932 with additional engineering advancements: a 6-cylinder model with "Floating Power" engine mounts; a safety steel body; free wheeling, hydraulic brakes; a double-drop rigid X-member frame; and a low center of gravity—practically a total redesign from the previous year.

As the depression took its full toll within American and world business, Chrysler, in fact, strengthened its place among other automobile manufacturers and gained a reputation for being vigorous, tough, and competitive. In 1933 Chrysler was the only automotive firm to surpass its sales record of 1929, which had been the boom sales year in the industry. Throughout the depression years the company never reduced research or investment expenditures, recognizing that engineering and research were the foundations upon which the company had been built and on which competitive advantage in the current marketplace and future growth would be founded.

In 1934, inspired by Carl Breer and influenced by Zeder and Skelton, Chrysler introduced the Chrysler and DeSoto Airflow cars. The Airflows embodied a new concept of weight distribution which reduced vibration frequencies to within a range more comfortable to passengers. Engineers moved the engine forward over the front axle, making it possible to shift the entire car body ahead and place the rear seat in front of the rear axle, producing a smoother, more comfortable ride. The quality of the car's ride was further enhanced by using smaller wheels and larger tires, a forerunner of today's low-pressure tires. The body featured an aerodynamic design made possible by unit body construction, a method which also provided greater strength, rigidity, and safety for passengers.

An almost endless stream of engineering innovations continued to pour from the Chrysler engineering department during the remainder of the pre-World War II years. More than fifty engineering changes or modifications appeared on Chrysler, Dodge, DeSoto, and Plymouth cars between 1934 and 1940. No other car manufacturer matched this record of technological development.

Between 1940 and 1945, when the U.S. government turned to the automobile industry for the war effort, Chrysler became a major manufacturer of urgently needed war materials for both the army and navy. Many considered Chrysler the mainstay of the government's war product needs; the company produced various types of trucks and vehicles, tanks, shells, bomber parts, gyroscopes, and scores of other items necessary to the nation's war effort. Chrysler's engineering department, under ZSB, was responsible for introducing engineering innovations and practices which improved designs as well as performance and often facilitated production quotas. One of their more notable achievements was the mass production of the navy's gyroscope, which no one believed could be produced on a mass scale. Not only did Chrysler produce the nearly 6,000 gyroscopes ordered, but it also came in ahead of schedule and below contracted costs. Chrysler's war production record, like that of the rest of the automobile industry, was impressive. Much of Chrysler's success was due to the engineering genius of Zeder, Skelton, and Breer.

The government lifted its ban on automobile production late in 1945. Prewar dies and drawings were pulled from storage, and the various product lines continued their customary minor differences in such areas as wheelbases and engine specifications while remaining stylistically similar. Chrysler produced only a few cars in the 1946 model year, conditions which prevailed for most other car manufacturers as well. Only Studebaker introduced an entirely newly designed car for 1946.

As other manufacturers introduced their first fully redesigned cars of the postwar era in 1949, Chrysler's models remained boxy and generally unattractive to the overanxious consumer, but they continued to sell to a car-starved market. But the seller's market did not last. Soon sleek, elongated, stylish cars were emerging from the engineering and styling departments of other carmakers, but at Chrysler engineering the emphasis remained on prewar styling. It appeared that the once-innovative Zeder, Skelton, and Breer could not adjust to the demands of the consumer. They continued to operate on the premise that they knew better than the customer what was best in Chrysler products. Zeder, for example, bluntly stated that Chrysler would not rush pell-mell into streamlining at the expense of comfort.

With this outlook Chrysler Corporation's 1949 models remained nondistinct. They were set apart only by traditional differences in wheelbases, body width, and under-the-hood embellishments that only the mechanics appreciated. But Chrysler still managed a good year despite its lack of trendy engineering and styling. As a matter of fact, sales were up for all divisions except DeSoto. The corporate model year total was close to 1 million units, some 110,000 more than in 1948. But while sales, profits, and dividends remained high due to product pricing, the competition was steadily developing automobiles that displayed performance and appearance—and at ever decreasing prices. At Chrysler cost was second to engineering.

Sales and profits continued to satisfy corporate executives and stockholders, and on the surface the collective decision to stick to "practicality" appeared to have been correct. In fact, the profit picture was so rosy that Walter Chrysler's handpicked successor to the presidency, K. T. Keller, decided to step aside in 1950 and allow Lester L. Colbert to assume the presidency of the corporation. Colbert's tenure, however, saw the underlying problems come to the fore. The problem was that Chrysler sales and profits were sustained not by its prewar engineering and design vitality but by high prices, which were rapidly being undercut by Ford and Chevrolet. Chrysler needed a shake-up in management and engineering in order to forestall inevitable sales declines and retain its share of the car market.

Perhaps Chrysler's loss of its engineering advantage and sales declines in the 1950s were due as much as anything else to the changing of the guard in top management. Surely, Keller's move from the presidency to chairman of the board removed one obstacle to the needed product changes that had been blocked by Keller's bias for practicality over style.

The other factors which facilitated the urgently needed product improvement were the departures of Zeder, Skelton, and Breer. Breer retired in 1949, Zeder died in 1951, and Skelton retired the same year. Until his death in 1970, Breer served as engineering consultant to Chrysler. Skelton did likewise until his death at Palm Beach, Florida, in 1969. Considering their outstanding past record, this, no doubt, left a void, if not a vacuum, at Chrys-

ler engineering. But it also offered opportunities for new ideas.

Without question there was ample talent left in the engineering department, but adjustment to the removal of design constraints imposed by both Keller's ideas and Zeder, Skelton, and Breer's preference for proven prewar concepts took time.

It is easy to understand why Chrysler referred to Zeder, Skelton, and Breer as the "Three Musketeers." For more than thirty-three years they performed as if their three minds were synchronized. Their engineering innovations ranged from the design of the original 1924 Chrysler Six with its advanced high-compression engine and 4-wheel hydraulic brakes to the 1934 Airflow with aerodynamic styling and radically new suspension and passenger comfort. They were widely acclaimed as the most creative engineers of their time. ZSB guided Chrysler Corporation from the beginning in all technical matters. Richard Langworth and Jan P. Norbye, in their *Complete History of Chrysler* (1985), state that "Chrysler was astounded by the natural way these three engineers worked together, communicating almost as if by a sixth sense to produce sound and often brilliant solutions to a variety of thorny problems." Whatever the cause, the chemistry between the three men existed, and Chrysler products and the car buyer were the beneficiaries of a better engineered, more comfortable, and safer car during the years when Zeder, Skelton, and Breer dominated the engineering department at Chrysler.

References:

Walter P. Chrysler, *Life of an American Workman* (New York: Dodd, Mead, 1937);

"Chrysler," *Fortune*, 12 (August 1935): 30-37;

Chrysler Corporation, *A Pictorial History of Chrysler Corporation Cars* (Detroit, 1975);

Beverly Rae Kimes, "Chrysler: From the Airflow," *Automobile Quarterly*, 7 (Fall 1968): 206-221;

Richard M. Langworth, "Town and Country: Chrysler's Beautiful Land Yacht," *Automobile Quarterly*, 11 (Third Quarter 1973): 298-309;

Langworth and Jan P. Norbye, *The Complete History of Chrysler Corporation, 1924-1985* (New York: Beekman, 1985);

Eugene W. Lewis, *Motor Memories* (Detroit: Alved, 1947);

Michael Moritz and Barrett Seaman, *Going for Broke: The Chrysler Story* (Garden City, N.Y.: Doubleday, 1981);

John B. Rae, *The American Automobile: A Brief History* (Chicago: University of Chicago Press, 1965);

Rae, *American Automobile Manufacturers* (Philadelphia: Chilton, 1959).

Archives:

The Chrysler Archives in Highland Park contain files and photographs and are available to the public by appointment. Especially useful are manuscripts written by Carl Breer, Owen Skelton, and Allen B. "Tobe" Couture, an early associate of ZSB Engineering. Material on Fred Zeder and Carl Breer is available in limited quantity. Reference to Owen Skelton is scarce.

Contributors

John Barnard–*Oakland University*
Michael L. Berger–*St. Mary's College of Maryland*
William R. Childs–*Ohio State University*
Kevin M. Dwyer–*George Washington University*
James J. Flink–*University of California, Irvine*
Mark S. Foster–*University of Colorado at Denver*
Gilbert J. Gall–*Pennsylvania State University*
E. Bruce Geelhoed–*Ball State University*
Northcoate Hamilton–*Columbia, South Carolina*
Beverly Rae Kimes–*New York, New York*
Robert J. Kothe–*Atlanta, Georgia*
Michael L. Lazare–*New Milford, Connecticut*
Stuart W. Leslie–*Johns Hopkins University*
George S. May–*Eastern Michigan University*
John B. Rae–*Harvey Mudd College*
Alan R. Raucher–*Wayne State University*
Richard P. Scharchburg–*GMI Engineering & Management Institute*
Genevieve Wren–*Creative Automotive Research*
James Wren–*Motor Vehicle Manufacturers Association*

Index

The following index includes names of people, corporations, organizations, laws, and technologies. It also includes key terms such as *engines*, *labor relations*, etc.

A page number in *italic* indicates the first page of an entry devoted to the subject. *Illus.* indicates a picture of the subject.

Index